STAR WARS

DARK EMPIRE II

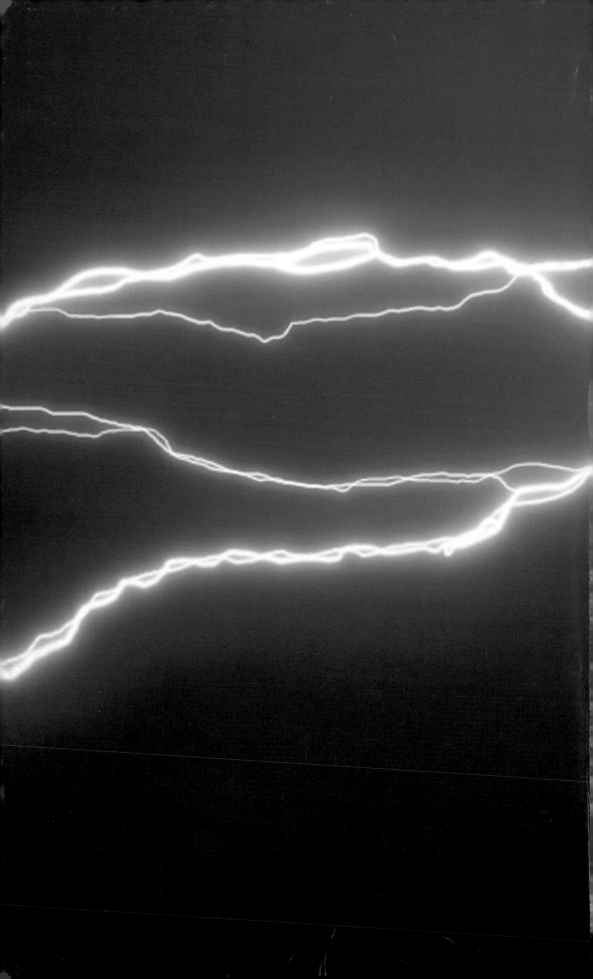

STAR WARS

DARK EMPIRE II

STORY **TOM VEITCH**   ART **CAM KENNEDY**

LETTERING **TODD KLEIN**

WITH

EMPIRE'S END

STORY **TOM VEITCH**   ART **JIM BAIKIE**

LETTERING **LOIS BUHALIS**

FRONT COVER **TSUNEO SANDA**

BACK COVER ART **DAVE DORMAN**

DARK HORSE BOOKS™

PUBLISHER
MIKE RICHARDSON

SERIES EDITORS
DAN THORSLAND.
RYDER WINDHAM. BOB COOPER

COLLECTIOVN EDITOR
RANDY STRADLEY

ASSISTANT EDITOR
DAVE MARSHALL

COLLECTION DESIGNER
DAVID NESTELLE

ART DIRECTOR
LIA RIBACCHI

SPECIAL THANKS TO LELAND CHEE,
SUE ROSTONI, AND AMY GARY AT LUCAS LICENSING

THE EVENTS IN THIS STORY TAKE PLACE
SEVEN YEARS AFTER THE BATTLE OF ENDOR

THIS VOLUME COLLECTS THE COMIC-BOOK SERIES STAR WARS: DARK EMPIRE II #1-6 AND STAR
WARS: EMPIRE'S END #1-2, BOTH ORIGINALLY PUBLISHED BY DARK HORSE COMICS.

PUBLISHED BY
DARK HORSE BOOKS
A DIVISION OF DARK HORSE COMICS, INC.
10956 SE MAIN STREET
MILWAUKIE, OR 97222

DARKHORSE.COM
STARWARS.COM

TO FIND A COMICS SHOP IN YOUR AREA, CALL THE COMIC
SHOP LOCATOR SERVICE TOLL-FREE AT 1-888-266-4226

SECOND EDITION: SEPTEMBER 2006
ISBN-10: 1-59307-526-X
ISBN-13: 978-1-59307-526-2

3 5 7 9 10 8 6 4 2
PRINTED IN CHINA

FOREWORD

BY RALPH MCQUARRIE

(From the first edition, originally published in 1995)

Since I am, aside from the vision in the mind of George Lucas, the first person to see Darth Vader, a lightsaber, Artoo-Detoo, and many other characters and things that make up the *Star Wars* world, I've decided to write this foreword.

I've had to think it over because, outside of that fact, my qualifications are sketchy. I cannot pontificate on theory relating to the art of sequential images or anything profound. I'm certain Cam Kennedy or any number of people could have read the script I read and listened to George talk about what he wanted to see, then gone ahead and designed the things as well or better. But, since I was the one there at the time, and I'd done a few things that could be called science fiction or fantasy art, I became the first *Star Wars* artist.

That was in December 1974, twenty years ago. And, after all this time, I'm still doing *Star Wars* illustrations, albeit after a long period of not doing *Star Wars* illustrations. It's just as interesting to me now as it was then, more so in a way. Rick McCallum [producer on Episodes I - III] had talked to me about maybe doing some work on it. I'd been thinking about what I would say if this came up, and I had to admit to myself first that the work I'd done on *Star Wars* was the best I've done. Second, I'd had the most fun doing it. So there wasn't much question about saying I'd like to work with Rick.

There is one thing out there though that has always haunted me. It gets back to the question, "What have you got to say, Ralph?" I've always worked on someone else's project, making their idea work if I can. I add my ideas, it's true but . . . I've always thought that to be a real artist, one has to originate one's own project and carry it through. That's why I'm full of admiration for the work of Moebius, Ken Steacy, and many others in that category.

I haven't been an avid collector of comics and science fiction or fantasy art, but I've seen quite a lot, and I'll say the work in the *Dark Empire* series is very impressive. I look with envy at the crisp, stylized drawings by Cam Kennedy, the rich color and painterly effects Dave Dorman gets into his work. In my own work, my approach has mainly been to simply make things look like the way I'd see them on the screen. I've shied away from attempts to achieve style. Perhaps I'm just a bit timid, afraid such efforts would only produce what would seem to be affectations of some sort. Style must just happen it seems to me. Where does one look for one's own style? It's great to see it when it's there though, and it certainly is there in the *Dark Empire* pages.

LUKE Skywalker's bold attempt to learn the secrets of the reborn Emperor Palpatine's power nearly ended in disaster for himself and the Alliance. But now, with the aid of information gleaned from a Jedi Holocron, Skywalker is prepared to search for Jedi who may still survive and who can aid him in his quest to destroy the Empire once and for all.

But even as hope seems to be rising, the Empire is extending its grasp beyond the boundaries of the Galactic Core . . .

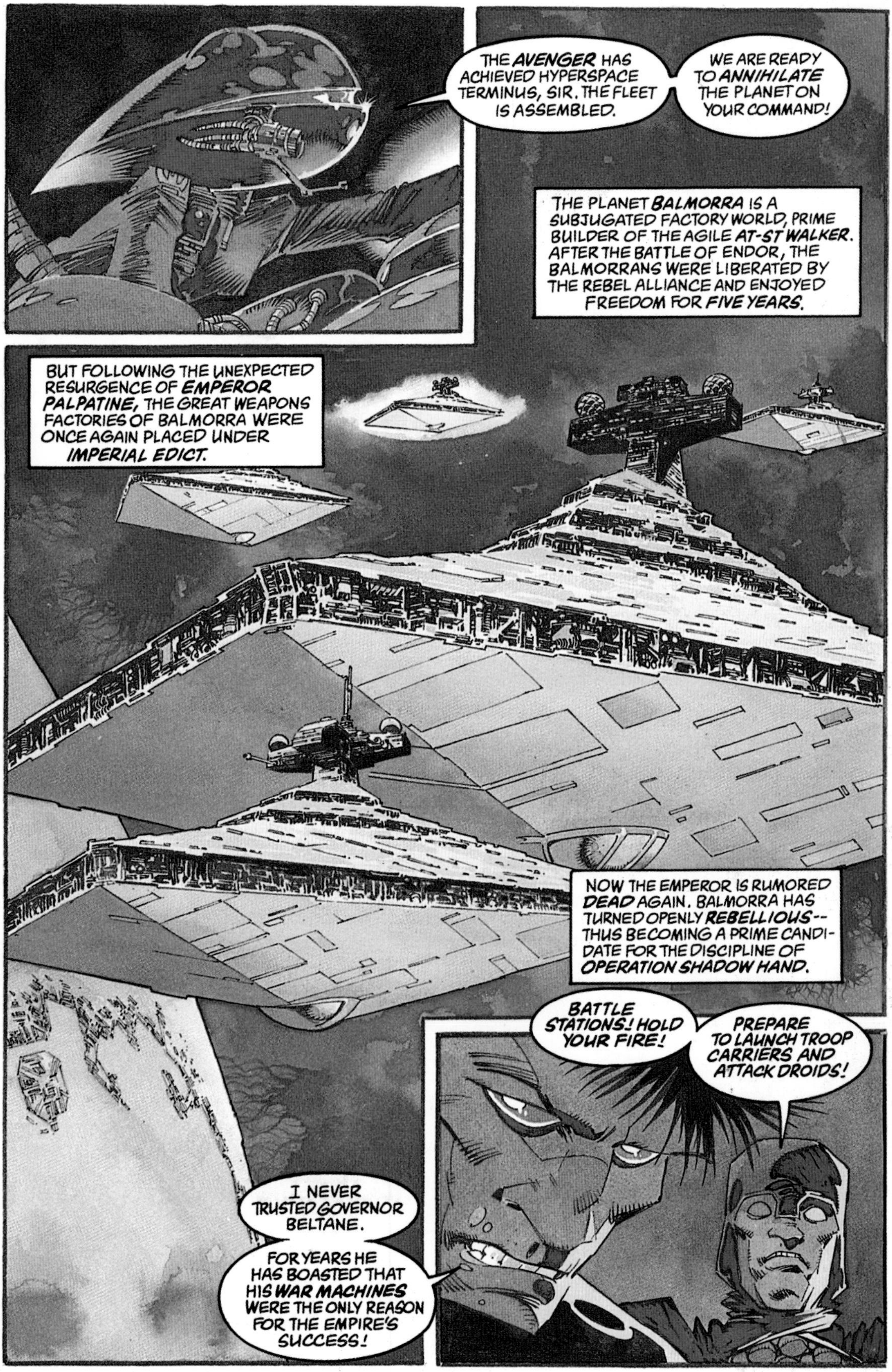
THE AVENGER HAS ACHIEVED HYPERSPACE TERMINUS, SIR. THE FLEET IS ASSEMBLED.
WE ARE READY TO ANNIHILATE THE PLANET ON YOUR COMMAND!
THE PLANET BALMORRA IS A SUBJUGATED FACTORY WORLD, PRIME BUILDER OF THE AGILE AT-ST WALKER. AFTER THE BATTLE OF ENDOR, THE BALMORRANS WERE LIBERATED BY THE REBEL ALLIANCE AND ENJOYED FREEDOM FOR FIVE YEARS.
BUT FOLLOWING THE UNEXPECTED RESURGENCE OF EMPEROR PALPATINE, THE GREAT WEAPONS FACTORIES OF BALMORRA WERE ONCE AGAIN PLACED UNDER IMPERIAL EDICT.
NOW THE EMPEROR IS RUMORED DEAD AGAIN. BALMORRA HAS TURNED OPENLY REBELLIOUS-- THUS BECOMING A PRIME CANDIDATE FOR THE DISCIPLINE OF OPERATION SHADOW HAND.
BATTLE STATIONS! HOLD YOUR FIRE!
PREPARE TO LAUNCH TROOP CARRIERS AND ATTACK DROIDS!
I NEVER TRUSTED GOVERNOR BELTANE.
FOR YEARS HE HAS BOASTED THAT HIS WAR MACHINES WERE THE ONLY REASON FOR THE EMPIRE'S SUCCESS!

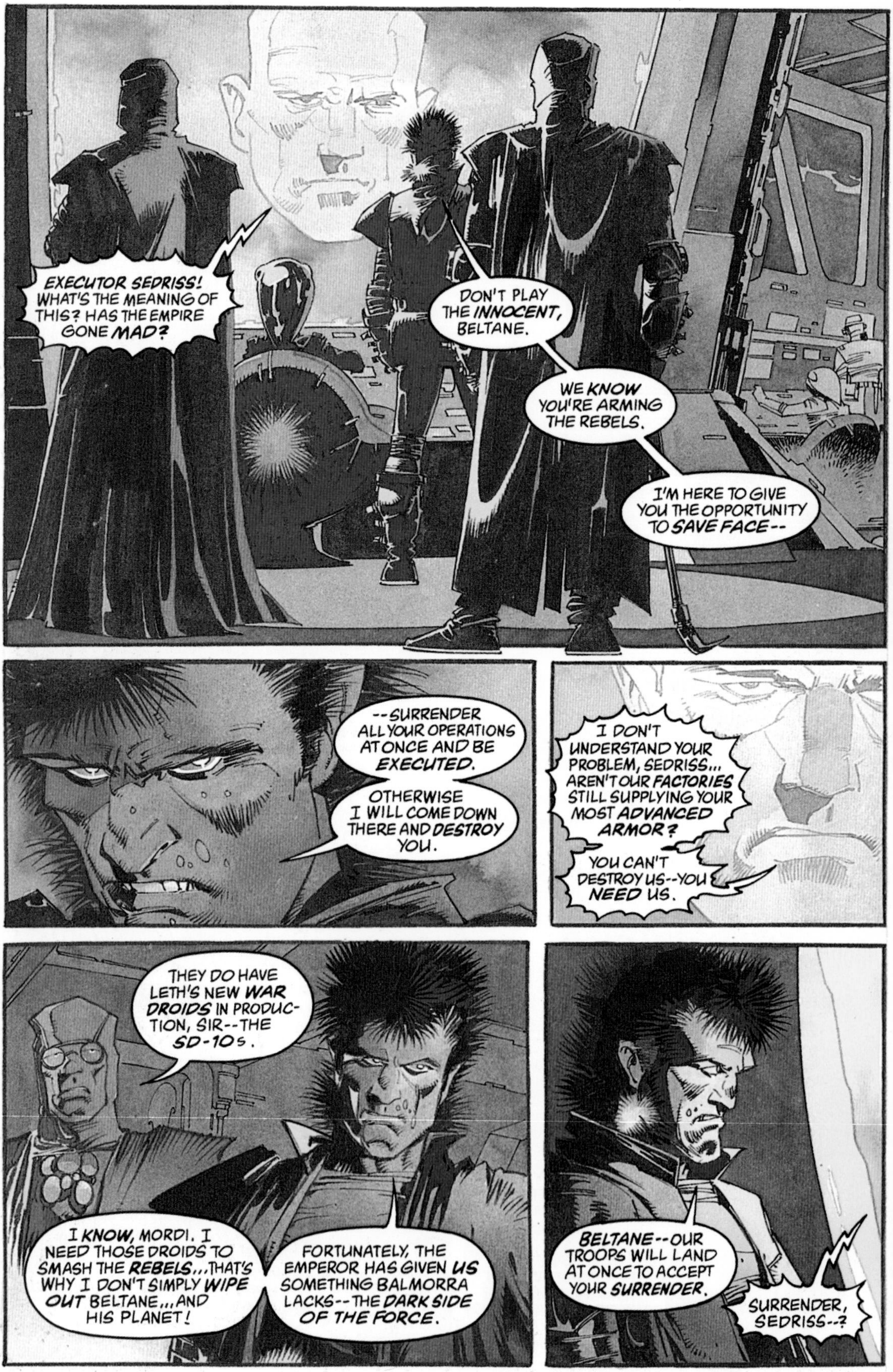
EXECUTOR SEDRISS! WHAT'S THE MEANING OF THIS? HAS THE EMPIRE GONE MAD?
DON'T PLAY THE INNOCENT, BELTANE.
WE KNOW YOU'RE ARMING THE REBELS.
I'M HERE TO GIVE YOU THE OPPORTUNITY TO SAVE FACE--
--SURRENDER ALL YOUR OPERATIONS AT ONCE AND BE EXECUTED.
OTHERWISE I WILL COME DOWN THERE AND DESTROY YOU.
I DON'T UNDERSTAND YOUR PROBLEM, SEDRISS... AREN'T OUR FACTORIES STILL SUPPLYING YOUR MOST ADVANCED ARMOR?
YOU CAN'T DESTROY US--YOU NEED US.
THEY DO HAVE LETH'S NEW WAR DROIDS IN PRODUCTION, SIR--THE SD-10s.
I KNOW, MORDI. I NEED THOSE DROIDS TO SMASH THE REBELS...THAT'S WHY I DON'T SIMPLY WIPE OUT BELTANE... AND HIS PLANET!
FORTUNATELY, THE EMPEROR HAS GIVEN US SOMETHING BALMORRA LACKS--THE DARK SIDE OF THE FORCE.
BELTANE--OUR TROOPS WILL LAND AT ONCE TO ACCEPT YOUR SURRENDER.
SURRENDER, SEDRISS--?

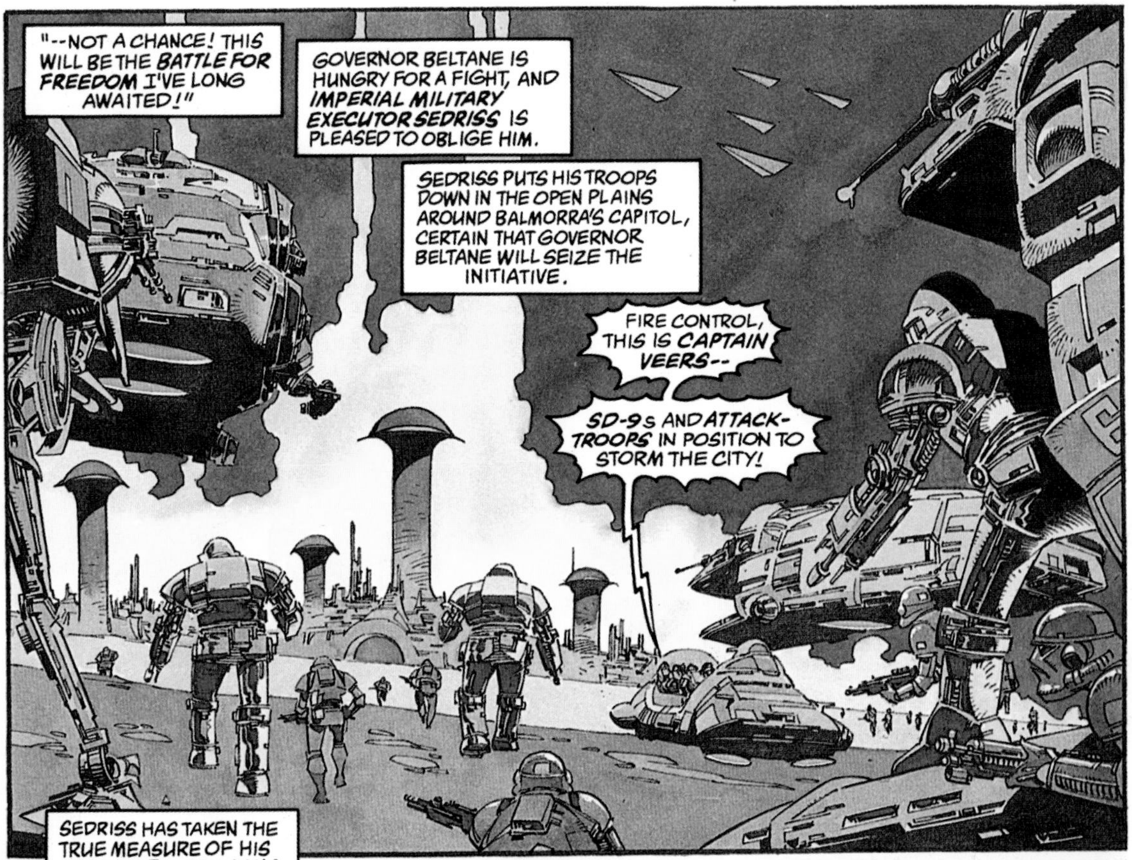
"--NOT A CHANCE! THIS WILL BE THE BATTLE FOR FREEDOM I'VE LONG AWAITED!"
GOVERNOR BELTANE IS HUNGRY FOR A FIGHT, AND IMPERIAL MILITARY EXECUTOR SEDRISS IS PLEASED TO OBLIGE HIM.
SEDRISS PUTS HIS TROOPS DOWN IN THE OPEN PLAINS AROUND BALMORRA'S CAPITOL, CERTAIN THAT GOVERNOR BELTANE WILL SEIZE THE INITIATIVE.
FIRE CONTROL, THIS IS CAPTAIN VEERS--
SD-9s AND ATTACK-TROOPS IN POSITION TO STORM THE CITY!

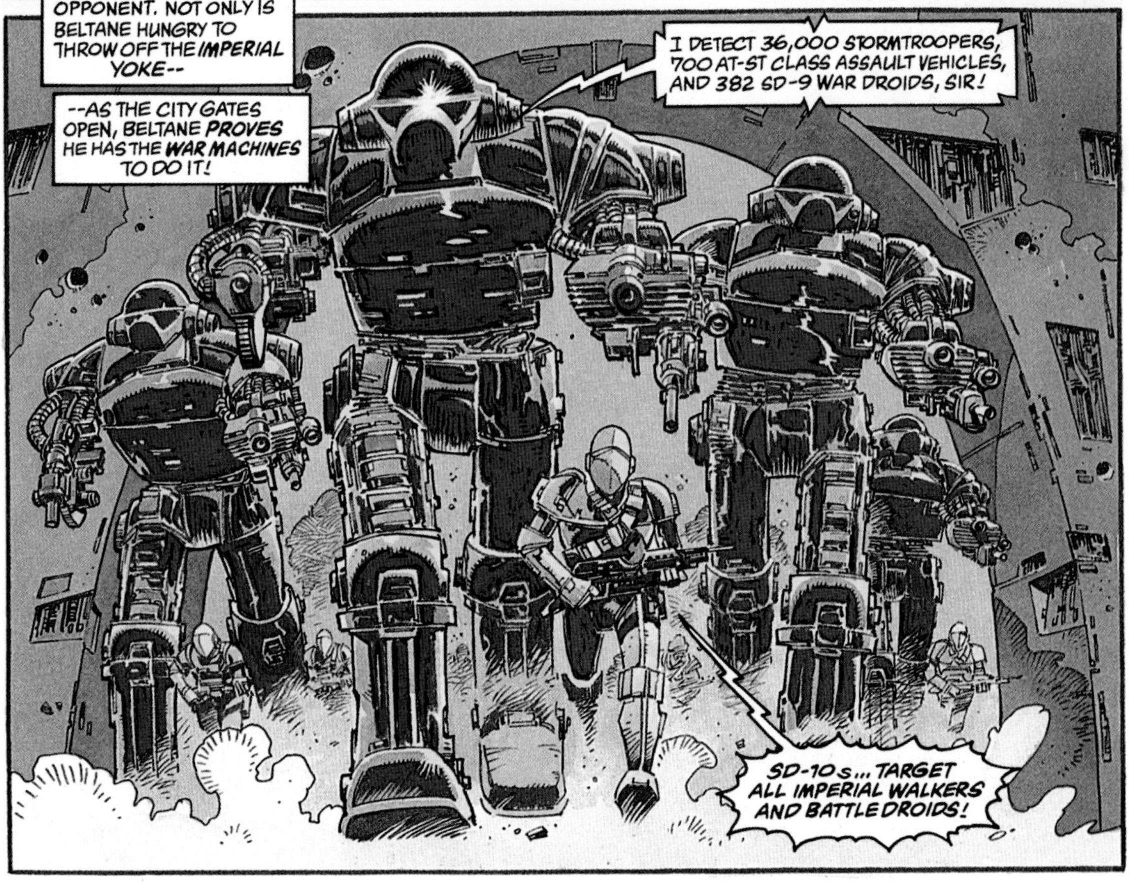
SEDRISS HAS TAKEN THE TRUE MEASURE OF HIS OPPONENT. NOT ONLY IS BELTANE HUNGRY TO THROW OFF THE IMPERIAL YOKE--
--AS THE CITY GATES OPEN, BELTANE PROVES HE HAS THE WAR MACHINES TO DO IT!
I DETECT 36,000 STORMTROOPERS, 700 AT-ST CLASS ASSAULT VEHICLES, AND 382 SD-9 WAR DROIDS, SIR!
SD-10s... TARGET ALL IMPERIAL WALKERS AND BATTLE DROIDS!

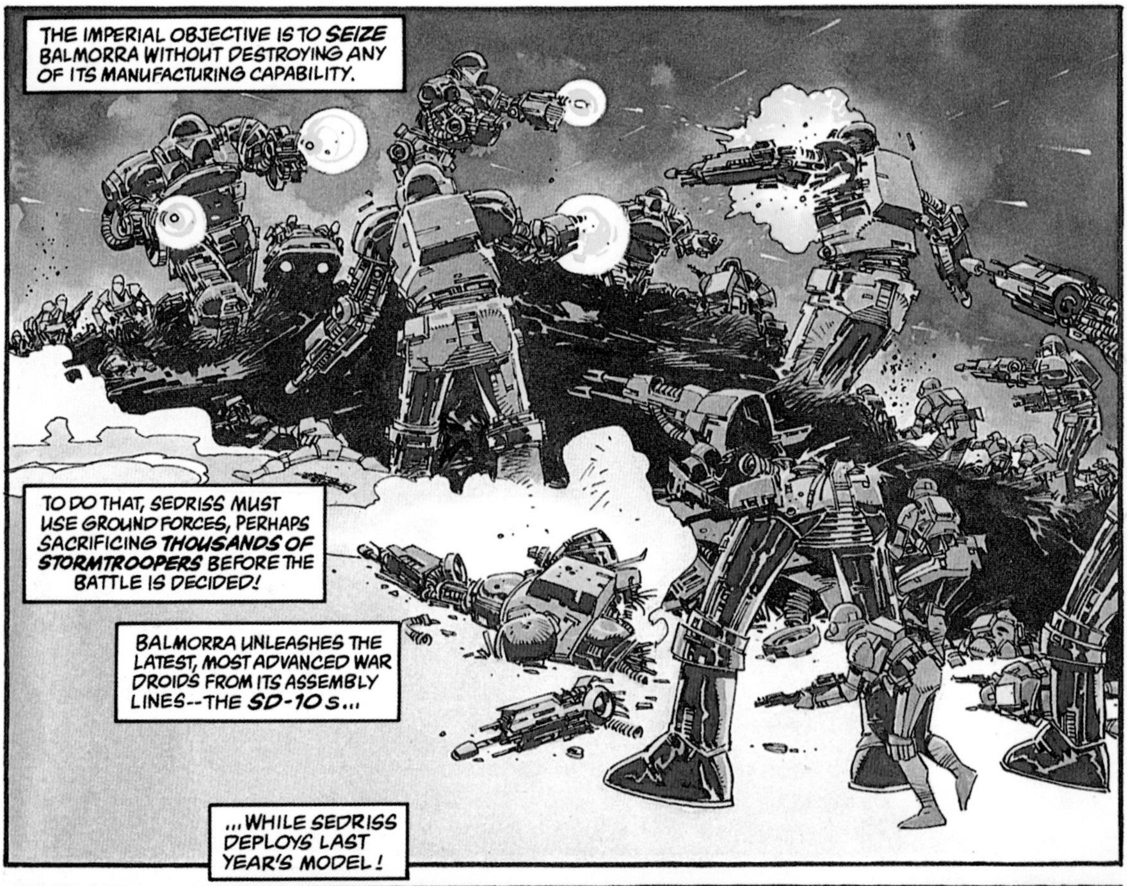
THE IMPERIAL OBJECTIVE IS TO SEIZE BALMORRA WITHOUT DESTROYING ANY OF ITS MANUFACTURING CAPABILITY.
TO DO THAT, SEDRISS MUST USE GROUND FORCES, PERHAPS SACRIFICING THOUSANDS OF STORMTROOPERS BEFORE THE BATTLE IS DECIDED!
BALMORRA UNLEASHES THE LATEST, MOST ADVANCED WAR DROIDS FROM ITS ASSEMBLY LINES--THE SD-10s...
...WHILE SEDRISS DEPLOYS LAST YEAR'S MODEL!

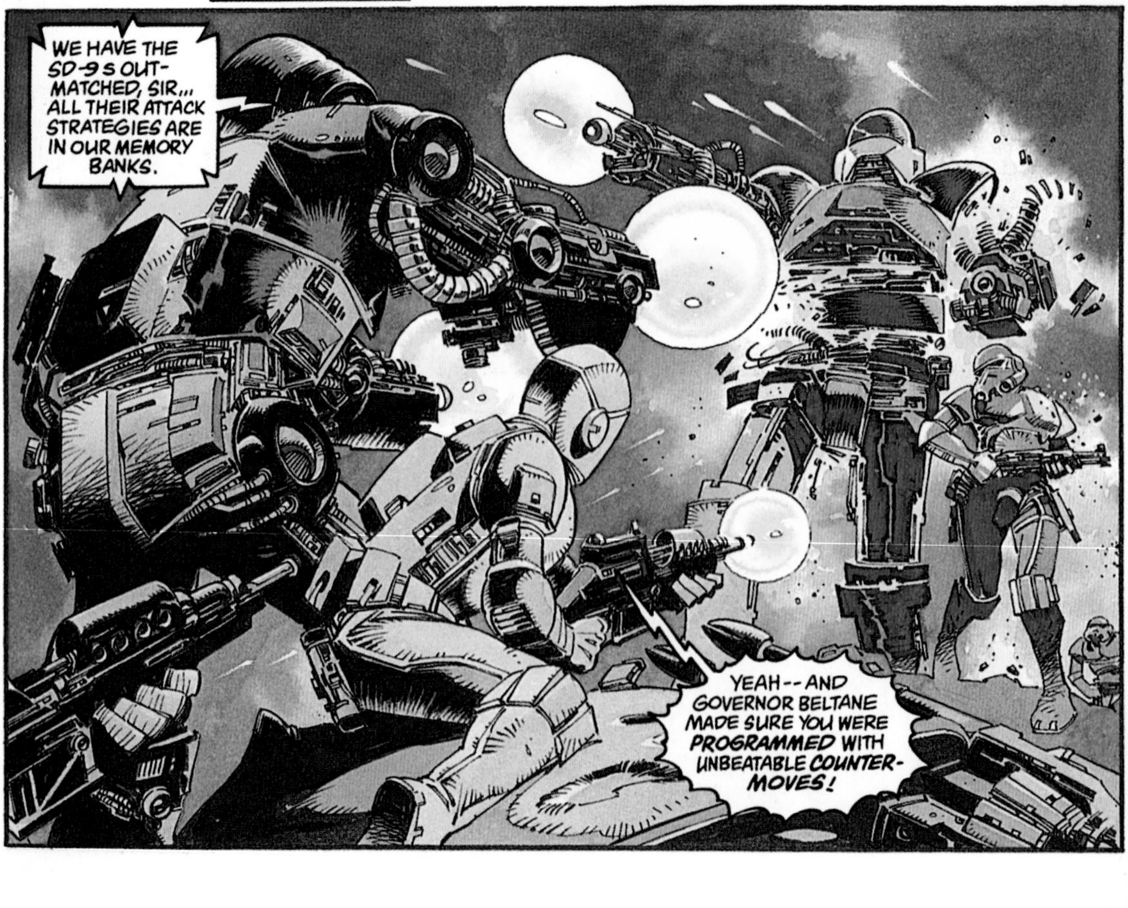
WE HAVE THE SD-9s OUT-MATCHED, SIR... ALL THEIR ATTACK STRATEGIES ARE IN OUR MEMORY BANKS.
YEAH--AND GOVERNOR BELTANE MADE SURE YOU WERE PROGRAMMED WITH UNBEATABLE COUNTER-MOVES!

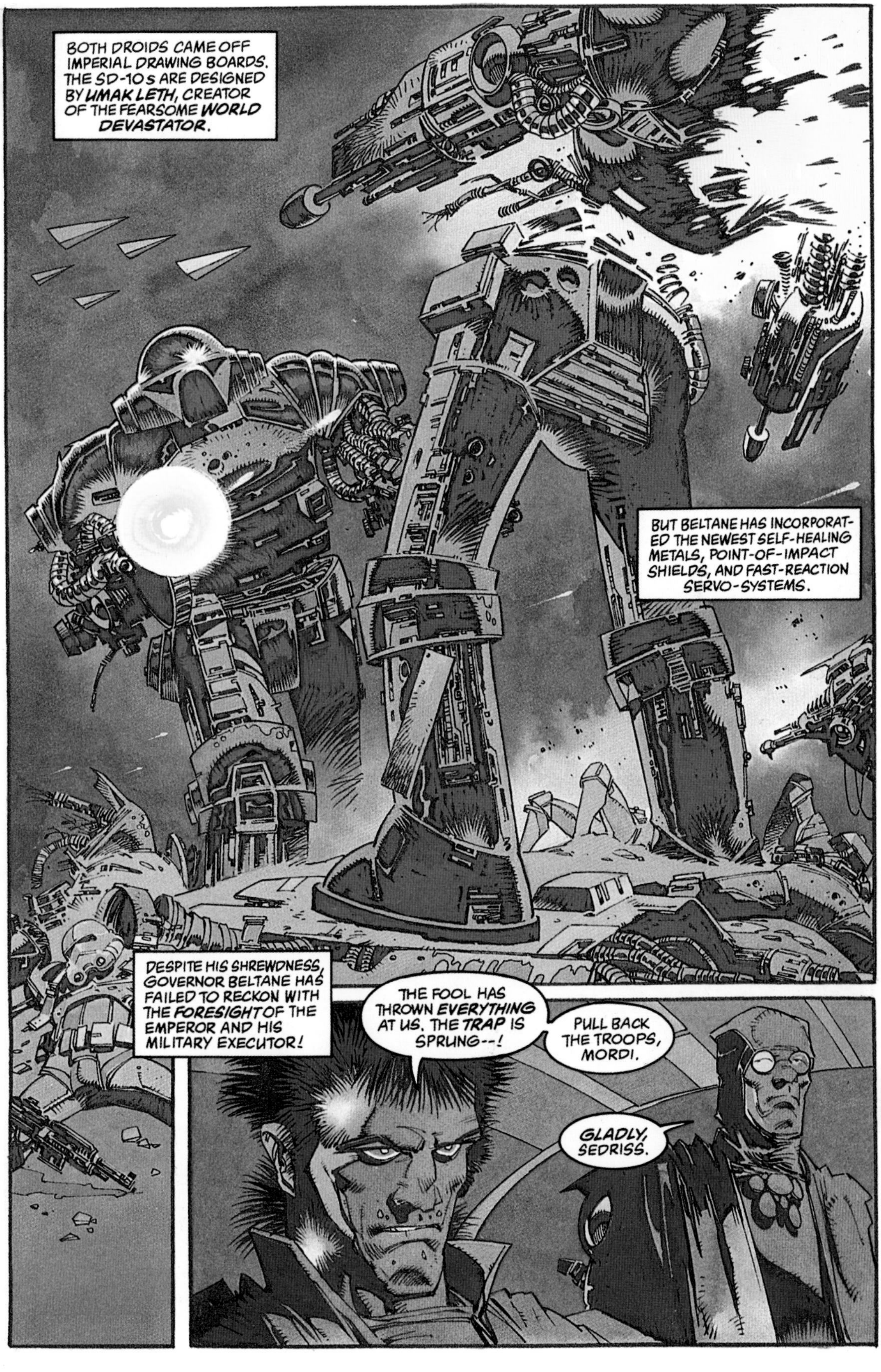
BOTH DROIDS CAME OFF IMPERIAL DRAWING BOARDS. THE SD-10s ARE DESIGNED BY UMAK LETH, CREATOR OF THE FEARSOME WORLD DEVASTATOR.
BUT BELTANE HAS INCORPORATED THE NEWEST SELF-HEALING METALS, POINT-OF-IMPACT SHIELDS, AND FAST-REACTION SERVO-SYSTEMS.
DESPITE HIS SHREWDNESS, GOVERNOR BELTANE HAS FAILED TO RECKON WITH THE FORESIGHT OF THE EMPEROR AND HIS MILITARY EXECUTOR!
THE FOOL HAS THROWN EVERYTHING AT US. THE TRAP IS SPRUNG--!
PULL BACK THE TROOPS, MORDI.
GLADLY, SEDRISS.

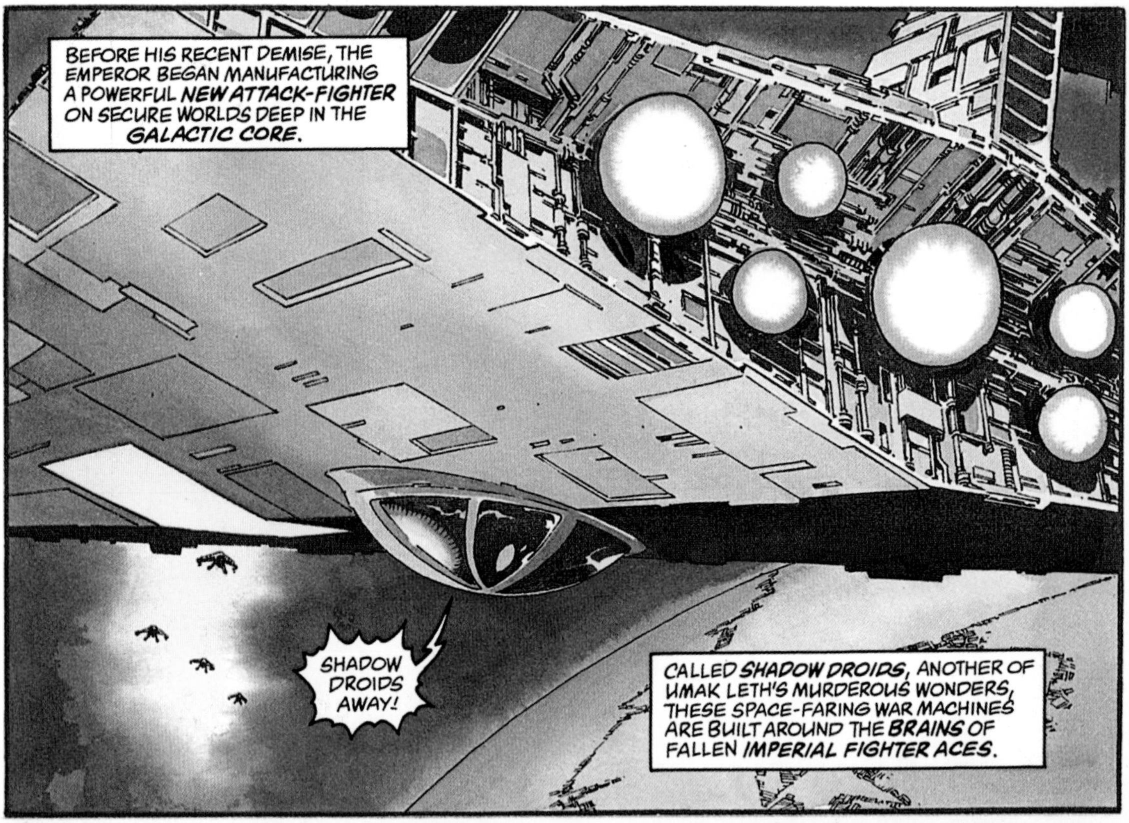
BEFORE HIS RECENT DEMISE, THE EMPEROR BEGAN MANUFACTURING A POWERFUL NEW ATTACK-FIGHTER ON SECURE WORLDS DEEP IN THE GALACTIC CORE.
SHADOW DROIDS AWAY!
CALLED SHADOW DROIDS, ANOTHER OF UMAK LETH'S MURDEROUS WONDERS, THESE SPACE-FARING WAR MACHINES ARE BUILT AROUND THE BRAINS OF FALLEN IMPERIAL FIGHTER ACES.

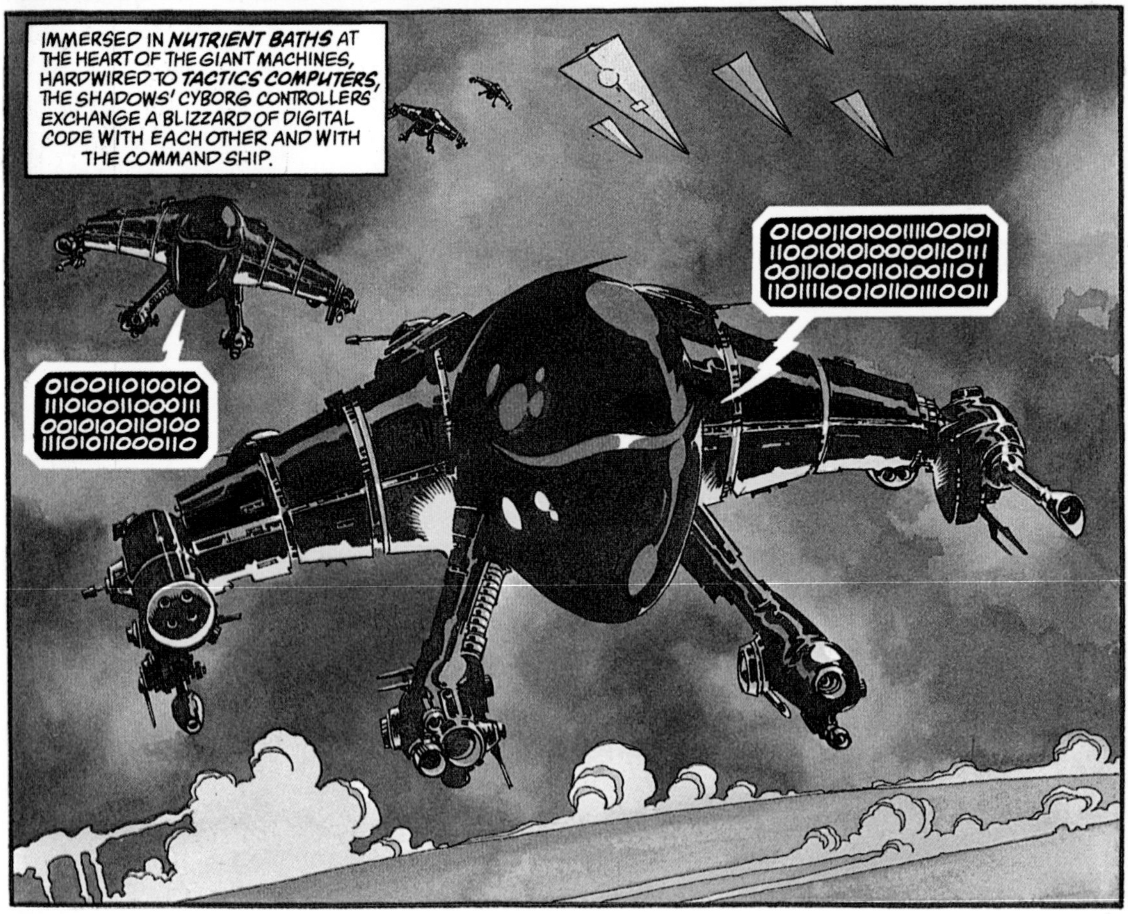
IMMERSED IN NUTRIENT BATHS AT THE HEART OF THE GIANT MACHINES, HARDWIRED TO TACTICS COMPUTERS, THE SHADOWS' CYBORG CONTROLLERS EXCHANGE A BLIZZARD OF DIGITAL CODE WITH EACH OTHER AND WITH THE COMMAND SHIP.
0100110100111100101 11001010100000110111 001101001101001101 110111100101101110011
010011010010 111010011000111 0010100110100 11101011000110

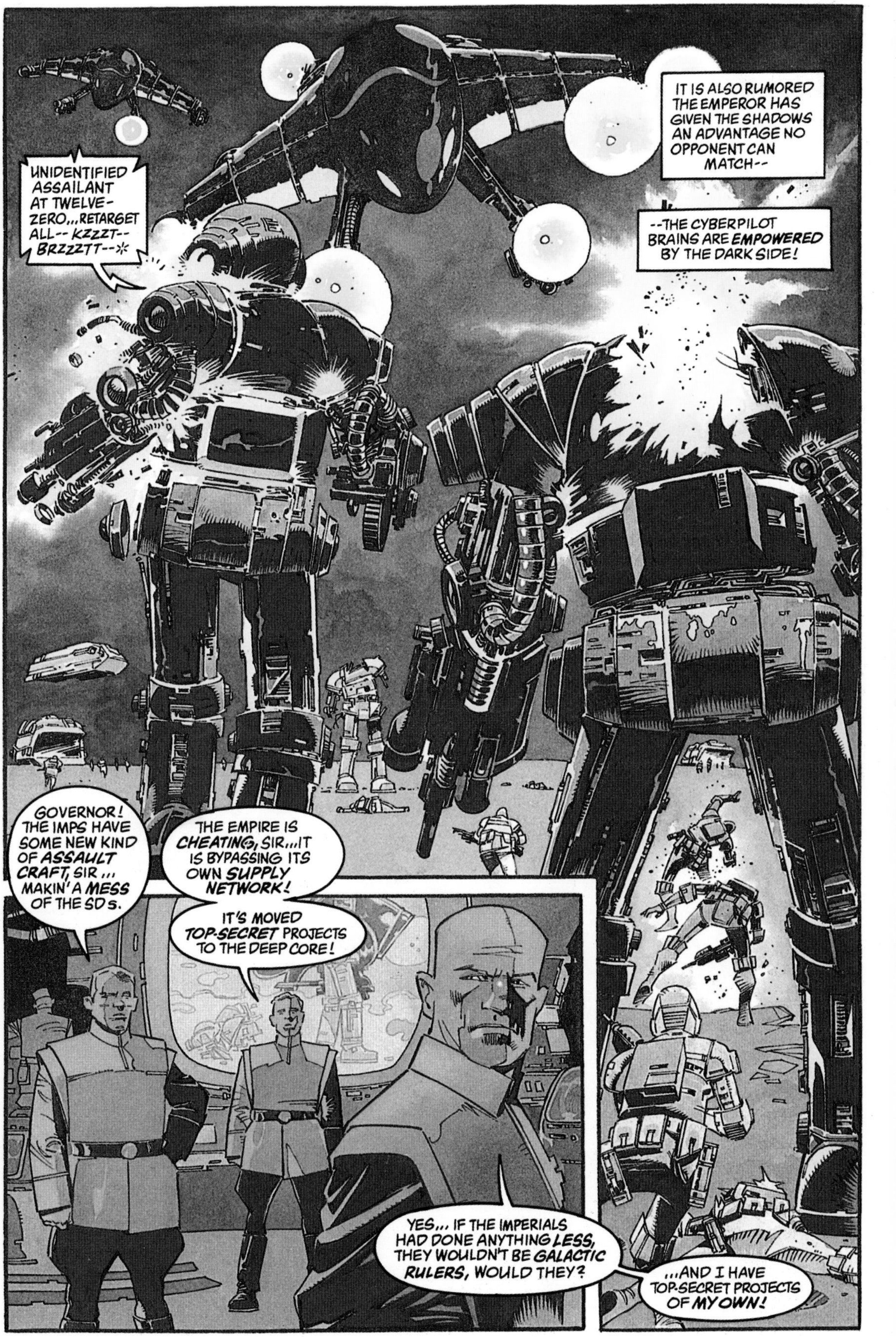

UNIDENTIFIED ASSAILANT AT TWELVE-ZERO... RETARGET ALL-- KZZZT-- BRZZZTT--
IT IS ALSO RUMORED THE EMPEROR HAS GIVEN THE SHADOWS AN ADVANTAGE NO OPPONENT CAN MATCH--
--THE CYBERPILOT BRAINS ARE EMPOWERED BY THE DARK SIDE!
GOVERNOR! THE IMPS HAVE SOME NEW KIND OF ASSAULT CRAFT, SIR... MAKIN' A MESS OF THE SDs.
THE EMPIRE IS CHEATING, SIR... IT IS BYPASSING ITS OWN SUPPLY NETWORK!
IT'S MOVED TOP-SECRET PROJECTS TO THE DEEP CORE!
YES... IF THE IMPERIALS HAD DONE ANYTHING LESS, THEY WOULDN'T BE GALACTIC RULERS, WOULD THEY?
...AND I HAVE TOP-SECRET PROJECTS OF MY OWN!

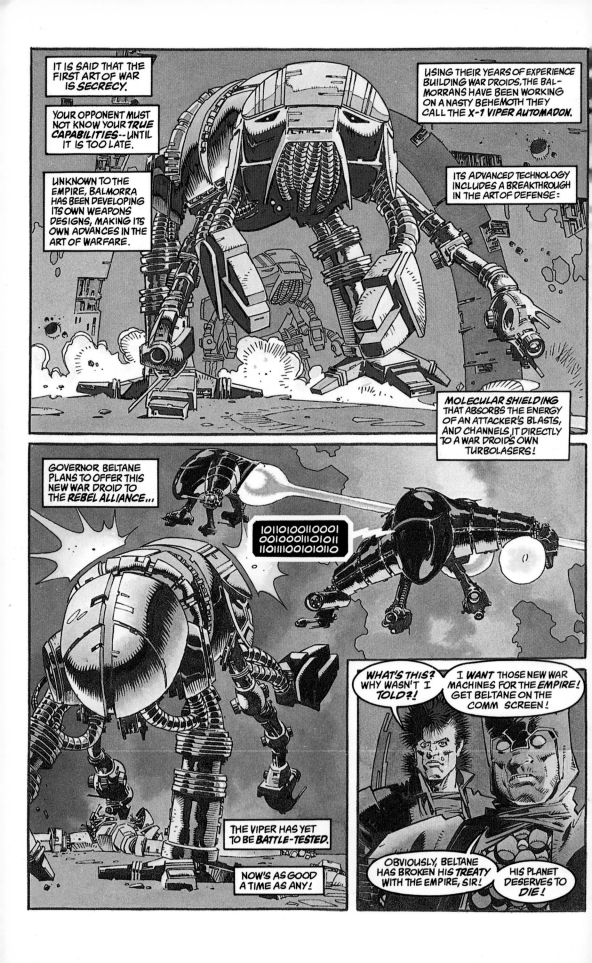

IT IS SAID THAT THE FIRST ART OF WAR IS *SECRECY.*

YOUR OPPONENT MUST NOT KNOW YOUR *TRUE CAPABILITIES*--UNTIL IT IS TOO LATE.

UNKNOWN TO THE EMPIRE, BALMORRA HAS BEEN DEVELOPING ITS OWN WEAPONS DESIGNS, MAKING ITS OWN ADVANCES IN THE ART OF WARFARE.

USING THEIR YEARS OF EXPERIENCE BUILDING WAR DROIDS, THE BAL-MORRANS HAVE BEEN WORKING ON A NASTY BEHEMOTH THEY CALL THE *X-1 VIPER AUTOMADON.*

ITS ADVANCED TECHNOLOGY INCLUDES A BREAKTHROUGH IN THE ART OF DEFENSE:

MOLECULAR SHIELDING THAT ABSORBS THE ENERGY OF AN ATTACKER'S BLASTS, AND CHANNELS IT DIRECTLY TO A WAR DROID'S OWN TURBOLASERS!

GOVERNOR BELTANE PLANS TO OFFER THIS NEW WAR DROID TO THE *REBEL ALLIANCE...*

IOIIOIOOIIOOOI OOIOOOIIIOIOII IIOIIIOOIOIOIIO

THE VIPER HAS YET TO BE *BATTLE-TESTED.*

NOW'S AS GOOD A TIME AS ANY!

WHAT'S THIS? WHY WASN'T I *TOLD?!*

I *WANT* THOSE NEW WAR MACHINES FOR THE *EMPIRE!* GET BELTANE ON THE COMM SCREEN!

OBVIOUSLY, BELTANE HAS BROKEN HIS *TREATY* WITH THE EMPIRE, SIR!

HIS PLANET DESERVES TO *DIE!*

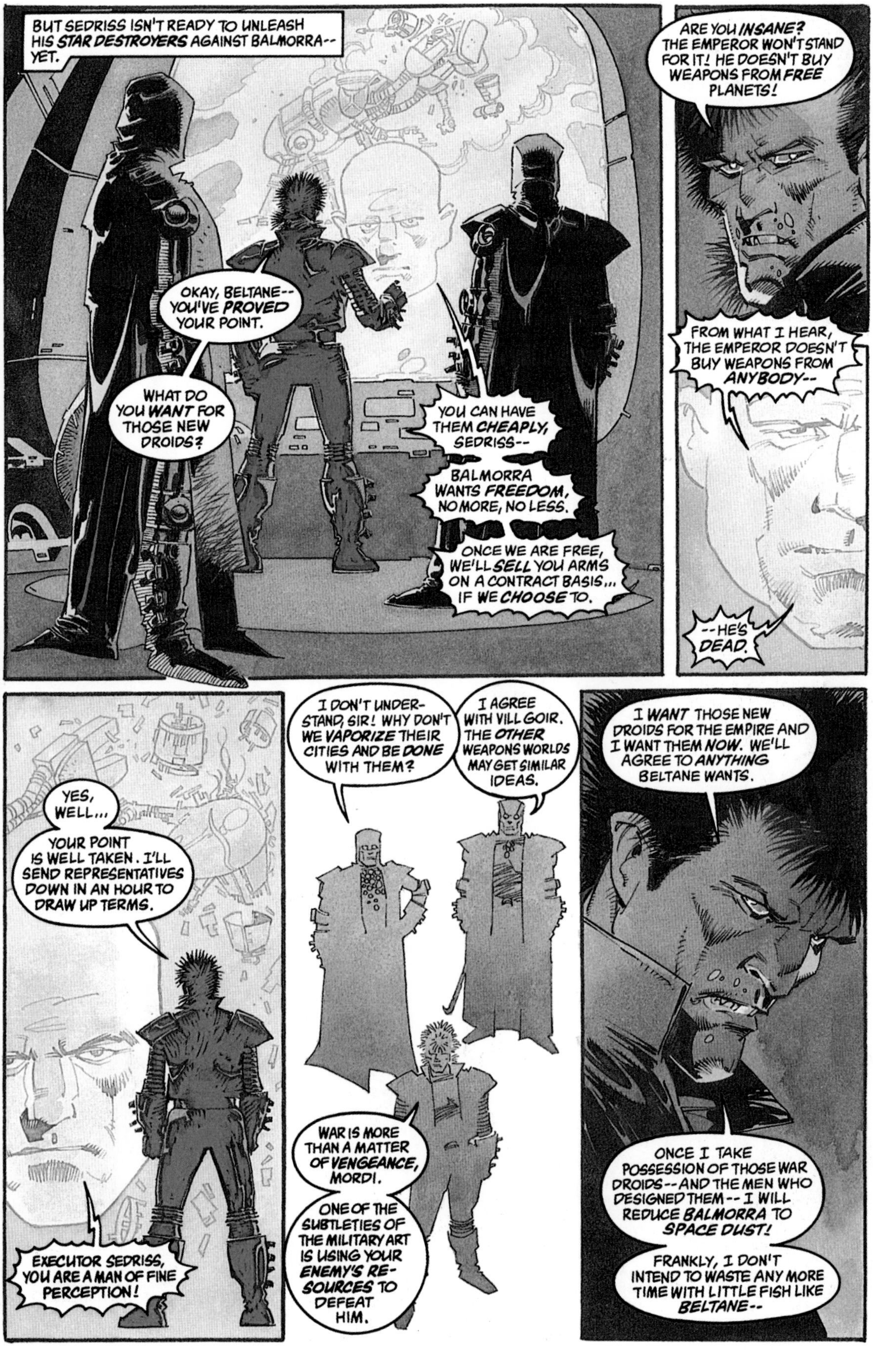

BUT SEDRISS ISN'T READY TO UNLEASH HIS STAR DESTROYERS AGAINST BALMORRA--YET.
OKAY, BELTANE--YOU'VE PROVED YOUR POINT.
WHAT DO YOU WANT FOR THOSE NEW DROIDS?
YOU CAN HAVE THEM CHEAPLY, SEDRISS--
BALMORRA WANTS FREEDOM, NO MORE, NO LESS.
ONCE WE ARE FREE, WE'LL SELL YOU ARMS ON A CONTRACT BASIS... IF WE CHOOSE TO.
ARE YOU INSANE? THE EMPEROR WON'T STAND FOR IT! HE DOESN'T BUY WEAPONS FROM FREE PLANETS!
FROM WHAT I HEAR, THE EMPEROR DOESN'T BUY WEAPONS FROM ANYBODY--
--HE'S DEAD.
YES, WELL...
YOUR POINT IS WELL TAKEN. I'LL SEND REPRESENTATIVES DOWN IN AN HOUR TO DRAW UP TERMS.
EXECUTOR SEDRISS, YOU ARE A MAN OF FINE PERCEPTION!
I DON'T UNDERSTAND, SIR! WHY DON'T WE VAPORIZE THEIR CITIES AND BE DONE WITH THEM?
I AGREE WITH VILL GOIR. THE OTHER WEAPONS WORLDS MAY GET SIMILAR IDEAS.
WAR IS MORE THAN A MATTER OF VENGEANCE, MORDI.
ONE OF THE SUBTLETIES OF THE MILITARY ART IS USING YOUR ENEMY'S RESOURCES TO DEFEAT HIM.
I WANT THOSE NEW DROIDS FOR THE EMPIRE AND I WANT THEM NOW. WE'LL AGREE TO ANYTHING BELTANE WANTS.
ONCE I TAKE POSSESSION OF THOSE WAR DROIDS--AND THE MEN WHO DESIGNED THEM--I WILL REDUCE BALMORRA TO SPACE DUST!
FRANKLY, I DON'T INTEND TO WASTE ANY MORE TIME WITH LITTLE FISH LIKE BELTANE--

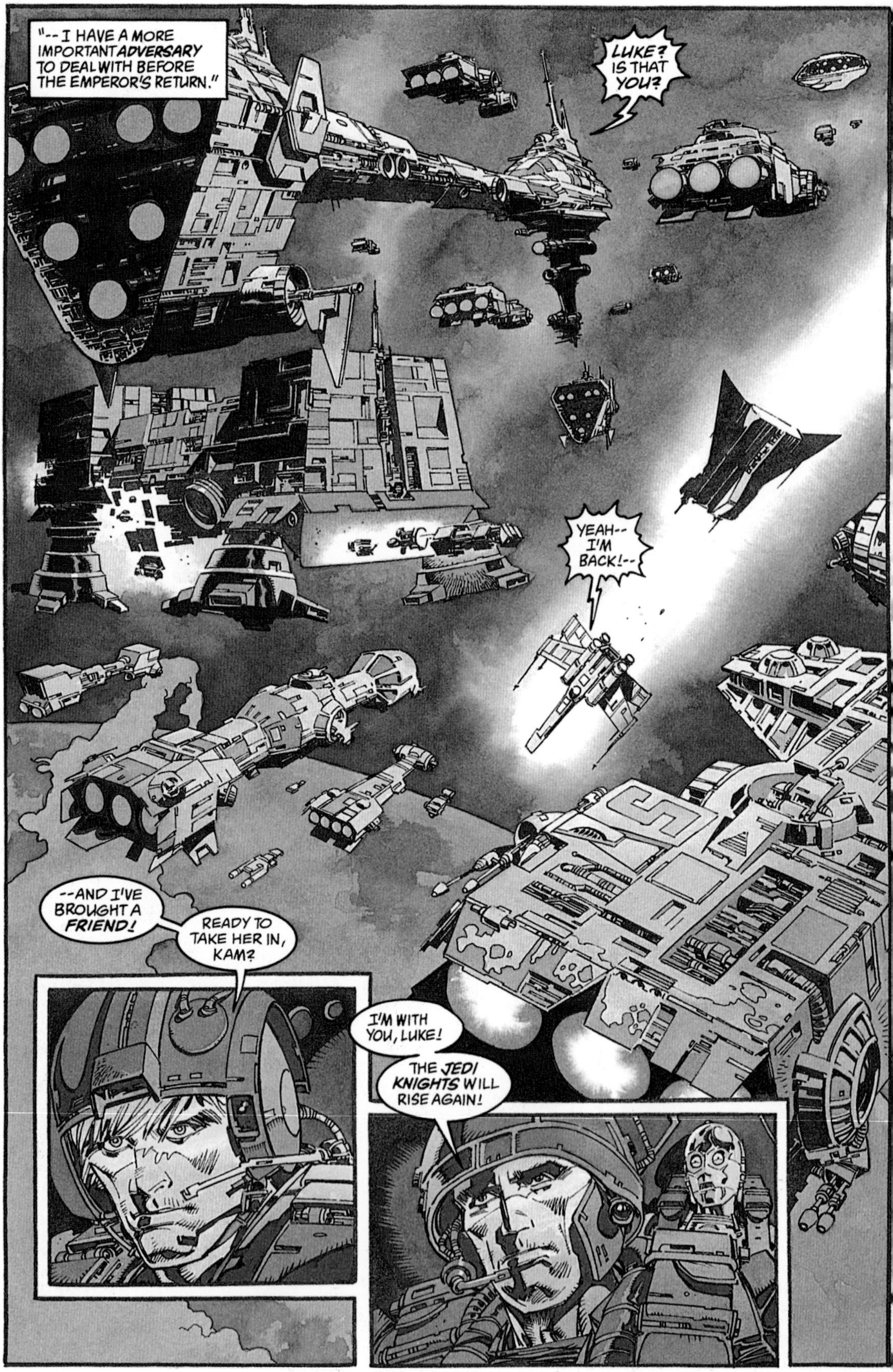
"-- I HAVE A MORE IMPORTANT ADVERSARY TO DEAL WITH BEFORE THE EMPEROR'S RETURN."
LUKE? IS THAT YOU?
YEAH-- I'M BACK!--
--AND I'VE BROUGHT A FRIEND!
READY TO TAKE HER IN, KAM?
I'M WITH YOU, LUKE!
THE JEDI KNIGHTS WILL RISE AGAIN!

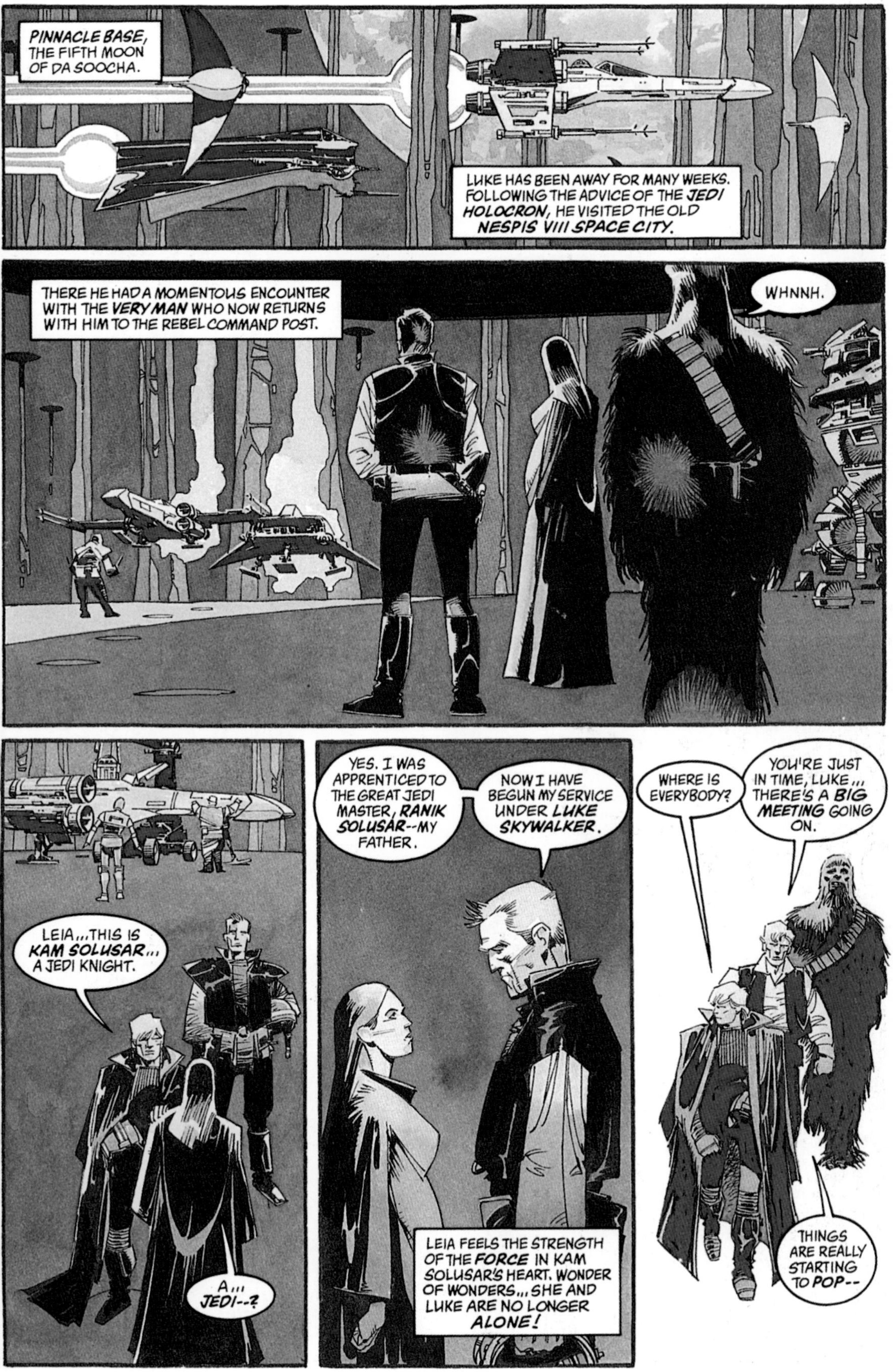
PINNACLE BASE, THE FIFTH MOON OF DA SOOCHA.
LUKE HAS BEEN AWAY FOR MANY WEEKS. FOLLOWING THE ADVICE OF THE JEDI HOLOCRON, HE VISITED THE OLD NESPIS VIII SPACE CITY.
THERE HE HAD A MOMENTOUS ENCOUNTER WITH THE VERY MAN WHO NOW RETURNS WITH HIM TO THE REBEL COMMAND POST.
WHNNH.
LEIA... THIS IS KAM SOLUSAR... A JEDI KNIGHT.
A... JEDI--?
YES. I WAS APPRENTICED TO THE GREAT JEDI MASTER, RANIK SOLUSAR--MY FATHER.
NOW I HAVE BEGUN MY SERVICE UNDER LUKE SKYWALKER.
LEIA FEELS THE STRENGTH OF THE FORCE IN KAM SOLUSAR'S HEART. WONDER OF WONDERS... SHE AND LUKE ARE NO LONGER ALONE!
WHERE IS EVERYBODY?
YOU'RE JUST IN TIME, LUKE... THERE'S A BIG MEETING GOING ON.
THINGS ARE REALLY STARTING TO POP--

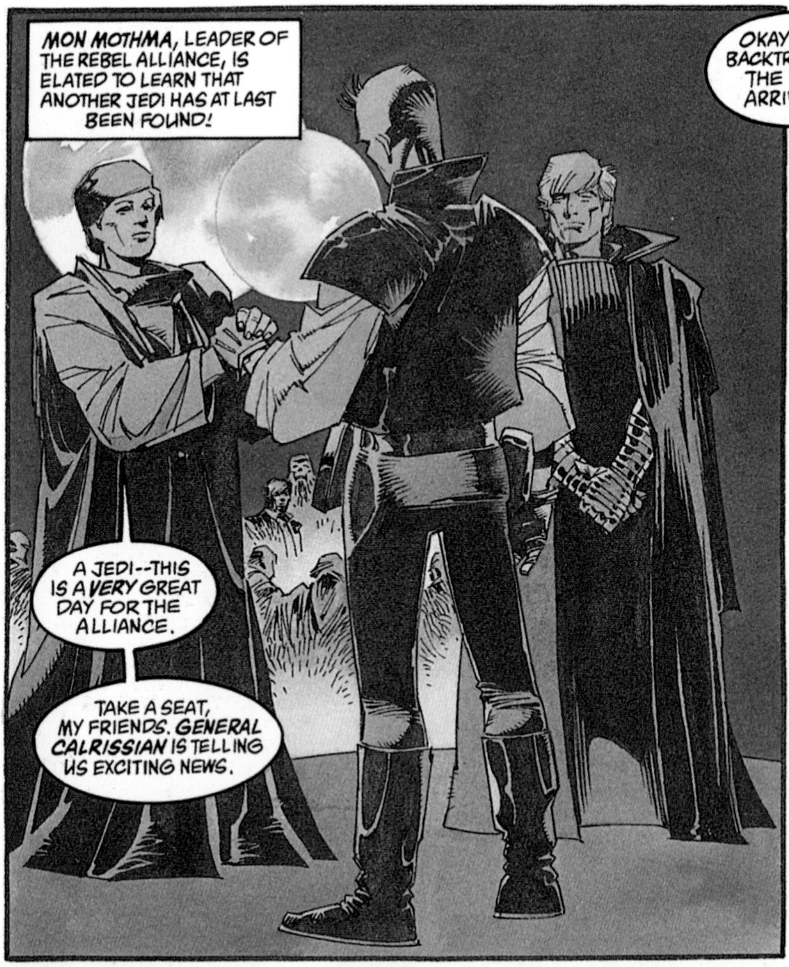
MON MOTHMA, LEADER OF THE REBEL ALLIANCE, IS ELATED TO LEARN THAT ANOTHER JEDI HAS AT LAST BEEN FOUND!
A JEDI--THIS IS A VERY GREAT DAY FOR THE ALLIANCE.
TAKE A SEAT, MY FRIENDS. GENERAL CALRISSIAN IS TELLING US EXCITING NEWS.

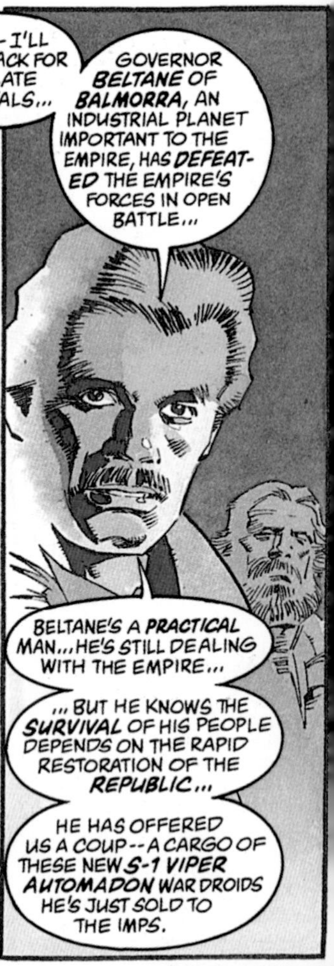
OKAY-- I'LL BACKTRACK FOR THE LATE ARRIVALS...
GOVERNOR BELTANE OF BALMORRA, AN INDUSTRIAL PLANET IMPORTANT TO THE EMPIRE, HAS DEFEATED THE EMPIRE'S FORCES IN OPEN BATTLE...
BELTANE'S A PRACTICAL MAN... HE'S STILL DEALING WITH THE EMPIRE...
... BUT HE KNOWS THE SURVIVAL OF HIS PEOPLE DEPENDS ON THE RAPID RESTORATION OF THE REPUBLIC...
HE HAS OFFERED US A COUP--A CARGO OF THESE NEW S-1 VIPER AUTOMADON WAR DROIDS HE'S JUST SOLD TO THE IMPS.

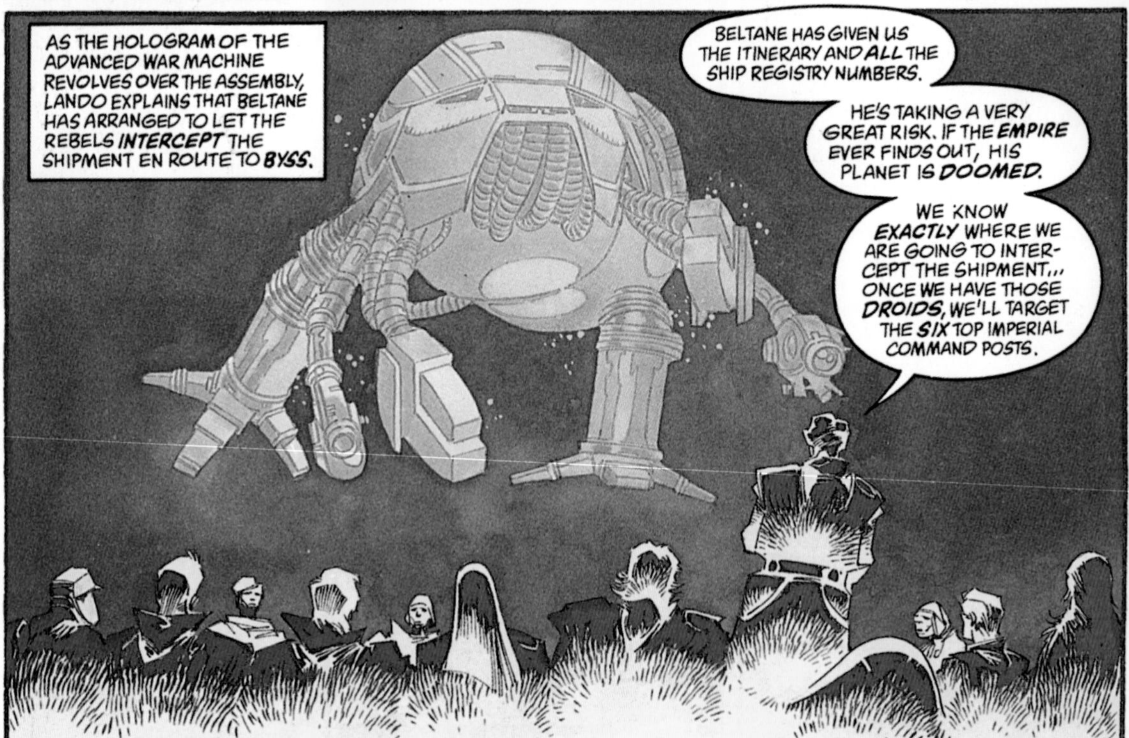
AS THE HOLOGRAM OF THE ADVANCED WAR MACHINE REVOLVES OVER THE ASSEMBLY, LANDO EXPLAINS THAT BELTANE HAS ARRANGED TO LET THE REBELS INTERCEPT THE SHIPMENT EN ROUTE TO BYSS.
BELTANE HAS GIVEN US THE ITINERARY AND ALL THE SHIP REGISTRY NUMBERS.
HE'S TAKING A VERY GREAT RISK. IF THE EMPIRE EVER FINDS OUT, HIS PLANET IS DOOMED.
WE KNOW EXACTLY WHERE WE ARE GOING TO INTERCEPT THE SHIPMENT... ONCE WE HAVE THOSE DROIDS, WE'LL TARGET THE SIX TOP IMPERIAL COMMAND POSTS.

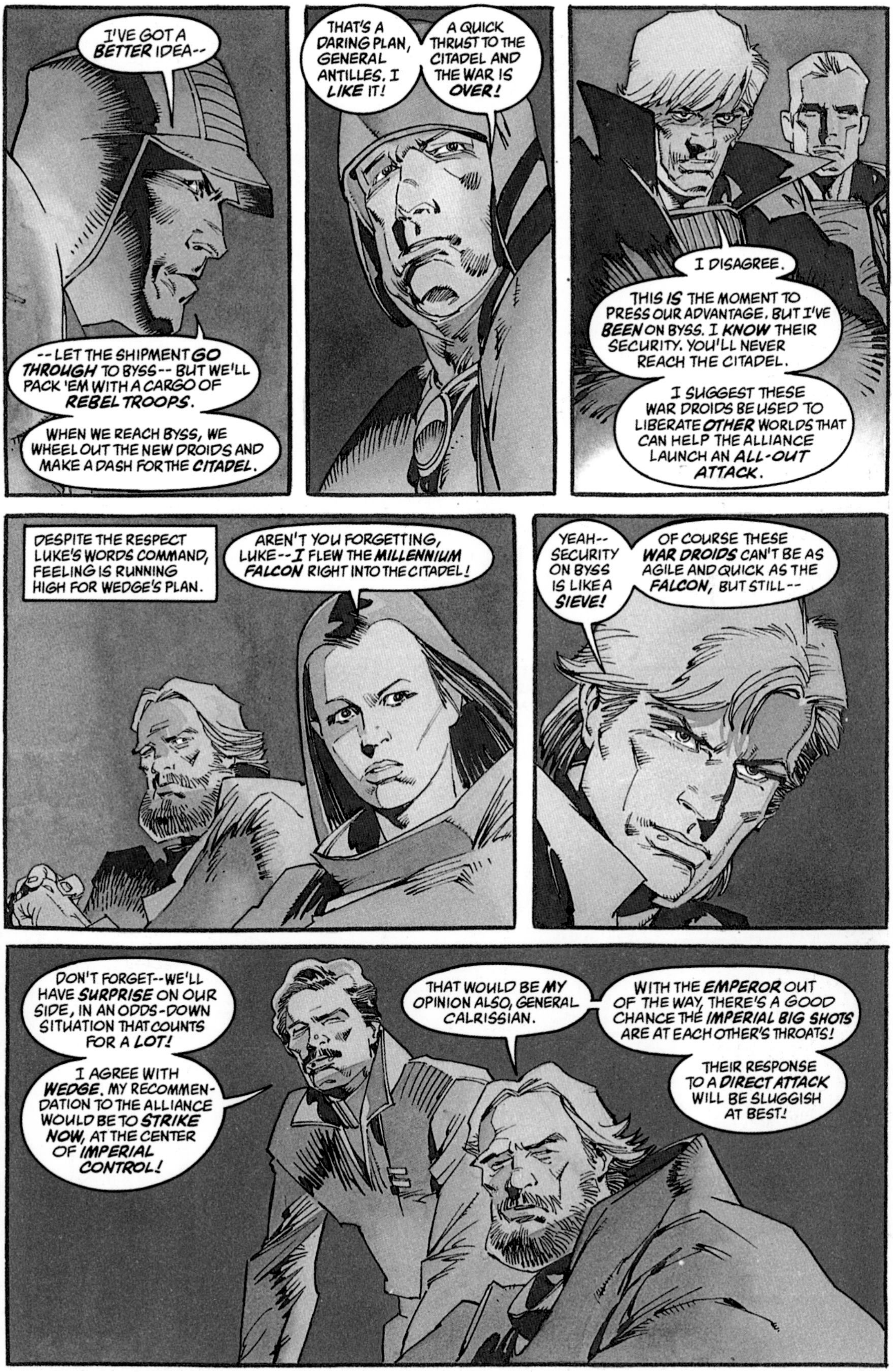
I'VE GOT A BETTER IDEA--
--LET THE SHIPMENT GO THROUGH TO BYSS-- BUT WE'LL PACK 'EM WITH A CARGO OF REBEL TROOPS.
WHEN WE REACH BYSS, WE WHEEL OUT THE NEW DROIDS AND MAKE A DASH FOR THE CITADEL.
THAT'S A DARING PLAN, GENERAL ANTILLES. I LIKE IT!
A QUICK THRUST TO THE CITADEL AND THE WAR IS OVER!
I DISAGREE.
THIS IS THE MOMENT TO PRESS OUR ADVANTAGE. BUT I'VE BEEN ON BYSS. I KNOW THEIR SECURITY. YOU'LL NEVER REACH THE CITADEL.
I SUGGEST THESE WAR DROIDS BE USED TO LIBERATE OTHER WORLDS THAT CAN HELP THE ALLIANCE LAUNCH AN ALL-OUT ATTACK.
DESPITE THE RESPECT LUKE'S WORDS COMMAND, FEELING IS RUNNING HIGH FOR WEDGE'S PLAN.
AREN'T YOU FORGETTING, LUKE--I FLEW THE MILLENNIUM FALCON RIGHT INTO THE CITADEL!
YEAH-- SECURITY ON BYSS IS LIKE A SIEVE!
OF COURSE THESE WAR DROIDS CAN'T BE AS AGILE AND QUICK AS THE FALCON, BUT STILL--
DON'T FORGET--WE'LL HAVE SURPRISE ON OUR SIDE, IN AN ODDS-DOWN SITUATION THAT COUNTS FOR A LOT!
I AGREE WITH WEDGE. MY RECOMMENDATION TO THE ALLIANCE WOULD BE TO STRIKE NOW, AT THE CENTER OF IMPERIAL CONTROL!
THAT WOULD BE MY OPINION ALSO, GENERAL CALRISSIAN.
WITH THE EMPEROR OUT OF THE WAY, THERE'S A GOOD CHANCE THE IMPERIAL BIG SHOTS ARE AT EACH OTHER'S THROATS!
THEIR RESPONSE TO A DIRECT ATTACK WILL BE SLUGGISH AT BEST!

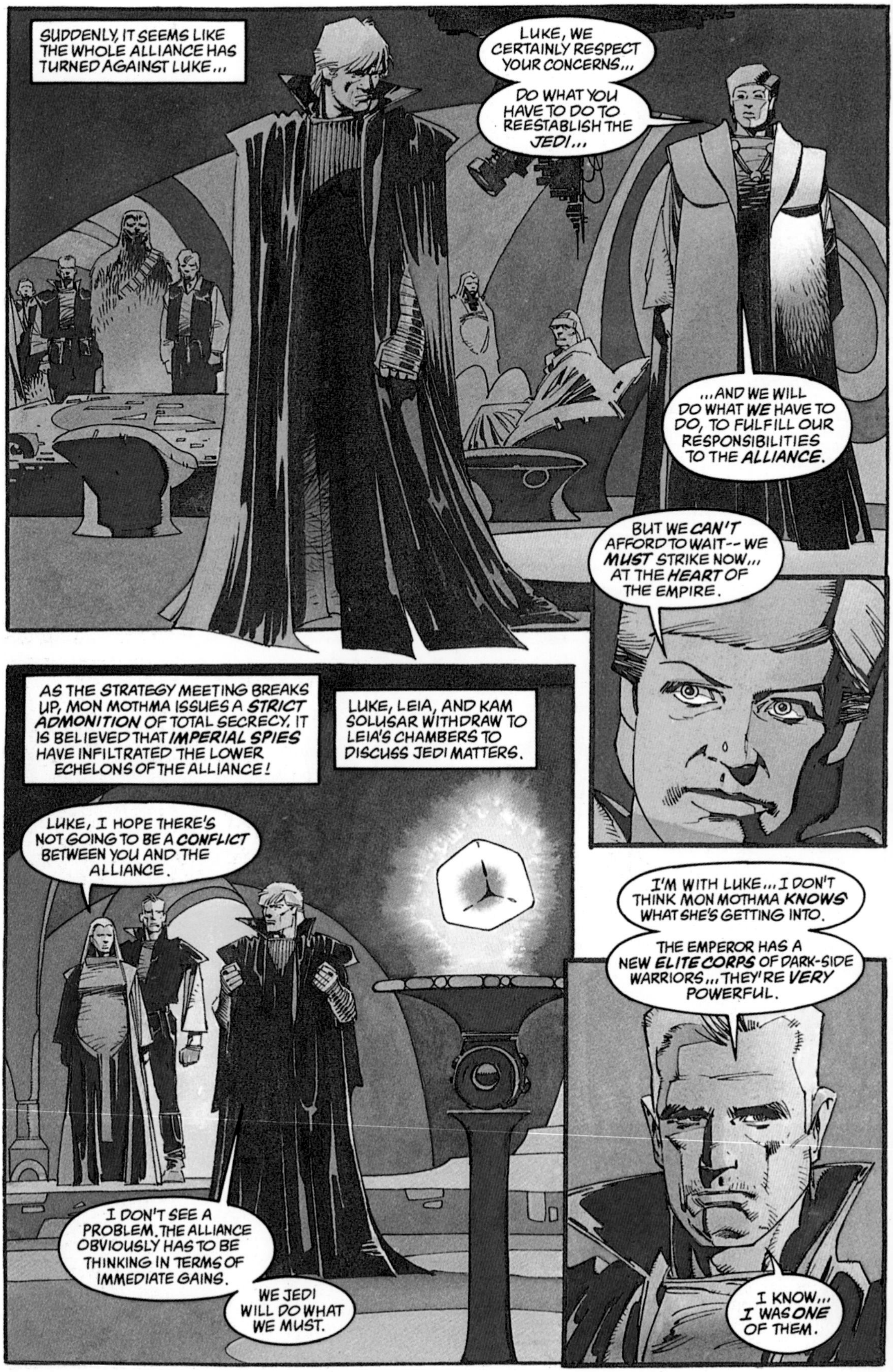
SUDDENLY, IT SEEMS LIKE THE WHOLE ALLIANCE HAS TURNED AGAINST LUKE...
LUKE, WE CERTAINLY RESPECT YOUR CONCERNS...
DO WHAT YOU HAVE TO DO TO REESTABLISH THE JEDI...
...AND WE WILL DO WHAT WE HAVE TO DO, TO FULFILL OUR RESPONSIBILITIES TO THE ALLIANCE.
BUT WE CAN'T AFFORD TO WAIT-- WE MUST STRIKE NOW... AT THE HEART OF THE EMPIRE.
AS THE STRATEGY MEETING BREAKS UP, MON MOTHMA ISSUES A STRICT ADMONITION OF TOTAL SECRECY. IT IS BELIEVED THAT IMPERIAL SPIES HAVE INFILTRATED THE LOWER ECHELONS OF THE ALLIANCE!
LUKE, LEIA, AND KAM SOLUSAR WITHDRAW TO LEIA'S CHAMBERS TO DISCUSS JEDI MATTERS.
LUKE, I HOPE THERE'S NOT GOING TO BE A CONFLICT BETWEEN YOU AND THE ALLIANCE.
I DON'T SEE A PROBLEM. THE ALLIANCE OBVIOUSLY HAS TO BE THINKING IN TERMS OF IMMEDIATE GAINS.
WE JEDI WILL DO WHAT WE MUST.
I'M WITH LUKE... I DON'T THINK MON MOTHMA KNOWS WHAT SHE'S GETTING INTO.
THE EMPEROR HAS A NEW ELITE CORPS OF DARK-SIDE WARRIORS... THEY'RE VERY POWERFUL.
I KNOW... I WAS ONE OF THEM.

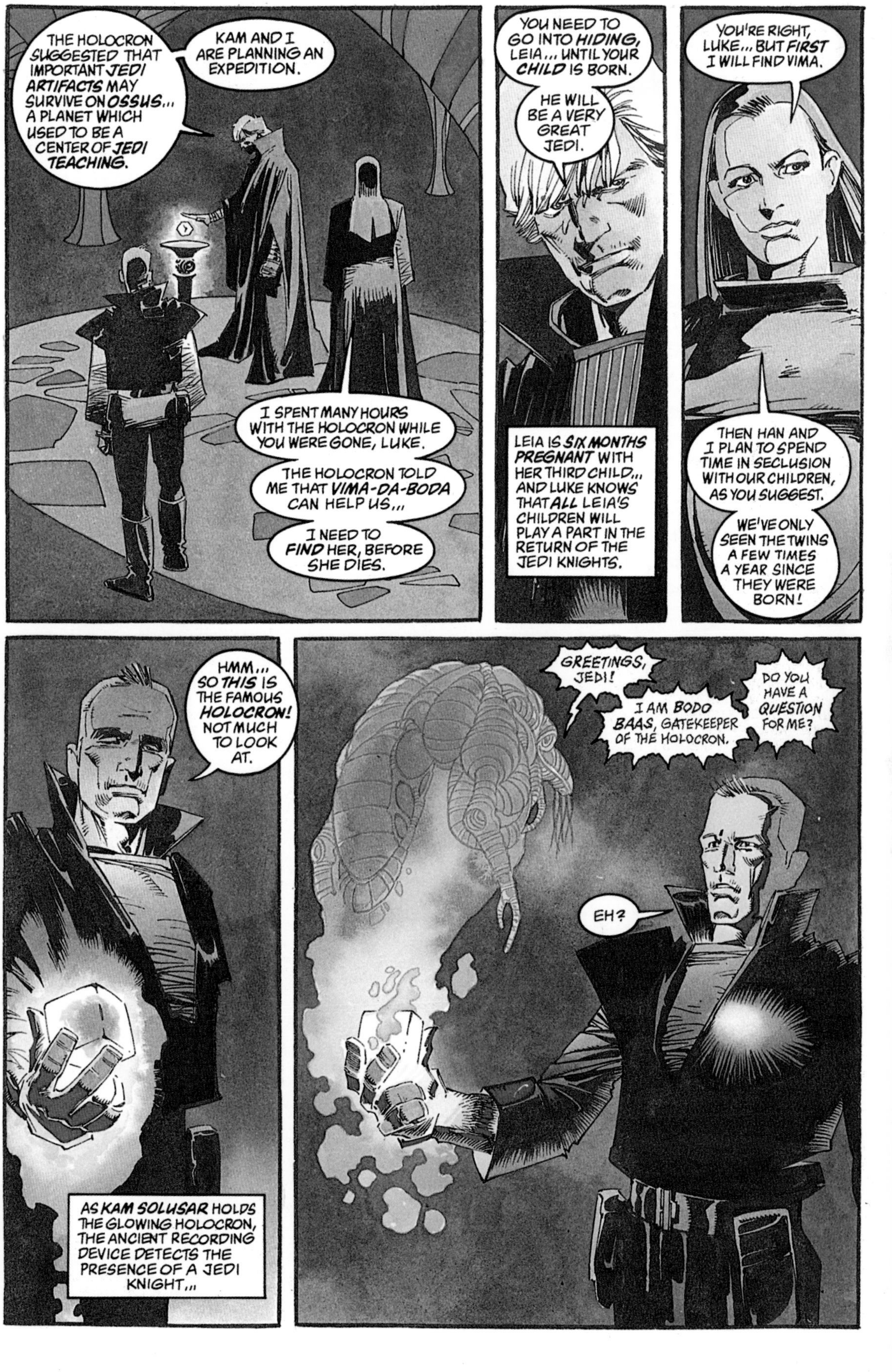
THE HOLOCRON SUGGESTED THAT IMPORTANT JEDI ARTIFACTS MAY SURVIVE ON OSSUS... A PLANET WHICH USED TO BE A CENTER OF JEDI TEACHING.
KAM AND I ARE PLANNING AN EXPEDITION.
I SPENT MANY HOURS WITH THE HOLOCRON WHILE YOU WERE GONE, LUKE.
THE HOLOCRON TOLD ME THAT VIMA-DA-BODA CAN HELP US...
I NEED TO FIND HER, BEFORE SHE DIES.
YOU NEED TO GO INTO HIDING, LEIA... UNTIL YOUR CHILD IS BORN.
HE WILL BE A VERY GREAT JEDI.
LEIA IS SIX MONTHS PREGNANT WITH HER THIRD CHILD... AND LUKE KNOWS THAT ALL LEIA'S CHILDREN WILL PLAY A PART IN THE RETURN OF THE JEDI KNIGHTS.
YOU'RE RIGHT, LUKE... BUT FIRST I WILL FIND VIMA.
THEN HAN AND I PLAN TO SPEND TIME IN SECLUSION WITH OUR CHILDREN, AS YOU SUGGEST.
WE'VE ONLY SEEN THE TWINS A FEW TIMES A YEAR SINCE THEY WERE BORN!
HMM... SO THIS IS THE FAMOUS HOLOCRON! NOT MUCH TO LOOK AT.
AS KAM SOLUSAR HOLDS THE GLOWING HOLOCRON, THE ANCIENT RECORDING DEVICE DETECTS THE PRESENCE OF A JEDI KNIGHT...
GREETINGS, JEDI!
I AM BODO BAAS, GATEKEEPER OF THE HOLOCRON.
DO YOU HAVE A QUESTION FOR ME?
EH?

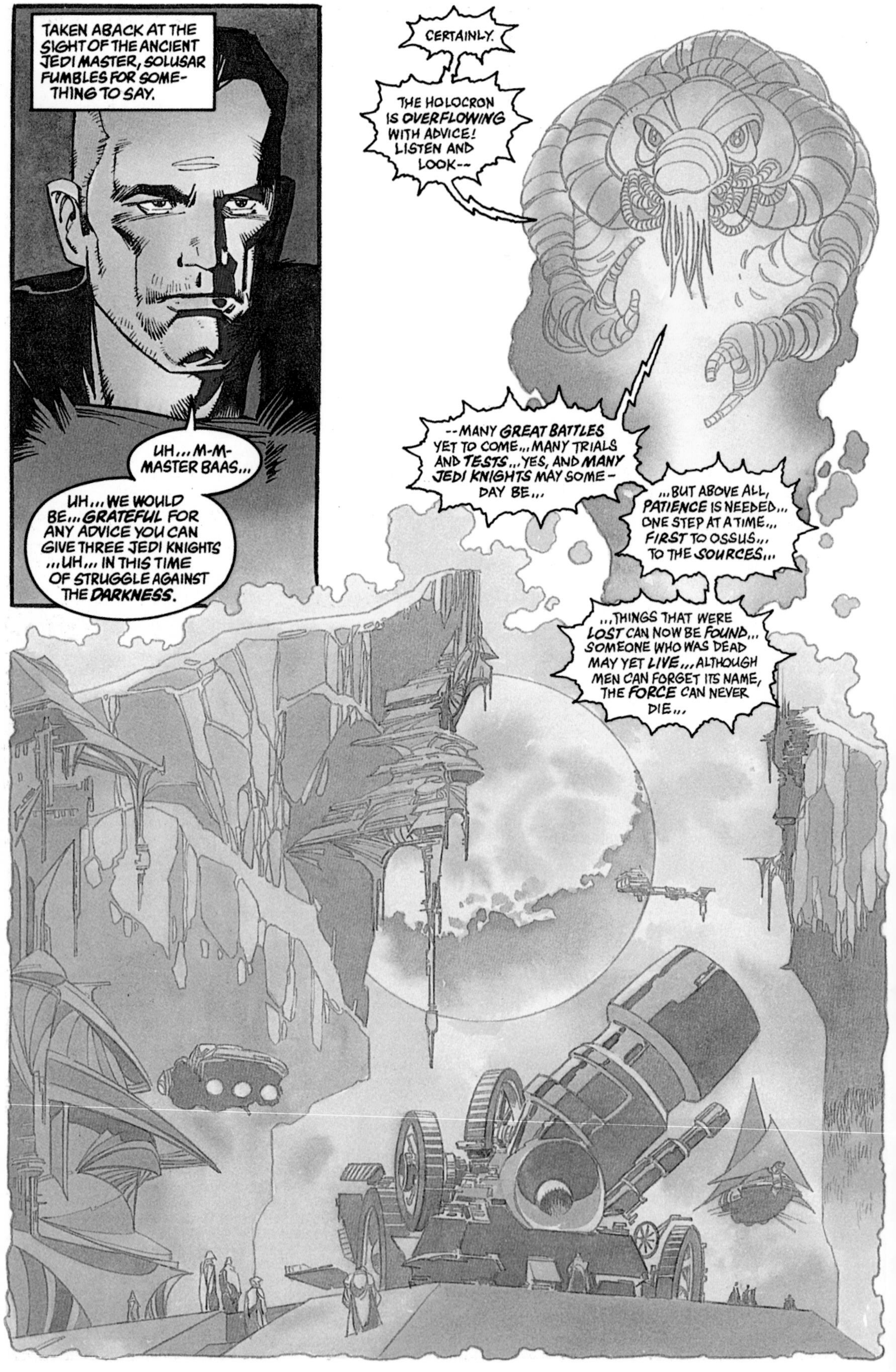
TAKEN ABACK AT THE SIGHT OF THE ANCIENT JEDI MASTER, SOLUSAR FUMBLES FOR SOMETHING TO SAY.
UH... M-M-MASTER BAAS...
UH... WE WOULD BE... GRATEFUL FOR ANY ADVICE YOU CAN GIVE THREE JEDI KNIGHTS ...UH... IN THIS TIME OF STRUGGLE AGAINST THE DARKNESS.
CERTAINLY.
THE HOLOCRON IS OVERFLOWING WITH ADVICE! LISTEN AND LOOK--
--MANY GREAT BATTLES YET TO COME... MANY TRIALS AND TESTS... YES, AND MANY JEDI KNIGHTS MAY SOME-DAY BE...
...BUT ABOVE ALL, PATIENCE IS NEEDED... ONE STEP AT A TIME... FIRST TO OSSUS... TO THE SOURCES...
...THINGS THAT WERE LOST CAN NOW BE FOUND... SOMEONE WHO WAS DEAD MAY YET LIVE... ALTHOUGH MEN CAN FORGET ITS NAME, THE FORCE CAN NEVER DIE...

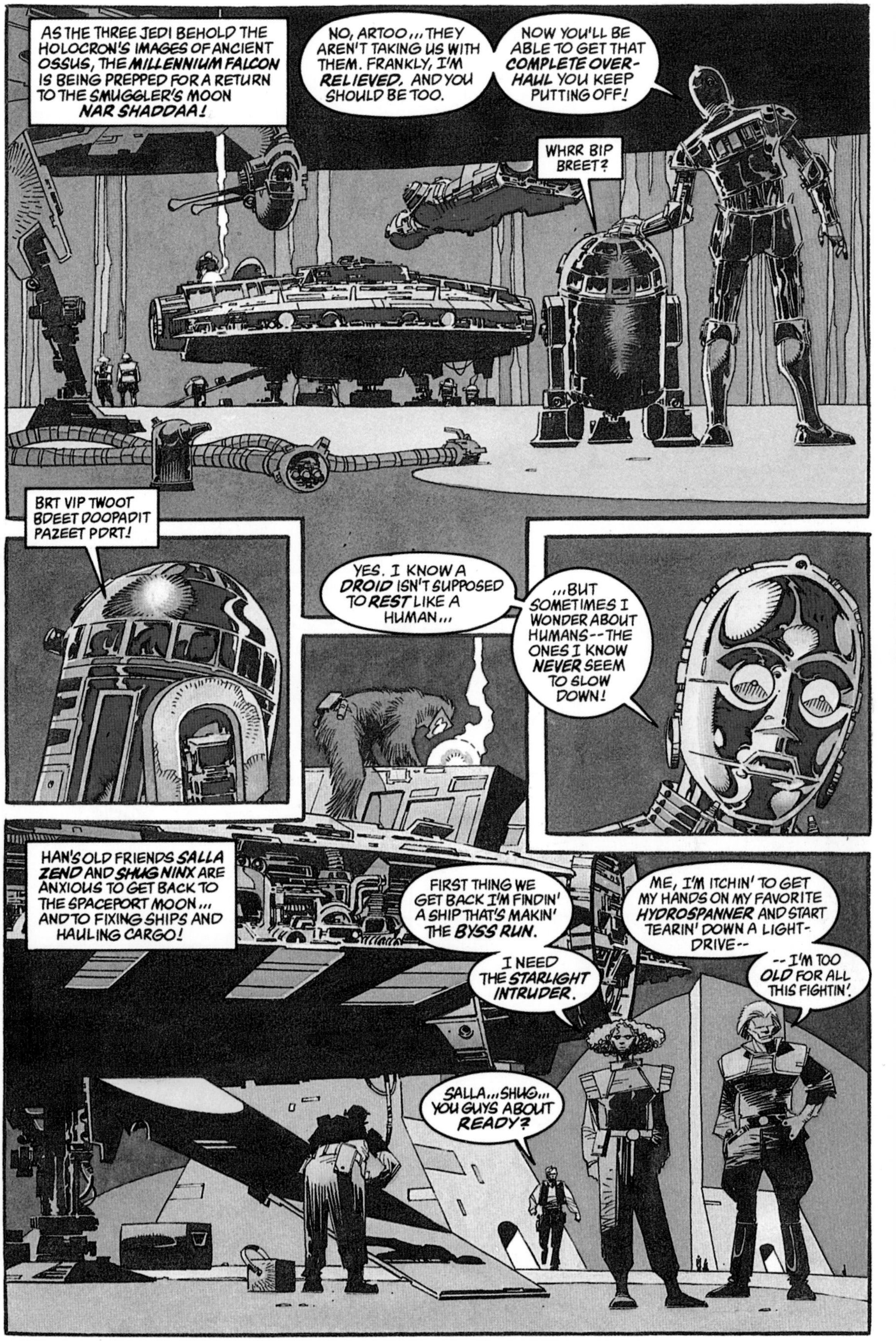

AS THE THREE JEDI BEHOLD THE HOLOCRON'S IMAGES OF ANCIENT OSSUS, THE MILLENNIUM FALCON IS BEING PREPPED FOR A RETURN TO THE SMUGGLER'S MOON NAR SHADDAA!
NO, ARTOO... THEY AREN'T TAKING US WITH THEM. FRANKLY, I'M RELIEVED. AND YOU SHOULD BE TOO.
NOW YOU'LL BE ABLE TO GET THAT COMPLETE OVER-HAUL YOU KEEP PUTTING OFF!
WHRR BIP BREET?
BRT VIP TWOOT BDEET DOOPADIT PAZEET PDRT!
YES. I KNOW A DROID ISN'T SUPPOSED TO REST LIKE A HUMAN...
...BUT SOMETIMES I WONDER ABOUT HUMANS--THE ONES I KNOW NEVER SEEM TO SLOW DOWN!
HAN'S OLD FRIENDS SALLA ZEND AND SHUG NINX ARE ANXIOUS TO GET BACK TO THE SPACEPORT MOON... AND TO FIXING SHIPS AND HAULING CARGO!
FIRST THING WE GET BACK I'M FINDIN' A SHIP THAT'S MAKIN' THE BYSS RUN.
I NEED THE STARLIGHT INTRUDER.
ME, I'M ITCHIN' TO GET MY HANDS ON MY FAVORITE HYDROSPANNER AND START TEARIN' DOWN A LIGHT-DRIVE--
--I'M TOO OLD FOR ALL THIS FIGHTIN'.
SALLA... SHUG... YOU GUYS ABOUT READY?

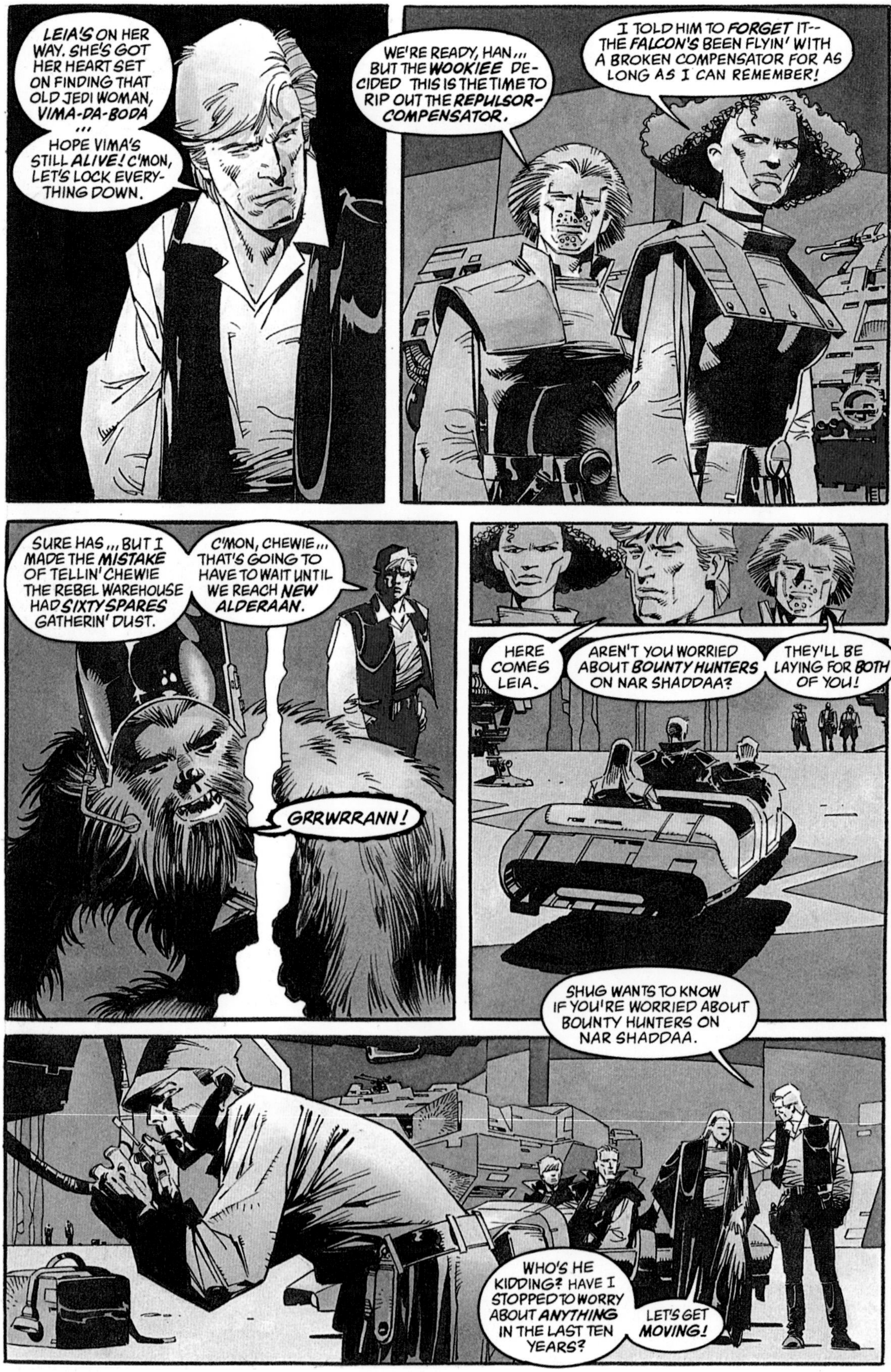
LEIA'S ON HER WAY. SHE'S GOT HER HEART SET ON FINDING THAT OLD JEDI WOMAN, VIMA-DA-BODA ...
HOPE VIMA'S STILL ALIVE! C'MON, LET'S LOCK EVERYTHING DOWN.
WE'RE READY, HAN... BUT THE WOOKIEE DECIDED THIS IS THE TIME TO RIP OUT THE REPULSOR-COMPENSATOR.
I TOLD HIM TO FORGET IT-- THE FALCON'S BEEN FLYIN' WITH A BROKEN COMPENSATOR FOR AS LONG AS I CAN REMEMBER!
SURE HAS... BUT I MADE THE MISTAKE OF TELLIN' CHEWIE THE REBEL WAREHOUSE HAD SIXTY SPARES GATHERIN' DUST.
C'MON, CHEWIE... THAT'S GOING TO HAVE TO WAIT UNTIL WE REACH NEW ALDERAAN.
GRRWRRANN!
HERE COMES LEIA.
AREN'T YOU WORRIED ABOUT BOUNTY HUNTERS ON NAR SHADDAA?
THEY'LL BE LAYING FOR BOTH OF YOU!
SHUG WANTS TO KNOW IF YOU'RE WORRIED ABOUT BOUNTY HUNTERS ON NAR SHADDAA.
WHO'S HE KIDDING? HAVE I STOPPED TO WORRY ABOUT ANYTHING IN THE LAST TEN YEARS?
LET'S GET MOVING!

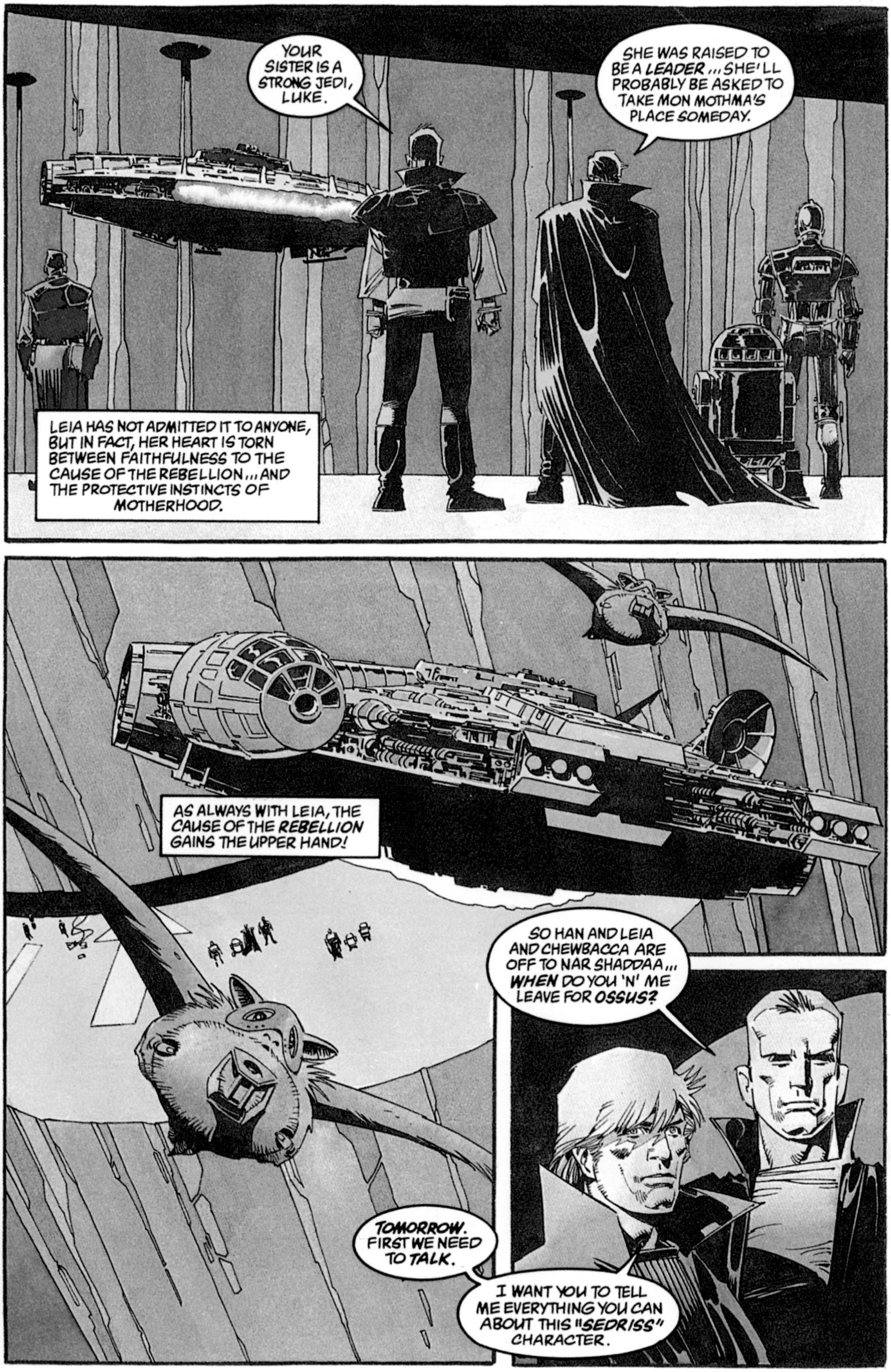
YOUR SISTER IS A STRONG JEDI, LUKE.
SHE WAS RAISED TO BE A LEADER... SHE'LL PROBABLY BE ASKED TO TAKE MON MOTHMA'S PLACE SOMEDAY.
LEIA HAS NOT ADMITTED IT TO ANYONE, BUT IN FACT, HER HEART IS TORN BETWEEN FAITHFULNESS TO THE CAUSE OF THE REBELLION... AND THE PROTECTIVE INSTINCTS OF MOTHERHOOD.
AS ALWAYS WITH LEIA, THE CAUSE OF THE REBELLION GAINS THE UPPER HAND!
SO HAN AND LEIA AND CHEWBACCA ARE OFF TO NAR SHADDAA... WHEN DO YOU 'N' ME LEAVE FOR OSSUS?
TOMORROW. FIRST WE NEED TO TALK.
I WANT YOU TO TELL ME EVERYTHING YOU CAN ABOUT THIS "SEDRISS" CHARACTER.

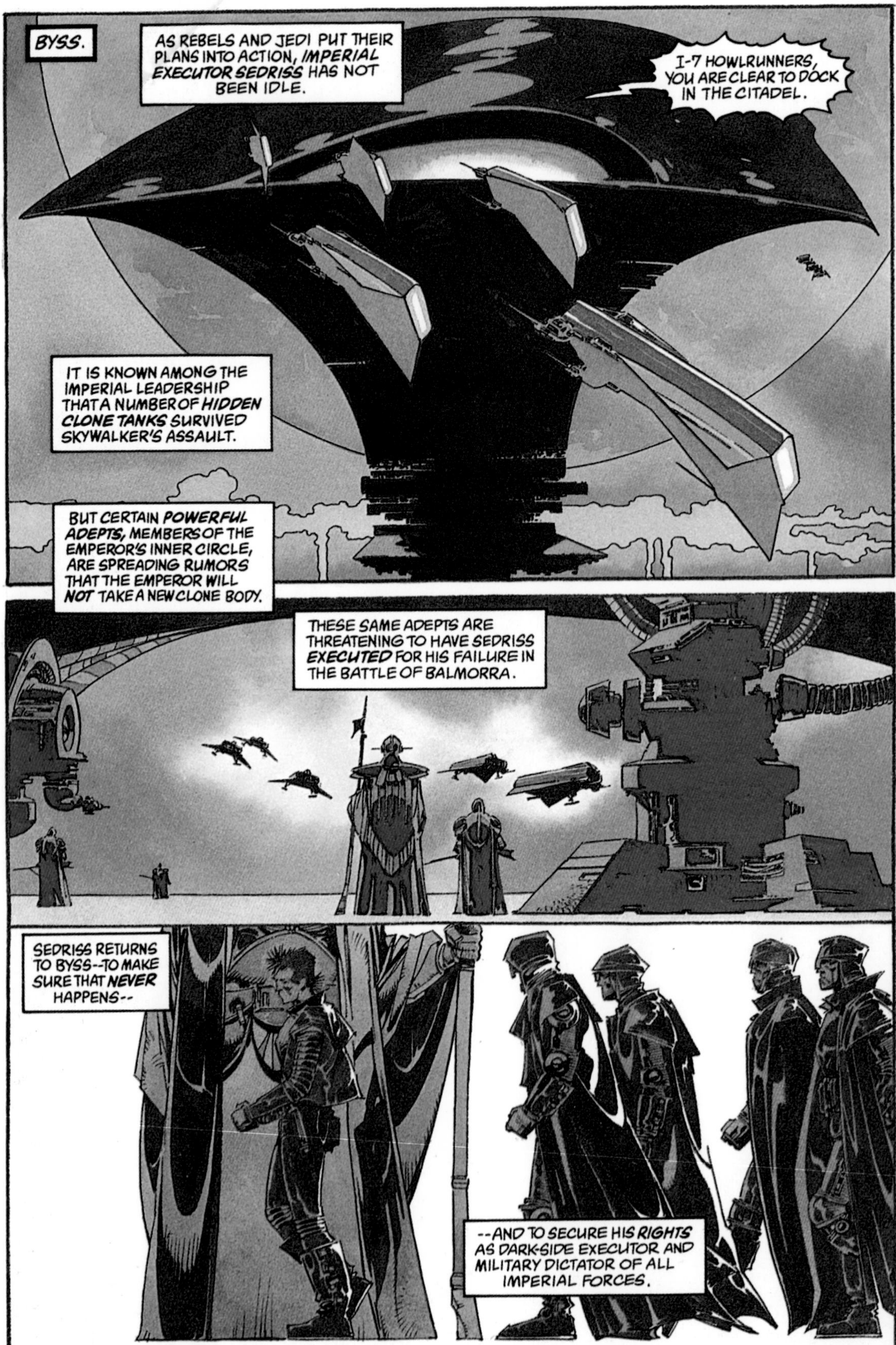
BYSS.
AS REBELS AND JEDI PUT THEIR PLANS INTO ACTION, IMPERIAL EXECUTOR SEDRISS HAS NOT BEEN IDLE.
I-7 HOWLRUNNERS, YOU ARE CLEAR TO DOCK IN THE CITADEL.
IT IS KNOWN AMONG THE IMPERIAL LEADERSHIP THAT A NUMBER OF HIDDEN CLONE TANKS SURVIVED SKYWALKER'S ASSAULT.
BUT CERTAIN POWERFUL ADEPTS, MEMBERS OF THE EMPEROR'S INNER CIRCLE, ARE SPREADING RUMORS THAT THE EMPEROR WILL NOT TAKE A NEW CLONE BODY.
THESE SAME ADEPTS ARE THREATENING TO HAVE SEDRISS EXECUTED FOR HIS FAILURE IN THE BATTLE OF BALMORRA.
SEDRISS RETURNS TO BYSS--TO MAKE SURE THAT NEVER HAPPENS--
--AND TO SECURE HIS RIGHTS AS DARK-SIDE EXECUTOR AND MILITARY DICTATOR OF ALL IMPERIAL FORCES.

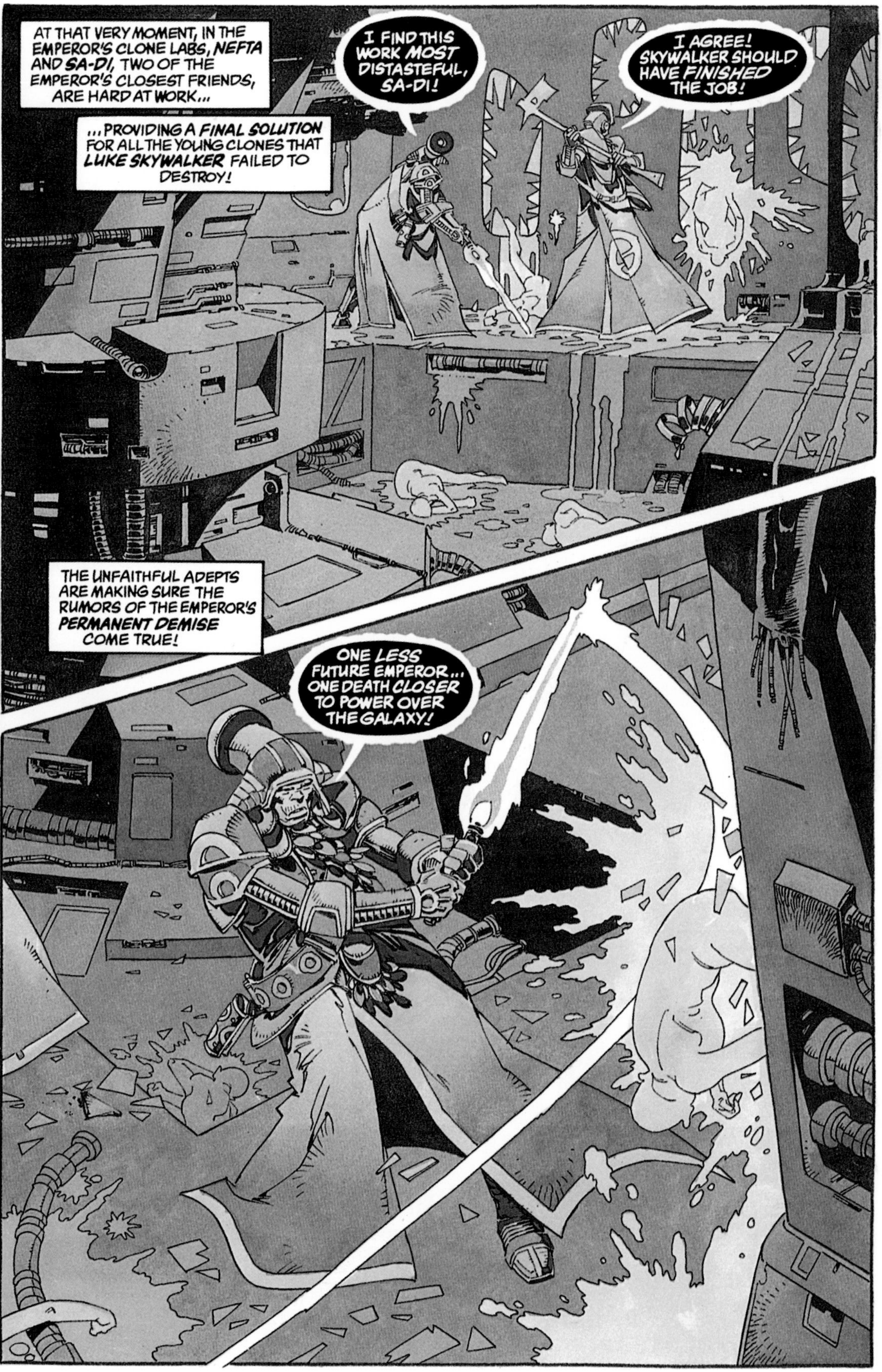
AT THAT VERY MOMENT, IN THE EMPEROR'S CLONE LABS, NEFTA AND SA-DI, TWO OF THE EMPEROR'S CLOSEST FRIENDS, ARE HARD AT WORK...
I FIND THIS WORK MOST DISTASTEFUL, SA-DI!
I AGREE! SKYWALKER SHOULD HAVE FINISHED THE JOB!
...PROVIDING A FINAL SOLUTION FOR ALL THE YOUNG CLONES THAT LUKE SKYWALKER FAILED TO DESTROY!
THE UNFAITHFUL ADEPTS ARE MAKING SURE THE RUMORS OF THE EMPEROR'S PERMANENT DEMISE COME TRUE!
ONE LESS FUTURE EMPEROR... ONE DEATH CLOSER TO POWER OVER THE GALAXY!

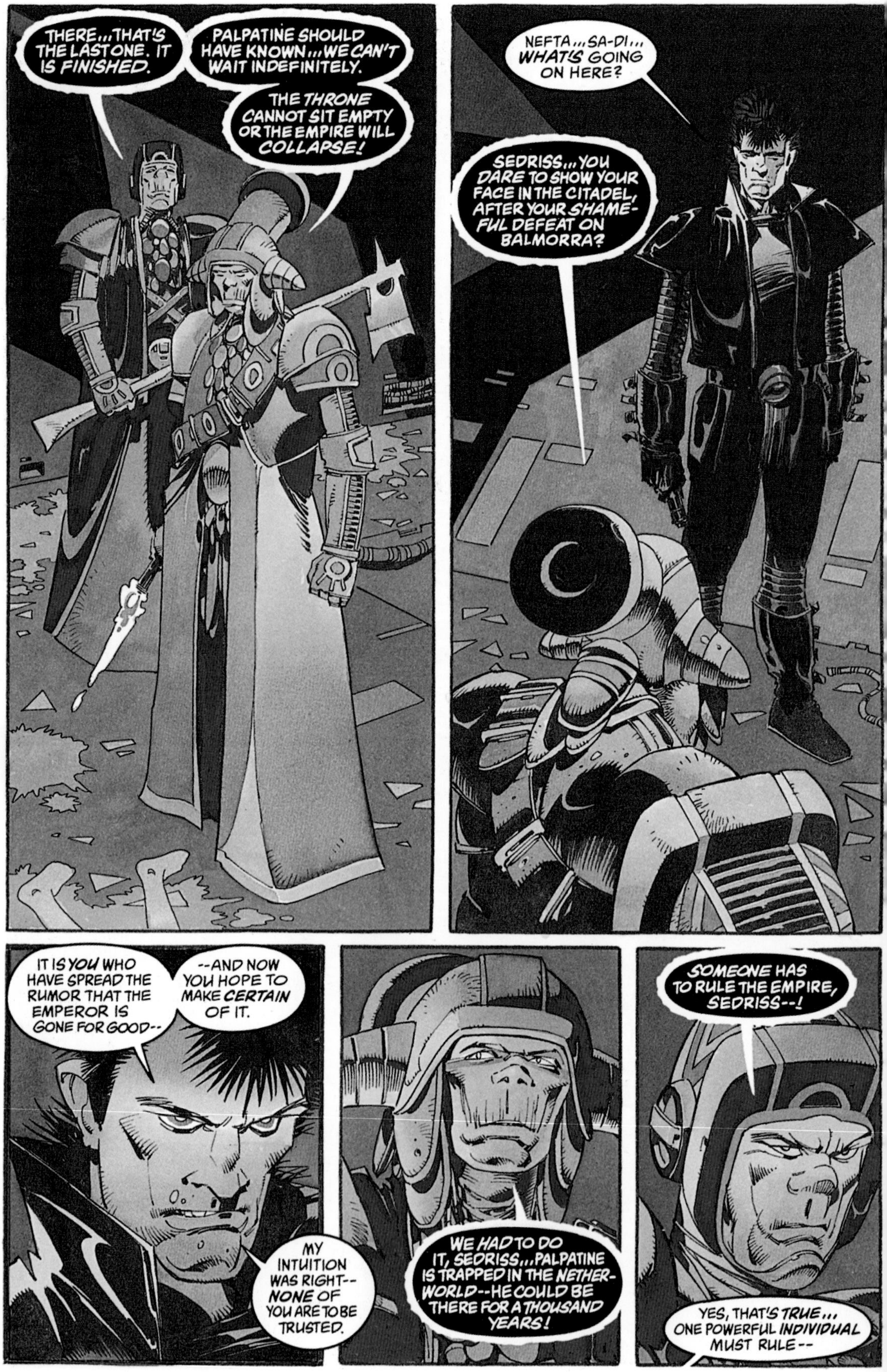

THERE... THAT'S THE LAST ONE. IT IS FINISHED.
PALPATINE SHOULD HAVE KNOWN... WE CAN'T WAIT INDEFINITELY.
THE THRONE CANNOT SIT EMPTY OR THE EMPIRE WILL COLLAPSE!
NEFTA... SA-DI... WHAT'S GOING ON HERE?
SEDRISS... YOU DARE TO SHOW YOUR FACE IN THE CITADEL, AFTER YOUR SHAME-FUL DEFEAT ON BALMORRA?
IT IS YOU WHO HAVE SPREAD THE RUMOR THAT THE EMPEROR IS GONE FOR GOOD--
--AND NOW YOU HOPE TO MAKE CERTAIN OF IT.
MY INTUITION WAS RIGHT-- NONE OF YOU ARE TO BE TRUSTED.
WE HAD TO DO IT, SEDRISS... PALPATINE IS TRAPPED IN THE NETHER-WORLD--HE COULD BE THERE FOR A THOUSAND YEARS!
SOMEONE HAS TO RULE THE EMPIRE, SEDRISS--!
YES, THAT'S TRUE... ONE POWERFUL INDIVIDUAL MUST RULE--

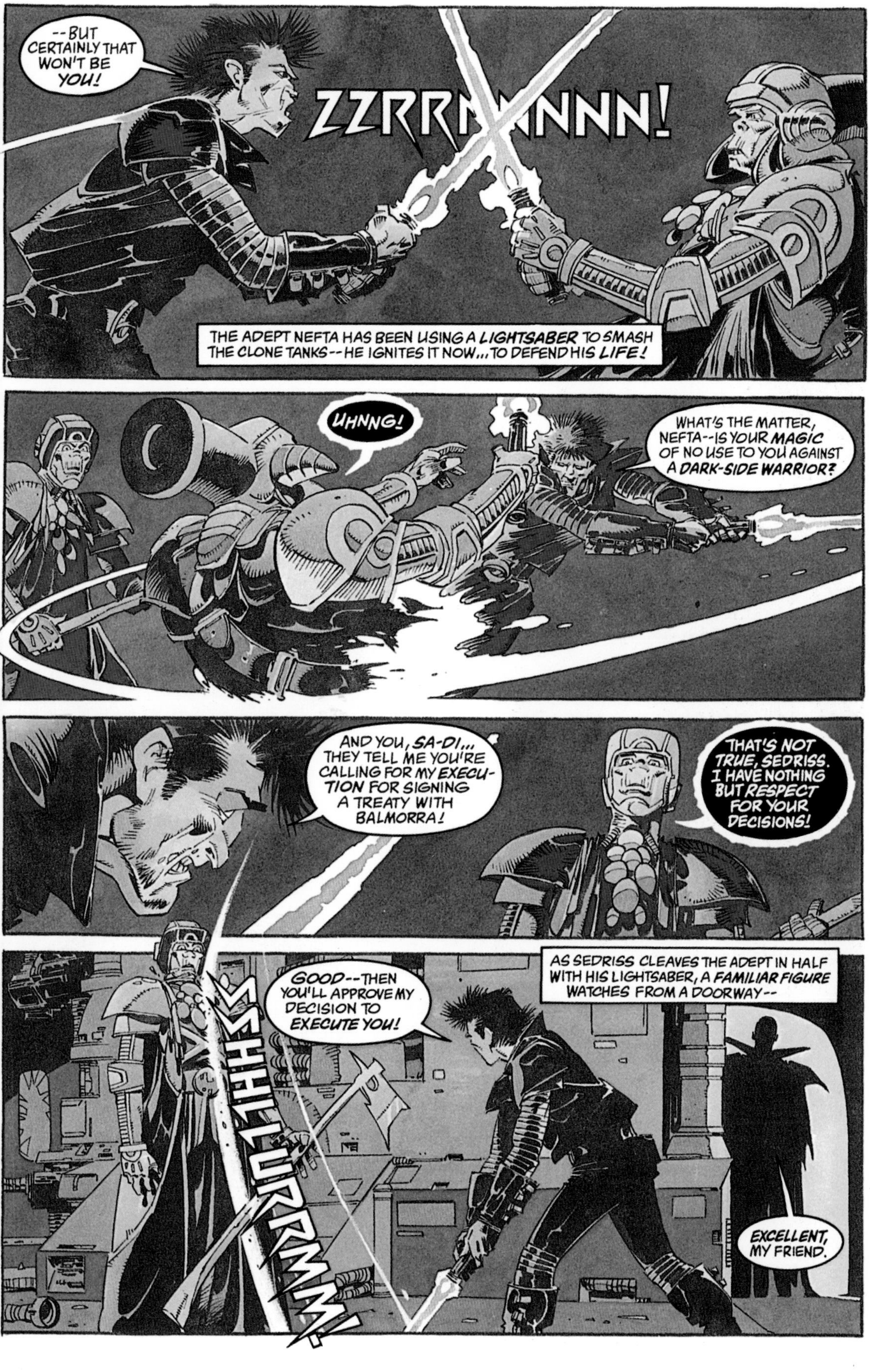
--BUT CERTAINLY THAT WON'T BE YOU!
ZZRRNNNNN!
THE ADEPT NEFTA HAS BEEN USING A LIGHTSABER TO SMASH THE CLONE TANKS--HE IGNITES IT NOW... TO DEFEND HIS LIFE!
UHNNG!
WHAT'S THE MATTER, NEFTA--IS YOUR MAGIC OF NO USE TO YOU AGAINST A DARK-SIDE WARRIOR?
AND YOU, SA-DI... THEY TELL ME YOU'RE CALLING FOR MY EXECUTION FOR SIGNING A TREATY WITH BALMORRA!
THAT'S NOT TRUE, SEDRISS. I HAVE NOTHING BUT RESPECT FOR YOUR DECISIONS!
AS SEDRISS CLEAVES THE ADEPT IN HALF WITH HIS LIGHTSABER, A FAMILIAR FIGURE WATCHES FROM A DOORWAY--
GOOD--THEN YOU'LL APPROVE MY DECISION TO EXECUTE YOU!
SHHLURRMM!
EXCELLENT, MY FRIEND.

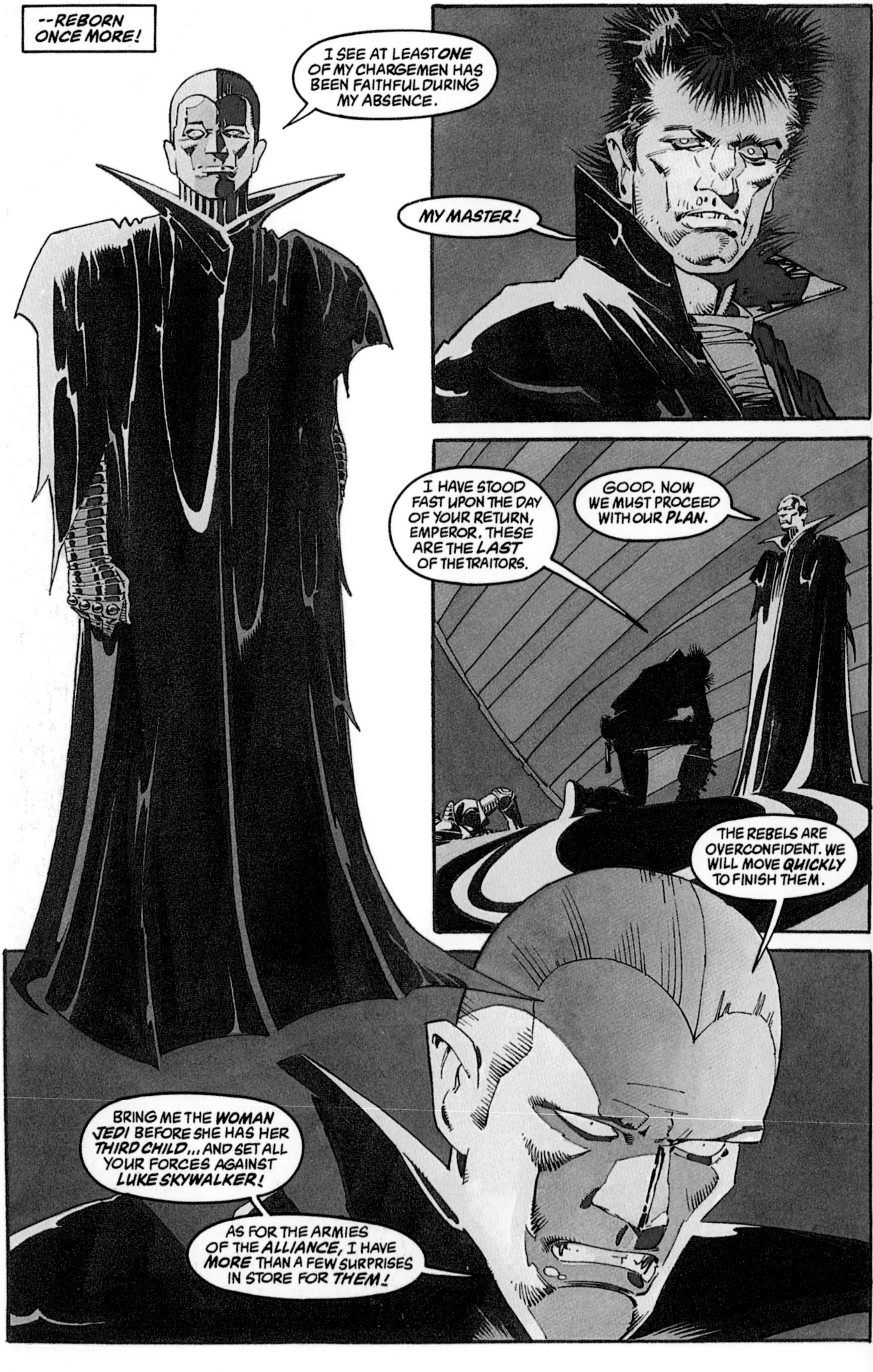
--REBORN ONCE MORE!
I SEE AT LEAST ONE OF MY CHARGEMEN HAS BEEN FAITHFUL DURING MY ABSENCE.
MY MASTER!
I HAVE STOOD FAST UPON THE DAY OF YOUR RETURN, EMPEROR. THESE ARE THE LAST OF THE TRAITORS.
GOOD. NOW WE MUST PROCEED WITH OUR PLAN.
THE REBELS ARE OVERCONFIDENT. WE WILL MOVE QUICKLY TO FINISH THEM.
BRING ME THE WOMAN JEDI BEFORE SHE HAS HER THIRD CHILD... AND SET ALL YOUR FORCES AGAINST LUKE SKYWALKER!
AS FOR THE ARMIES OF THE ALLIANCE, I HAVE MORE THAN A FEW SURPRISES IN STORE FOR THEM!

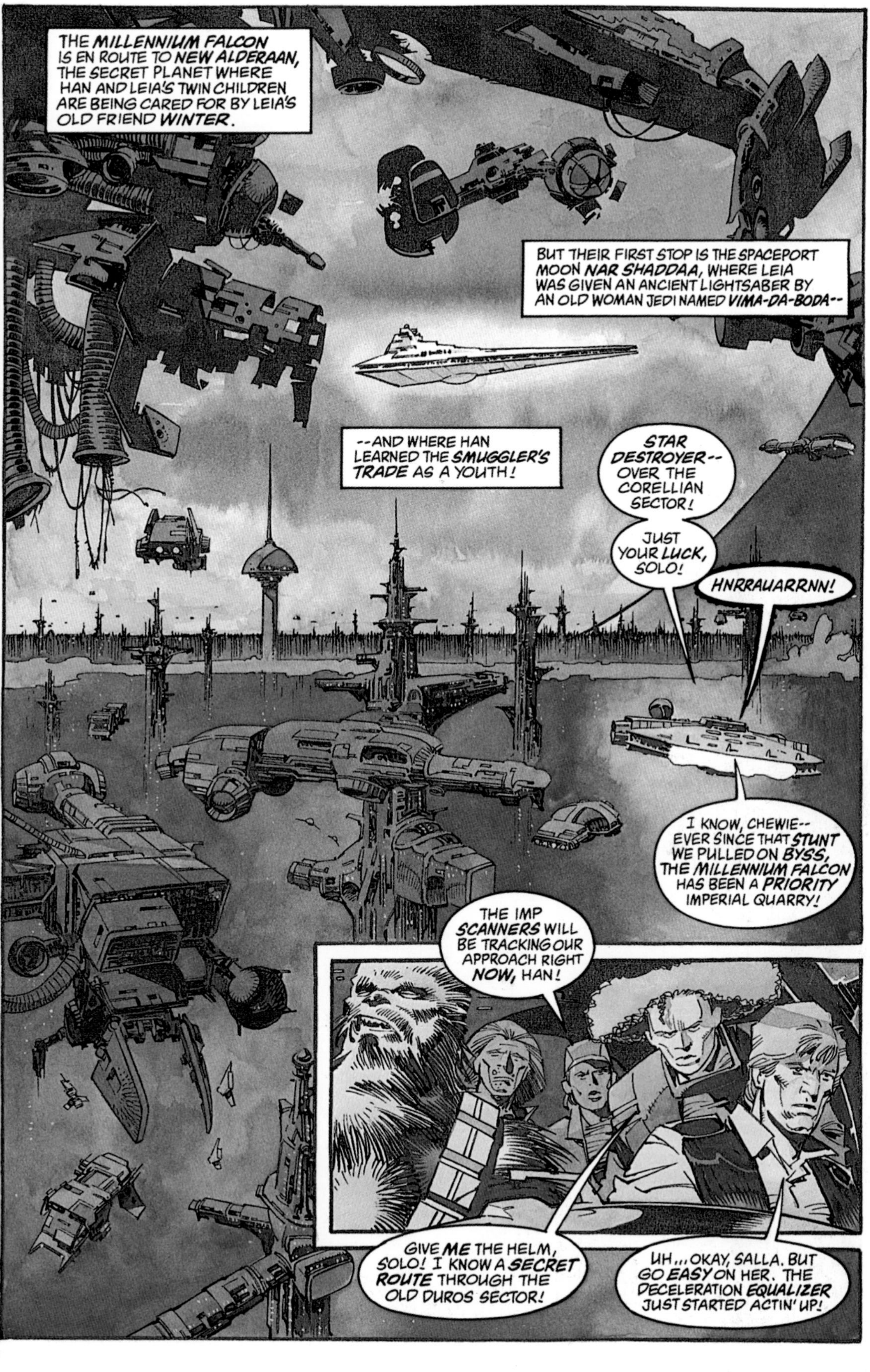
THE MILLENNIUM FALCON IS EN ROUTE TO NEW ALDERAAN, THE SECRET PLANET WHERE HAN AND LEIA'S TWIN CHILDREN ARE BEING CARED FOR BY LEIA'S OLD FRIEND WINTER.
BUT THEIR FIRST STOP IS THE SPACEPORT MOON NAR SHADDAA, WHERE LEIA WAS GIVEN AN ANCIENT LIGHTSABER BY AN OLD WOMAN JEDI NAMED VIMA-DA-BODA--
--AND WHERE HAN LEARNED THE SMUGGLER'S TRADE AS A YOUTH!
STAR DESTROYER-- OVER THE CORELLIAN SECTOR!
JUST YOUR LUCK, SOLO!
HNRRAUARRNN!
I KNOW, CHEWIE-- EVER SINCE THAT STUNT WE PULLED ON BYSS, THE MILLENNIUM FALCON HAS BEEN A PRIORITY IMPERIAL QUARRY!
THE IMP SCANNERS WILL BE TRACKING OUR APPROACH RIGHT NOW, HAN!
GIVE ME THE HELM, SOLO! I KNOW A SECRET ROUTE THROUGH THE OLD DUROS SECTOR!
UH... OKAY, SALLA. BUT GO EASY ON HER. THE DECELERATION EQUALIZER JUST STARTED ACTIN' UP!

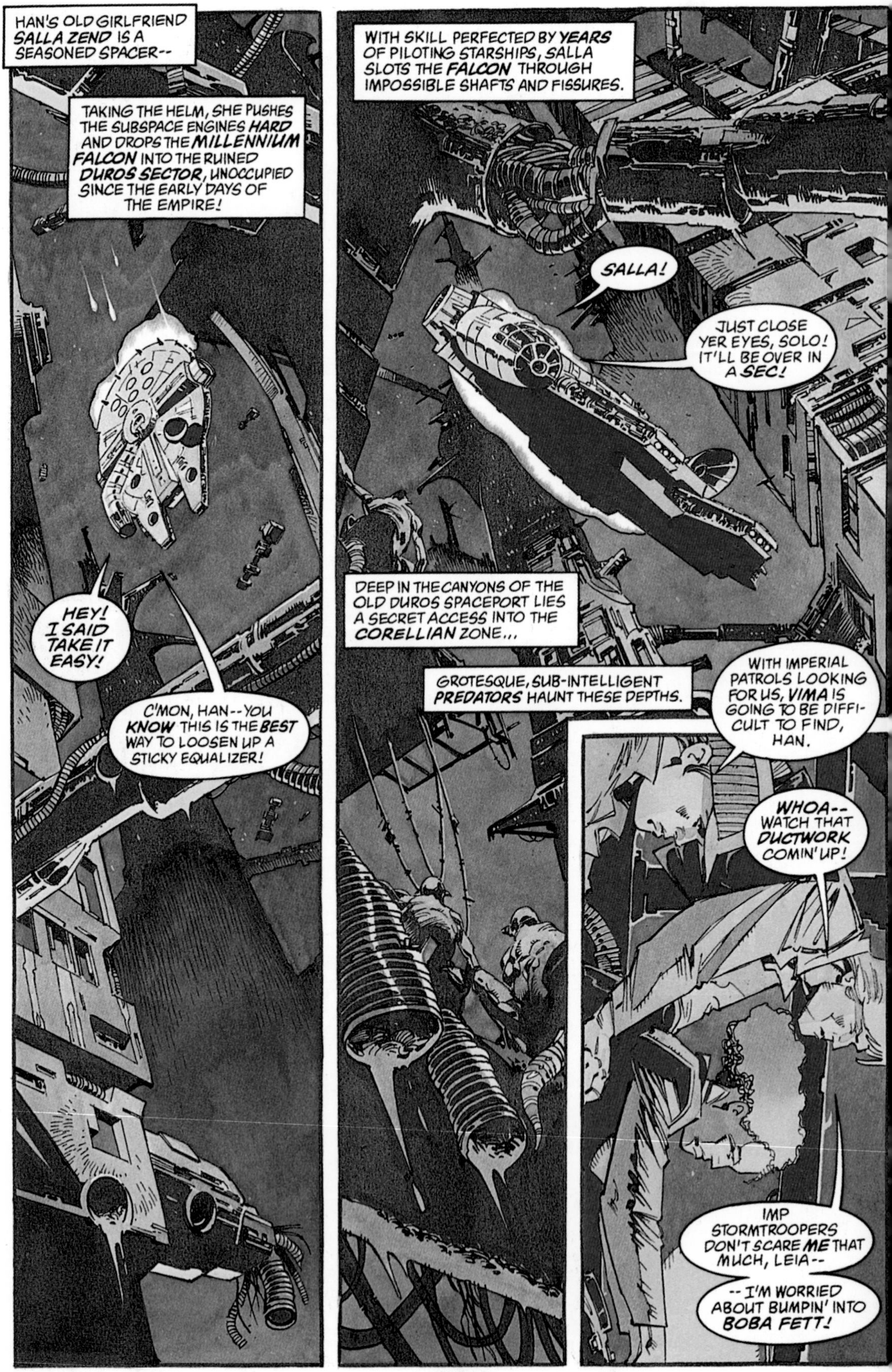
HAN'S OLD GIRLFRIEND SALLA ZEND IS A SEASONED SPACER--
TAKING THE HELM, SHE PUSHES THE SUBSPACE ENGINES HARD AND DROPS THE MILLENNIUM FALCON INTO THE RUINED DUROS SECTOR, UNOCCUPIED SINCE THE EARLY DAYS OF THE EMPIRE!
HEY! I SAID TAKE IT EASY!
C'MON, HAN--YOU KNOW THIS IS THE BEST WAY TO LOOSEN UP A STICKY EQUALIZER!
WITH SKILL PERFECTED BY YEARS OF PILOTING STARSHIPS, SALLA SLOTS THE FALCON THROUGH IMPOSSIBLE SHAFTS AND FISSURES.
SALLA!
JUST CLOSE YER EYES, SOLO! IT'LL BE OVER IN A SEC!
DEEP IN THE CANYONS OF THE OLD DUROS SPACEPORT LIES A SECRET ACCESS INTO THE CORELLIAN ZONE...
GROTESQUE, SUB-INTELLIGENT PREDATORS HAUNT THESE DEPTHS.
WITH IMPERIAL PATROLS LOOKING FOR US, VIMA IS GOING TO BE DIFFICULT TO FIND, HAN.
WHOA-- WATCH THAT DUCTWORK COMIN' UP!
IMP STORMTROOPERS DON'T SCARE ME THAT MUCH, LEIA--
--I'M WORRIED ABOUT BUMPIN' INTO BOBA FETT!

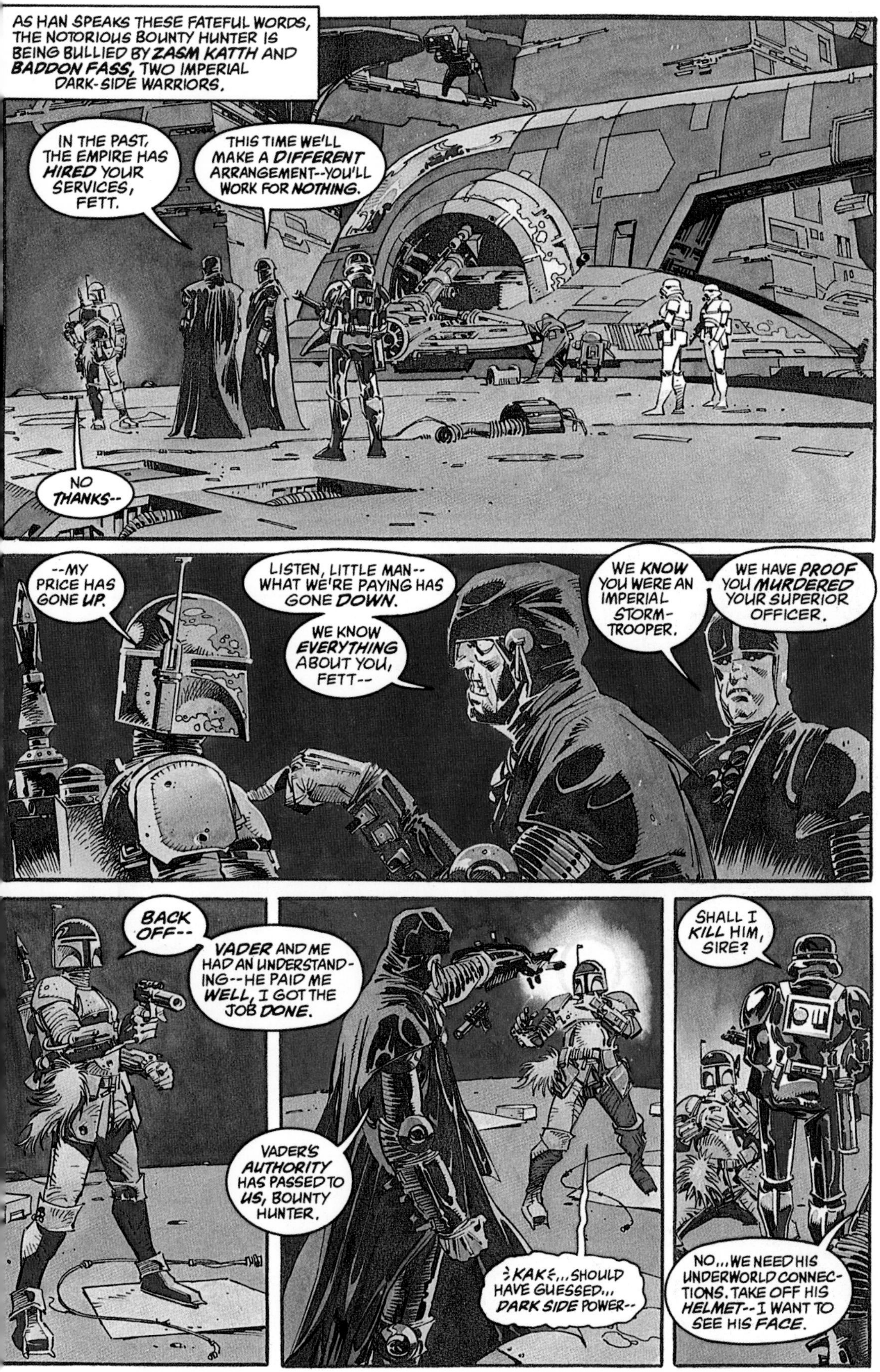

AS HAN SPEAKS THESE FATEFUL WORDS, THE NOTORIOUS BOUNTY HUNTER IS BEING BULLIED BY ZASM KATTH AND BADDON FASS, TWO IMPERIAL DARK-SIDE WARRIORS.
IN THE PAST, THE EMPIRE HAS HIRED YOUR SERVICES, FETT.
THIS TIME WE'LL MAKE A DIFFERENT ARRANGEMENT--YOU'LL WORK FOR NOTHING.
NO THANKS--
--MY PRICE HAS GONE UP.
LISTEN, LITTLE MAN--WHAT WE'RE PAYING HAS GONE DOWN.
WE KNOW EVERYTHING ABOUT YOU, FETT--
WE KNOW YOU WERE AN IMPERIAL STORM-TROOPER.
WE HAVE PROOF YOU MURDERED YOUR SUPERIOR OFFICER.
BACK OFF--
VADER AND ME HAD AN UNDERSTANDING--HE PAID ME WELL, I GOT THE JOB DONE.
VADER'S AUTHORITY HAS PASSED TO US, BOUNTY HUNTER.
KAK... SHOULD HAVE GUESSED... DARK SIDE POWER--
SHALL I KILL HIM, SIRE?
NO... WE NEED HIS UNDERWORLD CONNECTIONS. TAKE OFF HIS HELMET--I WANT TO SEE HIS FACE.

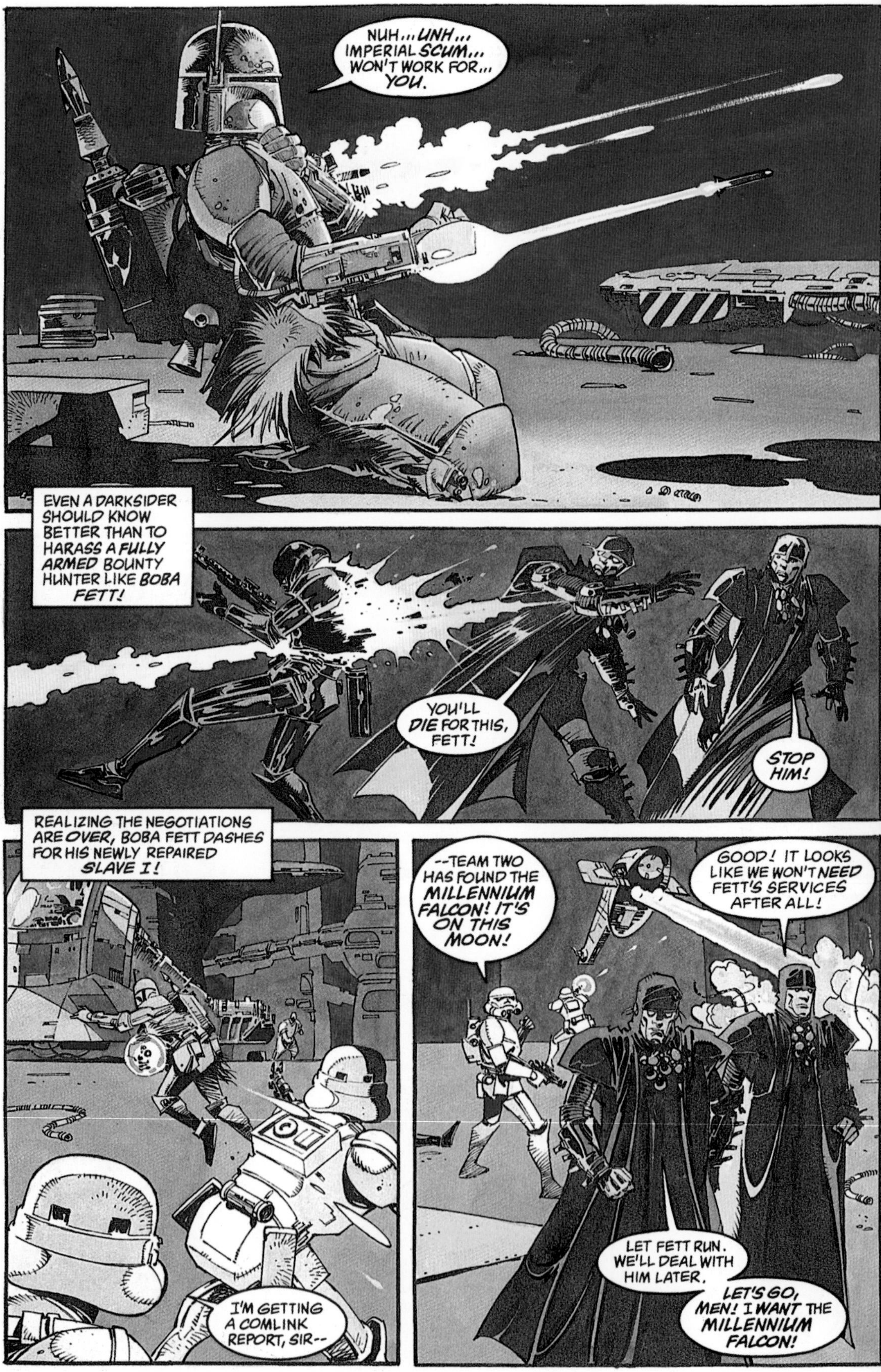
NUH... UNH... IMPERIAL SCUM... WON'T WORK FOR... YOU.
EVEN A DARKSIDER SHOULD KNOW BETTER THAN TO HARASS A FULLY ARMED BOUNTY HUNTER LIKE BOBA FETT!
YOU'LL DIE FOR THIS, FETT!
STOP HIM!
REALIZING THE NEGOTIATIONS ARE OVER, BOBA FETT DASHES FOR HIS NEWLY REPAIRED SLAVE I!
I'M GETTING A COMLINK REPORT, SIR--
--TEAM TWO HAS FOUND THE MILLENNIUM FALCON! IT'S ON THIS MOON!
GOOD! IT LOOKS LIKE WE WON'T NEED FETT'S SERVICES AFTER ALL!
LET FETT RUN. WE'LL DEAL WITH HIM LATER.
LET'S GO, MEN! I WANT THE MILLENNIUM FALCON!

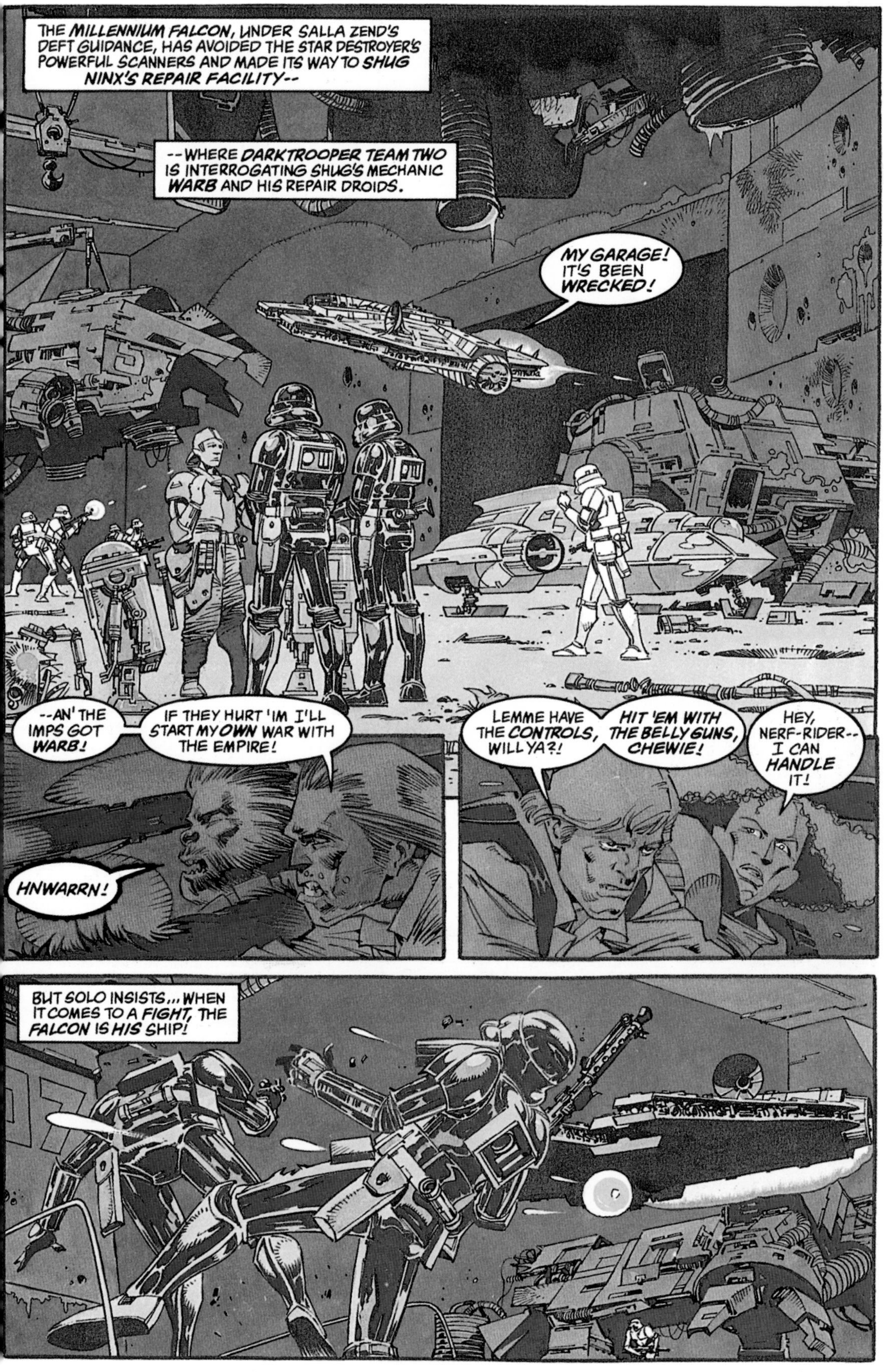
THE MILLENNIUM FALCON, UNDER SALLA ZEND'S DEFT GUIDANCE, HAS AVOIDED THE STAR DESTROYER'S POWERFUL SCANNERS AND MADE ITS WAY TO SHUG NINX'S REPAIR FACILITY--
--WHERE DARKTROOPER TEAM TWO IS INTERROGATING SHUG'S MECHANIC WARB AND HIS REPAIR DROIDS.
MY GARAGE! IT'S BEEN WRECKED!
--AN' THE IMPS GOT WARB!
IF THEY HURT 'IM I'LL START MY OWN WAR WITH THE EMPIRE!
HNWARRN!
LEMME HAVE THE CONTROLS, WILL YA?!
HIT 'EM WITH THE BELLY GUNS, CHEWIE!
HEY, NERF-RIDER-- I CAN HANDLE IT!
BUT SOLO INSISTS... WHEN IT COMES TO A FIGHT, THE FALCON IS HIS SHIP!

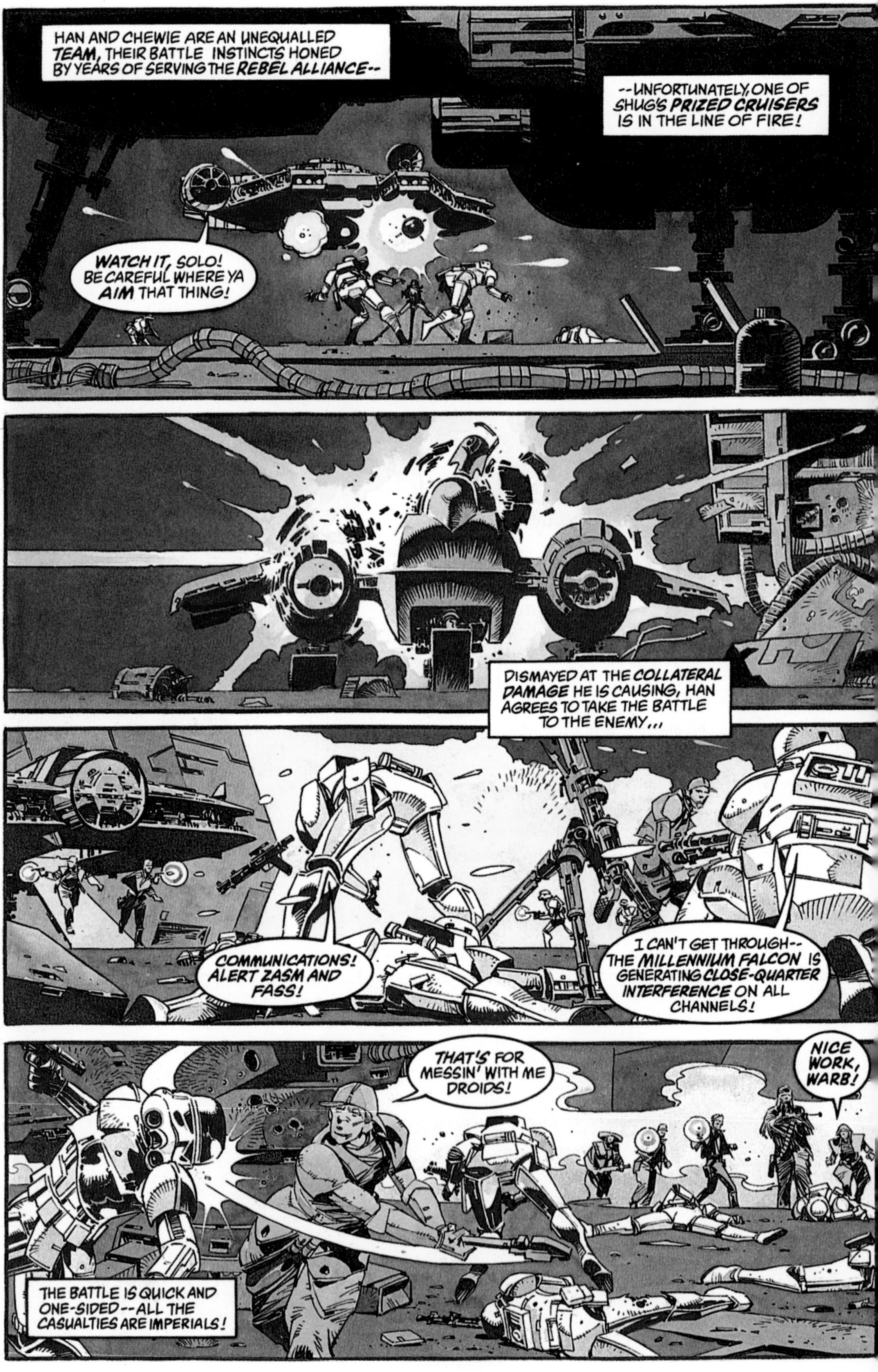
HAN AND CHEWIE ARE AN UNEQUALLED TEAM, THEIR BATTLE INSTINCTS HONED BY YEARS OF SERVING THE REBEL ALLIANCE--
--UNFORTUNATELY, ONE OF SHUG'S PRIZED CRUISERS IS IN THE LINE OF FIRE!
WATCH IT, SOLO! BE CAREFUL WHERE YA AIM THAT THING!
DISMAYED AT THE COLLATERAL DAMAGE HE IS CAUSING, HAN AGREES TO TAKE THE BATTLE TO THE ENEMY...
COMMUNICATIONS! ALERT ZASM AND FASS!
I CAN'T GET THROUGH-- THE MILLENNIUM FALCON IS GENERATING CLOSE-QUARTER INTERFERENCE ON ALL CHANNELS!
THAT'S FOR MESSIN' WITH ME DROIDS!
NICE WORK, WARB!
THE BATTLE IS QUICK AND ONE-SIDED--ALL THE CASUALTIES ARE IMPERIALS!

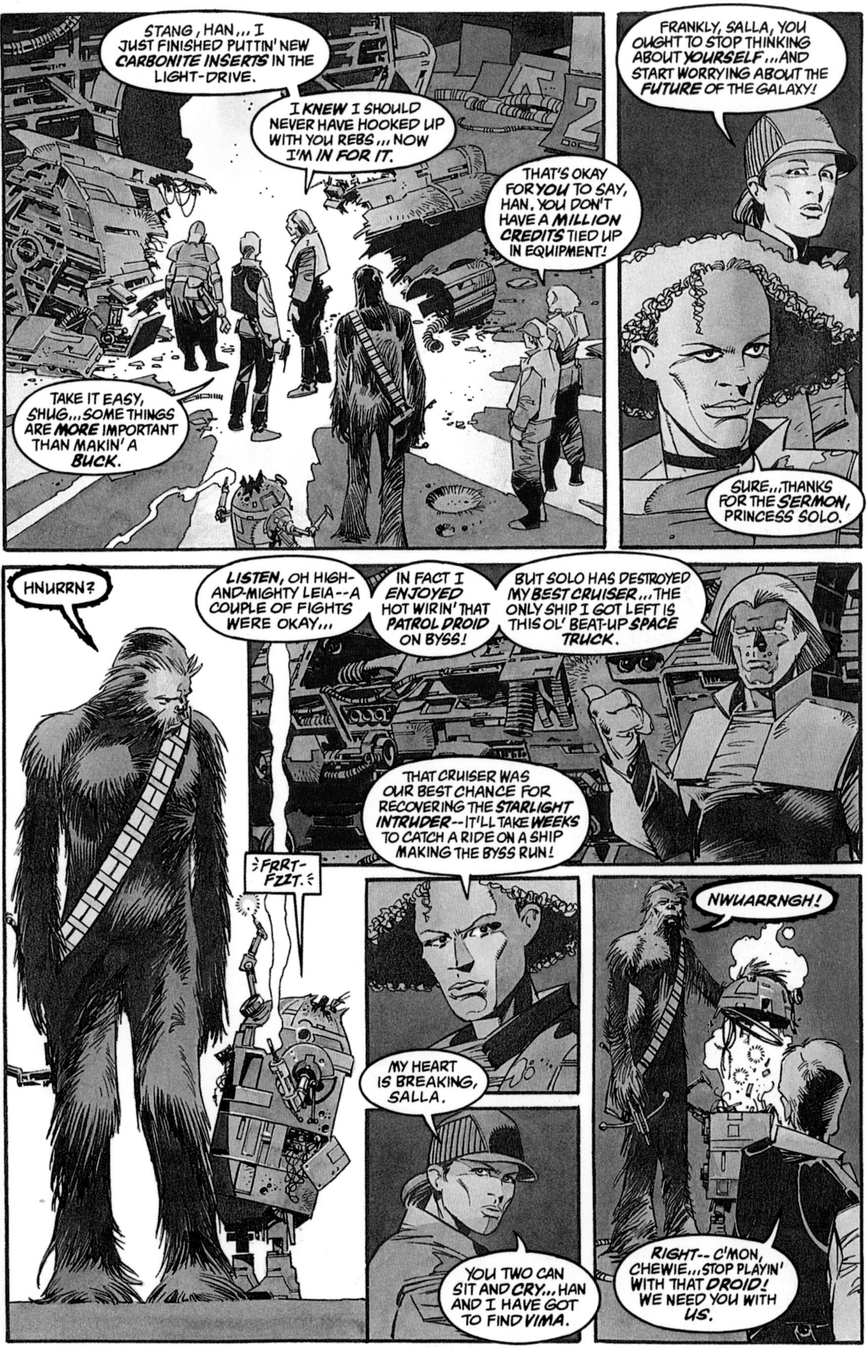
STANG, HAN... I JUST FINISHED PUTTIN' NEW CARBONITE INSERTS IN THE LIGHT-DRIVE.
I KNEW I SHOULD NEVER HAVE HOOKED UP WITH YOU REBS... NOW I'M IN FOR IT.
THAT'S OKAY FOR YOU TO SAY, HAN. YOU DON'T HAVE A MILLION CREDITS TIED UP IN EQUIPMENT!
TAKE IT EASY, SHUG... SOME THINGS ARE MORE IMPORTANT THAN MAKIN' A BUCK.
FRANKLY, SALLA, YOU OUGHT TO STOP THINKING ABOUT YOURSELF... AND START WORRYING ABOUT THE FUTURE OF THE GALAXY!
SURE... THANKS FOR THE SERMON, PRINCESS SOLO.
HNURRN?
LISTEN, OH HIGH-AND-MIGHTY LEIA--A COUPLE OF FIGHTS WERE OKAY...
IN FACT I ENJOYED HOT WIRIN' THAT PATROL DROID ON BYSS!
BUT SOLO HAS DESTROYED MY BEST CRUISER... THE ONLY SHIP I GOT LEFT IS THIS OL' BEAT-UP SPACE TRUCK.
THAT CRUISER WAS OUR BEST CHANCE FOR RECOVERING THE STARLIGHT INTRUDER--IT'LL TAKE WEEKS TO CATCH A RIDE ON A SHIP MAKING THE BYSS RUN!
FRRT-FZZT.
MY HEART IS BREAKING, SALLA.
YOU TWO CAN SIT AND CRY... HAN AND I HAVE GOT TO FIND VIMA.
NWUARRNGH!
RIGHT-- C'MON, CHEWIE... STOP PLAYIN' WITH THAT DROID! WE NEED YOU WITH US.

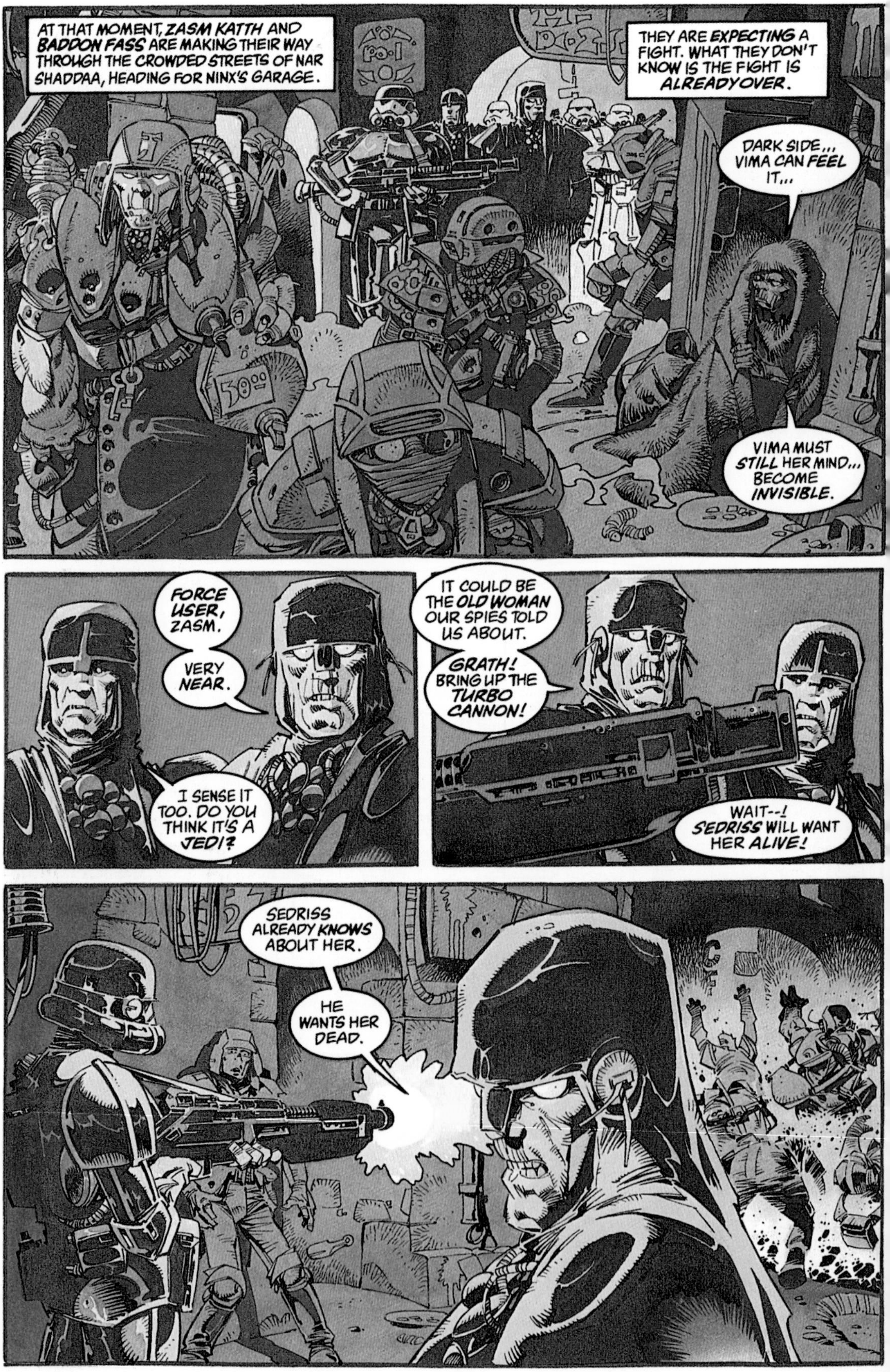
AT THAT MOMENT, ZASM KATTH AND BADDON FASS ARE MAKING THEIR WAY THROUGH THE CROWDED STREETS OF NAR SHADDAA, HEADING FOR NINX'S GARAGE.
THEY ARE EXPECTING A FIGHT. WHAT THEY DON'T KNOW IS THE FIGHT IS ALREADY OVER.
DARK SIDE... VIMA CAN FEEL IT...
VIMA MUST STILL HER MIND... BECOME INVISIBLE.
FORCE USER, ZASM.
VERY NEAR.
I SENSE IT TOO. DO YOU THINK IT'S A JEDI?
IT COULD BE THE OLD WOMAN OUR SPIES TOLD US ABOUT.
GRATH! BRING UP THE TURBO CANNON!
WAIT--! SEDRISS WILL WANT HER ALIVE!
SEDRISS ALREADY KNOWS ABOUT HER.
HE WANTS HER DEAD.

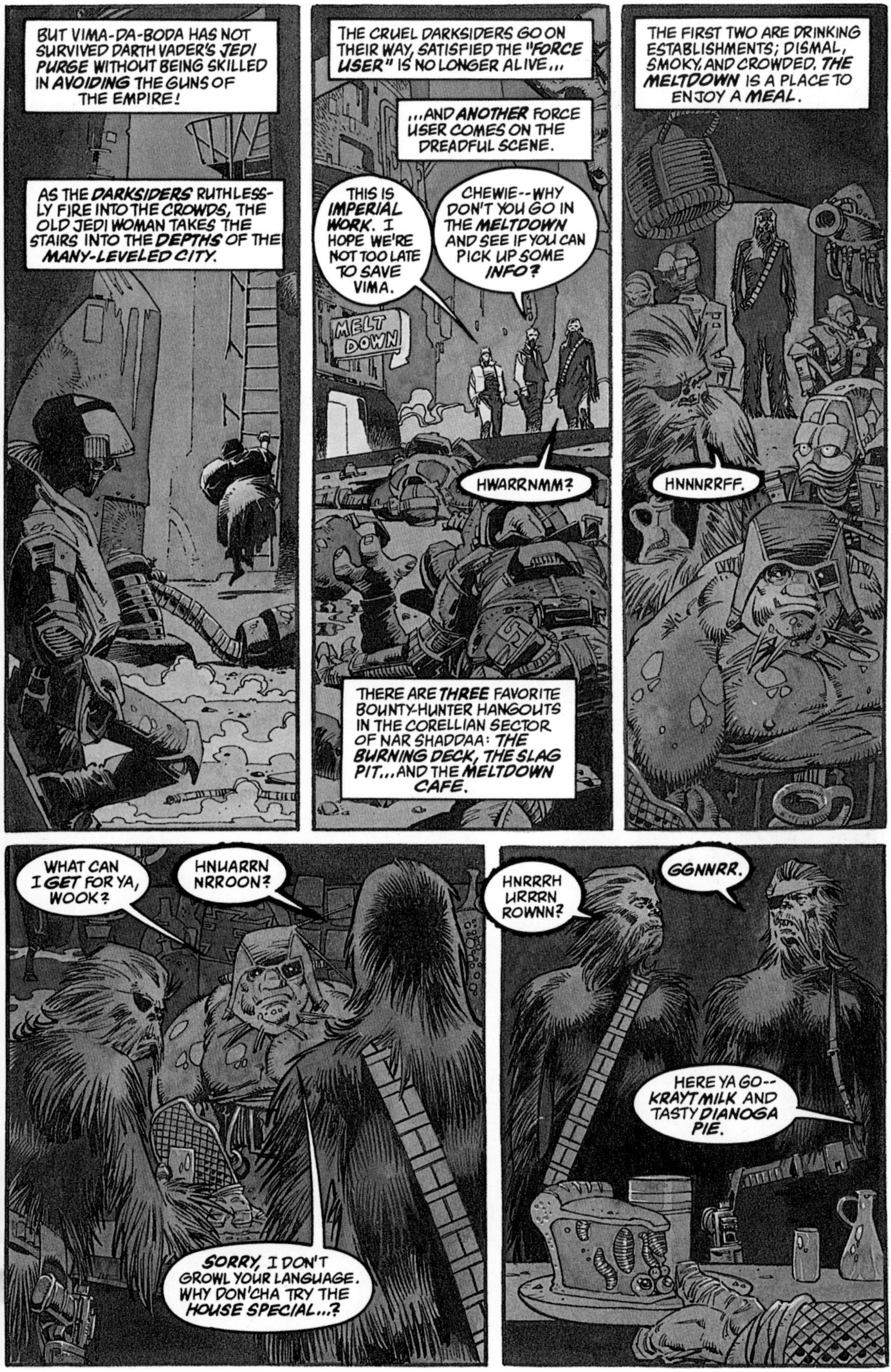
BUT VIMA-DA-BODA HAS NOT SURVIVED DARTH VADER'S JEDI PURGE WITHOUT BEING SKILLED IN AVOIDING THE GUNS OF THE EMPIRE!
AS THE DARKSIDERS RUTHLESSLY FIRE INTO THE CROWDS, THE OLD JEDI WOMAN TAKES THE STAIRS INTO THE DEPTHS OF THE MANY-LEVELED CITY.
THE CRUEL DARKSIDERS GO ON THEIR WAY, SATISFIED THE "FORCE USER" IS NO LONGER ALIVE...
...AND ANOTHER FORCE USER COMES ON THE DREADFUL SCENE.
THIS IS IMPERIAL WORK. I HOPE WE'RE NOT TOO LATE TO SAVE VIMA.
CHEWIE--WHY DON'T YOU GO IN THE MELTDOWN AND SEE IF YOU CAN PICK UP SOME INFO?
MELT DOWN
HWARRNMM?
THERE ARE THREE FAVORITE BOUNTY-HUNTER HANGOUTS IN THE CORELLIAN SECTOR OF NAR SHADDAA: THE BURNING DECK, THE SLAG PIT...AND THE MELTDOWN CAFE.
THE FIRST TWO ARE DRINKING ESTABLISHMENTS; DISMAL, SMOKY, AND CROWDED. THE MELTDOWN IS A PLACE TO ENJOY A MEAL.
HNNNRRFF.
WHAT CAN I GET FOR YA, WOOK?
HNUARRN NRROON?
SORRY, I DON'T GROWL YOUR LANGUAGE. WHY DON'CHA TRY THE HOUSE SPECIAL...?
HNRRRH URRRN ROWNN?
GGNNRR.
HERE YA GO--KRAYT MILK AND TASTY DIANOGA PIE.

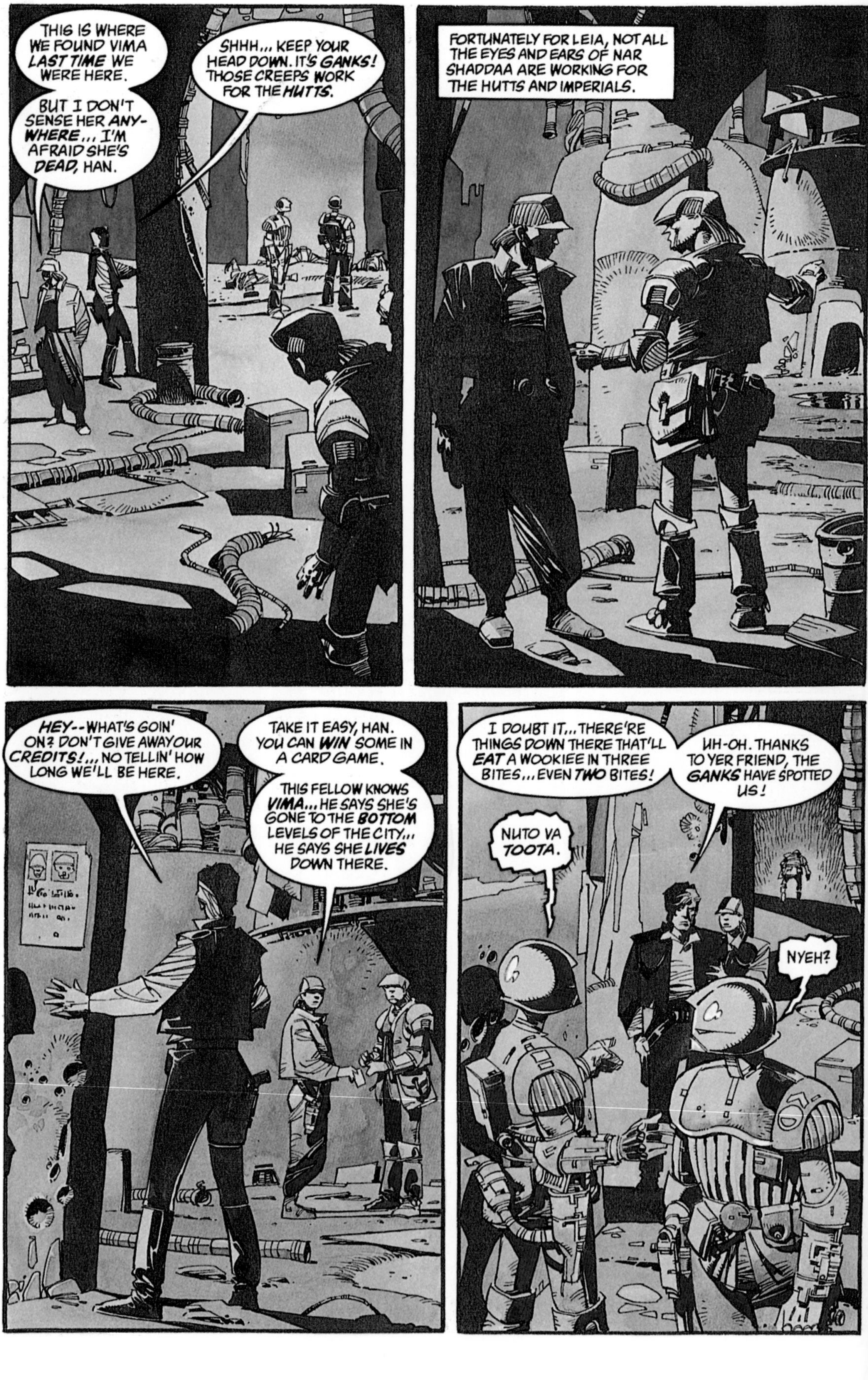
THIS IS WHERE WE FOUND VIMA LAST TIME WE WERE HERE.
BUT I DON'T SENSE HER ANYWHERE... I'M AFRAID SHE'S DEAD, HAN.
SHHH... KEEP YOUR HEAD DOWN. IT'S GANKS! THOSE CREEPS WORK FOR THE HUTTS.
FORTUNATELY FOR LEIA, NOT ALL THE EYES AND EARS OF NAR SHADDAA ARE WORKING FOR THE HUTTS AND IMPERIALS.
HEY--WHAT'S GOIN' ON? DON'T GIVE AWAY OUR CREDITS!... NO TELLIN' HOW LONG WE'LL BE HERE.
TAKE IT EASY, HAN. YOU CAN WIN SOME IN A CARD GAME.
THIS FELLOW KNOWS VIMA... HE SAYS SHE'S GONE TO THE BOTTOM LEVELS OF THE CITY... HE SAYS SHE LIVES DOWN THERE.
I DOUBT IT... THERE'RE THINGS DOWN THERE THAT'LL EAT A WOOKIEE IN THREE BITES... EVEN TWO BITES!
NUTO VA TOOTA.
UH-OH. THANKS TO YER FRIEND, THE GANKS HAVE SPOTTED US!
NYEH?

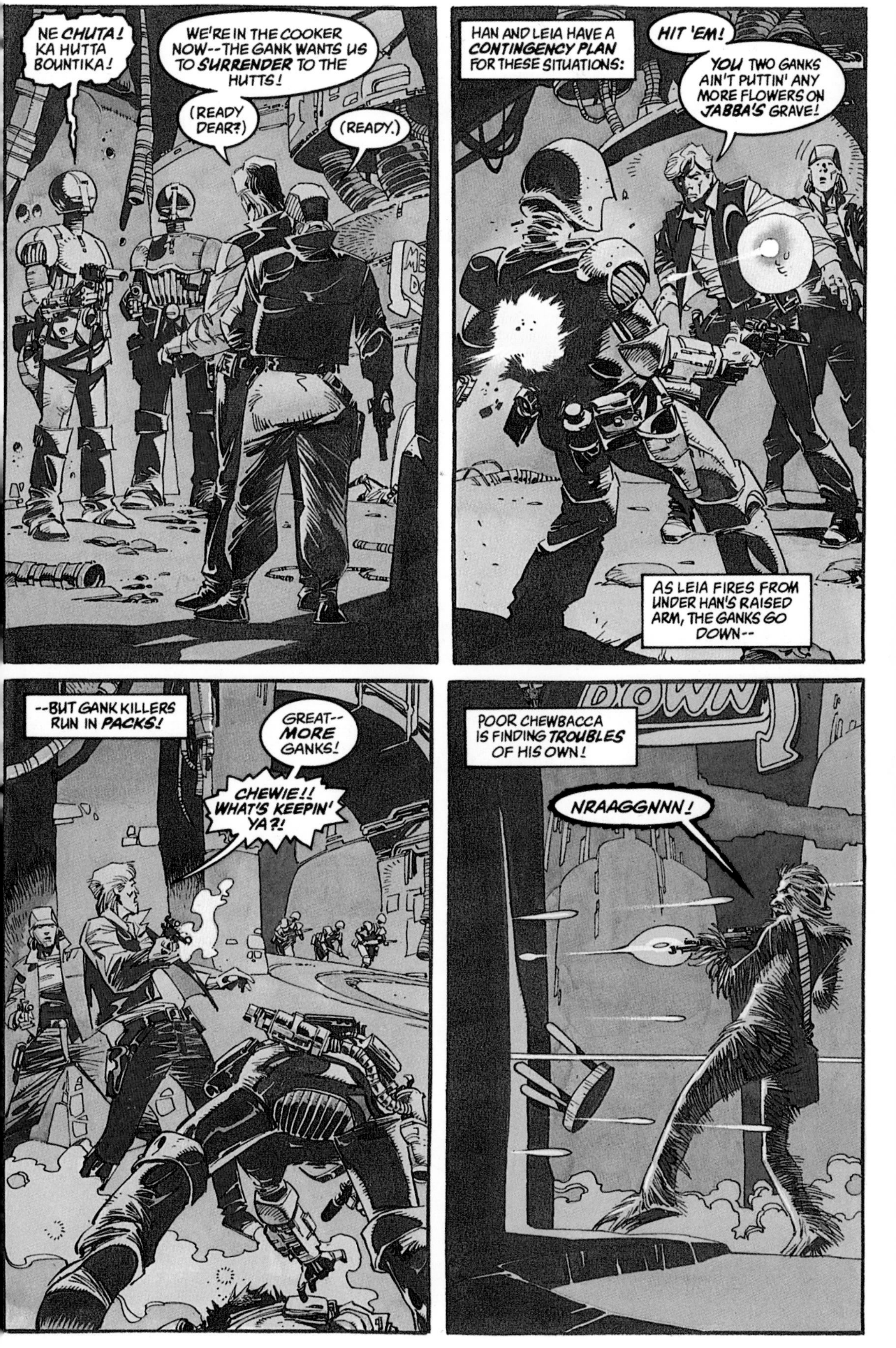
NE CHUTA! KA HUTTA BOUNTIKA!
WE'RE IN THE COOKER NOW--THE GANK WANTS US TO SURRENDER TO THE HUTTS!
(READY DEAR?)
(READY.)
HAN AND LEIA HAVE A CONTINGENCY PLAN FOR THESE SITUATIONS:
HIT 'EM!
YOU TWO GANKS AIN'T PUTTIN' ANY MORE FLOWERS ON JABBA'S GRAVE!
AS LEIA FIRES FROM UNDER HAN'S RAISED ARM, THE GANKS GO DOWN--
--BUT GANK KILLERS RUN IN PACKS!
GREAT--MORE GANKS!
CHEWIE!! WHAT'S KEEPIN' YA?!
DOWN
POOR CHEWBACCA IS FINDING TROUBLES OF HIS OWN!
NRAAGGNNN!

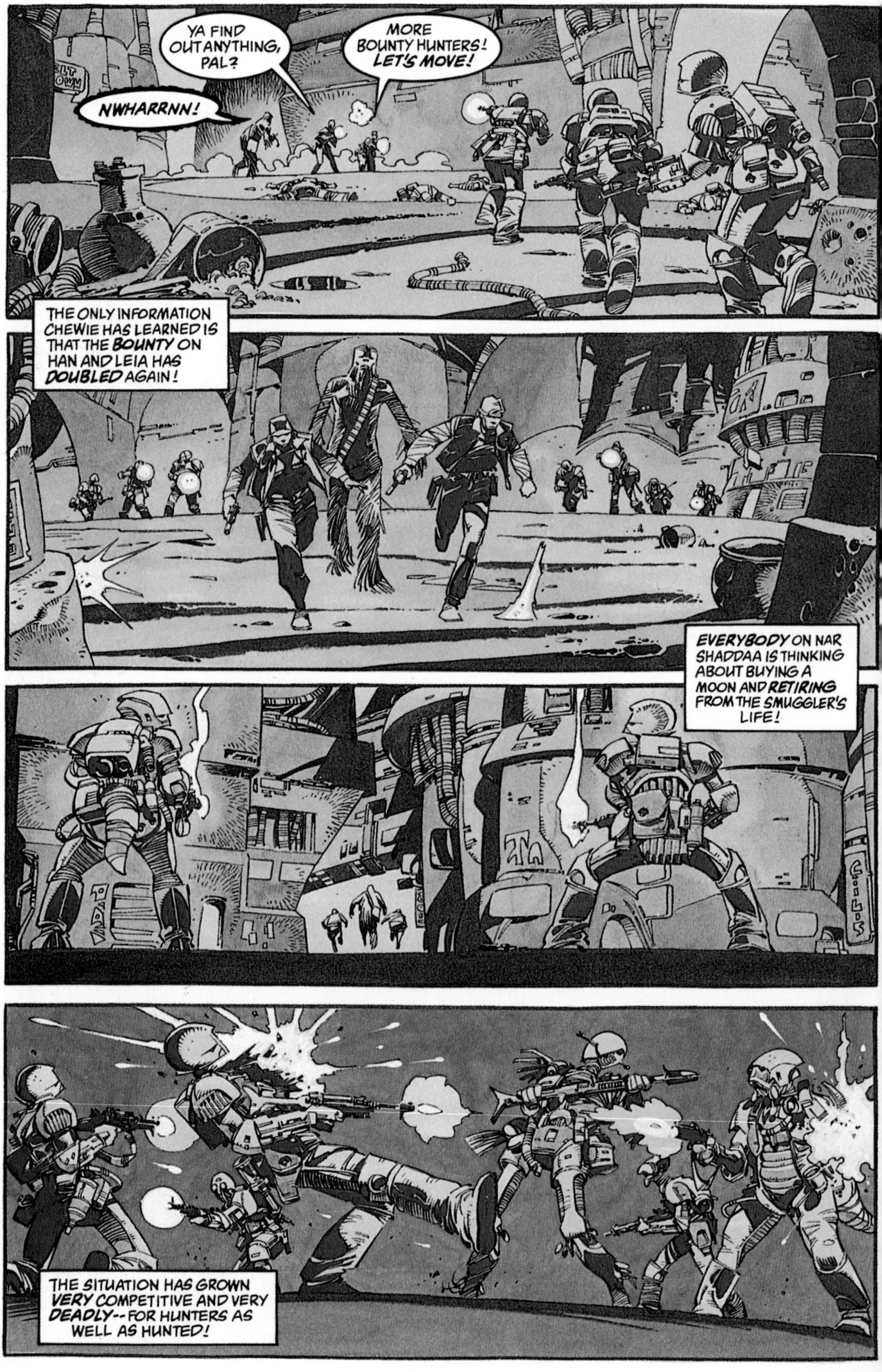
YA FIND OUT ANYTHING, PAL?
MORE BOUNTY HUNTERS! LET'S MOVE!
NWHARRNN!
THE ONLY INFORMATION CHEWIE HAS LEARNED IS THAT THE BOUNTY ON HAN AND LEIA HAS DOUBLED AGAIN!
EVERYBODY ON NAR SHADDAA IS THINKING ABOUT BUYING A MOON AND RETIRING FROM THE SMUGGLER'S LIFE!
THE SITUATION HAS GROWN VERY COMPETITIVE AND VERY DEADLY-- FOR HUNTERS AS WELL AS HUNTED!

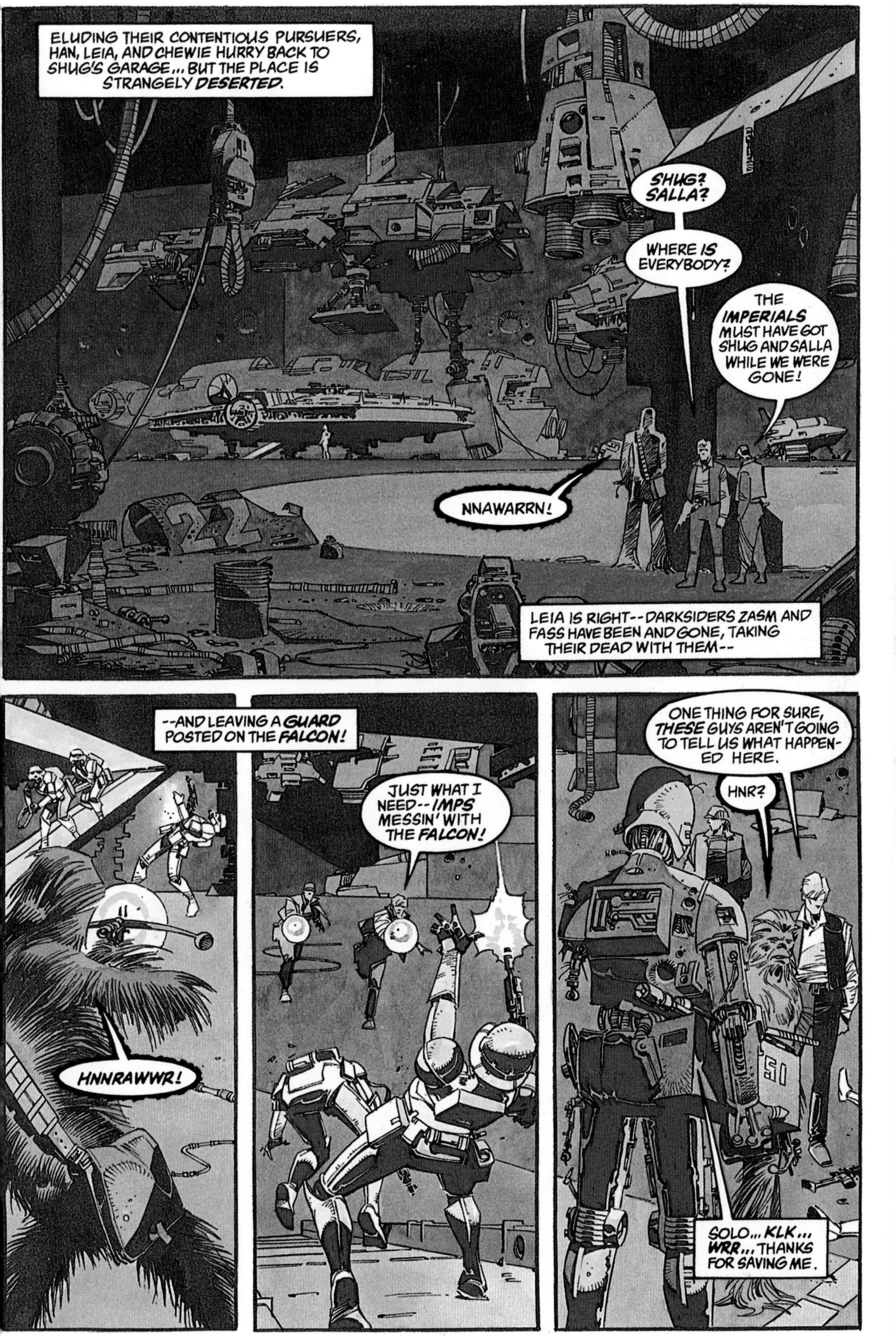
ELUDING THEIR CONTENTIOUS PURSUERS, HAN, LEIA, AND CHEWIE HURRY BACK TO SHUG'S GARAGE... BUT THE PLACE IS STRANGELY DESERTED.
SHUG? SALLA?
WHERE IS EVERYBODY?
THE IMPERIALS MUST HAVE GOT SHUG AND SALLA WHILE WE WERE GONE!
NNAWARRN!
LEIA IS RIGHT--DARKSIDERS ZASM AND FASS HAVE BEEN AND GONE, TAKING THEIR DEAD WITH THEM--
--AND LEAVING A GUARD POSTED ON THE FALCON!
HNNRAWWR!
JUST WHAT I NEED--IMPS MESSIN' WITH THE FALCON!
ONE THING FOR SURE, THESE GUYS AREN'T GOING TO TELL US WHAT HAPPENED HERE.
HNR?
SOLO... KLK... WRR... THANKS FOR SAVING ME.

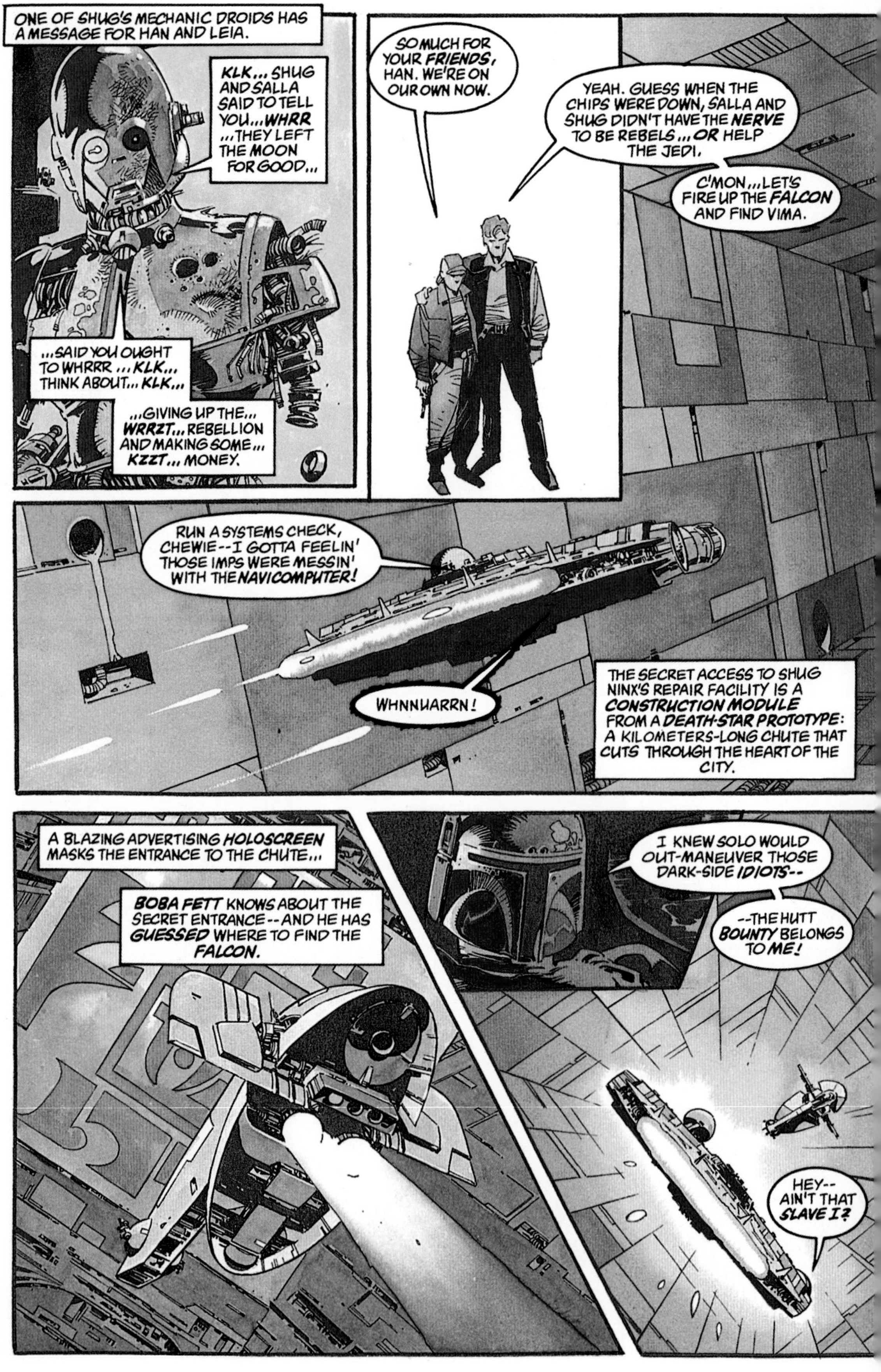
ONE OF SHUG'S MECHANIC DROIDS HAS A MESSAGE FOR HAN AND LEIA.
KLK... SHUG AND SALLA SAID TO TELL YOU... WHRR ...THEY LEFT THE MOON FOR GOOD...
...SAID YOU OUGHT TO WHRRR ... KLK... THINK ABOUT... KLK...
...GIVING UP THE... WRRZT... REBELLION AND MAKING SOME... KZZT... MONEY.
SO MUCH FOR YOUR FRIENDS, HAN. WE'RE ON OUR OWN NOW.
YEAH. GUESS WHEN THE CHIPS WERE DOWN, SALLA AND SHUG DIDN'T HAVE THE NERVE TO BE REBELS... OR HELP THE JEDI.
C'MON... LET'S FIRE UP THE FALCON AND FIND VIMA.
RUN A SYSTEMS CHECK, CHEWIE--I GOTTA FEELIN' THOSE IMPS WERE MESSIN' WITH THE NAVICOMPUTER!
WHNNUARRN!
THE SECRET ACCESS TO SHUG NINX'S REPAIR FACILITY IS A CONSTRUCTION MODULE FROM A DEATH-STAR PROTOTYPE: A KILOMETERS-LONG CHUTE THAT CUTS THROUGH THE HEART OF THE CITY.
A BLAZING ADVERTISING HOLOSCREEN MASKS THE ENTRANCE TO THE CHUTE...
BOBA FETT KNOWS ABOUT THE SECRET ENTRANCE--AND HE HAS GUESSED WHERE TO FIND THE FALCON.
I KNEW SOLO WOULD OUT-MANEUVER THOSE DARK-SIDE IDIOTS--
--THE HUTT BOUNTY BELONGS TO ME!
HEY-- AIN'T THAT SLAVE I?

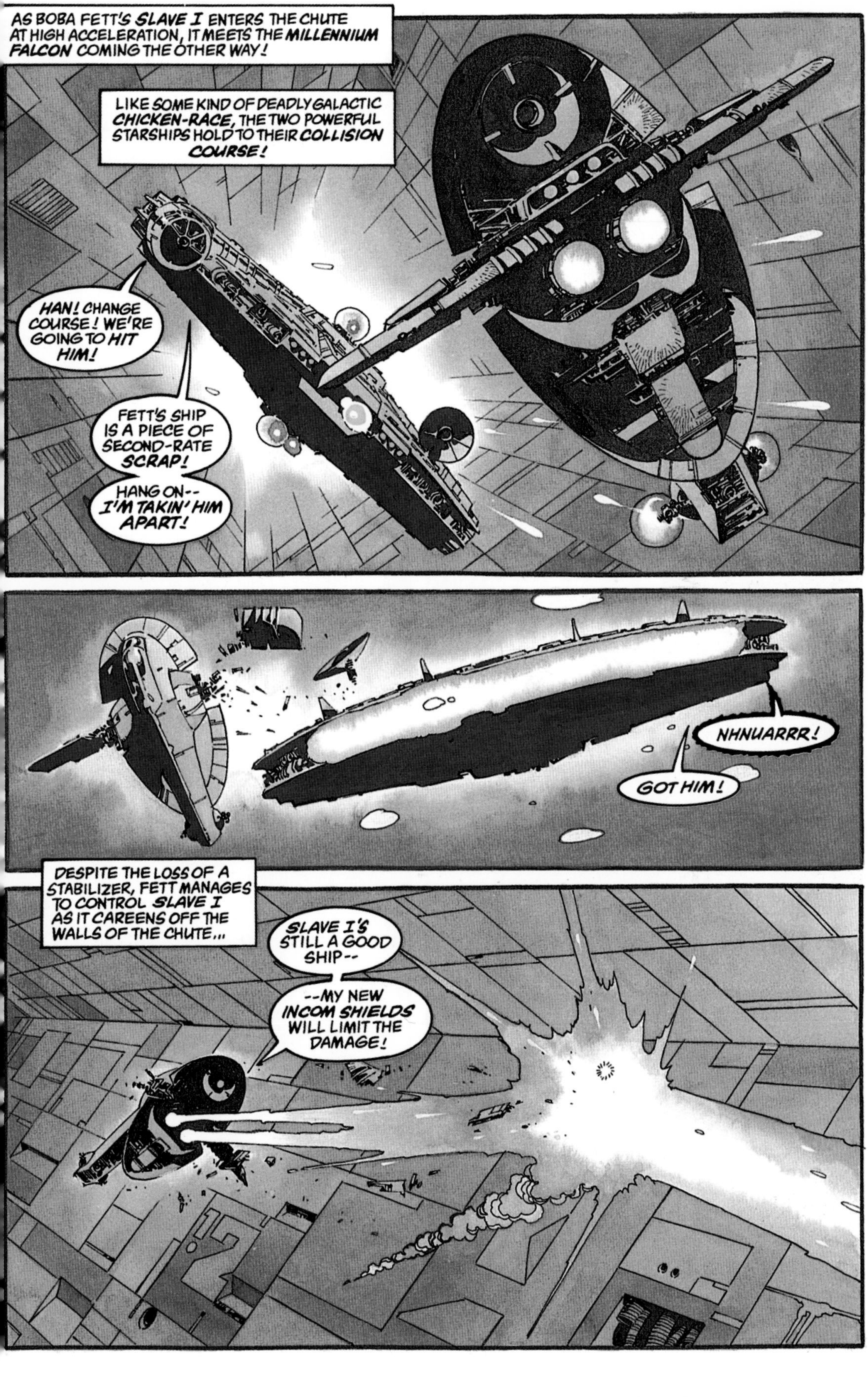
AS BOBA FETT'S SLAVE I ENTERS THE CHUTE AT HIGH ACCELERATION, IT MEETS THE MILLENNIUM FALCON COMING THE OTHER WAY!
LIKE SOME KIND OF DEADLY GALACTIC CHICKEN-RACE, THE TWO POWERFUL STARSHIPS HOLD TO THEIR COLLISION COURSE!
HAN! CHANGE COURSE! WE'RE GOING TO HIT HIM!
FETT'S SHIP IS A PIECE OF SECOND-RATE SCRAP!
HANG ON-- I'M TAKIN' HIM APART!
NHNUARRR!
GOT HIM!
DESPITE THE LOSS OF A STABILIZER, FETT MANAGES TO CONTROL SLAVE I AS IT CAREENS OFF THE WALLS OF THE CHUTE...
SLAVE I'S STILL A GOOD SHIP--
--MY NEW INCOM SHIELDS WILL LIMIT THE DAMAGE!

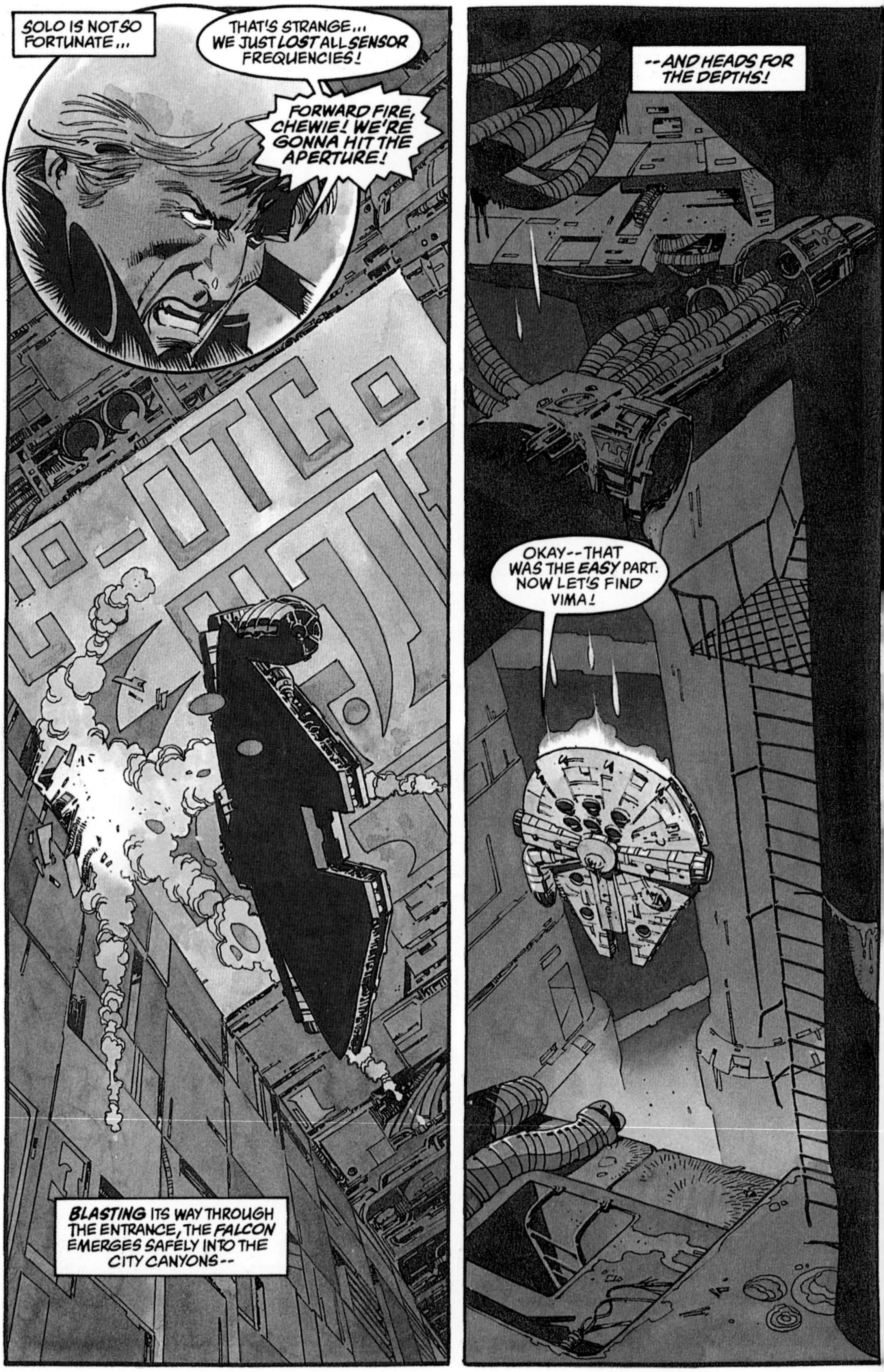
SOLO IS NOT SO FORTUNATE...
THAT'S STRANGE... WE JUST *LOST* ALL *SENSOR* FREQUENCIES!
FORWARD FIRE, CHEWIE! WE'RE GONNA HIT THE APERTURE!
BLASTING ITS WAY THROUGH THE ENTRANCE, THE *FALCON* EMERGES SAFELY INTO THE CITY CANYONS--
--AND HEADS FOR THE DEPTHS!
OKAY--THAT WAS THE *EASY* PART. NOW LET'S FIND VIMA!

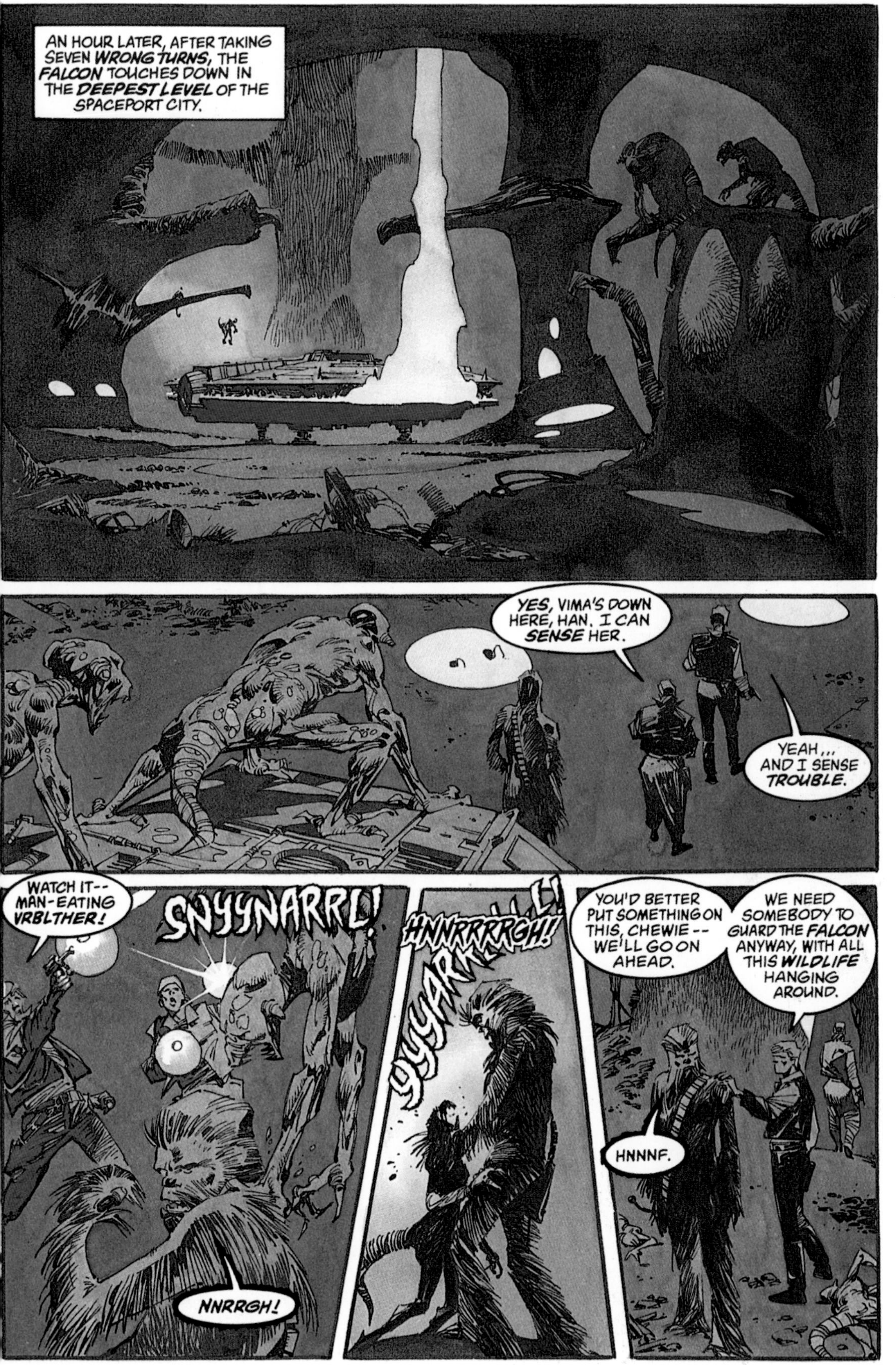
AN HOUR LATER, AFTER TAKING SEVEN WRONG TURNS, THE FALCON TOUCHES DOWN IN THE DEEPEST LEVEL OF THE SPACEPORT CITY.
YES, VIMA'S DOWN HERE, HAN. I CAN SENSE HER.
YEAH... AND I SENSE TROUBLE.
WATCH IT-- MAN-EATING VRBLTHER!
SNYYNARRL!
NNRRGH!
HNNRRRRGH!
YOU'D BETTER PUT SOMETHING ON THIS, CHEWIE -- WE'LL GO ON AHEAD.
WE NEED SOMEBODY TO GUARD THE FALCON ANYWAY, WITH ALL THIS WILDLIFE HANGING AROUND.
HNNNF.

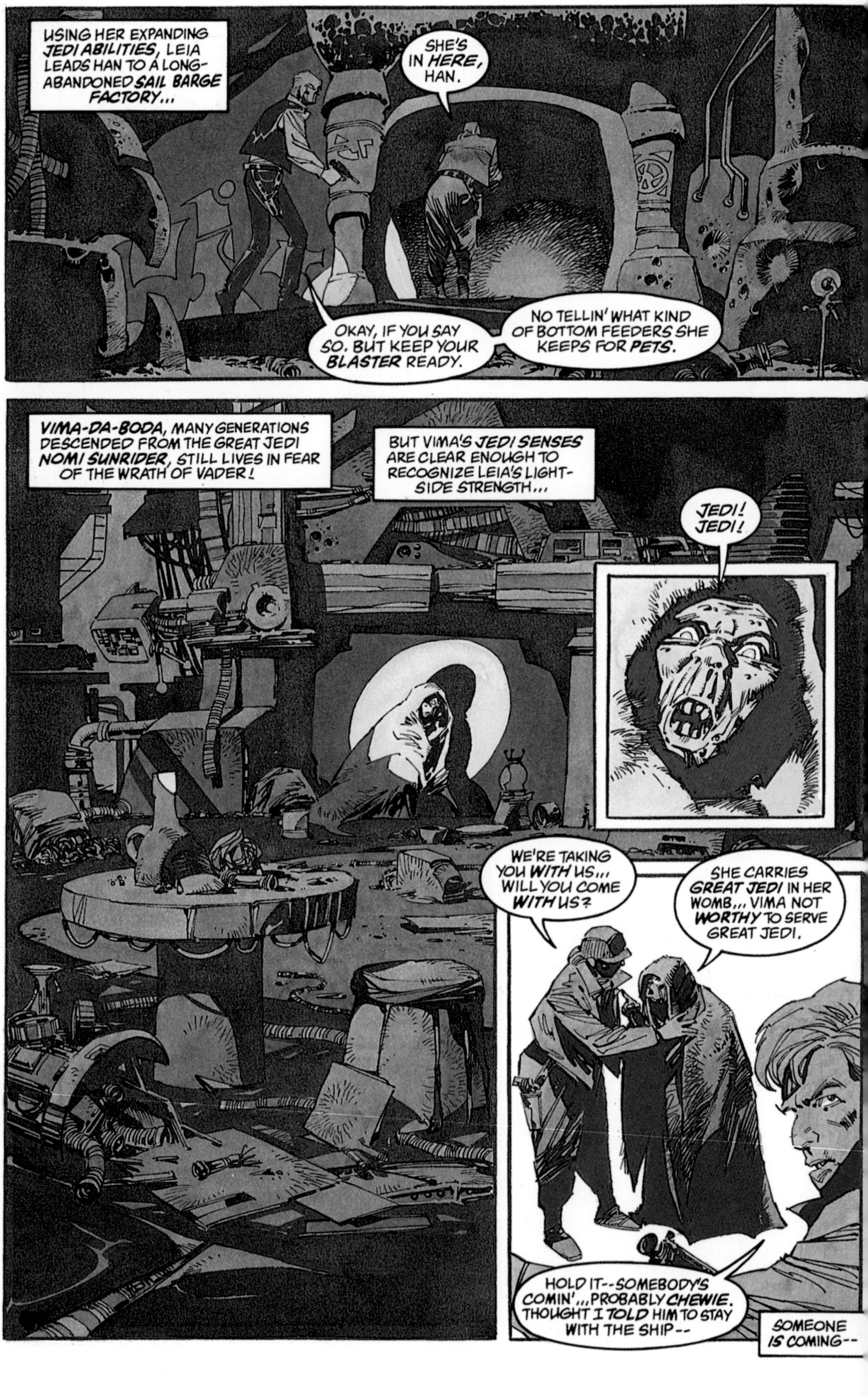
USING HER EXPANDING JEDI ABILITIES, LEIA LEADS HAN TO A LONG-ABANDONED SAIL BARGE FACTORY...
SHE'S IN HERE, HAN.
OKAY, IF YOU SAY SO. BUT KEEP YOUR BLASTER READY.
NO TELLIN' WHAT KIND OF BOTTOM FEEDERS SHE KEEPS FOR PETS.
VIMA-DA-BODA, MANY GENERATIONS DESCENDED FROM THE GREAT JEDI NOMI SUNRIDER, STILL LIVES IN FEAR OF THE WRATH OF VADER!
BUT VIMA'S JEDI SENSES ARE CLEAR ENOUGH TO RECOGNIZE LEIA'S LIGHT-SIDE STRENGTH...
JEDI! JEDI!
WE'RE TAKING YOU WITH US... WILL YOU COME WITH US?
SHE CARRIES GREAT JEDI IN HER WOMB... VIMA NOT WORTHY TO SERVE GREAT JEDI.
HOLD IT--SOMEBODY'S COMIN'... PROBABLY CHEWIE. THOUGHT I TOLD HIM TO STAY WITH THE SHIP--
SOMEONE IS COMING--

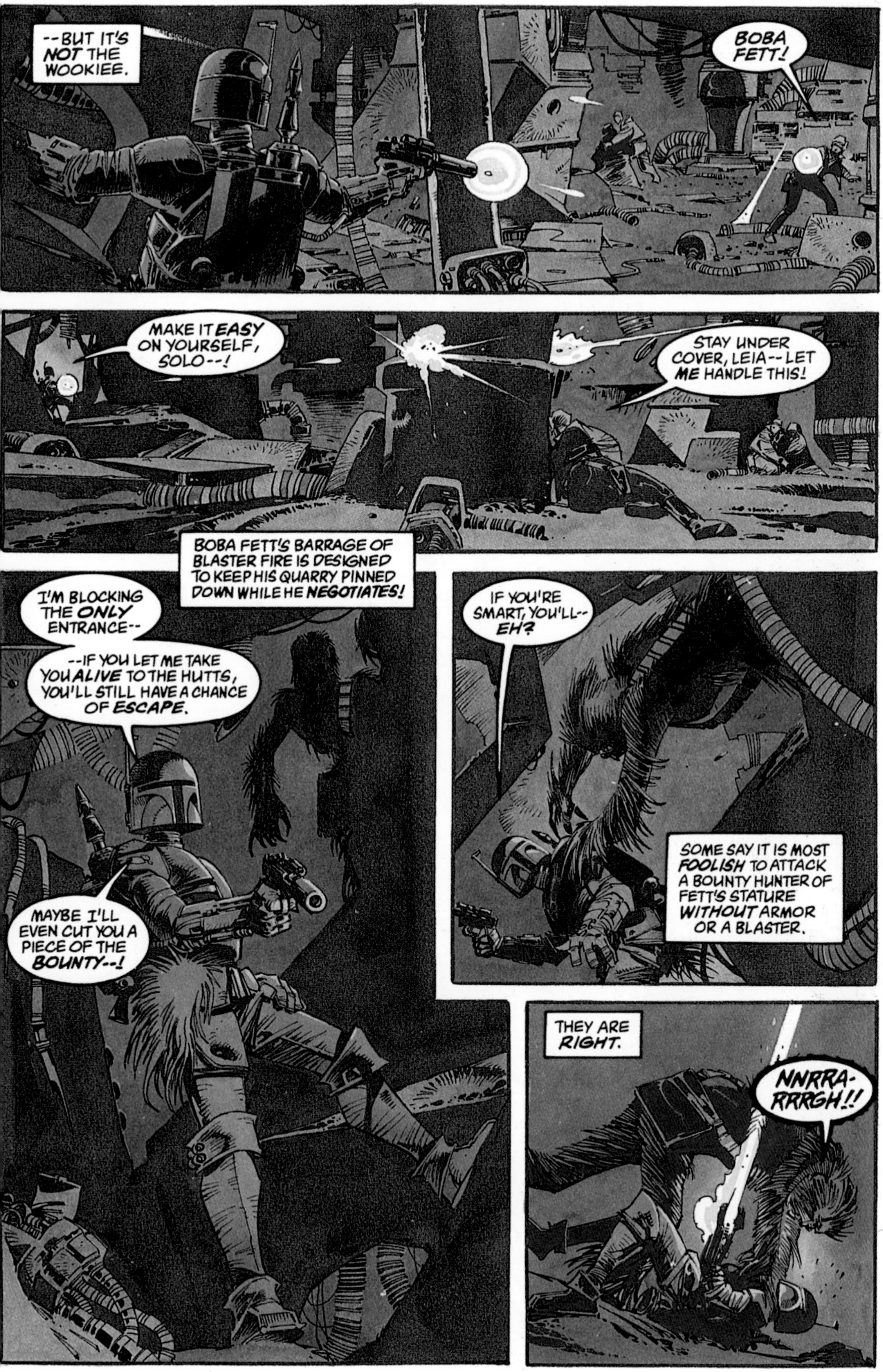

--BUT IT'S NOT THE WOOKIEE.
BOBA FETT!
MAKE IT EASY ON YOURSELF, SOLO--!
STAY UNDER COVER, LEIA--LET ME HANDLE THIS!
BOBA FETT'S BARRAGE OF BLASTER FIRE IS DESIGNED TO KEEP HIS QUARRY PINNED DOWN WHILE HE NEGOTIATES!
I'M BLOCKING THE ONLY ENTRANCE--
--IF YOU LET ME TAKE YOU ALIVE TO THE HUTTS, YOU'LL STILL HAVE A CHANCE OF ESCAPE.
MAYBE I'LL EVEN CUT YOU A PIECE OF THE BOUNTY--!
IF YOU'RE SMART, YOU'LL--EH?
SOME SAY IT IS MOST FOOLISH TO ATTACK A BOUNTY HUNTER OF FETT'S STATURE WITHOUT ARMOR OR A BLASTER.
THEY ARE RIGHT.
NNRRA-RRRGH!!

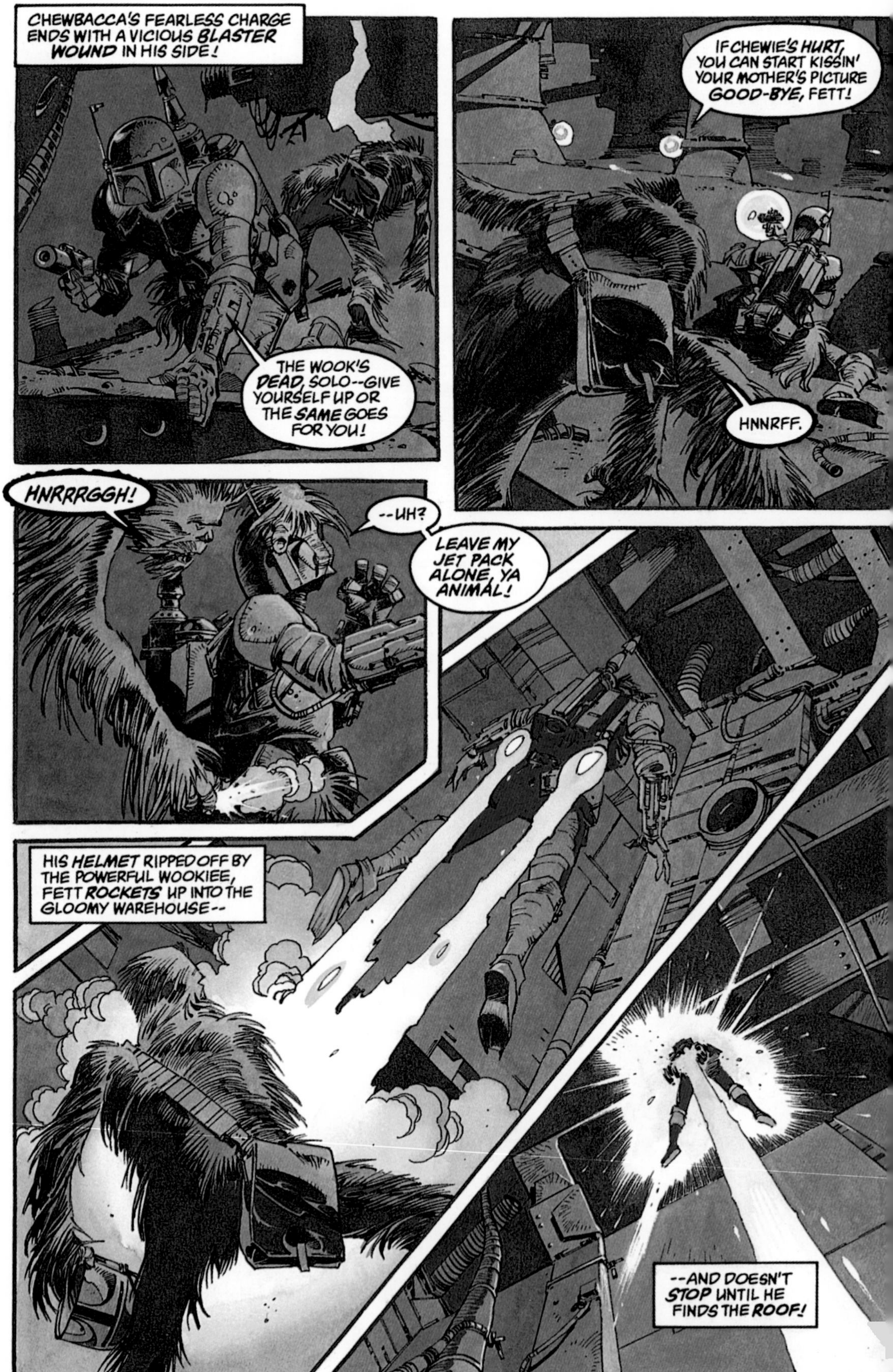
CHEWBACCA'S FEARLESS CHARGE ENDS WITH A VICIOUS BLASTER WOUND IN HIS SIDE!
THE WOOK'S DEAD, SOLO--GIVE YOURSELF UP OR THE SAME GOES FOR YOU!
IF CHEWIE'S HURT, YOU CAN START KISSIN' YOUR MOTHER'S PICTURE GOOD-BYE, FETT!
HNNRFF.
HNRRRGGH!
--UH?
LEAVE MY JET PACK ALONE, YA ANIMAL!
HIS HELMET RIPPED OFF BY THE POWERFUL WOOKIEE, FETT ROCKETS UP INTO THE GLOOMY WAREHOUSE--
--AND DOESN'T STOP UNTIL HE FINDS THE ROOF!

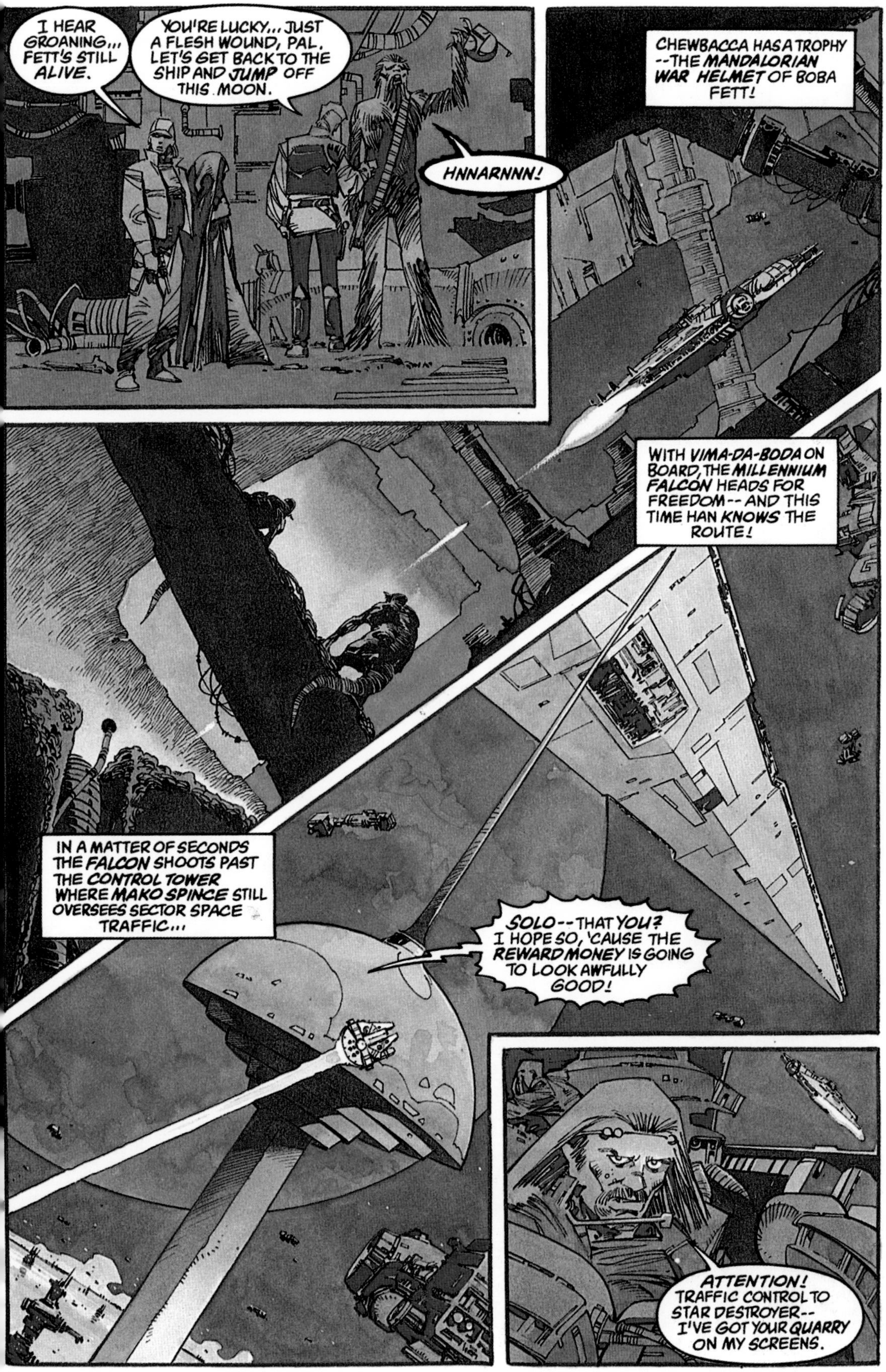
I HEAR GROANING... FETT'S STILL ALIVE.
YOU'RE LUCKY... JUST A FLESH WOUND, PAL. LET'S GET BACK TO THE SHIP AND JUMP OFF THIS MOON.
HNNARNNN!
CHEWBACCA HAS A TROPHY --THE MANDALORIAN WAR HELMET OF BOBA FETT!
WITH VIMA-DA-BODA ON BOARD, THE MILLENNIUM FALCON HEADS FOR FREEDOM -- AND THIS TIME HAN KNOWS THE ROUTE!
IN A MATTER OF SECONDS THE FALCON SHOOTS PAST THE CONTROL TOWER WHERE MAKO SPINCE STILL OVERSEES SECTOR SPACE TRAFFIC...
SOLO--THAT YOU? I HOPE SO, 'CAUSE THE REWARD MONEY IS GOING TO LOOK AWFULLY GOOD!
ATTENTION! TRAFFIC CONTROL TO STAR DESTROYER-- I'VE GOT YOUR QUARRY ON MY SCREENS.

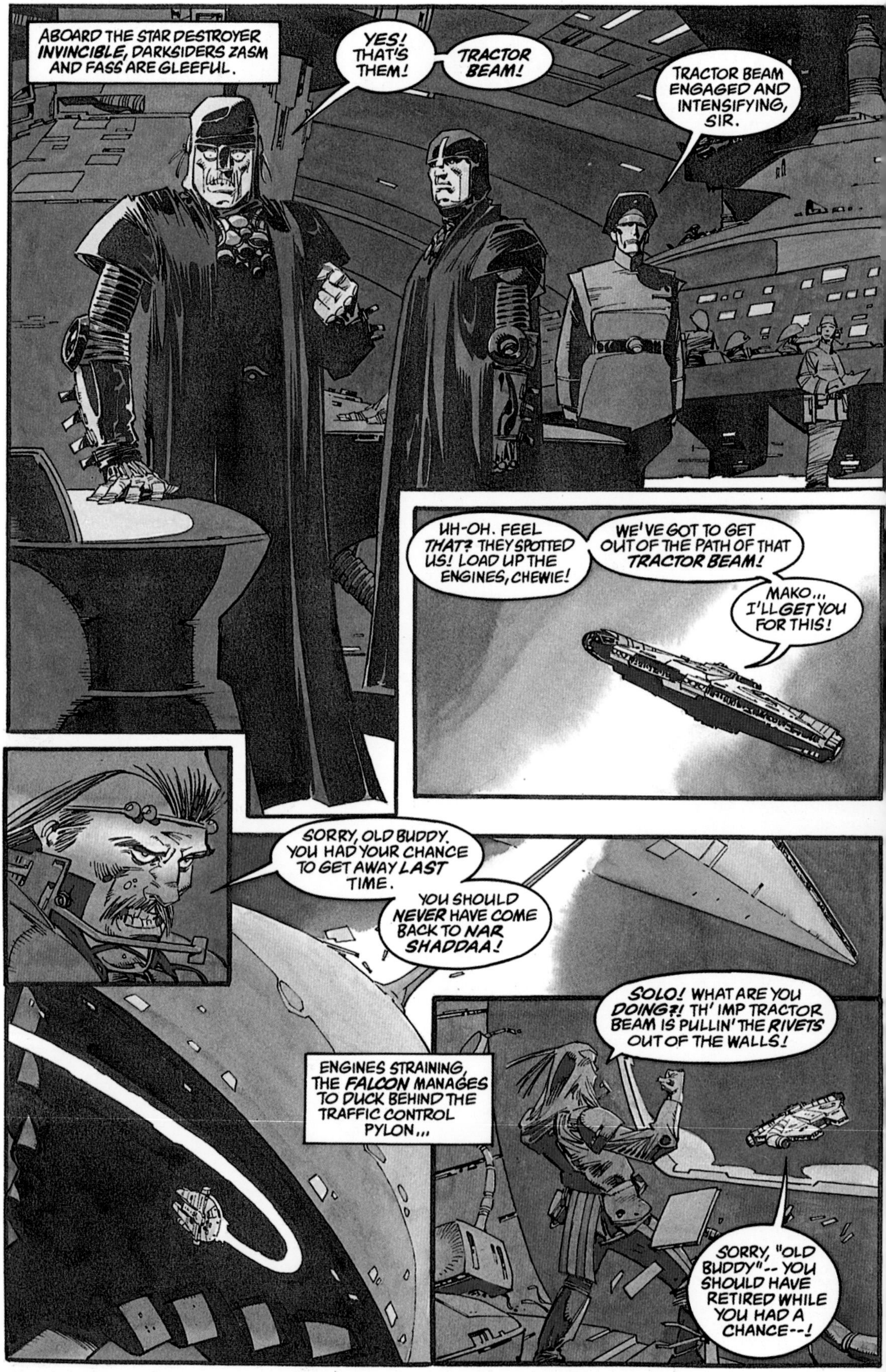

ABOARD THE STAR DESTROYER INVINCIBLE, DARKSIDERS ZASM AND FASS ARE GLEEFUL.
YES! THAT'S THEM!
TRACTOR BEAM!
TRACTOR BEAM ENGAGED AND INTENSIFYING, SIR.
UH-OH. FEEL THAT? THEY SPOTTED US! LOAD UP THE ENGINES, CHEWIE!
WE'VE GOT TO GET OUT OF THE PATH OF THAT TRACTOR BEAM!
MAKO... I'LL GET YOU FOR THIS!
SORRY, OLD BUDDY. YOU HAD YOUR CHANCE TO GET AWAY LAST TIME.
YOU SHOULD NEVER HAVE COME BACK TO NAR SHADDAA!
ENGINES STRAINING, THE FALCON MANAGES TO DUCK BEHIND THE TRAFFIC CONTROL PYLON...
SOLO! WHAT ARE YOU DOING?! TH' IMP TRACTOR BEAM IS PULLIN' THE RIVETS OUT OF THE WALLS!
SORRY, "OLD BUDDY"-- YOU SHOULD HAVE RETIRED WHILE YOU HAD A CHANCE--!

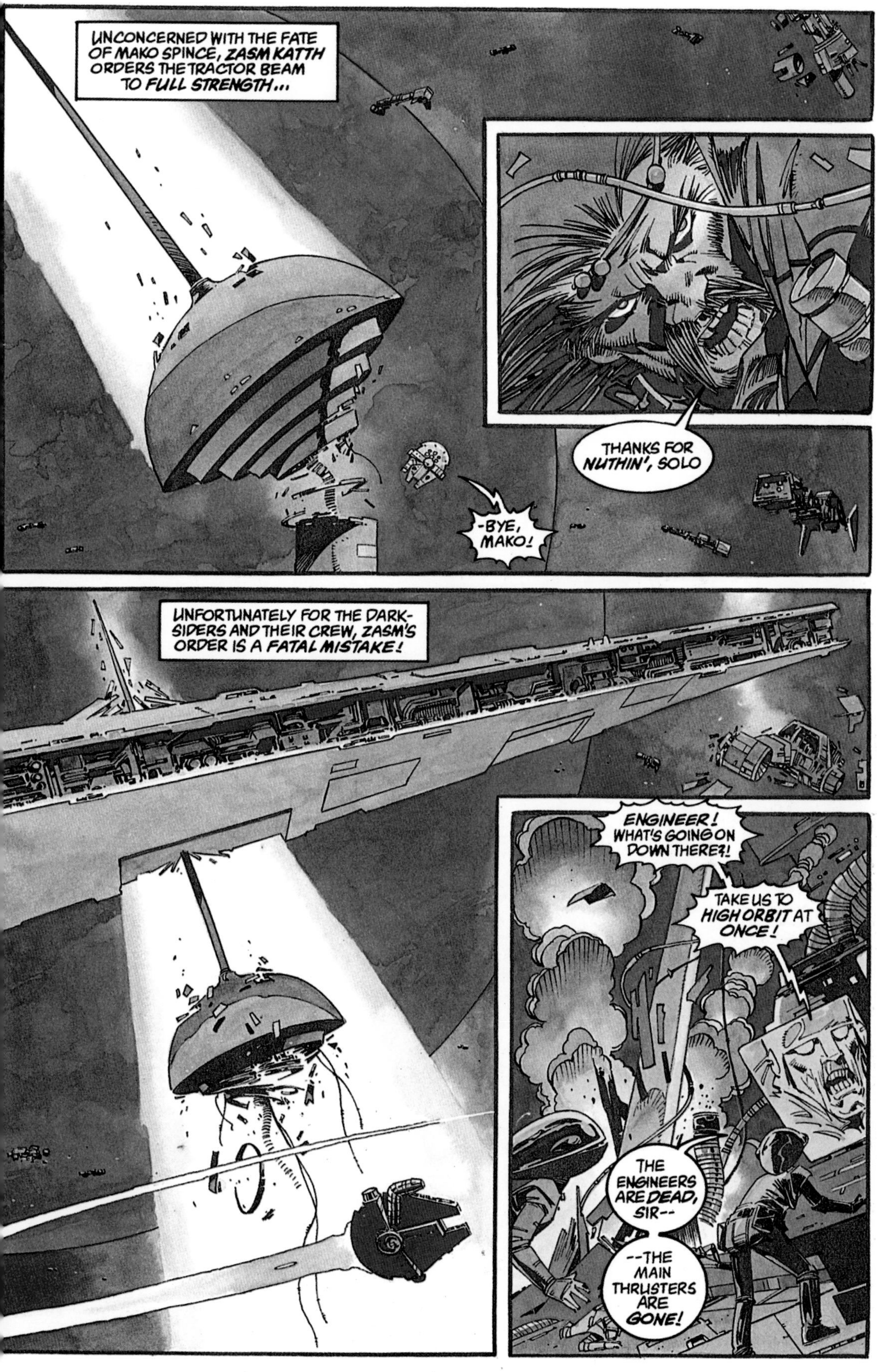
UNCONCERNED WITH THE FATE OF MAKO SPINCE, ZASM KATTH ORDERS THE TRACTOR BEAM TO FULL STRENGTH...
THANKS FOR NUTHIN', SOLO
-BYE, MAKO!
UNFORTUNATELY FOR THE DARK-SIDERS AND THEIR CREW, ZASM'S ORDER IS A FATAL MISTAKE!
ENGINEER! WHAT'S GOING ON DOWN THERE?!
TAKE US TO HIGH ORBIT AT ONCE!
THE ENGINEERS ARE DEAD, SIR--
--THE MAIN THRUSTERS ARE GONE!

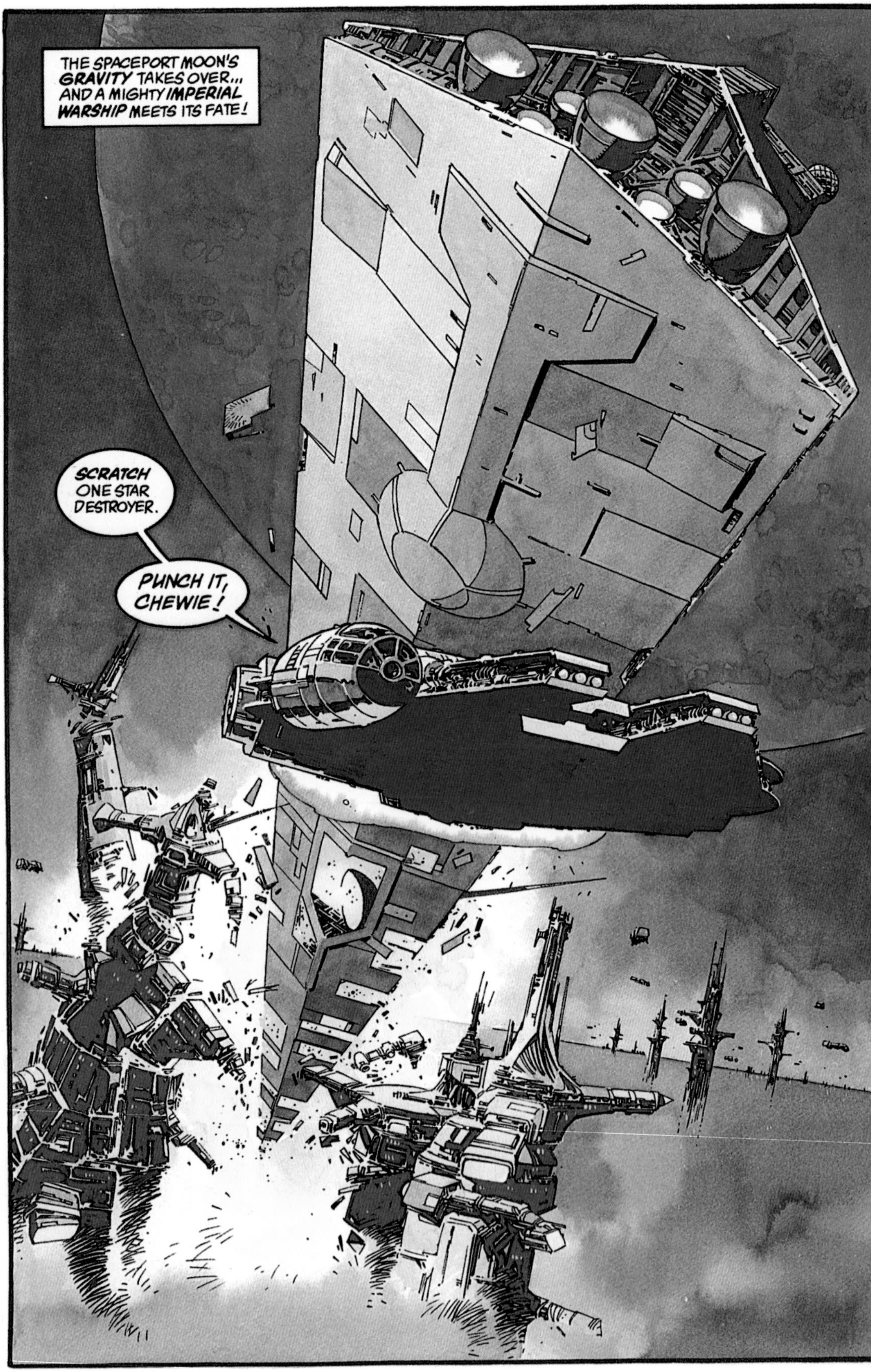
THE SPACEPORT MOON'S GRAVITY TAKES OVER... AND A MIGHTY IMPERIAL WARSHIP MEETS ITS FATE!
SCRATCH ONE STAR DESTROYER.
PUNCH IT, CHEWIE!

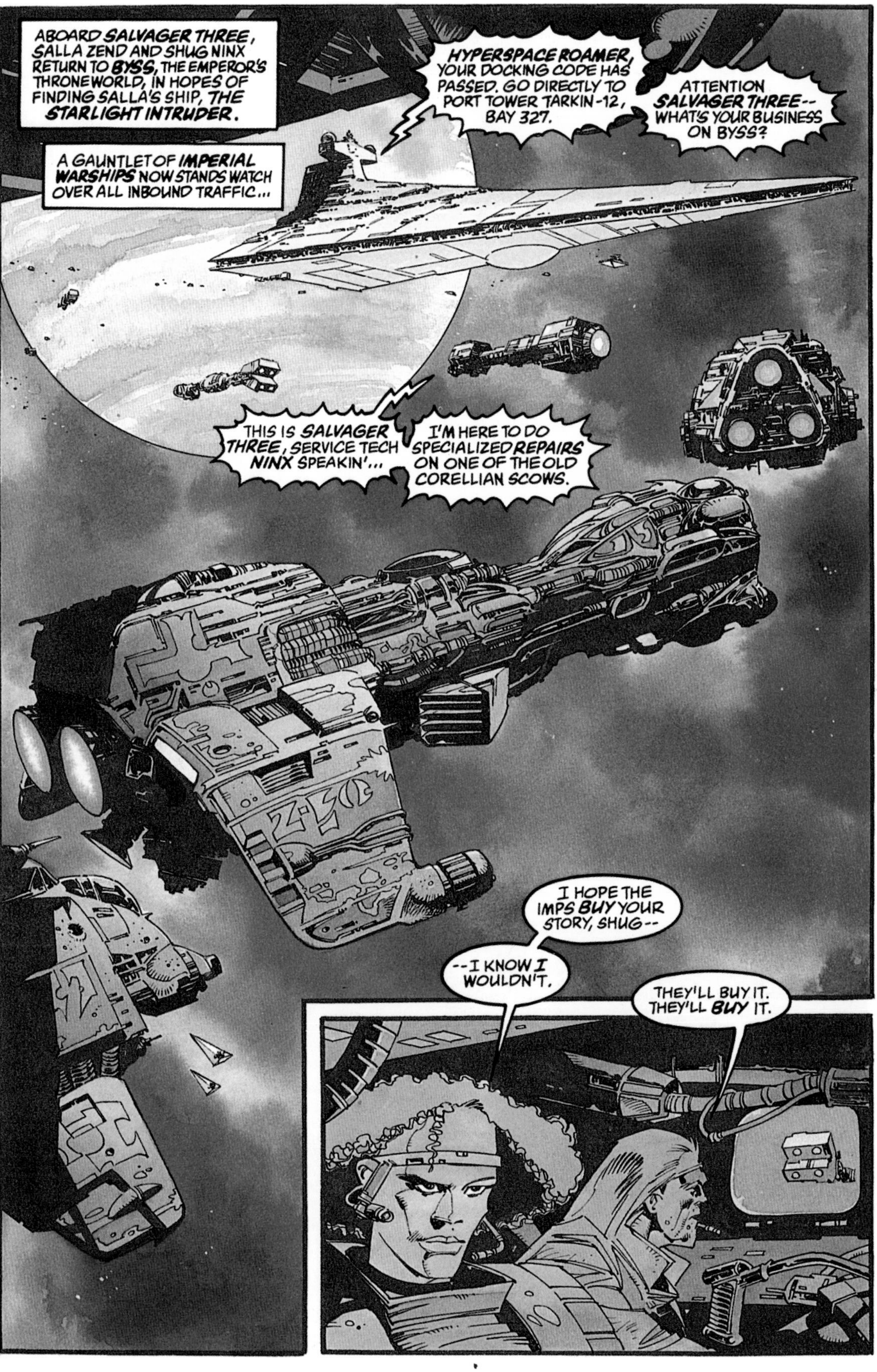

ABOARD SALVAGER THREE, SALLA ZEND AND SHUG NINX RETURN TO BYSS, THE EMPEROR'S THRONEWORLD, IN HOPES OF FINDING SALLA'S SHIP, THE STARLIGHT INTRUDER.
A GAUNTLET OF IMPERIAL WARSHIPS NOW STANDS WATCH OVER ALL INBOUND TRAFFIC...
HYPERSPACE ROAMER, YOUR DOCKING CODE HAS PASSED. GO DIRECTLY TO PORT TOWER TARKIN-12, BAY 327.
ATTENTION SALVAGER THREE-- WHAT'S YOUR BUSINESS ON BYSS?
THIS IS SALVAGER THREE, SERVICE TECH NINX SPEAKIN'...
I'M HERE TO DO SPECIALIZED REPAIRS ON ONE OF THE OLD CORELLIAN SCOWS.
I HOPE THE IMPS BUY YOUR STORY, SHUG--
--I KNOW I WOULDN'T.
THEY'LL BUY IT. THEY'LL BUY IT.

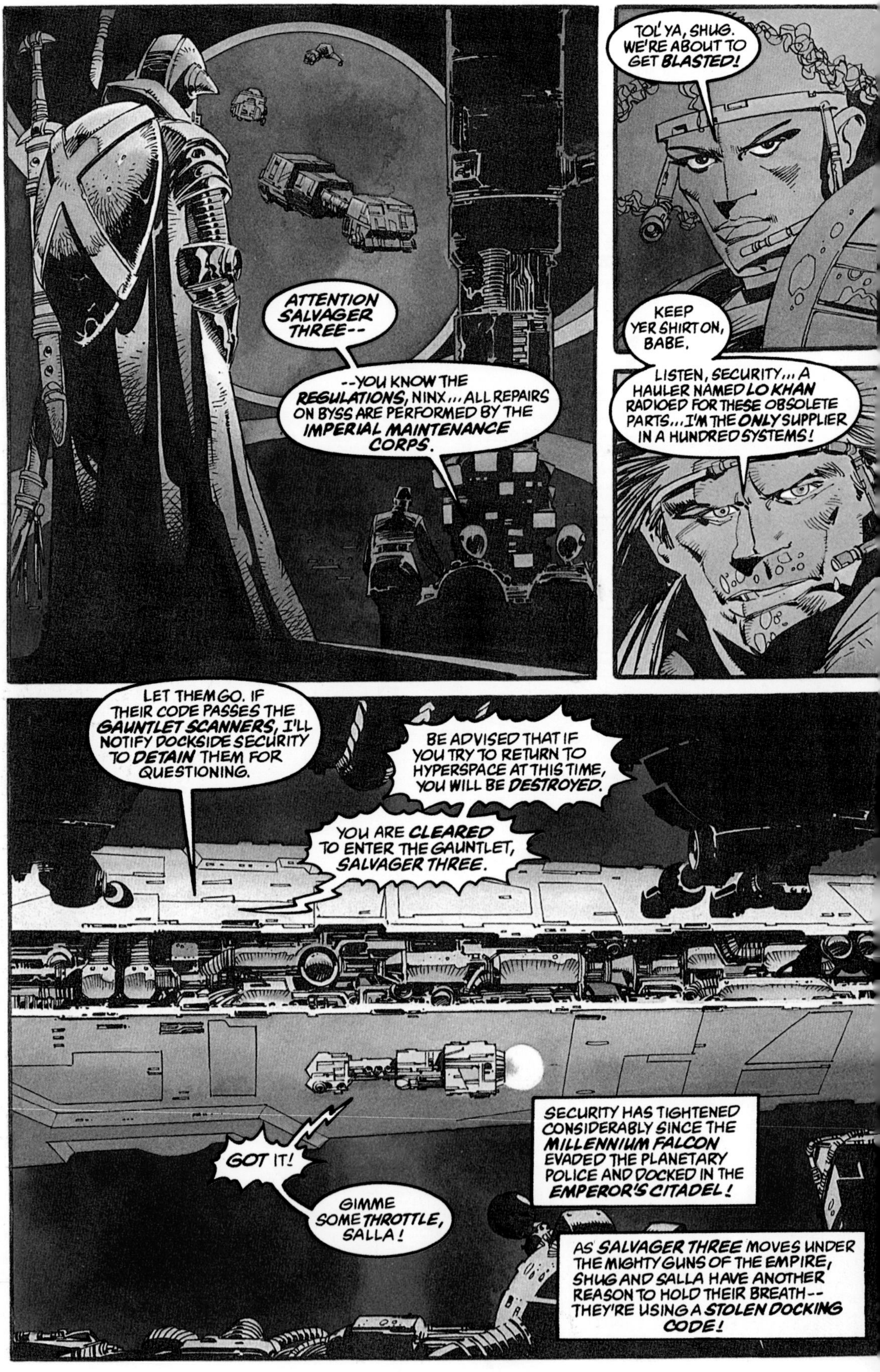

ATTENTION SALVAGER THREE--
--YOU KNOW THE REGULATIONS, NINX... ALL REPAIRS ON BYSS ARE PERFORMED BY THE IMPERIAL MAINTENANCE CORPS.
TOL'YA, SHUG. WE'RE ABOUT TO GET BLASTED!
KEEP YER SHIRT ON, BABE.
LISTEN, SECURITY... A HAULER NAMED LO KHAN RADIOED FOR THESE OBSOLETE PARTS... I'M THE ONLY SUPPLIER IN A HUNDRED SYSTEMS!
LET THEM GO. IF THEIR CODE PASSES THE GAUNTLET SCANNERS, I'LL NOTIFY DOCKSIDE SECURITY TO DETAIN THEM FOR QUESTIONING.
BE ADVISED THAT IF YOU TRY TO RETURN TO HYPERSPACE AT THIS TIME, YOU WILL BE DESTROYED.
YOU ARE CLEARED TO ENTER THE GAUNTLET, SALVAGER THREE.
SECURITY HAS TIGHTENED CONSIDERABLY SINCE THE MILLENNIUM FALCON EVADED THE PLANETARY POLICE AND DOCKED IN THE EMPEROR'S CITADEL!
GOT IT!
GIMME SOME THROTTLE, SALLA!
AS SALVAGER THREE MOVES UNDER THE MIGHTY GUNS OF THE EMPIRE, SHUG AND SALLA HAVE ANOTHER REASON TO HOLD THEIR BREATH-- THEY'RE USING A STOLEN DOCKING CODE!

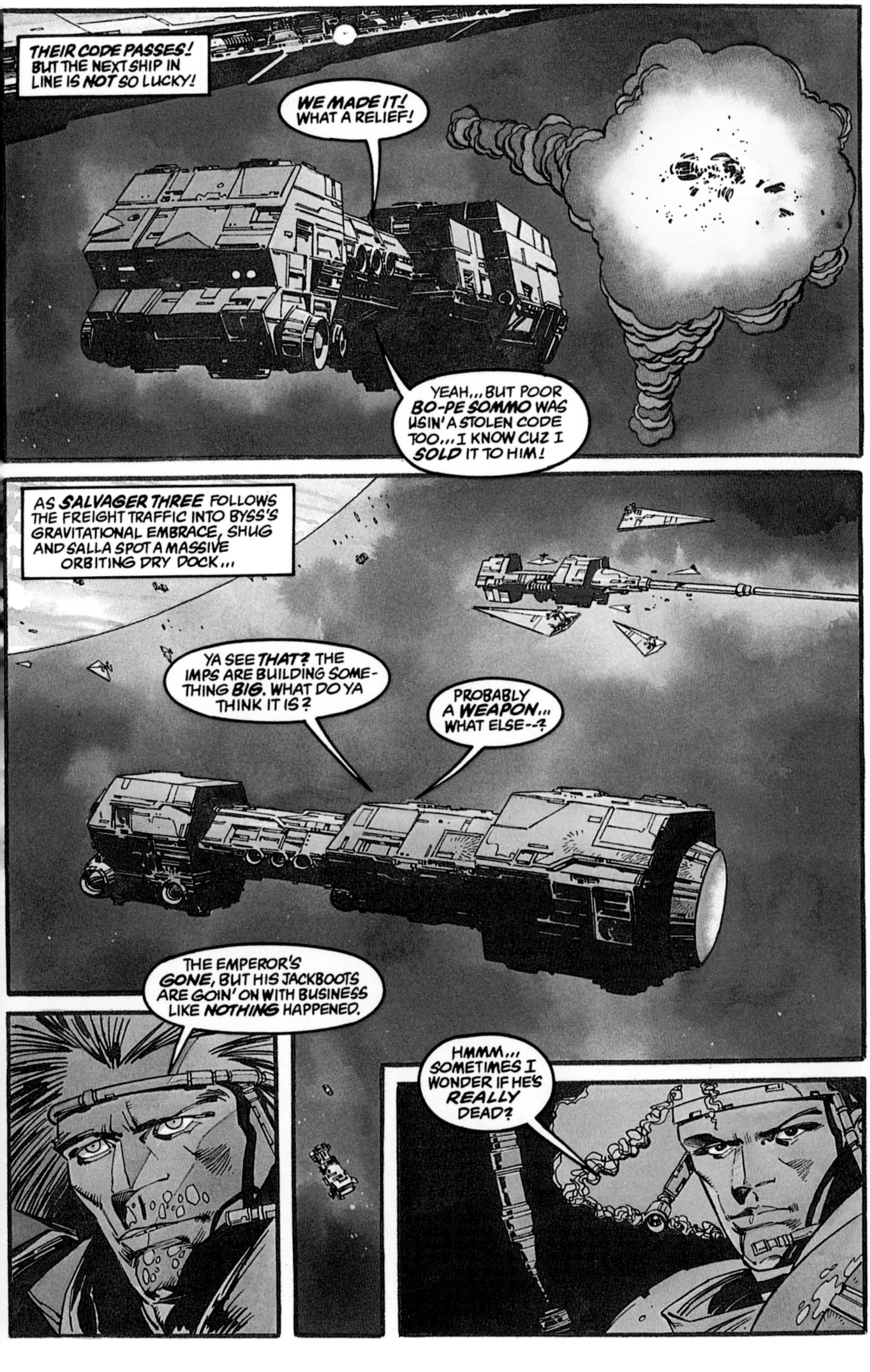
THEIR CODE PASSES! BUT THE NEXT SHIP IN LINE IS NOT SO LUCKY!
WE MADE IT! WHAT A RELIEF!
YEAH... BUT POOR BO-PE SOMMO WAS USIN' A STOLEN CODE TOO... I KNOW CUZ I SOLD IT TO HIM!
AS SALVAGER THREE FOLLOWS THE FREIGHT TRAFFIC INTO BYSS'S GRAVITATIONAL EMBRACE, SHUG AND SALLA SPOT A MASSIVE ORBITING DRY DOCK...
YA SEE THAT? THE IMPS ARE BUILDING SOMETHING BIG. WHAT DO YA THINK IT IS?
PROBABLY A WEAPON... WHAT ELSE--?
THE EMPEROR'S GONE, BUT HIS JACKBOOTS ARE GOIN' ON WITH BUSINESS LIKE NOTHING HAPPENED.
HMMM... SOMETIMES I WONDER IF HE'S REALLY DEAD?

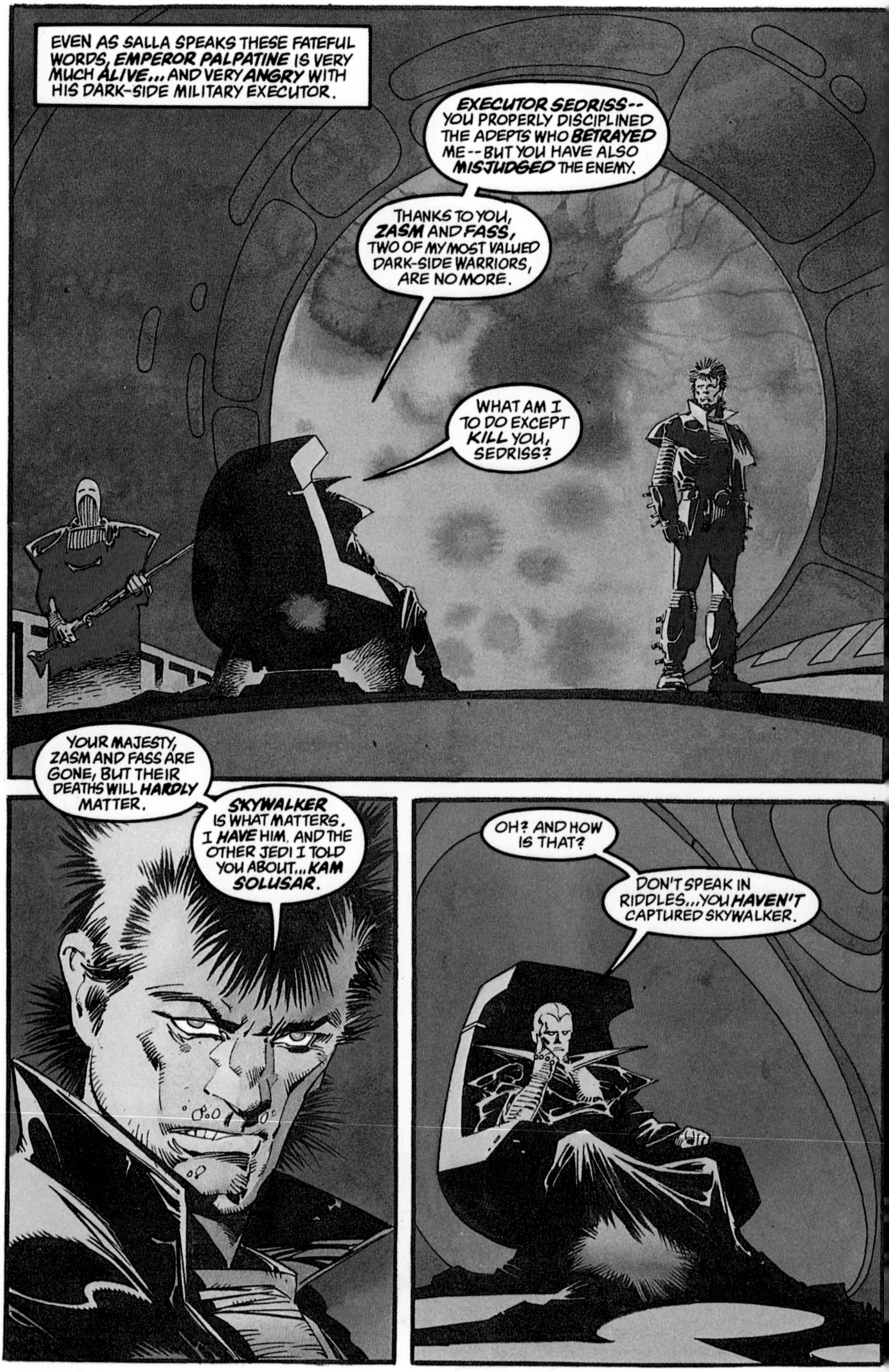
EVEN AS SALLA SPEAKS THESE FATEFUL WORDS, EMPEROR PALPATINE IS VERY MUCH ALIVE... AND VERY ANGRY WITH HIS DARK-SIDE MILITARY EXECUTOR.
EXECUTOR SEDRISS-- YOU PROPERLY DISCIPLINED THE ADEPTS WHO BETRAYED ME--BUT YOU HAVE ALSO MISJUDGED THE ENEMY.
THANKS TO YOU, ZASM AND FASS, TWO OF MY MOST VALUED DARK-SIDE WARRIORS, ARE NO MORE.
WHAT AM I TO DO EXCEPT KILL YOU, SEDRISS?
YOUR MAJESTY, ZASM AND FASS ARE GONE, BUT THEIR DEATHS WILL HARDLY MATTER.
SKYWALKER IS WHAT MATTERS. I HAVE HIM, AND THE OTHER JEDI I TOLD YOU ABOUT... KAM SOLUSAR.
OH? AND HOW IS THAT?
DON'T SPEAK IN RIDDLES... YOU HAVEN'T CAPTURED SKYWALKER.

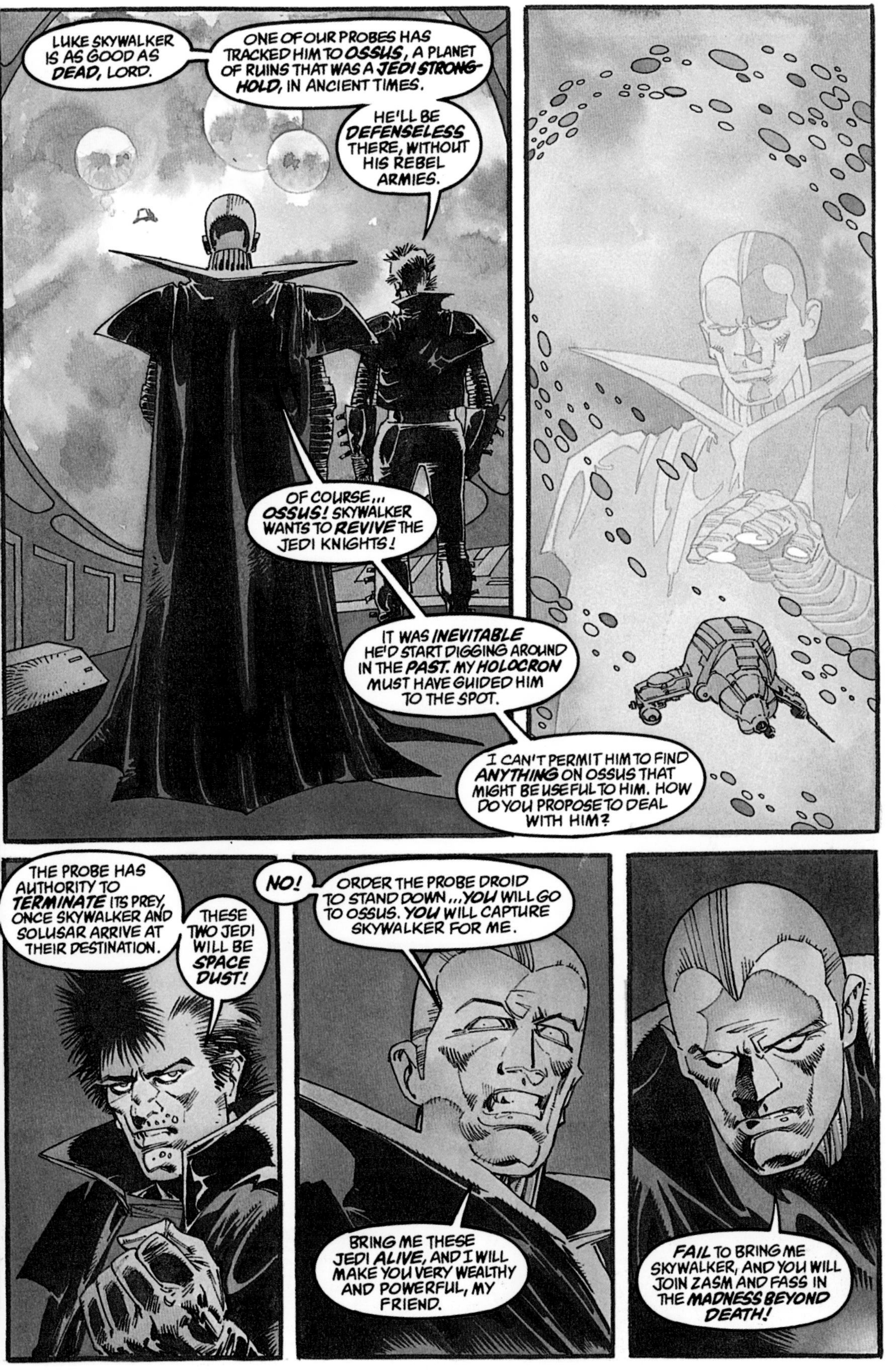
LUKE SKYWALKER IS AS GOOD AS DEAD, LORD.
ONE OF OUR PROBES HAS TRACKED HIM TO OSSUS, A PLANET OF RUINS THAT WAS A JEDI STRONGHOLD, IN ANCIENT TIMES.
HE'LL BE DEFENSELESS THERE, WITHOUT HIS REBEL ARMIES.
OF COURSE... OSSUS! SKYWALKER WANTS TO REVIVE THE JEDI KNIGHTS!
IT WAS INEVITABLE HE'D START DIGGING AROUND IN THE PAST. MY HOLOCRON MUST HAVE GUIDED HIM TO THE SPOT.
I CAN'T PERMIT HIM TO FIND ANYTHING ON OSSUS THAT MIGHT BE USEFUL TO HIM. HOW DO YOU PROPOSE TO DEAL WITH HIM?
THE PROBE HAS AUTHORITY TO TERMINATE ITS PREY, ONCE SKYWALKER AND SOLUSAR ARRIVE AT THEIR DESTINATION.
THESE TWO JEDI WILL BE SPACE DUST!
NO!
ORDER THE PROBE DROID TO STAND DOWN... YOU WILL GO TO OSSUS. YOU WILL CAPTURE SKYWALKER FOR ME.
BRING ME THESE JEDI ALIVE, AND I WILL MAKE YOU VERY WEALTHY AND POWERFUL, MY FRIEND.
FAIL TO BRING ME SKYWALKER, AND YOU WILL JOIN ZASM AND FASS IN THE MADNESS BEYOND DEATH!

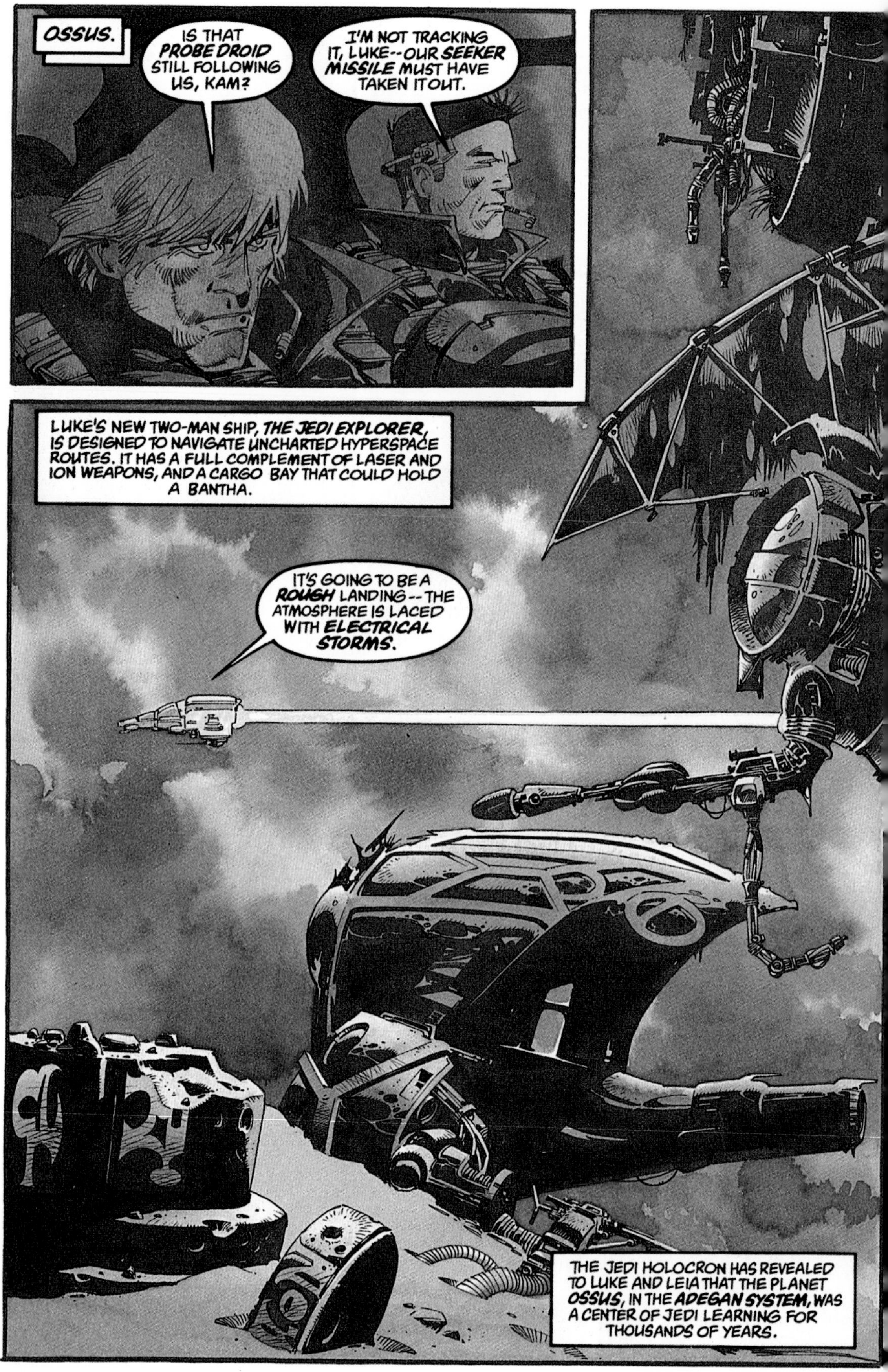
OSSUS.
IS THAT PROBE DROID STILL FOLLOWING US, KAM?
I'M NOT TRACKING IT, LUKE--OUR SEEKER MISSILE MUST HAVE TAKEN IT OUT.
LUKE'S NEW TWO-MAN SHIP, THE JEDI EXPLORER, IS DESIGNED TO NAVIGATE UNCHARTED HYPERSPACE ROUTES. IT HAS A FULL COMPLEMENT OF LASER AND ION WEAPONS, AND A CARGO BAY THAT COULD HOLD A BANTHA.
IT'S GOING TO BE A ROUGH LANDING--THE ATMOSPHERE IS LACED WITH ELECTRICAL STORMS.
THE JEDI HOLOCRON HAS REVEALED TO LUKE AND LEIA THAT THE PLANET OSSUS, IN THE ADEGAN SYSTEM, WAS A CENTER OF JEDI LEARNING FOR THOUSANDS OF YEARS.

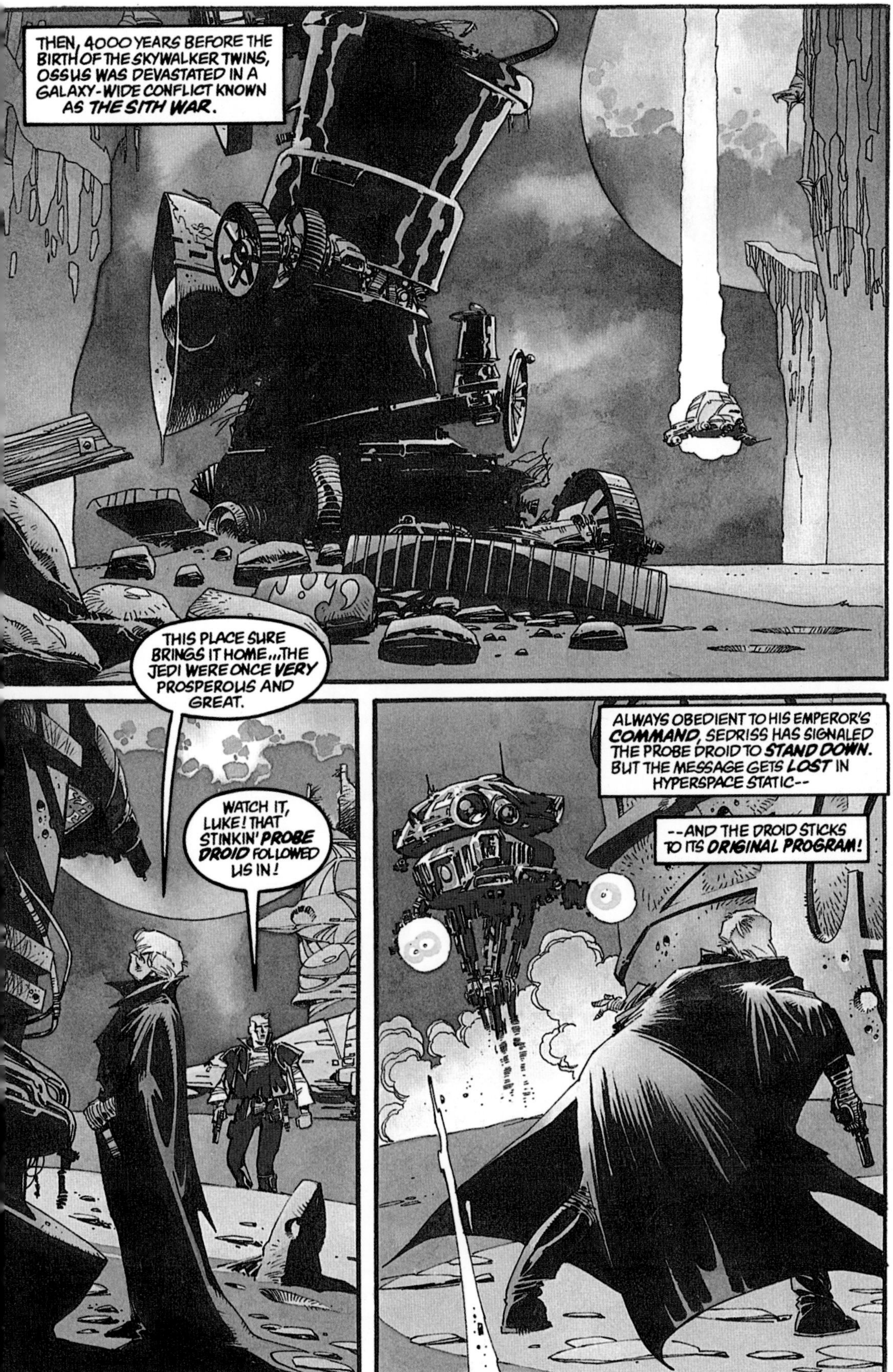

THEN, 4000 YEARS BEFORE THE BIRTH OF THE SKYWALKER TWINS, OSSUS WAS DEVASTATED IN A GALAXY-WIDE CONFLICT KNOWN AS THE SITH WAR.
THIS PLACE SURE BRINGS IT HOME... THE JEDI WERE ONCE VERY PROSPEROUS AND GREAT.
WATCH IT, LUKE! THAT STINKIN' PROBE DROID FOLLOWED US IN!
ALWAYS OBEDIENT TO HIS EMPEROR'S COMMAND, SEDRISS HAS SIGNALED THE PROBE DROID TO STAND DOWN. BUT THE MESSAGE GETS LOST IN HYPERSPACE STATIC--
--AND THE DROID STICKS TO ITS ORIGINAL PROGRAM!

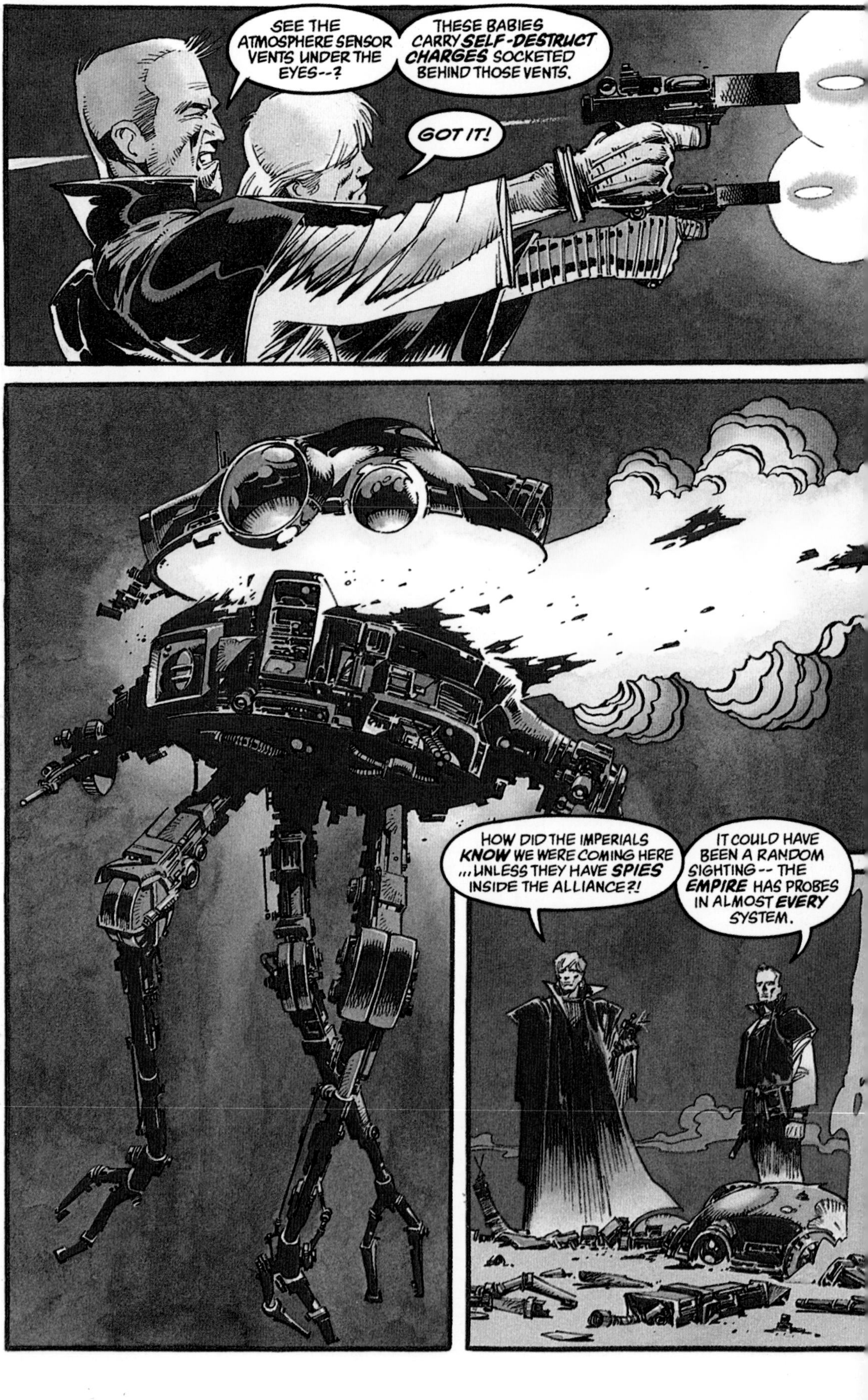

SEE THE ATMOSPHERE SENSOR VENTS UNDER THE EYES--?
THESE BABIES CARRY SELF-DESTRUCT CHARGES SOCKETED BEHIND THOSE VENTS.
GOT IT!
HOW DID THE IMPERIALS KNOW WE WERE COMING HERE ...UNLESS THEY HAVE SPIES INSIDE THE ALLIANCE?!
IT COULD HAVE BEEN A RANDOM SIGHTING -- THE EMPIRE HAS PROBES IN ALMOST EVERY SYSTEM.

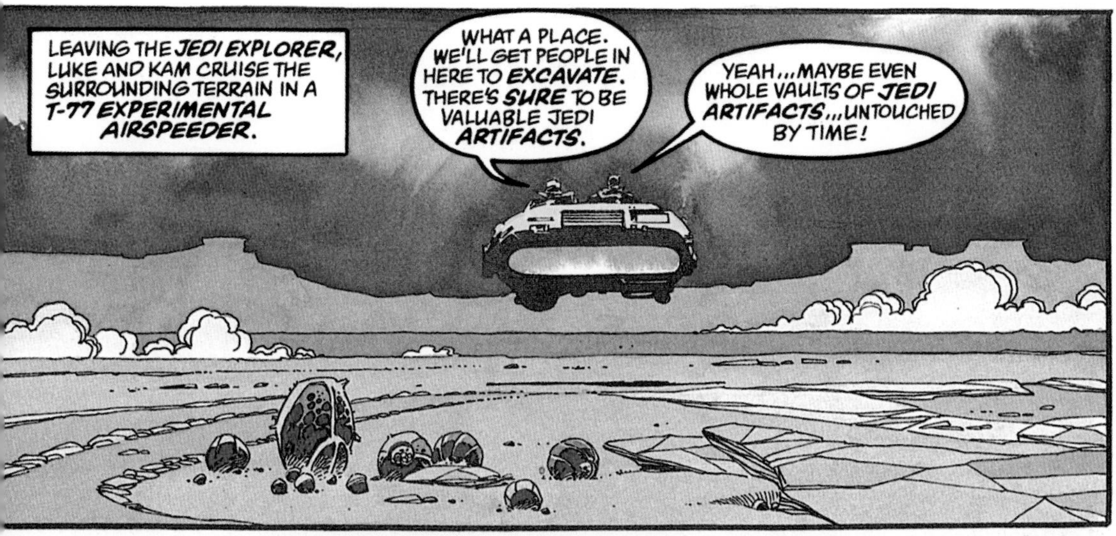
LEAVING THE JEDI EXPLORER, LUKE AND KAM CRUISE THE SURROUNDING TERRAIN IN A T-77 EXPERIMENTAL AIRSPEEDER.
WHAT A PLACE. WE'LL GET PEOPLE IN HERE TO EXCAVATE. THERE'S SURE TO BE VALUABLE JEDI ARTIFACTS.
YEAH... MAYBE EVEN WHOLE VAULTS OF JEDI ARTIFACTS... UNTOUCHED BY TIME!

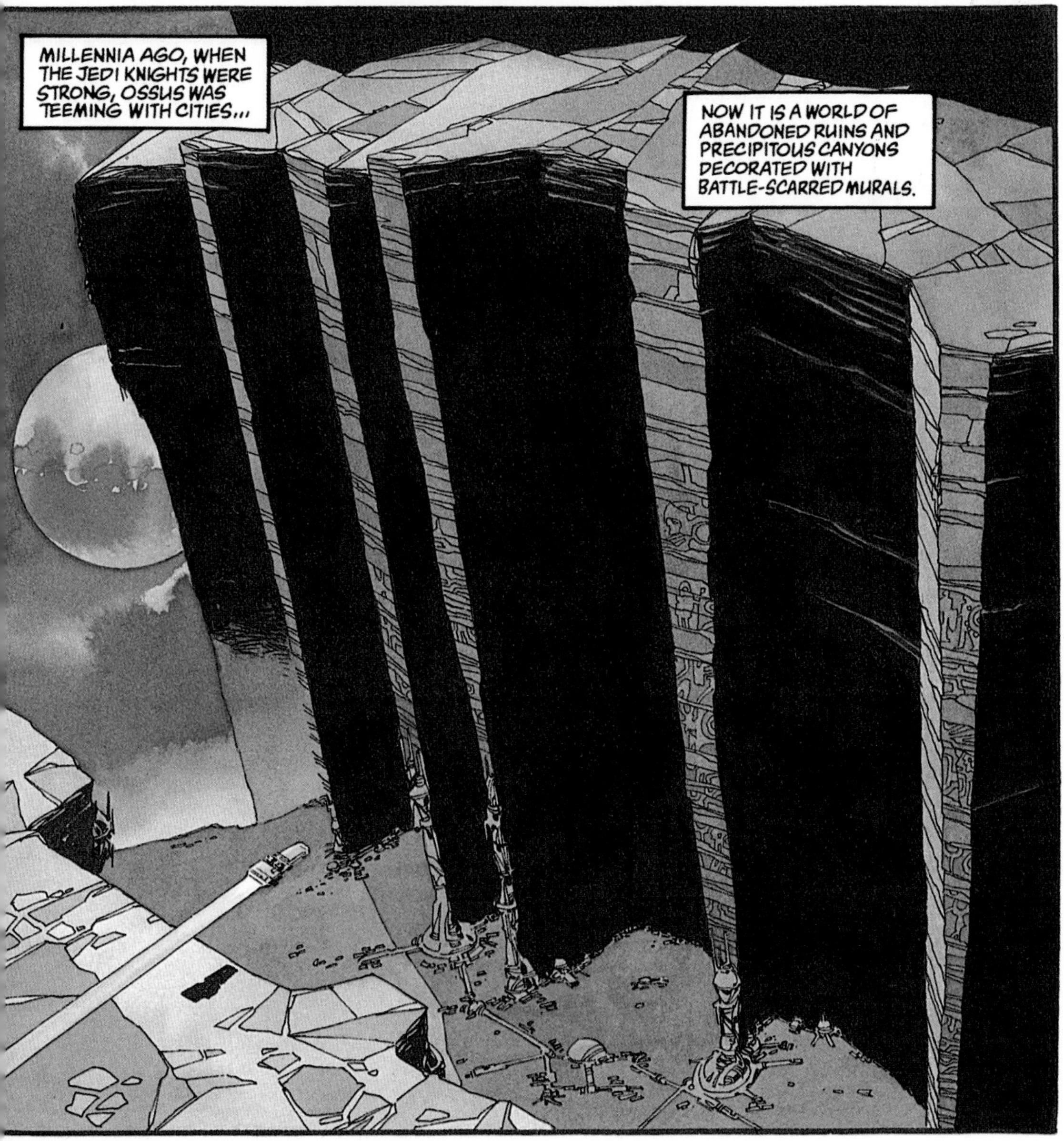
MILLENNIA AGO, WHEN THE JEDI KNIGHTS WERE STRONG, OSSUS WAS TEEMING WITH CITIES...
NOW IT IS A WORLD OF ABANDONED RUINS AND PRECIPITOUS CANYONS DECORATED WITH BATTLE-SCARRED MURALS.

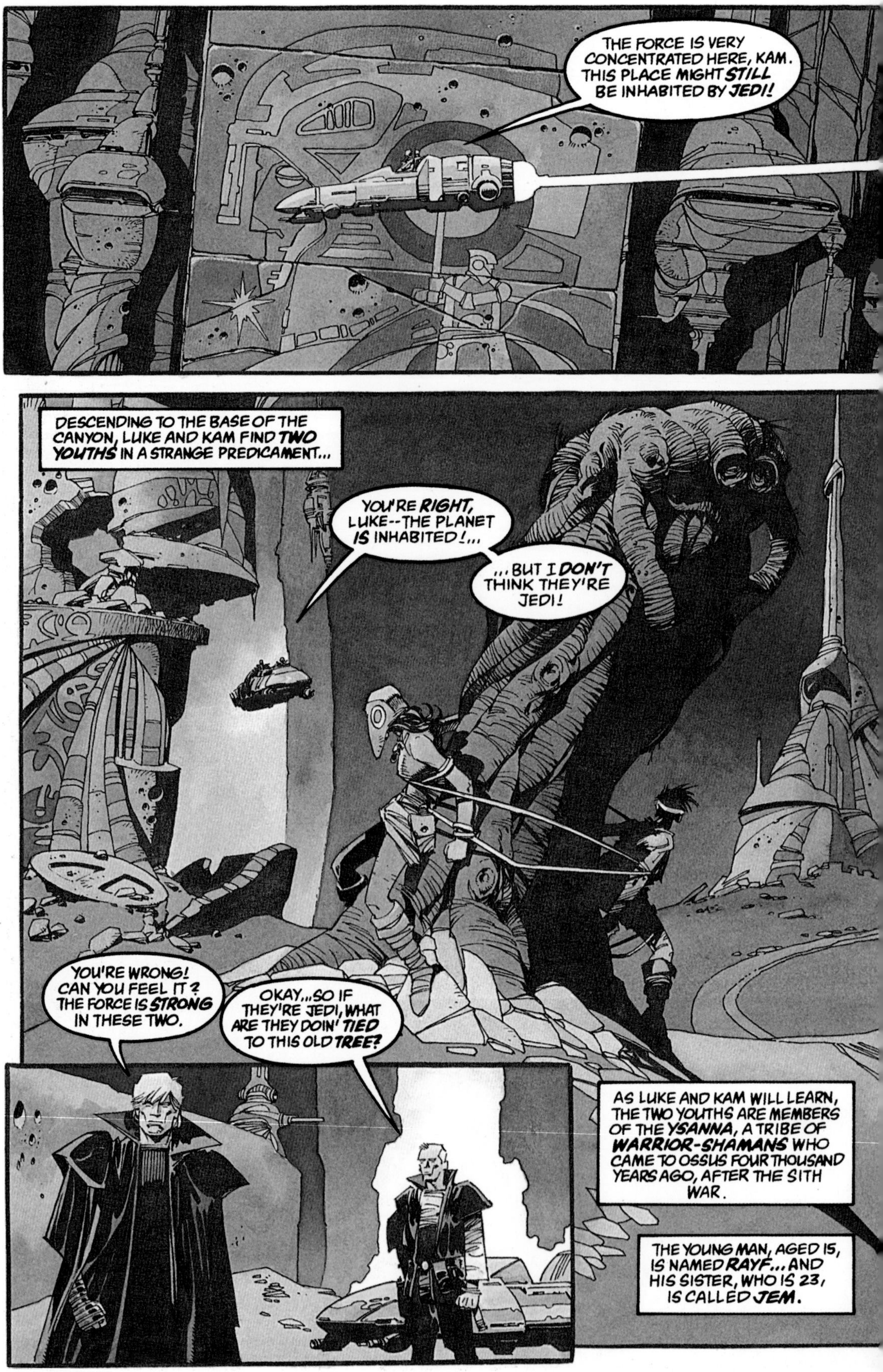
THE FORCE IS VERY CONCENTRATED HERE, KAM. THIS PLACE MIGHT STILL BE INHABITED BY JEDI!
DESCENDING TO THE BASE OF THE CANYON, LUKE AND KAM FIND TWO YOUTHS IN A STRANGE PREDICAMENT...
YOU'RE RIGHT, LUKE--THE PLANET IS INHABITED!...
...BUT I DON'T THINK THEY'RE JEDI!
YOU'RE WRONG! CAN YOU FEEL IT? THE FORCE IS STRONG IN THESE TWO.
OKAY...SO IF THEY'RE JEDI, WHAT ARE THEY DOIN' TIED TO THIS OLD TREE?
AS LUKE AND KAM WILL LEARN, THE TWO YOUTHS ARE MEMBERS OF THE YSANNA, A TRIBE OF WARRIOR-SHAMANS WHO CAME TO OSSUS FOUR THOUSAND YEARS AGO, AFTER THE SITH WAR.
THE YOUNG MAN, AGED 15, IS NAMED RAYF... AND HIS SISTER, WHO IS 23, IS CALLED JEM.

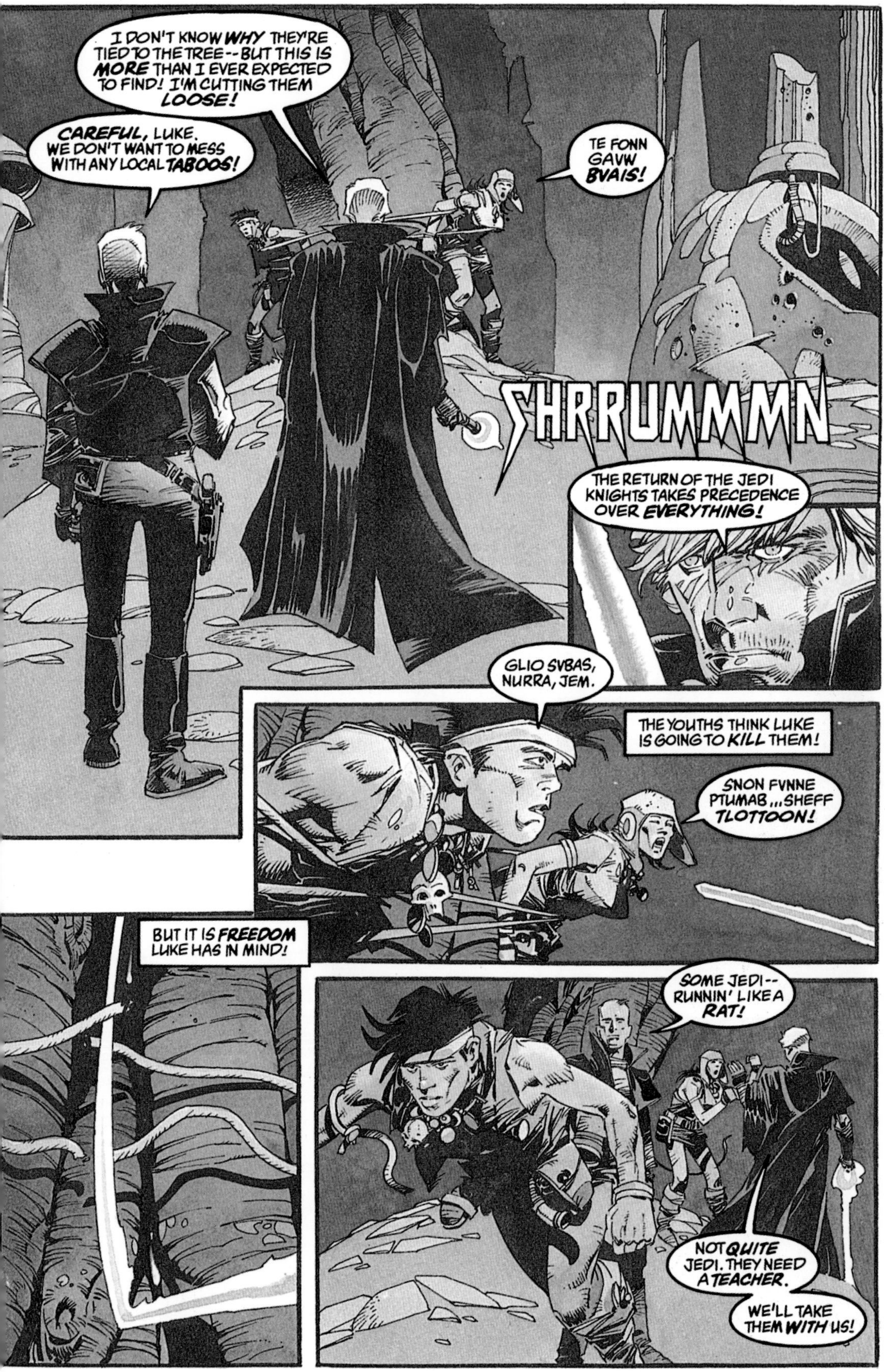

I DON'T KNOW WHY THEY'RE TIED TO THE TREE--BUT THIS IS MORE THAN I EVER EXPECTED TO FIND! I'M CUTTING THEM LOOSE!
CAREFUL, LUKE. WE DON'T WANT TO MESS WITH ANY LOCAL TABOOS!
TE FONN GAVW BVAIS!
SHRRUMMMN
THE RETURN OF THE JEDI KNIGHTS TAKES PRECEDENCE OVER EVERYTHING!
GLIO SVBAS, NURRA, JEM.
THE YOUTHS THINK LUKE IS GOING TO KILL THEM!
SNON FVNNE PTUMAB ... SHEFF TLOTTOON!
BUT IT IS FREEDOM LUKE HAS IN MIND!
SOME JEDI-- RUNNIN' LIKE A RAT!
NOT QUITE JEDI. THEY NEED A TEACHER.
WE'LL TAKE THEM WITH US!

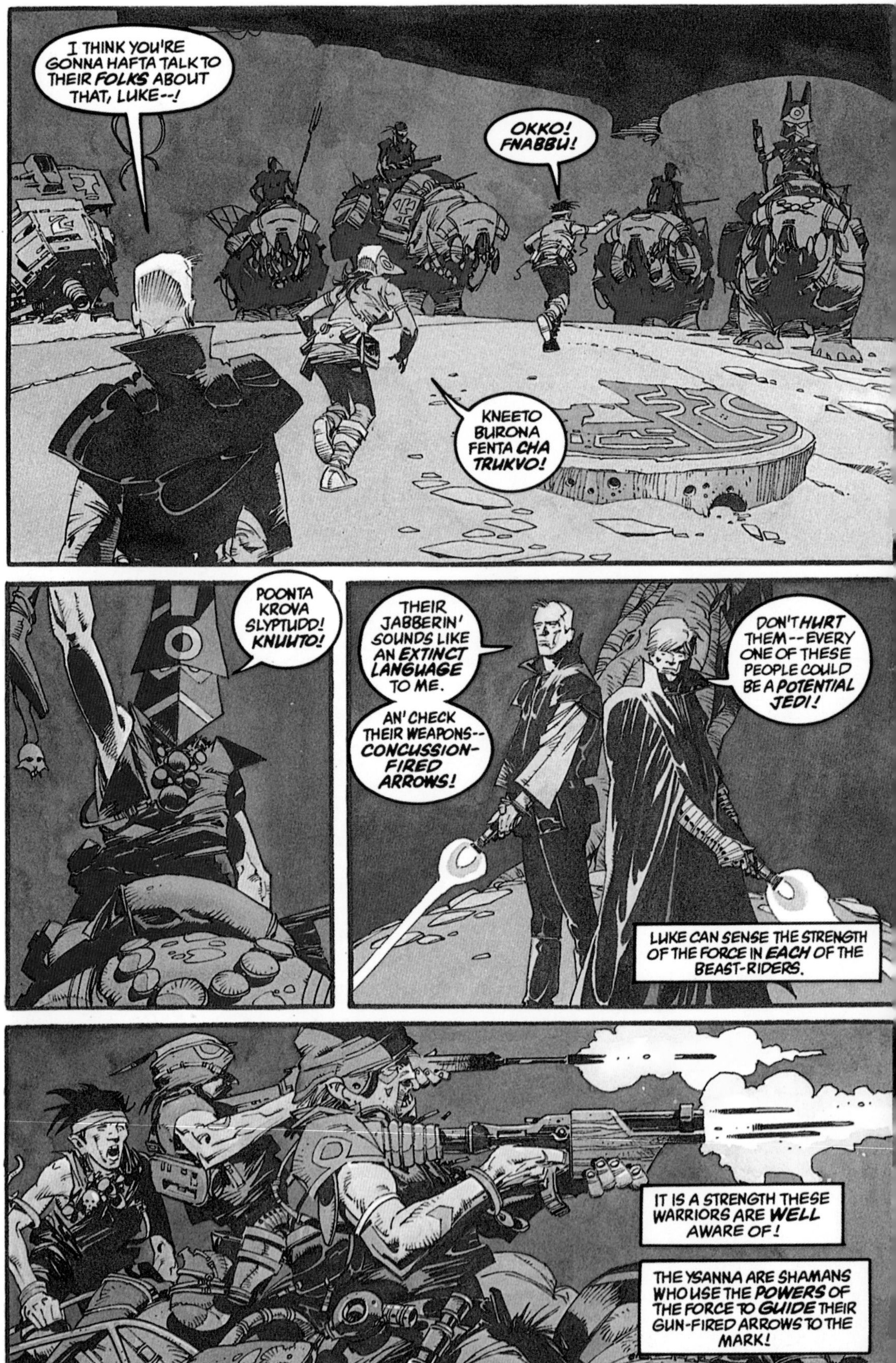

I THINK YOU'RE GONNA HAFTA TALK TO THEIR FOLKS ABOUT THAT, LUKE--!
OKKO! FNABBU!
KNEETO BURONA FENTA CHA TRUKVO!
POONTA KROVA SLYPTUDD! KNUUTO!
THEIR JABBERIN' SOUNDS LIKE AN EXTINCT LANGUAGE TO ME.
AN' CHECK THEIR WEAPONS-- CONCUSSION-FIRED ARROWS!
DON'T HURT THEM--EVERY ONE OF THESE PEOPLE COULD BE A POTENTIAL JEDI!
LUKE CAN SENSE THE STRENGTH OF THE FORCE IN EACH OF THE BEAST-RIDERS.
IT IS A STRENGTH THESE WARRIORS ARE WELL AWARE OF!
THE YSANNA ARE SHAMANS WHO USE THE POWERS OF THE FORCE TO GUIDE THEIR GUN-FIRED ARROWS TO THE MARK!

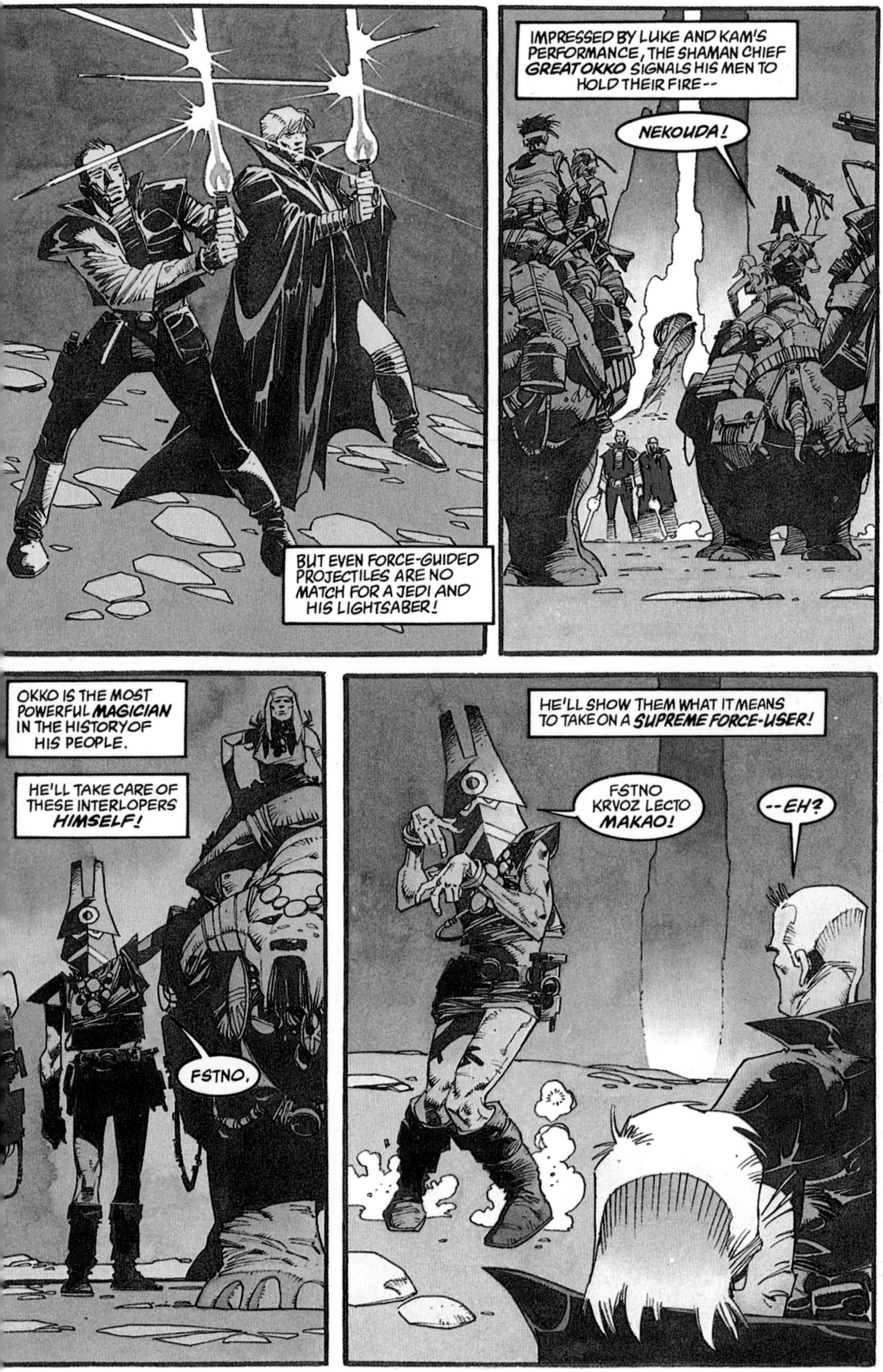

BUT EVEN FORCE-GUIDED PROJECTILES ARE NO MATCH FOR A JEDI AND HIS LIGHTSABER!
IMPRESSED BY LUKE AND KAM'S PERFORMANCE, THE SHAMAN CHIEF GREAT OKKO SIGNALS HIS MEN TO HOLD THEIR FIRE--
NEKOUDA!
OKKO IS THE MOST POWERFUL MAGICIAN IN THE HISTORY OF HIS PEOPLE.
HE'LL TAKE CARE OF THESE INTERLOPERS HIMSELF!
FSTNO.
HE'LL SHOW THEM WHAT IT MEANS TO TAKE ON A SUPREME FORCE-USER!
FSTNO KRVOZ LECTO MAKAO!
--EH?

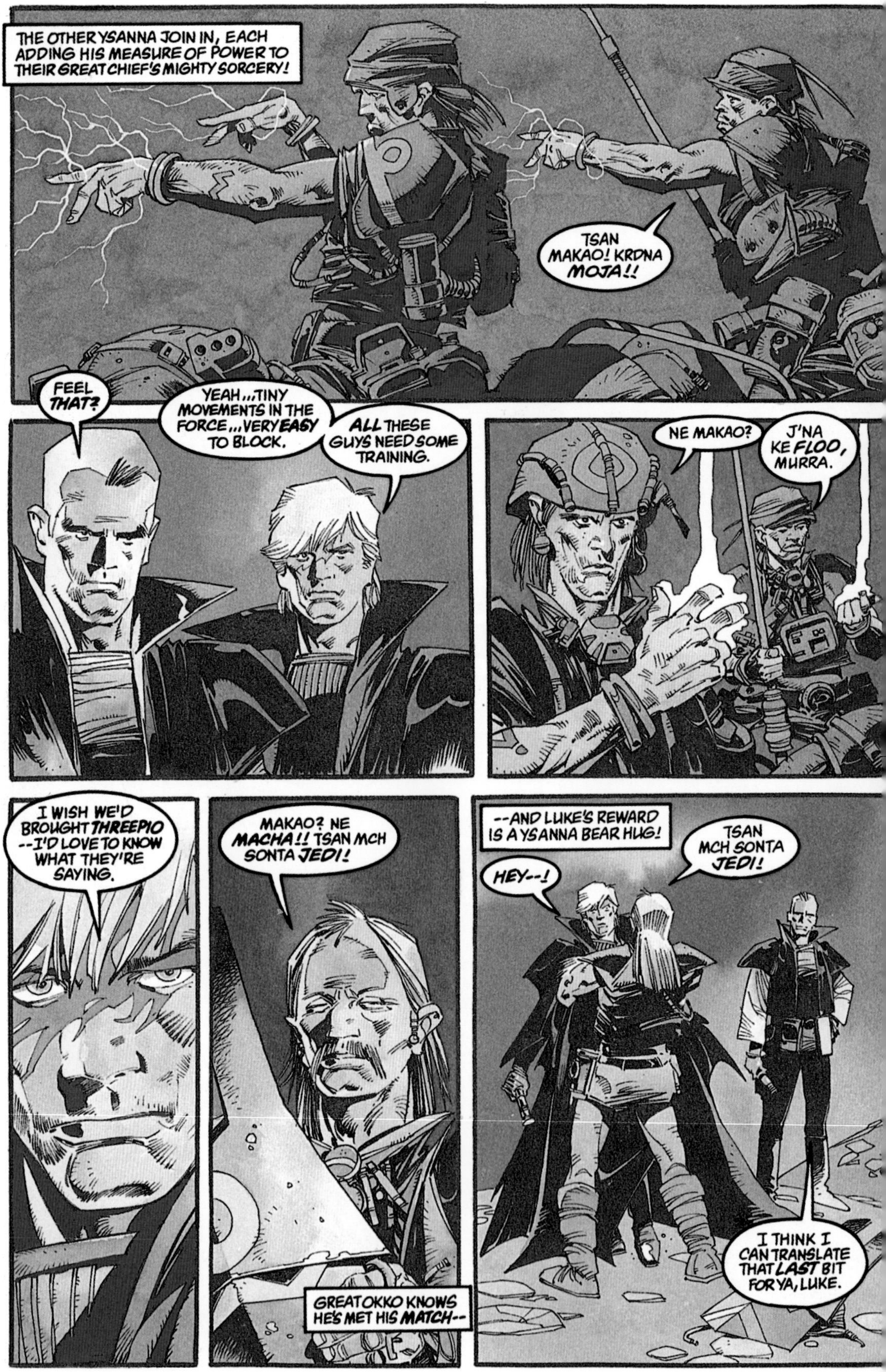
THE OTHER YSANNA JOIN IN, EACH ADDING HIS MEASURE OF POWER TO THEIR GREAT CHIEF'S MIGHTY SORCERY!
TSAN MAKAO! KRDNA MOJA!!
FEEL THAT?
YEAH...TINY MOVEMENTS IN THE FORCE...VERY EASY TO BLOCK.
ALL THESE GUYS NEED SOME TRAINING.
NE MAKAO?
J'NA KE FLOO, MURRA.
I WISH WE'D BROUGHT THREEPIO --I'D LOVE TO KNOW WHAT THEY'RE SAYING.
MAKAO? NE MACHA!! TSAN MCH SONTA JEDI!
GREAT OKKO KNOWS HE'S MET HIS MATCH--
--AND LUKE'S REWARD IS A YSANNA BEAR HUG!
TSAN MCH SONTA JEDI!
HEY--!
I THINK I CAN TRANSLATE THAT LAST BIT FOR YA, LUKE.

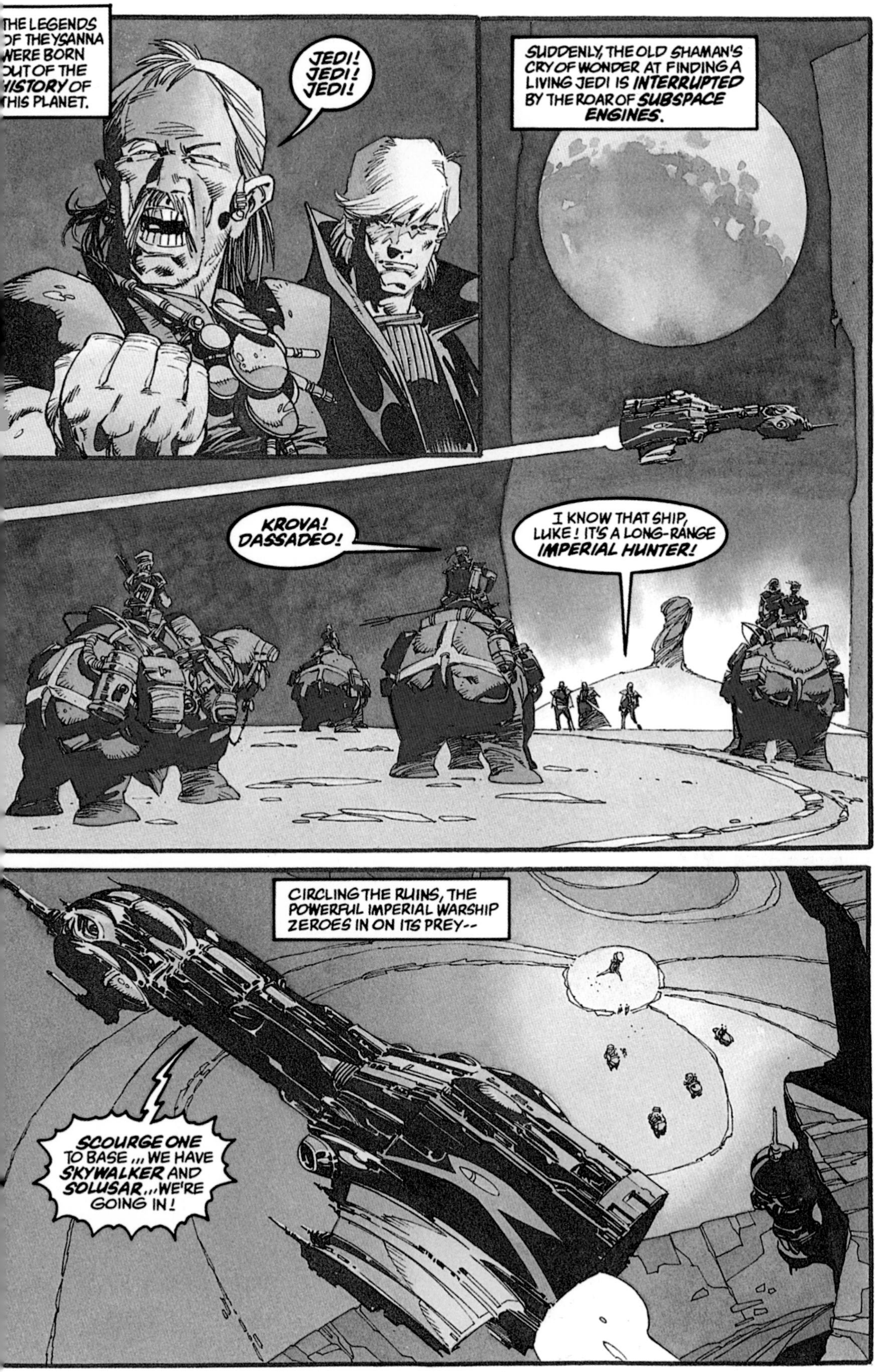
THE LEGENDS OF THE YSANNA WERE BORN OUT OF THE HISTORY OF THIS PLANET.
JEDI! JEDI! JEDI!
SUDDENLY, THE OLD SHAMAN'S CRY OF WONDER AT FINDING A LIVING JEDI IS INTERRUPTED BY THE ROAR OF SUBSPACE ENGINES.
KROVA! DASSADEO!
I KNOW THAT SHIP, LUKE! IT'S A LONG-RANGE IMPERIAL HUNTER!
CIRCLING THE RUINS, THE POWERFUL IMPERIAL WARSHIP ZEROES IN ON ITS PREY--
SCOURGE ONE TO BASE ... WE HAVE SKYWALKER AND SOLUSAR ... WE'RE GOING IN!

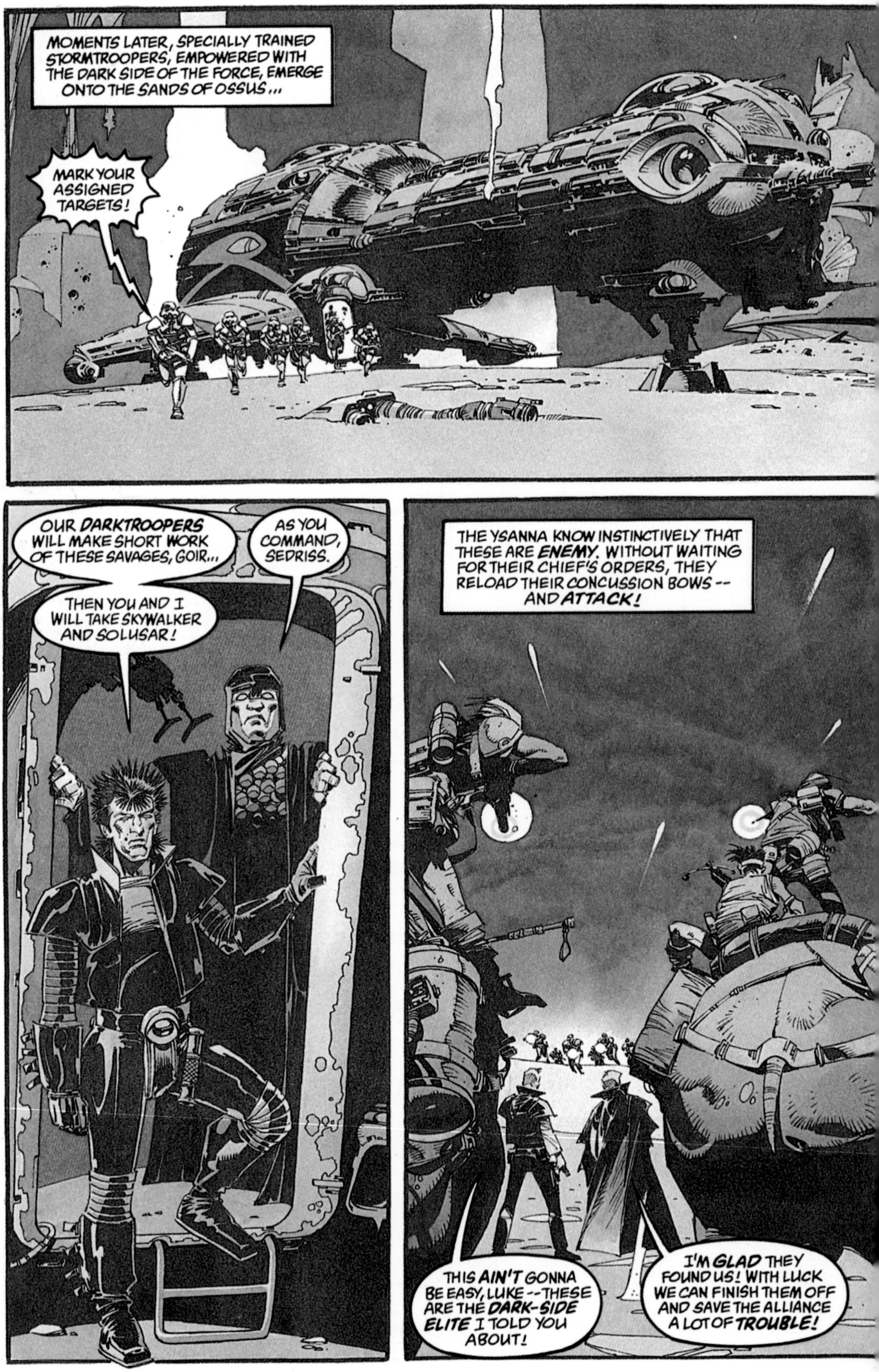
MOMENTS LATER, SPECIALLY TRAINED STORMTROOPERS, EMPOWERED WITH THE DARK SIDE OF THE FORCE, EMERGE ONTO THE SANDS OF OSSUS...
MARK YOUR ASSIGNED TARGETS!
OUR DARKTROOPERS WILL MAKE SHORT WORK OF THESE SAVAGES, GOIR...
THEN YOU AND I WILL TAKE SKYWALKER AND SOLUSAR!
AS YOU COMMAND, SEDRISS.
THE YSANNA KNOW INSTINCTIVELY THAT THESE ARE ENEMY. WITHOUT WAITING FOR THEIR CHIEF'S ORDERS, THEY RELOAD THEIR CONCUSSION BOWS -- AND ATTACK!
THIS AIN'T GONNA BE EASY, LUKE -- THESE ARE THE DARK-SIDE ELITE I TOLD YOU ABOUT!
I'M GLAD THEY FOUND US! WITH LUCK WE CAN FINISH THEM OFF AND SAVE THE ALLIANCE A LOT OF TROUBLE!

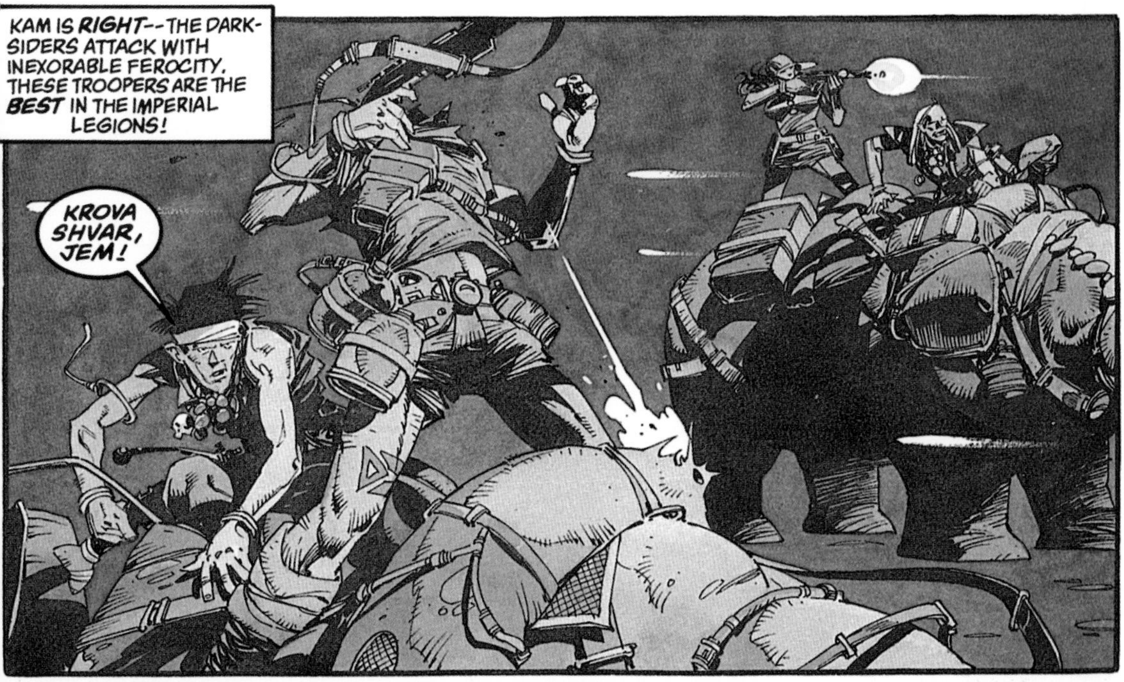
KAM IS RIGHT--THE DARK-SIDERS ATTACK WITH INEXORABLE FEROCITY. THESE TROOPERS ARE THE BEST IN THE IMPERIAL LEGIONS!
KROVA SHVAR, JEM!
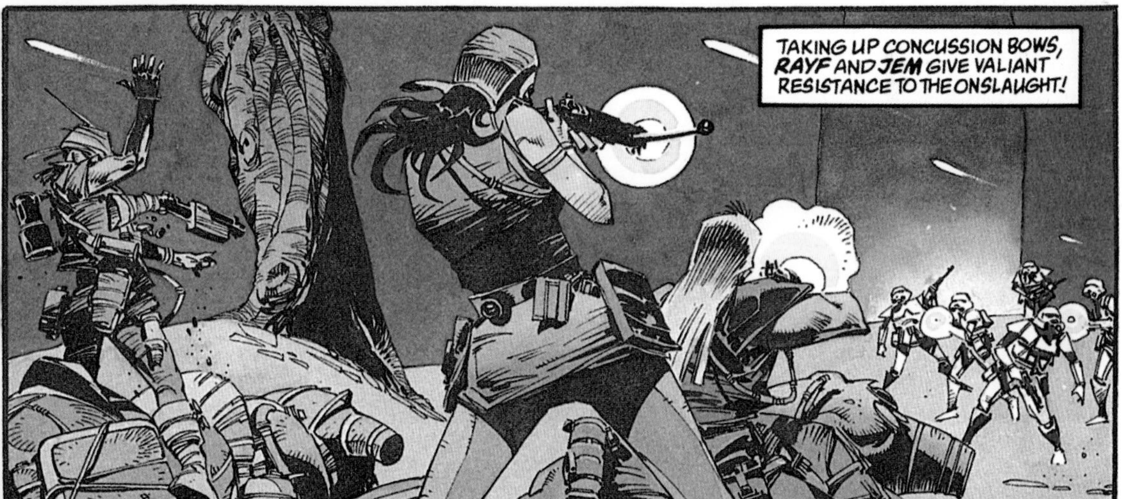
TAKING UP CONCUSSION BOWS, RAYF AND JEM GIVE VALIANT RESISTANCE TO THE ONSLAUGHT!
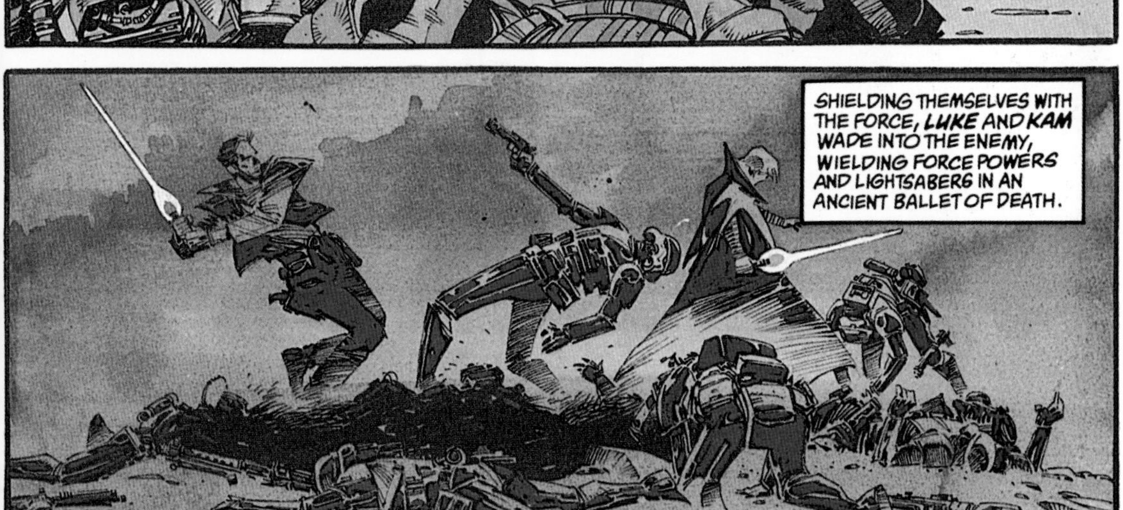
SHIELDING THEMSELVES WITH THE FORCE, LUKE AND KAM WADE INTO THE ENEMY, WIELDING FORCE POWERS AND LIGHTSABERS IN AN ANCIENT BALLET OF DEATH.

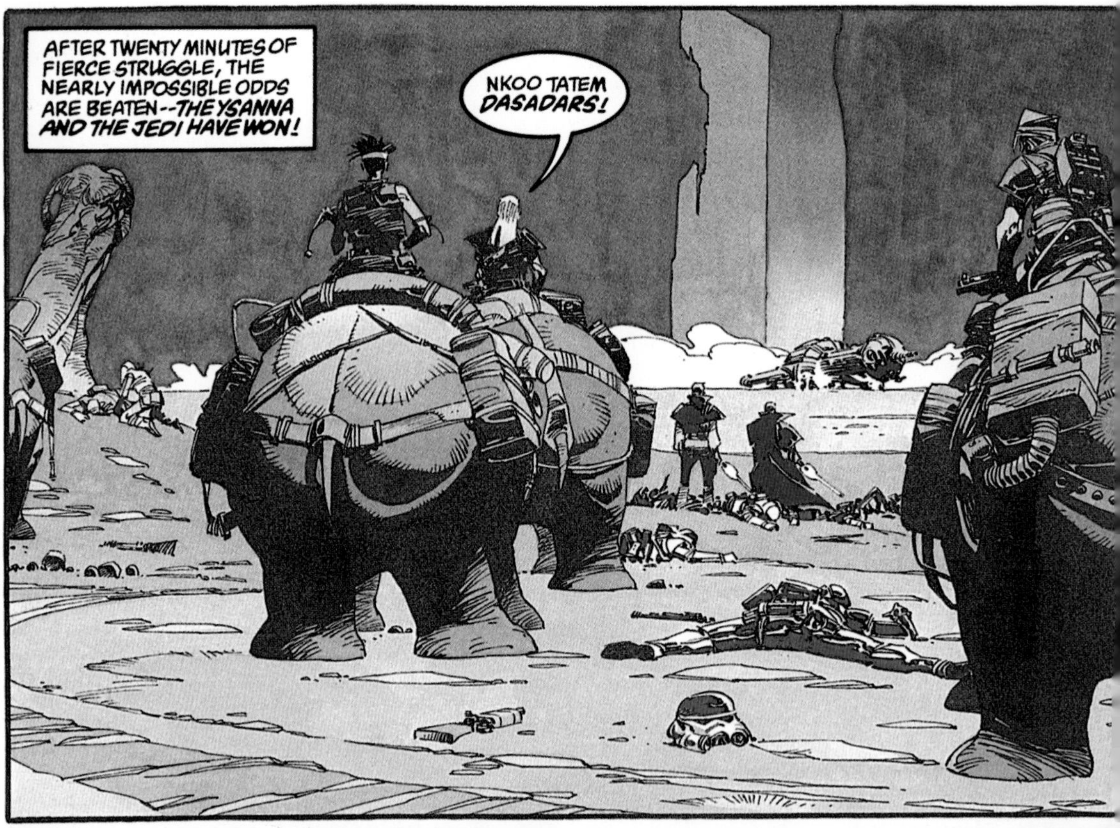
AFTER TWENTY MINUTES OF FIERCE STRUGGLE, THE NEARLY IMPOSSIBLE ODDS ARE BEATEN--THE YSANNA AND THE JEDI HAVE WON!
NKOO TATEM DASADARS!

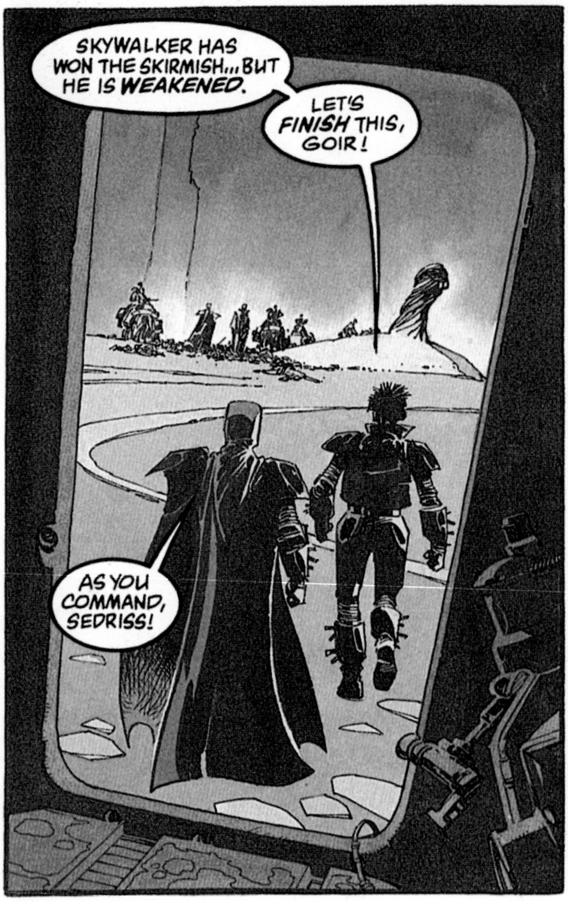
SKYWALKER HAS WON THE SKIRMISH... BUT HE IS WEAKENED.
LET'S FINISH THIS, GOIR!
AS YOU COMMAND, SEDRISS!

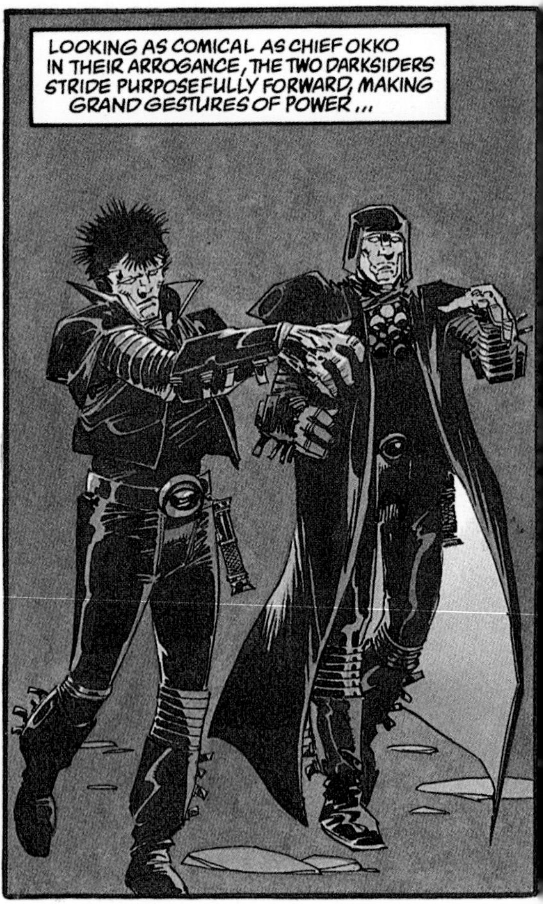
LOOKING AS COMICAL AS CHIEF OKKO IN THEIR ARROGANCE, THE TWO DARKSIDERS STRIDE PURPOSEFULLY FORWARD, MAKING GRAND GESTURES OF POWER...

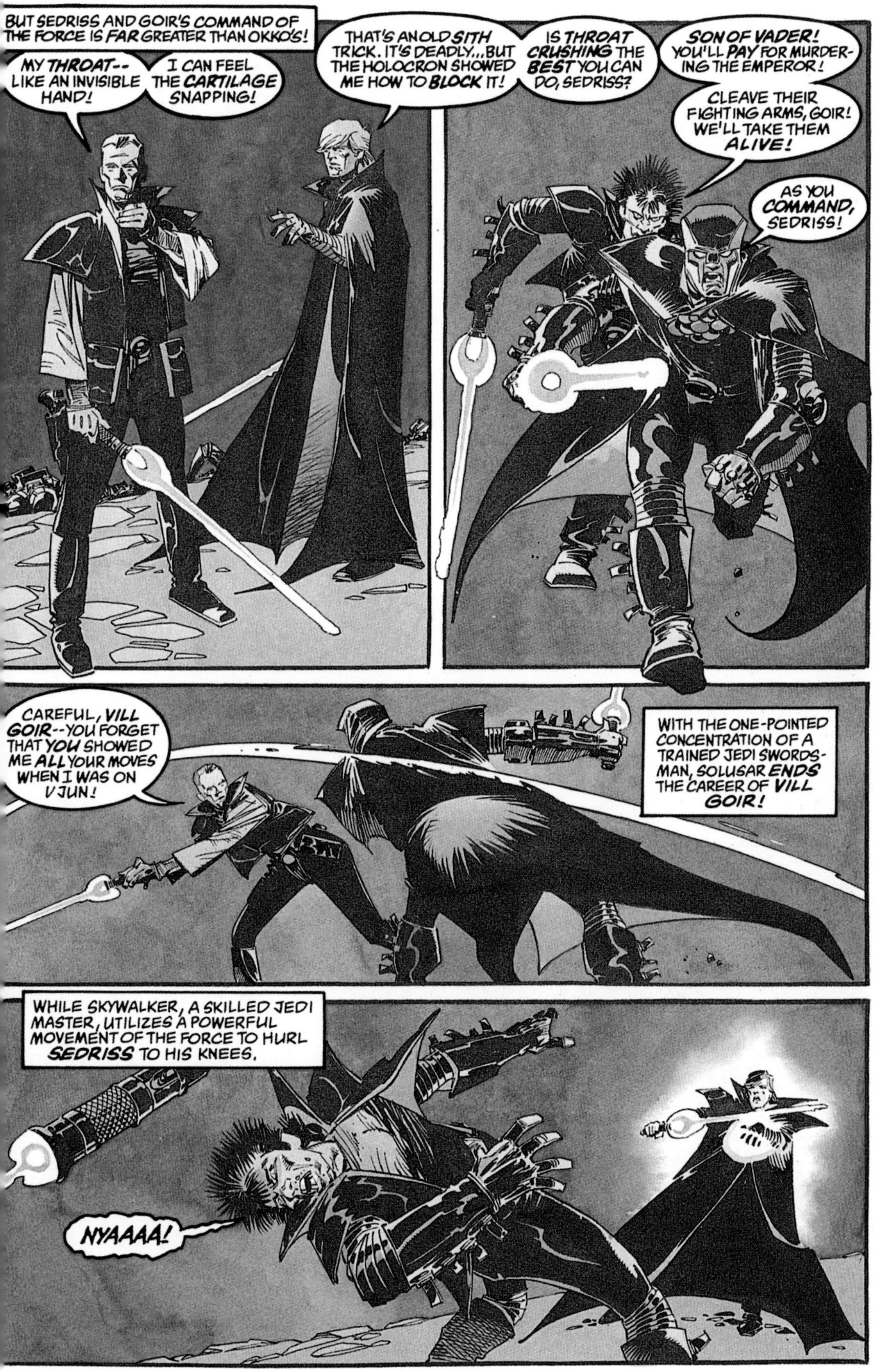
BUT SEDRISS AND GOIR'S COMMAND OF THE FORCE IS FAR GREATER THAN OKKO'S!
MY THROAT-- LIKE AN INVISIBLE HAND!
I CAN FEEL THE CARTILAGE SNAPPING!
THAT'S AN OLD SITH TRICK. IT'S DEADLY... BUT THE HOLOCRON SHOWED ME HOW TO BLOCK IT!
IS THROAT CRUSHING THE BEST YOU CAN DO, SEDRISS?
SON OF VADER! YOU'LL PAY FOR MURDERING THE EMPEROR!
CLEAVE THEIR FIGHTING ARMS, GOIR! WE'LL TAKE THEM ALIVE!
AS YOU COMMAND, SEDRISS!
CAREFUL, VILL GOIR--YOU FORGET THAT YOU SHOWED ME ALL YOUR MOVES WHEN I WAS ON VJUN!
WITH THE ONE-POINTED CONCENTRATION OF A TRAINED JEDI SWORDSMAN, SOLUSAR ENDS THE CAREER OF VILL GOIR!
WHILE SKYWALKER, A SKILLED JEDI MASTER, UTILIZES A POWERFUL MOVEMENT OF THE FORCE TO HURL SEDRISS TO HIS KNEES.
NYAAAA!

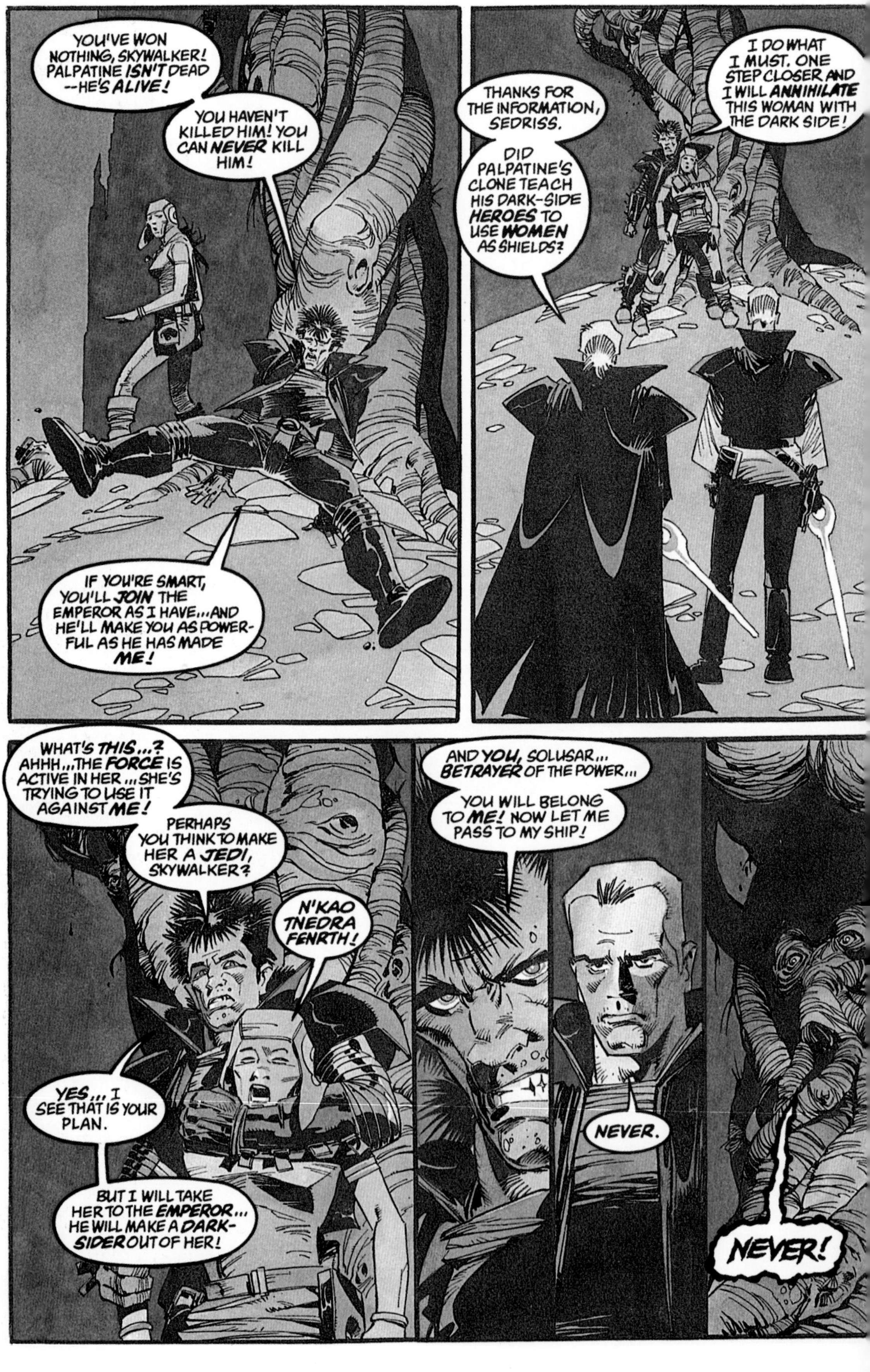
YOU'VE WON NOTHING, SKYWALKER! PALPATINE ISN'T DEAD --HE'S ALIVE!
YOU HAVEN'T KILLED HIM! YOU CAN NEVER KILL HIM!
IF YOU'RE SMART, YOU'LL JOIN THE EMPEROR AS I HAVE... AND HE'LL MAKE YOU AS POWERFUL AS HE HAS MADE ME!
THANKS FOR THE INFORMATION, SEDRISS.
DID PALPATINE'S CLONE TEACH HIS DARK-SIDE HEROES TO USE WOMEN AS SHIELDS?
I DO WHAT I MUST. ONE STEP CLOSER AND I WILL ANNIHILATE THIS WOMAN WITH THE DARK SIDE!
WHAT'S THIS...? AHHH... THE FORCE IS ACTIVE IN HER... SHE'S TRYING TO USE IT AGAINST ME!
PERHAPS YOU THINK TO MAKE HER A JEDI, SKYWALKER?
N'KAO TNEDRA FENRTH!
YES... I SEE THAT IS YOUR PLAN.
BUT I WILL TAKE HER TO THE EMPEROR... HE WILL MAKE A DARK-SIDER OUT OF HER!
AND YOU, SOLUSAR... BETRAYER OF THE POWER...
YOU WILL BELONG TO ME! NOW LET ME PASS TO MY SHIP!
NEVER.
NEVER!

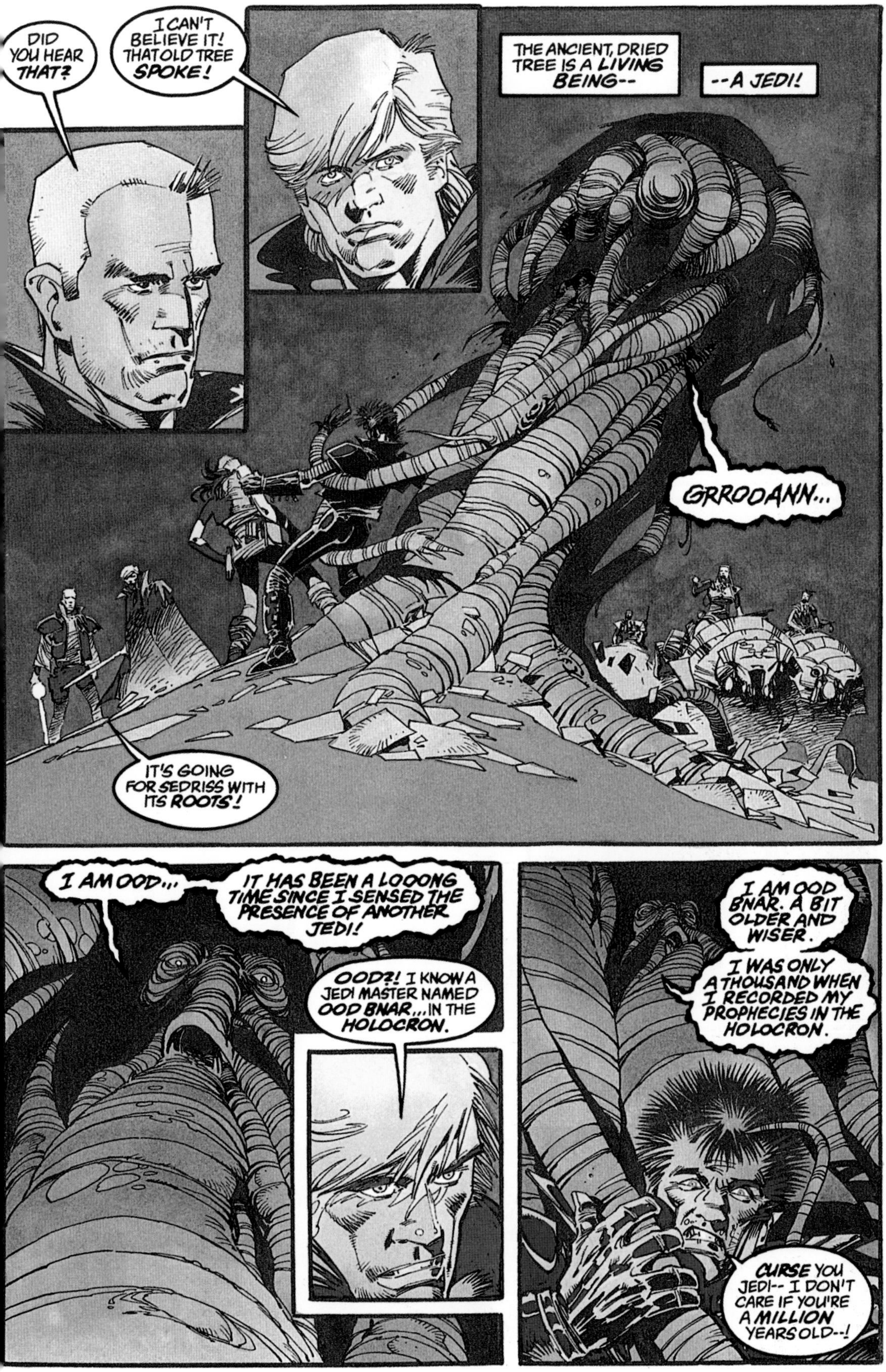
DID YOU HEAR THAT?
I CAN'T BELIEVE IT! THAT OLD TREE SPOKE!
THE ANCIENT, DRIED TREE IS A LIVING BEING--
--A JEDI!
GRROOANN...
IT'S GOING FOR SEDRISS WITH ITS ROOTS!
I AM OOD...
IT HAS BEEN A LOOONG TIME SINCE I SENSED THE PRESENCE OF ANOTHER JEDI!
OOD?! I KNOW A JEDI MASTER NAMED OOD BNAR... IN THE HOLOCRON.
I AM OOD BNAR. A BIT OLDER AND WISER.
I WAS ONLY A THOUSAND WHEN I RECORDED MY PROPHECIES IN THE HOLOCRON.
CURSE YOU JEDI-- I DON'T CARE IF YOU'RE A MILLION YEARS OLD--!

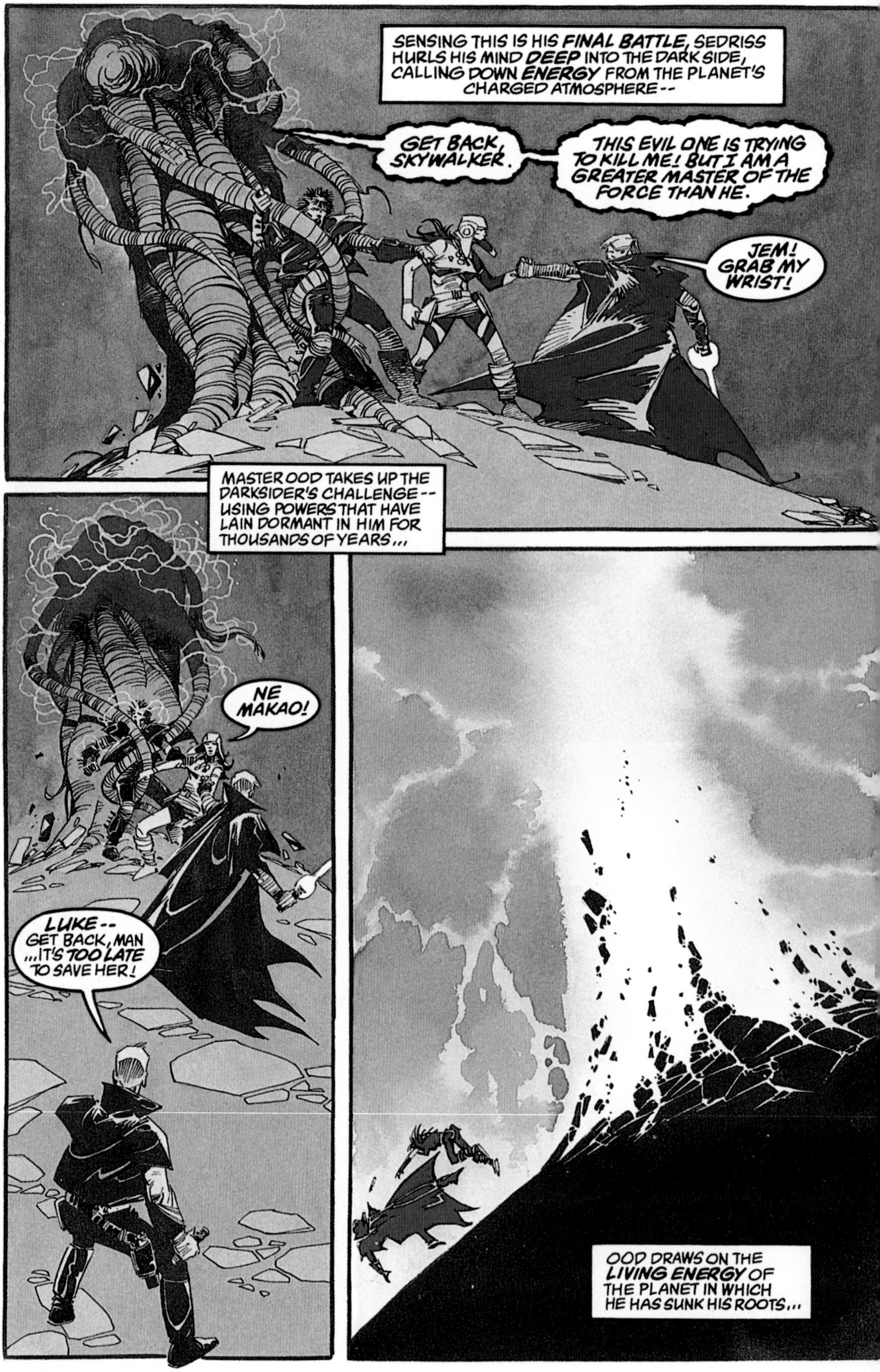
SENSING THIS IS HIS FINAL BATTLE, SEDRISS HURLS HIS MIND DEEP INTO THE DARK SIDE, CALLING DOWN ENERGY FROM THE PLANET'S CHARGED ATMOSPHERE --
GET BACK, SKYWALKER.
THIS EVIL ONE IS TRYING TO KILL ME! BUT I AM A GREATER MASTER OF THE FORCE THAN HE.
JEM! GRAB MY WRIST!
MASTER OOD TAKES UP THE DARKSIDER'S CHALLENGE -- USING POWERS THAT HAVE LAIN DORMANT IN HIM FOR THOUSANDS OF YEARS...
NE MAKAO!
LUKE -- GET BACK, MAN ...IT'S TOO LATE TO SAVE HER!
OOD DRAWS ON THE LIVING ENERGY OF THE PLANET IN WHICH HE HAS SUNK HIS ROOTS...

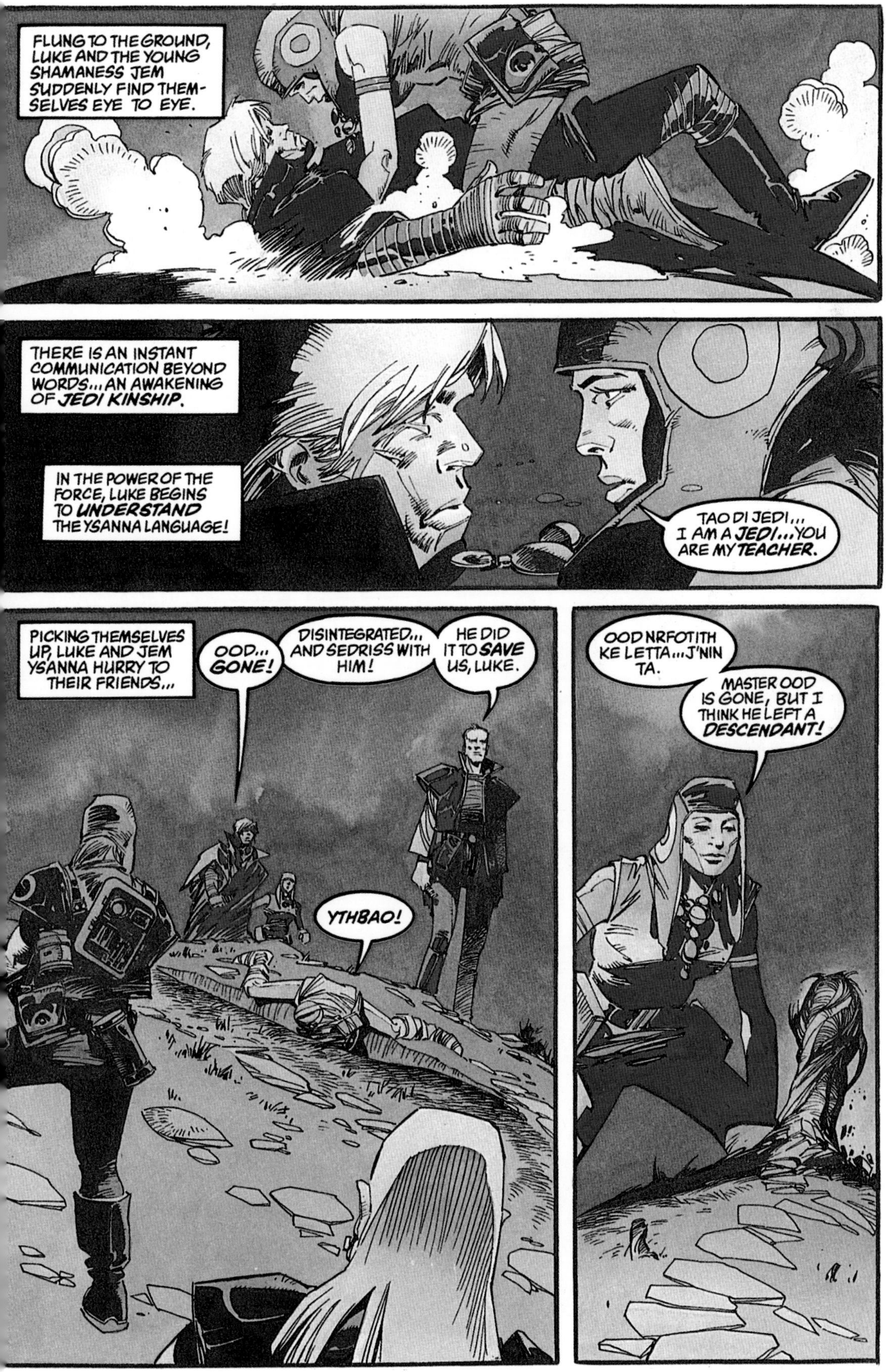
FLUNG TO THE GROUND, LUKE AND THE YOUNG SHAMANESS JEM SUDDENLY FIND THEMSELVES EYE TO EYE.
THERE IS AN INSTANT COMMUNICATION BEYOND WORDS... AN AWAKENING OF JEDI KINSHIP.
IN THE POWER OF THE FORCE, LUKE BEGINS TO UNDERSTAND THE YSANNA LANGUAGE!
TAO DI JEDI... I AM A JEDI... YOU ARE MY TEACHER.
PICKING THEMSELVES UP, LUKE AND JEM YSANNA HURRY TO THEIR FRIENDS...
OOD... GONE!
DISINTEGRATED... AND SEDRISS WITH HIM!
HE DID IT TO SAVE US, LUKE.
YTHBAO!
OOD NRFOTITH KE LETTA... J'NIN TA.
MASTER OOD IS GONE, BUT I THINK HE LEFT A DESCENDANT!

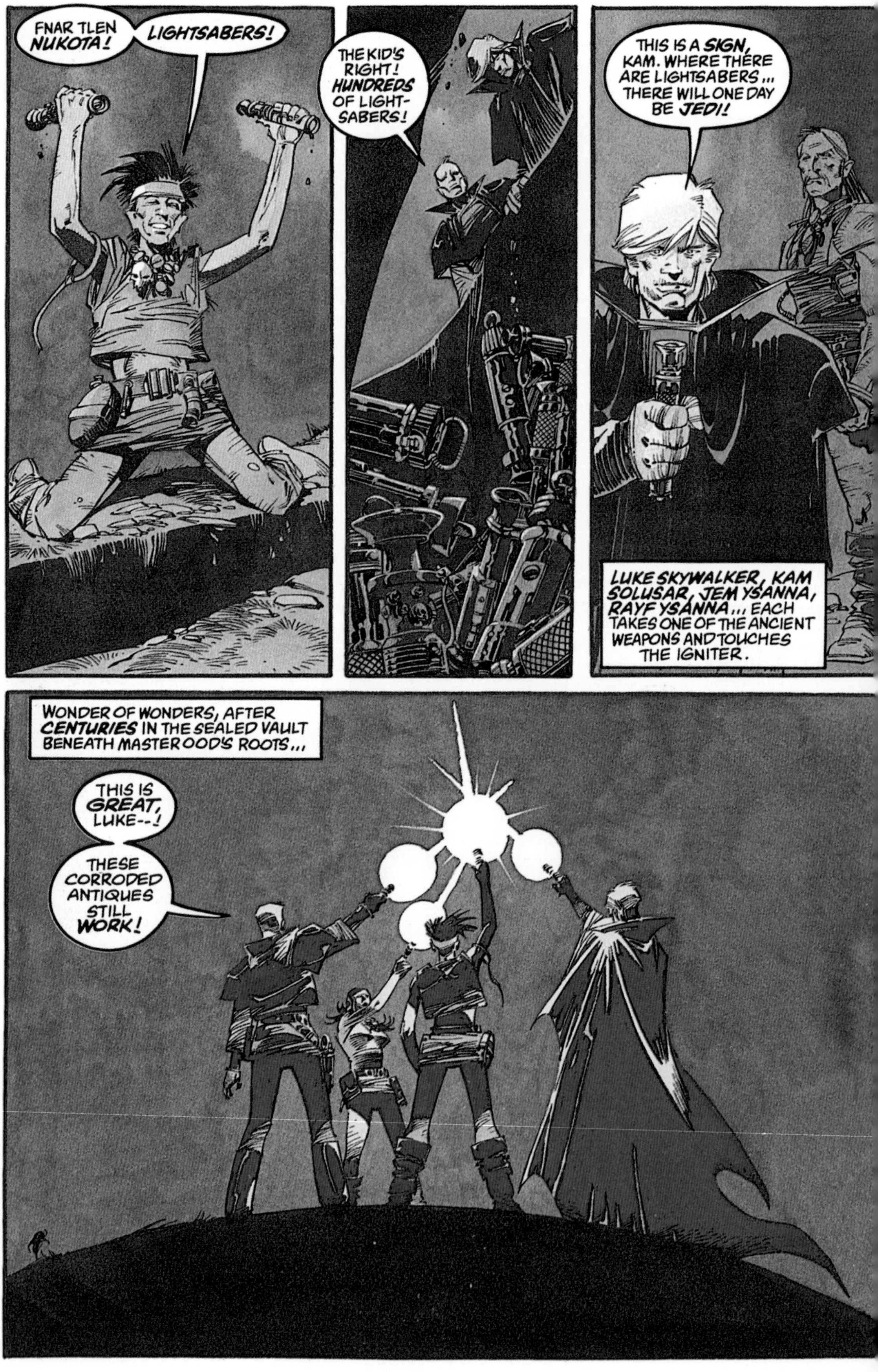

FNAR TLEN NUKOTA!
LIGHTSABERS!
THE KID'S RIGHT! HUNDREDS OF LIGHT-SABERS!
THIS IS A SIGN, KAM. WHERE THERE ARE LIGHTSABERS... THERE WILL ONE DAY BE JEDI!
LUKE SKYWALKER, KAM SOLUSAR, JEM YSANNA, RAYF YSANNA... EACH TAKES ONE OF THE ANCIENT WEAPONS AND TOUCHES THE IGNITER.
WONDER OF WONDERS, AFTER CENTURIES IN THE SEALED VAULT BENEATH MASTER OOD'S ROOTS...
THIS IS GREAT, LUKE--!
THESE CORRODED ANTIQUES STILL WORK!

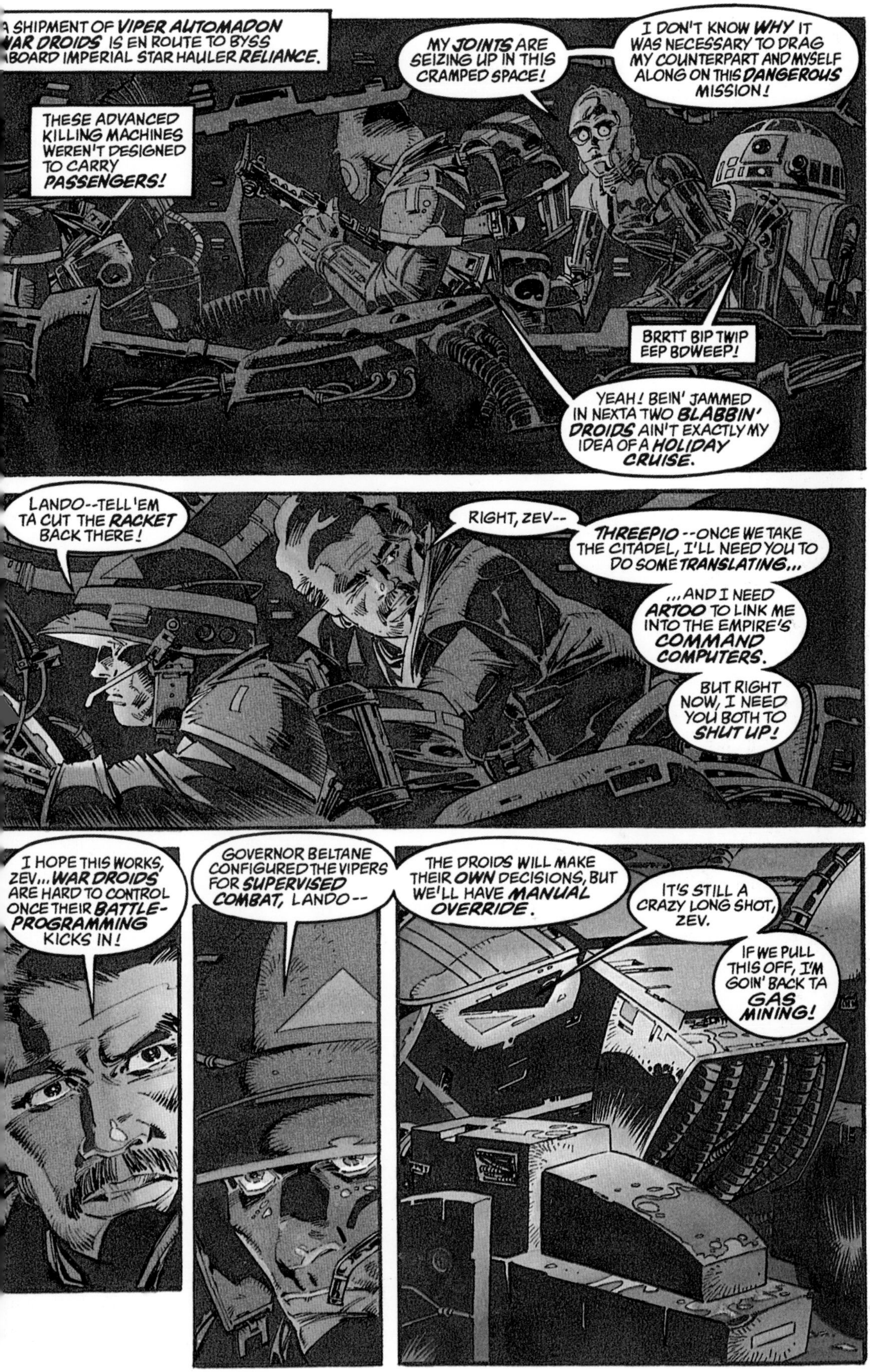
A SHIPMENT OF VIPER AUTOMADON WAR DROIDS IS EN ROUTE TO BYSS ABOARD IMPERIAL STAR HAULER RELIANCE.
MY JOINTS ARE SEIZING UP IN THIS CRAMPED SPACE!
I DON'T KNOW WHY IT WAS NECESSARY TO DRAG MY COUNTERPART AND MYSELF ALONG ON THIS DANGEROUS MISSION!
THESE ADVANCED KILLING MACHINES WEREN'T DESIGNED TO CARRY PASSENGERS!
BRRTT BIP TWIP EEP BDWEEP!
YEAH! BEIN' JAMMED IN NEXTA TWO BLABBIN' DROIDS AIN'T EXACTLY MY IDEA OF A HOLIDAY CRUISE.
LANDO--TELL'EM TA CUT THE RACKET BACK THERE!
RIGHT, ZEV--
THREEPIO--ONCE WE TAKE THE CITADEL, I'LL NEED YOU TO DO SOME TRANSLATING...
...AND I NEED ARTOO TO LINK ME INTO THE EMPIRE'S COMMAND COMPUTERS.
BUT RIGHT NOW, I NEED YOU BOTH TO SHUT UP!
I HOPE THIS WORKS, ZEV...WAR DROIDS ARE HARD TO CONTROL ONCE THEIR BATTLE-PROGRAMMING KICKS IN!
GOVERNOR BELTANE CONFIGURED THE VIPERS FOR SUPERVISED COMBAT, LANDO--
THE DROIDS WILL MAKE THEIR OWN DECISIONS, BUT WE'LL HAVE MANUAL OVERRIDE.
IT'S STILL A CRAZY LONG SHOT, ZEV.
IF WE PULL THIS OFF, I'M GOIN' BACK TA GAS MINING!

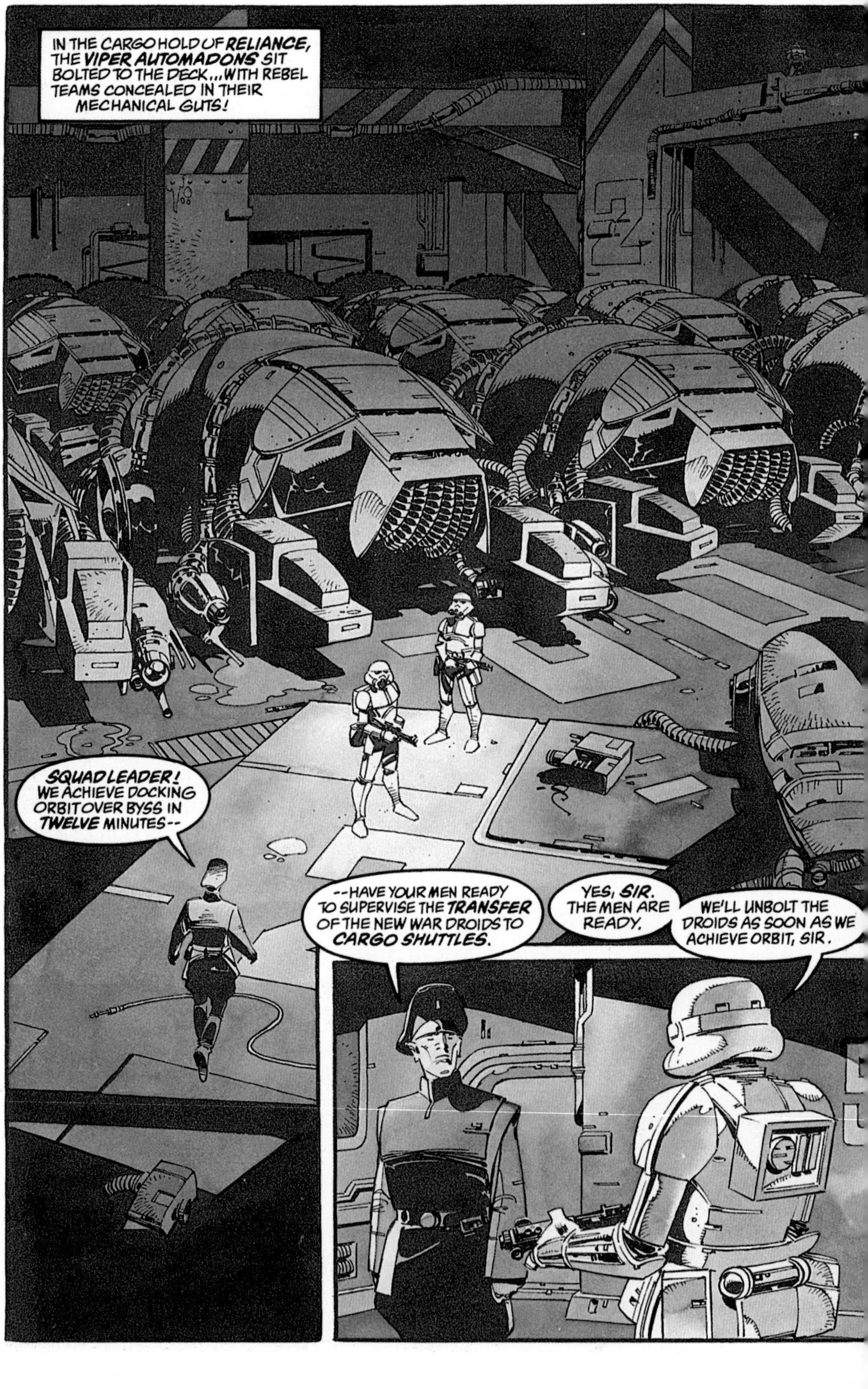
IN THE CARGO HOLD OF RELIANCE, THE VIPER AUTOMADONS SIT BOLTED TO THE DECK...WITH REBEL TEAMS CONCEALED IN THEIR MECHANICAL GUTS!
SQUAD LEADER! WE ACHIEVE DOCKING ORBIT OVER BYSS IN TWELVE MINUTES--
--HAVE YOUR MEN READY TO SUPERVISE THE TRANSFER OF THE NEW WAR DROIDS TO CARGO SHUTTLES.
YES, SIR. THE MEN ARE READY.
WE'LL UNBOLT THE DROIDS AS SOON AS WE ACHIEVE ORBIT, SIR.

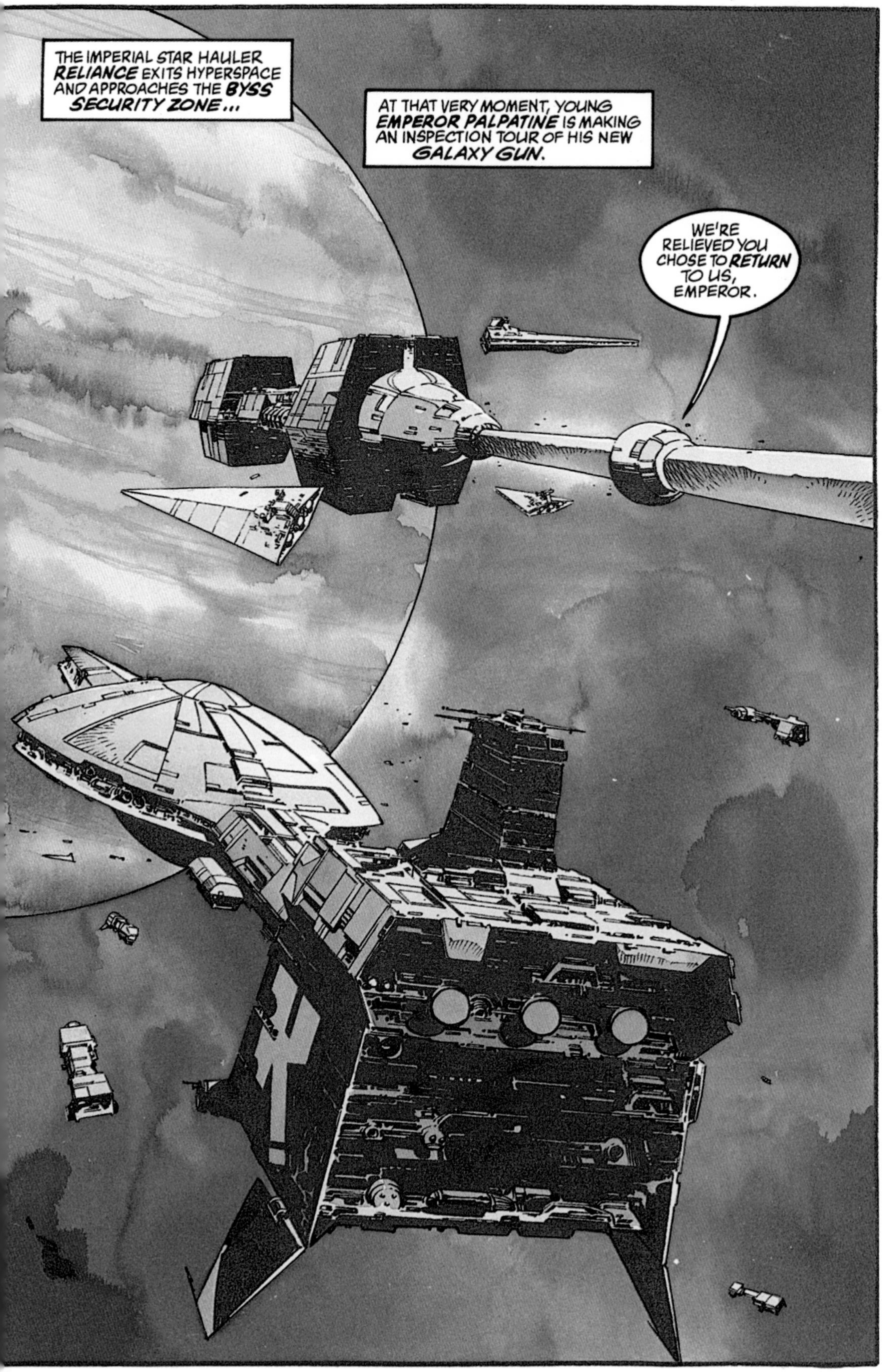
THE IMPERIAL STAR HAULER RELIANCE EXITS HYPERSPACE AND APPROACHES THE BYSS SECURITY ZONE...
AT THAT VERY MOMENT, YOUNG EMPEROR PALPATINE IS MAKING AN INSPECTION TOUR OF HIS NEW GALAXY GUN.
WE'RE RELIEVED YOU CHOSE TO RETURN TO US, EMPEROR.

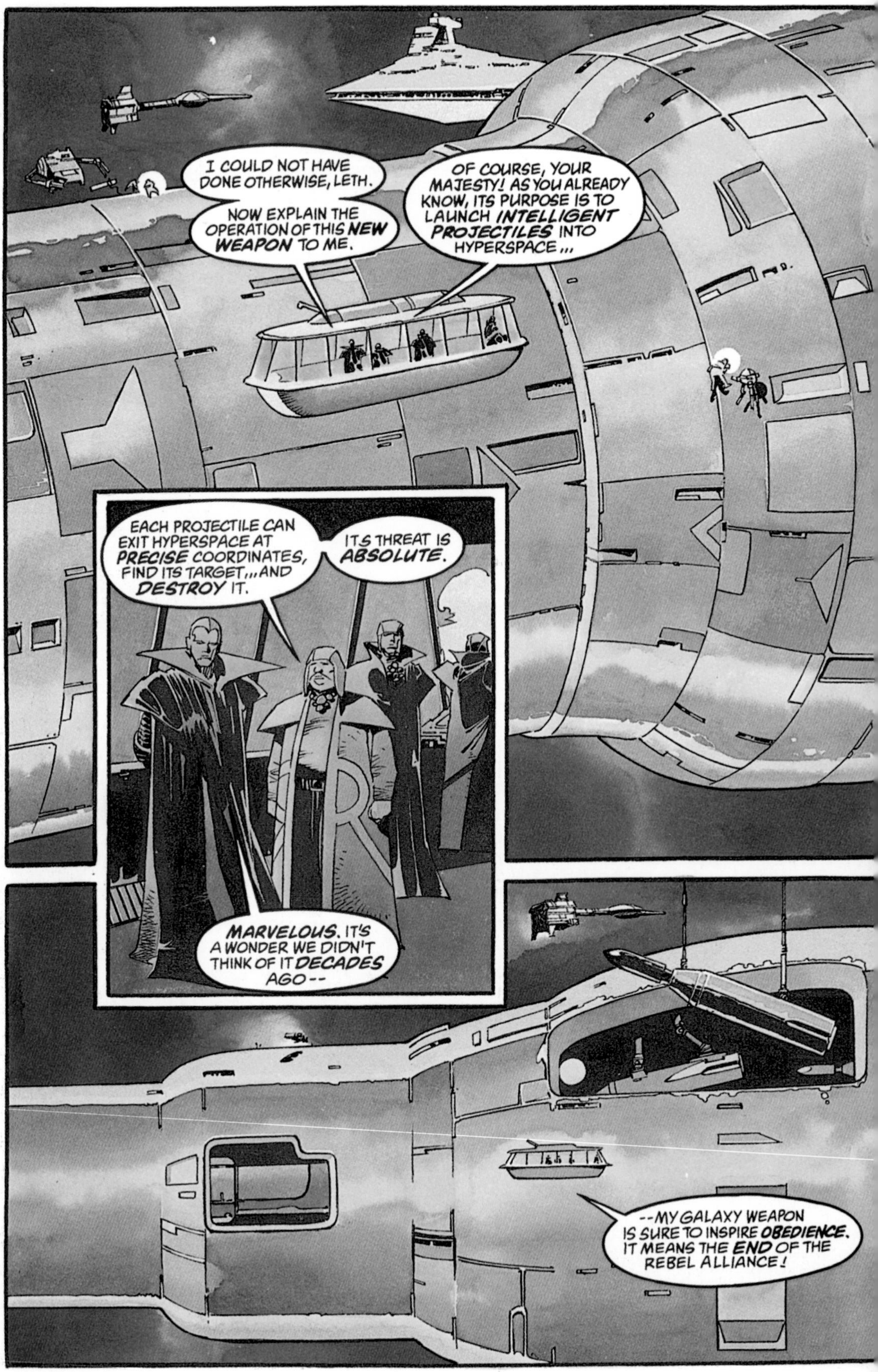

I COULD NOT HAVE DONE OTHERWISE, LETH.
NOW EXPLAIN THE OPERATION OF THIS NEW WEAPON TO ME.
OF COURSE, YOUR MAJESTY! AS YOU ALREADY KNOW, ITS PURPOSE IS TO LAUNCH INTELLIGENT PROJECTILES INTO HYPERSPACE...
EACH PROJECTILE CAN EXIT HYPERSPACE AT PRECISE COORDINATES, FIND ITS TARGET... AND DESTROY IT.
IT'S THREAT IS ABSOLUTE.
MARVELOUS. IT'S A WONDER WE DIDN'T THINK OF IT DECADES AGO--
--MY GALAXY WEAPON IS SURE TO INSPIRE OBEDIENCE. IT MEANS THE END OF THE REBEL ALLIANCE!

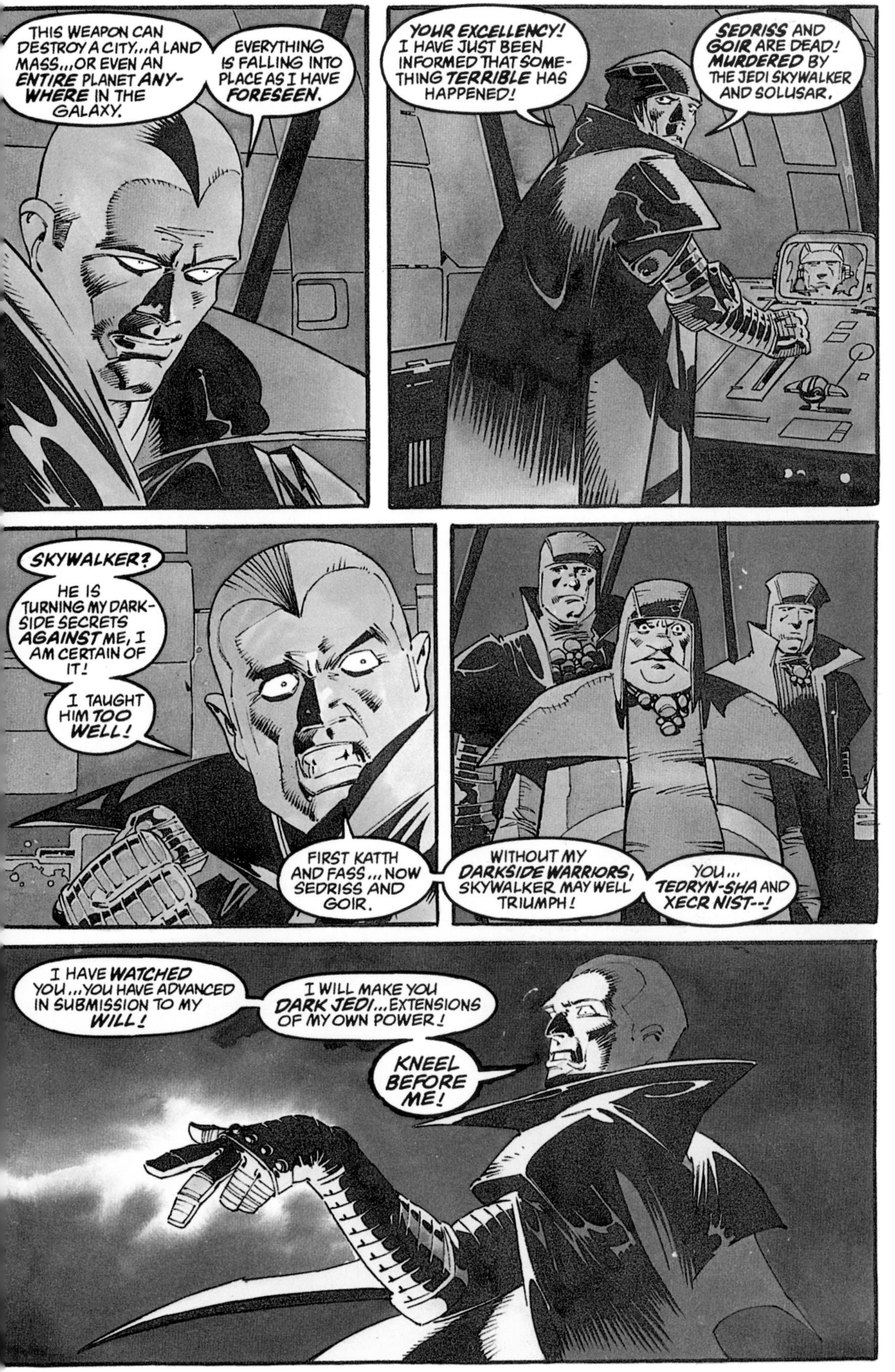

THIS WEAPON CAN DESTROY A CITY...A LAND MASS...OR EVEN AN ENTIRE PLANET ANYWHERE IN THE GALAXY.
EVERYTHING IS FALLING INTO PLACE AS I HAVE FORESEEN.
YOUR EXCELLENCY! I HAVE JUST BEEN INFORMED THAT SOMETHING TERRIBLE HAS HAPPENED!
SEDRISS AND GOIR ARE DEAD! MURDERED BY THE JEDI SKYWALKER AND SOLUSAR.
SKYWALKER?
HE IS TURNING MY DARKSIDE SECRETS AGAINST ME, I AM CERTAIN OF IT!
I TAUGHT HIM TOO WELL!
FIRST KATTH AND FASS... NOW SEDRISS AND GOIR.
WITHOUT MY DARKSIDE WARRIORS, SKYWALKER MAY WELL TRIUMPH!
YOU... TEDRYN-SHA AND XECR NIST--!
I HAVE WATCHED YOU...YOU HAVE ADVANCED IN SUBMISSION TO MY WILL!
I WILL MAKE YOU DARK JEDI...EXTENSIONS OF MY OWN POWER!
KNEEL BEFORE ME!

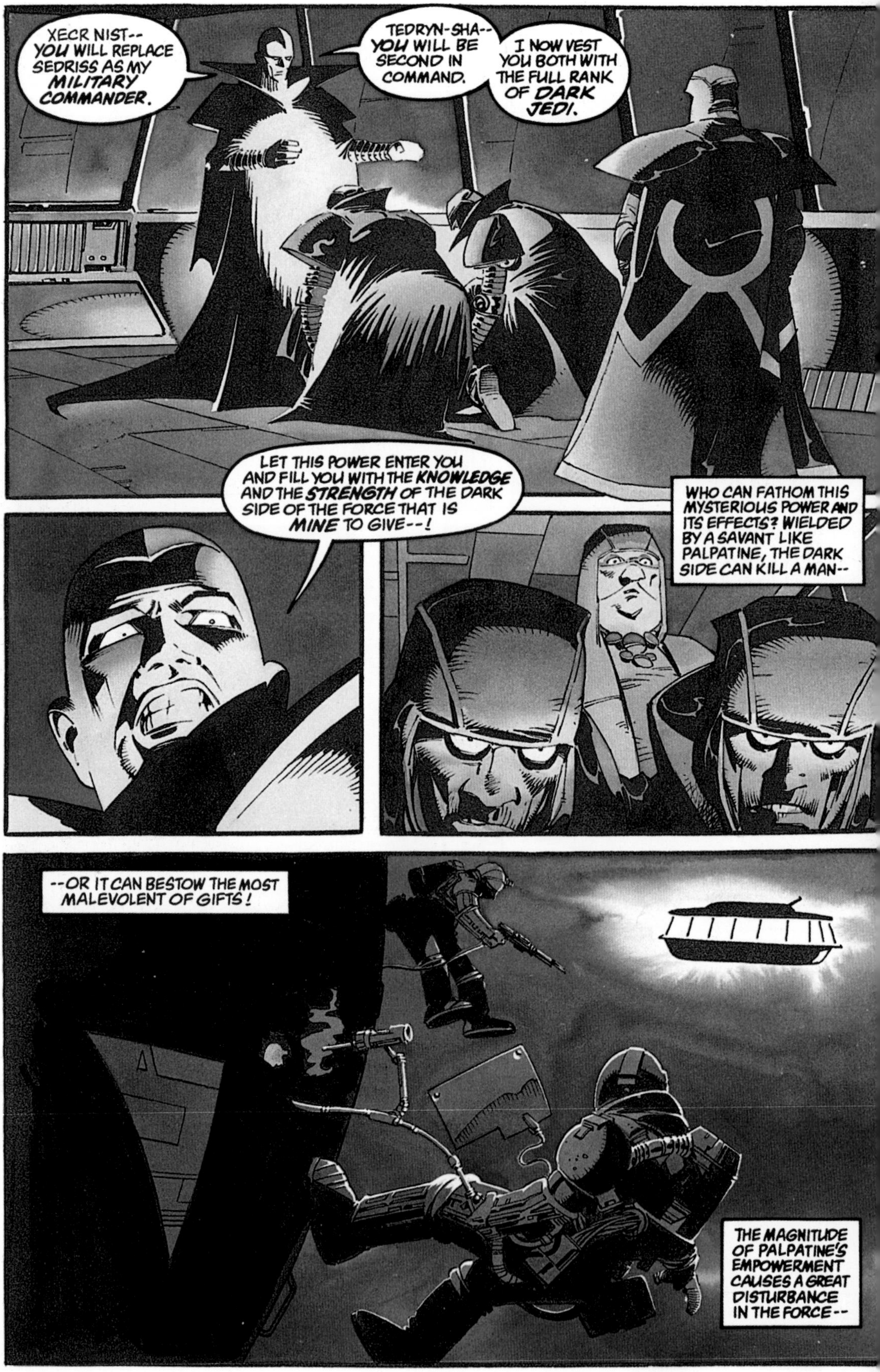

XECR NIST-- YOU WILL REPLACE SEDRISS AS MY MILITARY COMMANDER.
TEDRYN-SHA-- YOU WILL BE SECOND IN COMMAND.
I NOW VEST YOU BOTH WITH THE FULL RANK OF DARK JEDI.
LET THIS POWER ENTER YOU AND FILL YOU WITH THE KNOWLEDGE AND THE STRENGTH OF THE DARK SIDE OF THE FORCE THAT IS MINE TO GIVE--!
WHO CAN FATHOM THIS MYSTERIOUS POWER AND ITS EFFECTS? WIELDED BY A SAVANT LIKE PALPATINE, THE DARK SIDE CAN KILL A MAN--
--OR IT CAN BESTOW THE MOST MALEVOLENT OF GIFTS!
THE MAGNITUDE OF PALPATINE'S EMPOWERMENT CAUSES A GREAT DISTURBANCE IN THE FORCE--

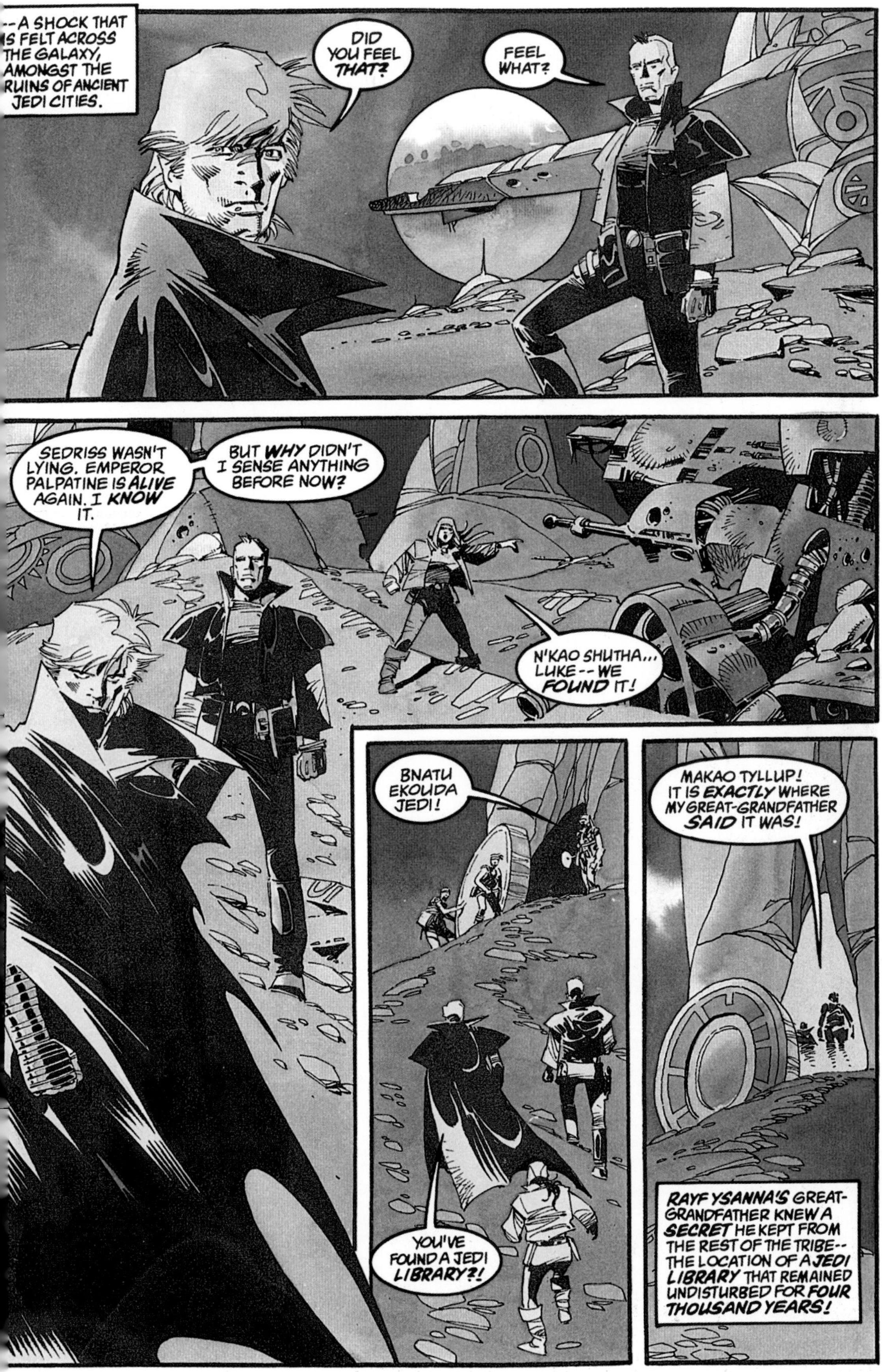
--A SHOCK THAT IS FELT ACROSS THE GALAXY, AMONGST THE RUINS OF ANCIENT JEDI CITIES.
DID YOU FEEL THAT?
FEEL WHAT?
SEDRISS WASN'T LYING. EMPEROR PALPATINE IS ALIVE AGAIN. I KNOW IT.
BUT WHY DIDN'T I SENSE ANYTHING BEFORE NOW?
N'KAO SHUTHA... LUKE-- WE FOUND IT!
BNATU EKOUDA JEDI!
YOU'VE FOUND A JEDI LIBRARY?!
MAKAO TYLLUP! IT IS EXACTLY WHERE MY GREAT-GRANDFATHER SAID IT WAS!
RAYF YSANNA'S GREAT-GRANDFATHER KNEW A SECRET HE KEPT FROM THE REST OF THE TRIBE-- THE LOCATION OF A JEDI LIBRARY THAT REMAINED UNDISTURBED FOR FOUR THOUSAND YEARS!

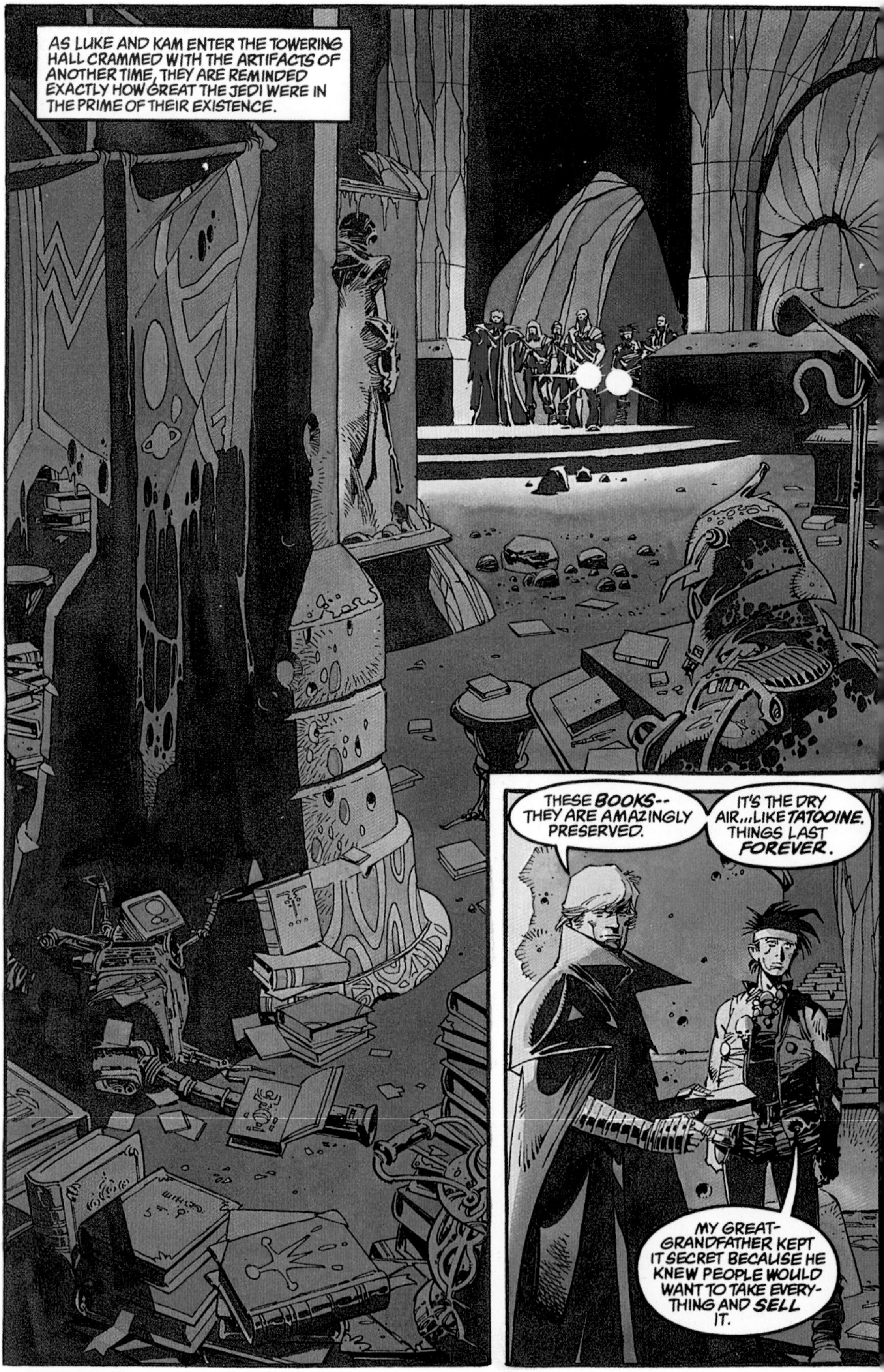
AS LUKE AND KAM ENTER THE TOWERING HALL CRAMMED WITH THE ARTIFACTS OF ANOTHER TIME, THEY ARE REMINDED EXACTLY HOW GREAT THE JEDI WERE IN THE PRIME OF THEIR EXISTENCE.
THESE BOOKS-- THEY ARE AMAZINGLY PRESERVED.
IT'S THE DRY AIR...LIKE TATOOINE. THINGS LAST FOREVER.
MY GREAT-GRANDFATHER KEPT IT SECRET BECAUSE HE KNEW PEOPLE WOULD WANT TO TAKE EVERY-THING AND SELL IT.

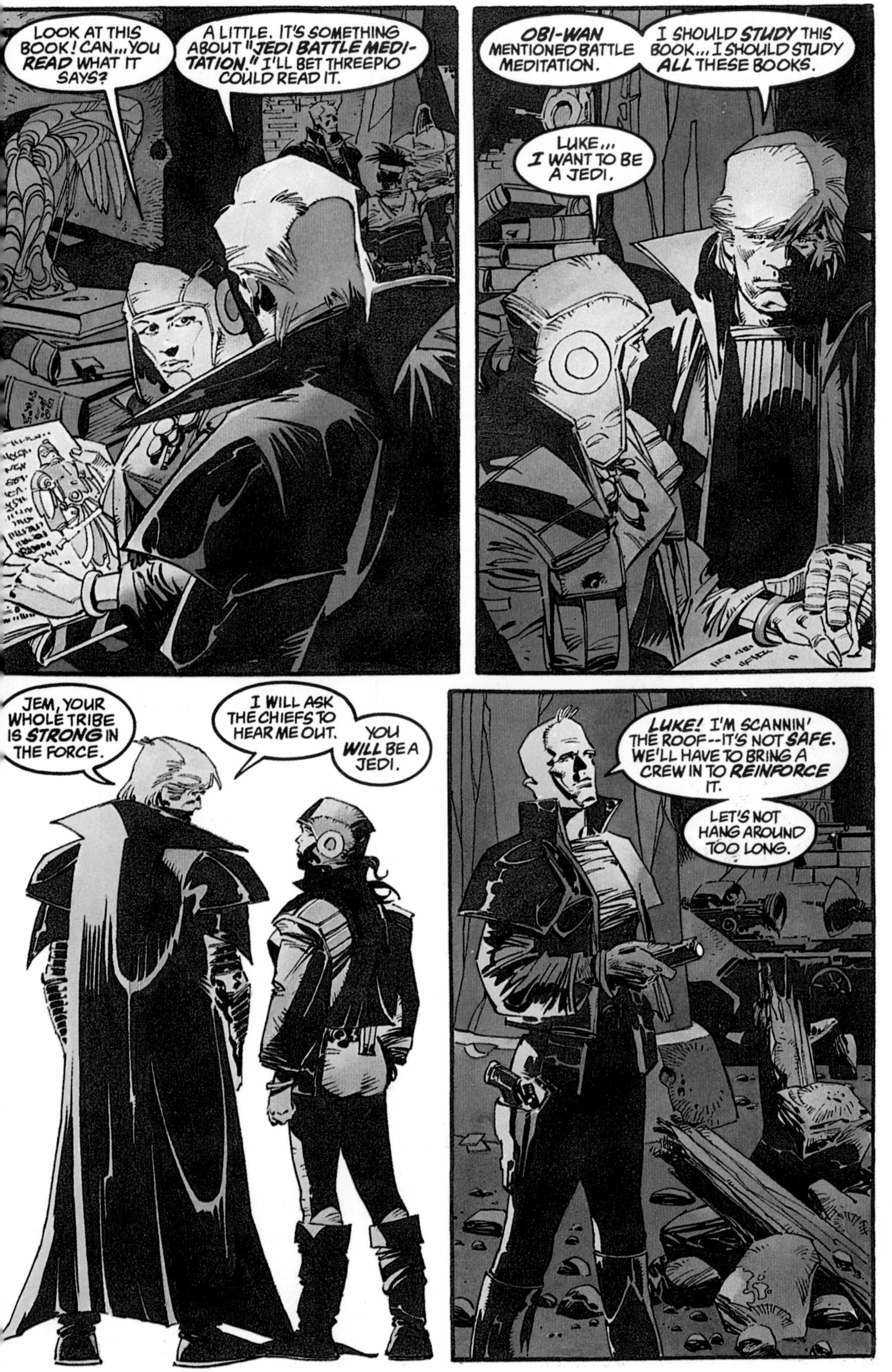

LOOK AT THIS BOOK! CAN... YOU READ WHAT IT SAYS?
A LITTLE. IT'S SOMETHING ABOUT "JEDI BATTLE MEDITATION." I'LL BET THREEPIO COULD READ IT.
OBI-WAN MENTIONED BATTLE MEDITATION.
I SHOULD STUDY THIS BOOK... I SHOULD STUDY ALL THESE BOOKS.
LUKE... I WANT TO BE A JEDI.
JEM, YOUR WHOLE TRIBE IS STRONG IN THE FORCE.
I WILL ASK THE CHIEFS TO HEAR ME OUT.
YOU WILL BE A JEDI.
LUKE! I'M SCANNIN' THE ROOF--IT'S NOT SAFE. WE'LL HAVE TO BRING A CREW IN TO REINFORCE IT.
LET'S NOT HANG AROUND TOO LONG.

THE *HOLOCRON* WAS RIGHT-- LUKE HAS FOUND IMPORTANT JEDI ARTIFACTS ON OSSUS. HE HAS ALSO FOUND SOMETHING *GREATER*...

CHIEF OKKO, I BELIEVE YOUR ANCESTORS WERE *JEDI*....YOU CAN BE JEDI.

WE ARE *NOT* JEDI. WE ARE *YSANNA*.

WE DO NOT NEED *YOU* TO TEACH US ANYTHING. YSANNA MAGIC IS *STRONG*.

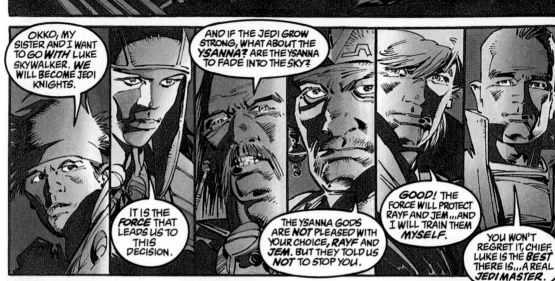

OKKO, MY SISTER AND I WANT TO GO *WITH* LUKE SKYWALKER. *WE* WILL BECOME JEDI KNIGHTS.

IT IS THE *FORCE* THAT LEADS US TO THIS DECISION.

AND IF THE JEDI *GROW* STRONG, WHAT ABOUT THE *YSANNA*? ARE THE YSANNA TO FADE INTO THE SKY?

THE YSANNA GODS ARE *NOT* PLEASED WITH YOUR CHOICE, *RAYF* AND *JEM*. BUT THEY TOLD US *NOT* TO STOP YOU.

GOOD! THE FORCE WILL PROTECT RAYF AND JEM...AND I WILL TRAIN THEM *MYSELF*.

YOU WON'T REGRET IT, CHIEF. LUKE IS THE *BEST* THERE IS...A REAL *JEDI MASTER*.

THE YSANNA AGREE TO *STAND WATCH* OVER THE JEDI RUINS UNTIL THE REBEL ALLIANCE SENDS IN THEIR EXCAVATION TEAMS.

WITH THE TWO YOUNG YSANNA WARRIORS ABOARD, THE *JEDI EXPLORER* COMPLETES ITS MISSION TO OSSUS--AND BEGINS THE RETURN TO *PINNACLE BASE!*

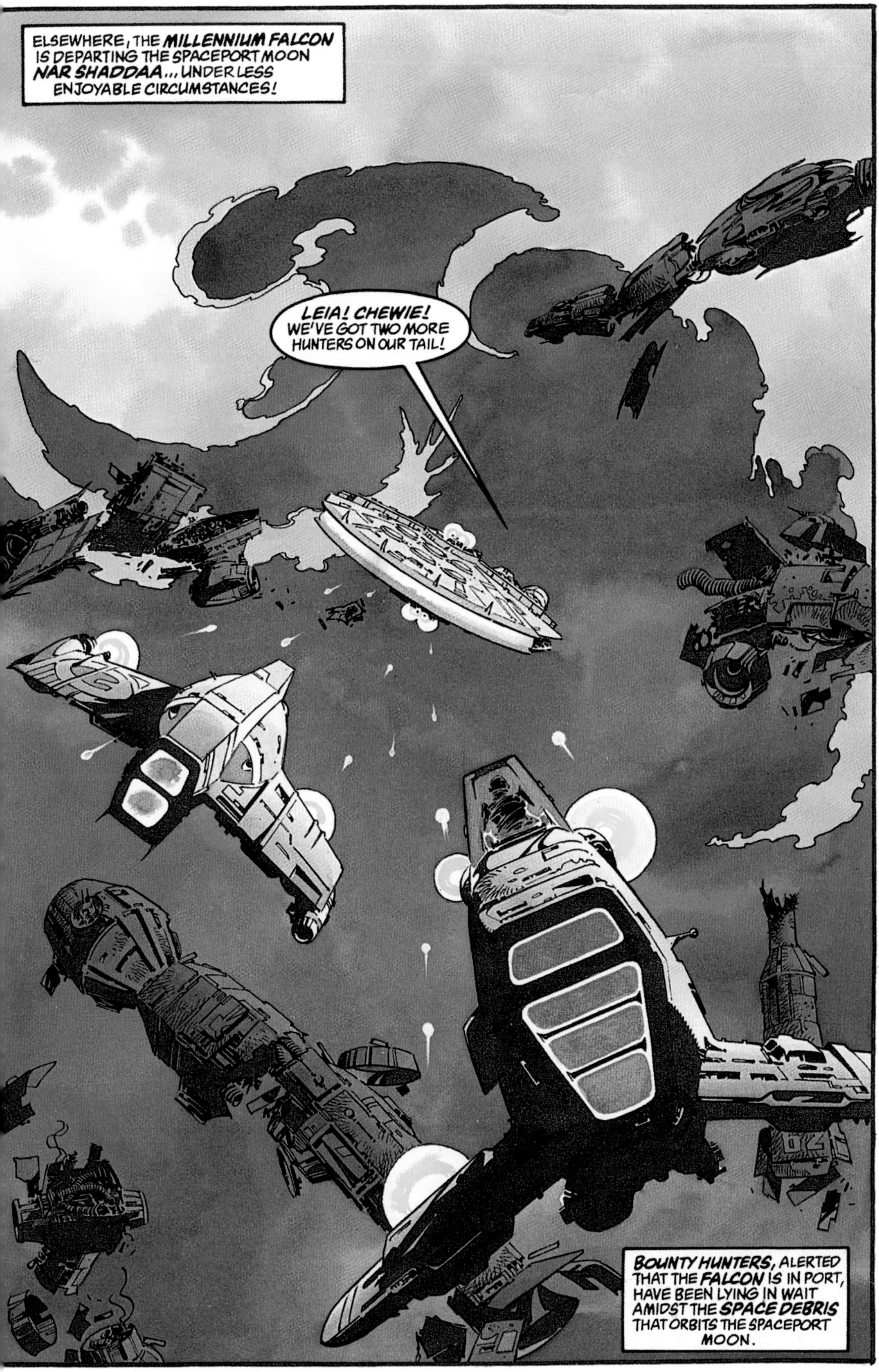
ELSEWHERE, THE MILLENNIUM FALCON IS DEPARTING THE SPACEPORT MOON NAR SHADDAA... UNDER LESS ENJOYABLE CIRCUMSTANCES!
LEIA! CHEWIE! WE'VE GOT TWO MORE HUNTERS ON OUR TAIL!
BOUNTY HUNTERS, ALERTED THAT THE FALCON IS IN PORT, HAVE BEEN LYING IN WAIT AMIDST THE SPACE DEBRIS THAT ORBITS THE SPACEPORT MOON.

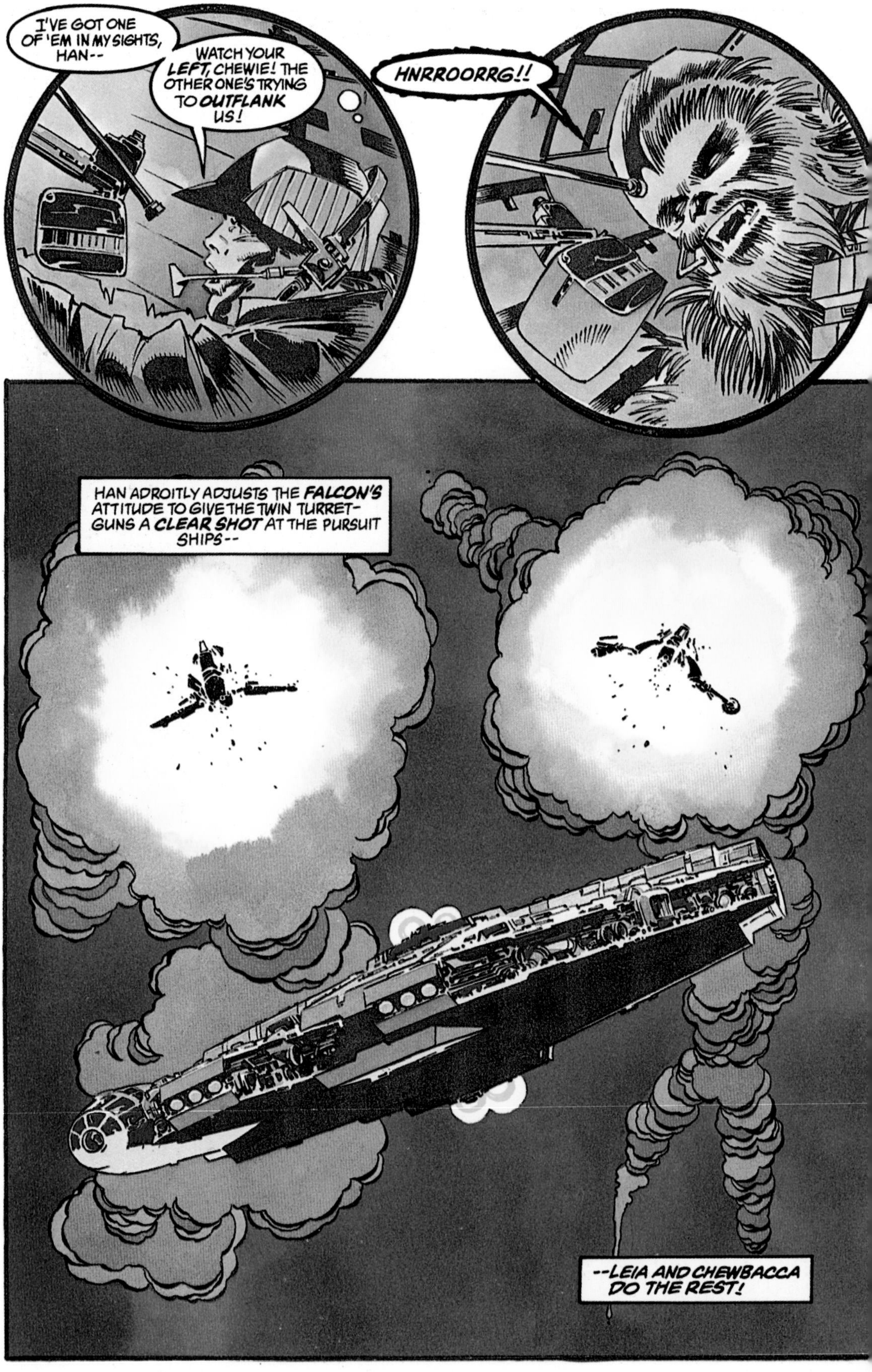

I'VE GOT ONE OF 'EM IN MY SIGHTS, HAN--
WATCH YOUR LEFT, CHEWIE! THE OTHER ONE'S TRYING TO OUTFLANK US!
HNRROORRG!!
HAN ADROITLY ADJUSTS THE FALCON'S ATTITUDE TO GIVE THE TWIN TURRET-GUNS A CLEAR SHOT AT THE PURSUIT SHIPS--
--LEIA AND CHEWBACCA DO THE REST!

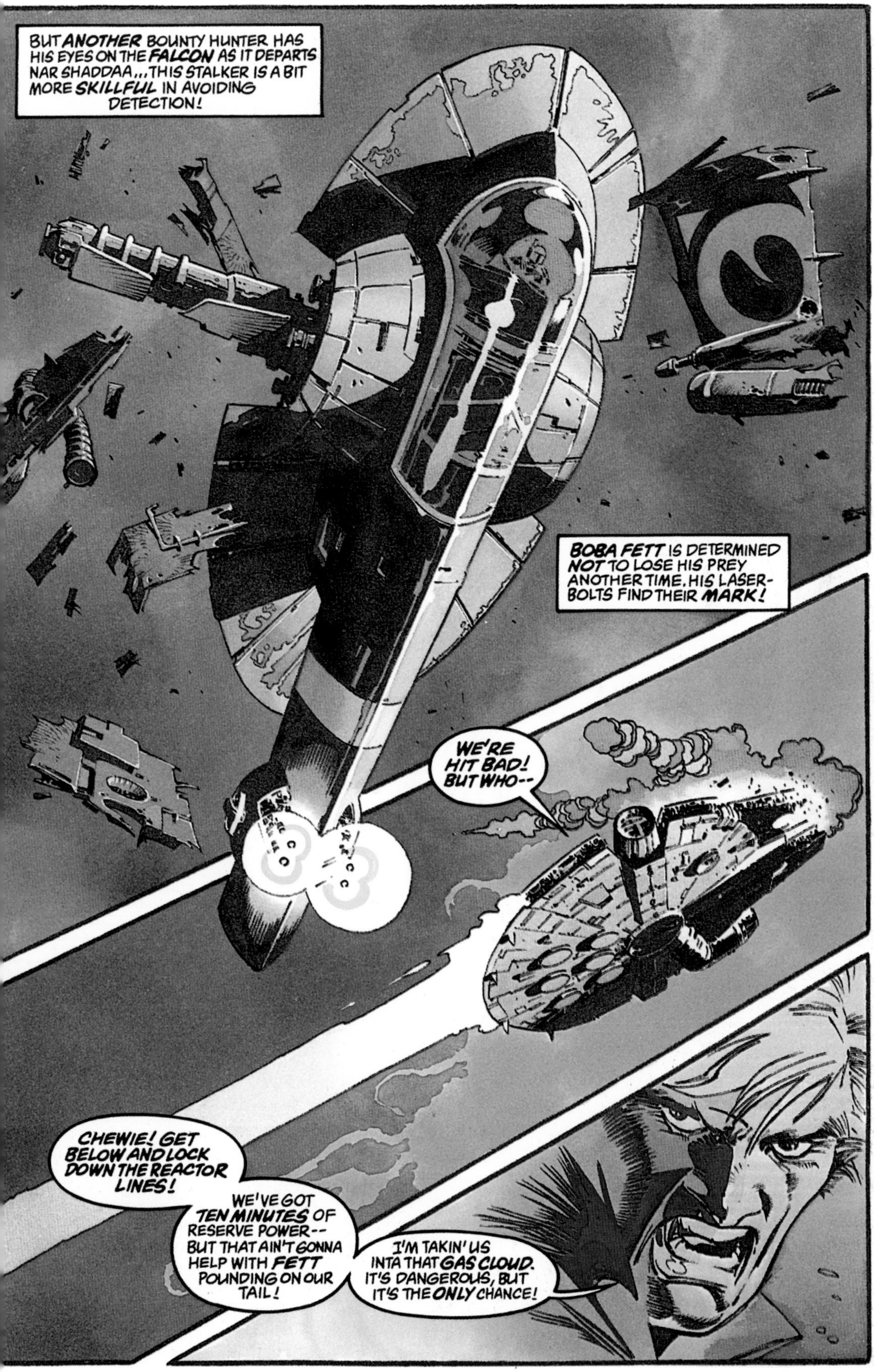
BUT **ANOTHER** BOUNTY HUNTER HAS HIS EYES ON THE **FALCON** AS IT DEPARTS NAR SHADDAA... THIS STALKER IS A BIT MORE **SKILLFUL** IN AVOIDING DETECTION!
BOBA FETT IS DETERMINED **NOT** TO LOSE HIS PREY ANOTHER TIME. HIS LASER-BOLTS FIND THEIR **MARK!**
WE'RE HIT BAD! BUT WHO--
CHEWIE! GET BELOW AND LOCK DOWN THE REACTOR LINES!
WE'VE GOT **TEN MINUTES** OF RESERVE POWER-- BUT THAT AIN'T GONNA HELP WITH **FETT** POUNDING ON OUR TAIL!
I'M TAKIN' US INTA THAT **GAS CLOUD**. IT'S DANGEROUS, BUT IT'S THE **ONLY** CHANCE!

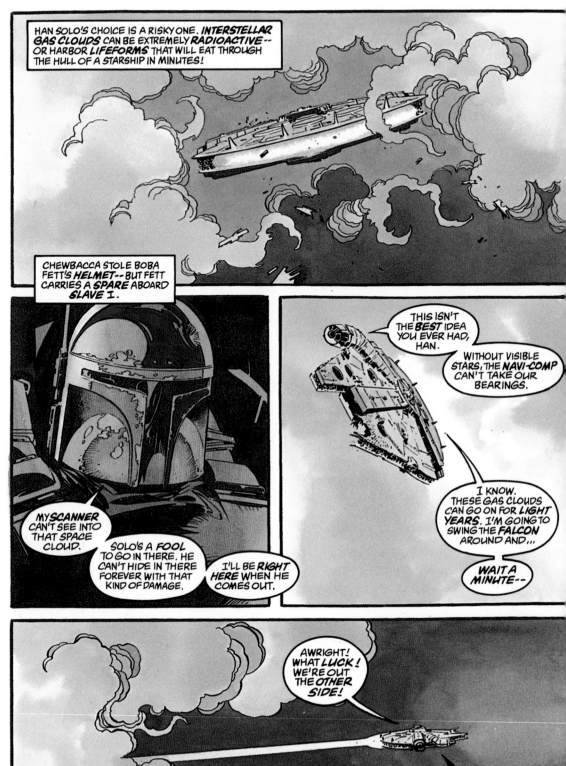

HAN SOLO'S CHOICE IS A RISKY ONE. *INTERSTELLAR GAS CLOUDS* CAN BE EXTREMELY *RADIOACTIVE*-- OR HARBOR *LIFEFORMS* THAT WILL EAT THROUGH THE HULL OF A STARSHIP IN MINUTES!

CHEWBACCA STOLE BOBA FETT'S *HELMET*--BUT FETT CARRIES A *SPARE* ABOARD *SLAVE* I.

THIS ISN'T THE *BEST* IDEA YOU EVER HAD, HAN.

WITHOUT VISIBLE STARS, THE *NAVI-COMP* CAN'T TAKE OUR BEARINGS.

I KNOW. THESE GAS CLOUDS CAN GO ON FOR *LIGHT YEARS.* I'M GOING TO SWING THE *FALCON* AROUND AND...

WAIT A MINUTE--

MY *SCANNER* CAN'T SEE INTO THAT SPACE CLOUD.

SOLO'S A *FOOL* TO GO IN THERE. HE CAN'T HIDE IN THERE FOREVER WITH THAT KIND OF DAMAGE.

I'LL BE *RIGHT HERE* WHEN HE COMES OUT.

AWRIGHT! WHAT *LUCK!* WE'RE OUT THE *OTHER SIDE!*

NRROWWNN!

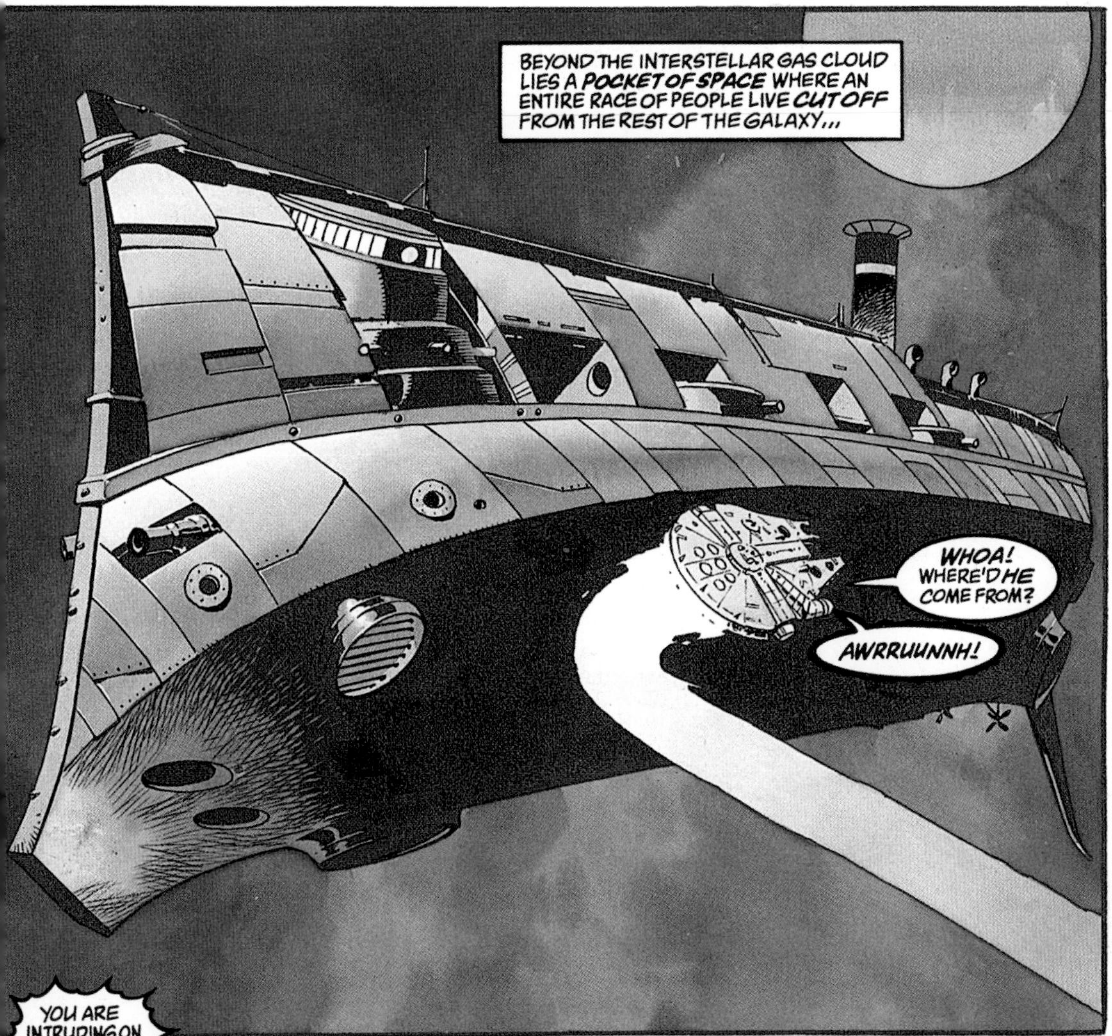
BEYOND THE INTERSTELLAR GAS CLOUD LIES A POCKET OF SPACE WHERE AN ENTIRE RACE OF PEOPLE LIVE CUT OFF FROM THE REST OF THE GALAXY...
WHOA! WHERE'D HE COME FROM?
AWRRUUNNH!

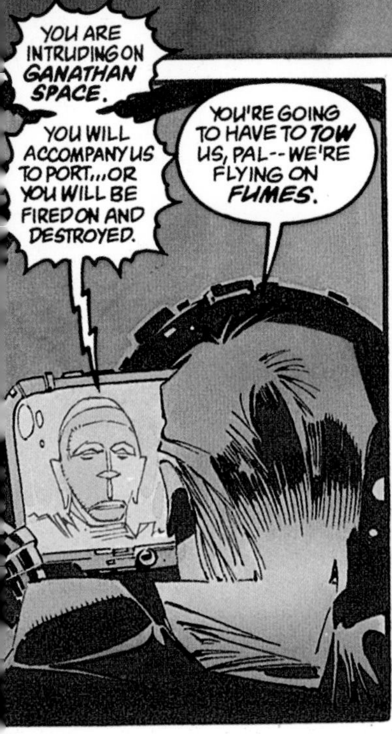
YOU ARE INTRUDING ON GANATHAN SPACE.
YOU WILL ACCOMPANY US TO PORT...OR YOU WILL BE FIRED ON AND DESTROYED.
YOU'RE GOING TO HAVE TO TOW US, PAL-- WE'RE FLYING ON FUMES.

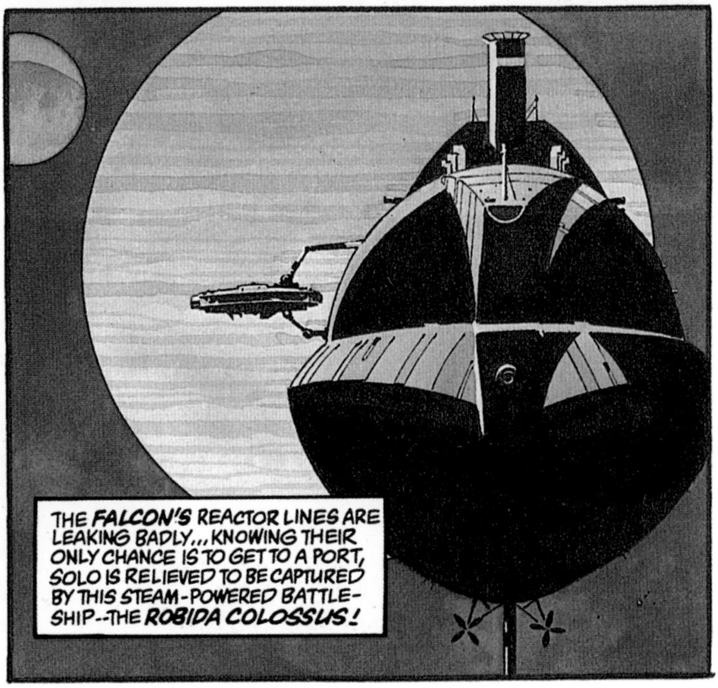
THE FALCON'S REACTOR LINES ARE LEAKING BADLY... KNOWING THEIR ONLY CHANCE IS TO GET TO A PORT, SOLO IS RELIEVED TO BE CAPTURED BY THIS STEAM-POWERED BATTLE-SHIP--THE ROBIDA COLOSSUS!

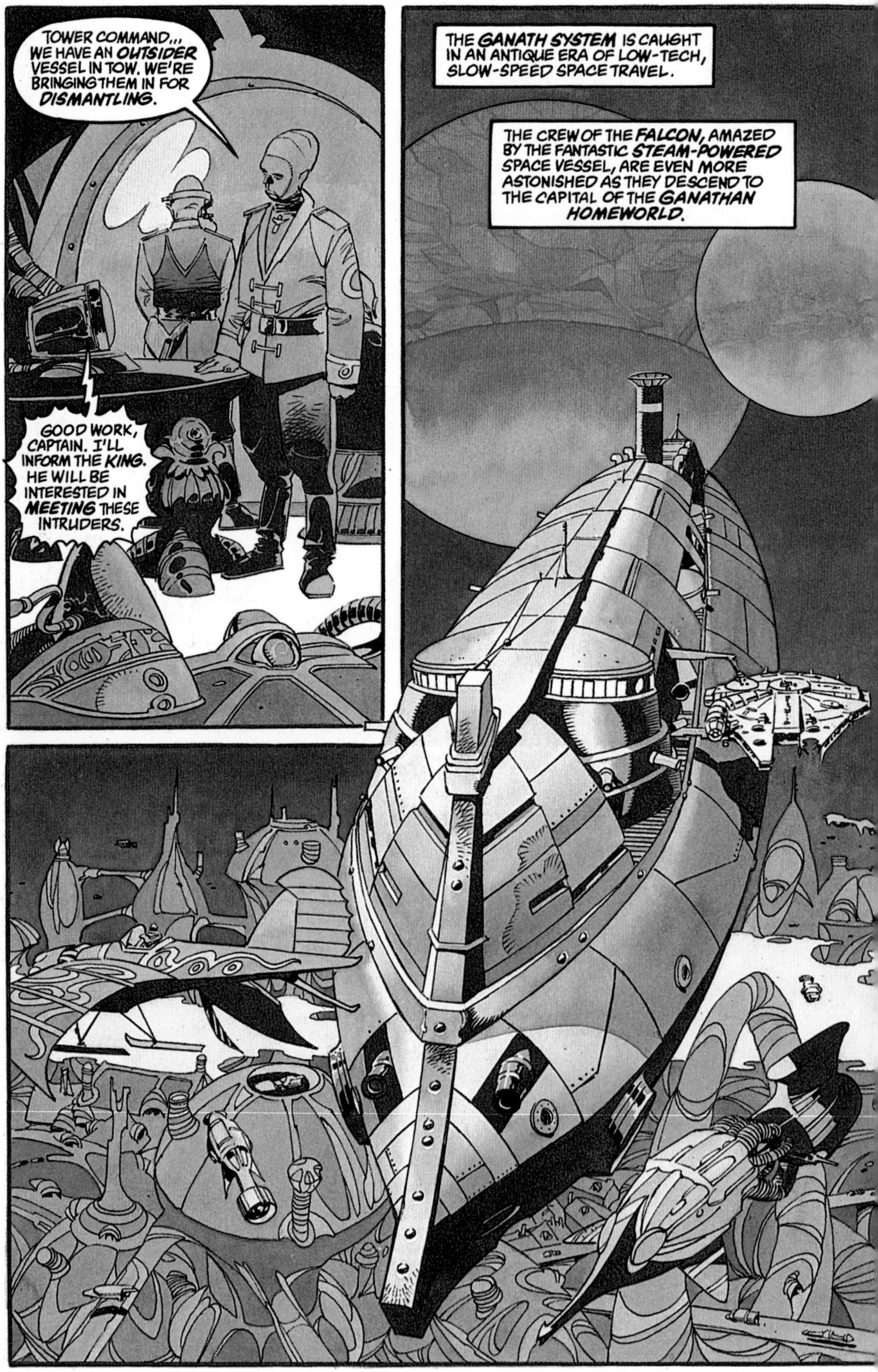
TOWER COMMAND... WE HAVE AN OUTSIDER VESSEL IN TOW. WE'RE BRINGING THEM IN FOR DISMANTLING.
GOOD WORK, CAPTAIN. I'LL INFORM THE KING. HE WILL BE INTERESTED IN MEETING THESE INTRUDERS.
THE GANATH SYSTEM IS CAUGHT IN AN ANTIQUE ERA OF LOW-TECH, SLOW-SPEED SPACE TRAVEL.
THE CREW OF THE FALCON, AMAZED BY THE FANTASTIC STEAM-POWERED SPACE VESSEL, ARE EVEN MORE ASTONISHED AS THEY DESCEND TO THE CAPITAL OF THE GANATHAN HOMEWORLD.

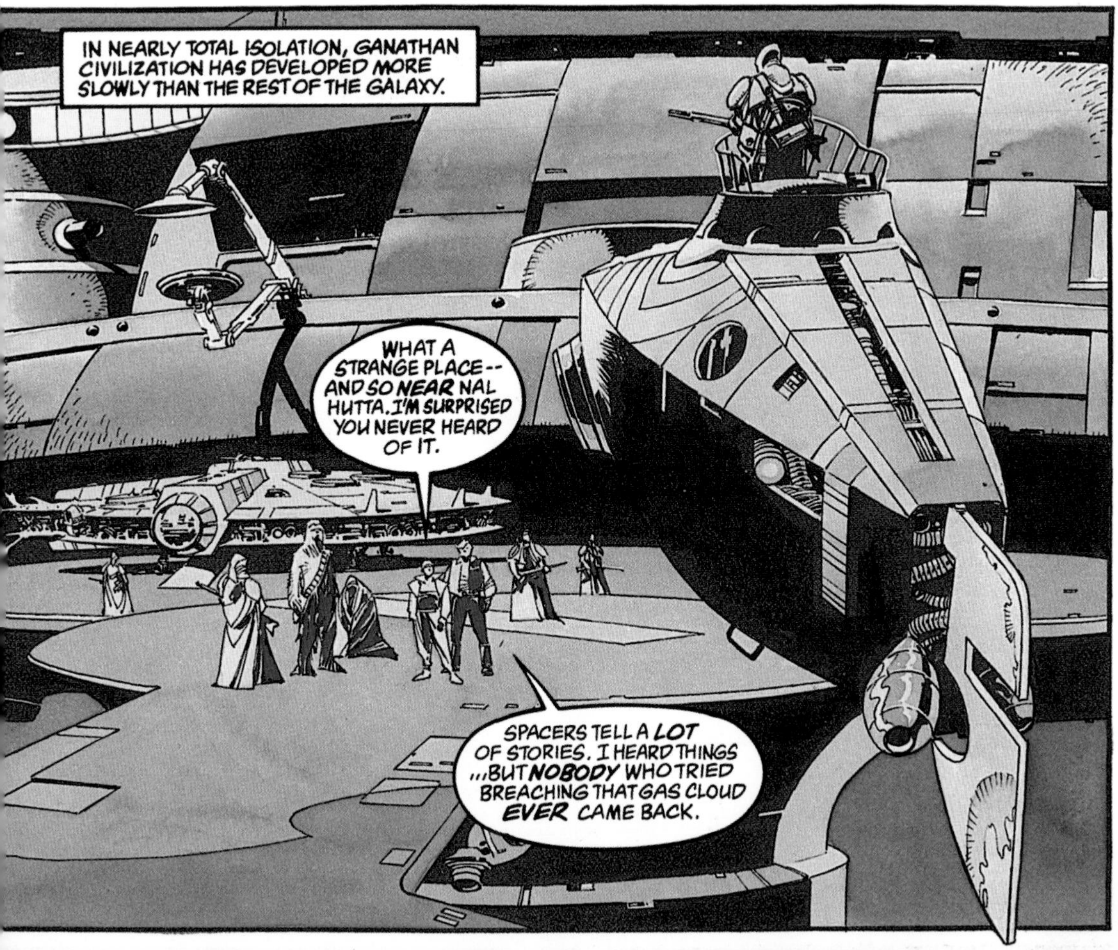
IN NEARLY TOTAL ISOLATION, GANATHAN CIVILIZATION HAS DEVELOPED MORE SLOWLY THAN THE REST OF THE GALAXY.
WHAT A STRANGE PLACE-- AND SO NEAR NAL HUTTA. I'M SURPRISED YOU NEVER HEARD OF IT.
SPACERS TELL A LOT OF STORIES. I HEARD THINGS ...BUT NOBODY WHO TRIED BREACHING THAT GAS CLOUD EVER CAME BACK.
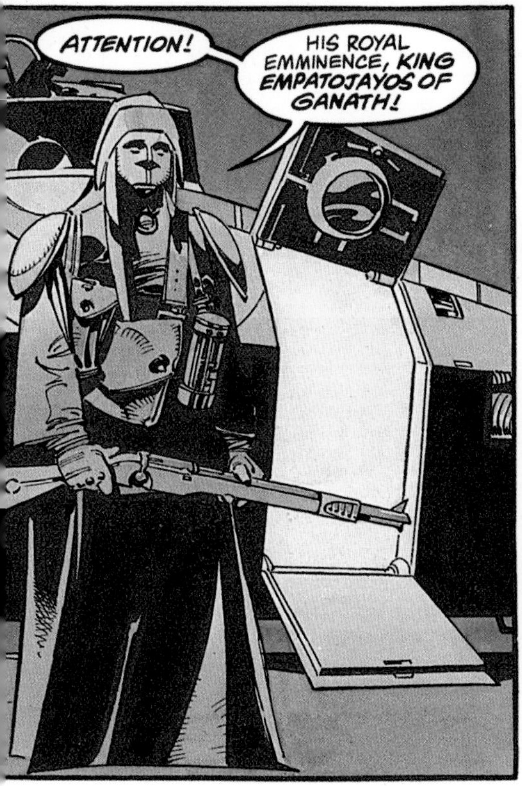
ATTENTION!
HIS ROYAL EMMINENCE, KING EMPATOJAYOS OF GANATH!
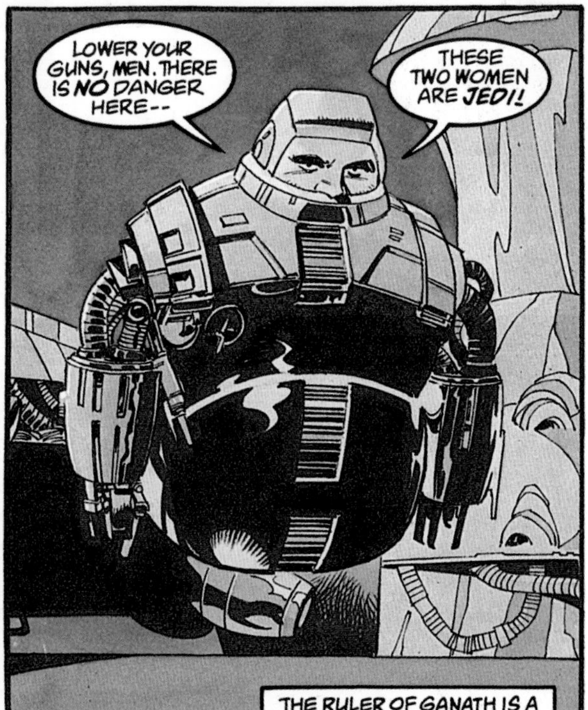
LOWER YOUR GUNS, MEN. THERE IS NO DANGER HERE--
THESE TWO WOMEN ARE JEDI!
THE RULER OF GANATH IS A HALF-MAN ENCASED IN PROSTHETIC MACHINERY!

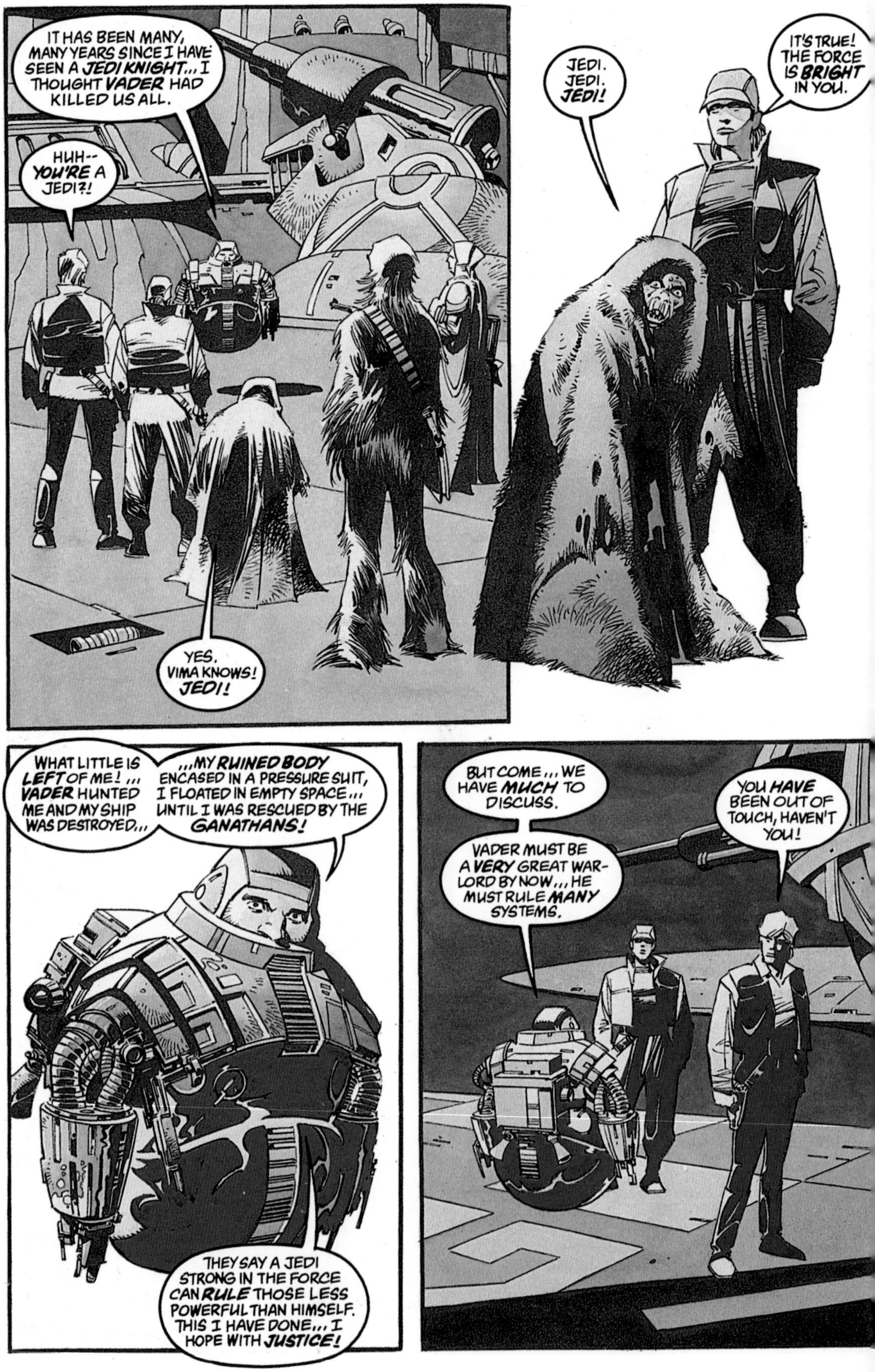

IT HAS BEEN MANY, MANY YEARS SINCE I HAVE SEEN A JEDI KNIGHT... I THOUGHT VADER HAD KILLED US ALL.
HUH-- YOU'RE A JEDI?!
JEDI. JEDI. JEDI!
IT'S TRUE! THE FORCE IS BRIGHT IN YOU.
YES. VIMA KNOWS! JEDI!
WHAT LITTLE IS LEFT OF ME! ... VADER HUNTED ME AND MY SHIP WAS DESTROYED...
...MY RUINED BODY ENCASED IN A PRESSURE SUIT, I FLOATED IN EMPTY SPACE... UNTIL I WAS RESCUED BY THE GANATHANS!
THEY SAY A JEDI STRONG IN THE FORCE CAN RULE THOSE LESS POWERFUL THAN HIMSELF. THIS I HAVE DONE... I HOPE WITH JUSTICE!
BUT COME... WE HAVE MUCH TO DISCUSS.
VADER MUST BE A VERY GREAT WARLORD BY NOW... HE MUST RULE MANY SYSTEMS.
YOU HAVE BEEN OUT OF TOUCH, HAVEN'T YOU!

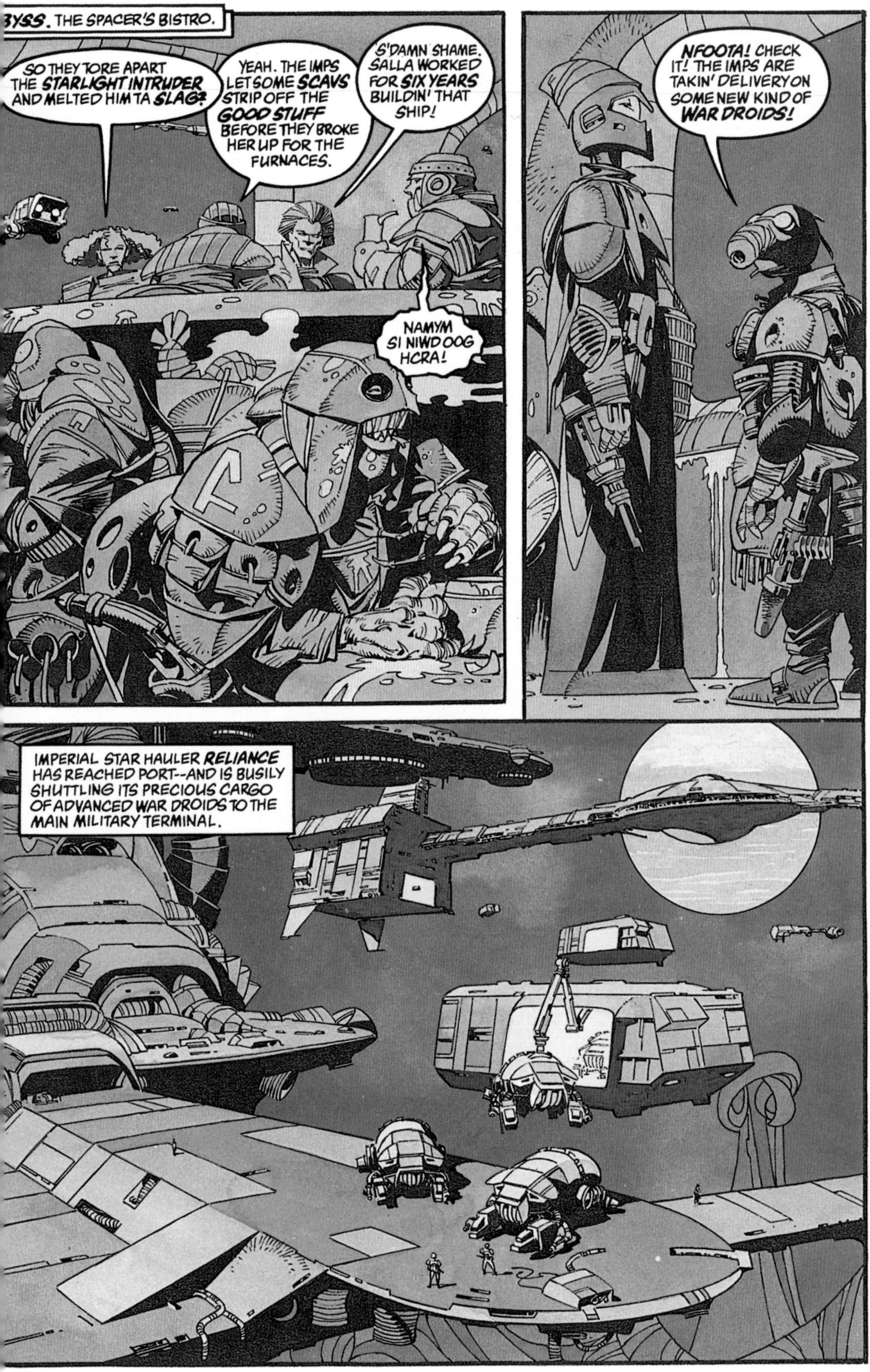
BYSS. THE SPACER'S BISTRO.
SO THEY TORE APART THE STARLIGHT INTRUDER AND MELTED HIM TA SLAG?
YEAH. THE IMPS LET SOME SCAVS STRIP OFF THE GOOD STUFF BEFORE THEY BROKE HER UP FOR THE FURNACES.
S'DAMN SHAME. SALLA WORKED FOR SIX YEARS BUILDIN' THAT SHIP!
NAMYM SI NIWD OOG HCRA!
NFOOTA! CHECK IT! THE IMPS ARE TAKIN' DELIVERY ON SOME NEW KIND OF WAR DROIDS!
IMPERIAL STAR HAULER RELIANCE HAS REACHED PORT--AND IS BUSILY SHUTTLING ITS PRECIOUS CARGO OF ADVANCED WAR DROIDS TO THE MAIN MILITARY TERMINAL.

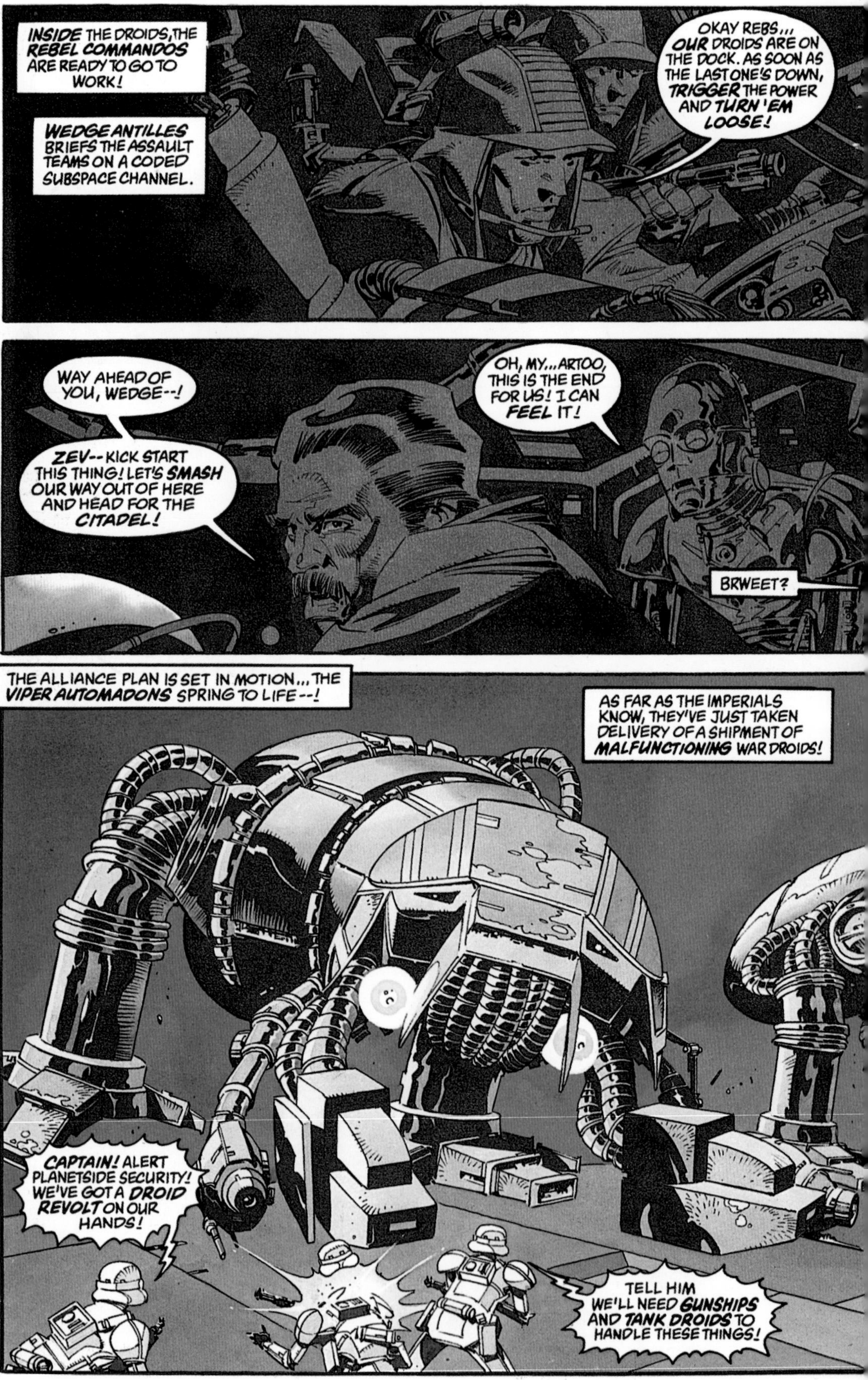
INSIDE THE DROIDS, THE REBEL COMMANDOS ARE READY TO GO TO WORK!
WEDGE ANTILLES BRIEFS THE ASSAULT TEAMS ON A CODED SUBSPACE CHANNEL.
OKAY REBS... OUR DROIDS ARE ON THE DOCK. AS SOON AS THE LAST ONE'S DOWN, TRIGGER THE POWER AND TURN 'EM LOOSE!
WAY AHEAD OF YOU, WEDGE--!
ZEV--KICK START THIS THING! LET'S SMASH OUR WAY OUT OF HERE AND HEAD FOR THE CITADEL!
OH, MY... ARTOO, THIS IS THE END FOR US! I CAN FEEL IT!
BRWEET?
THE ALLIANCE PLAN IS SET IN MOTION... THE VIPER AUTOMADONS SPRING TO LIFE--!
AS FAR AS THE IMPERIALS KNOW, THEY'VE JUST TAKEN DELIVERY OF A SHIPMENT OF MALFUNCTIONING WAR DROIDS!
CAPTAIN! ALERT PLANETSIDE SECURITY! WE'VE GOT A DROID REVOLT ON OUR HANDS!
TELL HIM WE'LL NEED GUNSHIPS AND TANK DROIDS TO HANDLE THESE THINGS!

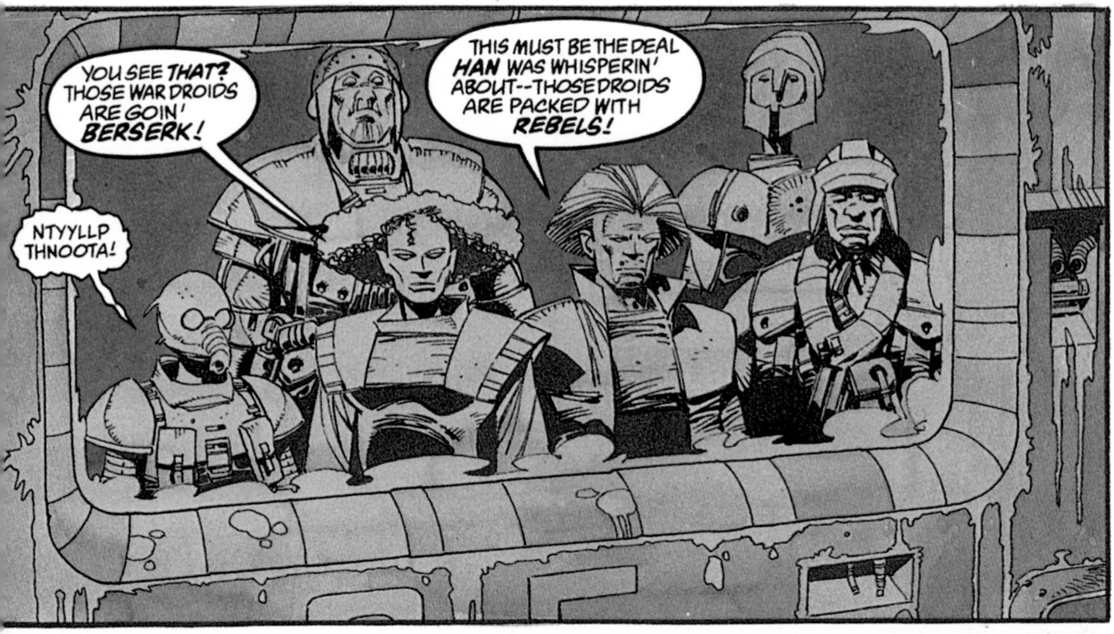
YOU SEE THAT? THOSE WAR DROIDS ARE GOIN' BERSERK!
THIS MUST BE THE DEAL HAN WAS WHISPERIN' ABOUT--THOSE DROIDS ARE PACKED WITH REBELS!
NTYYLLP THNOOTA!

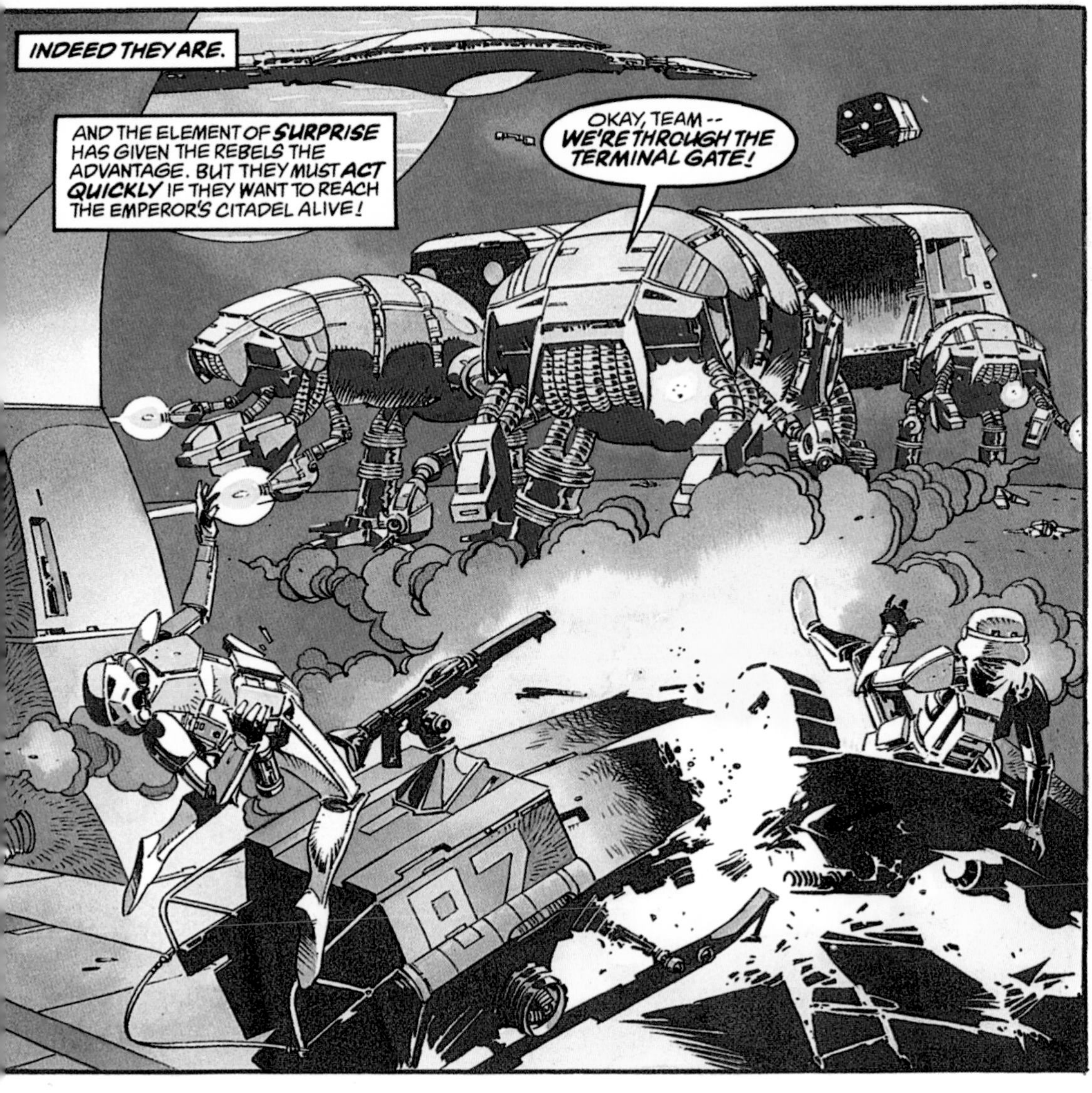
INDEED THEY ARE.
AND THE ELEMENT OF SURPRISE HAS GIVEN THE REBELS THE ADVANTAGE. BUT THEY MUST ACT QUICKLY IF THEY WANT TO REACH THE EMPEROR'S CITADEL ALIVE!
OKAY, TEAM -- WE'RE THROUGH THE TERMINAL GATE!

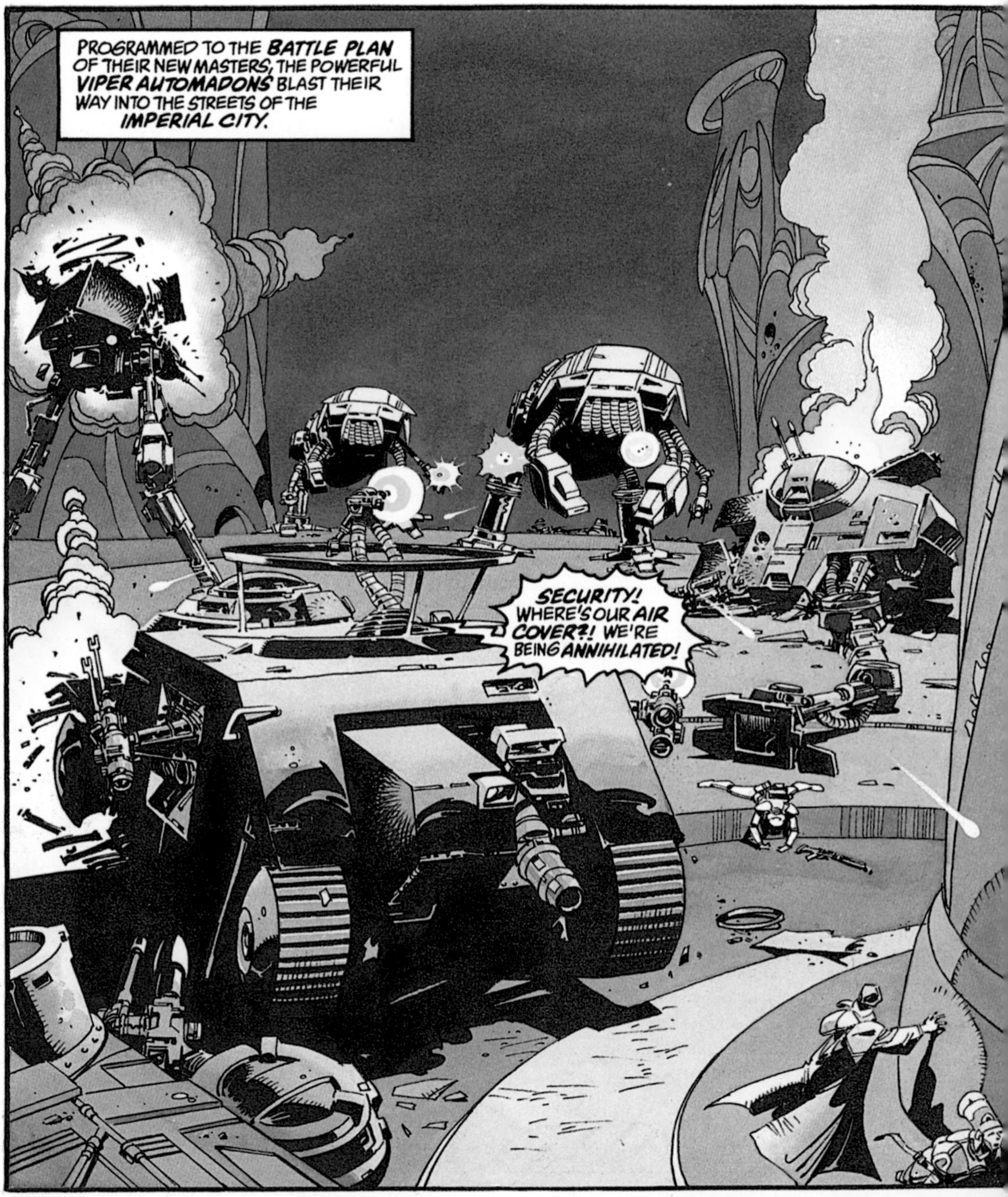
PROGRAMMED TO THE BATTLE PLAN OF THEIR NEW MASTERS, THE POWERFUL VIPER AUTOMADONS BLAST THEIR WAY INTO THE STREETS OF THE IMPERIAL CITY.
SECURITY! WHERE'S OUR AIR COVER?! WE'RE BEING ANNIHILATED!

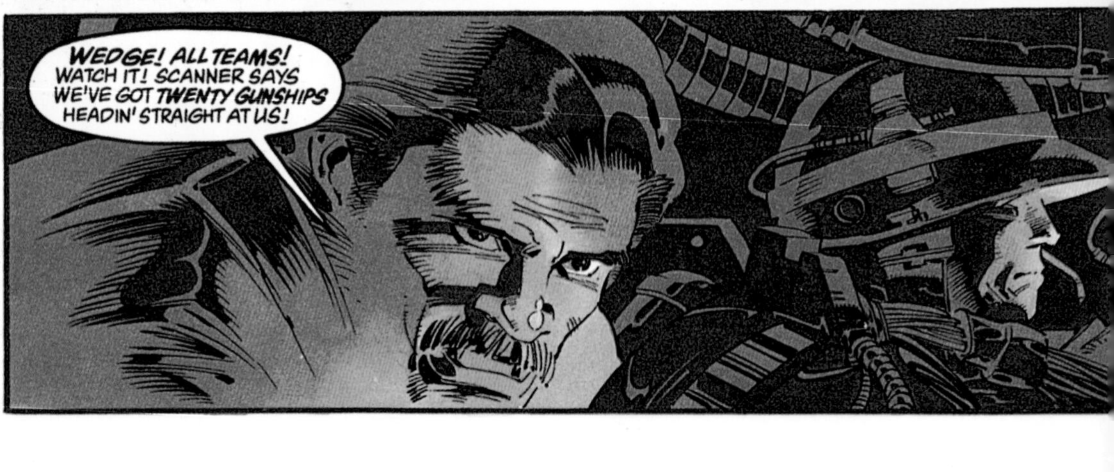
WEDGE! ALL TEAMS! WATCH IT! SCANNER SAYS WE'VE GOT TWENTY GUNSHIPS HEADIN' STRAIGHT AT US!

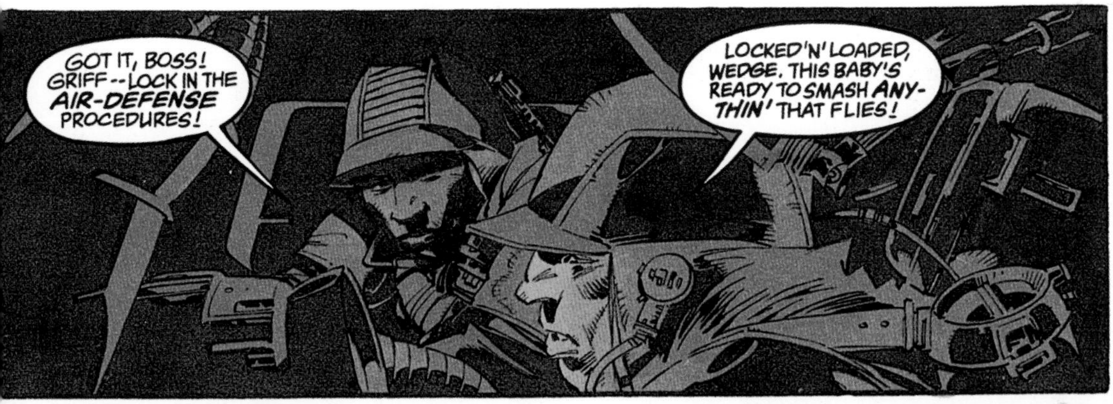
GOT IT, BOSS! GRIFF--LOCK IN THE AIR-DEFENSE PROCEDURES!
LOCKED 'N' LOADED, WEDGE. THIS BABY'S READY TO SMASH ANY-THIN' THAT FLIES!

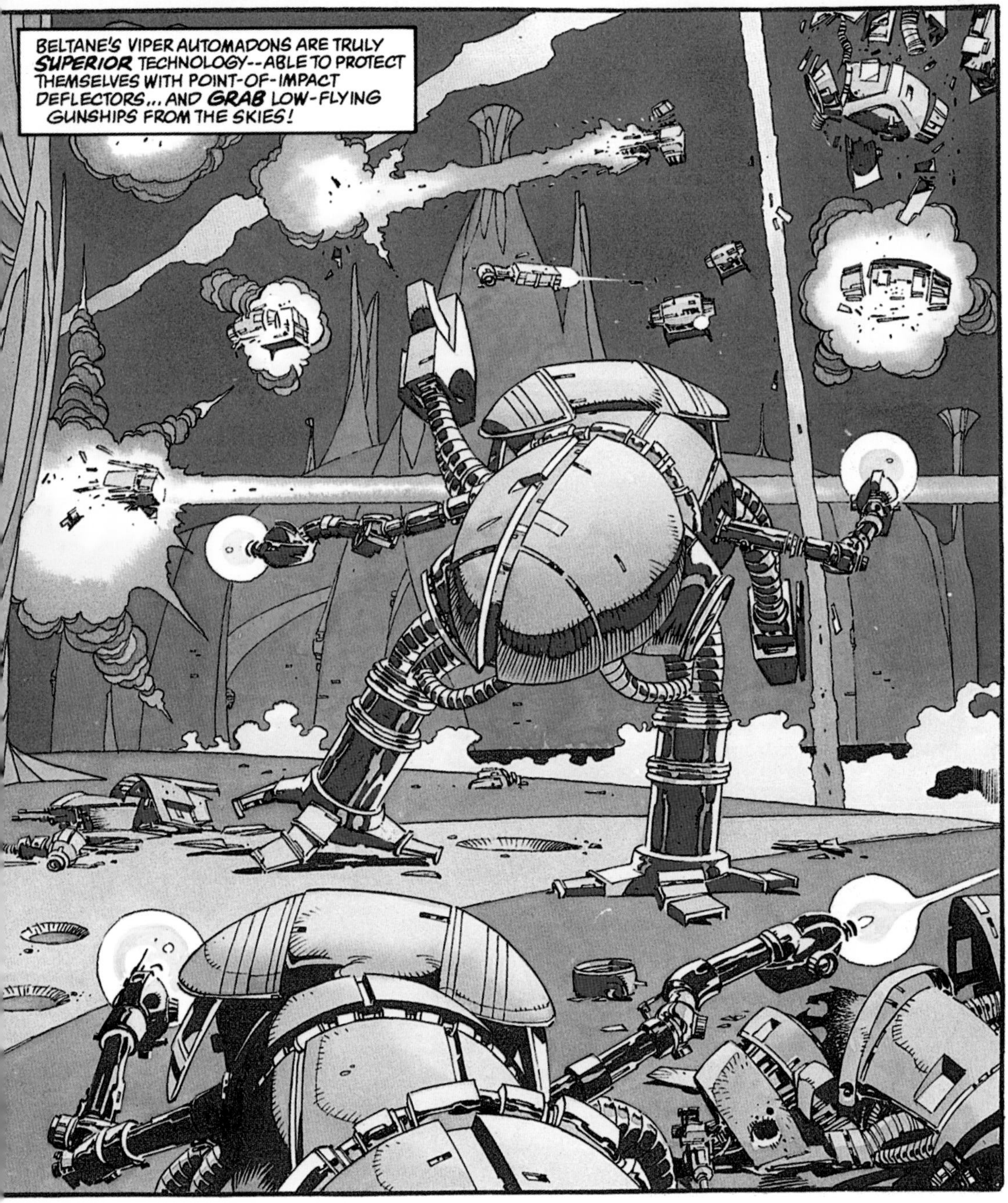
BELTANE'S VIPER AUTOMADONS ARE TRULY SUPERIOR TECHNOLOGY--ABLE TO PROTECT THEMSELVES WITH POINT-OF-IMPACT DEFLECTORS... AND GRAB LOW-FLYING GUNSHIPS FROM THE SKIES!

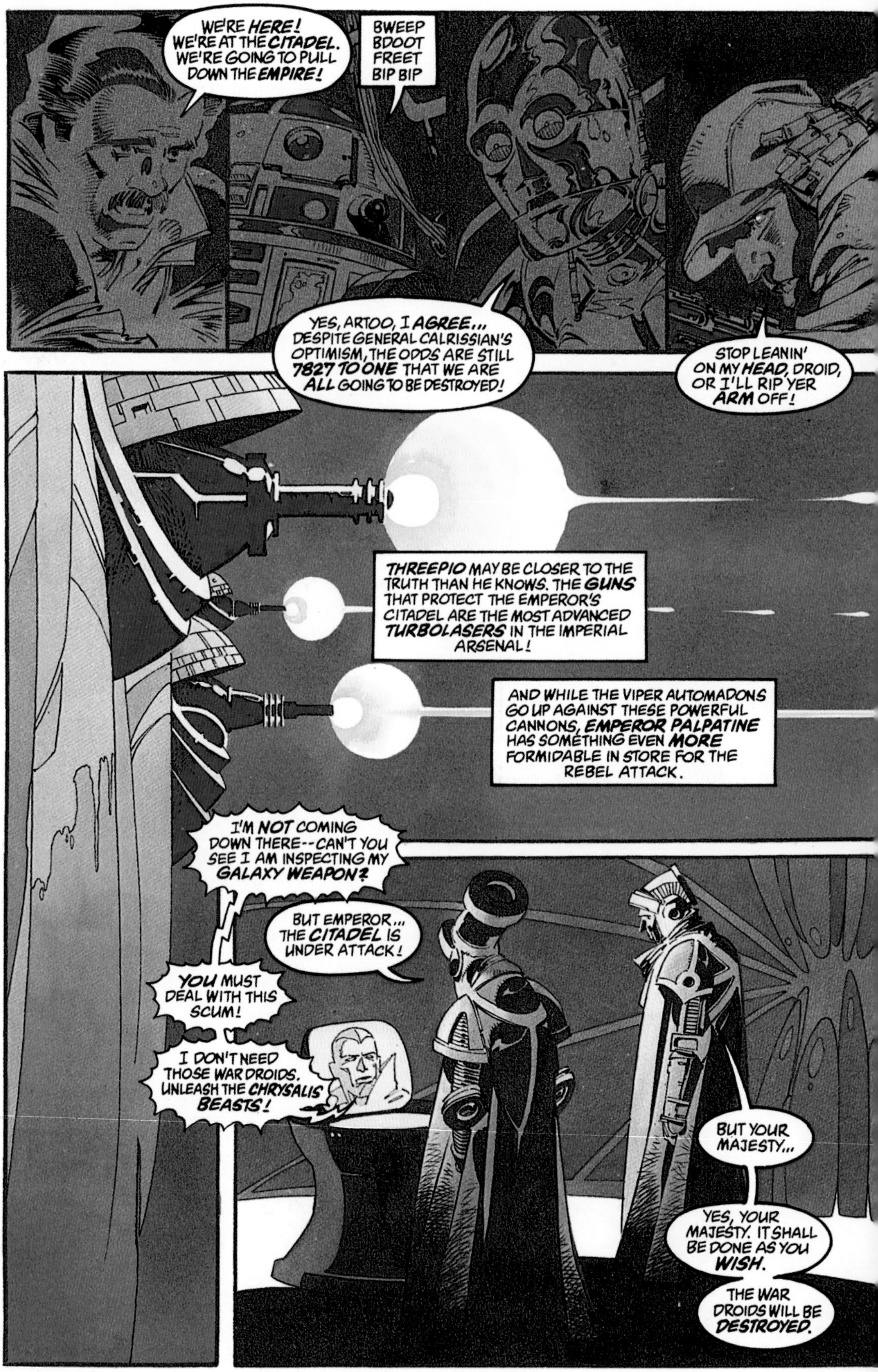
WE'RE HERE! WE'RE AT THE CITADEL. WE'RE GOING TO PULL DOWN THE EMPIRE!
BWEEP BDOOT FREET BIP BIP
YES, ARTOO, I AGREE... DESPITE GENERAL CALRISSIAN'S OPTIMISM, THE ODDS ARE STILL 7827 TO ONE THAT WE ARE ALL GOING TO BE DESTROYED!
STOP LEANIN' ON MY HEAD, DROID, OR I'LL RIP YER ARM OFF!
THREEPIO MAY BE CLOSER TO THE TRUTH THAN HE KNOWS. THE GUNS THAT PROTECT THE EMPEROR'S CITADEL ARE THE MOST ADVANCED TURBOLASERS IN THE IMPERIAL ARSENAL!
AND WHILE THE VIPER AUTOMADONS GO UP AGAINST THESE POWERFUL CANNONS, EMPEROR PALPATINE HAS SOMETHING EVEN MORE FORMIDABLE IN STORE FOR THE REBEL ATTACK.
I'M NOT COMING DOWN THERE--CAN'T YOU SEE I AM INSPECTING MY GALAXY WEAPON?
BUT EMPEROR... THE CITADEL IS UNDER ATTACK!
YOU MUST DEAL WITH THIS SCUM!
I DON'T NEED THOSE WAR DROIDS. UNLEASH THE CHRYSALIS BEASTS!
BUT YOUR MAJESTY...
YES, YOUR MAJESTY. IT SHALL BE DONE AS YOU WISH.
THE WAR DROIDS WILL BE DESTROYED.

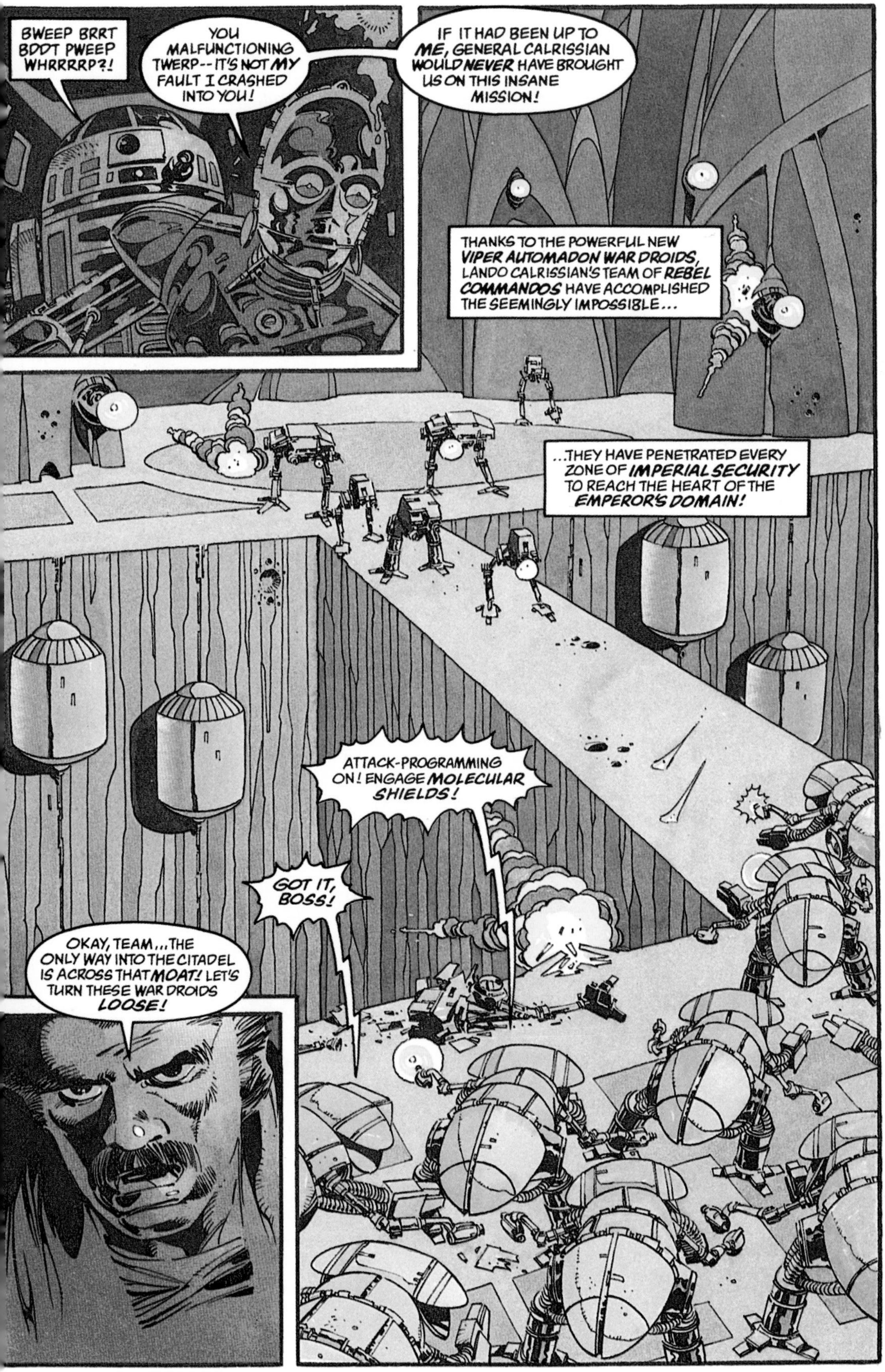
BWEEP BRRT BDDT PWEEP WHRRRRP?!
YOU MALFUNCTIONING TWERP--IT'S NOT MY FAULT I CRASHED INTO YOU!
IF IT HAD BEEN UP TO ME, GENERAL CALRISSIAN WOULD NEVER HAVE BROUGHT US ON THIS INSANE MISSION!
THANKS TO THE POWERFUL NEW VIPER AUTOMADON WAR DROIDS, LANDO CALRISSIAN'S TEAM OF REBEL COMMANDOS HAVE ACCOMPLISHED THE SEEMINGLY IMPOSSIBLE...
...THEY HAVE PENETRATED EVERY ZONE OF IMPERIAL SECURITY TO REACH THE HEART OF THE EMPEROR'S DOMAIN!
ATTACK-PROGRAMMING ON! ENGAGE MOLECULAR SHIELDS!
GOT IT, BOSS!
OKAY, TEAM...THE ONLY WAY INTO THE CITADEL IS ACROSS THAT MOAT! LET'S TURN THESE WAR DROIDS LOOSE!

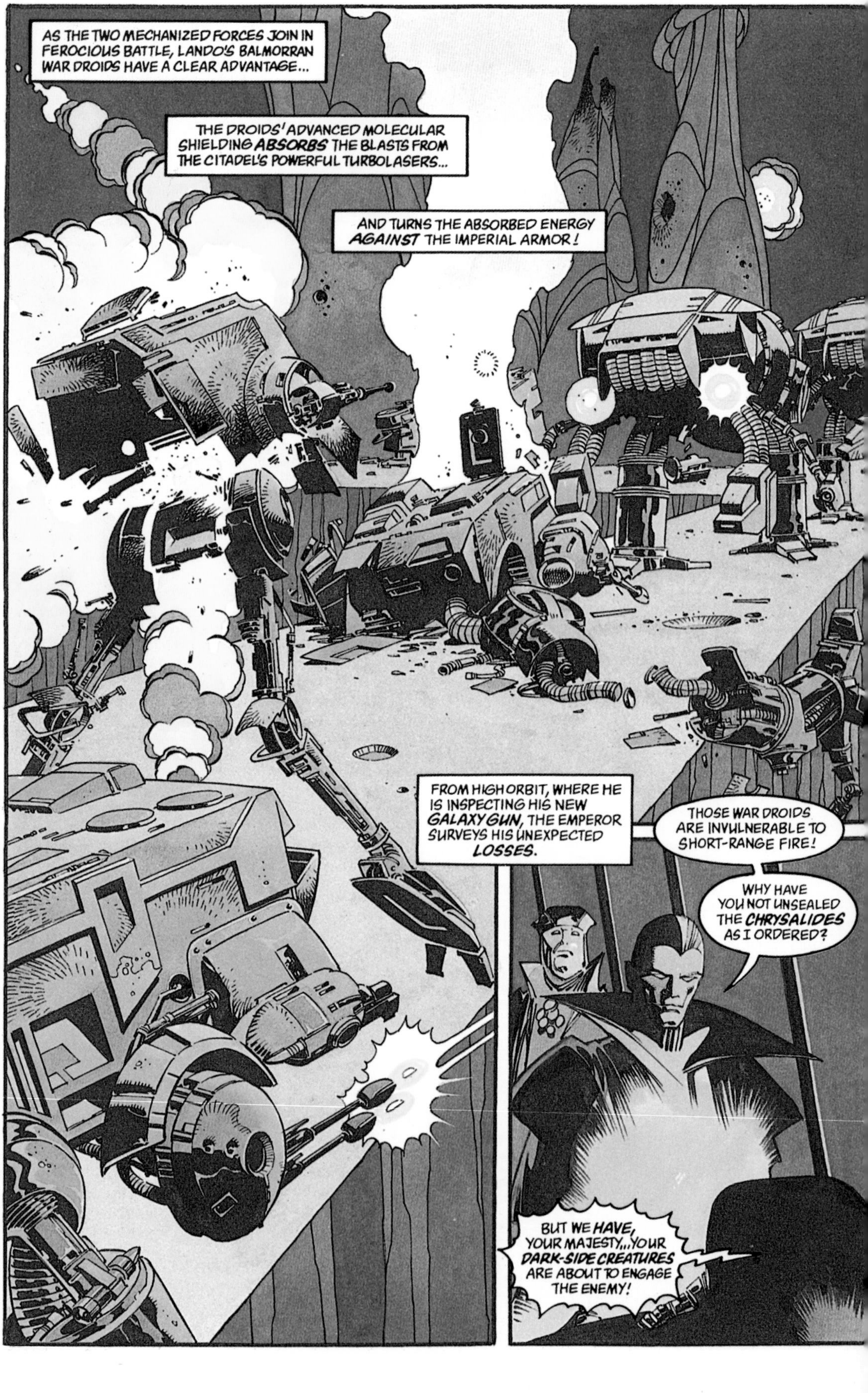
AS THE TWO MECHANIZED FORCES JOIN IN FEROCIOUS BATTLE, LANDO'S BALMORRAN WAR DROIDS HAVE A CLEAR ADVANTAGE...
THE DROIDS' ADVANCED MOLECULAR SHIELDING ABSORBS THE BLASTS FROM THE CITADEL'S POWERFUL TURBOLASERS...
AND TURNS THE ABSORBED ENERGY AGAINST THE IMPERIAL ARMOR!
FROM HIGH ORBIT, WHERE HE IS INSPECTING HIS NEW GALAXY GUN, THE EMPEROR SURVEYS HIS UNEXPECTED LOSSES.
THOSE WAR DROIDS ARE INVULNERABLE TO SHORT-RANGE FIRE!
WHY HAVE YOU NOT UNSEALED THE CHRYSALIDES AS I ORDERED?
BUT WE HAVE, YOUR MAJESTY... YOUR DARK-SIDE CREATURES ARE ABOUT TO ENGAGE THE ENEMY!

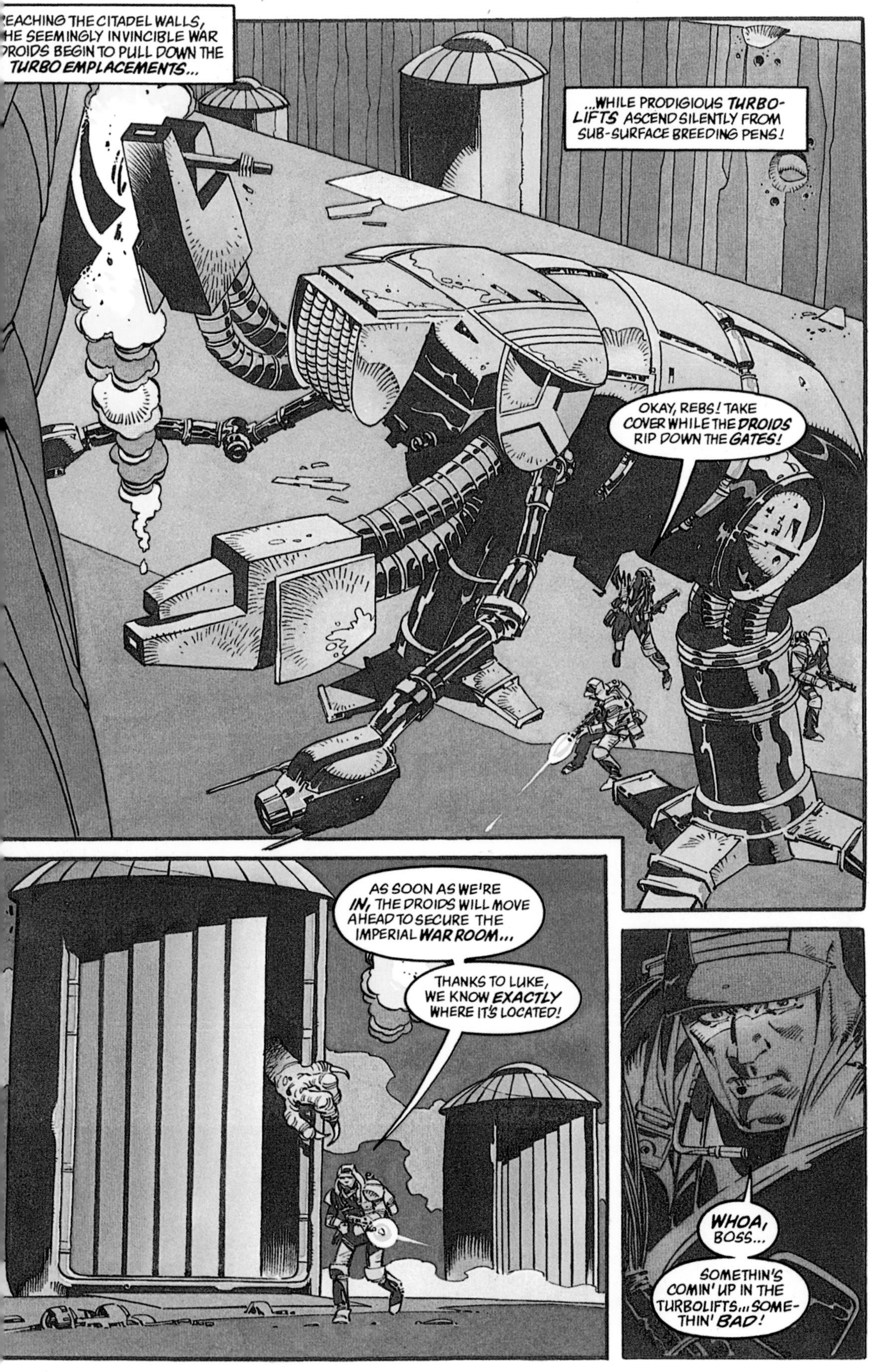
REACHING THE CITADEL WALLS, THE SEEMINGLY INVINCIBLE WAR DROIDS BEGIN TO PULL DOWN THE TURBO EMPLACEMENTS...
...WHILE PRODIGIOUS TURBO-LIFTS ASCEND SILENTLY FROM SUB-SURFACE BREEDING PENS!
OKAY, REBS! TAKE COVER WHILE THE DROIDS RIP DOWN THE GATES!
AS SOON AS WE'RE IN, THE DROIDS WILL MOVE AHEAD TO SECURE THE IMPERIAL WAR ROOM...
THANKS TO LUKE, WE KNOW EXACTLY WHERE IT'S LOCATED!
WHOA, BOSS...
SOMETHIN'S COMIN' UP IN THE TURBOLIFTS... SOME-THIN' BAD!

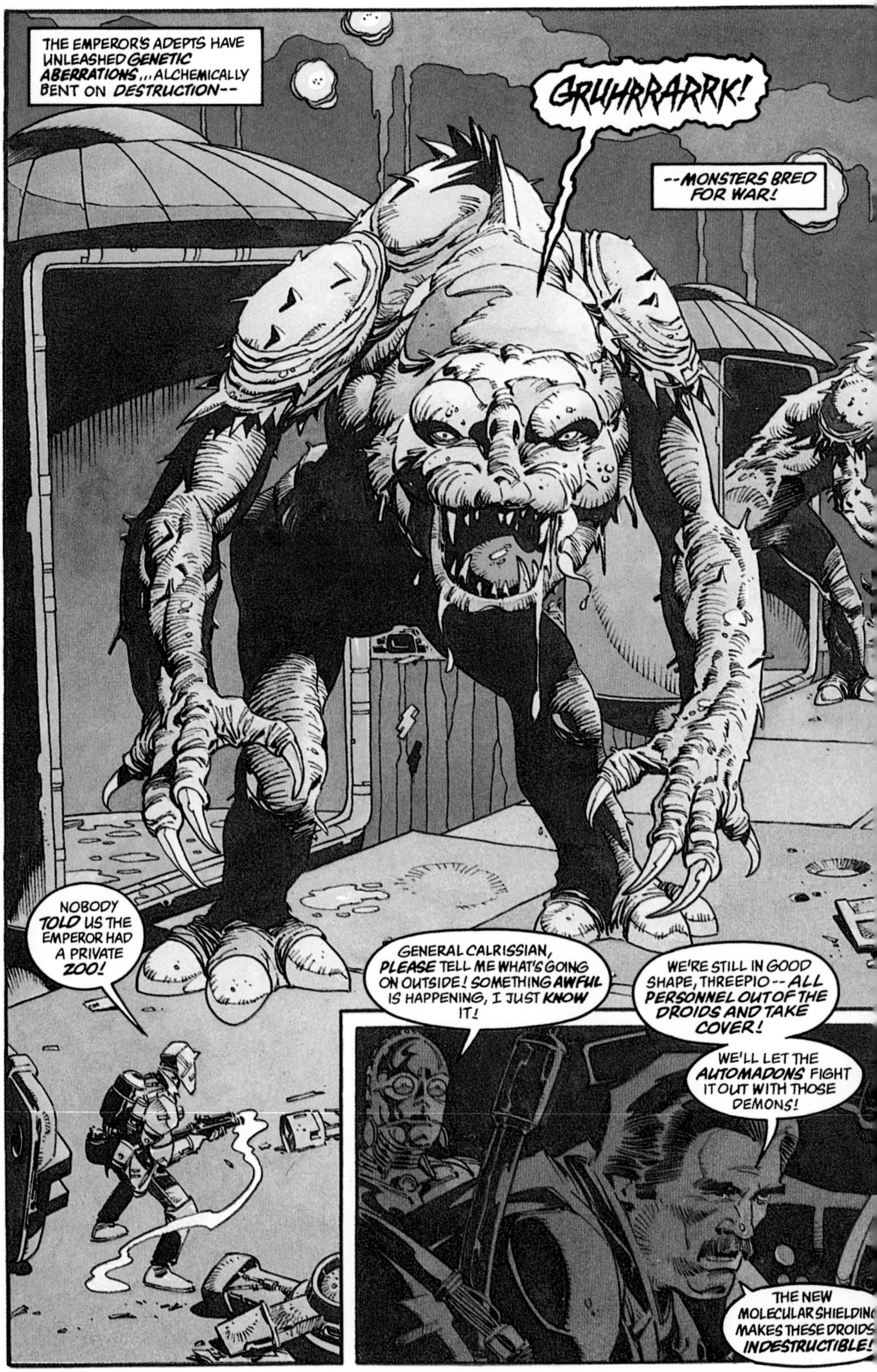
THE EMPEROR'S ADEPTS HAVE UNLEASHED GENETIC ABERRATIONS... ALCHEMICALLY BENT ON DESTRUCTION--
GRUHRRARRK!
--MONSTERS BRED FOR WAR!
NOBODY TOLD US THE EMPEROR HAD A PRIVATE ZOO!
GENERAL CALRISSIAN, PLEASE TELL ME WHAT'S GOING ON OUTSIDE! SOMETHING AWFUL IS HAPPENING, I JUST KNOW IT!
WE'RE STILL IN GOOD SHAPE, THREEPIO -- ALL PERSONNEL OUT OF THE DROIDS AND TAKE COVER!
WE'LL LET THE AUTOMADONS FIGHT IT OUT WITH THOSE DEMONS!
THE NEW MOLECULAR SHIELDING MAKES THESE DROIDS INDESTRUCTIBLE!

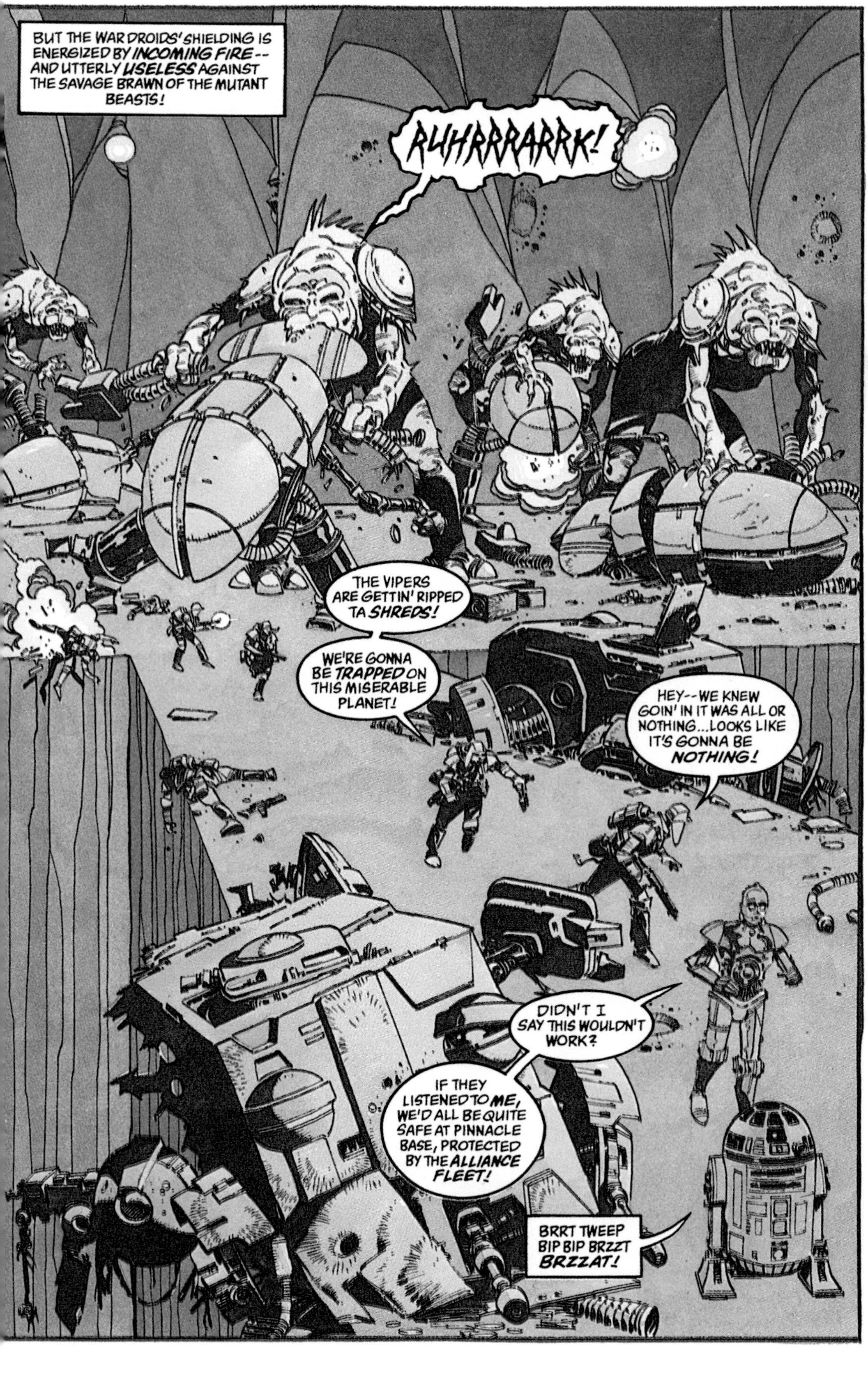
BUT THE WAR DROIDS' SHIELDING IS ENERGIZED BY INCOMING FIRE-- AND UTTERLY USELESS AGAINST THE SAVAGE BRAWN OF THE MUTANT BEASTS!
RUHRRRARRK!
THE VIPERS ARE GETTIN' RIPPED TA SHREDS!
WE'RE GONNA BE TRAPPED ON THIS MISERABLE PLANET!
HEY--WE KNEW GOIN' IN IT WAS ALL OR NOTHING...LOOKS LIKE IT'S GONNA BE NOTHING!
DIDN'T I SAY THIS WOULDN'T WORK?
IF THEY LISTENED TO ME, WE'D ALL BE QUITE SAFE AT PINNACLE BASE, PROTECTED BY THE ALLIANCE FLEET!
BRRT TWEEP BIP BIP BRZZT BRZZAT!

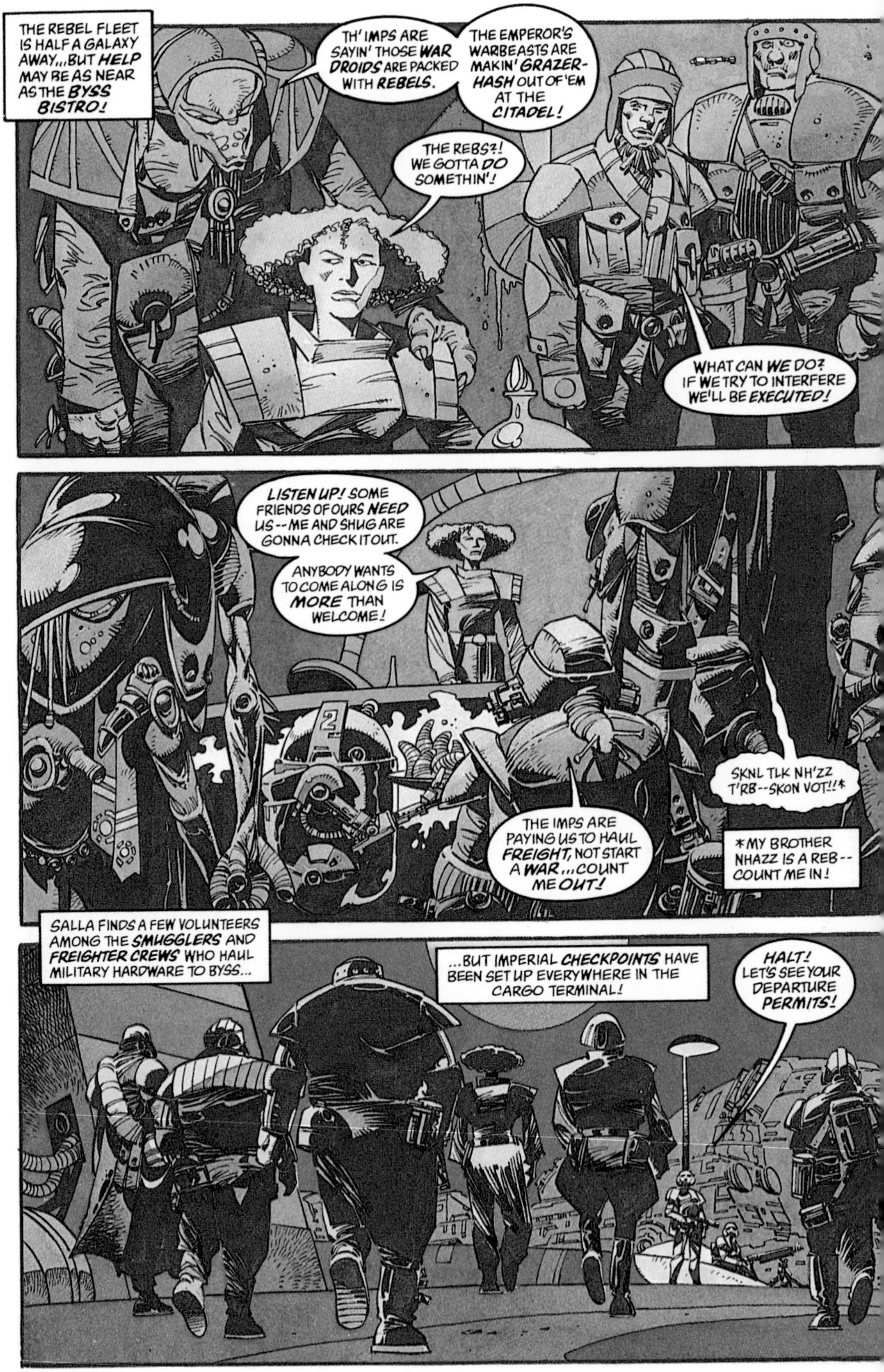
THE REBEL FLEET IS HALF A GALAXY AWAY... BUT HELP MAY BE AS NEAR AS THE BYSS BISTRO!
TH' IMPS ARE SAYIN' THOSE WAR DROIDS ARE PACKED WITH REBELS.
THE EMPEROR'S WARBEASTS ARE MAKIN' GRAZER-HASH OUT OF 'EM AT THE CITADEL!
THE REBS?! WE GOTTA DO SOMETHIN'!
WHAT CAN WE DO? IF WE TRY TO INTERFERE WE'LL BE EXECUTED!
LISTEN UP! SOME FRIENDS OF OURS NEED US -- ME AND SHUG ARE GONNA CHECK IT OUT.
ANYBODY WANTS TO COME ALONG IS MORE THAN WELCOME!
THE IMPS ARE PAYING US TO HAUL FREIGHT, NOT START A WAR... COUNT ME OUT!
SKNL TLK NH'ZZ T'RB--SKON VOT!!*
*MY BROTHER NHAZZ IS A REB -- COUNT ME IN!
SALLA FINDS A FEW VOLUNTEERS AMONG THE SMUGGLERS AND FREIGHTER CREWS WHO HAUL MILITARY HARDWARE TO BYSS...
...BUT IMPERIAL CHECKPOINTS HAVE BEEN SET UP EVERYWHERE IN THE CARGO TERMINAL!
HALT! LET'S SEE YOUR DEPARTURE PERMITS!
2

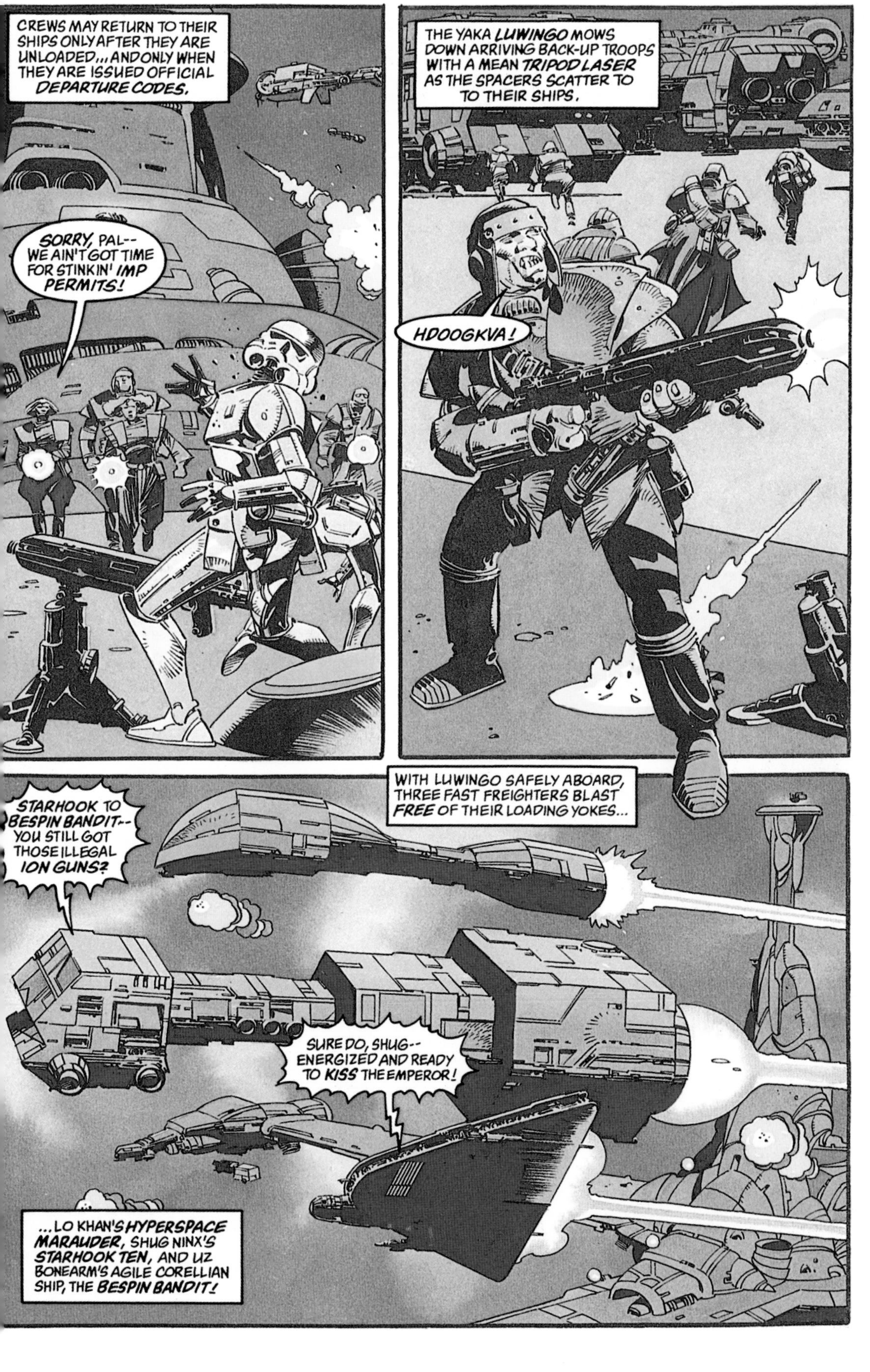

CREWS MAY RETURN TO THEIR SHIPS ONLY AFTER THEY ARE UNLOADED... AND ONLY WHEN THEY ARE ISSUED OFFICIAL DEPARTURE CODES.
SORRY, PAL-- WE AIN'T GOT TIME FOR STINKIN' IMP PERMITS!
THE YAKA LUWINGO MOWS DOWN ARRIVING BACK-UP TROOPS WITH A MEAN TRIPOD LASER AS THE SPACERS SCATTER TO TO THEIR SHIPS.
HDOOGKVA!
WITH LUWINGO SAFELY ABOARD, THREE FAST FREIGHTERS BLAST FREE OF THEIR LOADING YOKES...
STARHOOK TO BESPIN BANDIT-- YOU STILL GOT THOSE ILLEGAL ION GUNS?
SURE DO, SHUG-- ENERGIZED AND READY TO KISS THE EMPEROR!
...LO KHAN'S HYPERSPACE MARAUDER, SHUG NINX'S STARHOOK TEN, AND UZ BONEARM'S AGILE CORELLIAN SHIP, THE BESPIN BANDIT!

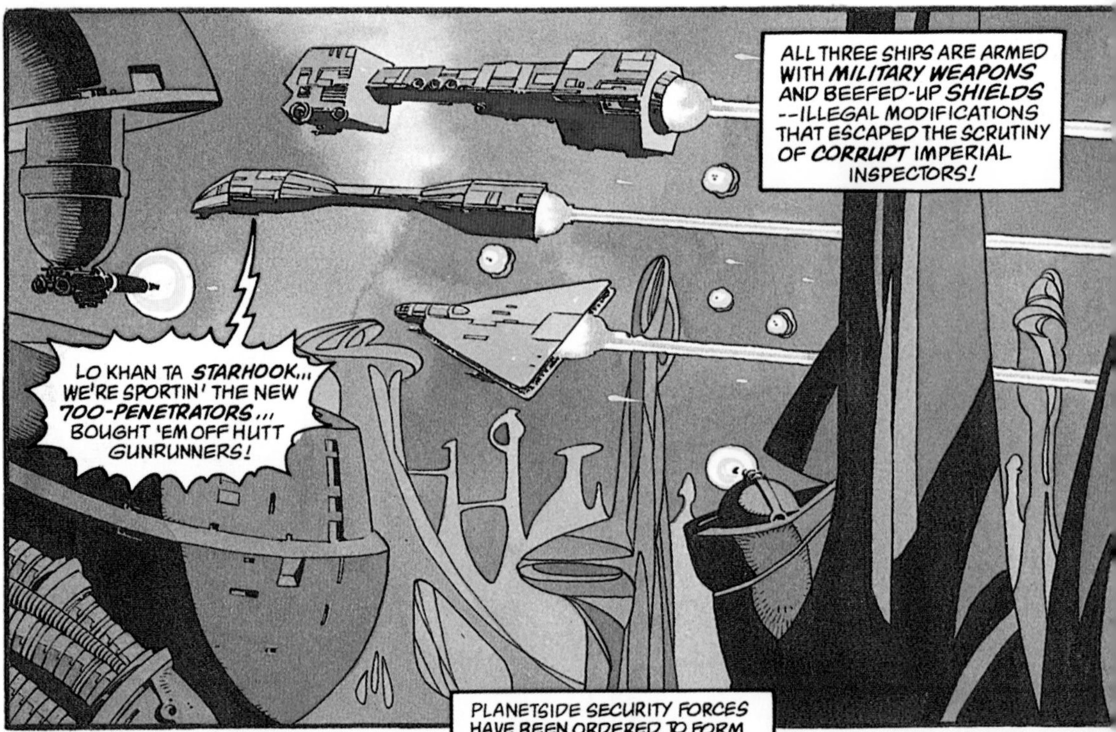
ALL THREE SHIPS ARE ARMED WITH MILITARY WEAPONS AND BEEFED-UP SHIELDS --ILLEGAL MODIFICATIONS THAT ESCAPED THE SCRUTINY OF CORRUPT IMPERIAL INSPECTORS!
LO KHAN TA STARHOOK... WE'RE SPORTIN' THE NEW 700-PENETRATORS... BOUGHT 'EM OFF HUTT GUNRUNNERS!

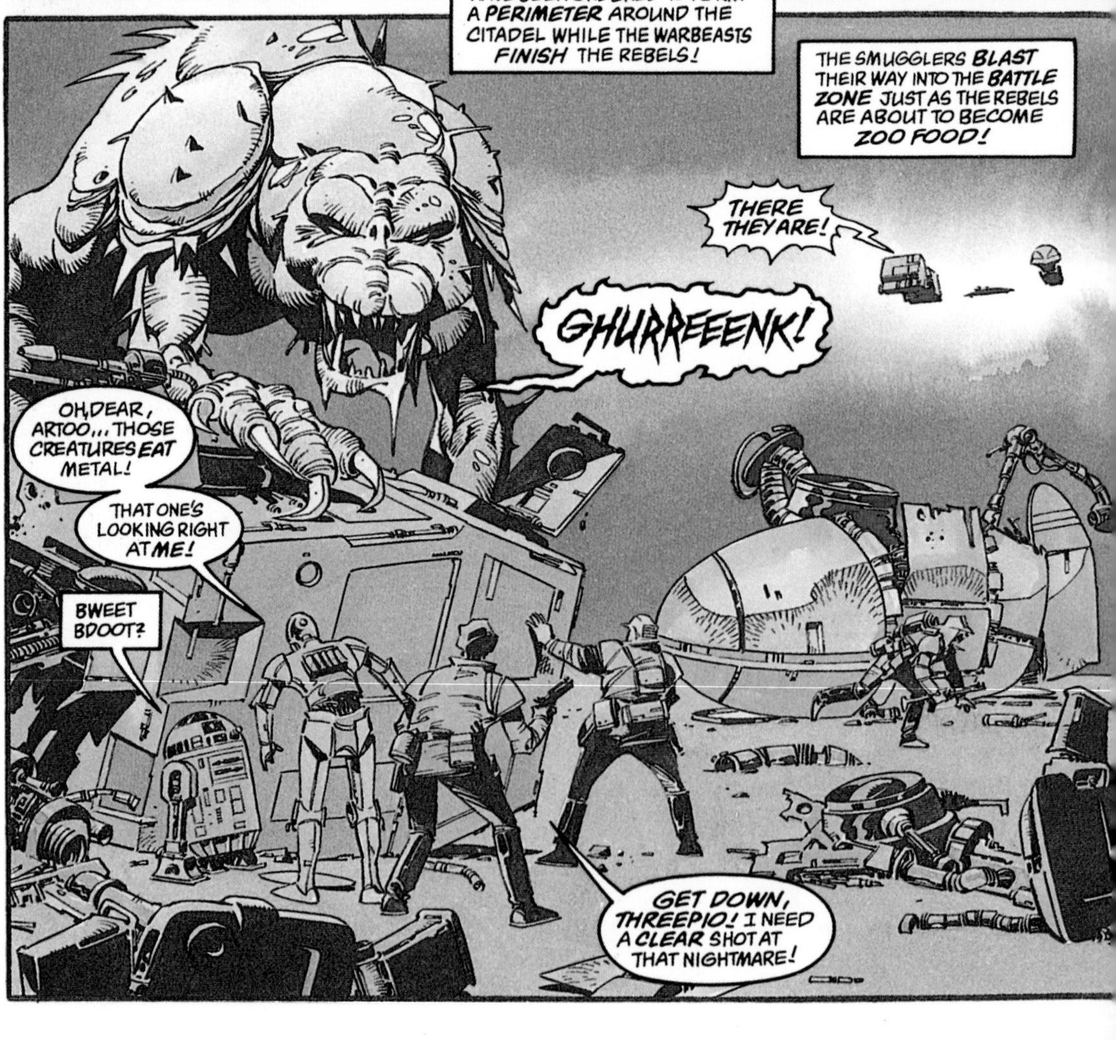
PLANETSIDE SECURITY FORCES HAVE BEEN ORDERED TO FORM A PERIMETER AROUND THE CITADEL WHILE THE WARBEASTS FINISH THE REBELS!
THE SMUGGLERS BLAST THEIR WAY INTO THE BATTLE ZONE JUST AS THE REBELS ARE ABOUT TO BECOME ZOO FOOD!
THERE THEY ARE!
GHURREEENK!
OH, DEAR, ARTOO... THOSE CREATURES EAT METAL!
THAT ONE'S LOOKING RIGHT AT ME!
BWEET BDOOT?
GET DOWN, THREEPIO! I NEED A CLEAR SHOT AT THAT NIGHTMARE!

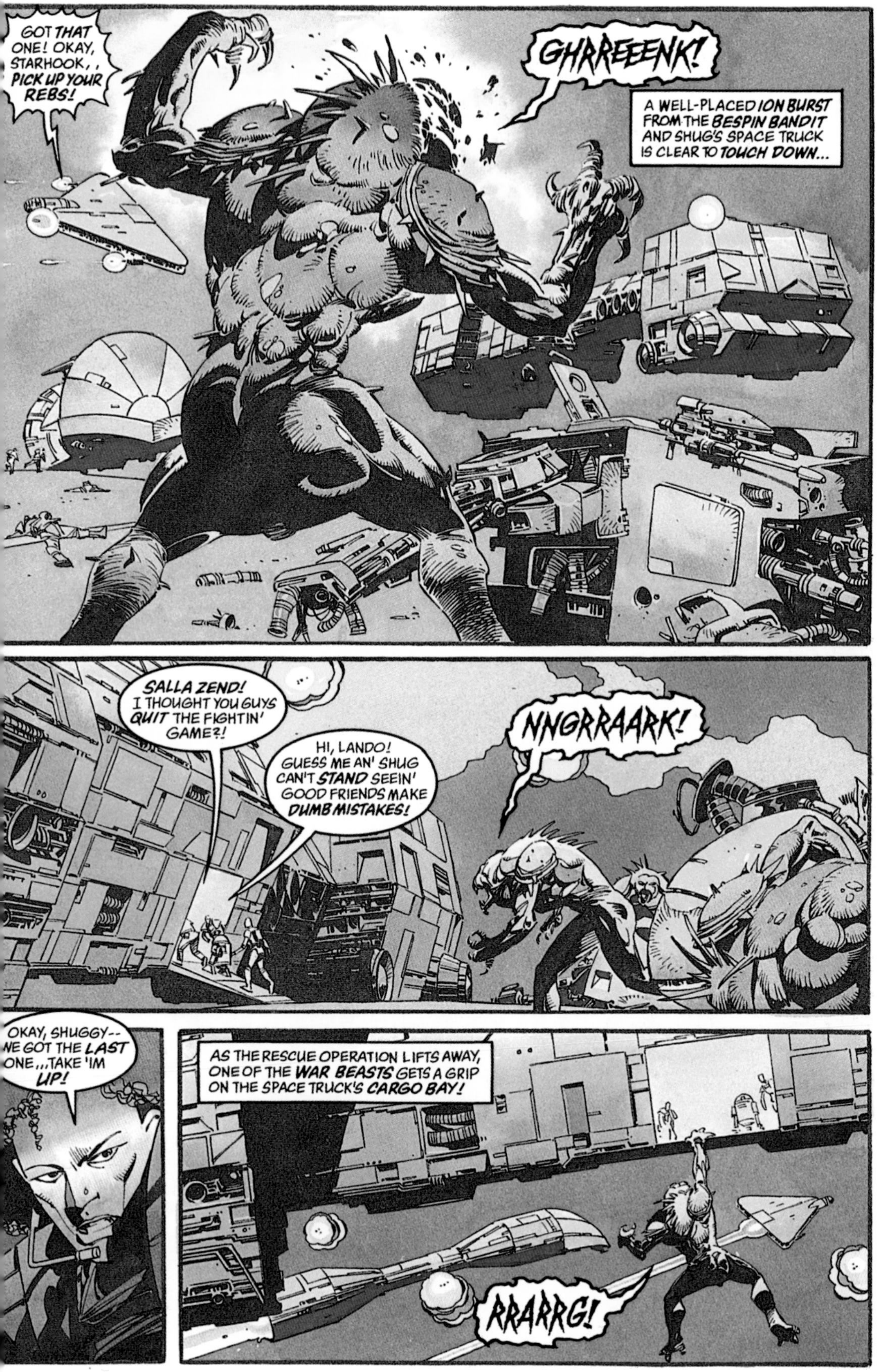

GOT THAT ONE! OKAY, STARHOOK,, PICK UP YOUR REBS!
GHRREEENK!
A WELL-PLACED ION BURST FROM THE BESPIN BANDIT AND SHUG'S SPACE TRUCK IS CLEAR TO TOUCH DOWN...
SALLA ZEND! I THOUGHT YOU GUYS QUIT THE FIGHTIN' GAME?!
HI, LANDO! GUESS ME AN' SHUG CAN'T STAND SEEIN' GOOD FRIENDS MAKE DUMB MISTAKES!
NNGRRAARK!
OKAY, SHUGGY-- WE GOT THE LAST ONE,,,TAKE 'IM UP!
AS THE RESCUE OPERATION LIFTS AWAY, ONE OF THE WAR BEASTS GETS A GRIP ON THE SPACE TRUCK'S CARGO BAY!
RRARRG!

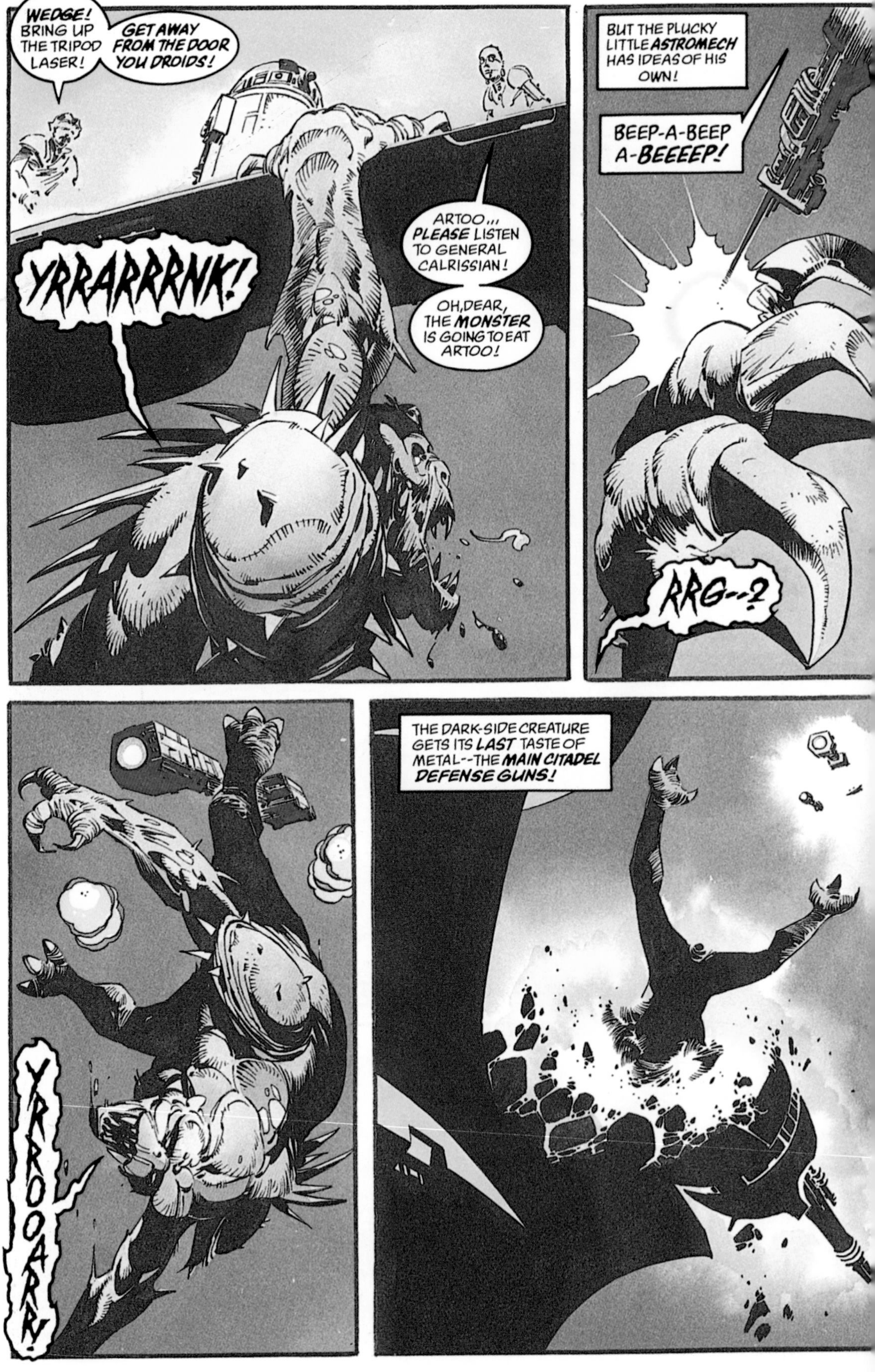
WEDGE! BRING UP THE TRIPOD LASER!
GET AWAY FROM THE DOOR YOU DROIDS!
YRRARRRNK!
ARTOO... PLEASE LISTEN TO GENERAL CALRISSIAN!
OH, DEAR, THE MONSTER IS GOING TO EAT ARTOO!
BUT THE PLUCKY LITTLE ASTROMECH HAS IDEAS OF HIS OWN!
BEEP-A-BEEP A-BEEEEP!
RRG--?
YRROOARRN!
THE DARK-SIDE CREATURE GETS ITS LAST TASTE OF METAL--THE MAIN CITADEL DEFENSE GUNS!

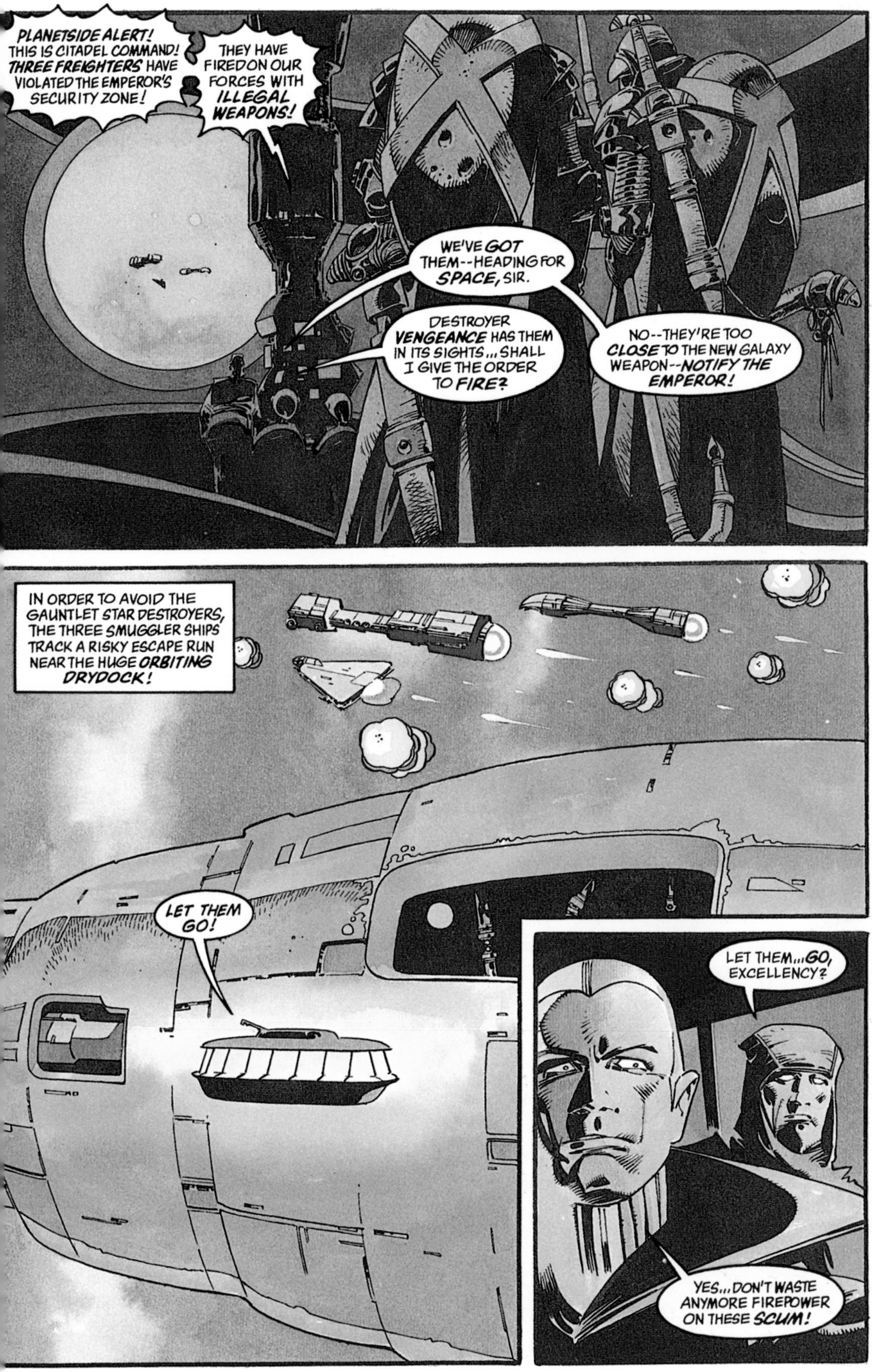
PLANETSIDE ALERT! THIS IS CITADEL COMMAND! THREE FREIGHTERS HAVE VIOLATED THE EMPEROR'S SECURITY ZONE!
THEY HAVE FIRED ON OUR FORCES WITH ILLEGAL WEAPONS!
WE'VE GOT THEM--HEADING FOR SPACE, SIR.
DESTROYER VENGEANCE HAS THEM IN ITS SIGHTS... SHALL I GIVE THE ORDER TO FIRE?
NO--THEY'RE TOO CLOSE TO THE NEW GALAXY WEAPON--NOTIFY THE EMPEROR!
IN ORDER TO AVOID THE GAUNTLET STAR DESTROYERS, THE THREE SMUGGLER SHIPS TRACK A RISKY ESCAPE RUN NEAR THE HUGE ORBITING DRYDOCK!
LET THEM GO!
LET THEM... GO, EXCELLENCY?
YES... DON'T WASTE ANYMORE FIREPOWER ON THESE SCUM!

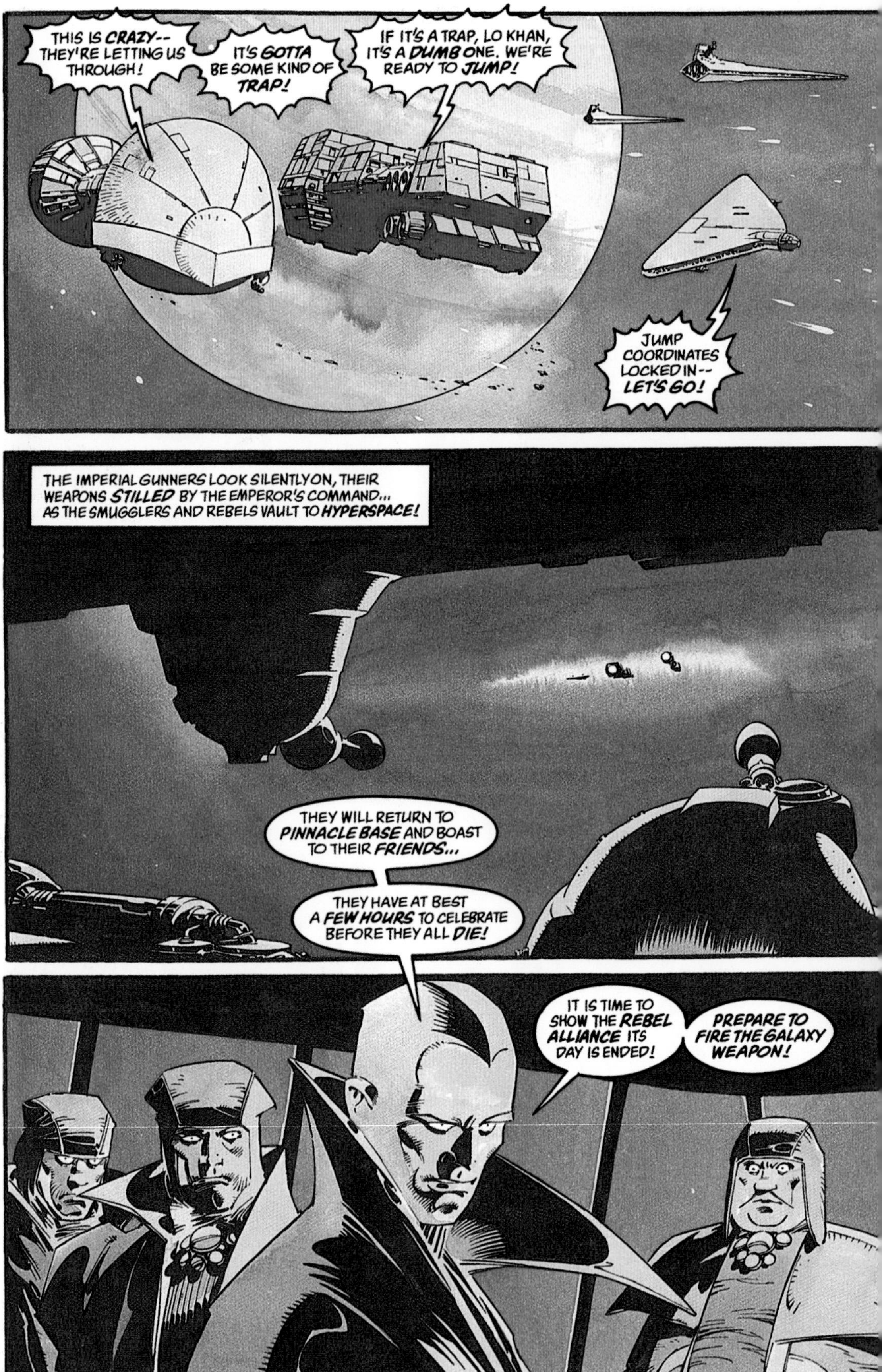
THIS IS CRAZY-- THEY'RE LETTING US THROUGH!
IT'S GOTTA BE SOME KIND OF TRAP!
IF IT'S A TRAP, LO KHAN, IT'S A DUMB ONE. WE'RE READY TO JUMP!
JUMP COORDINATES LOCKED IN-- LET'S GO!
THE IMPERIAL GUNNERS LOOK SILENTLY ON, THEIR WEAPONS STILLED BY THE EMPEROR'S COMMAND... AS THE SMUGGLERS AND REBELS VAULT TO HYPERSPACE!
THEY WILL RETURN TO PINNACLE BASE AND BOAST TO THEIR FRIENDS...
THEY HAVE AT BEST A FEW HOURS TO CELEBRATE BEFORE THEY ALL DIE!
IT IS TIME TO SHOW THE REBEL ALLIANCE ITS DAY IS ENDED!
PREPARE TO FIRE THE GALAXY WEAPON!

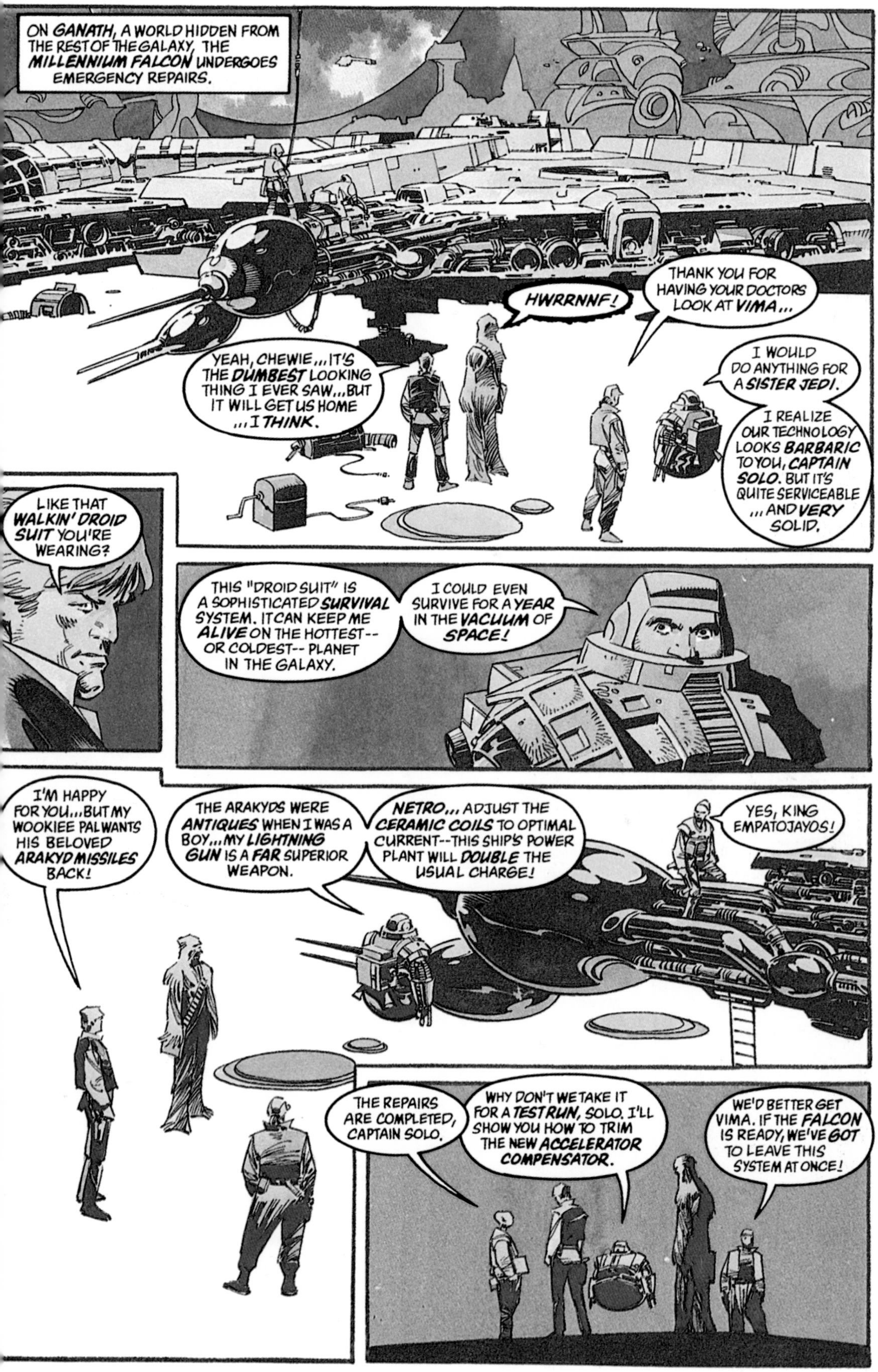
ON GANATH, A WORLD HIDDEN FROM THE REST OF THE GALAXY, THE MILLENNIUM FALCON UNDERGOES EMERGENCY REPAIRS.
HWRRNNF!
YEAH, CHEWIE... IT'S THE DUMBEST LOOKING THING I EVER SAW... BUT IT WILL GET US HOME ... I THINK.
THANK YOU FOR HAVING YOUR DOCTORS LOOK AT VIMA...
I WOULD DO ANYTHING FOR A SISTER JEDI.
I REALIZE OUR TECHNOLOGY LOOKS BARBARIC TO YOU, CAPTAIN SOLO. BUT IT'S QUITE SERVICEABLE ... AND VERY SOLID.
LIKE THAT WALKIN' DROID SUIT YOU'RE WEARING?
THIS "DROID SUIT" IS A SOPHISTICATED SURVIVAL SYSTEM. IT CAN KEEP ME ALIVE ON THE HOTTEST-- OR COLDEST-- PLANET IN THE GALAXY.
I COULD EVEN SURVIVE FOR A YEAR IN THE VACUUM OF SPACE!
I'M HAPPY FOR YOU... BUT MY WOOKIEE PAL WANTS HIS BELOVED ARAKYD MISSILES BACK!
THE ARAKYDS WERE ANTIQUES WHEN I WAS A BOY... MY LIGHTNING GUN IS A FAR SUPERIOR WEAPON.
NETRO... ADJUST THE CERAMIC COILS TO OPTIMAL CURRENT--THIS SHIP'S POWER PLANT WILL DOUBLE THE USUAL CHARGE!
YES, KING EMPATOJAYOS!
THE REPAIRS ARE COMPLETED, CAPTAIN SOLO.
WHY DON'T WE TAKE IT FOR A TEST RUN, SOLO. I'LL SHOW YOU HOW TO TRIM THE NEW ACCELERATOR COMPENSATOR.
WE'D BETTER GET VIMA. IF THE FALCON IS READY, WE'VE GOT TO LEAVE THIS SYSTEM AT ONCE!

SOLO AND CHEWBACCA ARE GREATLY RELIEVED TO FIND THE *FALCON* STILL FLIES, DESPITE THE CLUNKY-LOOKING REPAIRS!

I DON'T KNOW, KING BRAND... THE CONTROLS ARE ACTIN' *WEIRD*...SHE'S GOT A TENDENCY TO *ROLL*.

CHEWIE...BETTER RECALIBRATE THE FLUX STABILIZER.

RHNURF.

LOOKS LIKE YOU'VE GOT THE IDEA, SOLO...*ENJOY* YOURSELF.

I'M GOING BACK AND TALK TO MY *FELLOW JEDI*.

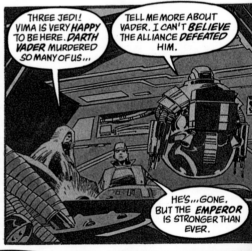

THREE JEDI! VIMA IS VERY *HAPPY* TO BE HERE. *DARTH VADER* MURDERED SO MANY OF US...

TELL ME MORE ABOUT VADER. I CAN'T *BELIEVE* THE ALLIANCE *DEFEATED* HIM.

HE'S...GONE. BUT THE *EMPEROR* IS STRONGER THAN EVER.

IS IT TRUE VADER WAS *KILLED* BY THE EMPEROR HIMSELF? WAS HE *REALLY*...YOUR *FATHER*?

YES, BUT *ANAKIN SKYWALKER*...MY FATHER...IS *FREE* OF THE DARK SIDE.

MY BROTHER *LUKE* IS A JEDI MASTER...HE HAS VOWED TO *RESTORE* THE JEDI TO THEIR FORMER GLORY.

I WILL *JOIN* YOU IN THIS FIGHT. THE *JEDI KNIGHTS MUST RISE AGAIN.*

THE *FORCE* CAN *NEVER* DIE. THE *JEDI* KNOW THE FORCE...AND VIMA KNOWS THE JEDI ARE *FOREVER.*

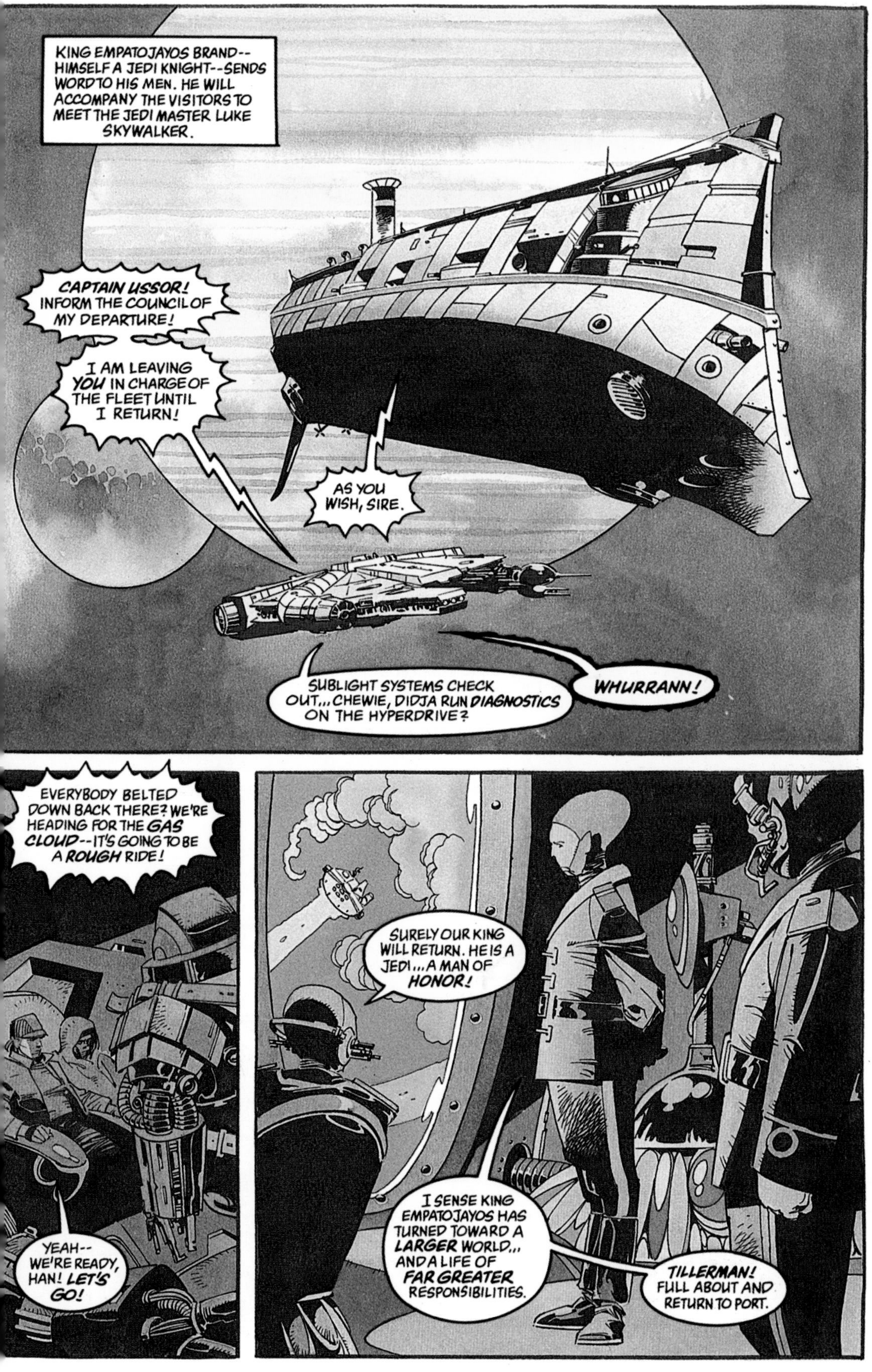
KING EMPATOJAYOS BRAND--HIMSELF A JEDI KNIGHT--SENDS WORD TO HIS MEN. HE WILL ACCOMPANY THE VISITORS TO MEET THE JEDI MASTER LUKE SKYWALKER.
CAPTAIN USSOR! INFORM THE COUNCIL OF MY DEPARTURE!
I AM LEAVING YOU IN CHARGE OF THE FLEET UNTIL I RETURN!
AS YOU WISH, SIRE.
SUBLIGHT SYSTEMS CHECK OUT... CHEWIE, DIDJA RUN DIAGNOSTICS ON THE HYPERDRIVE?
WHURRANN!
EVERYBODY BELTED DOWN BACK THERE? WE'RE HEADING FOR THE GAS CLOUD--IT'S GOING TO BE A ROUGH RIDE!
YEAH--WE'RE READY, HAN! LET'S GO!
SURELY OUR KING WILL RETURN. HE IS A JEDI... A MAN OF HONOR!
I SENSE KING EMPATOJAYOS HAS TURNED TOWARD A LARGER WORLD... AND A LIFE OF FAR GREATER RESPONSIBILITIES.
TILLERMAN! FULL ABOUT AND RETURN TO PORT.

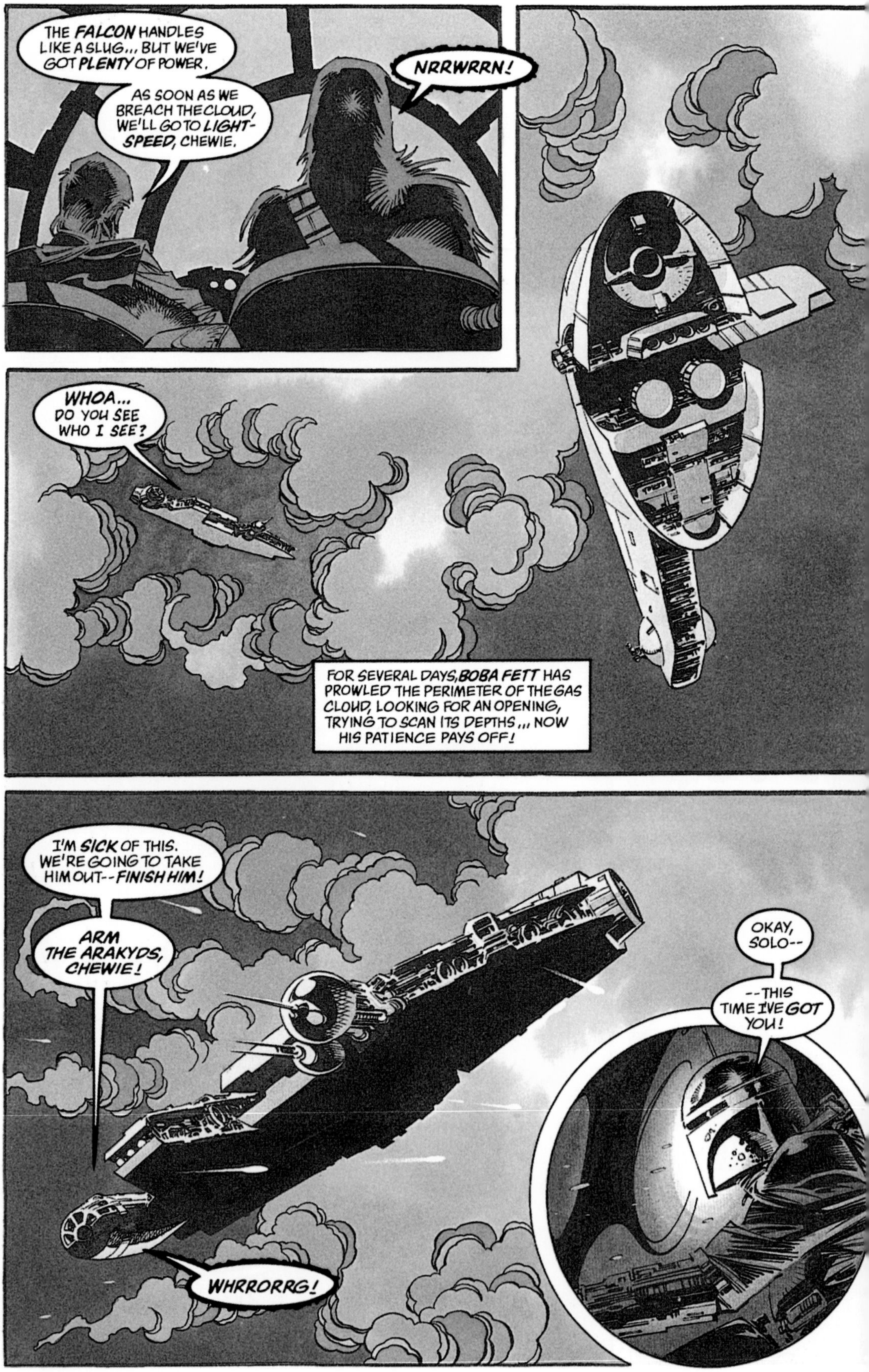
THE FALCON HANDLES LIKE A SLUG... BUT WE'VE GOT PLENTY OF POWER.
AS SOON AS WE BREACH THE CLOUD, WE'LL GO TO LIGHT-SPEED, CHEWIE.
NRRWRRN!
WHOA... DO YOU SEE WHO I SEE?
FOR SEVERAL DAYS, BOBA FETT HAS PROWLED THE PERIMETER OF THE GAS CLOUD, LOOKING FOR AN OPENING, TRYING TO SCAN ITS DEPTHS... NOW HIS PATIENCE PAYS OFF!
I'M SICK OF THIS. WE'RE GOING TO TAKE HIM OUT--FINISH HIM!
ARM THE ARAKYDS, CHEWIE!
WHRRORRG!
OKAY, SOLO--
--THIS TIME I'VE GOT YOU!

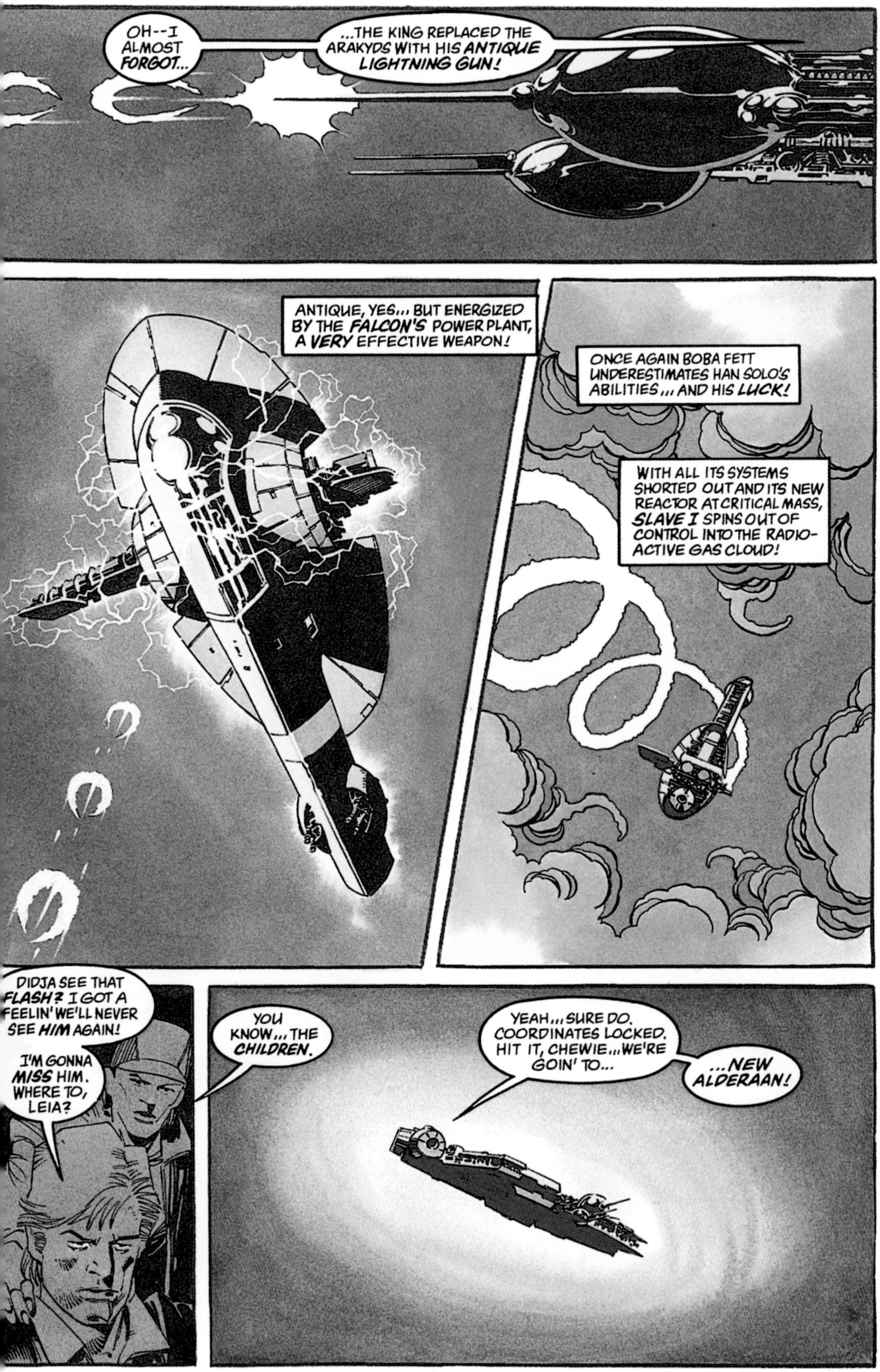
OH--I ALMOST FORGOT...
...THE KING REPLACED THE ARAKYDS WITH HIS ANTIQUE LIGHTNING GUN!
ANTIQUE, YES... BUT ENERGIZED BY THE FALCON'S POWER PLANT, A VERY EFFECTIVE WEAPON!
ONCE AGAIN BOBA FETT UNDERESTIMATES HAN SOLO'S ABILITIES... AND HIS LUCK!
WITH ALL ITS SYSTEMS SHORTED OUT AND ITS NEW REACTOR AT CRITICAL MASS, SLAVE I SPINS OUT OF CONTROL INTO THE RADIO-ACTIVE GAS CLOUD!
DIDJA SEE THAT FLASH? I GOT A FEELIN' WE'LL NEVER SEE HIM AGAIN!
I'M GONNA MISS HIM. WHERE TO, LEIA?
YOU KNOW... THE CHILDREN.
YEAH... SURE DO. COORDINATES LOCKED. HIT IT, CHEWIE... WE'RE GOIN' TO...
...NEW ALDERAAN!

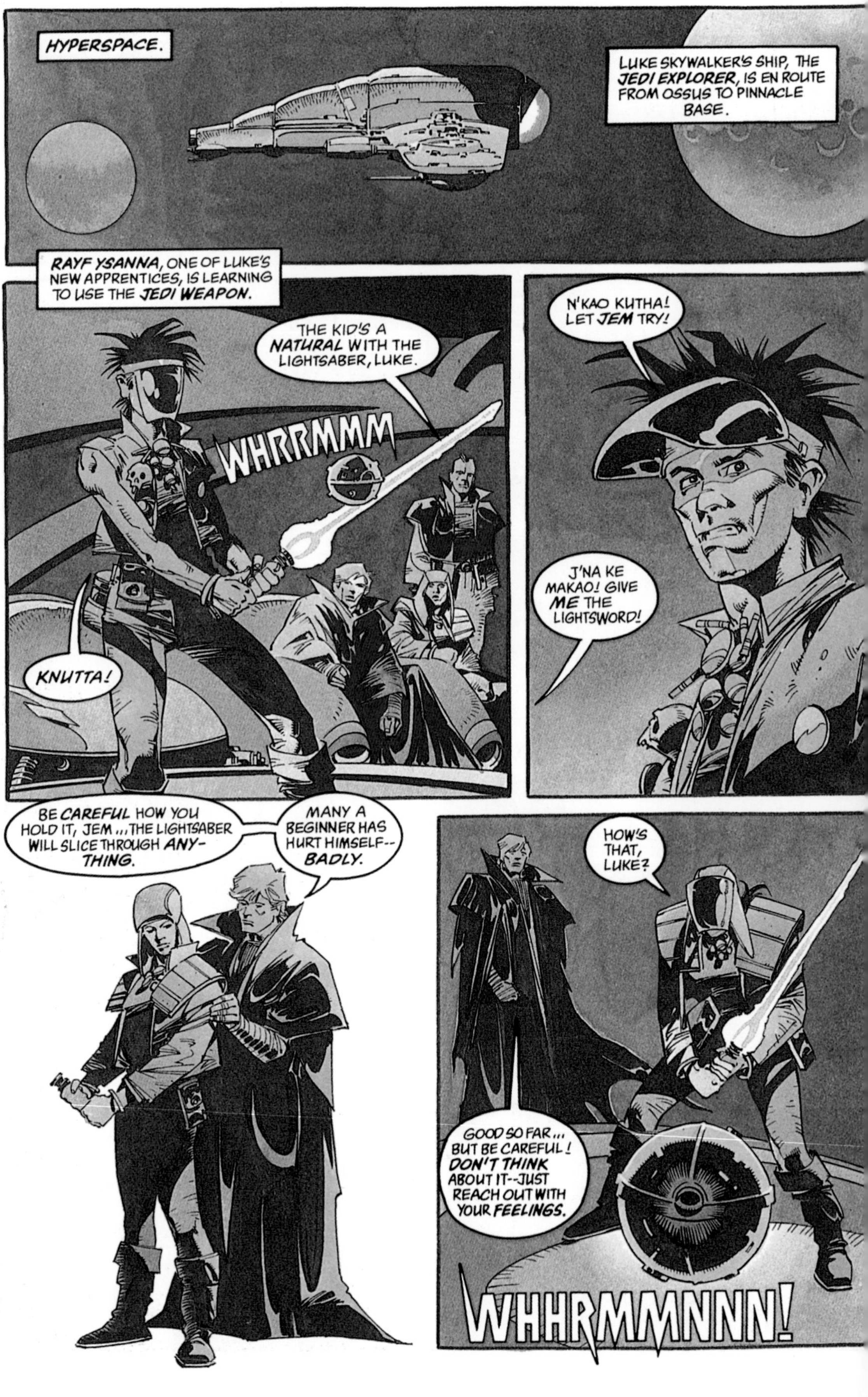

HYPERSPACE.
LUKE SKYWALKER'S SHIP, THE JEDI EXPLORER, IS EN ROUTE FROM OSSUS TO PINNACLE BASE.
RAYF YSANNA, ONE OF LUKE'S NEW APPRENTICES, IS LEARNING TO USE THE JEDI WEAPON.
THE KID'S A NATURAL WITH THE LIGHTSABER, LUKE.
WHRRMMM
KNUTTA!
N'KAO KUTHA! LET JEM TRY!
J'NA KE MAKAO! GIVE ME THE LIGHTSWORD!
BE CAREFUL HOW YOU HOLD IT, JEM ... THE LIGHTSABER WILL SLICE THROUGH ANY-THING.
MANY A BEGINNER HAS HURT HIMSELF-- BADLY.
HOW'S THAT, LUKE?
GOOD SO FAR ... BUT BE CAREFUL! DON'T THINK ABOUT IT--JUST REACH OUT WITH YOUR FEELINGS.
WHRMMNNN!

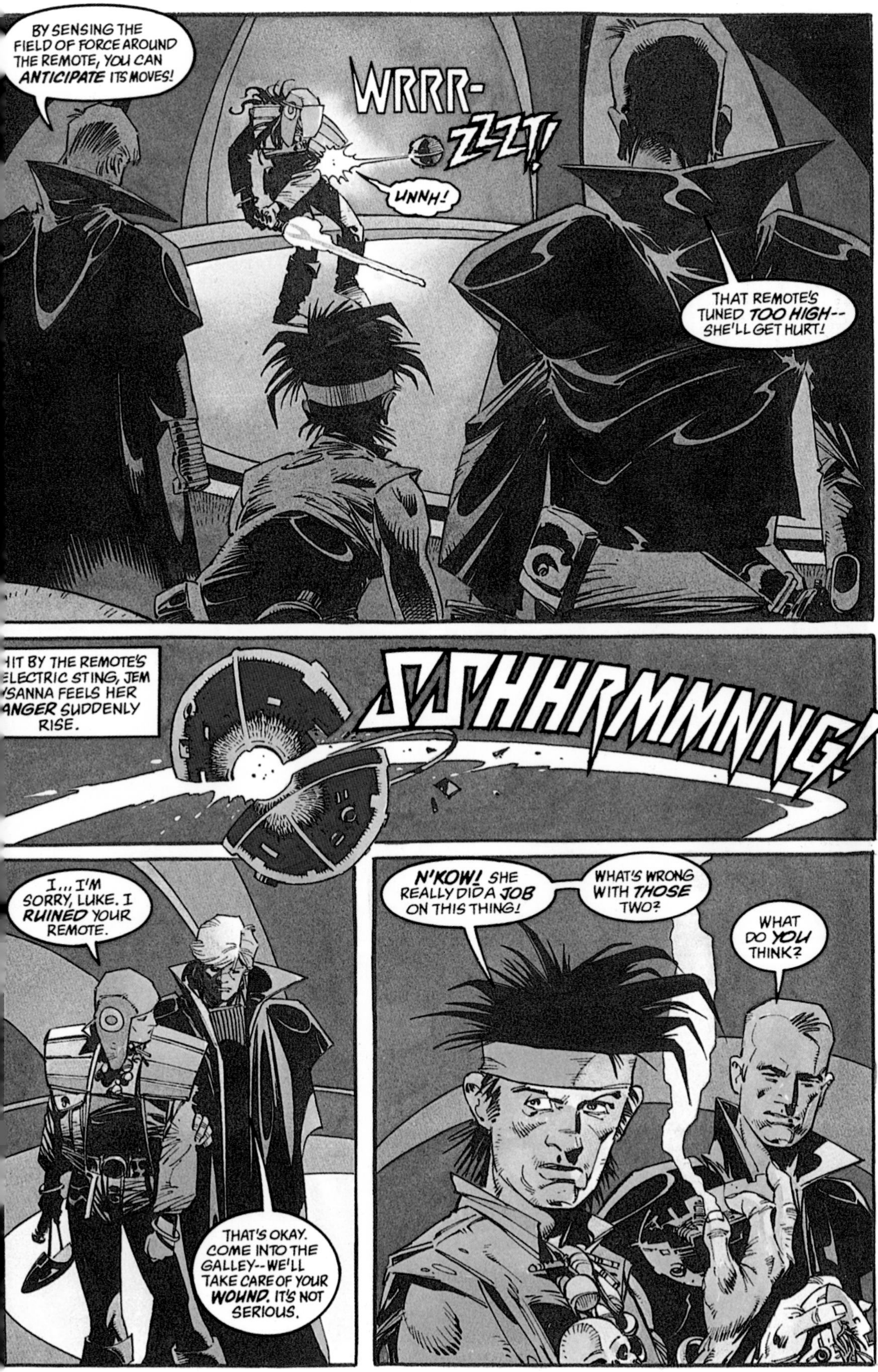

BY SENSING THE FIELD OF FORCE AROUND THE REMOTE, YOU CAN ANTICIPATE ITS MOVES!
WRRR-ZZZT!
UNNH!
THAT REMOTE'S TUNED TOO HIGH--SHE'LL GET HURT!
HIT BY THE REMOTE'S ELECTRIC STING, JEM YSANNA FEELS HER ANGER SUDDENLY RISE.
SSHHRMMNNG!
I... I'M SORRY, LUKE. I RUINED YOUR REMOTE.
THAT'S OKAY. COME INTO THE GALLEY--WE'LL TAKE CARE OF YOUR WOUND. IT'S NOT SERIOUS.
N'KOW! SHE REALLY DID A JOB ON THIS THING!
WHAT'S WRONG WITH THOSE TWO?
WHAT DO YOU THINK?

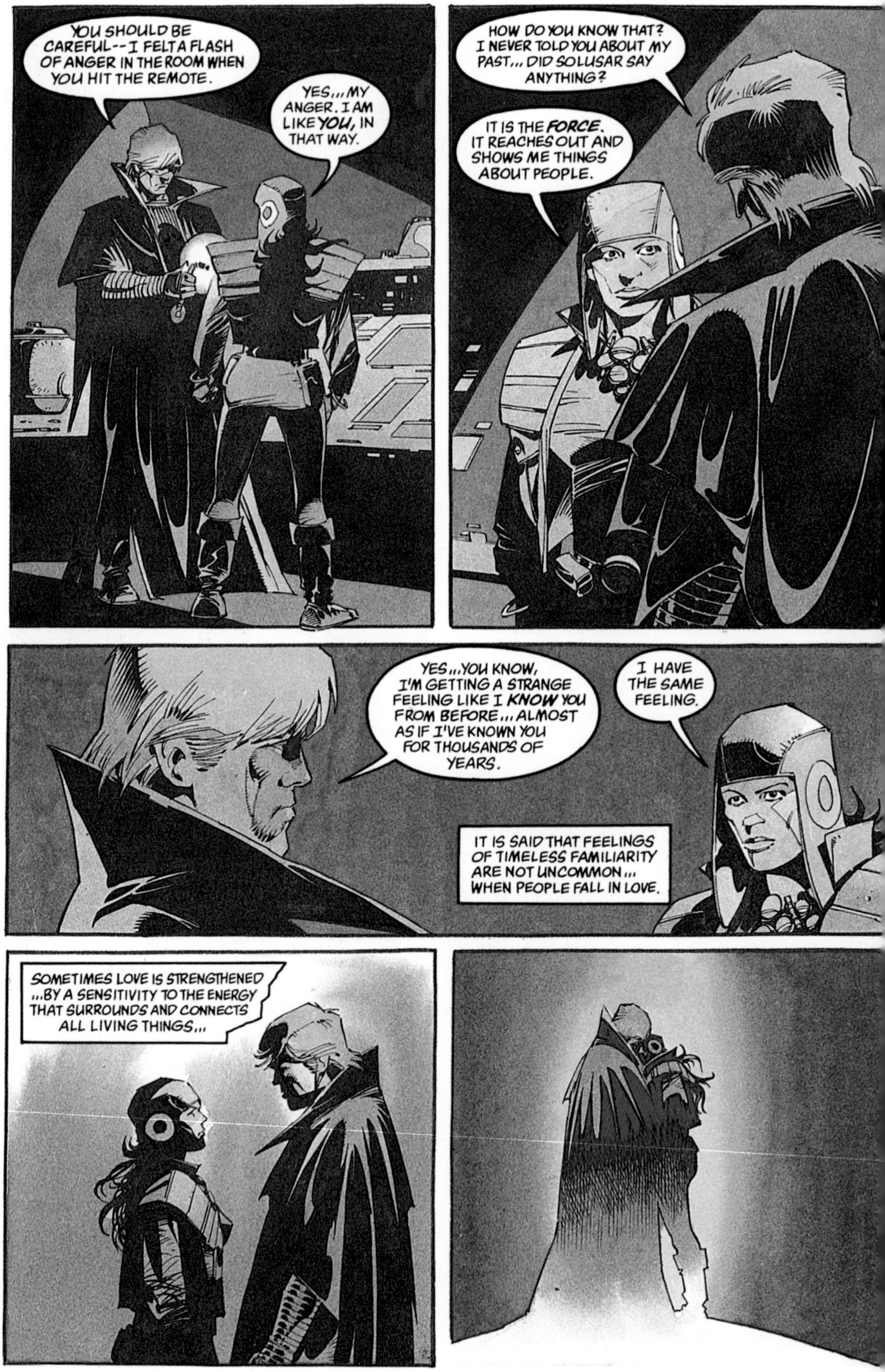

YOU SHOULD BE CAREFUL--I FELT A FLASH OF ANGER IN THE ROOM WHEN YOU HIT THE REMOTE.
YES... MY ANGER. I AM LIKE *YOU,* IN THAT WAY.
HOW DO YOU KNOW THAT? I NEVER TOLD YOU ABOUT MY PAST... DID SOLUSAR SAY ANYTHING?
IT IS THE *FORCE*. IT REACHES OUT AND SHOWS ME THINGS ABOUT PEOPLE.
YES... YOU KNOW, I'M GETTING A STRANGE FEELING LIKE I *KNOW* YOU FROM BEFORE... ALMOST AS IF I'VE KNOWN YOU FOR THOUSANDS OF YEARS.
I HAVE THE SAME FEELING.
IT IS SAID THAT FEELINGS OF TIMELESS FAMILIARITY ARE NOT UNCOMMON... WHEN PEOPLE FALL IN LOVE.
SOMETIMES LOVE IS STRENGTHENED ...BY A SENSITIVITY TO THE ENERGY THAT SURROUNDS AND CONNECTS ALL LIVING THINGS...

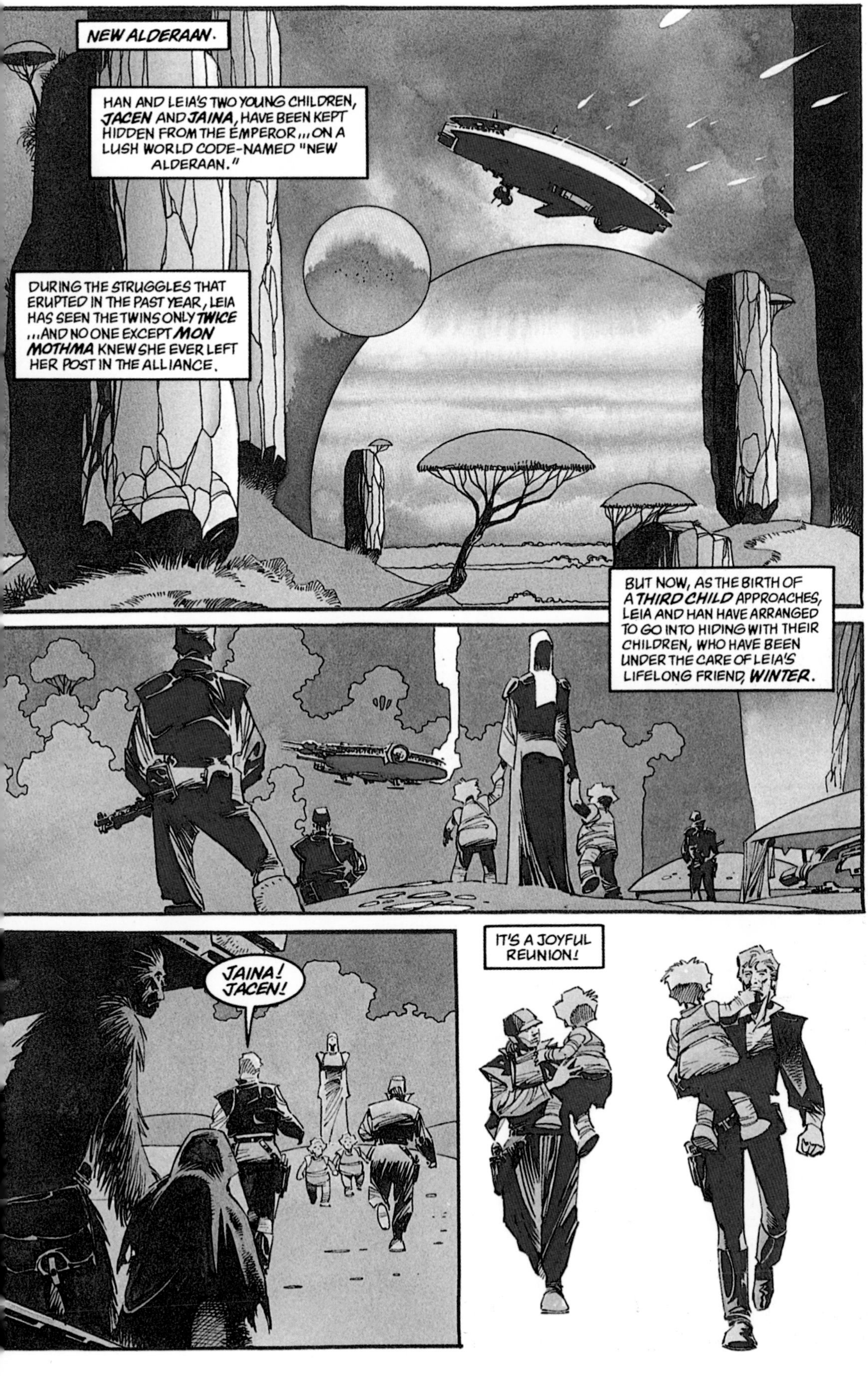
NEW ALDERAAN.
HAN AND LEIA'S TWO YOUNG CHILDREN, JACEN AND JAINA, HAVE BEEN KEPT HIDDEN FROM THE EMPEROR,...ON A LUSH WORLD CODE-NAMED "NEW ALDERAAN."
DURING THE STRUGGLES THAT ERUPTED IN THE PAST YEAR, LEIA HAS SEEN THE TWINS ONLY TWICE ...AND NO ONE EXCEPT MON MOTHMA KNEW SHE EVER LEFT HER POST IN THE ALLIANCE.
BUT NOW, AS THE BIRTH OF A THIRD CHILD APPROACHES, LEIA AND HAN HAVE ARRANGED TO GO INTO HIDING WITH THEIR CHILDREN, WHO HAVE BEEN UNDER THE CARE OF LEIA'S LIFELONG FRIEND, WINTER.
JAINA! JACEN!
IT'S A JOYFUL REUNION!

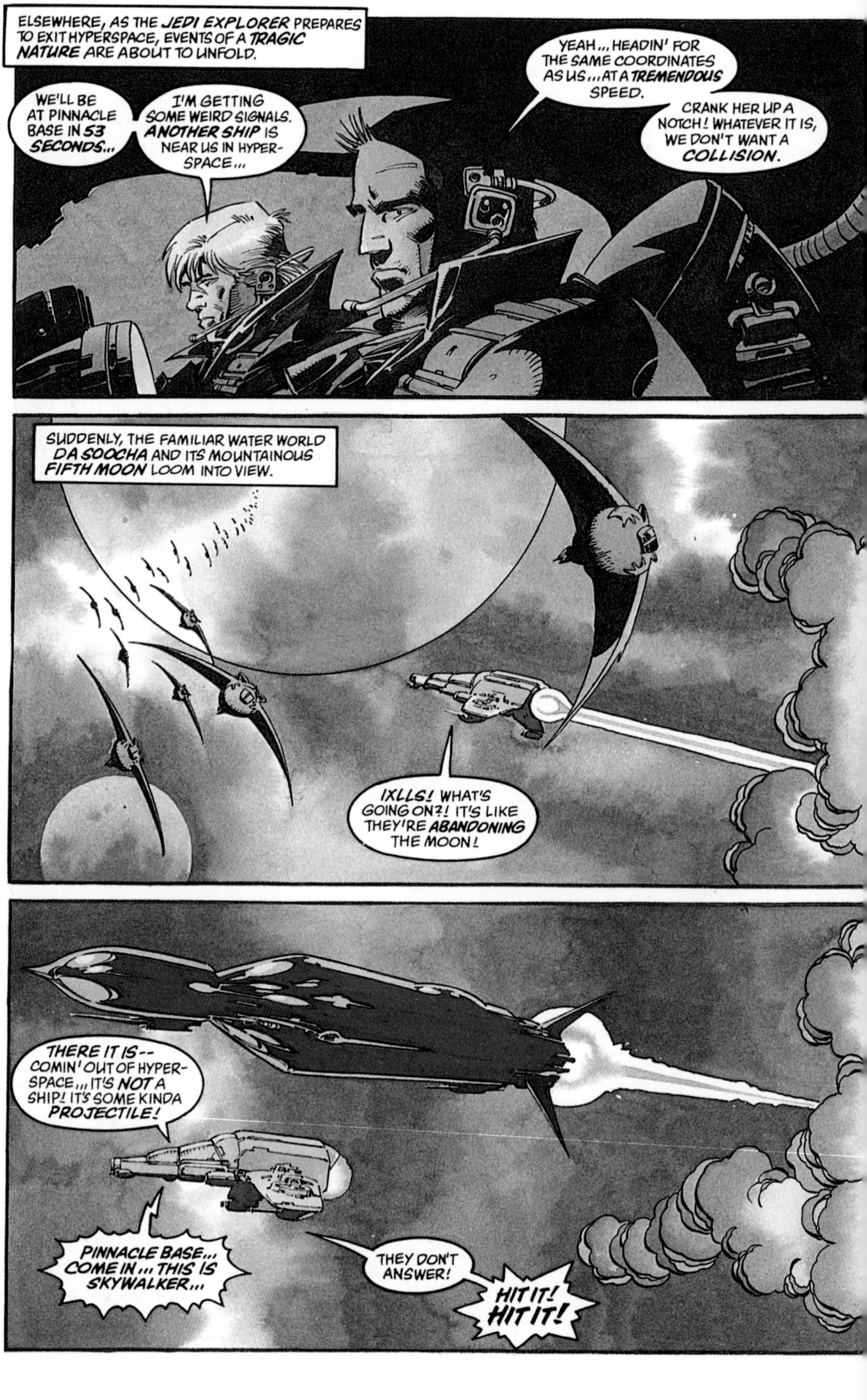
ELSEWHERE, AS THE JEDI EXPLORER PREPARES TO EXIT HYPERSPACE, EVENTS OF A TRAGIC NATURE ARE ABOUT TO UNFOLD.
WE'LL BE AT PINNACLE BASE IN 53 SECONDS...
I'M GETTING SOME WEIRD SIGNALS. ANOTHER SHIP IS NEAR US IN HYPER-SPACE...
YEAH... HEADIN' FOR THE SAME COORDINATES AS US... AT A TREMENDOUS SPEED.
CRANK HER UP A NOTCH! WHATEVER IT IS, WE DON'T WANT A COLLISION.
SUDDENLY, THE FAMILIAR WATER WORLD DA SOOCHA AND ITS MOUNTAINOUS FIFTH MOON LOOM INTO VIEW.
IXLLS! WHAT'S GOING ON?! IT'S LIKE THEY'RE ABANDONING THE MOON!
THERE IT IS-- COMIN' OUT OF HYPER-SPACE... IT'S NOT A SHIP! IT'S SOME KINDA PROJECTILE!
PINNACLE BASE... COME IN... THIS IS SKYWALKER...
THEY DON'T ANSWER!
HIT IT! HIT IT!

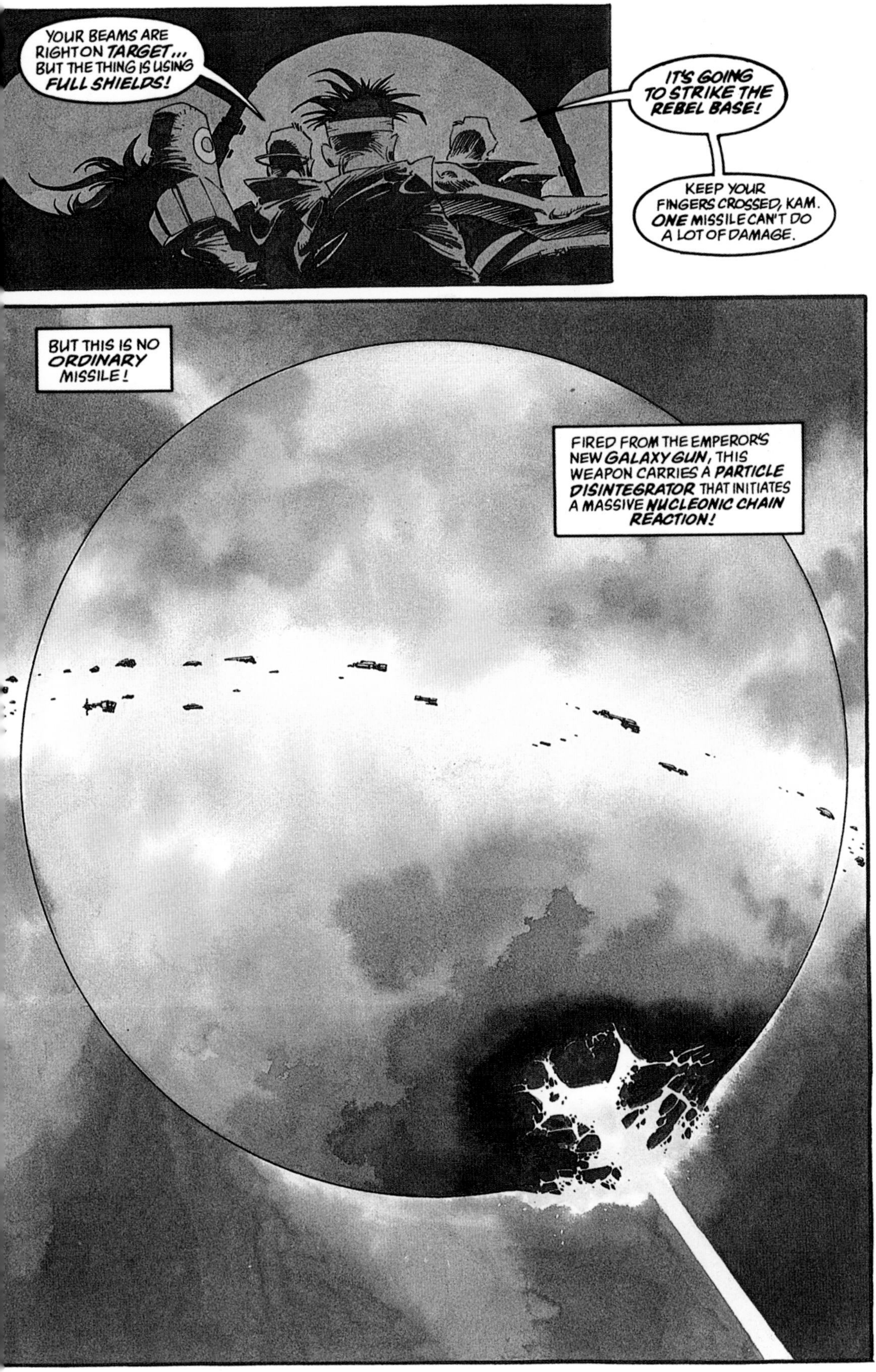

YOUR BEAMS ARE RIGHT ON TARGET... BUT THE THING IS USING FULL SHIELDS!
IT'S GOING TO STRIKE THE REBEL BASE!
KEEP YOUR FINGERS CROSSED, KAM. ONE MISSILE CAN'T DO A LOT OF DAMAGE.
BUT THIS IS NO ORDINARY MISSILE!
FIRED FROM THE EMPEROR'S NEW GALAXY GUN, THIS WEAPON CARRIES A PARTICLE DISINTEGRATOR THAT INITIATES A MASSIVE NUCLEONIC CHAIN REACTION!

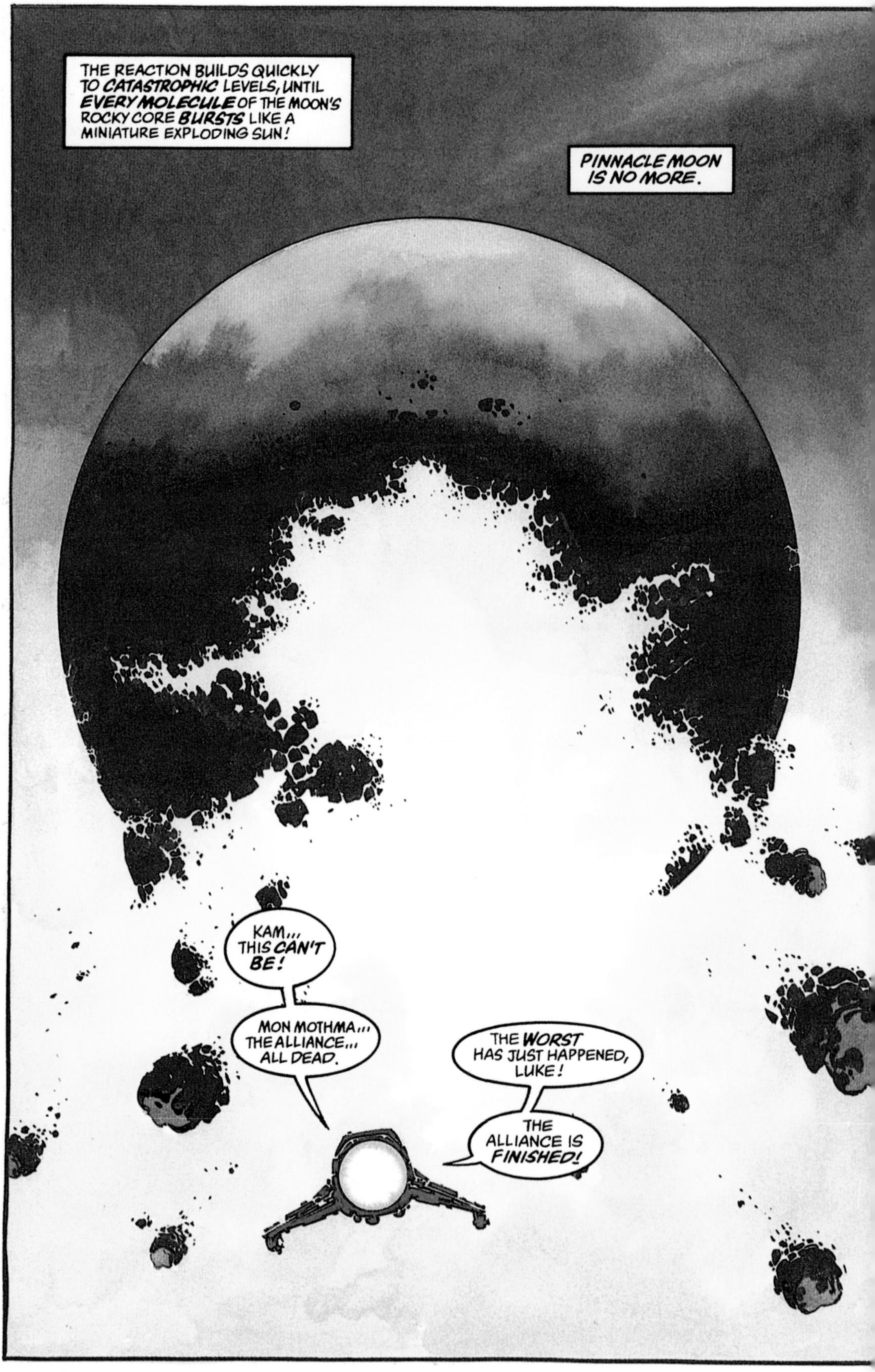
THE REACTION BUILDS QUICKLY TO CATASTROPHIC LEVELS, UNTIL EVERY MOLECULE OF THE MOON'S ROCKY CORE BURSTS LIKE A MINIATURE EXPLODING SUN!
PINNACLE MOON IS NO MORE.
KAM... THIS CAN'T BE!
MON MOTHMA... THE ALLIANCE... ALL DEAD.
THE WORST HAS JUST HAPPENED, LUKE!
THE ALLIANCE IS FINISHED!

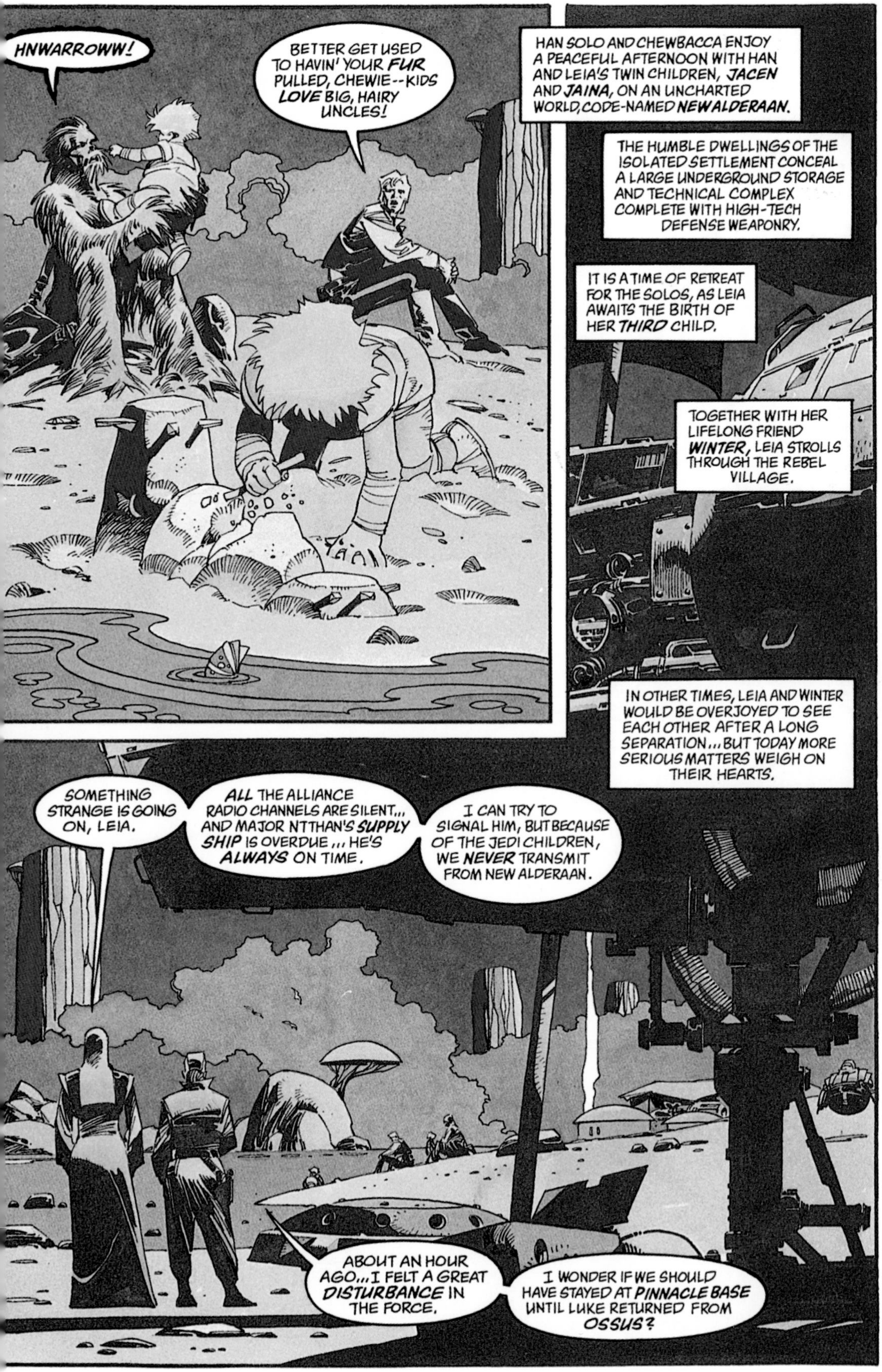
HNWARROWW!
BETTER GET USED TO HAVIN' YOUR FUR PULLED, CHEWIE--KIDS LOVE BIG, HAIRY UNCLES!
HAN SOLO AND CHEWBACCA ENJOY A PEACEFUL AFTERNOON WITH HAN AND LEIA'S TWIN CHILDREN, JACEN AND JAINA, ON AN UNCHARTED WORLD, CODE-NAMED NEW ALDERAAN.
THE HUMBLE DWELLINGS OF THE ISOLATED SETTLEMENT CONCEAL A LARGE UNDERGROUND STORAGE AND TECHNICAL COMPLEX COMPLETE WITH HIGH-TECH DEFENSE WEAPONRY.
IT IS A TIME OF RETREAT FOR THE SOLOS, AS LEIA AWAITS THE BIRTH OF HER THIRD CHILD.
TOGETHER WITH HER LIFELONG FRIEND WINTER, LEIA STROLLS THROUGH THE REBEL VILLAGE.
IN OTHER TIMES, LEIA AND WINTER WOULD BE OVERJOYED TO SEE EACH OTHER AFTER A LONG SEPARATION... BUT TODAY MORE SERIOUS MATTERS WEIGH ON THEIR HEARTS.
SOMETHING STRANGE IS GOING ON, LEIA.
ALL THE ALLIANCE RADIO CHANNELS ARE SILENT... AND MAJOR NTHAN'S SUPPLY SHIP IS OVERDUE... HE'S ALWAYS ON TIME.
I CAN TRY TO SIGNAL HIM, BUT BECAUSE OF THE JEDI CHILDREN, WE NEVER TRANSMIT FROM NEW ALDERAAN.
ABOUT AN HOUR AGO... I FELT A GREAT DISTURBANCE IN THE FORCE.
I WONDER IF WE SHOULD HAVE STAYED AT PINNACLE BASE UNTIL LUKE RETURNED FROM OSSUS?

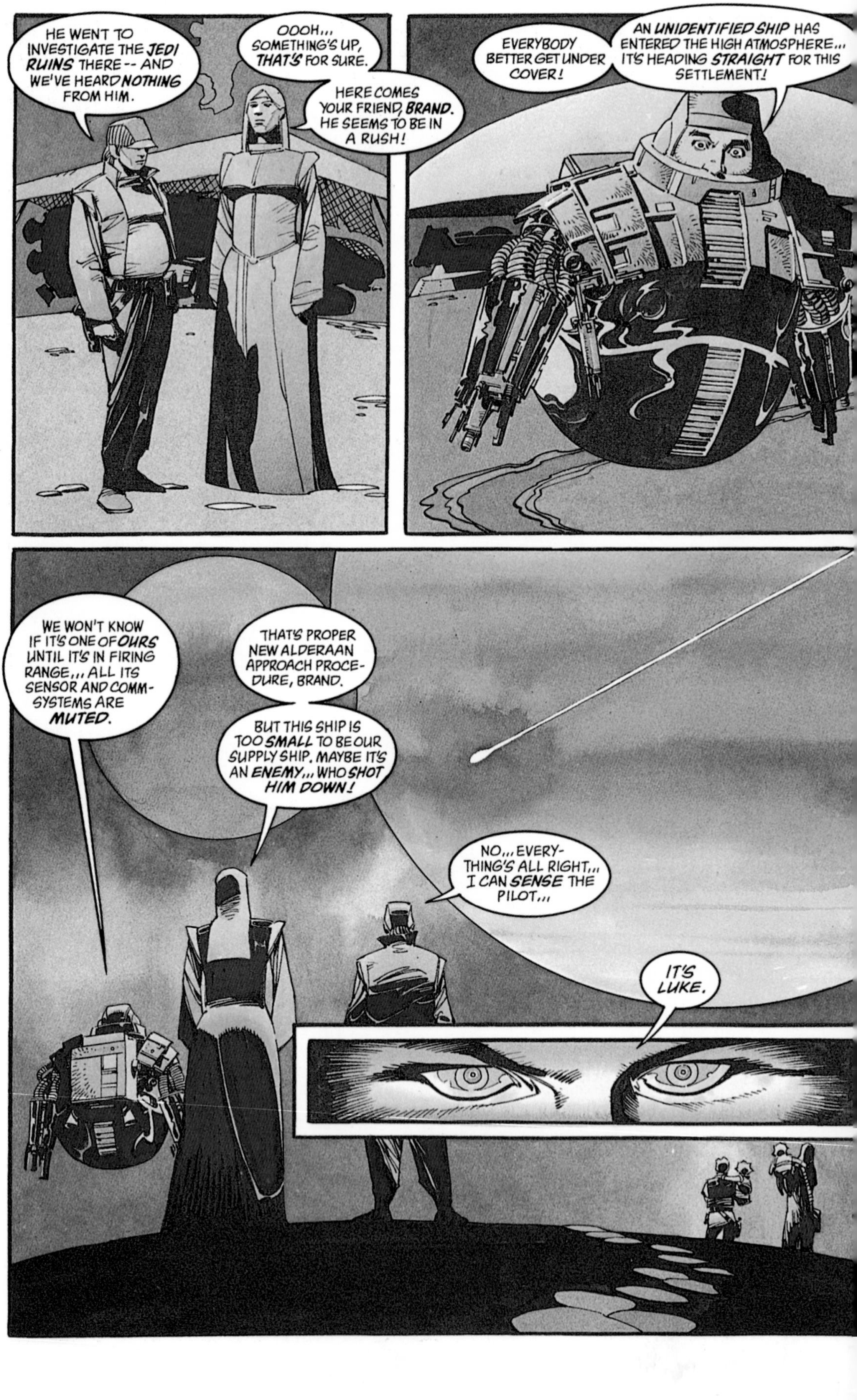
HE WENT TO INVESTIGATE THE JEDI RUINS THERE -- AND WE'VE HEARD NOTHING FROM HIM.
OOOH... SOMETHING'S UP, THAT'S FOR SURE.
HERE COMES YOUR FRIEND, BRAND. HE SEEMS TO BE IN A RUSH!
EVERYBODY BETTER GET UNDER COVER!
AN UNIDENTIFIED SHIP HAS ENTERED THE HIGH ATMOSPHERE... IT'S HEADING STRAIGHT FOR THIS SETTLEMENT!
WE WON'T KNOW IF IT'S ONE OF OURS UNTIL IT'S IN FIRING RANGE... ALL ITS SENSOR AND COMM-SYSTEMS ARE MUTED.
THAT'S PROPER NEW ALDERAAN APPROACH PROCEDURE, BRAND.
BUT THIS SHIP IS TOO SMALL TO BE OUR SUPPLY SHIP. MAYBE IT'S AN ENEMY... WHO SHOT HIM DOWN!
NO... EVERYTHING'S ALL RIGHT... I CAN SENSE THE PILOT...
IT'S LUKE.

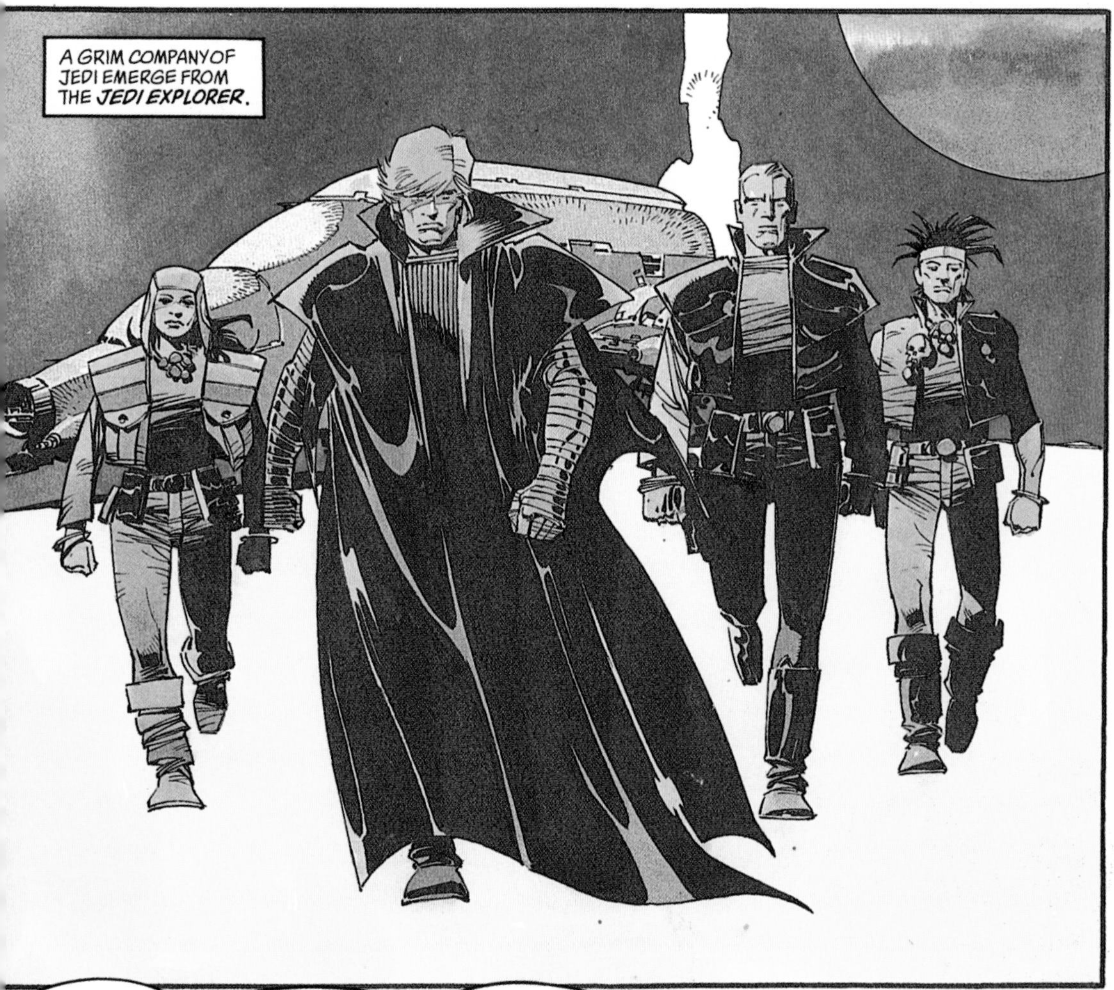
A GRIM COMPANY OF JEDI EMERGE FROM THE JEDI EXPLORER.

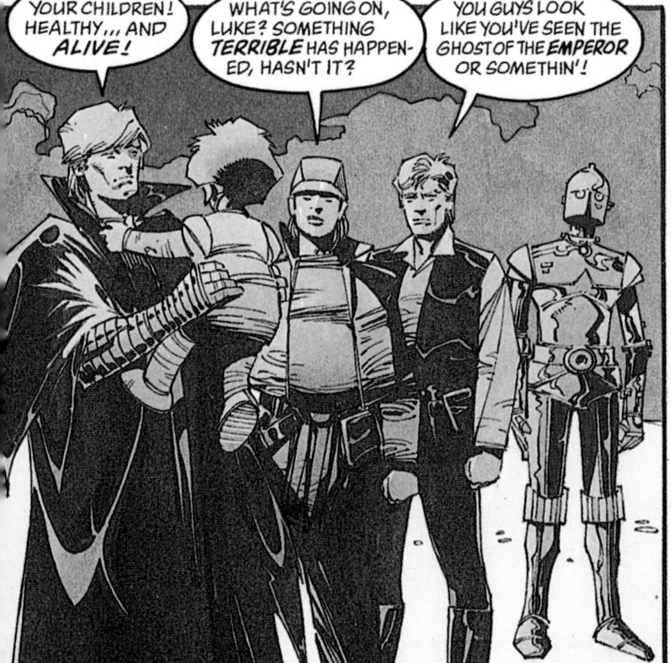
YOUR CHILDREN! HEALTHY,,, AND ALIVE!
WHAT'S GOING ON, LUKE? SOMETHING TERRIBLE HAS HAPPENED, HASN'T IT?
YOU GUYS LOOK LIKE YOU'VE SEEN THE GHOST OF THE EMPEROR OR SOMETHIN'!

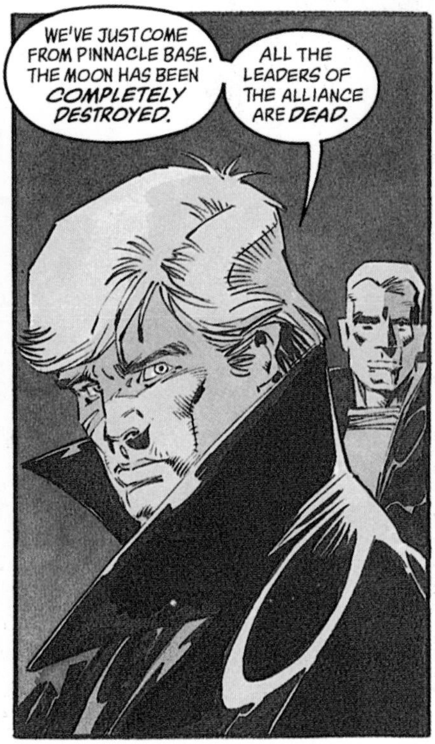
WE'VE JUST COME FROM PINNACLE BASE. THE MOON HAS BEEN COMPLETELY DESTROYED.
ALL THE LEADERS OF THE ALLIANCE ARE DEAD.

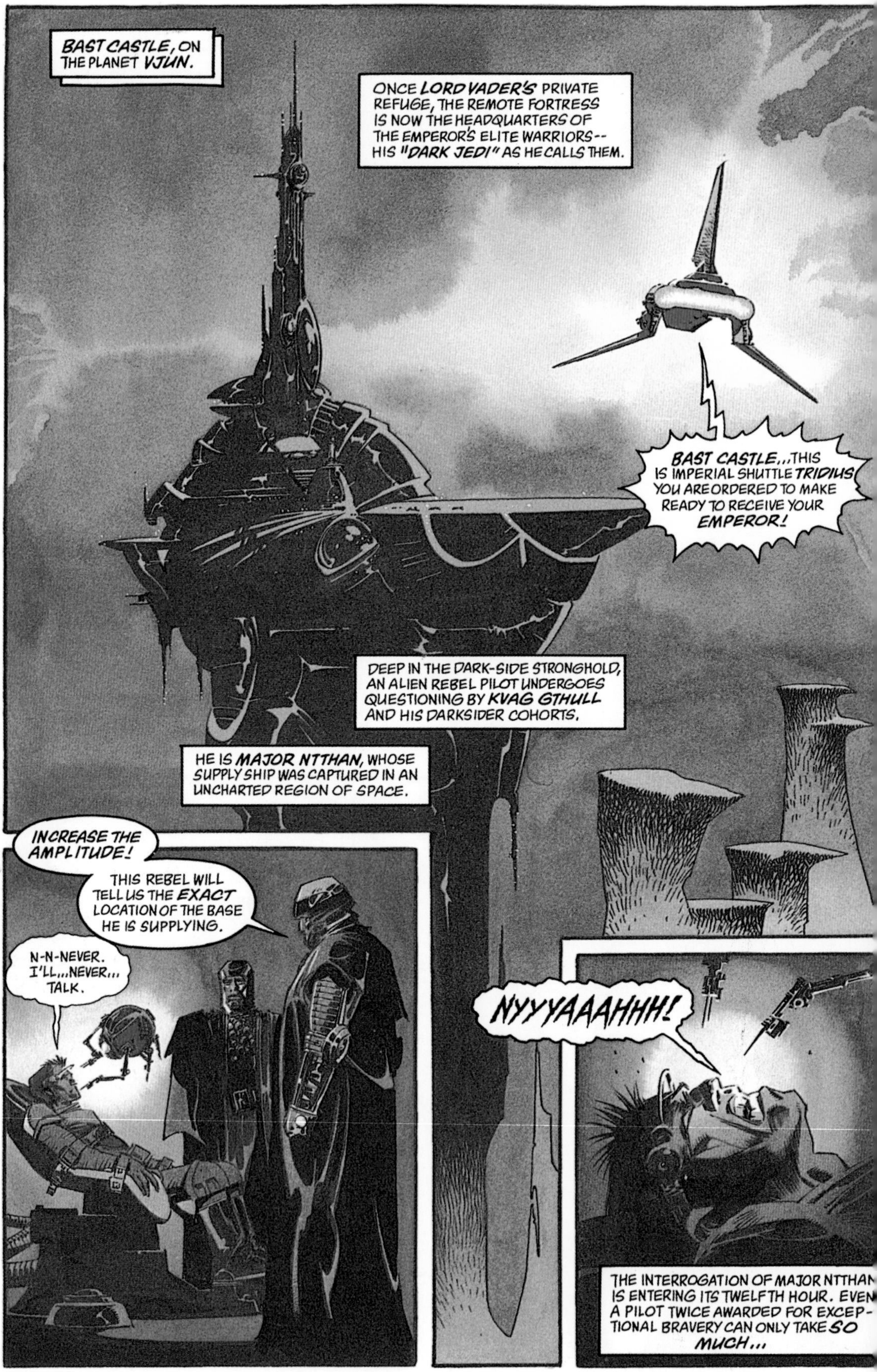
BAST CASTLE, ON THE PLANET VJUN.
ONCE LORD VADER'S PRIVATE REFUGE, THE REMOTE FORTRESS IS NOW THE HEADQUARTERS OF THE EMPEROR'S ELITE WARRIORS-- HIS "DARK JEDI" AS HE CALLS THEM.
BAST CASTLE... THIS IS IMPERIAL SHUTTLE TRIDIUS. YOU ARE ORDERED TO MAKE READY TO RECEIVE YOUR EMPEROR!
DEEP IN THE DARK-SIDE STRONGHOLD, AN ALIEN REBEL PILOT UNDERGOES QUESTIONING BY KVAG GTHULL AND HIS DARKSIDER COHORTS.
HE IS MAJOR NTTHAN, WHOSE SUPPLY SHIP WAS CAPTURED IN AN UNCHARTED REGION OF SPACE.
INCREASE THE AMPLITUDE!
THIS REBEL WILL TELL US THE EXACT LOCATION OF THE BASE HE IS SUPPLYING.
N-N-NEVER. I'LL... NEVER... TALK.
NYYYAAAHHH!
THE INTERROGATION OF MAJOR NTTHAN IS ENTERING ITS TWELFTH HOUR. EVEN A PILOT TWICE AWARDED FOR EXCEPTIONAL BRAVERY CAN ONLY TAKE SO MUCH...

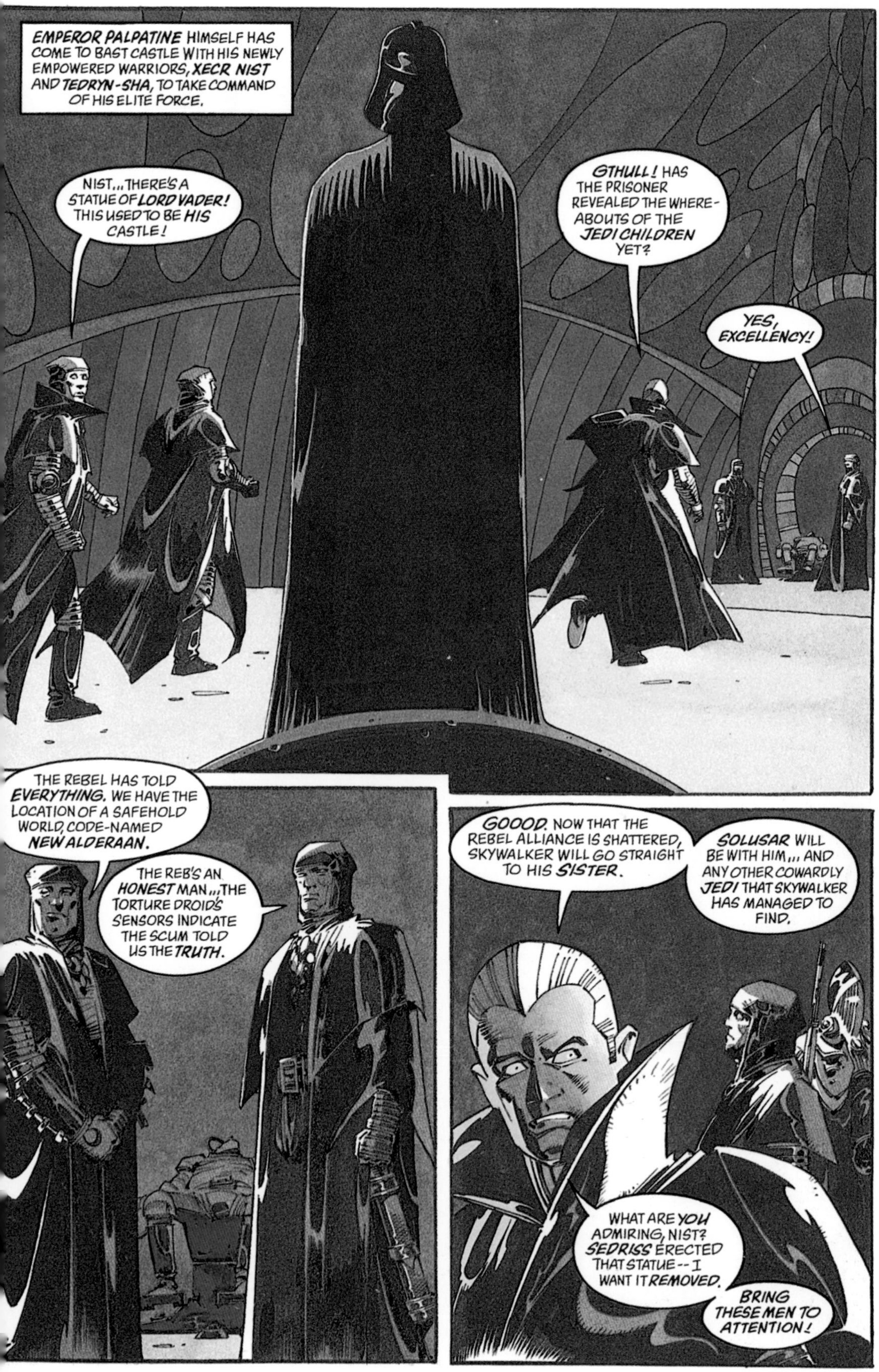
EMPEROR PALPATINE HIMSELF HAS COME TO BAST CASTLE WITH HIS NEWLY EMPOWERED WARRIORS, XECR NIST AND TEDRYN-SHA, TO TAKE COMMAND OF HIS ELITE FORCE.
NIST... THERE'S A STATUE OF LORD VADER! THIS USED TO BE HIS CASTLE!
GTHULL! HAS THE PRISONER REVEALED THE WHEREABOUTS OF THE JEDI CHILDREN YET?
YES, EXCELLENCY!
THE REBEL HAS TOLD EVERYTHING. WE HAVE THE LOCATION OF A SAFEHOLD WORLD, CODE-NAMED NEW ALDERAAN.
THE REB'S AN HONEST MAN... THE TORTURE DROID'S SENSORS INDICATE THE SCUM TOLD US THE TRUTH.
GOOOD. NOW THAT THE REBEL ALLIANCE IS SHATTERED, SKYWALKER WILL GO STRAIGHT TO HIS SISTER.
SOLUSAR WILL BE WITH HIM... AND ANY OTHER COWARDLY JEDI THAT SKYWALKER HAS MANAGED TO FIND.
WHAT ARE YOU ADMIRING, NIST? SEDRISS ERECTED THAT STATUE -- I WANT IT REMOVED.
BRING THESE MEN TO ATTENTION!

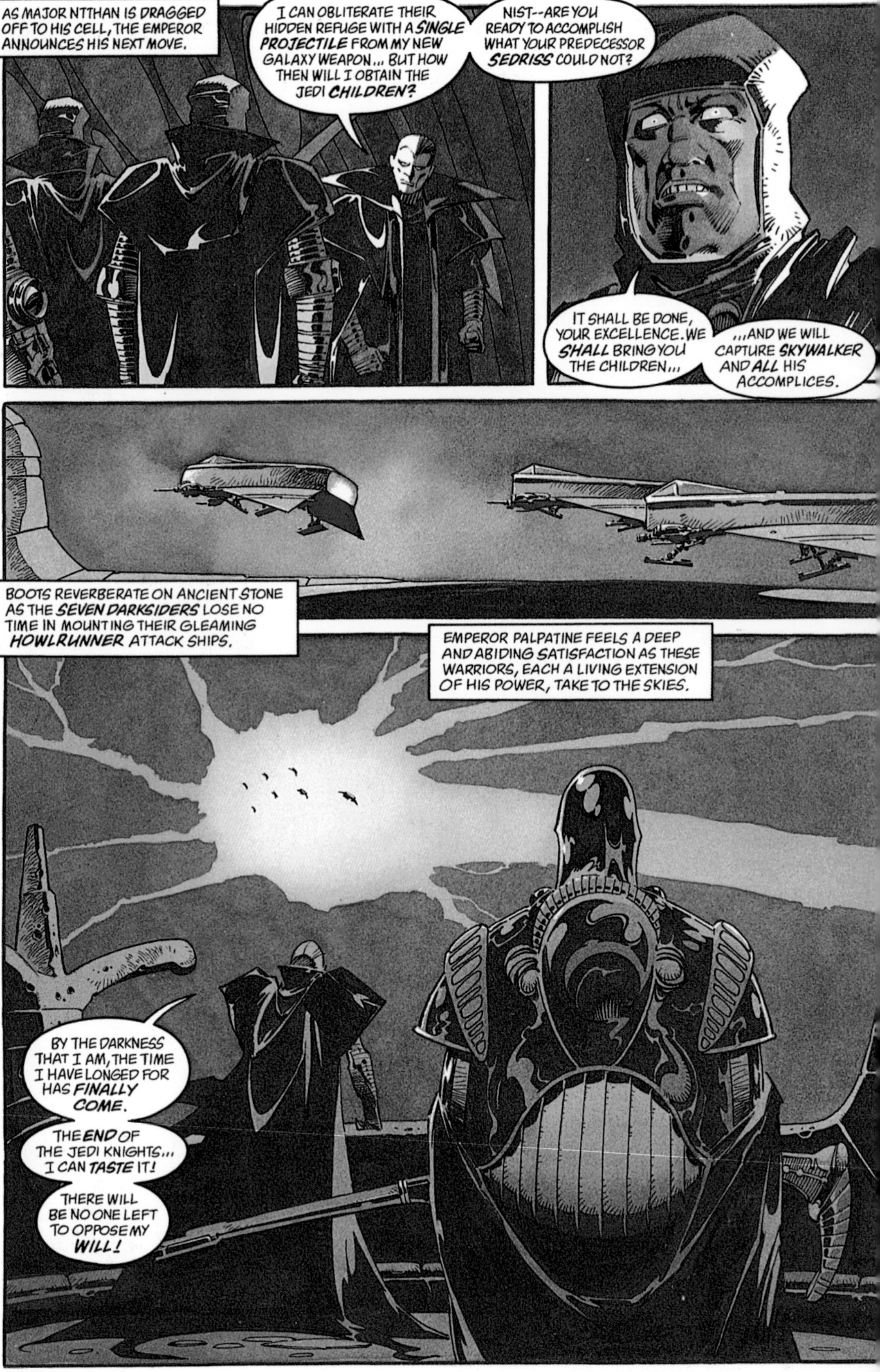
AS MAJOR NTTHAN IS DRAGGED OFF TO HIS CELL, THE EMPEROR ANNOUNCES HIS NEXT MOVE.
I CAN OBLITERATE THEIR HIDDEN REFUGE WITH A SINGLE PROJECTILE FROM MY NEW GALAXY WEAPON... BUT HOW THEN WILL I OBTAIN THE JEDI CHILDREN?
NIST--ARE YOU READY TO ACCOMPLISH WHAT YOUR PREDECESSOR SEDRISS COULD NOT?
IT SHALL BE DONE, YOUR EXCELLENCE. WE SHALL BRING YOU THE CHILDREN...
...AND WE WILL CAPTURE SKYWALKER AND ALL HIS ACCOMPLICES.
BOOTS REVERBERATE ON ANCIENT STONE AS THE SEVEN DARKSIDERS LOSE NO TIME IN MOUNTING THEIR GLEAMING HOWLRUNNER ATTACK SHIPS.
EMPEROR PALPATINE FEELS A DEEP AND ABIDING SATISFACTION AS THESE WARRIORS, EACH A LIVING EXTENSION OF HIS POWER, TAKE TO THE SKIES.
BY THE DARKNESS THAT I AM, THE TIME I HAVE LONGED FOR HAS FINALLY COME.
THE END OF THE JEDI KNIGHTS... I CAN TASTE IT!
THERE WILL BE NO ONE LEFT TO OPPOSE MY WILL!

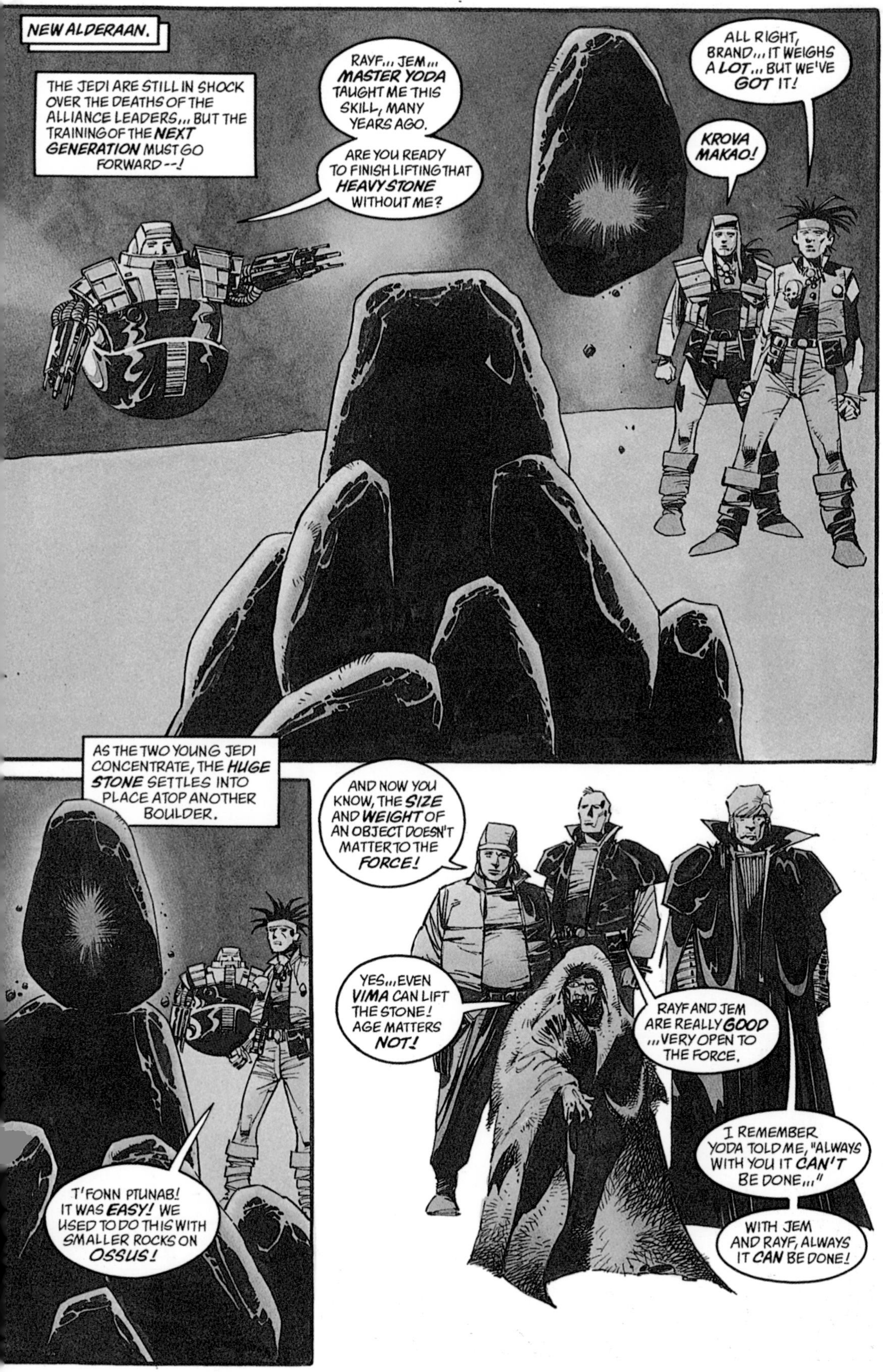
NEW ALDERAAN.
THE JEDI ARE STILL IN SHOCK OVER THE DEATHS OF THE ALLIANCE LEADERS... BUT THE TRAINING OF THE NEXT GENERATION MUST GO FORWARD--!
RAYF... JEM... MASTER YODA TAUGHT ME THIS SKILL, MANY YEARS AGO.
ARE YOU READY TO FINISH LIFTING THAT HEAVY STONE WITHOUT ME?
ALL RIGHT, BRAND... IT WEIGHS A LOT... BUT WE'VE GOT IT!
KROVA MAKAO!
AS THE TWO YOUNG JEDI CONCENTRATE, THE HUGE STONE SETTLES INTO PLACE ATOP ANOTHER BOULDER.
T'FONN PTUNAB! IT WAS EASY! WE USED TO DO THIS WITH SMALLER ROCKS ON OSSUS!
AND NOW YOU KNOW, THE SIZE AND WEIGHT OF AN OBJECT DOESN'T MATTER TO THE FORCE!
YES... EVEN VIMA CAN LIFT THE STONE! AGE MATTERS NOT!
RAYF AND JEM ARE REALLY GOOD ...VERY OPEN TO THE FORCE.
I REMEMBER YODA TOLD ME, "ALWAYS WITH YOU IT CAN'T BE DONE..."
WITH JEM AND RAYF, ALWAYS IT CAN BE DONE!

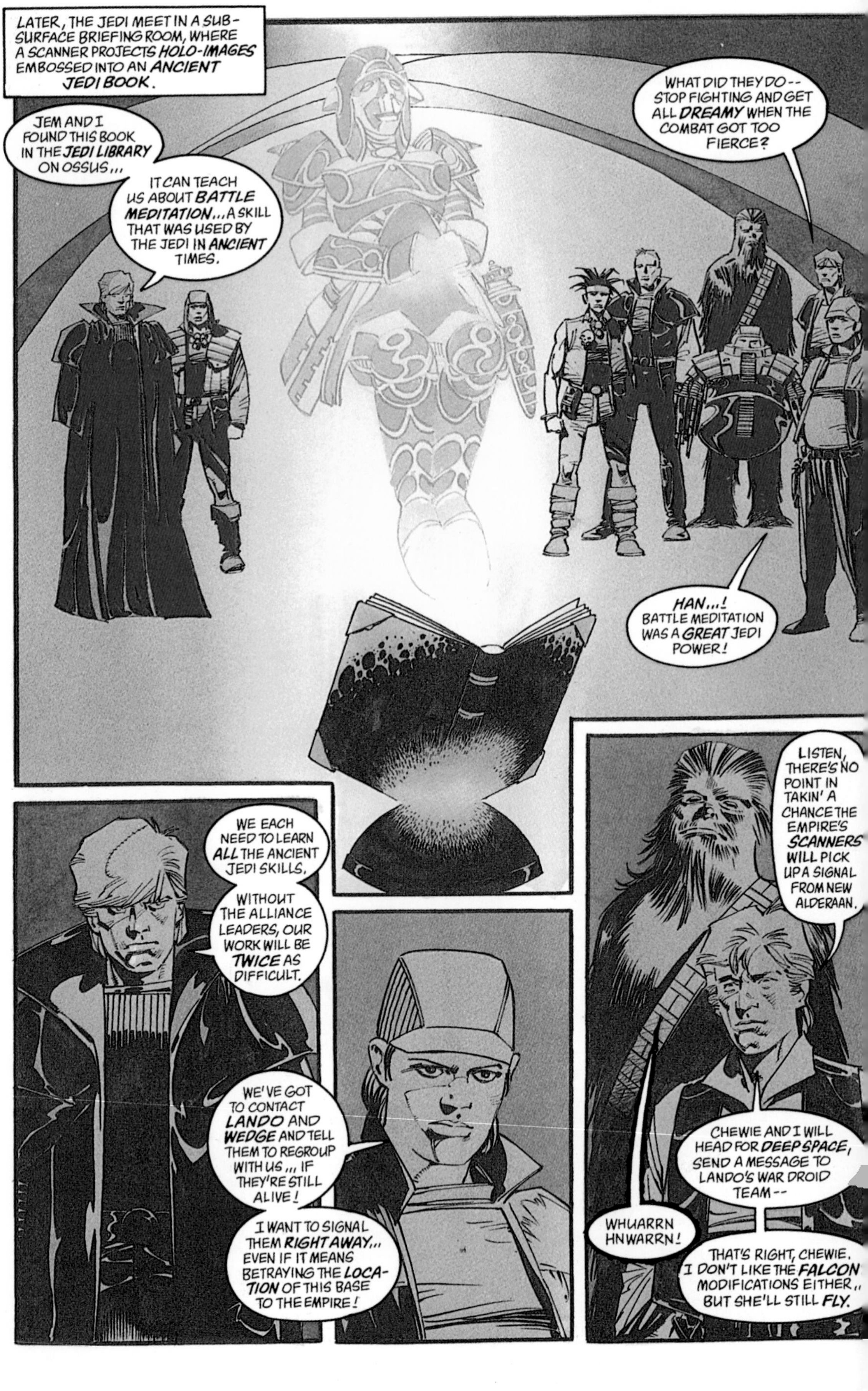
LATER, THE JEDI MEET IN A SUB-SURFACE BRIEFING ROOM, WHERE A SCANNER PROJECTS HOLO-IMAGES EMBOSSED INTO AN ANCIENT JEDI BOOK.
JEM AND I FOUND THIS BOOK IN THE JEDI LIBRARY ON OSSUS...
IT CAN TEACH US ABOUT BATTLE MEDITATION... A SKILL THAT WAS USED BY THE JEDI IN ANCIENT TIMES.
WHAT DID THEY DO -- STOP FIGHTING AND GET ALL DREAMY WHEN THE COMBAT GOT TOO FIERCE?
HAN...! BATTLE MEDITATION WAS A GREAT JEDI POWER!
WE EACH NEED TO LEARN ALL THE ANCIENT JEDI SKILLS.
WITHOUT THE ALLIANCE LEADERS, OUR WORK WILL BE TWICE AS DIFFICULT.
WE'VE GOT TO CONTACT LANDO AND WEDGE AND TELL THEM TO REGROUP WITH US... IF THEY'RE STILL ALIVE!
I WANT TO SIGNAL THEM RIGHT AWAY... EVEN IF IT MEANS BETRAYING THE LOCATION OF THIS BASE TO THE EMPIRE!
LISTEN, THERE'S NO POINT IN TAKIN' A CHANCE THE EMPIRE'S SCANNERS WILL PICK UP A SIGNAL FROM NEW ALDERAAN.
CHEWIE AND I WILL HEAD FOR DEEP SPACE, SEND A MESSAGE TO LANDO'S WAR DROID TEAM --
WHUARRN HNWARRN!
THAT'S RIGHT, CHEWIE. I DON'T LIKE THE FALCON MODIFICATIONS EITHER... BUT SHE'LL STILL FLY.

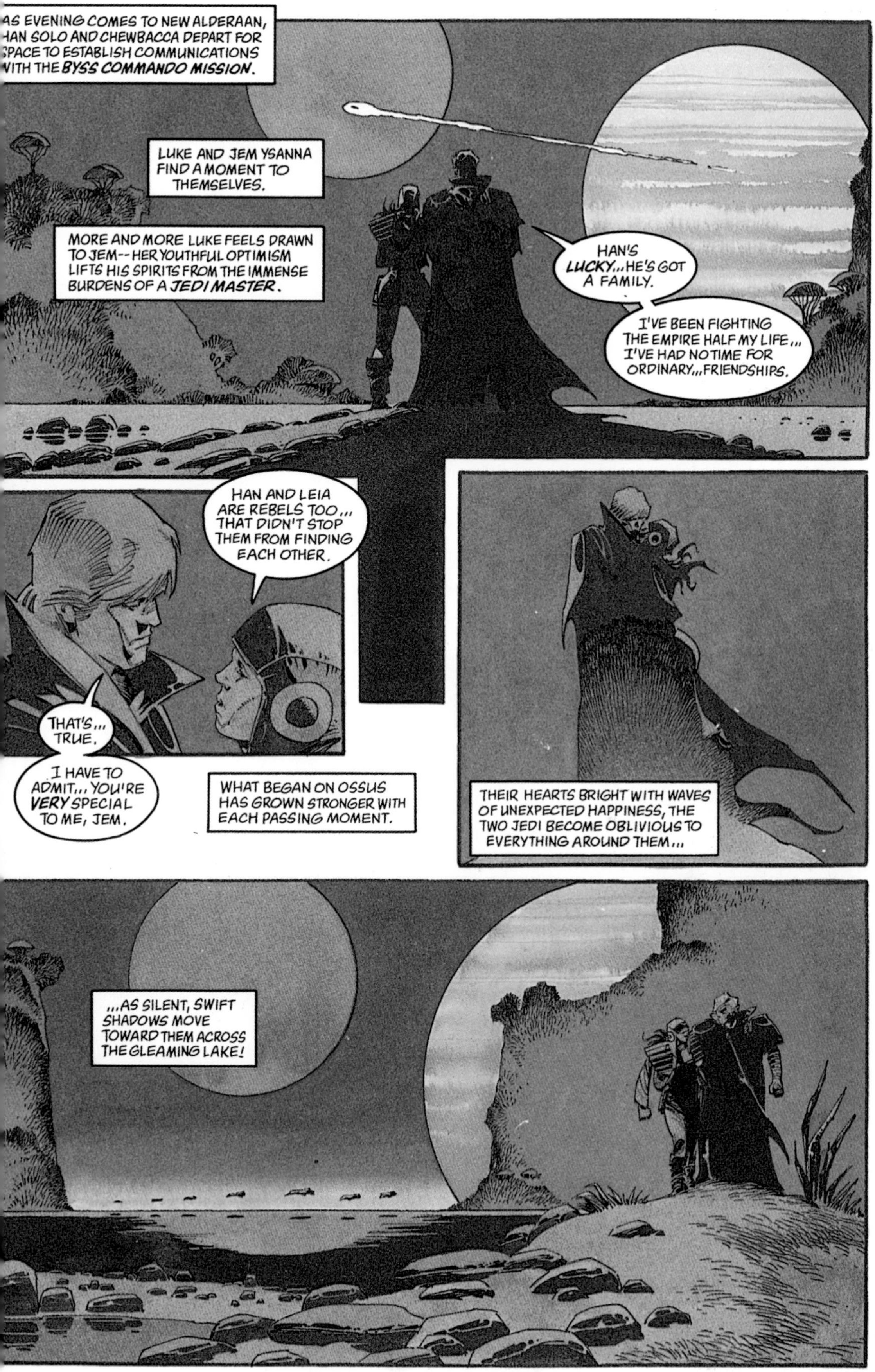
AS EVENING COMES TO NEW ALDERAAN, HAN SOLO AND CHEWBACCA DEPART FOR SPACE TO ESTABLISH COMMUNICATIONS WITH THE BYSS COMMANDO MISSION.
LUKE AND JEM YSANNA FIND A MOMENT TO THEMSELVES.
MORE AND MORE LUKE FEELS DRAWN TO JEM-- HER YOUTHFUL OPTIMISM LIFTS HIS SPIRITS FROM THE IMMENSE BURDENS OF A JEDI MASTER.
HAN'S LUCKY... HE'S GOT A FAMILY.
I'VE BEEN FIGHTING THE EMPIRE HALF MY LIFE... I'VE HAD NO TIME FOR ORDINARY... FRIENDSHIPS.
HAN AND LEIA ARE REBELS TOO... THAT DIDN'T STOP THEM FROM FINDING EACH OTHER.
THAT'S... TRUE.
I HAVE TO ADMIT... YOU'RE VERY SPECIAL TO ME, JEM.
WHAT BEGAN ON OSSUS HAS GROWN STRONGER WITH EACH PASSING MOMENT.
THEIR HEARTS BRIGHT WITH WAVES OF UNEXPECTED HAPPINESS, THE TWO JEDI BECOME OBLIVIOUS TO EVERYTHING AROUND THEM...
...AS SILENT, SWIFT SHADOWS MOVE TOWARD THEM ACROSS THE GLEAMING LAKE!

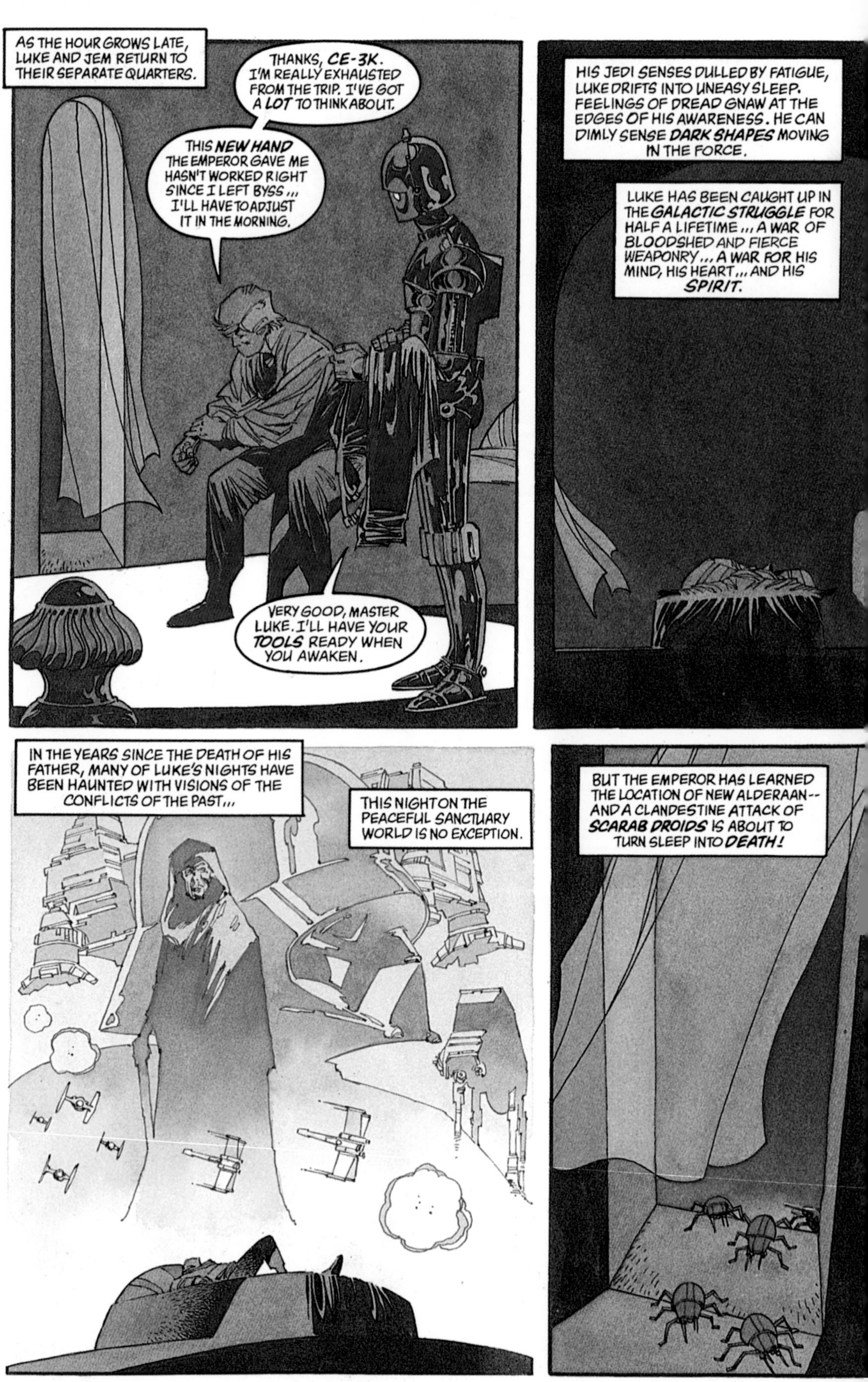

AS THE HOUR GROWS LATE, LUKE AND JEM RETURN TO THEIR SEPARATE QUARTERS.
THANKS, CE-3K. I'M REALLY EXHAUSTED FROM THE TRIP. I'VE GOT A LOT TO THINK ABOUT.
THIS NEW HAND THE EMPEROR GAVE ME HASN'T WORKED RIGHT SINCE I LEFT BYSS... I'LL HAVE TO ADJUST IT IN THE MORNING.
VERY GOOD, MASTER LUKE. I'LL HAVE YOUR TOOLS READY WHEN YOU AWAKEN.
HIS JEDI SENSES DULLED BY FATIGUE, LUKE DRIFTS INTO UNEASY SLEEP. FEELINGS OF DREAD GNAW AT THE EDGES OF HIS AWARENESS. HE CAN DIMLY SENSE DARK SHAPES MOVING IN THE FORCE.
LUKE HAS BEEN CAUGHT UP IN THE GALACTIC STRUGGLE FOR HALF A LIFETIME... A WAR OF BLOODSHED AND FIERCE WEAPONRY... A WAR FOR HIS MIND, HIS HEART... AND HIS SPIRIT.
IN THE YEARS SINCE THE DEATH OF HIS FATHER, MANY OF LUKE'S NIGHTS HAVE BEEN HAUNTED WITH VISIONS OF THE CONFLICTS OF THE PAST...
THIS NIGHT ON THE PEACEFUL SANCTUARY WORLD IS NO EXCEPTION.
BUT THE EMPEROR HAS LEARNED THE LOCATION OF NEW ALDERAAN-- AND A CLANDESTINE ATTACK OF SCARAB DROIDS IS ABOUT TO TURN SLEEP INTO DEATH!

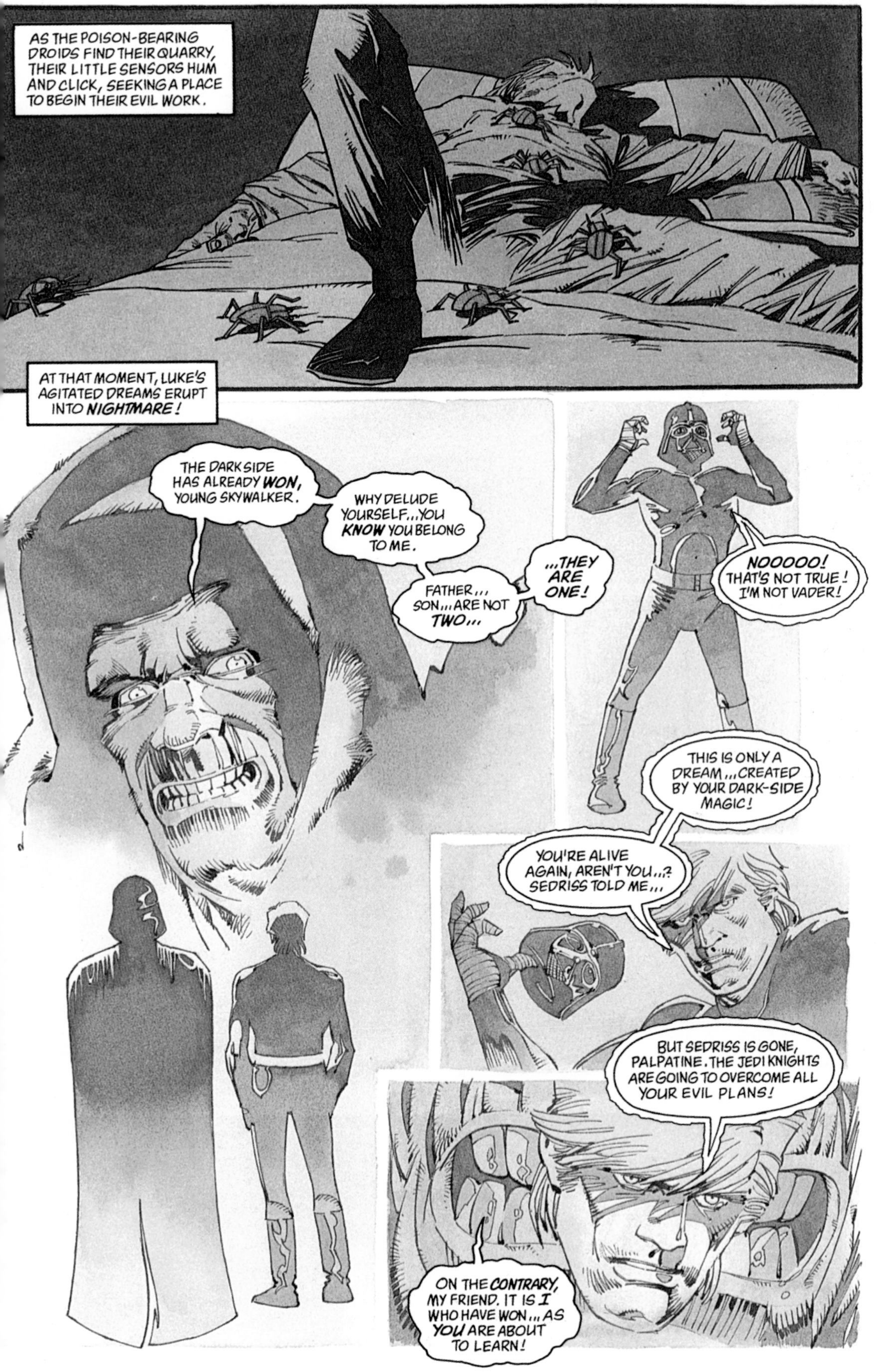
AS THE POISON-BEARING DROIDS FIND THEIR QUARRY, THEIR LITTLE SENSORS HUM AND CLICK, SEEKING A PLACE TO BEGIN THEIR EVIL WORK.
AT THAT MOMENT, LUKE'S AGITATED DREAMS ERUPT INTO NIGHTMARE!
THE DARK SIDE HAS ALREADY WON, YOUNG SKYWALKER.
WHY DELUDE YOURSELF... YOU KNOW YOU BELONG TO ME.
FATHER... SON... ARE NOT TWO...
...THEY ARE ONE!
NOOOOO! THAT'S NOT TRUE! I'M NOT VADER!
THIS IS ONLY A DREAM... CREATED BY YOUR DARK-SIDE MAGIC!
YOU'RE ALIVE AGAIN, AREN'T YOU...? SEDRISS TOLD ME...
BUT SEDRISS IS GONE, PALPATINE. THE JEDI KNIGHTS ARE GOING TO OVERCOME ALL YOUR EVIL PLANS!
ON THE CONTRARY, MY FRIEND. IT IS I WHO HAVE WON... AS YOU ARE ABOUT TO LEARN!

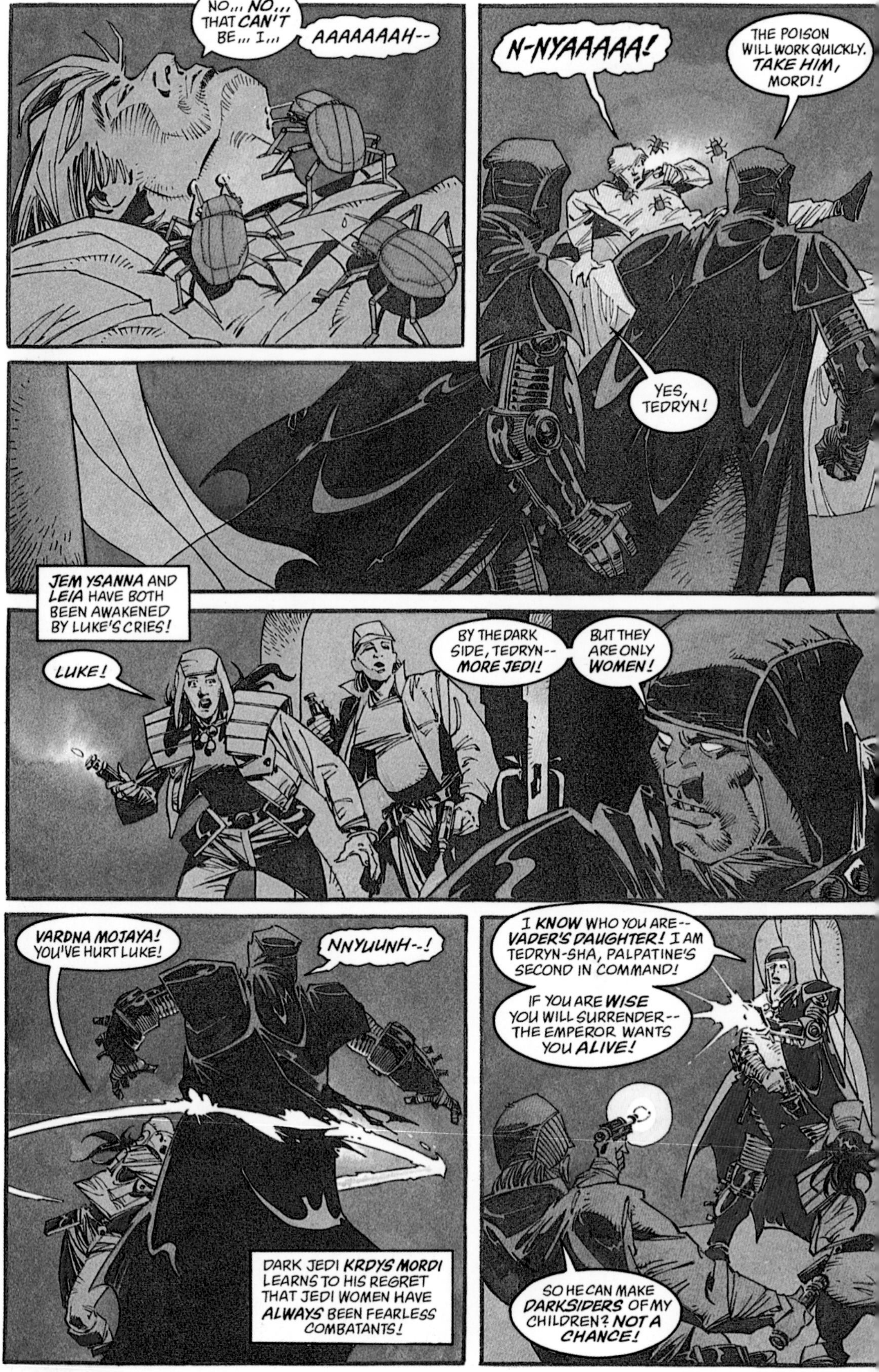

NO... NO... THAT CAN'T BE... I...
AAAAAAAH--
N-NYAAAAA!
THE POISON WILL WORK QUICKLY. TAKE HIM, MORDI!
YES, TEDRYN!
JEM YSANNA AND LEIA HAVE BOTH BEEN AWAKENED BY LUKE'S CRIES!
LUKE!
BY THE DARK SIDE, TEDRYN-- MORE JEDI!
BUT THEY ARE ONLY WOMEN!
VARDNA MOJAYA! YOU'VE HURT LUKE!
NNYUUNH--!
DARK JEDI KRDYS MORDI LEARNS TO HIS REGRET THAT JEDI WOMEN HAVE ALWAYS BEEN FEARLESS COMBATANTS!
I KNOW WHO YOU ARE-- VADER'S DAUGHTER! I AM TEDRYN-SHA, PALPATINE'S SECOND IN COMMAND!
IF YOU ARE WISE YOU WILL SURRENDER-- THE EMPEROR WANTS YOU ALIVE!
SO HE CAN MAKE DARKSIDERS OF MY CHILDREN? NOT A CHANCE!

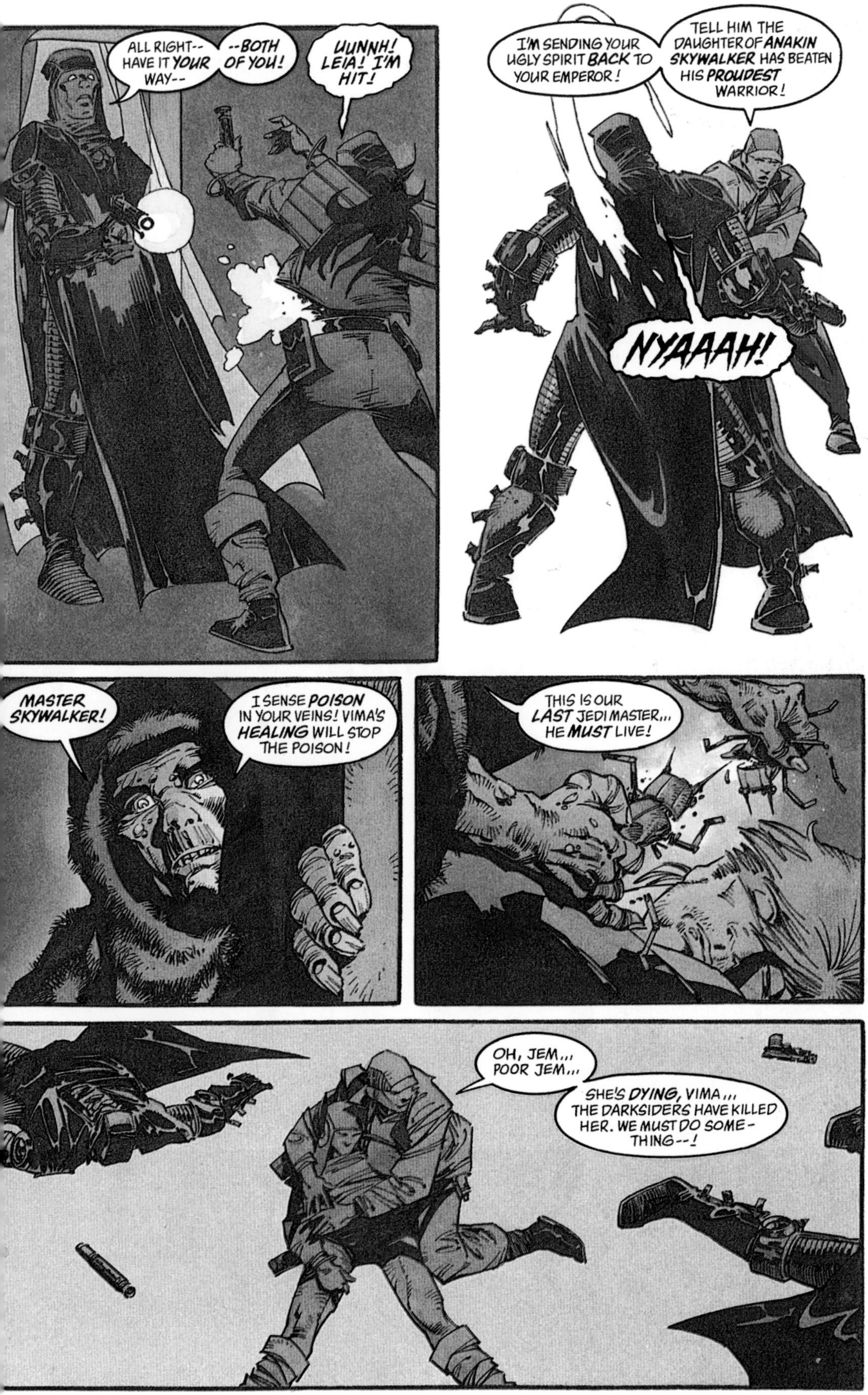
ALL RIGHT-- HAVE IT YOUR WAY--
--BOTH OF YOU!
UUNNH! LEIA! I'M HIT!
I'M SENDING YOUR UGLY SPIRIT BACK TO YOUR EMPEROR!
TELL HIM THE DAUGHTER OF ANAKIN SKYWALKER HAS BEATEN HIS PROUDEST WARRIOR!
NYAAAH!
MASTER SKYWALKER!
I SENSE POISON IN YOUR VEINS! VIMA'S HEALING WILL STOP THE POISON!
THIS IS OUR LAST JEDI MASTER... HE MUST LIVE!
OH, JEM... POOR JEM...
SHE'S DYING, VIMA... THE DARKSIDERS HAVE KILLED HER. WE MUST DO SOME-THING--!

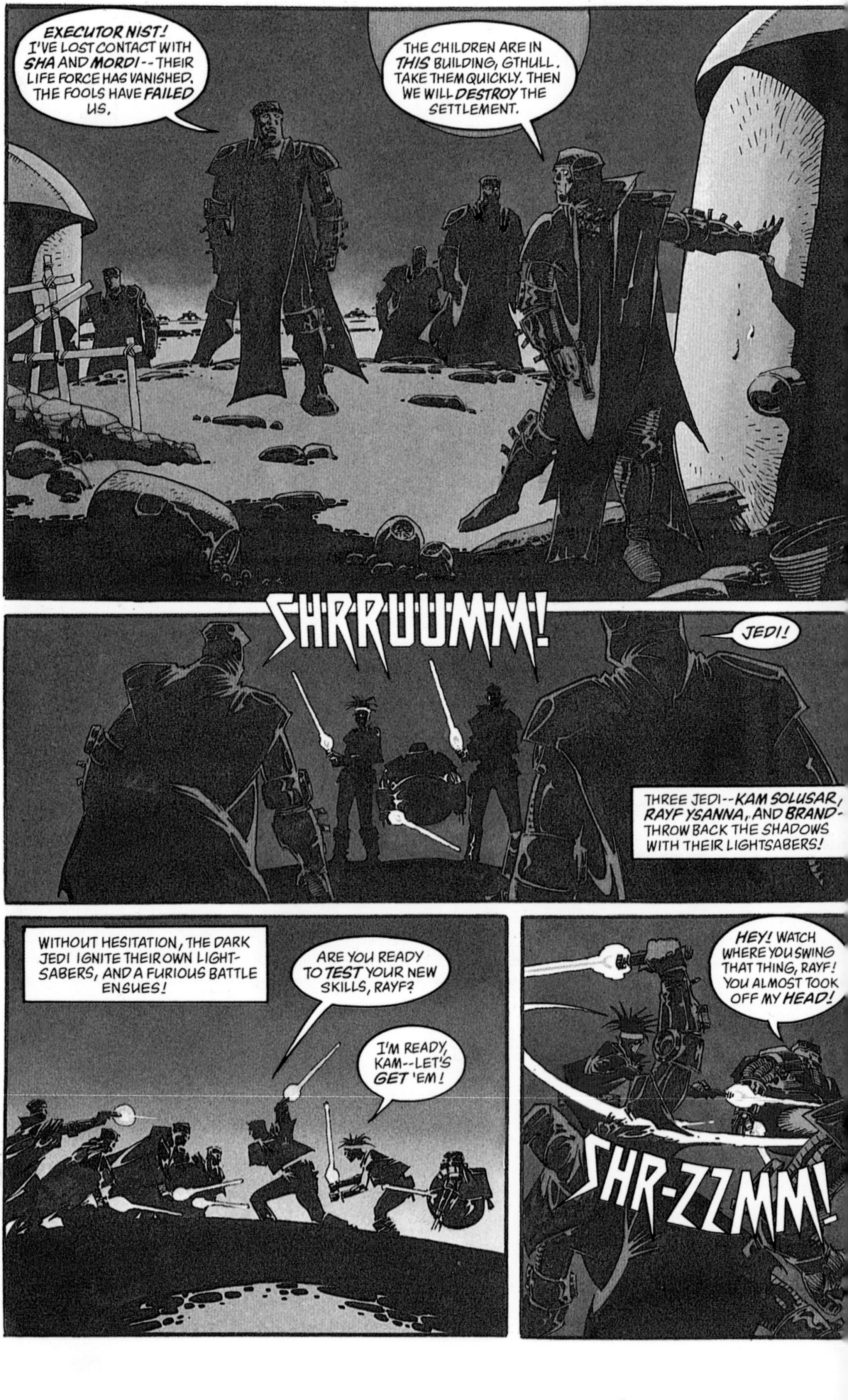
EXECUTOR NIST! I'VE LOST CONTACT WITH SHA AND MORDI--THEIR LIFE FORCE HAS VANISHED. THE FOOLS HAVE FAILED US.
THE CHILDREN ARE IN THIS BUILDING, GTHULL. TAKE THEM QUICKLY. THEN WE WILL DESTROY THE SETTLEMENT.
SHRRUUMM!
JEDI!
THREE JEDI--KAM SOLUSAR, RAYF YSANNA, AND BRAND-THROW BACK THE SHADOWS WITH THEIR LIGHTSABERS!
WITHOUT HESITATION, THE DARK JEDI IGNITE THEIR OWN LIGHT-SABERS, AND A FURIOUS BATTLE ENSUES!
ARE YOU READY TO TEST YOUR NEW SKILLS, RAYF?
I'M READY, KAM--LET'S GET 'EM!
HEY! WATCH WHERE YOU SWING THAT THING, RAYF! YOU ALMOST TOOK OFF MY HEAD!
SHR-ZZMM!

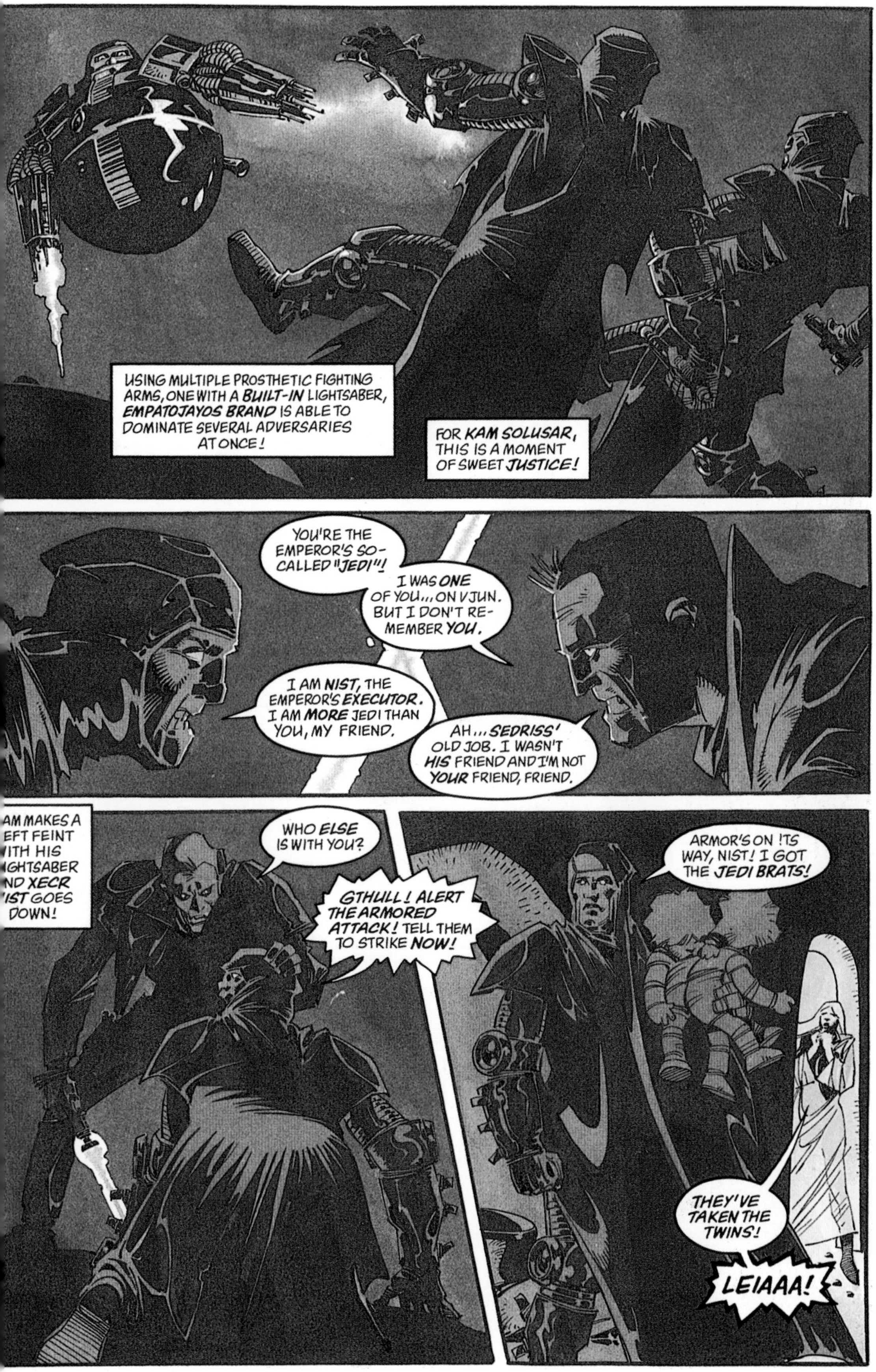

USING MULTIPLE PROSTHETIC FIGHTING ARMS, ONE WITH A BUILT-IN LIGHTSABER, EMPATOJAYOS BRAND IS ABLE TO DOMINATE SEVERAL ADVERSARIES AT ONCE!
FOR KAM SOLUSAR, THIS IS A MOMENT OF SWEET JUSTICE!
YOU'RE THE EMPEROR'S SO-CALLED "JEDI"!
I WAS ONE OF YOU... ON VJUN. BUT I DON'T RE-MEMBER YOU.
I AM NIST, THE EMPEROR'S EXECUTOR. I AM MORE JEDI THAN YOU, MY FRIEND.
AH... SEDRISS' OLD JOB. I WASN'T HIS FRIEND AND I'M NOT YOUR FRIEND, FRIEND.
AM MAKES A EFT FEINT WITH HIS IGHTSABER ND XECR IST GOES DOWN!
WHO ELSE IS WITH YOU?
GTHULL! ALERT THE ARMORED ATTACK! TELL THEM TO STRIKE NOW!
ARMOR'S ON ITS WAY, NIST! I GOT THE JEDI BRATS!
THEY'VE TAKEN THE TWINS!
LEIAAA!

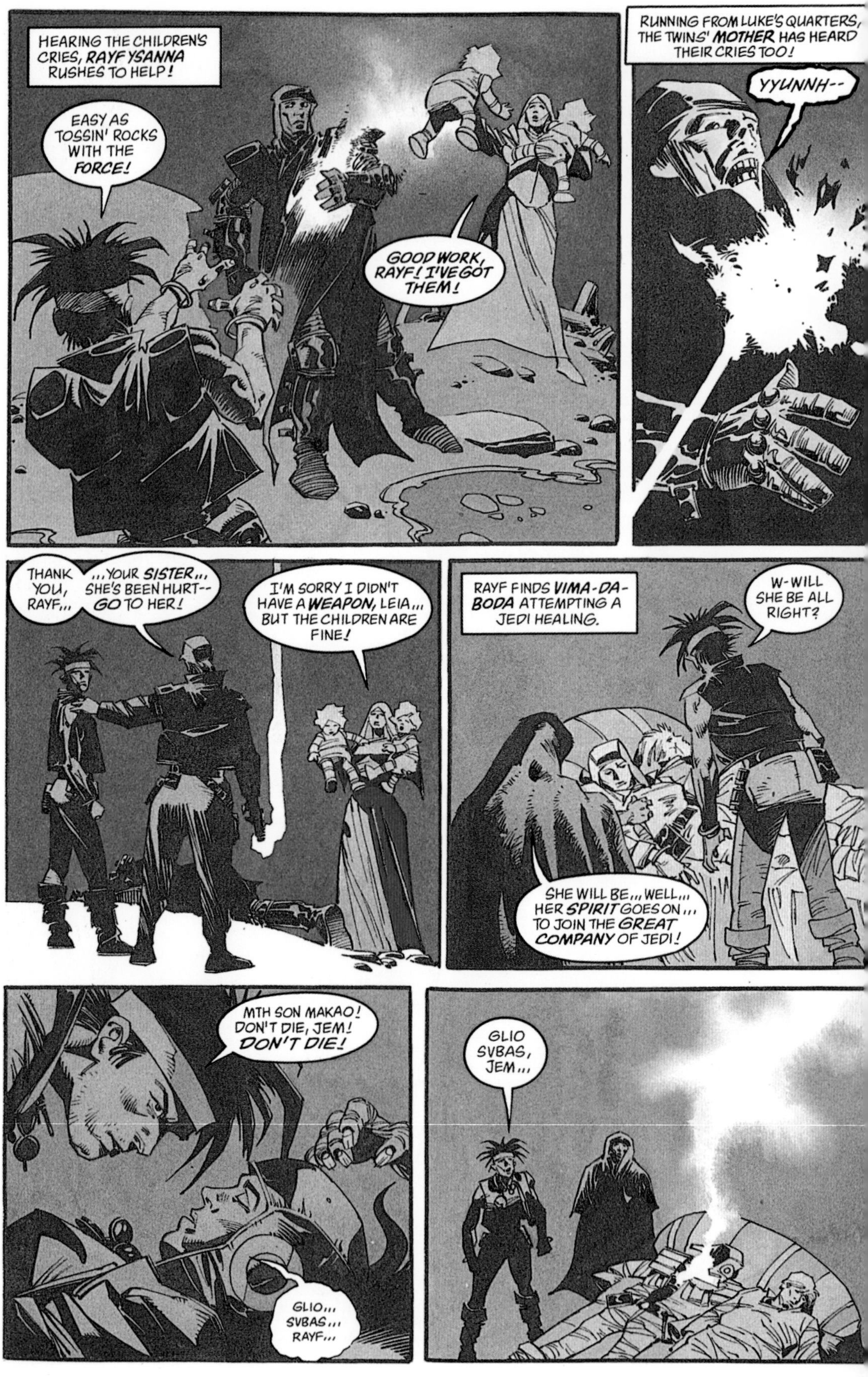

HEARING THE CHILDREN'S CRIES, RAYF YSANNA RUSHES TO HELP!
EASY AS TOSSIN' ROCKS WITH THE FORCE!
GOOD WORK, RAYF! I'VE GOT THEM!
RUNNING FROM LUKE'S QUARTERS, THE TWINS' MOTHER HAS HEARD THEIR CRIES TOO!
YYUNNH--
THANK YOU, RAYF,,,
,,,YOUR SISTER,,, SHE'S BEEN HURT-- GO TO HER!
I'M SORRY I DIDN'T HAVE A WEAPON, LEIA,,, BUT THE CHILDREN ARE FINE!
RAYF FINDS VIMA-DA-BODA ATTEMPTING A JEDI HEALING.
W-WILL SHE BE ALL RIGHT?
SHE WILL BE,,, WELL,,, HER SPIRIT GOES ON,,, TO JOIN THE GREAT COMPANY OF JEDI!
MTH SON MAKAO! DON'T DIE, JEM! DON'T DIE!
GLIO,,, SVBAS,,, RAYF,,,
GLIO SVBAS, JEM,,,

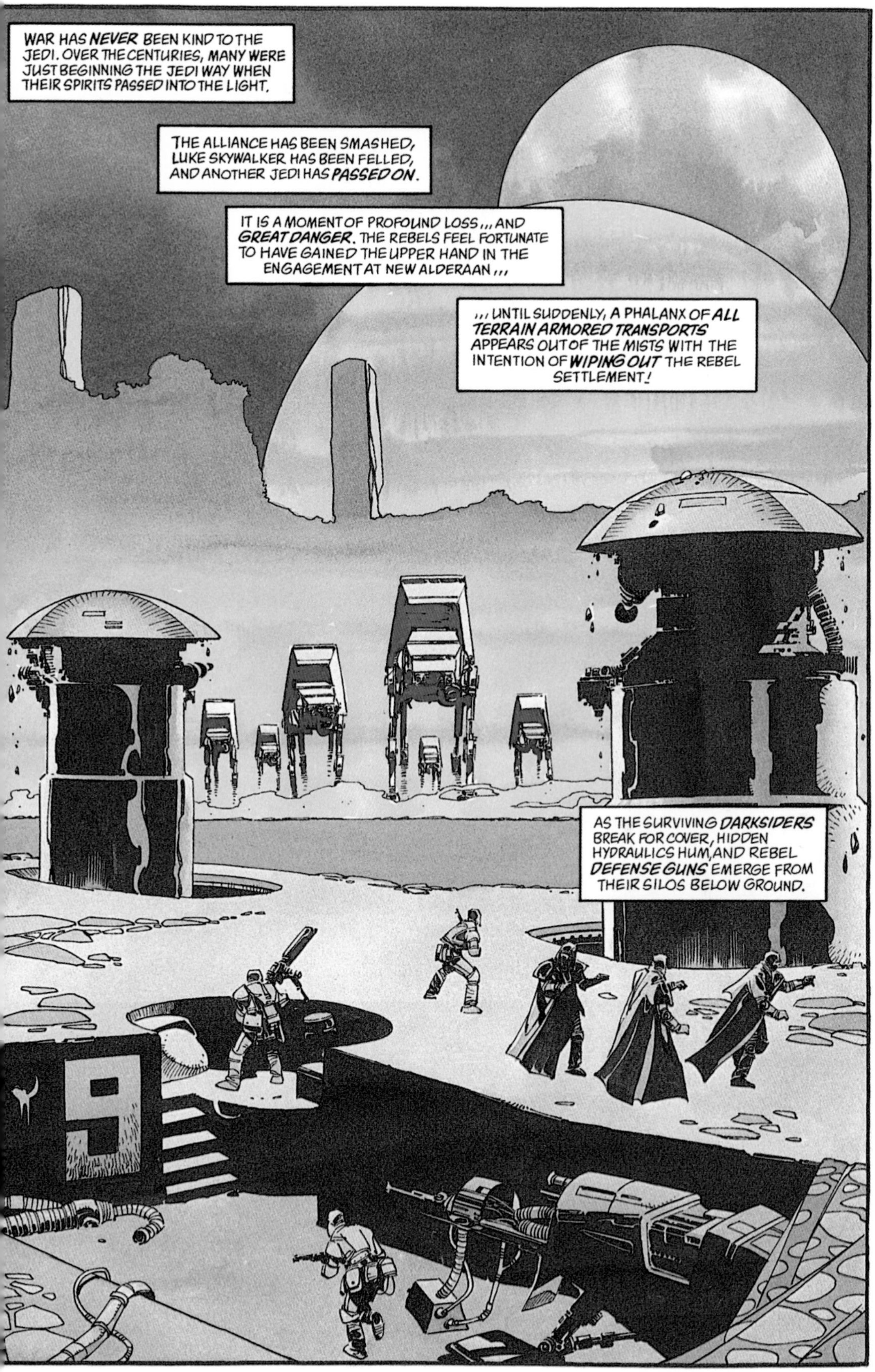
WAR HAS NEVER BEEN KIND TO THE JEDI. OVER THE CENTURIES, MANY WERE JUST BEGINNING THE JEDI WAY WHEN THEIR SPIRITS PASSED INTO THE LIGHT.
THE ALLIANCE HAS BEEN SMASHED, LUKE SKYWALKER HAS BEEN FELLED, AND ANOTHER JEDI HAS PASSED ON.
IT IS A MOMENT OF PROFOUND LOSS... AND GREAT DANGER. THE REBELS FEEL FORTUNATE TO HAVE GAINED THE UPPER HAND IN THE ENGAGEMENT AT NEW ALDERAAN...
...UNTIL SUDDENLY, A PHALANX OF ALL TERRAIN ARMORED TRANSPORTS APPEARS OUT OF THE MISTS WITH THE INTENTION OF WIPING OUT THE REBEL SETTLEMENT!
AS THE SURVIVING DARKSIDERS BREAK FOR COVER, HIDDEN HYDRAULICS HUM, AND REBEL DEFENSE GUNS EMERGE FROM THEIR SILOS BELOW GROUND.
9

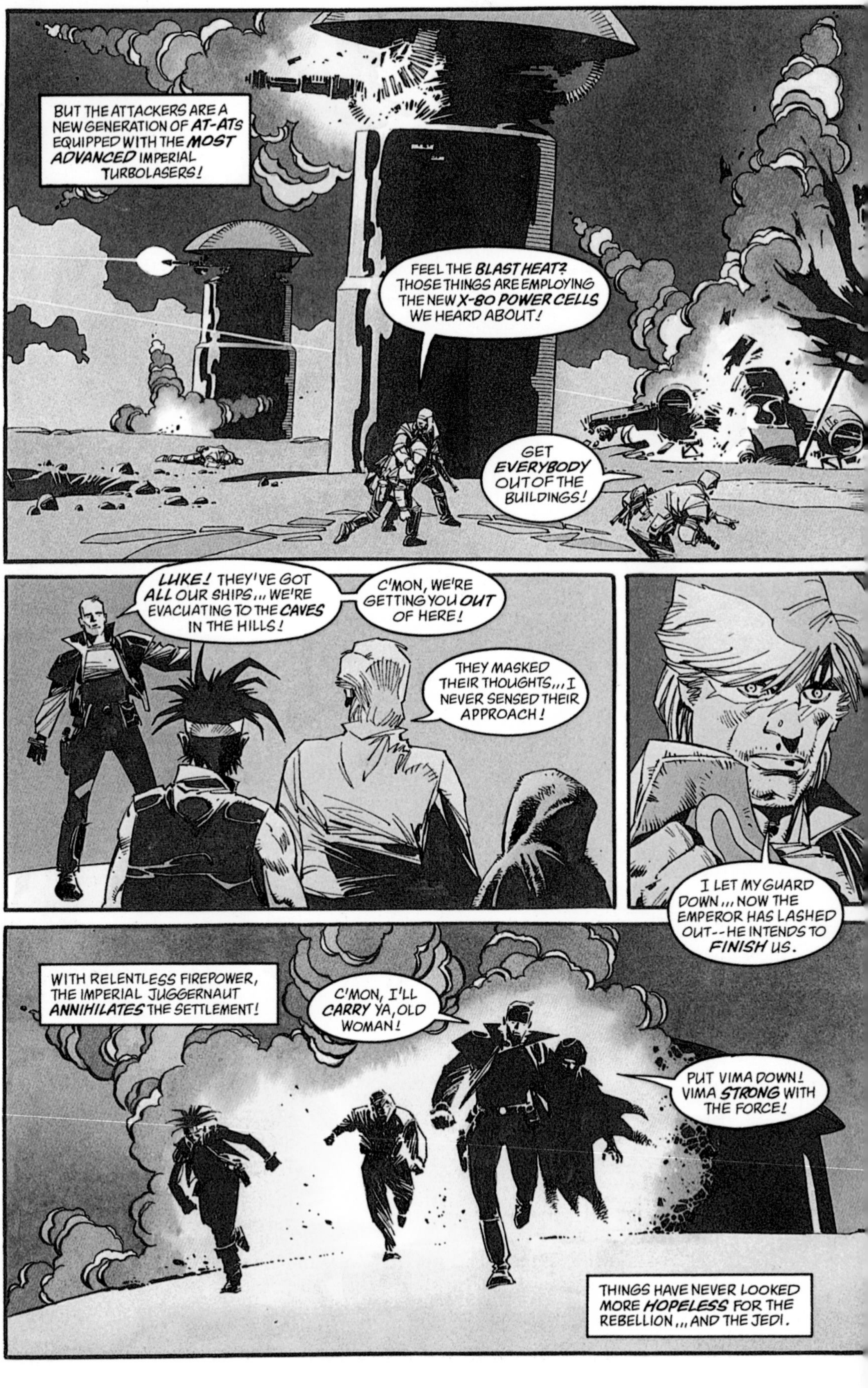

BUT THE ATTACKERS ARE A NEW GENERATION OF AT-ATs EQUIPPED WITH THE MOST ADVANCED IMPERIAL TURBOLASERS!
FEEL THE BLAST HEAT? THOSE THINGS ARE EMPLOYING THE NEW X-80 POWER CELLS WE HEARD ABOUT!
GET EVERYBODY OUT OF THE BUILDINGS!
LUKE! THEY'VE GOT ALL OUR SHIPS... WE'RE EVACUATING TO THE CAVES IN THE HILLS!
C'MON, WE'RE GETTING YOU OUT OF HERE!
THEY MASKED THEIR THOUGHTS... I NEVER SENSED THEIR APPROACH!
I LET MY GUARD DOWN... NOW THE EMPEROR HAS LASHED OUT--HE INTENDS TO FINISH US.
WITH RELENTLESS FIREPOWER, THE IMPERIAL JUGGERNAUT ANNIHILATES THE SETTLEMENT!
C'MON, I'LL CARRY YA, OLD WOMAN!
PUT VIMA DOWN! VIMA STRONG WITH THE FORCE!
THINGS HAVE NEVER LOOKED MORE HOPELESS FOR THE REBELLION... AND THE JEDI.

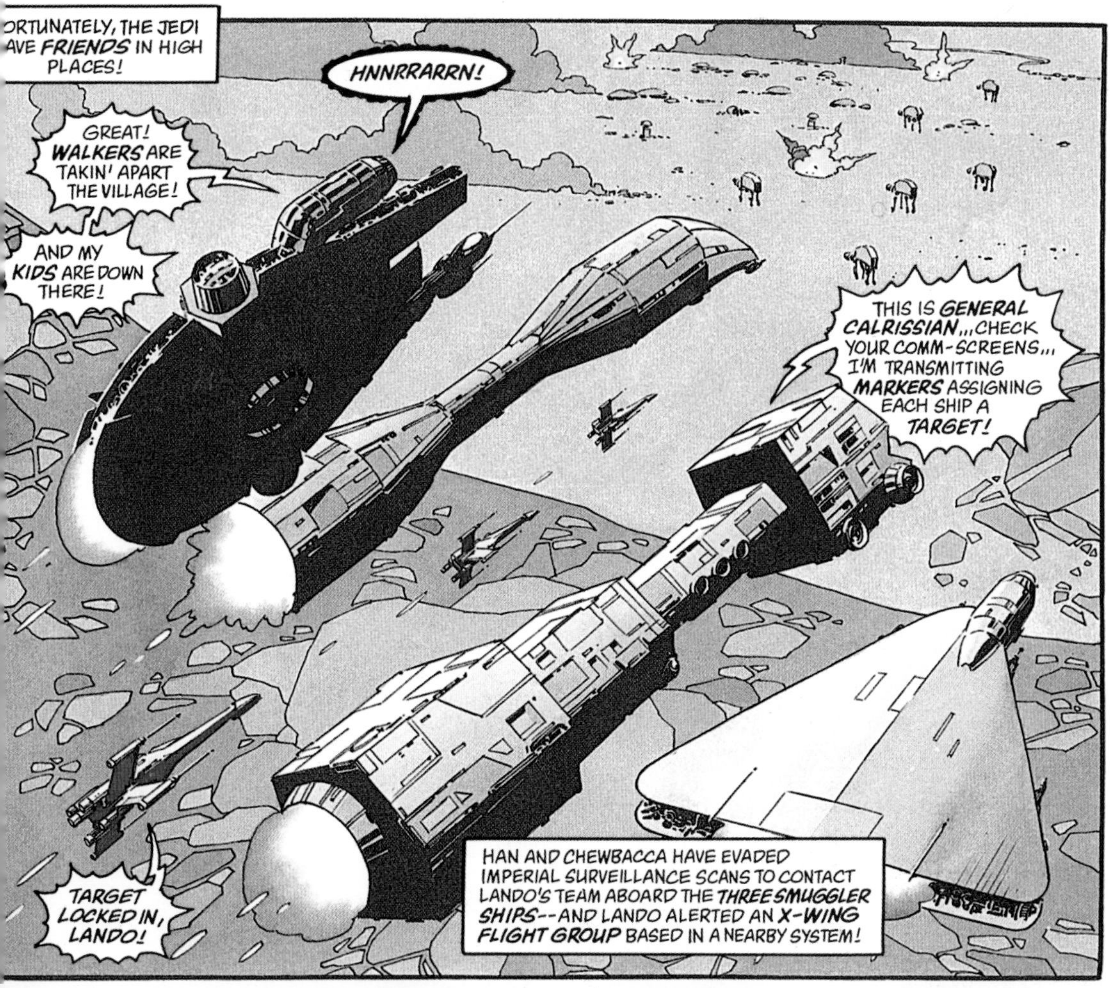
ORTUNATELY, THE JEDI AVE FRIENDS IN HIGH PLACES!
HNNRRARRN!
GREAT! WALKERS ARE TAKIN' APART THE VILLAGE!
AND MY KIDS ARE DOWN THERE!
THIS IS GENERAL CALRISSIAN... CHECK YOUR COMM-SCREENS... I'M TRANSMITTING MARKERS ASSIGNING EACH SHIP A TARGET!
TARGET LOCKED IN, LANDO!
HAN AND CHEWBACCA HAVE EVADED IMPERIAL SURVEILLANCE SCANS TO CONTACT LANDO'S TEAM ABOARD THE THREE SMUGGLER SHIPS--AND LANDO ALERTED AN X-WING FLIGHT GROUP BASED IN A NEARBY SYSTEM!

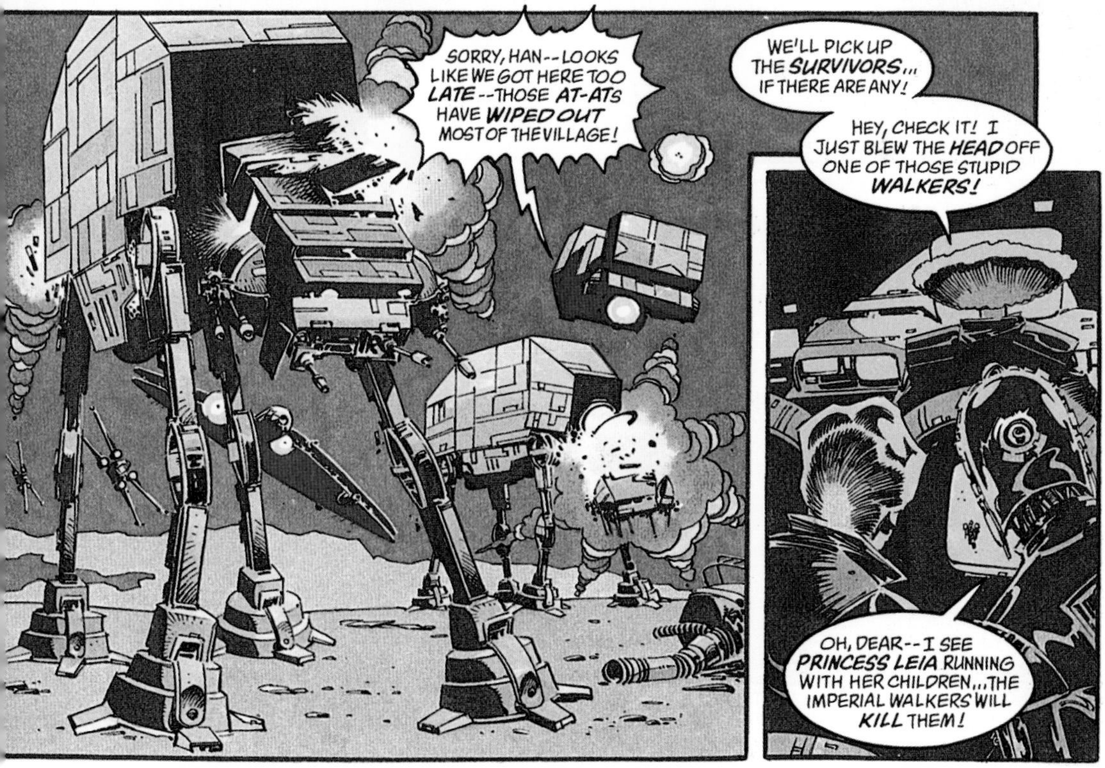
SORRY, HAN--LOOKS LIKE WE GOT HERE TOO LATE--THOSE AT-ATs HAVE WIPED OUT MOST OF THE VILLAGE!
WE'LL PICK UP THE SURVIVORS... IF THERE ARE ANY!
HEY, CHECK IT! I JUST BLEW THE HEAD OFF ONE OF THOSE STUPID WALKERS!
OH, DEAR--I SEE PRINCESS LEIA RUNNING WITH HER CHILDREN... THE IMPERIAL WALKERS WILL KILL THEM!

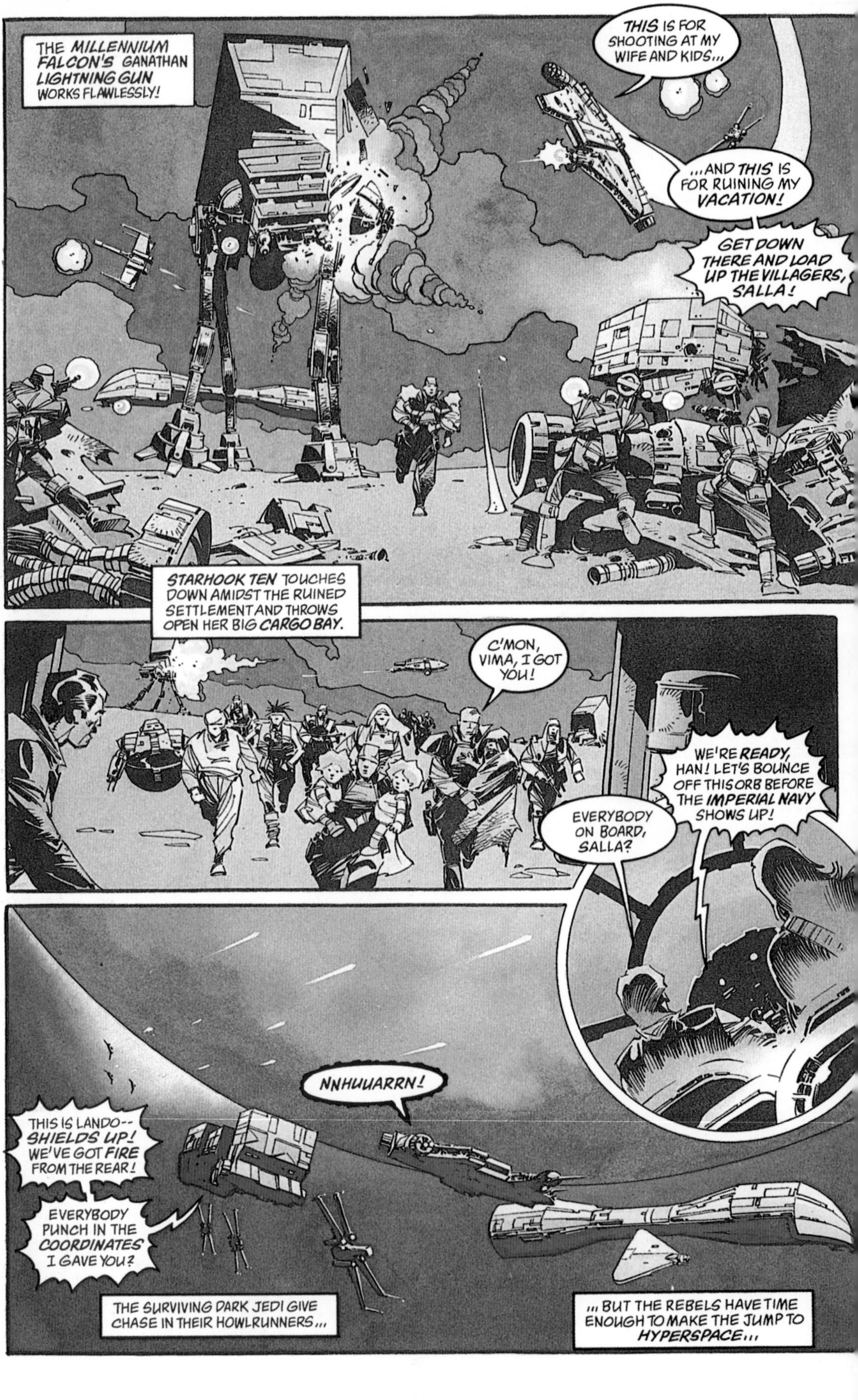
THE MILLENNIUM FALCON'S GANATHAN LIGHTNING GUN WORKS FLAWLESSLY!
THIS IS FOR SHOOTING AT MY WIFE AND KIDS...
...AND THIS IS FOR RUINING MY VACATION!
GET DOWN THERE AND LOAD UP THE VILLAGERS, SALLA!
STARHOOK TEN TOUCHES DOWN AMIDST THE RUINED SETTLEMENT AND THROWS OPEN HER BIG CARGO BAY.
C'MON, VIMA, I GOT YOU!
EVERYBODY ON BOARD, SALLA?
WE'RE READY, HAN! LET'S BOUNCE OFF THIS ORB BEFORE THE IMPERIAL NAVY SHOWS UP!
NNHUUARRN!
THIS IS LANDO-- SHIELDS UP! WE'VE GOT FIRE FROM THE REAR!
EVERYBODY PUNCH IN THE COORDINATES I GAVE YOU?
THE SURVIVING DARK JEDI GIVE CHASE IN THEIR HOWLRUNNERS...
...BUT THE REBELS HAVE TIME ENOUGH TO MAKE THE JUMP TO HYPERSPACE...

TO THE DISTANT *AURIL* SYSTEMS AND A DERELICT *CITY IN SPACE.*

I...*KNOW* THIS PLACE...THE OLD *NESPIS* SPACE-PORT.

YEAH...WHERE YOU AND I HAD OUR FATEFUL *MEETING.*

BUT WHY DID LANDO BRING US *HERE?*

ARE YOU OKAY, LEIA?

I'M...I FEEL MY TIME IS NEAR. WE NEED TO LAND....*SOON.*

PRINCESS LEIA... OH, DEAR.... I DON'T KNOW *HOW* YOU HUMANS MANAGE. IT'S SO MUCH *EASIER* TO CREATE A DROID!

BRRT-BEEP-BDEET?

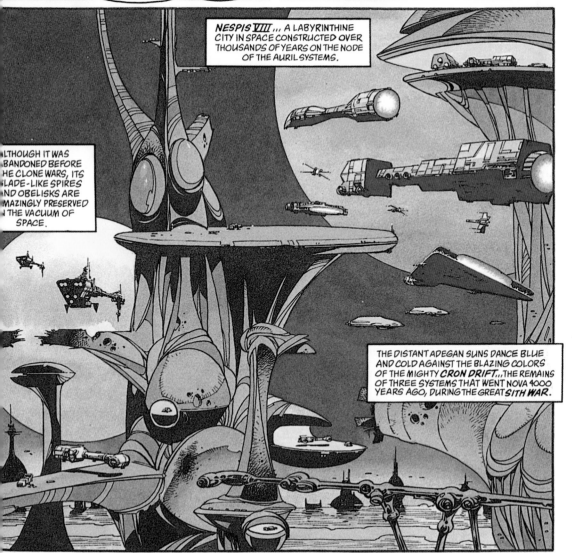

NESPIS VIII ..., A LABYRINTHINE CITY IN SPACE CONSTRUCTED OVER THOUSANDS OF YEARS ON THE NODE OF THE AURIL SYSTEMS.

ALTHOUGH IT WAS ABANDONED BEFORE THE CLONE WARS, ITS BLADE-LIKE SPIRES AND OBELISKS ARE AMAZINGLY PRESERVED IN THE VACUUM OF SPACE.

THE DISTANT ADEGAN SUNS DANCE BLUE AND COLD AGAINST THE BLAZING COLORS OF THE MIGHTY *CRON DRIFT...*THE REMAINS OF THREE SYSTEMS THAT WENT NOVA 4000 YEARS AGO, DURING THE GREAT *SITH WAR.*

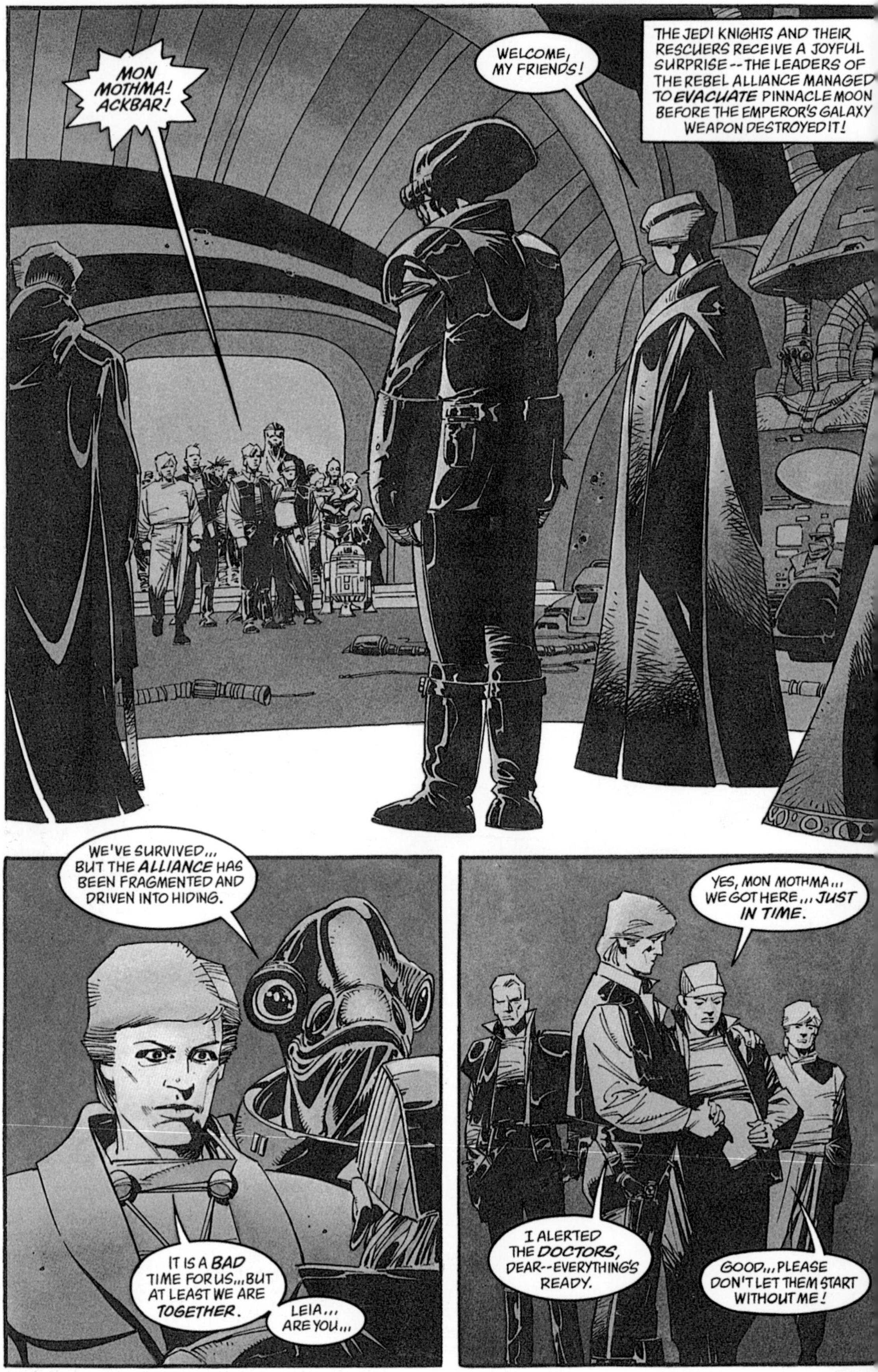
MON MOTHMA! ACKBAR!
WELCOME, MY FRIENDS!
THE JEDI KNIGHTS AND THEIR RESCUERS RECEIVE A JOYFUL SURPRISE--THE LEADERS OF THE REBEL ALLIANCE MANAGED TO EVACUATE PINNACLE MOON BEFORE THE EMPEROR'S GALAXY WEAPON DESTROYED IT!
WE'VE SURVIVED... BUT THE ALLIANCE HAS BEEN FRAGMENTED AND DRIVEN INTO HIDING.
IT IS A BAD TIME FOR US... BUT AT LEAST WE ARE TOGETHER.
LEIA... ARE YOU...
YES, MON MOTHMA... WE GOT HERE... JUST IN TIME.
I ALERTED THE DOCTORS, DEAR--EVERYTHING'S READY.
GOOD... PLEASE DON'T LET THEM START WITHOUT ME!

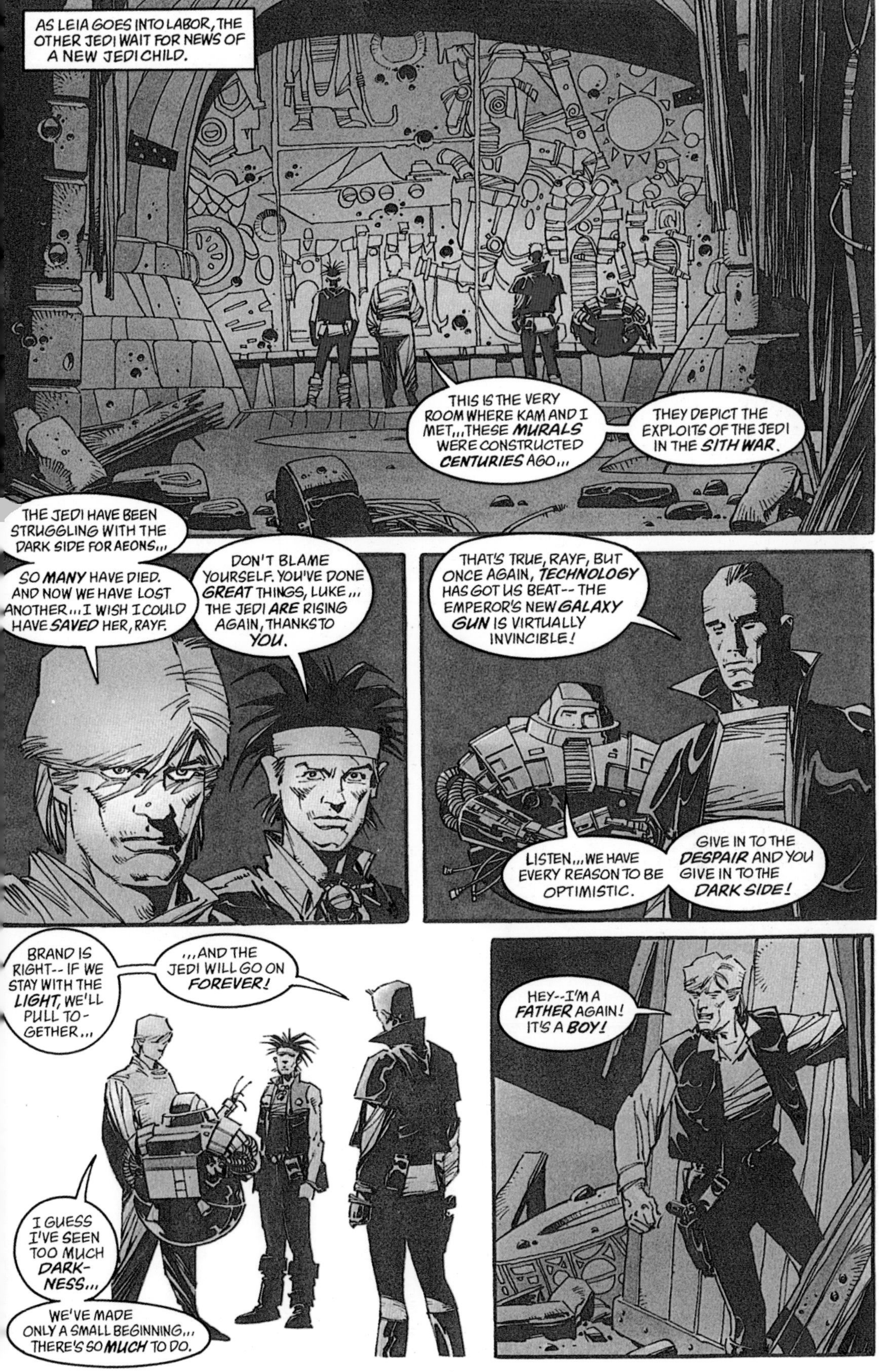

AS LEIA GOES INTO LABOR, THE OTHER JEDI WAIT FOR NEWS OF A NEW JEDI CHILD.
THIS IS THE VERY ROOM WHERE KAM AND I MET,,, THESE MURALS WERE CONSTRUCTED CENTURIES AGO,,,
THEY DEPICT THE EXPLOITS OF THE JEDI IN THE SITH WAR.
THE JEDI HAVE BEEN STRUGGLING WITH THE DARK SIDE FOR AEONS,,,
SO MANY HAVE DIED. AND NOW WE HAVE LOST ANOTHER... I WISH I COULD HAVE SAVED HER, RAYF.
DON'T BLAME YOURSELF. YOU'VE DONE GREAT THINGS, LUKE... THE JEDI ARE RISING AGAIN, THANKS TO YOU.
THAT'S TRUE, RAYF, BUT ONCE AGAIN, TECHNOLOGY HAS GOT US BEAT-- THE EMPEROR'S NEW GALAXY GUN IS VIRTUALLY INVINCIBLE!
LISTEN,,, WE HAVE EVERY REASON TO BE OPTIMISTIC.
GIVE IN TO THE DESPAIR AND YOU GIVE IN TO THE DARK SIDE!
BRAND IS RIGHT-- IF WE STAY WITH THE LIGHT, WE'LL PULL TO-GETHER...
,,,AND THE JEDI WILL GO ON FOREVER!
I GUESS I'VE SEEN TOO MUCH DARK-NESS...
WE'VE MADE ONLY A SMALL BEGINNING... THERE'S SO MUCH TO DO.
HEY--I'M A FATHER AGAIN! IT'S A BOY!

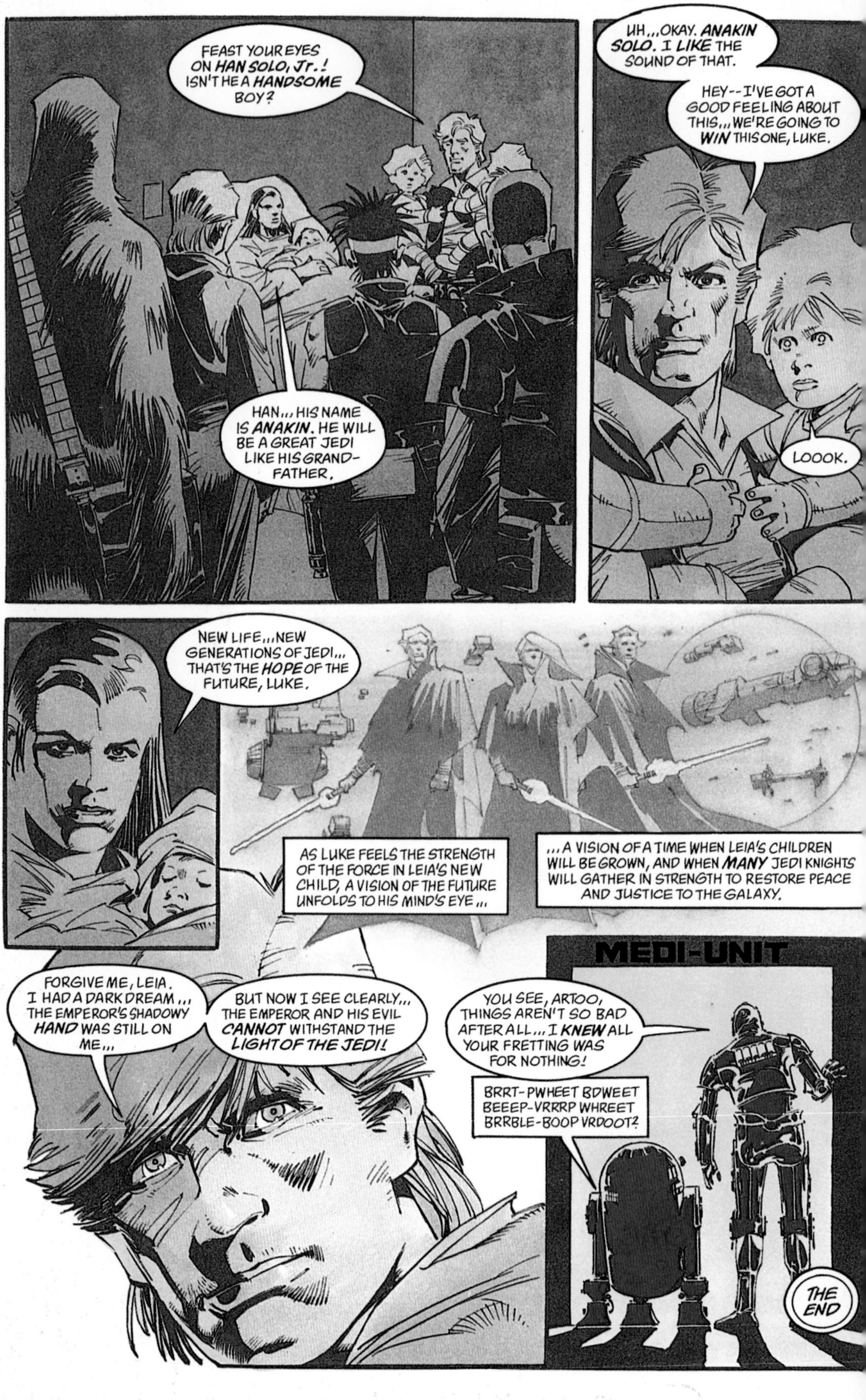

FEAST YOUR EYES ON HAN SOLO, Jr.! ISN'T HE A HANDSOME BOY?
HAN... HIS NAME IS ANAKIN. HE WILL BE A GREAT JEDI LIKE HIS GRAND-FATHER.
UH... OKAY. ANAKIN SOLO. I LIKE THE SOUND OF THAT.
HEY--I'VE GOT A GOOD FEELING ABOUT THIS... WE'RE GOING TO WIN THIS ONE, LUKE.
LOOOK.
NEW LIFE... NEW GENERATIONS OF JEDI... THAT'S THE HOPE OF THE FUTURE, LUKE.
AS LUKE FEELS THE STRENGTH OF THE FORCE IN LEIA'S NEW CHILD, A VISION OF THE FUTURE UNFOLDS TO HIS MIND'S EYE...
...A VISION OF A TIME WHEN LEIA'S CHILDREN WILL BE GROWN, AND WHEN MANY JEDI KNIGHTS WILL GATHER IN STRENGTH TO RESTORE PEACE AND JUSTICE TO THE GALAXY.
FORGIVE ME, LEIA. I HAD A DARK DREAM... THE EMPEROR'S SHADOWY HAND WAS STILL ON ME...
BUT NOW I SEE CLEARLY... THE EMPEROR AND HIS EVIL CANNOT WITHSTAND THE LIGHT OF THE JEDI!
MEDI-UNIT
YOU SEE, ARTOO, THINGS AREN'T SO BAD AFTER ALL... I KNEW ALL YOUR FRETTING WAS FOR NOTHING!
BRRT-PWHEET BDWEET BEEEP-VRRRP WHREET BRRBLE-BOOP VRDOOT?
THE END

STAR WARS®

EMPIRE'S END

EMPEROR

Palpatine has deployed a terrible new weapon, once again asserting his dominance over the galaxy. With the Alliance base destroyed, and its leaders driven into hiding, many worlds sympathetic to the Alliance have been forced to capitulate to the Empire or risk annihilation.

Luke Skywalker and his small band of Jedi have but one hope: draw the Emperor into a face-to-face confrontation, end his dark reign, and restore peace to the galaxy . . .

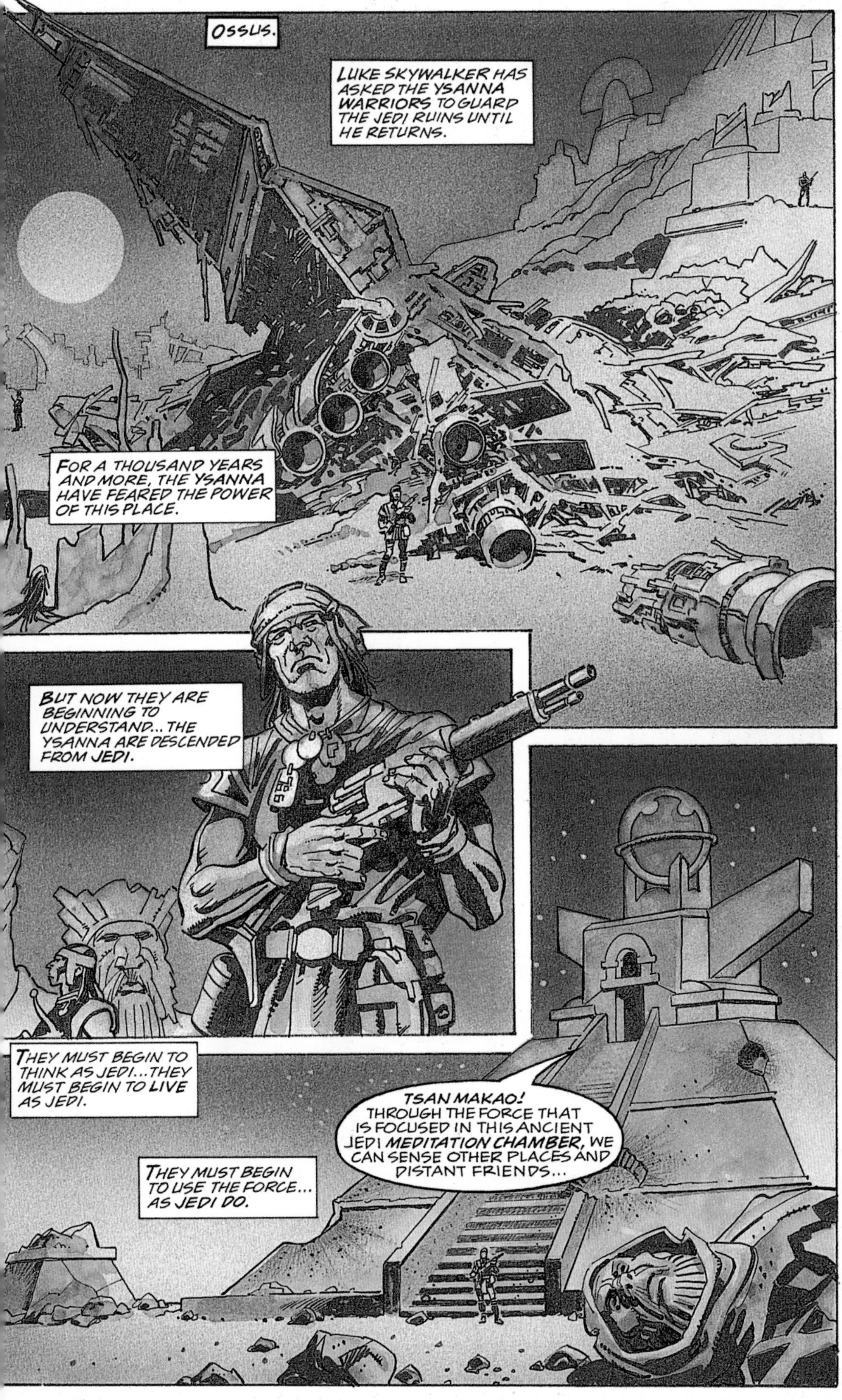
OSSUS.
LUKE SKYWALKER HAS ASKED THE YSANNA WARRIORS TO GUARD THE JEDI RUINS UNTIL HE RETURNS.
FOR A THOUSAND YEARS AND MORE, THE YSANNA HAVE FEARED THE POWER OF THIS PLACE.
BUT NOW THEY ARE BEGINNING TO UNDERSTAND... THE YSANNA ARE DESCENDED FROM JEDI.
THEY MUST BEGIN TO THINK AS JEDI... THEY MUST BEGIN TO LIVE AS JEDI.
THEY MUST BEGIN TO USE THE FORCE... AS JEDI DO.
TSAN MAKAO! THROUGH THE FORCE THAT IS FOCUSED IN THIS ANCIENT JEDI MEDITATION CHAMBER, WE CAN SENSE OTHER PLACES AND DISTANT FRIENDS...

MY BROTHERS, I SEE *TERRIBLE EVENTS,* THINGS WHICH MAKE MY HEART CRY OUT--

--I FEAR WE MADE A *GRAVE ERROR* WHEN WE ALLOWED OUR CHILDREN, *JEM* AND *RAYF,* TO GO WITH LUKE SKYWALKER.

BUT *CHIEF OKKO...* HOW CAN THAT BE? TELL US WHAT YOU SEE!

PASSAPEO KROVA! MY DAUGHTER... JEM... *DEAD.*

NEKOUDA! JEM IS *DEAD?*

SURELY, OKKO, YOU DO *NOT* SEE CLEARLY, BEING LITTLE ADVANCED IN JEDI MEDITATION.

NO, I SEE IT, TO THE *DARK SIDE* OF THE FORCE GROWS *STRONGER* THROUGH OUT THE GALAXY.

SKYWALKER WAS *FOOLISH* TO THINK HE COULD REVIVE THE JEDI... I KNOW THAT NOW.

WAIT... I SEE SOMETHING ELSE... THE REBEL ALLIANCE IS IN *GREAT* DANGER...

A *HUNDRED THOUSAND* REBEL WARRIORS ARE ABOUT TO *DIE...*

...BY ONE *BLOW* OF THE *EMPEROR'S FIST!*

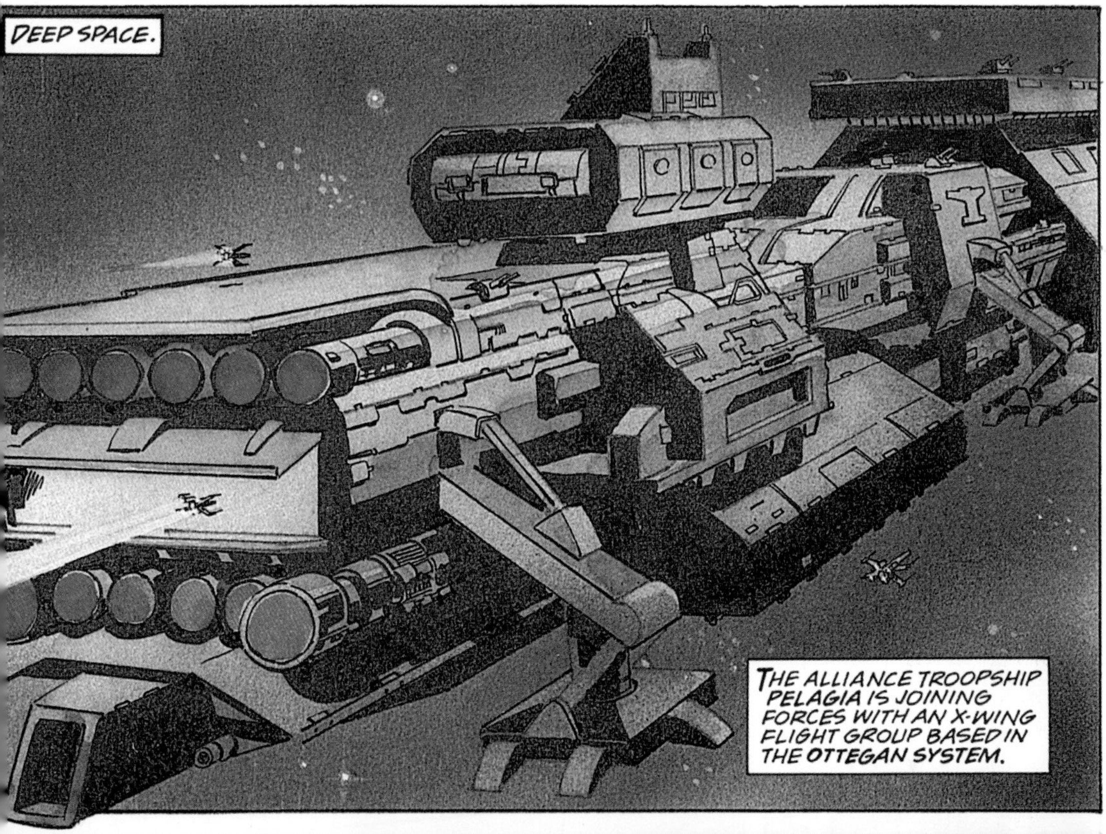
DEEP SPACE.
THE ALLIANCE TROOPSHIP PELAGIA IS JOINING FORCES WITH AN X-WING FLIGHT GROUP BASED IN THE OTTEGAN SYSTEM.

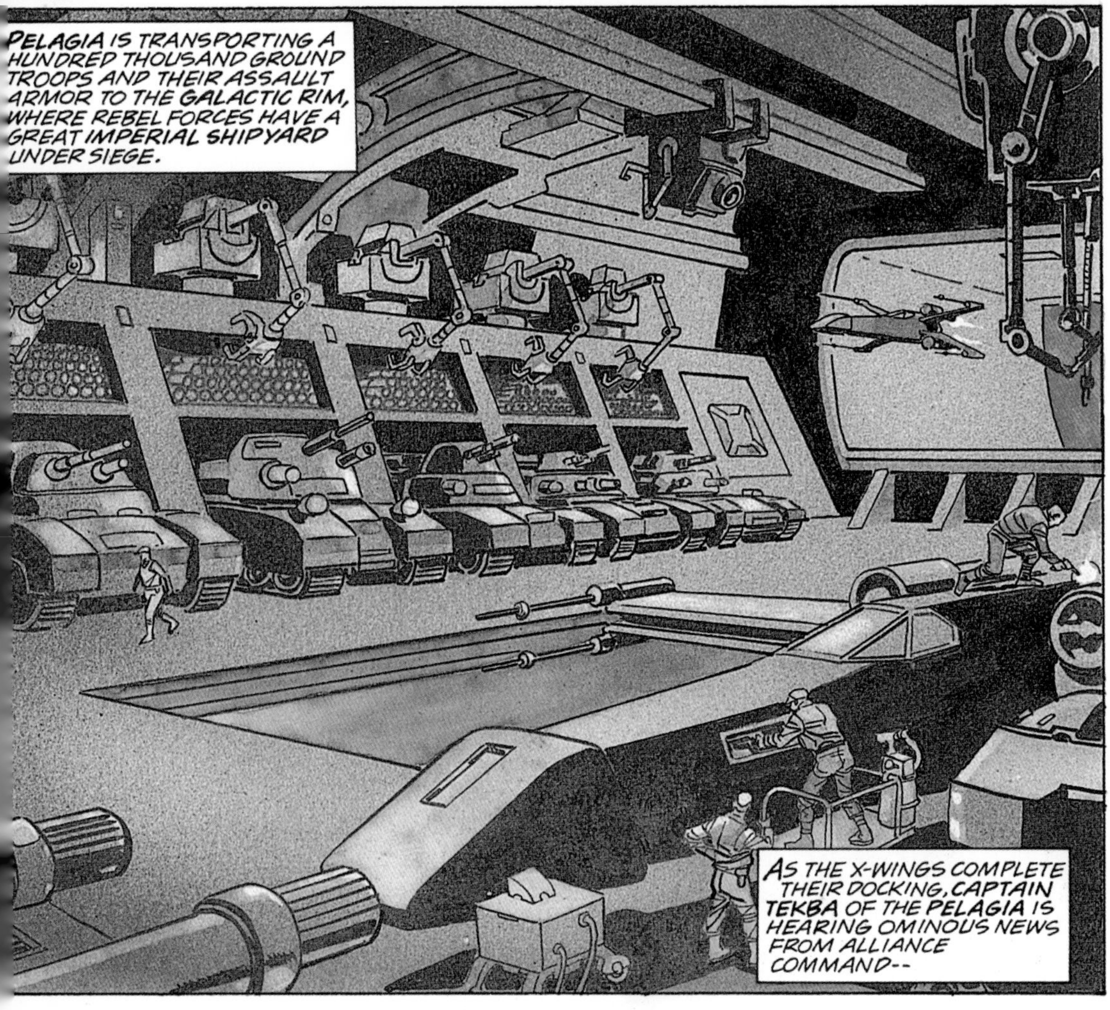
PELAGIA IS TRANSPORTING A HUNDRED THOUSAND GROUND TROOPS AND THEIR ASSAULT ARMOR TO THE GALACTIC RIM, WHERE REBEL FORCES HAVE A GREAT IMPERIAL SHIPYARD UNDER SIEGE.
AS THE X-WINGS COMPLETE THEIR DOCKING, CAPTAIN TEKBA OF THE PELAGIA IS HEARING OMINOUS NEWS FROM ALLIANCE COMMAND--

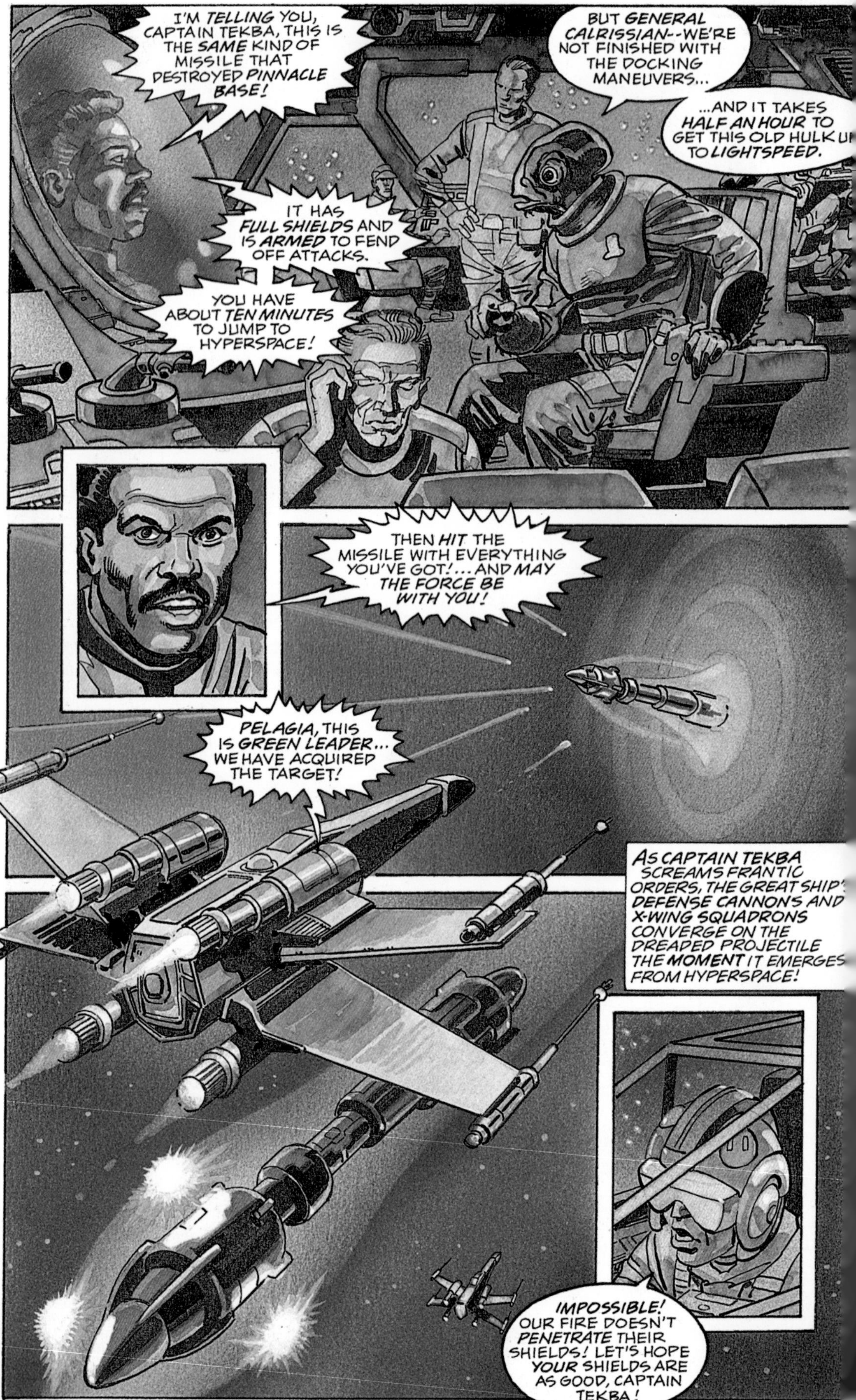
I'M TELLING YOU, CAPTAIN TEKBA, THIS IS THE SAME KIND OF MISSILE THAT DESTROYED PINNACLE BASE!
BUT GENERAL CALRISSIAN--WE'RE NOT FINISHED WITH THE DOCKING MANEUVERS...
...AND IT TAKES HALF AN HOUR TO GET THIS OLD HULK UP TO LIGHTSPEED.
IT HAS FULL SHIELDS AND IS ARMED TO FEND OFF ATTACKS.
YOU HAVE ABOUT TEN MINUTES TO JUMP TO HYPERSPACE!
THEN HIT THE MISSILE WITH EVERYTHING YOU'VE GOT!... AND MAY THE FORCE BE WITH YOU!
PELAGIA, THIS IS GREEN LEADER... WE HAVE ACQUIRED THE TARGET!
AS CAPTAIN TEKBA SCREAMS FRANTIC ORDERS, THE GREAT SHIP'S DEFENSE CANNONS AND X-WING SQUADRONS CONVERGE ON THE DREADED PROJECTILE THE MOMENT IT EMERGES FROM HYPERSPACE!
IMPOSSIBLE! OUR FIRE DOESN'T PENETRATE THEIR SHIELDS! LET'S HOPE YOUR SHIELDS ARE AS GOOD, CAPTAIN TEKBA!

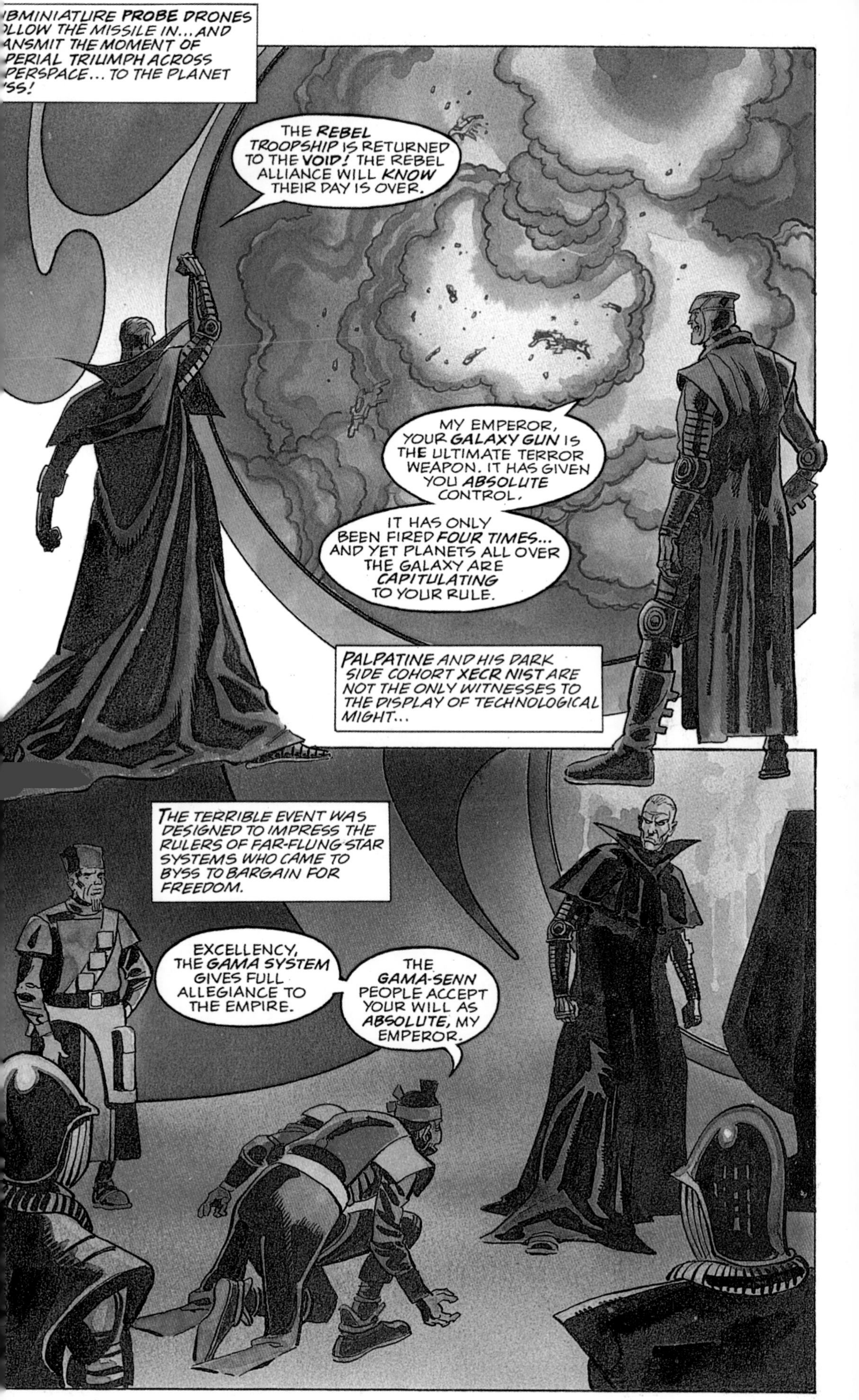

UBMINIATURE PROBE DRONES OLLOW THE MISSILE IN... AND ANSMIT THE MOMENT OF PERIAL TRIUMPH ACROSS PERSPACE... TO THE PLANET YSS!
THE REBEL TROOPSHIP IS RETURNED TO THE VOID! THE REBEL ALLIANCE WILL KNOW THEIR DAY IS OVER.
MY EMPEROR, YOUR GALAXY GUN IS THE ULTIMATE TERROR WEAPON. IT HAS GIVEN YOU ABSOLUTE CONTROL.
IT HAS ONLY BEEN FIRED FOUR TIMES... AND YET PLANETS ALL OVER THE GALAXY ARE CAPITULATING TO YOUR RULE.
PALPATINE AND HIS DARK SIDE COHORT XECR NIST ARE NOT THE ONLY WITNESSES TO THE DISPLAY OF TECHNOLOGICAL MIGHT...
THE TERRIBLE EVENT WAS DESIGNED TO IMPRESS THE RULERS OF FAR-FLUNG STAR SYSTEMS WHO CAME TO BYSS TO BARGAIN FOR FREEDOM.
EXCELLENCY, THE GAMA SYSTEM GIVES FULL ALLEGIANCE TO THE EMPIRE.
THE GAMA-SENN PEOPLE ACCEPT YOUR WILL AS ABSOLUTE, MY EMPEROR.

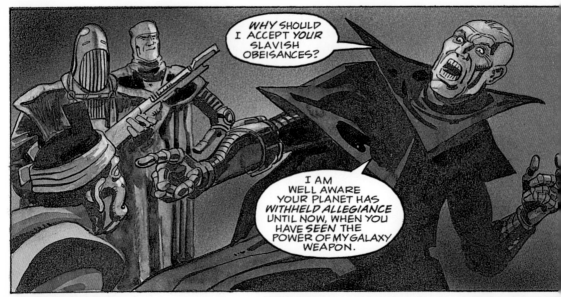

WHY SHOULD I ACCEPT *YOUR* SLAVISH OBEISANCES?

I AM WELL AWARE YOUR PLANET HAS *WITHHELD ALLEGIANCE* UNTIL NOW, WHEN YOU HAVE *SEEN* THE POWER OF MY *GALAXY WEAPON.*

I CAN *EASILY* ANNIHILATE YOUR WORLD AND ALL ITS INHABITANTS--

EMPEROR *PALPATINE!* AS YOUR *PHYSICIAN,* I MUST ADVISE YOU TO *CONTROL* YOUR EMOTIONS!

¿Unh?... JUST... AS I OBLITERATED THAT... REBEL *TROOPSHIP!*

YOUR *CLONE BODY* IS AGING *FAR* TOO FAST. WE NEED TO TAKE CELL SCRAPINGS TO TEST YOUR *LIFESPAN.*

CURSE THAT SKYWALKER... HE DESTROYED *ALL* MY BEST CLONES... I WAS FORCED TO TAKE ONE THAT WAS GENETICALLY *UNSTABLE.*

EMPEROR! OUR *SPIES* WITHIN THE REBEL ALLIANCE HAVE JUST REPORTED THE LOCATION OF THE *REBEL COMMAND BASE*... THE DERELICT *NESPIS VIII* SPACE CITY, NEAR THE CRON DRIFT.

EXCELLENT. ARM MY GALAXY WEAPON... *TARGET* THE COORDI-NATES OF THE NEW REBEL BASE.

THERE WILL BE *NO MORE* "DEMONSTRA-TIONS."

IT IS *TIME TO END* THIS WAR.

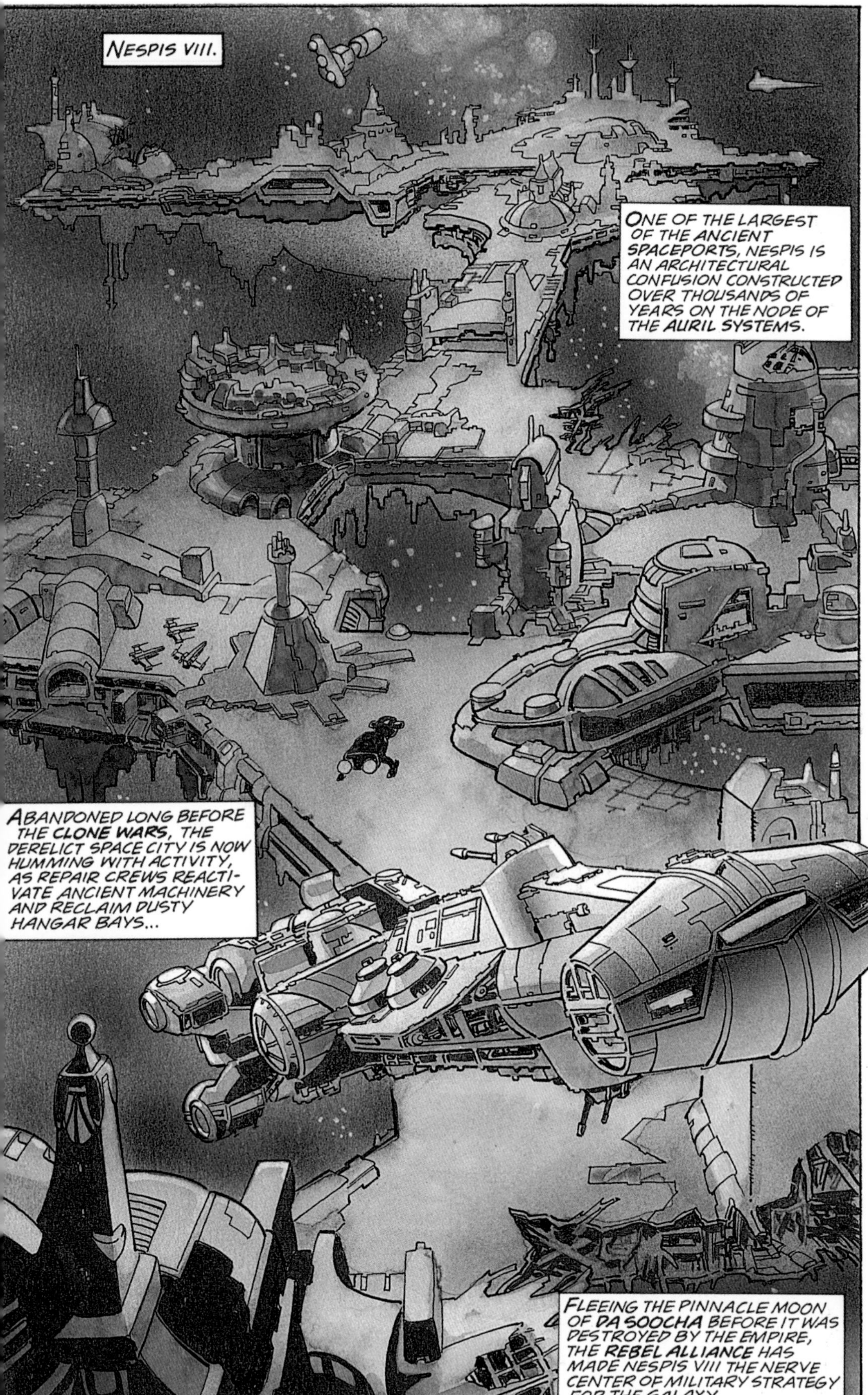
NESPIS VIII.
ONE OF THE LARGEST OF THE ANCIENT SPACEPORTS, NESPIS IS AN ARCHITECTURAL CONFUSION CONSTRUCTED OVER THOUSANDS OF YEARS ON THE NODE OF THE AURIL SYSTEMS.
ABANDONED LONG BEFORE THE CLONE WARS, THE DERELICT SPACE CITY IS NOW HUMMING WITH ACTIVITY, AS REPAIR CREWS REACTIVATE ANCIENT MACHINERY AND RECLAIM DUSTY HANGAR BAYS...
FLEEING THE PINNACLE MOON OF DA SOOCHA BEFORE IT WAS DESTROYED BY THE EMPIRE, THE REBEL ALLIANCE HAS MADE NESPIS VIII THE NERVE CENTER OF MILITARY STRATEGY FOR THE GALAXY.

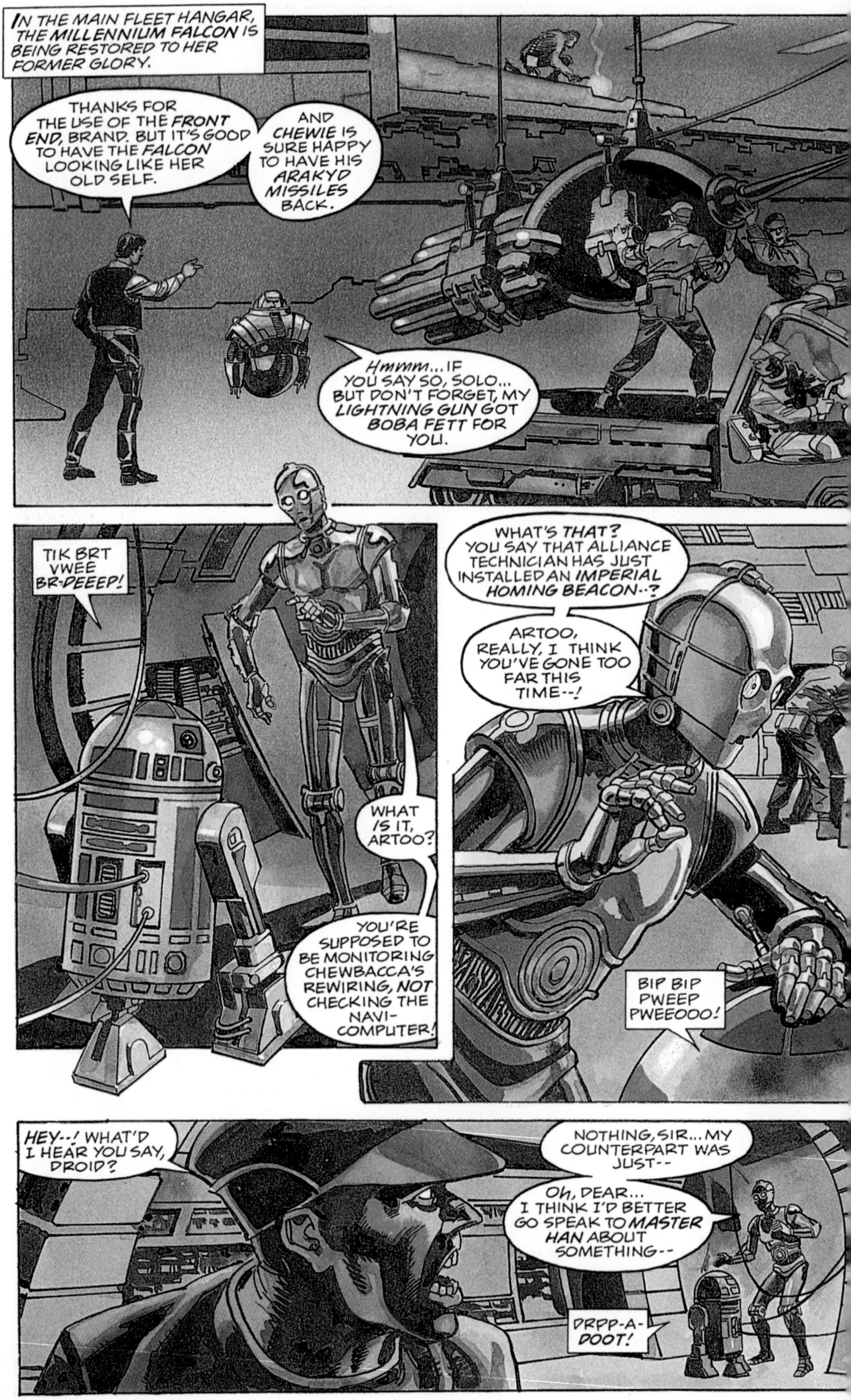
IN THE MAIN FLEET HANGAR, THE MILLENNIUM FALCON IS BEING RESTORED TO HER FORMER GLORY.
THANKS FOR THE USE OF THE FRONT END, BRAND. BUT IT'S GOOD TO HAVE THE FALCON LOOKING LIKE HER OLD SELF.
AND CHEWIE IS SURE HAPPY TO HAVE HIS ARAKYD MISSILES BACK.
Hmmm... IF YOU SAY SO, SOLO... BUT DON'T FORGET, MY LIGHTNING GUN GOT BOBA FETT FOR YOU.
TIK BRT VWEE BR-DEEEP!
WHAT IS IT, ARTOO?
YOU'RE SUPPOSED TO BE MONITORING CHEWBACCA'S REWIRING, NOT CHECKING THE NAVI-COMPUTER!
WHAT'S THAT? YOU SAY THAT ALLIANCE TECHNICIAN HAS JUST INSTALLED AN IMPERIAL HOMING BEACON--?
ARTOO, REALLY, I THINK YOU'VE GONE TOO FAR THIS TIME--!
BIP BIP PWEEP PWEEOOO!
HEY--! WHAT'D I HEAR YOU SAY, DROID?
NOTHING, SIR... MY COUNTERPART WAS JUST--
Oh, DEAR... I THINK I'D BETTER GO SPEAK TO MASTER HAN ABOUT SOMETHING--
DRPP-A-DOOT!

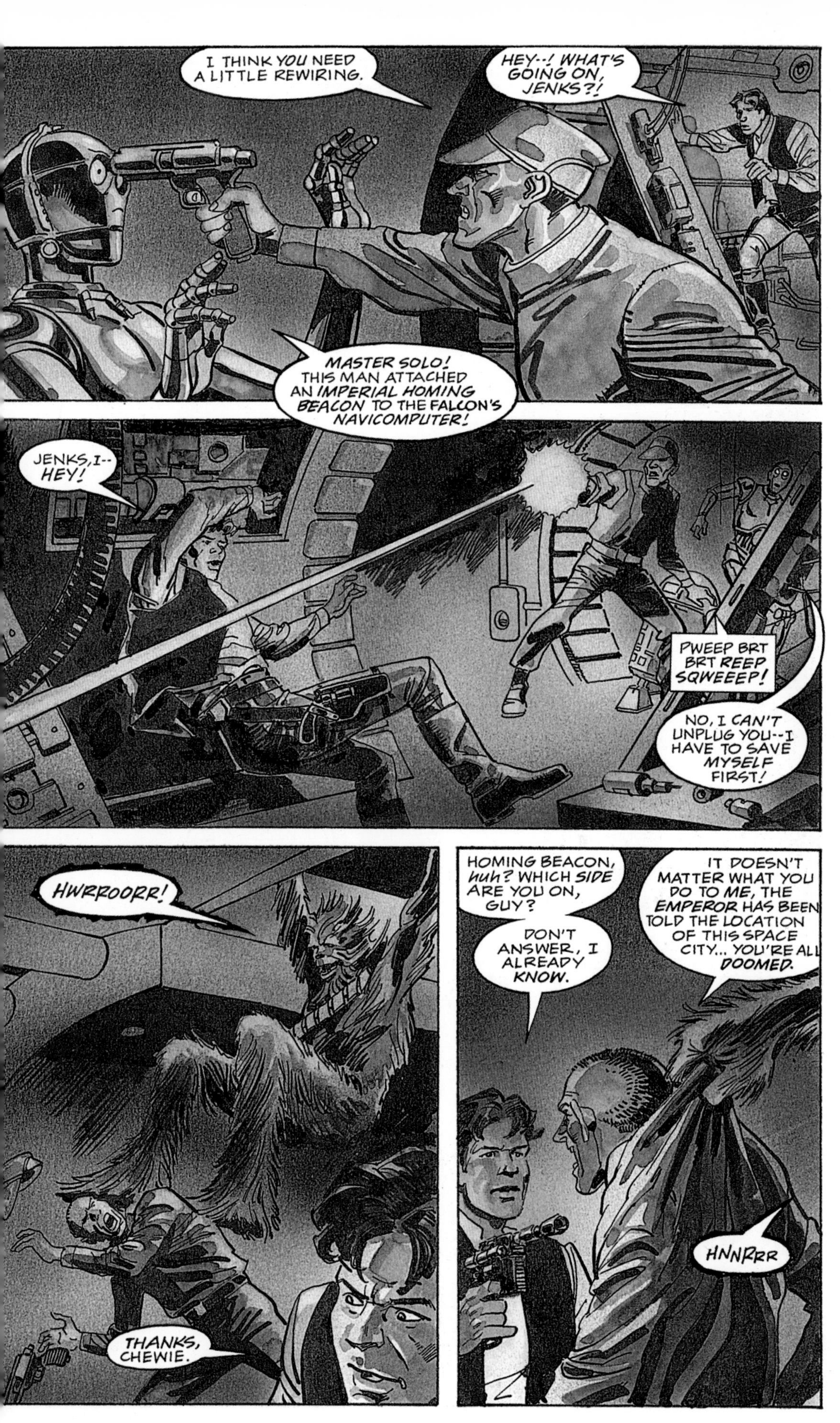
I THINK YOU NEED A LITTLE REWIRING.
HEY--! WHAT'S GOING ON, JENKS?!
MASTER SOLO! THIS MAN ATTACHED AN IMPERIAL HOMING BEACON TO THE FALCON'S NAVICOMPUTER!
JENKS, I-- HEY!
PWEEP BRT BRT REEP SQWEEEP!
NO, I CAN'T UNPLUG YOU--I HAVE TO SAVE MYSELF FIRST!
HWRROORR!
THANKS, CHEWIE.
HOMING BEACON, huh? WHICH SIDE ARE YOU ON, GUY?
DON'T ANSWER, I ALREADY KNOW.
IT DOESN'T MATTER WHAT YOU DO TO ME, THE EMPEROR HAS BEEN TOLD THE LOCATION OF THIS SPACE CITY... YOU'RE ALL DOOMED.
HNNRrr

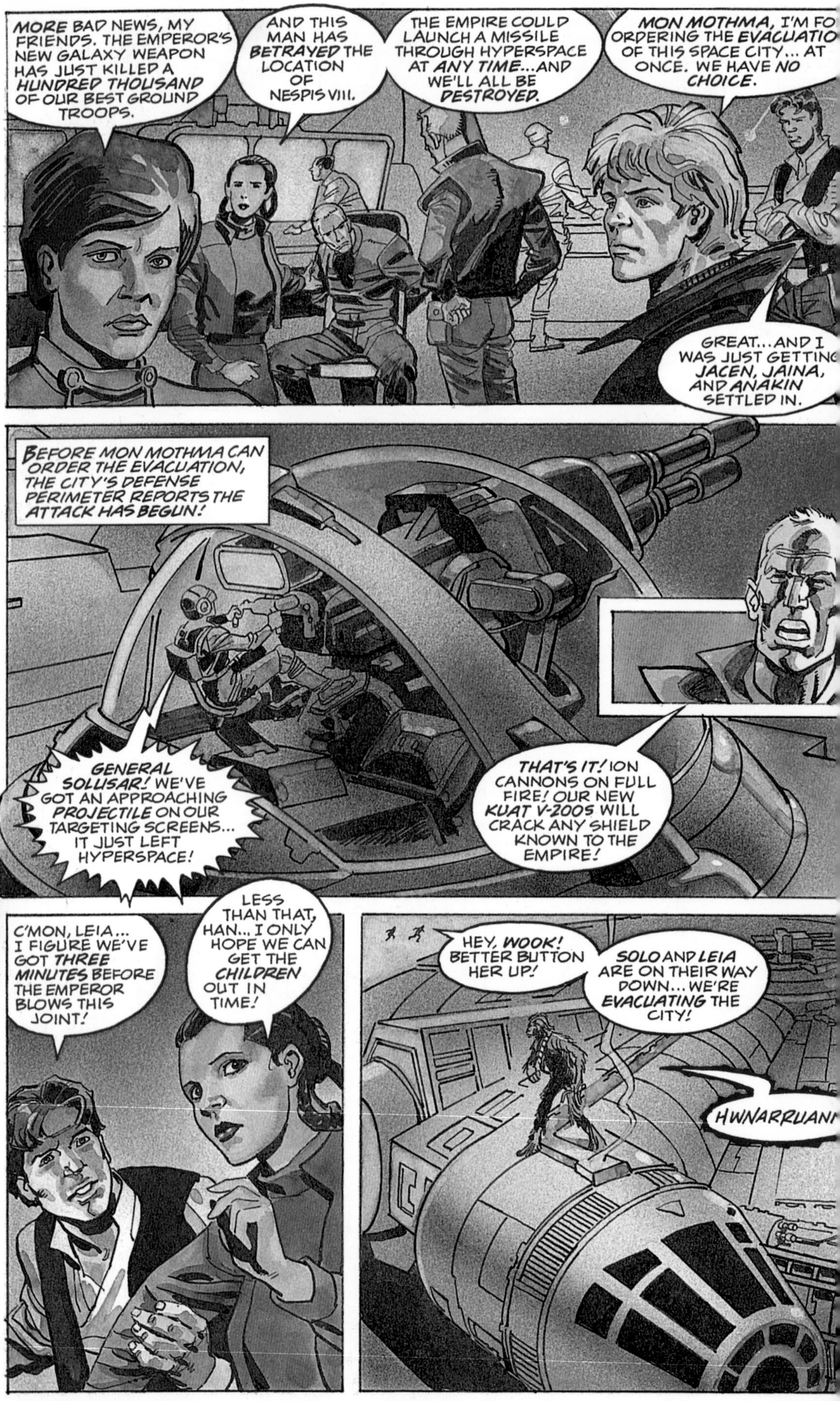
MORE BAD NEWS, MY FRIENDS. THE EMPEROR'S NEW GALAXY WEAPON HAS JUST KILLED A HUNDRED THOUSAND OF OUR BEST GROUND TROOPS.
AND THIS MAN HAS BETRAYED THE LOCATION OF NESPIS VIII.
THE EMPIRE COULD LAUNCH A MISSILE THROUGH HYPERSPACE AT ANY TIME... AND WE'LL ALL BE DESTROYED.
MON MOTHMA, I'M FO ORDERING THE EVACUATIO OF THIS SPACE CITY... AT ONCE. WE HAVE NO CHOICE.
GREAT... AND I WAS JUST GETTING JACEN, JAINA, AND ANAKIN SETTLED IN.
BEFORE MON MOTHMA CAN ORDER THE EVACUATION, THE CITY'S DEFENSE PERIMETER REPORTS THE ATTACK HAS BEGUN!
GENERAL SOLUSAR! WE'VE GOT AN APPROACHING PROJECTILE ON OUR TARGETING SCREENS... IT JUST LEFT HYPERSPACE!
THAT'S IT! ION CANNONS ON FULL FIRE! OUR NEW KUAT V-200S WILL CRACK ANY SHIELD KNOWN TO THE EMPIRE!
C'MON, LEIA... I FIGURE WE'VE GOT THREE MINUTES BEFORE THE EMPEROR BLOWS THIS JOINT!
LESS THAN THAT, HAN... I ONLY HOPE WE CAN GET THE CHILDREN OUT IN TIME!
HEY, WOOK! BETTER BUTTON HER UP!
SOLO AND LEIA ARE ON THEIR WAY DOWN... WE'RE EVACUATING THE CITY!
HWNARRUANN

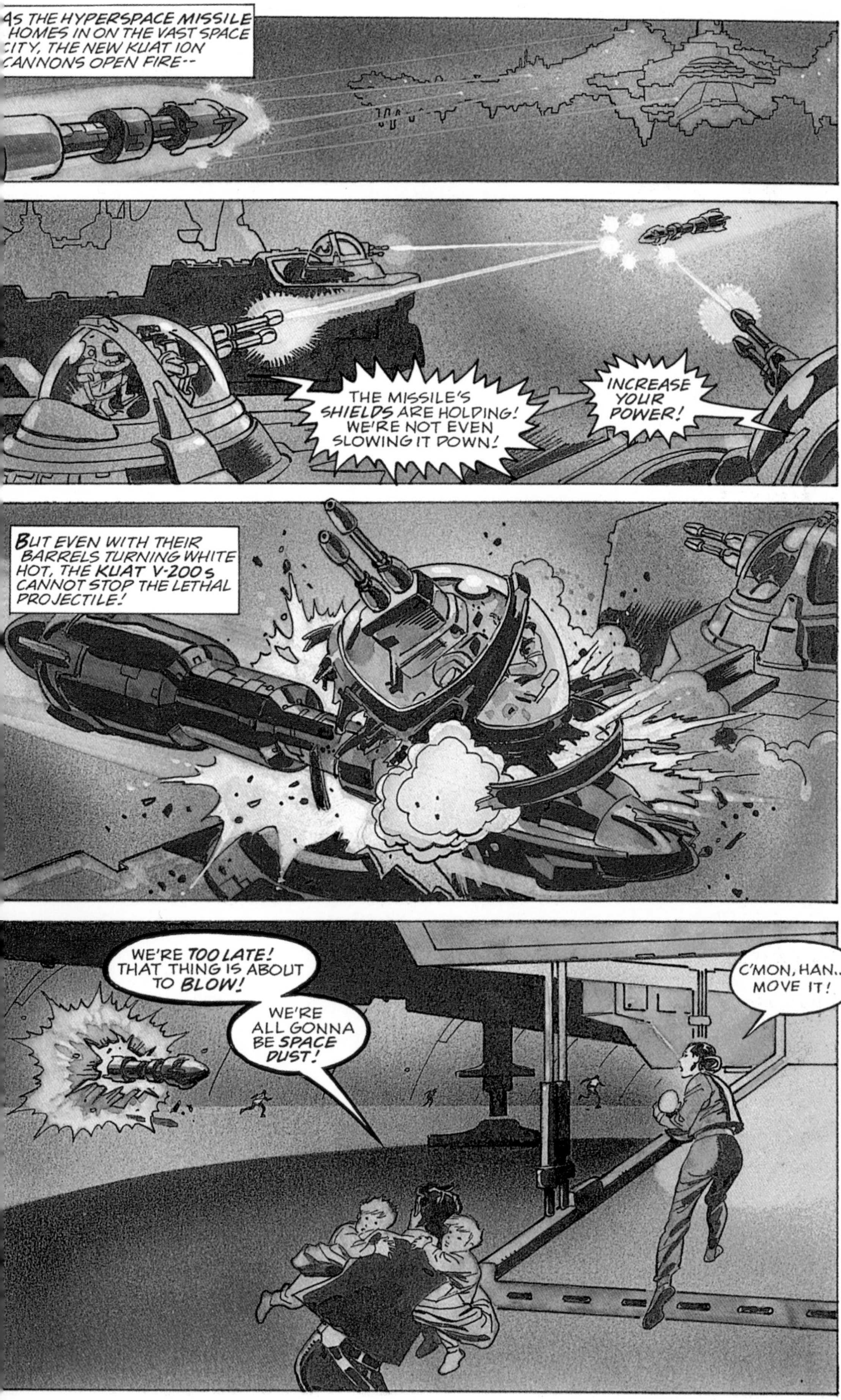
AS THE HYPERSPACE MISSILE HOMES IN ON THE VAST SPACE CITY, THE NEW KUAT ION CANNONS OPEN FIRE--
THE MISSILE'S SHIELDS ARE HOLDING! WE'RE NOT EVEN SLOWING IT DOWN!
INCREASE YOUR POWER!
BUT EVEN WITH THEIR BARRELS TURNING WHITE HOT, THE KUAT V-200s CANNOT STOP THE LETHAL PROJECTILE!
WE'RE TOO LATE! THAT THING IS ABOUT TO BLOW!
WE'RE ALL GONNA BE SPACE DUST!
C'MON, HAN... MOVE IT!

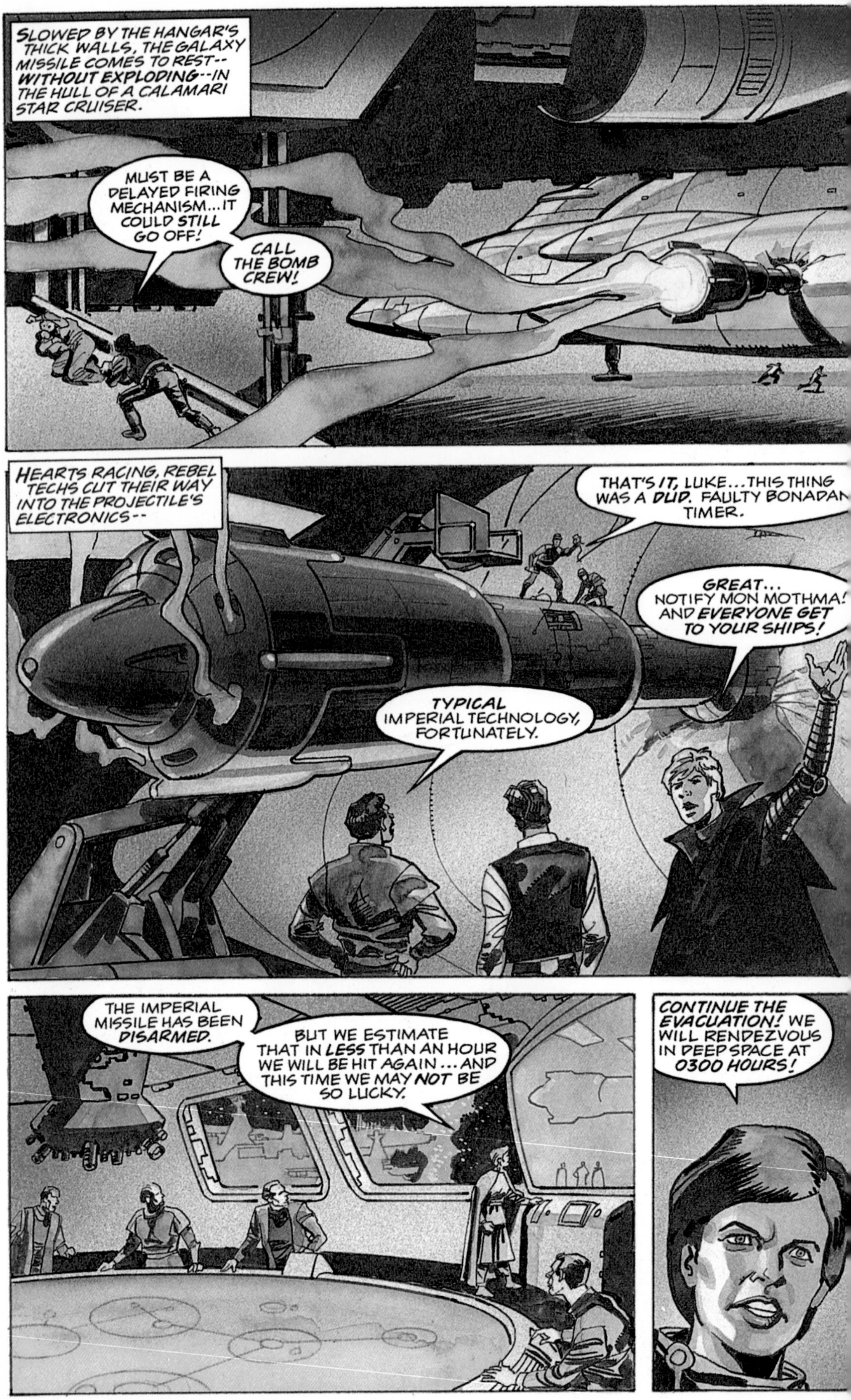
SLOWED BY THE HANGAR'S THICK WALLS, THE GALAXY MISSILE COMES TO REST-- WITHOUT EXPLODING--IN THE HULL OF A CALAMARI STAR CRUISER.
MUST BE A DELAYED FIRING MECHANISM... IT COULD STILL GO OFF!
CALL THE BOMB CREW!
HEARTS RACING, REBEL TECHS CUT THEIR WAY INTO THE PROJECTILE'S ELECTRONICS--
THAT'S IT, LUKE... THIS THING WAS A DUD. FAULTY BONADAN TIMER.
GREAT... NOTIFY MON MOTHMA! AND EVERYONE GET TO YOUR SHIPS!
TYPICAL IMPERIAL TECHNOLOGY, FORTUNATELY.
THE IMPERIAL MISSILE HAS BEEN DISARMED.
BUT WE ESTIMATE THAT IN LESS THAN AN HOUR WE WILL BE HIT AGAIN ... AND THIS TIME WE MAY NOT BE SO LUCKY.
CONTINUE THE EVACUATION! WE WILL RENDEZVOUS IN DEEP SPACE AT 0300 HOURS!

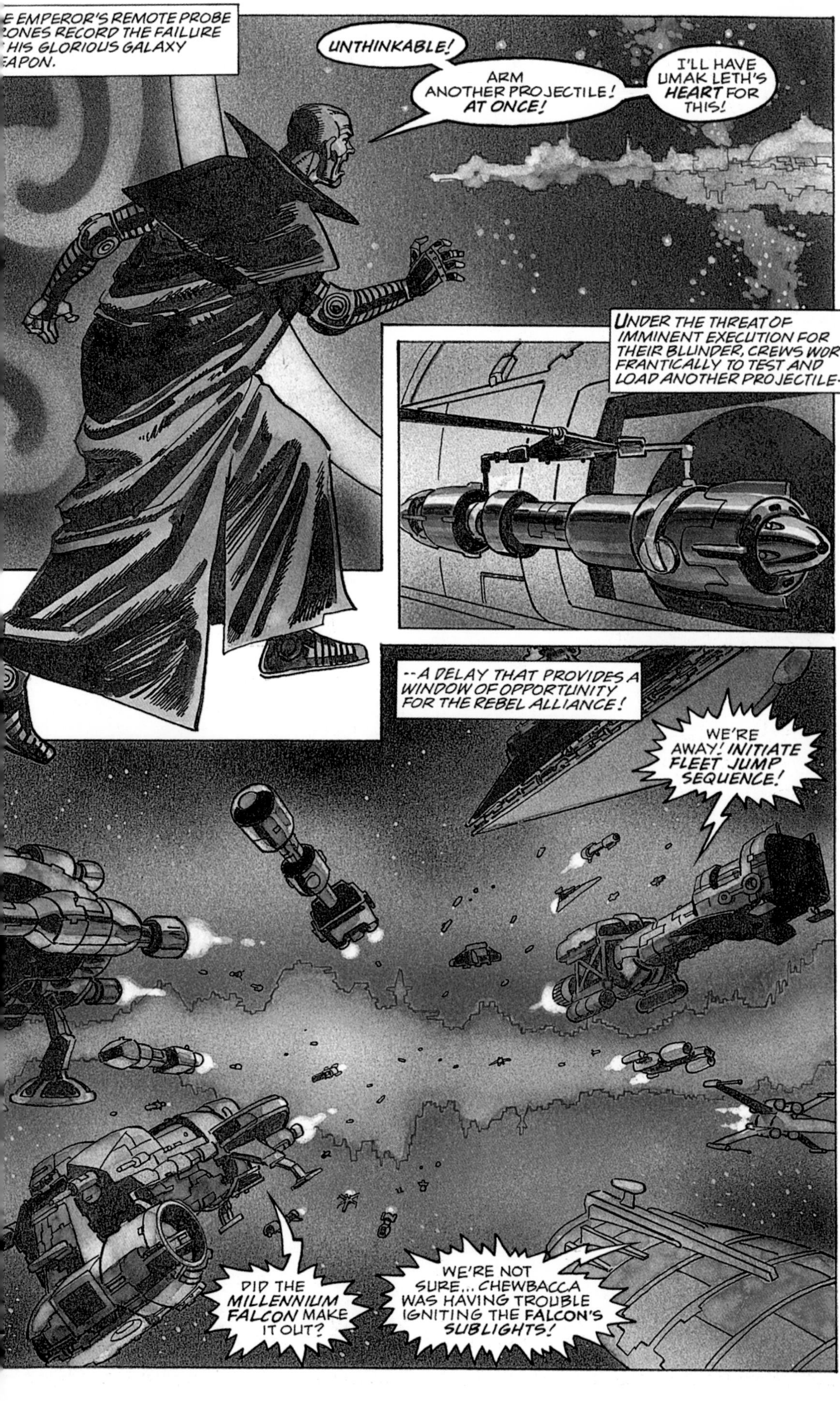
E EMPEROR'S REMOTE PROBE
ZONES RECORD THE FAILURE
HIS GLORIOUS GALAXY
EAPON.
UNTHINKABLE!
ARM ANOTHER PROJECTILE! AT ONCE!
I'LL HAVE UMAK LETH'S HEART FOR THIS!
UNDER THE THREAT OF IMMINENT EXECUTION FOR THEIR BLUNDER, CREWS WORK FRANTICALLY TO TEST AND LOAD ANOTHER PROJECTILE--
--A DELAY THAT PROVIDES A WINDOW OF OPPORTUNITY FOR THE REBEL ALLIANCE!
WE'RE AWAY! INITIATE FLEET JUMP SEQUENCE!
DID THE MILLENNIUM FALCON MAKE IT OUT?
WE'RE NOT SURE... CHEWBACCA WAS HAVING TROUBLE IGNITING THE FALCON'S SUBLIGHTS!

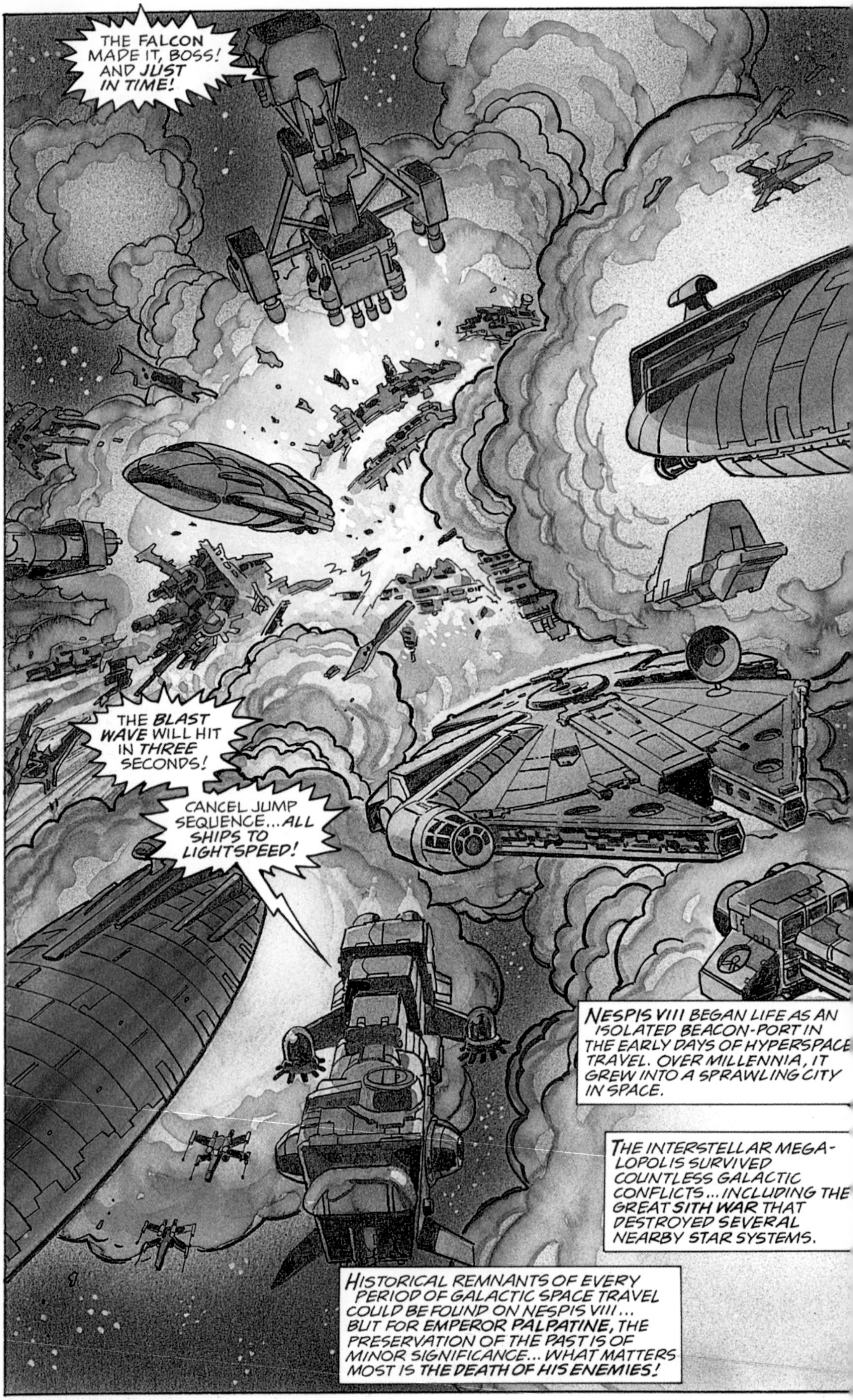
THE FALCON MADE IT, BOSS! AND JUST IN TIME!
THE BLAST WAVE WILL HIT IN THREE SECONDS!
CANCEL JUMP SEQUENCE... ALL SHIPS TO LIGHTSPEED!
NESPIS VIII BEGAN LIFE AS AN ISOLATED BEACON-PORT IN THE EARLY DAYS OF HYPERSPACE TRAVEL. OVER MILLENNIA, IT GREW INTO A SPRAWLING CITY IN SPACE.
THE INTERSTELLAR MEGA-LOPOLIS SURVIVED COUNTLESS GALACTIC CONFLICTS... INCLUDING THE GREAT SITH WAR THAT DESTROYED SEVERAL NEARBY STAR SYSTEMS.
HISTORICAL REMNANTS OF EVERY PERIOD OF GALACTIC SPACE TRAVEL COULD BE FOUND ON NESPIS VIII... BUT FOR EMPEROR PALPATINE, THE PRESERVATION OF THE PAST IS OF MINOR SIGNIFICANCE... WHAT MATTERS MOST IS THE DEATH OF HIS ENEMIES!

IS WAS TO BE MY MOMENT F *TRIUMPH*, LETH! YOUR COMPETENCE HAS LOWED THE REBELS TO ESCAPE!

IF I DID NOT *NEED* YOU TO OPERATE THIS SUPREME WEAPON YOU DESIGNED, I WOULD HAVE YOU *DESTROYED!*

I *WILL* HAVE YOU DESTROYED!

OTHERS ARE AT FAULT, SIRE... DEFECTIVE TIMING MECHANISMS FROM *BONADAN.* NEW PARTS ARE ON THE WAY!

HE RESPONSIBILITY IS OURS! YOU HAVE *THREE* AYS TO PUT THE GALAXY EAPON'S SYSTEMS IN ORDER.

WHEN WE RESUME FIRING, THE GUN WILL WORK *PERFECTLY...* OR YOU WILL *DIE.*

IT WILL BE AS YOU COMMAND, MY EMPEROR.

EXCELLENCE... PLEASE *CALM* YOURSELF!

THE *CELL TESTS* INDICATE YOUR PRESENT CLONE BODY IS IN *ACCELERATED DECAY.*

AS YOU KNOW, THERE ARE *NO OTHER CLONES* AVAILABLE.

SIRE, CALMNESS CAN *LENGTHEN* THE LIFESPAN OF THE CLONE...

...*ANGER* WILL ONLY *HASTEN* THE CLONE'S DESTRUCTION!

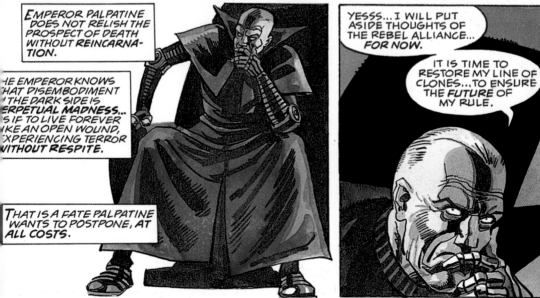

EMPEROR PALPATINE DOES NOT RELISH THE PROSPECT OF DEATH WITHOUT *REINCARNA-TION.*

HE EMPEROR KNOWS HAT DISEMBODIMENT THE DARK SIDE IS ERPETUAL MADNESS... S IF TO LIVE FOREVER KE AN OPEN WOUND, XPERIENCING TERROR ITHOUT RESPITE.

THAT IS A FATE PALPATINE WANTS TO POSTPONE, AT ALL COSTS.

YESSS... I WILL PUT ASIDE THOUGHTS OF THE REBEL ALLIANCE... *FOR NOW.*

IT IS TIME TO RESTORE MY LINE OF CLONES...TO ENSURE THE *FUTURE* OF MY RULE.

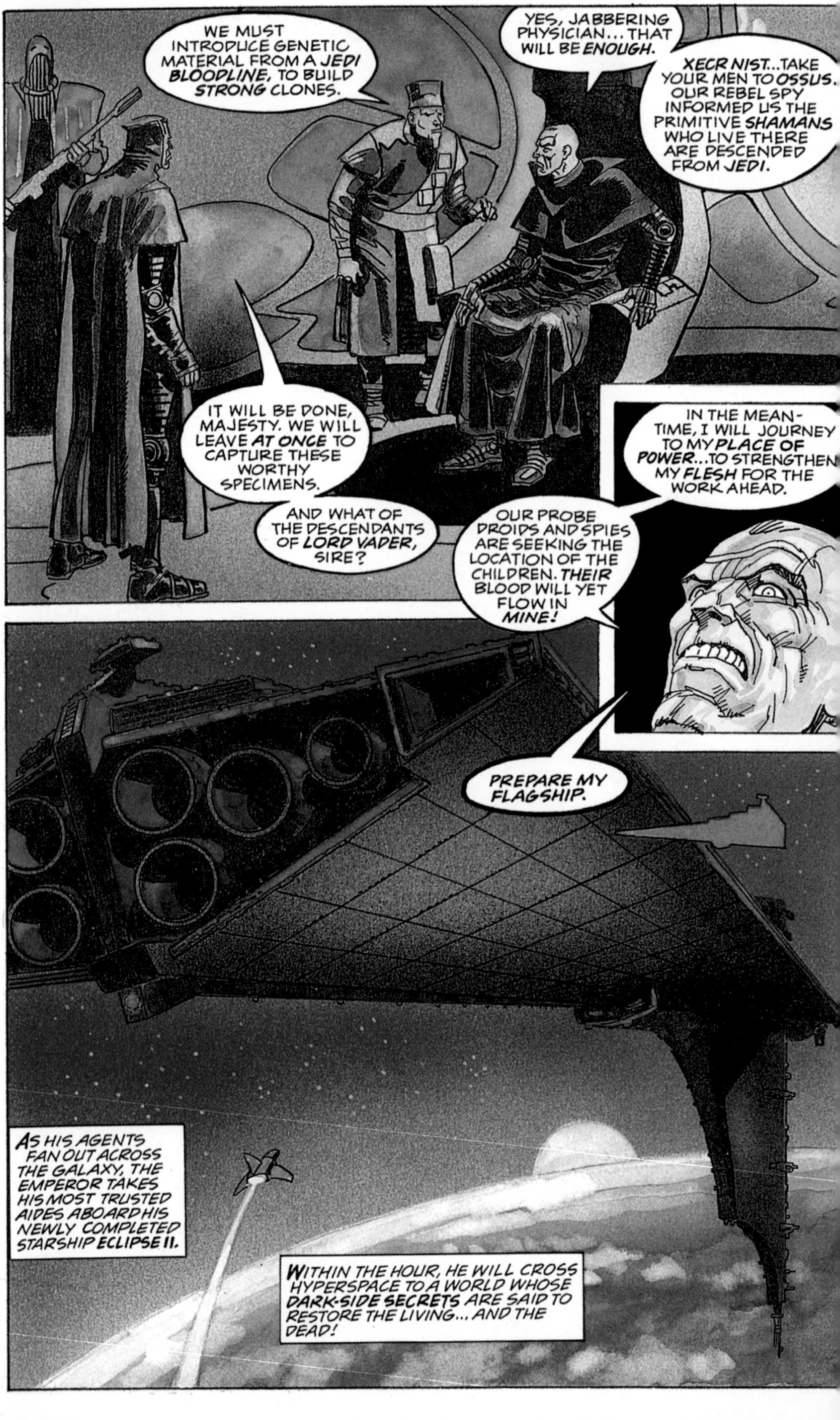

WE MUST INTRODUCE GENETIC MATERIAL FROM A JEDI BLOODLINE, TO BUILD STRONG CLONES.
YES, JABBERING PHYSICIAN... THAT WILL BE ENOUGH.
XECR NIST...TAKE YOUR MEN TO OSSUS. OUR REBEL SPY INFORMED US THE PRIMITIVE SHAMANS WHO LIVE THERE ARE DESCENDED FROM JEDI.
IT WILL BE DONE, MAJESTY. WE WILL LEAVE AT ONCE TO CAPTURE THESE WORTHY SPECIMENS.
AND WHAT OF THE DESCENDANTS OF LORD VADER, SIRE?
OUR PROBE DROIDS AND SPIES ARE SEEKING THE LOCATION OF THE CHILDREN. THEIR BLOOD WILL YET FLOW IN MINE!
IN THE MEAN-TIME, I WILL JOURNEY TO MY PLACE OF POWER...TO STRENGTHEN MY FLESH FOR THE WORK AHEAD.
PREPARE MY FLAGSHIP.
AS HIS AGENTS FAN OUT ACROSS THE GALAXY, THE EMPEROR TAKES HIS MOST TRUSTED AIDES ABOARD HIS NEWLY COMPLETED STARSHIP ECLIPSE II.
WITHIN THE HOUR, HE WILL CROSS HYPERSPACE TO A WORLD WHOSE DARK-SIDE SECRETS ARE SAID TO RESTORE THE LIVING... AND THE DEAD!

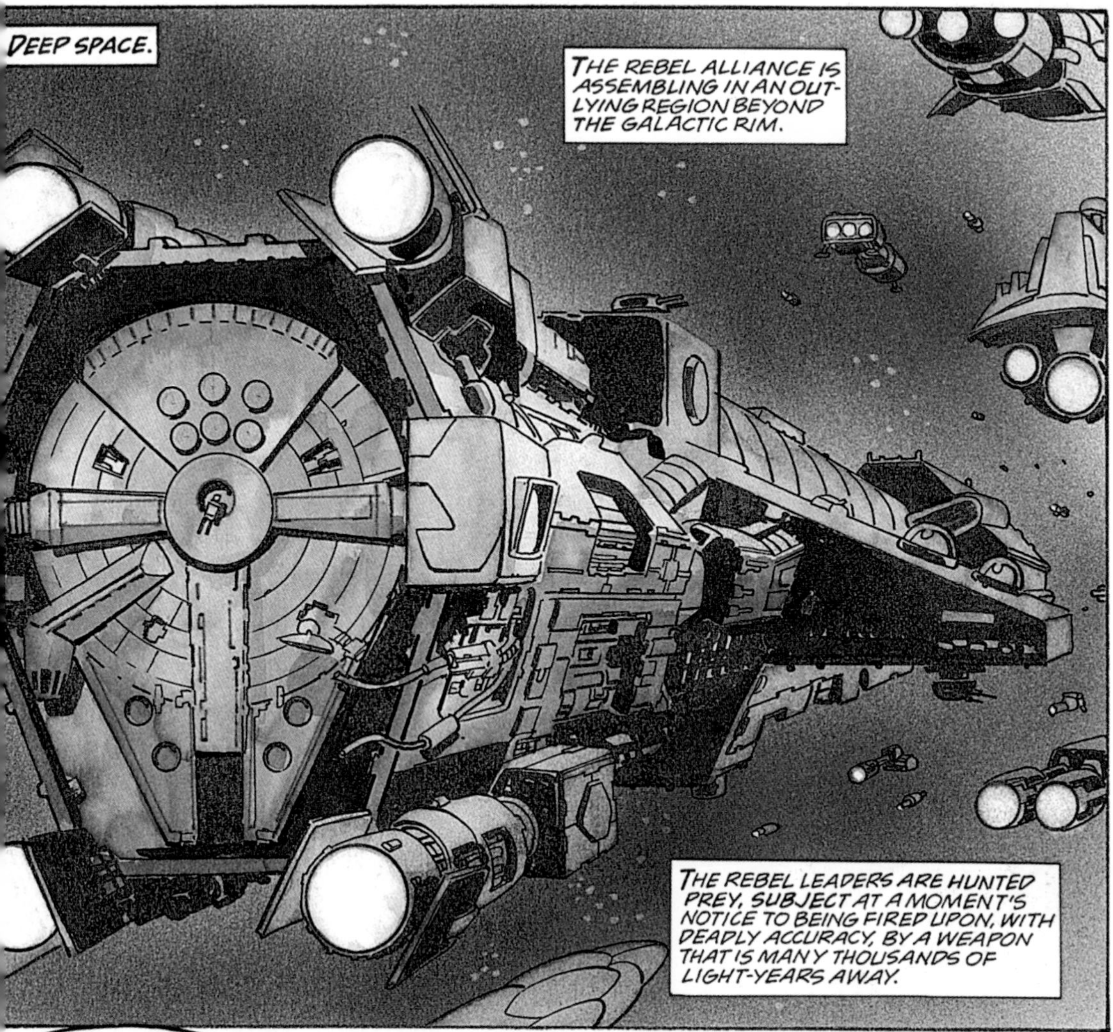
DEEP SPACE.
THE REBEL ALLIANCE IS ASSEMBLING IN AN OUT-LYING REGION BEYOND THE GALACTIC RIM.
THE REBEL LEADERS ARE HUNTED PREY, SUBJECT AT A MOMENT'S NOTICE TO BEING FIRED UPON, WITH DEADLY ACCURACY, BY A WEAPON THAT IS MANY THOUSANDS OF LIGHT-YEARS AWAY.

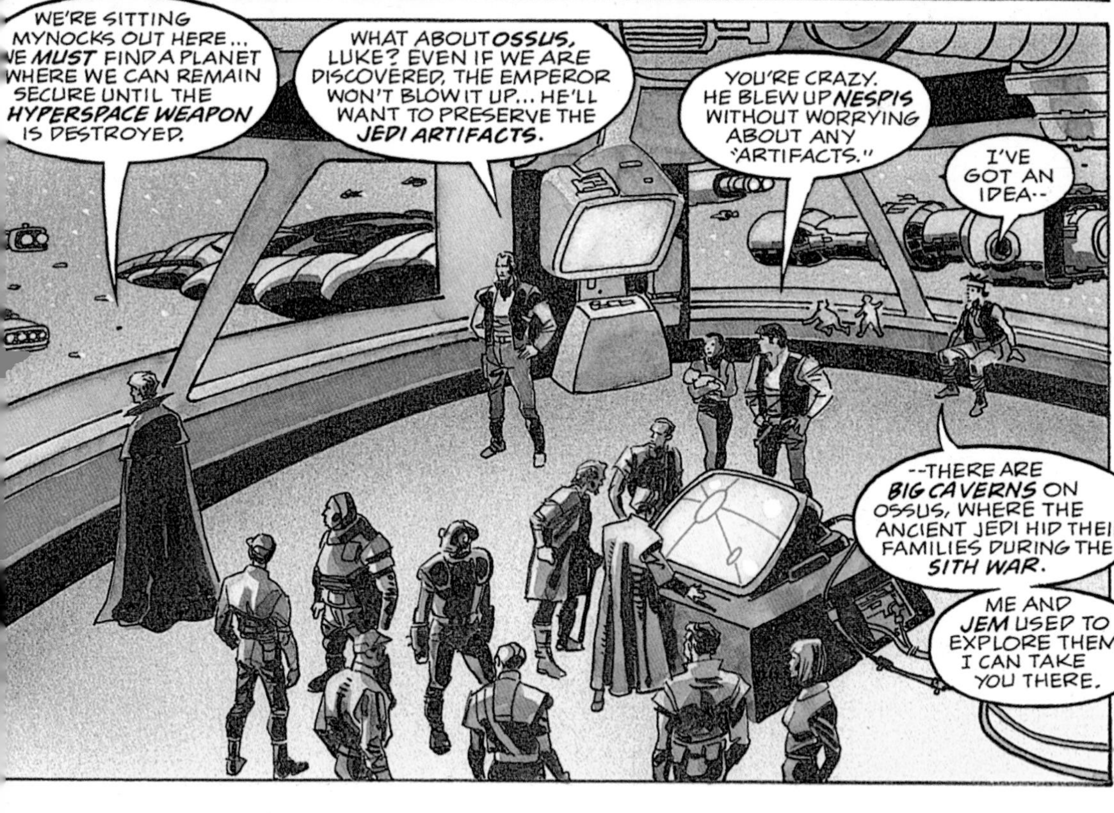
WE'RE SITTING MYNOCKS OUT HERE... WE MUST FIND A PLANET WHERE WE CAN REMAIN SECURE UNTIL THE HYPERSPACE WEAPON IS DESTROYED.
WHAT ABOUT OSSUS, LUKE? EVEN IF WE ARE DISCOVERED, THE EMPEROR WON'T BLOW IT UP... HE'LL WANT TO PRESERVE THE JEDI ARTIFACTS.
YOU'RE CRAZY. HE BLEW UP NESPIS WITHOUT WORRYING ABOUT ANY "ARTIFACTS."
I'VE GOT AN IDEA--
--THERE ARE BIG CAVERNS ON OSSUS, WHERE THE ANCIENT JEDI HID THEIR FAMILIES DURING THE SITH WAR.
ME AND JEM USED TO EXPLORE THEM... I CAN TAKE YOU THERE.

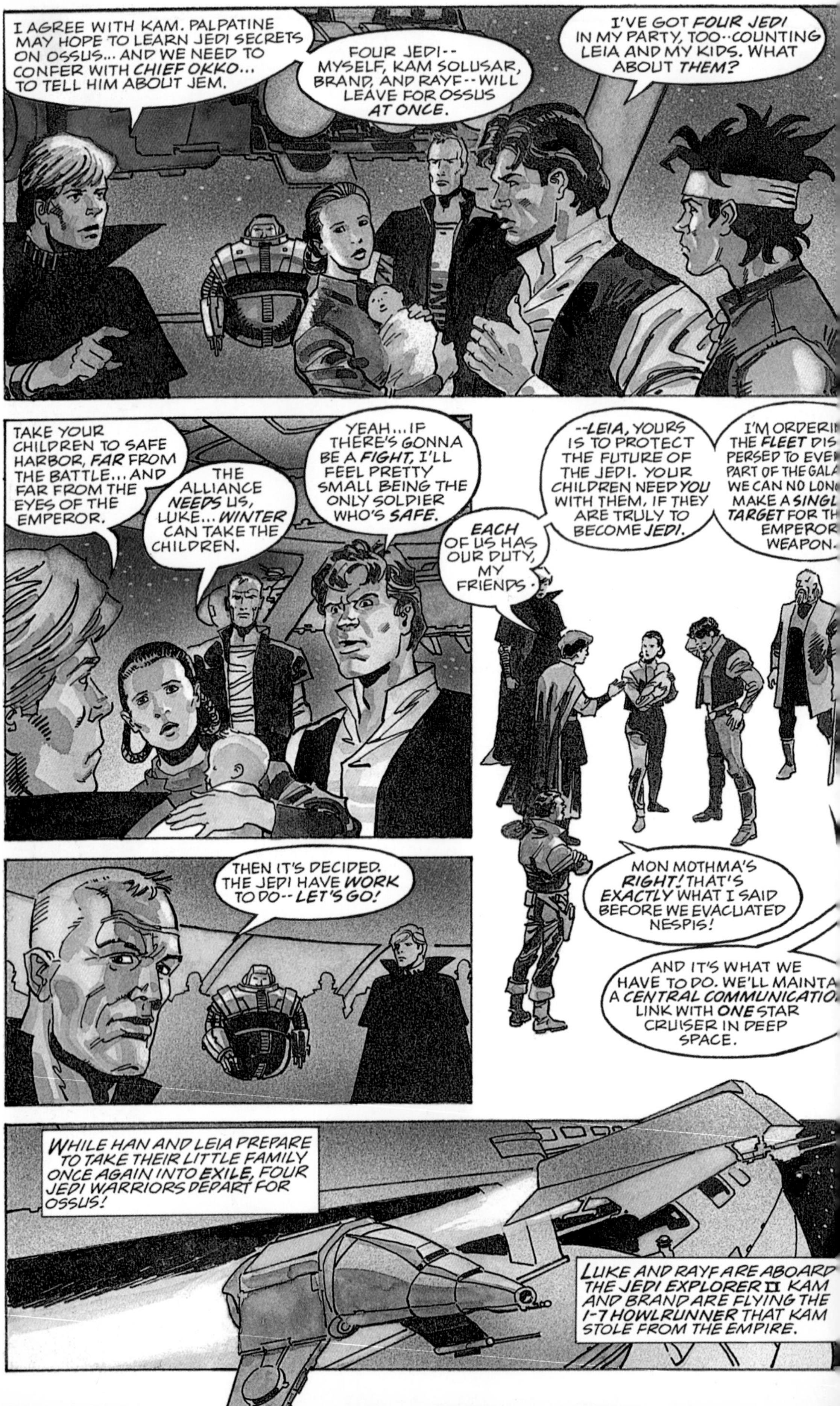
I AGREE WITH KAM. PALPATINE MAY HOPE TO LEARN JEDI SECRETS ON OSSUS... AND WE NEED TO CONFER WITH CHIEF OKKO... TO TELL HIM ABOUT JEM.
FOUR JEDI-- MYSELF, KAM SOLUSAR, BRAND, AND RAYF--WILL LEAVE FOR OSSUS AT ONCE.
I'VE GOT FOUR JEDI IN MY PARTY, TOO--COUNTING LEIA AND MY KIDS. WHAT ABOUT THEM?
TAKE YOUR CHILDREN TO SAFE HARBOR, FAR FROM THE BATTLE... AND FAR FROM THE EYES OF THE EMPEROR.
THE ALLIANCE NEEDS US, LUKE... WINTER CAN TAKE THE CHILDREN.
YEAH... IF THERE'S GONNA BE A FIGHT, I'LL FEEL PRETTY SMALL BEING THE ONLY SOLDIER WHO'S SAFE.
EACH OF US HAS OUR DUTY, MY FRIENDS--
--LEIA, YOURS IS TO PROTECT THE FUTURE OF THE JEDI. YOUR CHILDREN NEED YOU WITH THEM, IF THEY ARE TRULY TO BECOME JEDI.
I'M ORDERI THE FLEET DIS PERSED TO EVE PART OF THE GALA WE CAN NO LON MAKE A SINGL TARGET FOR TH EMPEROR WEAPON.
MON MOTHMA'S RIGHT! THAT'S EXACTLY WHAT I SAID BEFORE WE EVACUATED NESPIS!
AND IT'S WHAT WE HAVE TO DO. WE'LL MAINTA A CENTRAL COMMUNICATIO LINK WITH ONE STAR CRUISER IN DEEP SPACE.
THEN IT'S DECIDED. THE JEDI HAVE WORK TO DO--LET'S GO!
WHILE HAN AND LEIA PREPARE TO TAKE THEIR LITTLE FAMILY ONCE AGAIN INTO EXILE, FOUR JEDI WARRIORS DEPART FOR OSSUS!
LUKE AND RAYF ARE ABOARD THE JEDI EXPLORER II. KAM AND BRAND ARE FLYING THE I-7 HOWLRUNNER THAT KAM STOLE FROM THE EMPIRE.

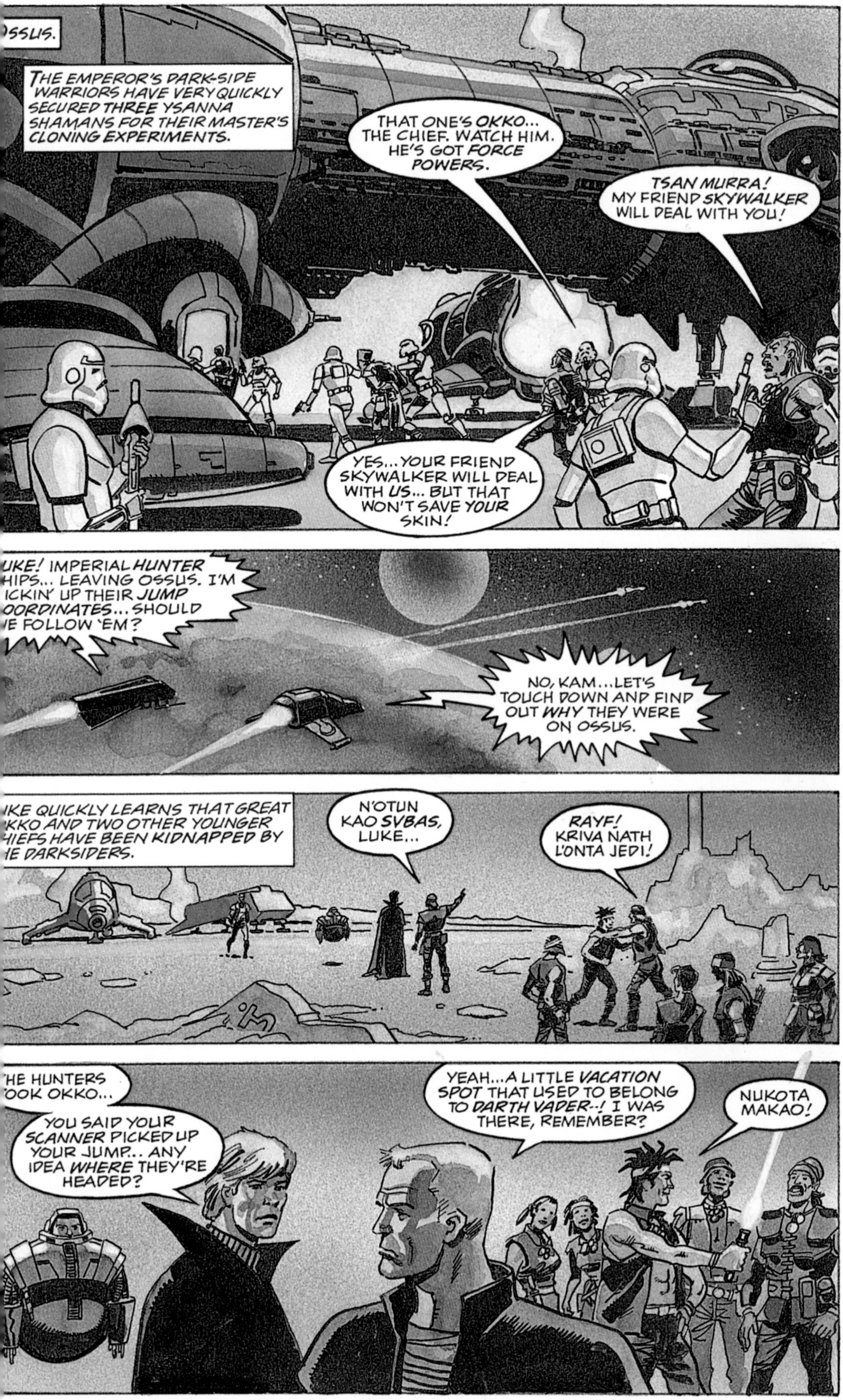

OSSUS.
THE EMPEROR'S DARK-SIDE WARRIORS HAVE VERY QUICKLY SECURED THREE YSANNA SHAMANS FOR THEIR MASTER'S CLONING EXPERIMENTS.
THAT ONE'S OKKO... THE CHIEF. WATCH HIM. HE'S GOT FORCE POWERS.
TSAN MURRA! MY FRIEND SKYWALKER WILL DEAL WITH YOU!
YES... YOUR FRIEND SKYWALKER WILL DEAL WITH US... BUT THAT WON'T SAVE YOUR SKIN!
UKE! IMPERIAL HUNTER HIPS... LEAVING OSSUS. I'M ICKIN' UP THEIR JUMP OORDINATES... SHOULD E FOLLOW 'EM?
NO, KAM... LET'S TOUCH DOWN AND FIND OUT WHY THEY WERE ON OSSUS.
UKE QUICKLY LEARNS THAT GREAT KKO AND TWO OTHER YOUNGER HIEFS HAVE BEEN KIDNAPPED BY HE DARKSIDERS.
N'OTUN KAO SVBAS, LUKE...
RAYF! KRIVA NATH L'ONTA JEDI!
HE HUNTERS OOK OKKO...
YOU SAID YOUR SCANNER PICKED UP YOUR JUMP... ANY IDEA WHERE THEY'RE HEADED?
YEAH... A LITTLE VACATION SPOT THAT USED TO BELONG TO DARTH VADER--! I WAS THERE, REMEMBER?
NUKOTA MAKAO!

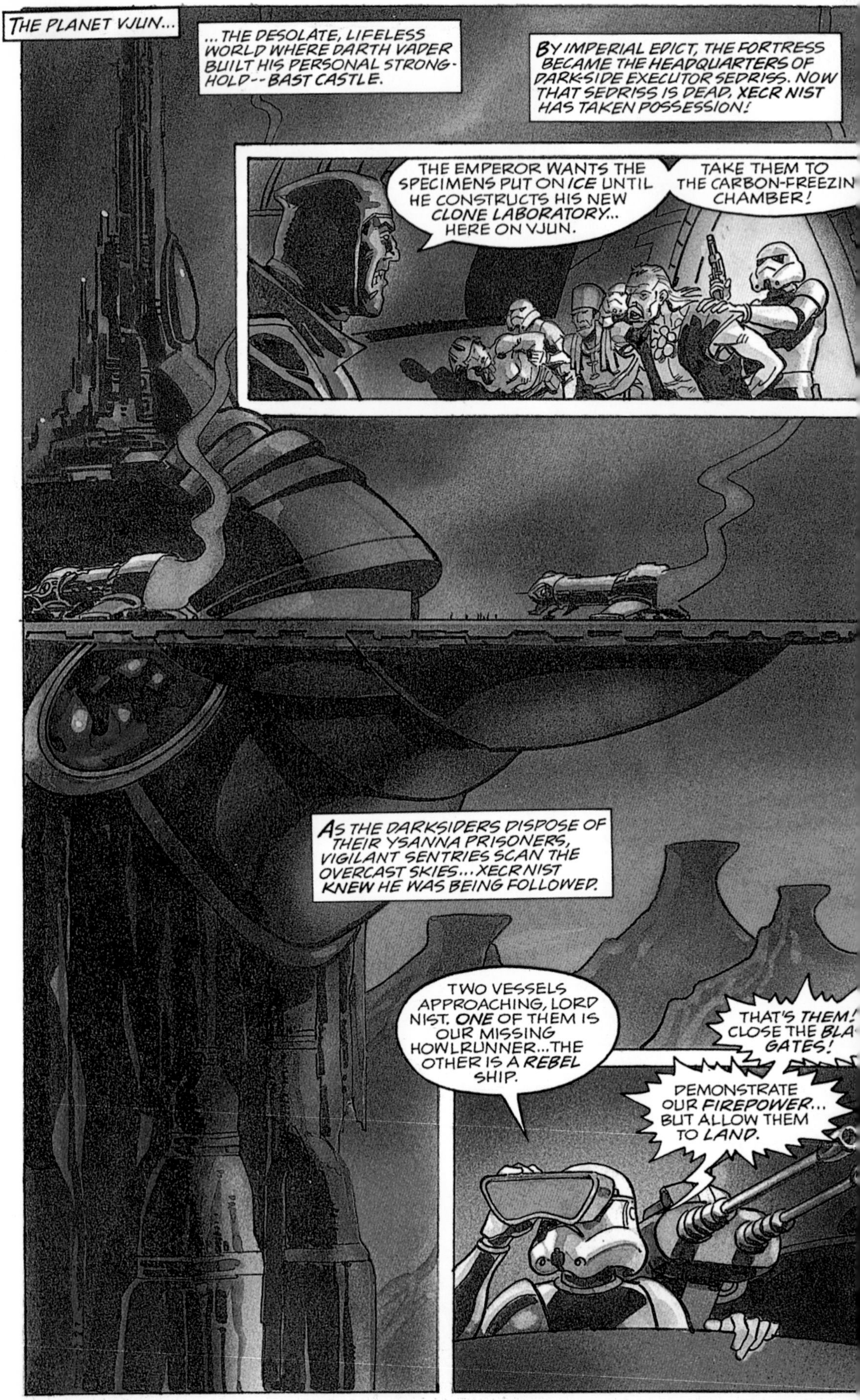
THE PLANET VJUN...
...THE DESOLATE, LIFELESS WORLD WHERE DARTH VADER BUILT HIS PERSONAL STRONG-HOLD--BAST CASTLE.
BY IMPERIAL EDICT, THE FORTRESS BECAME THE HEADQUARTERS OF DARK-SIDE EXECUTOR SEDRISS. NOW THAT SEDRISS IS DEAD, XECR NIST HAS TAKEN POSSESSION!
THE EMPEROR WANTS THE SPECIMENS PUT ON ICE UNTIL HE CONSTRUCTS HIS NEW CLONE LABORATORY... HERE ON VJUN.
TAKE THEM TO THE CARBON-FREEZIN CHAMBER!
AS THE DARKSIDERS DISPOSE OF THEIR YSANNA PRISONERS, VIGILANT SENTRIES SCAN THE OVERCAST SKIES... XECR NIST KNEW HE WAS BEING FOLLOWED.
TWO VESSELS APPROACHING, LORD NIST. ONE OF THEM IS OUR MISSING HOWLRUNNER...THE OTHER IS A REBEL SHIP.
THAT'S THEM! CLOSE THE BLA GATES!
DEMONSTRATE OUR FIREPOWER... BUT ALLOW THEM TO LAND.

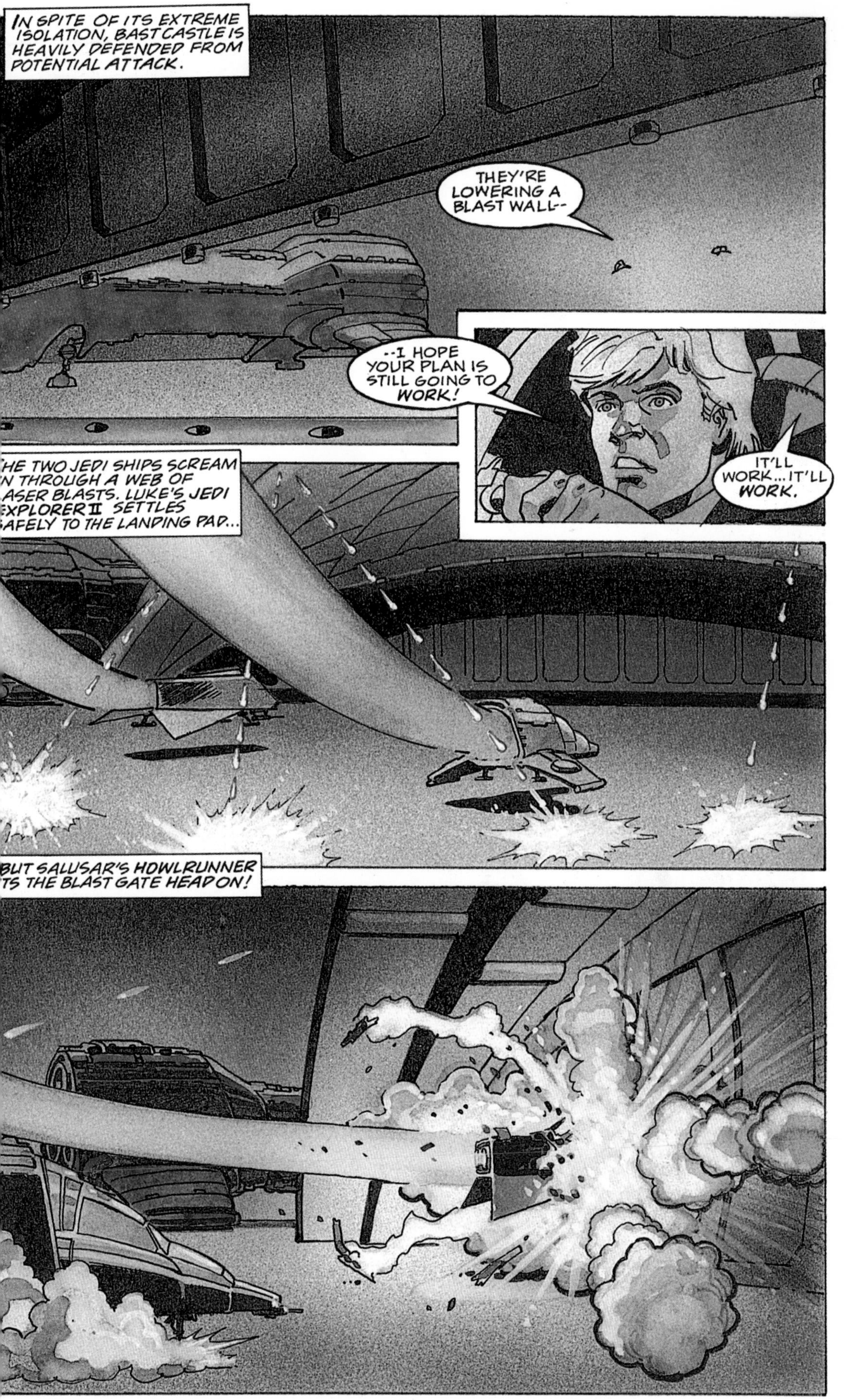
IN SPITE OF ITS EXTREME ISOLATION, BAST CASTLE IS HEAVILY DEFENDED FROM POTENTIAL ATTACK.
THEY'RE LOWERING A BLAST WALL--
--I HOPE YOUR PLAN IS STILL GOING TO WORK!
IT'LL WORK... IT'LL WORK.
THE TWO JEDI SHIPS SCREAM N THROUGH A WEB OF ASER BLASTS. LUKE'S JEDI EXPLORER II SETTLES AFELY TO THE LANDING PAD...
BUT SALUSAR'S HOWLRUNNER TS THE BLAST GATE HEAD ON!

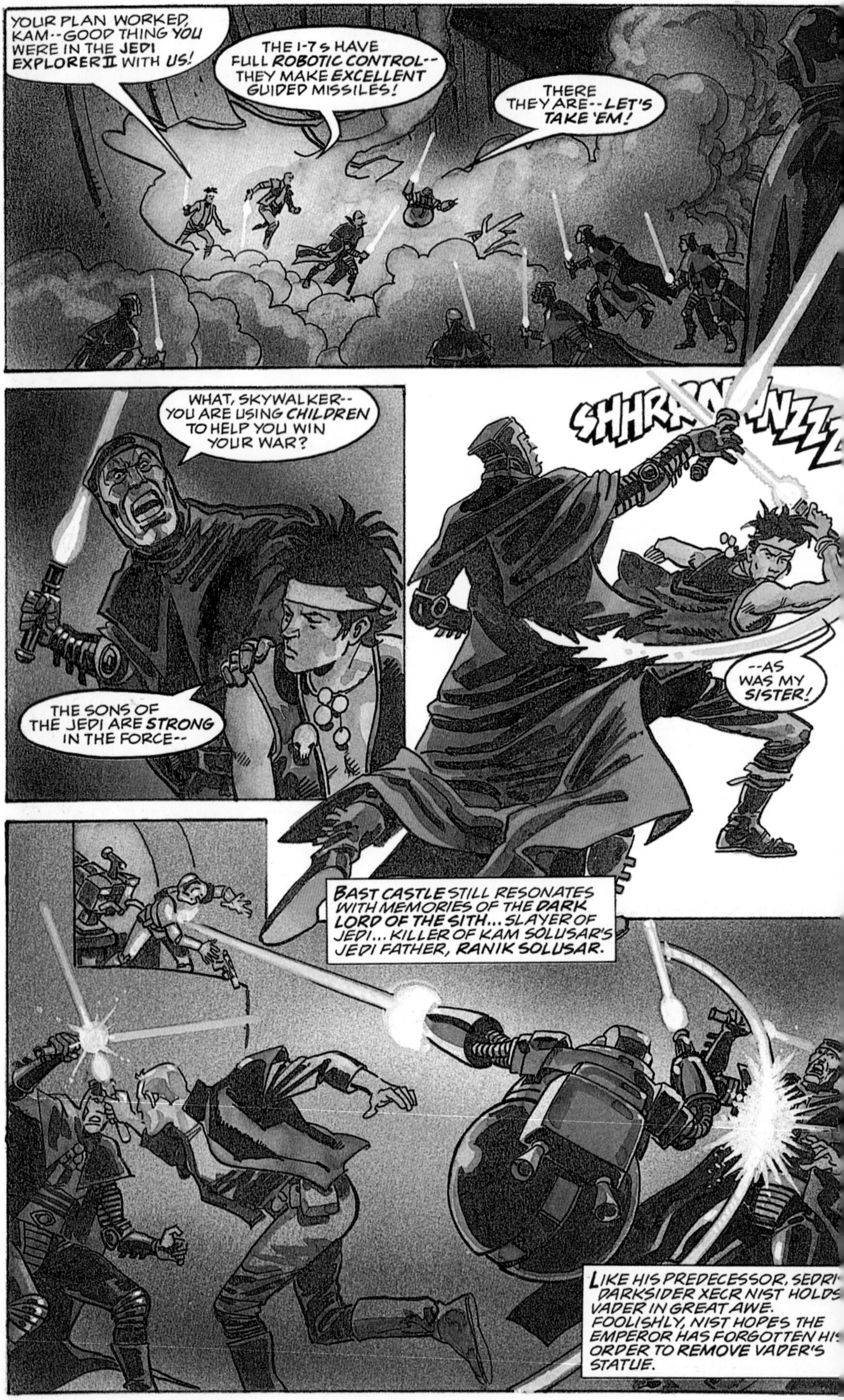

YOUR PLAN WORKED, KAM--GOOD THING YOU WERE IN THE JEDI EXPLORER II WITH US!
THE I-7s HAVE FULL ROBOTIC CONTROL--THEY MAKE EXCELLENT GUIDED MISSILES!
THERE THEY ARE--LET'S TAKE 'EM!
WHAT, SKYWALKER--YOU ARE USING CHILDREN TO HELP YOU WIN YOUR WAR?
THE SONS OF THE JEDI ARE STRONG IN THE FORCE--
--AS WAS MY SISTER!
BAST CASTLE STILL RESONATES WITH MEMORIES OF THE DARK LORD OF THE SITH... SLAYER OF JEDI... KILLER OF KAM SOLUSAR'S JEDI FATHER, RANIK SOLUSAR.
LIKE HIS PREDECESSOR, SEDRI DARKSIDER XECR NIST HOLDS VADER IN GREAT AWE. FOOLISHLY, NIST HOPES THE EMPEROR HAS FORGOTTEN HIS ORDER TO REMOVE VADER'S STATUE.

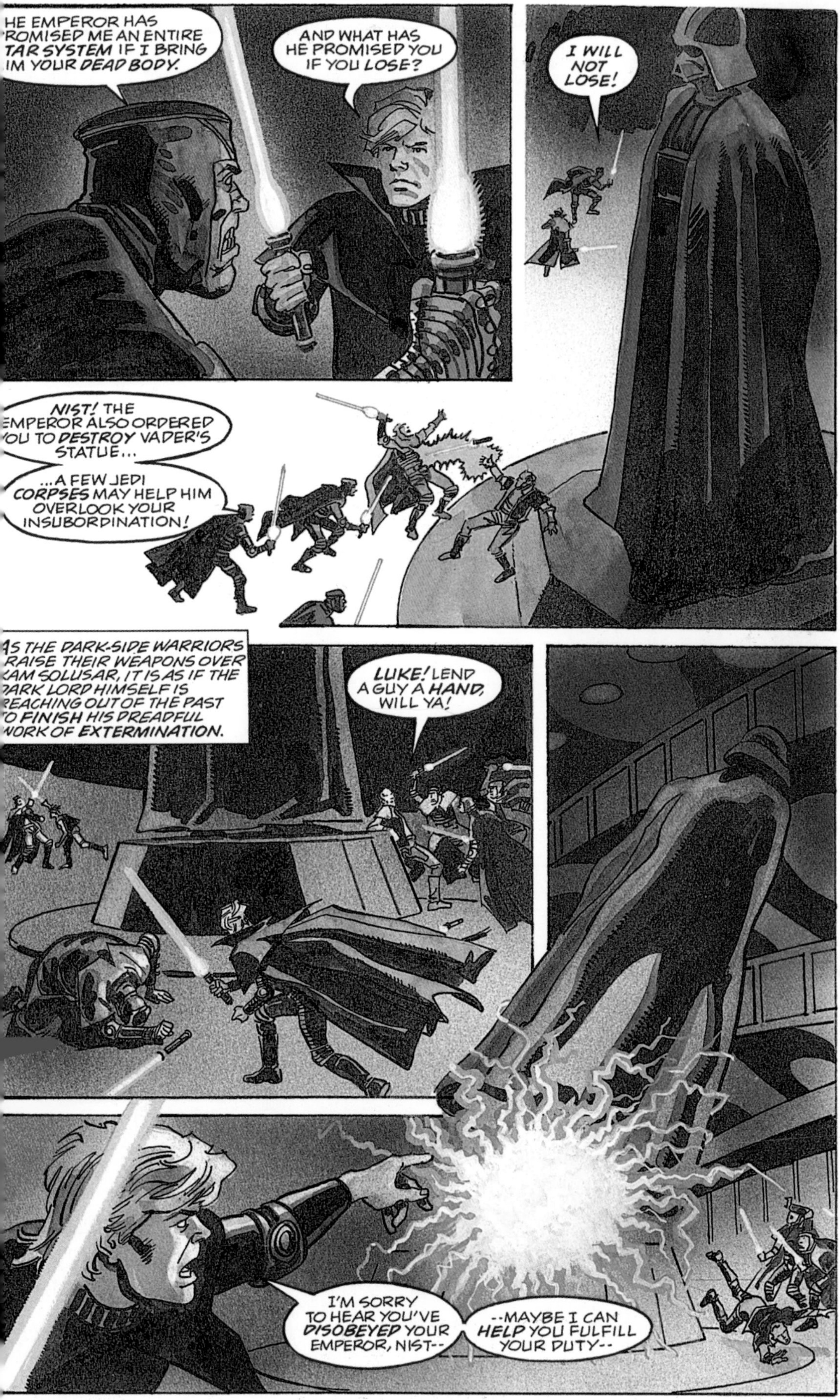
HE EMPEROR HAS ROMISED ME AN ENTIRE TAR SYSTEM IF I BRING IM YOUR DEAD BODY.
AND WHAT HAS HE PROMISED YOU IF YOU LOSE?
I WILL NOT LOSE!
NIST! THE EMPEROR ALSO ORDERED YOU TO DESTROY VADER'S STATUE...
...A FEW JEDI CORPSES MAY HELP HIM OVERLOOK YOUR INSUBORDINATION!
AS THE DARK-SIDE WARRIORS RAISE THEIR WEAPONS OVER KAM SOLUSAR, IT IS AS IF THE DARK LORD HIMSELF IS REACHING OUT OF THE PAST TO FINISH HIS DREADFUL WORK OF EXTERMINATION.
LUKE! LEND A GUY A HAND, WILL YA!
I'M SORRY TO HEAR YOU'VE DISOBEYED YOUR EMPEROR, NIST--
--MAYBE I CAN HELP YOU FULFILL YOUR DUTY--

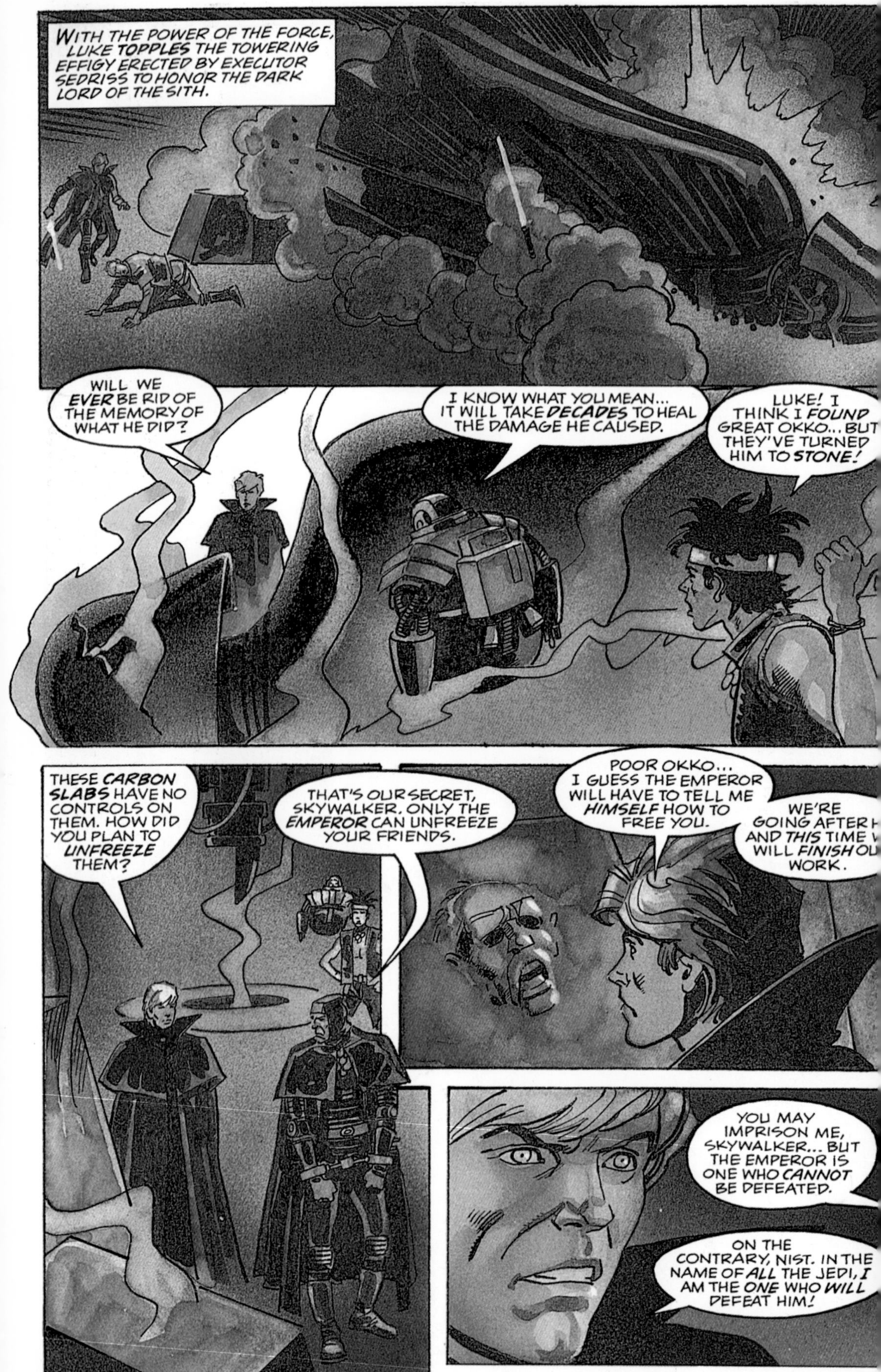
WITH THE POWER OF THE FORCE, LUKE TOPPLES THE TOWERING EFFIGY ERECTED BY EXECUTOR SEDRISS TO HONOR THE DARK LORD OF THE SITH.
WILL WE EVER BE RID OF THE MEMORY OF WHAT HE DID?
I KNOW WHAT YOU MEAN... IT WILL TAKE DECADES TO HEAL THE DAMAGE HE CAUSED.
LUKE! I THINK I FOUND GREAT OKKO... BUT THEY'VE TURNED HIM TO STONE!
THESE CARBON SLABS HAVE NO CONTROLS ON THEM. HOW DID YOU PLAN TO UNFREEZE THEM?
THAT'S OUR SECRET, SKYWALKER. ONLY THE EMPEROR CAN UNFREEZE YOUR FRIENDS.
POOR OKKO... I GUESS THE EMPEROR WILL HAVE TO TELL ME HIMSELF HOW TO FREE YOU.
YOU MAY IMPRISON ME, SKYWALKER... BUT THE EMPEROR IS ONE WHO CANNOT BE DEFEATED.
ON THE CONTRARY, NIST. IN THE NAME OF ALL THE JEDI, I AM THE ONE WHO WILL DEFEAT HIM!

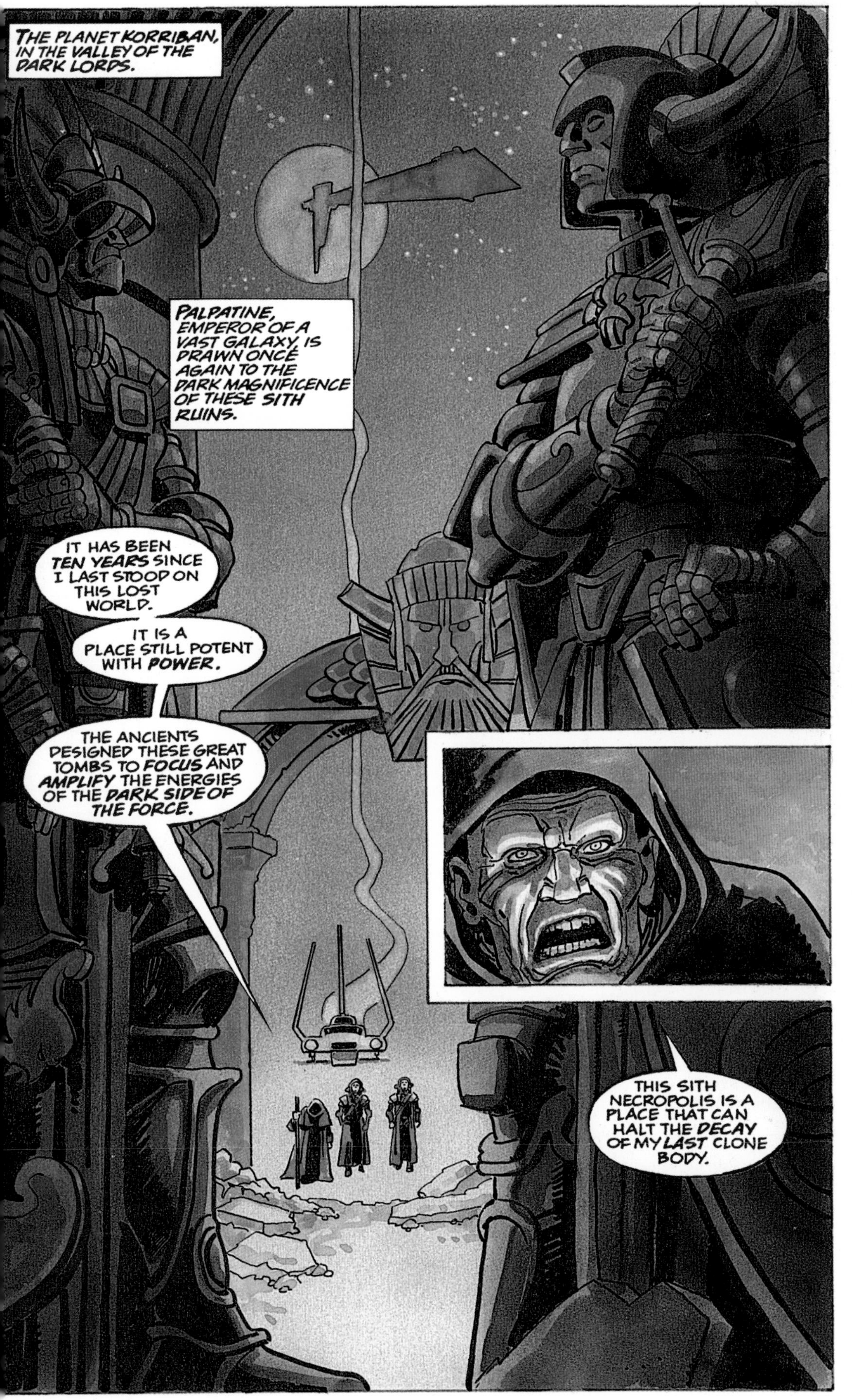
THE PLANET KORRIBAN, IN THE VALLEY OF THE DARK LORDS.
PALPATINE, EMPEROR OF A VAST GALAXY, IS DRAWN ONCE AGAIN TO THE DARK MAGNIFICENCE OF THESE SITH RUINS.
IT HAS BEEN TEN YEARS SINCE I LAST STOOD ON THIS LOST WORLD.
IT IS A PLACE STILL POTENT WITH POWER.
THE ANCIENTS DESIGNED THESE GREAT TOMBS TO FOCUS AND AMPLIFY THE ENERGIES OF THE DARK SIDE OF THE FORCE.
THIS SITH NECROPOLIS IS A PLACE THAT CAN HALT THE DECAY OF MY LAST CLONE BODY.

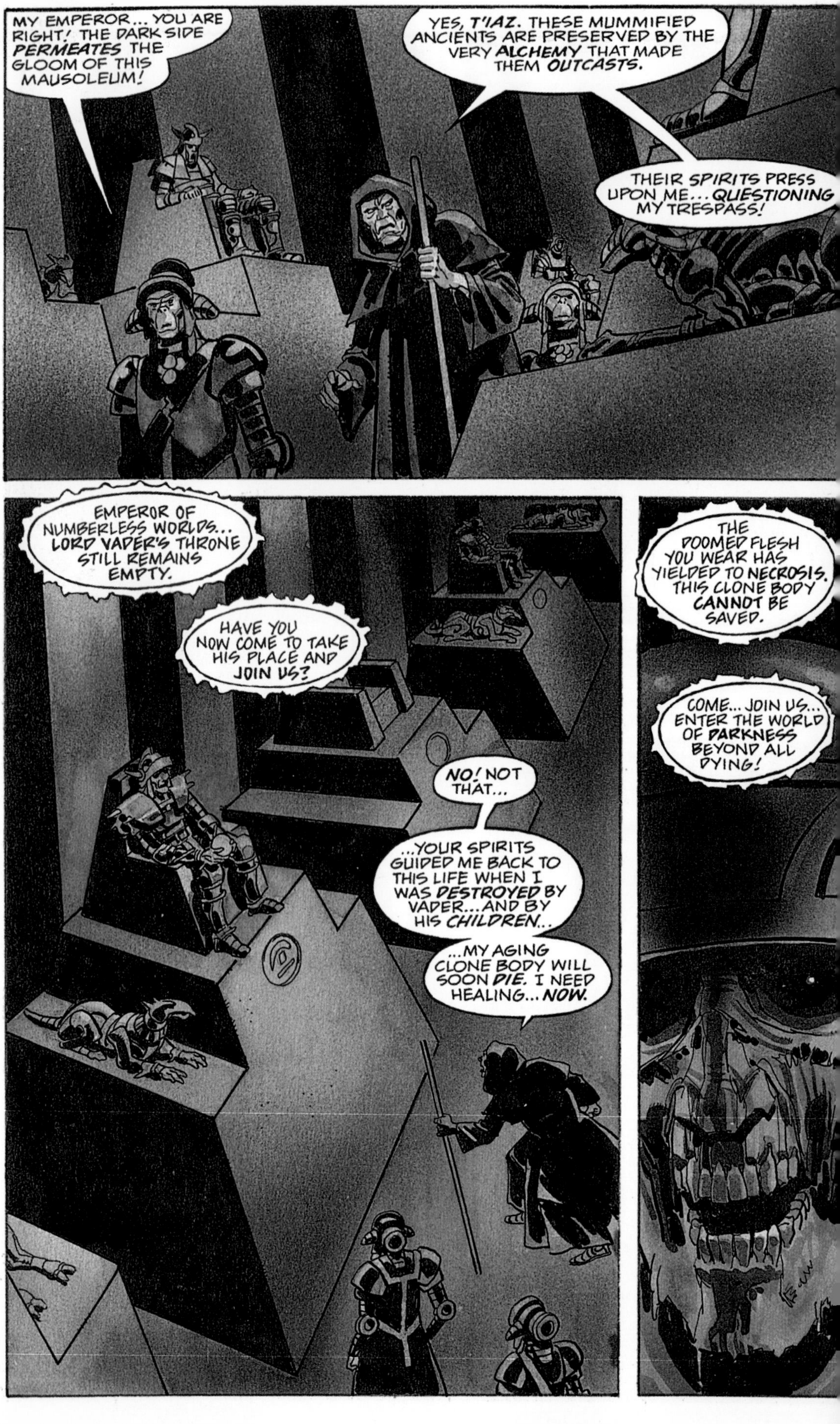
MY EMPEROR... YOU ARE RIGHT! THE DARK SIDE PERMEATES THE GLOOM OF THIS MAUSOLEUM!
YES, T'IAZ. THESE MUMMIFIED ANCIENTS ARE PRESERVED BY THE VERY ALCHEMY THAT MADE THEM OUTCASTS.
THEIR SPIRITS PRESS UPON ME... QUESTIONING MY TRESPASS!
EMPEROR OF NUMBERLESS WORLDS... LORD VADER'S THRONE STILL REMAINS EMPTY.
HAVE YOU NOW COME TO TAKE HIS PLACE AND JOIN US?
NO! NOT THAT...
...YOUR SPIRITS GUIDED ME BACK TO THIS LIFE WHEN I WAS DESTROYED BY VADER... AND BY HIS CHILDREN...
...MY AGING CLONE BODY WILL SOON DIE. I NEED HEALING... NOW.
THE DOOMED FLESH YOU WEAR HAS YIELDED TO NECROSIS. THIS CLONE BODY CANNOT BE SAVED.
COME... JOIN US... ENTER THE WORLD OF DARKNESS BEYOND ALL DYING!

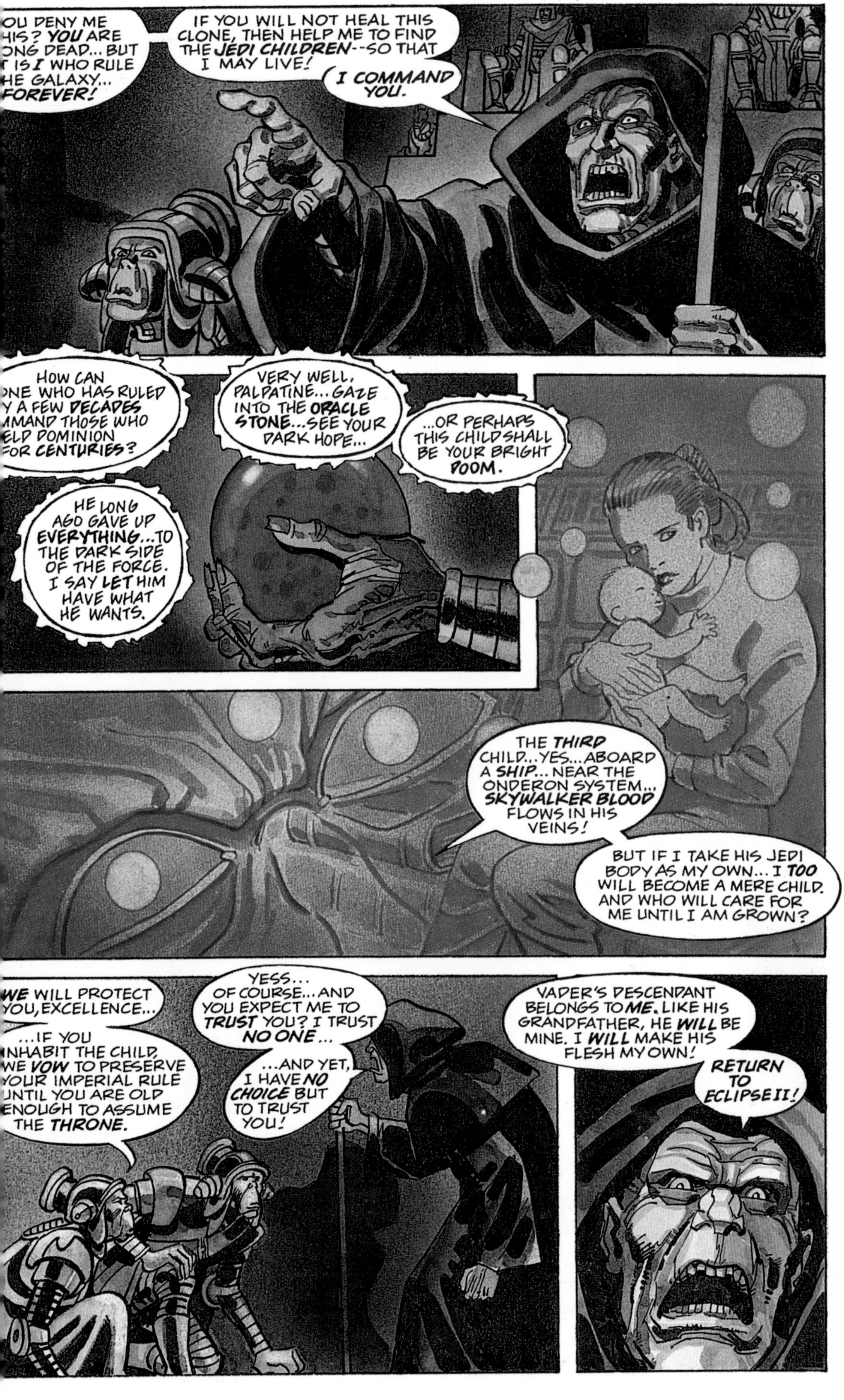
OU DENY ME HIS? YOU ARE ONG DEAD... BUT T IS I WHO RULE HE GALAXY... FOREVER!
IF YOU WILL NOT HEAL THIS CLONE, THEN HELP ME TO FIND THE JEDI CHILDREN--SO THAT I MAY LIVE!
I COMMAND YOU.
HOW CAN ONE WHO HAS RULED Y A FEW DECADES MMAND THOSE WHO ELD DOMINION FOR CENTURIES?
VERY WELL, PALPATINE... GAZE INTO THE ORACLE STONE...SEE YOUR DARK HOPE...
...OR PERHAPS THIS CHILD SHALL BE YOUR BRIGHT DOOM.
HE LONG AGO GAVE UP EVERYTHING...TO THE DARK SIDE OF THE FORCE. I SAY LET HIM HAVE WHAT HE WANTS.
THE THIRD CHILD...YES...ABOARD A SHIP...NEAR THE ONDERON SYSTEM... SKYWALKER BLOOD FLOWS IN HIS VEINS!
BUT IF I TAKE HIS JEDI BODY AS MY OWN... I TOO WILL BECOME A MERE CHILD. AND WHO WILL CARE FOR ME UNTIL I AM GROWN?
WE WILL PROTECT YOU, EXCELLENCE...
...IF YOU NHABIT THE CHILD, WE VOW TO PRESERVE YOUR IMPERIAL RULE UNTIL YOU ARE OLD ENOUGH TO ASSUME THE THRONE.
YESS... OF COURSE... AND YOU EXPECT ME TO TRUST YOU? I TRUST NO ONE...
...AND YET, I HAVE NO CHOICE BUT TO TRUST YOU!
VADER'S DESCENDANT BELONGS TO ME. LIKE HIS GRANDFATHER, HE WILL BE MINE. I WILL MAKE HIS FLESH MY OWN!
RETURN TO ECLIPSE II!

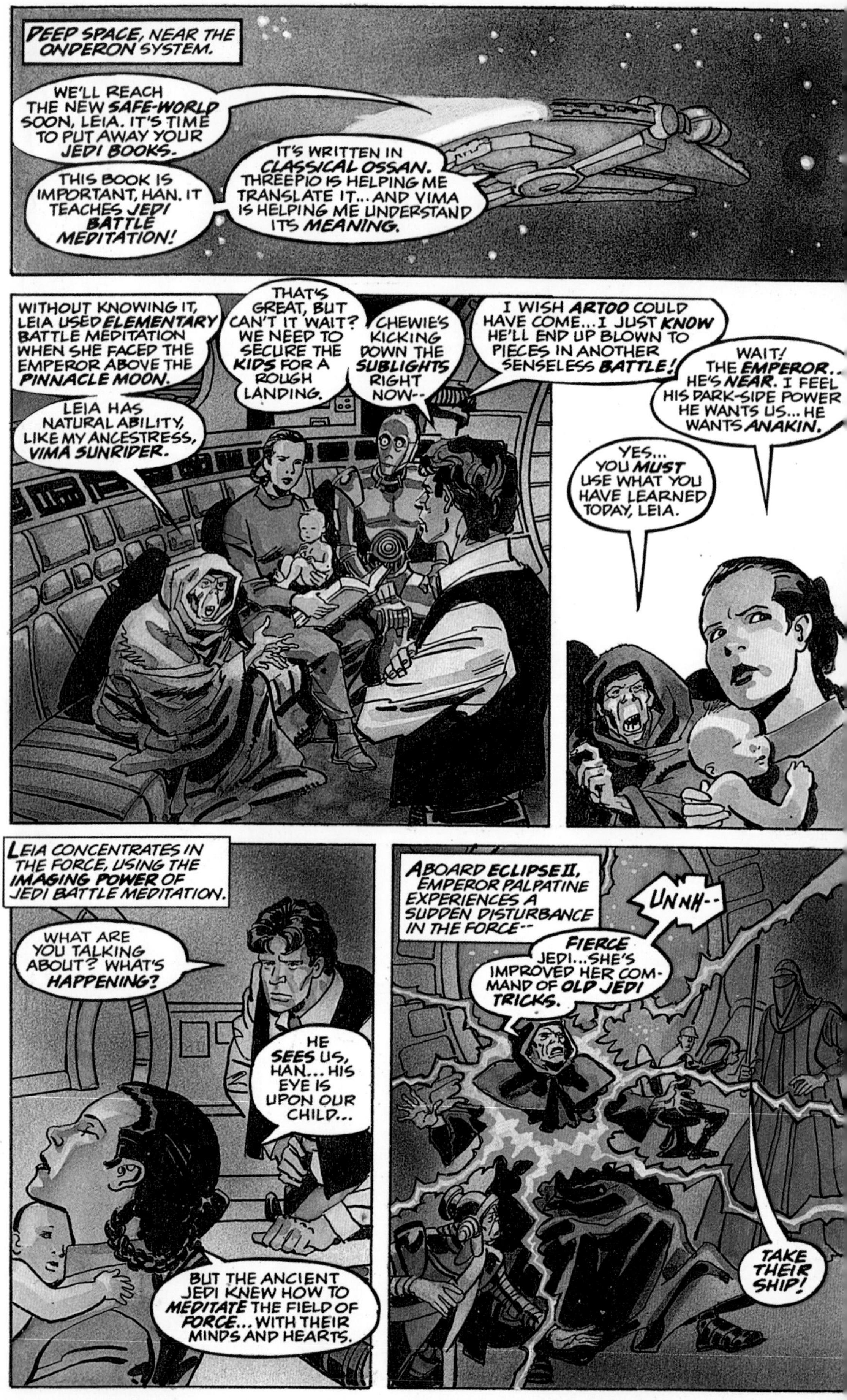
DEEP SPACE, NEAR THE ONDERON SYSTEM.
WE'LL REACH THE NEW SAFE-WORLD SOON, LEIA. IT'S TIME TO PUT AWAY YOUR JEDI BOOKS.
THIS BOOK IS IMPORTANT, HAN. IT TEACHES JEDI BATTLE MEDITATION!
IT'S WRITTEN IN CLASSICAL OSSAN. THREEPIO IS HELPING ME TRANSLATE IT... AND VIMA IS HELPING ME UNDERSTAND ITS MEANING.
WITHOUT KNOWING IT, LEIA USED ELEMENTARY BATTLE MEDITATION WHEN SHE FACED THE EMPEROR ABOVE THE PINNACLE MOON.
LEIA HAS NATURAL ABILITY, LIKE MY ANCESTRESS, VIMA SUNRIDER.
THAT'S GREAT, BUT CAN'T IT WAIT? WE NEED TO SECURE THE KIDS FOR A ROUGH LANDING.
CHEWIE'S KICKING DOWN THE SUBLIGHTS RIGHT NOW--
I WISH ARTOO COULD HAVE COME... I JUST KNOW HE'LL END UP BLOWN TO PIECES IN ANOTHER SENSELESS BATTLE!
WAIT! THE EMPEROR.. HE'S NEAR. I FEEL HIS DARK-SIDE POWER HE WANTS US... HE WANTS ANAKIN.
YES... YOU MUST USE WHAT YOU HAVE LEARNED TODAY, LEIA.
LEIA CONCENTRATES IN THE FORCE, USING THE IMAGING POWER OF JEDI BATTLE MEDITATION.
WHAT ARE YOU TALKING ABOUT? WHAT'S HAPPENING?
HE SEES US, HAN... HIS EYE IS UPON OUR CHILD...
BUT THE ANCIENT JEDI KNEW HOW TO MEDITATE THE FIELD OF FORCE... WITH THEIR MINDS AND HEARTS.
ABOARD ECLIPSE II, EMPEROR PALPATINE EXPERIENCES A SUDDEN DISTURBANCE IN THE FORCE--
UNNH--
FIERCE JEDI... SHE'S IMPROVED HER COMMAND OF OLD JEDI TRICKS.
TAKE THEIR SHIP!

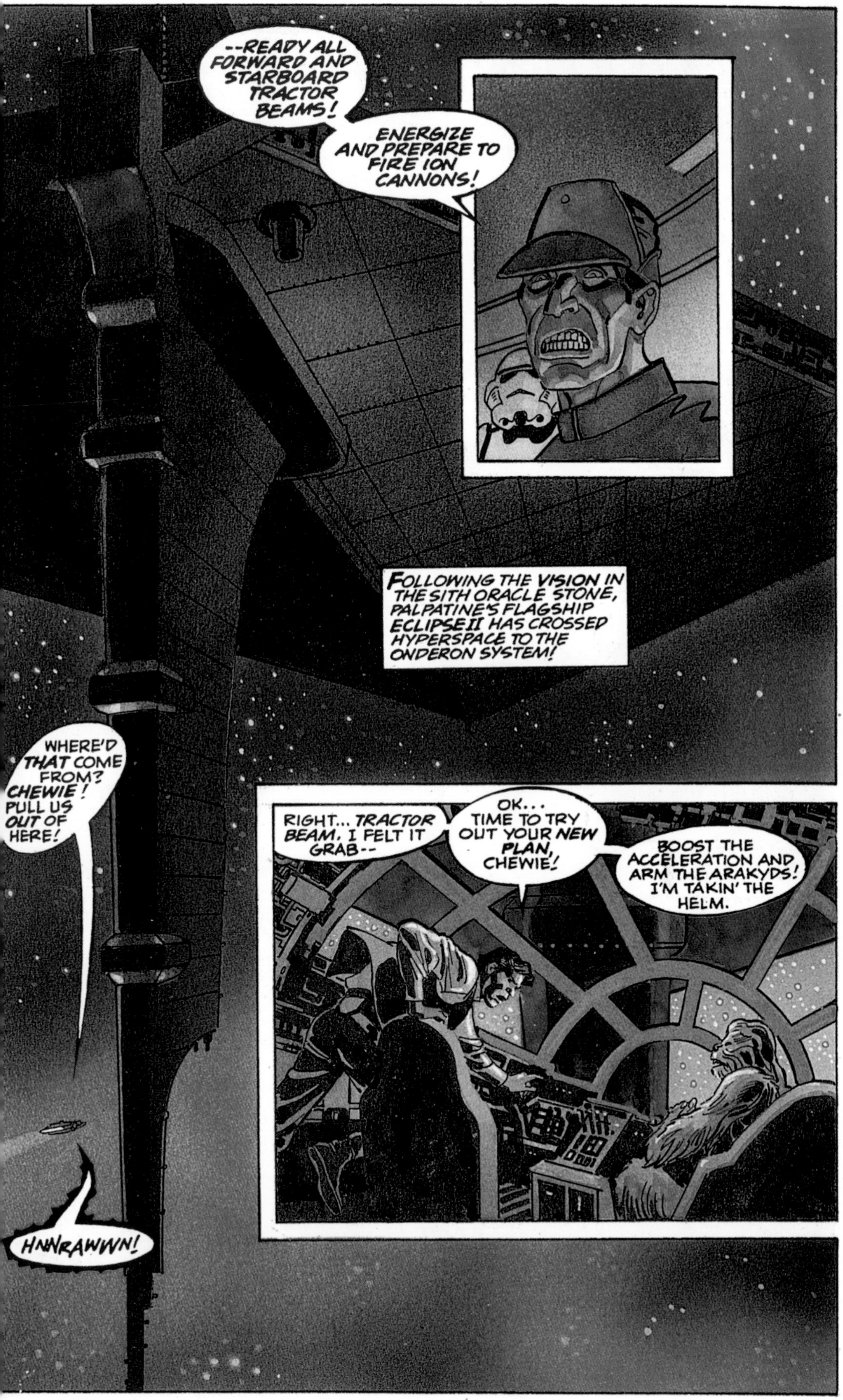
--READY ALL FORWARD AND STARBOARD TRACTOR BEAMS!
ENERGIZE AND PREPARE TO FIRE ION CANNONS!
FOLLOWING THE VISION IN THE SITH ORACLE STONE, PALPATINE'S FLAGSHIP ECLIPSE II HAS CROSSED HYPERSPACE TO THE ONDERON SYSTEM!
WHERE'D THAT COME FROM? CHEWIE! PULL US OUT OF HERE!
HNNRAWWN!
RIGHT... TRACTOR BEAM. I FELT IT GRAB--
OK... TIME TO TRY OUT YOUR NEW PLAN, CHEWIE!
BOOST THE ACCELERATION AND ARM THE ARAKYDS! I'M TAKIN' THE HELM.

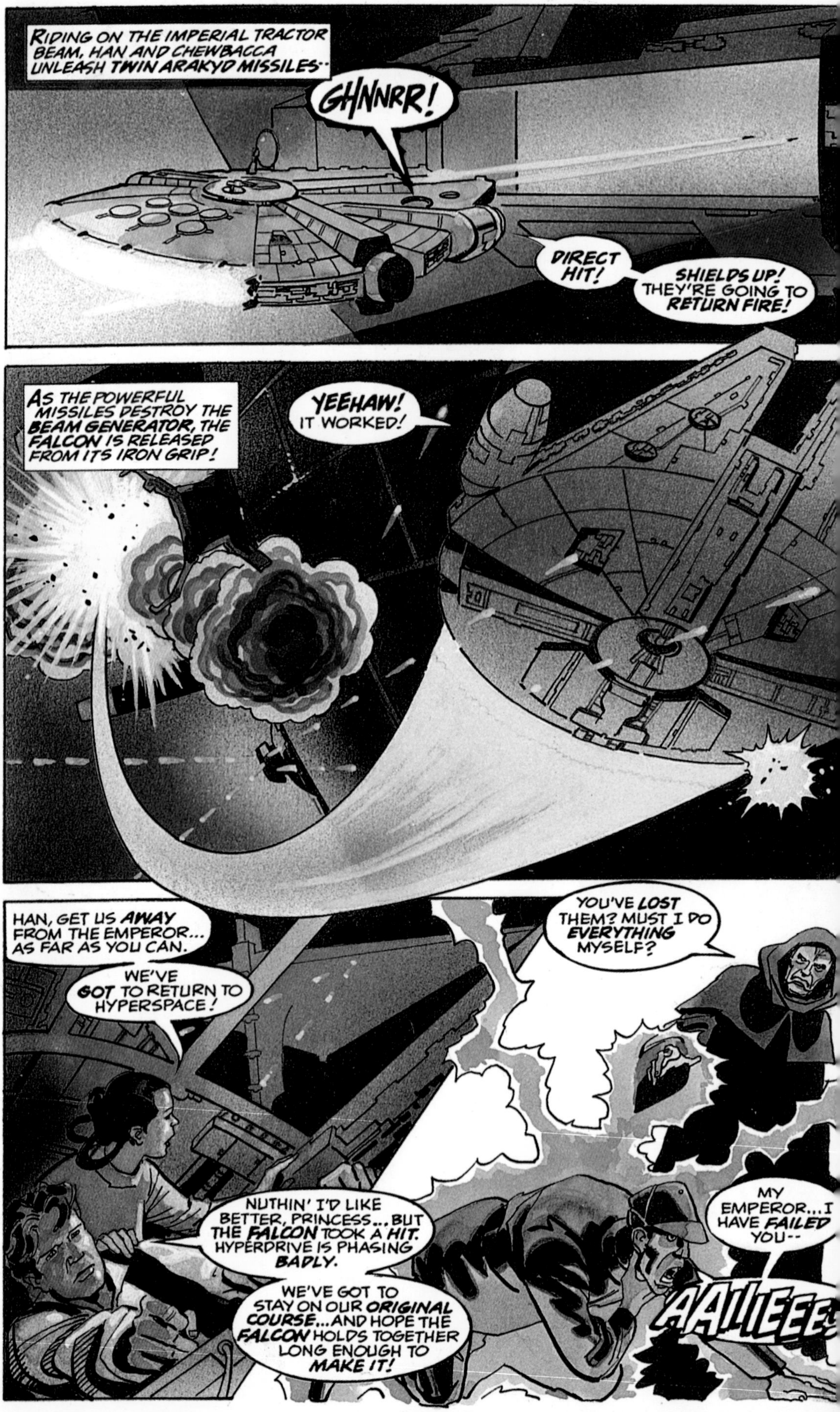
RIDING ON THE IMPERIAL TRACTOR BEAM, HAN AND CHEWBACCA UNLEASH TWIN ARAKYD MISSILES..
GHNNRR!
DIRECT HIT!
SHIELDS UP! THEY'RE GOING TO RETURN FIRE!
AS THE POWERFUL MISSILES DESTROY THE BEAM GENERATOR, THE FALCON IS RELEASED FROM ITS IRON GRIP!
YEEHAW! IT WORKED!
HAN, GET US AWAY FROM THE EMPEROR... AS FAR AS YOU CAN.
WE'VE GOT TO RETURN TO HYPERSPACE!
YOU'VE LOST THEM? MUST I DO EVERYTHING MYSELF?
NUTHIN' I'D LIKE BETTER, PRINCESS... BUT THE FALCON TOOK A HIT. HYPERDRIVE IS PHASING BADLY.
WE'VE GOT TO STAY ON OUR ORIGINAL COURSE...AND HOPE THE FALCON HOLDS TOGETHER LONG ENOUGH TO MAKE IT!
MY EMPEROR...I HAVE FAILED YOU--
AAIIEEE

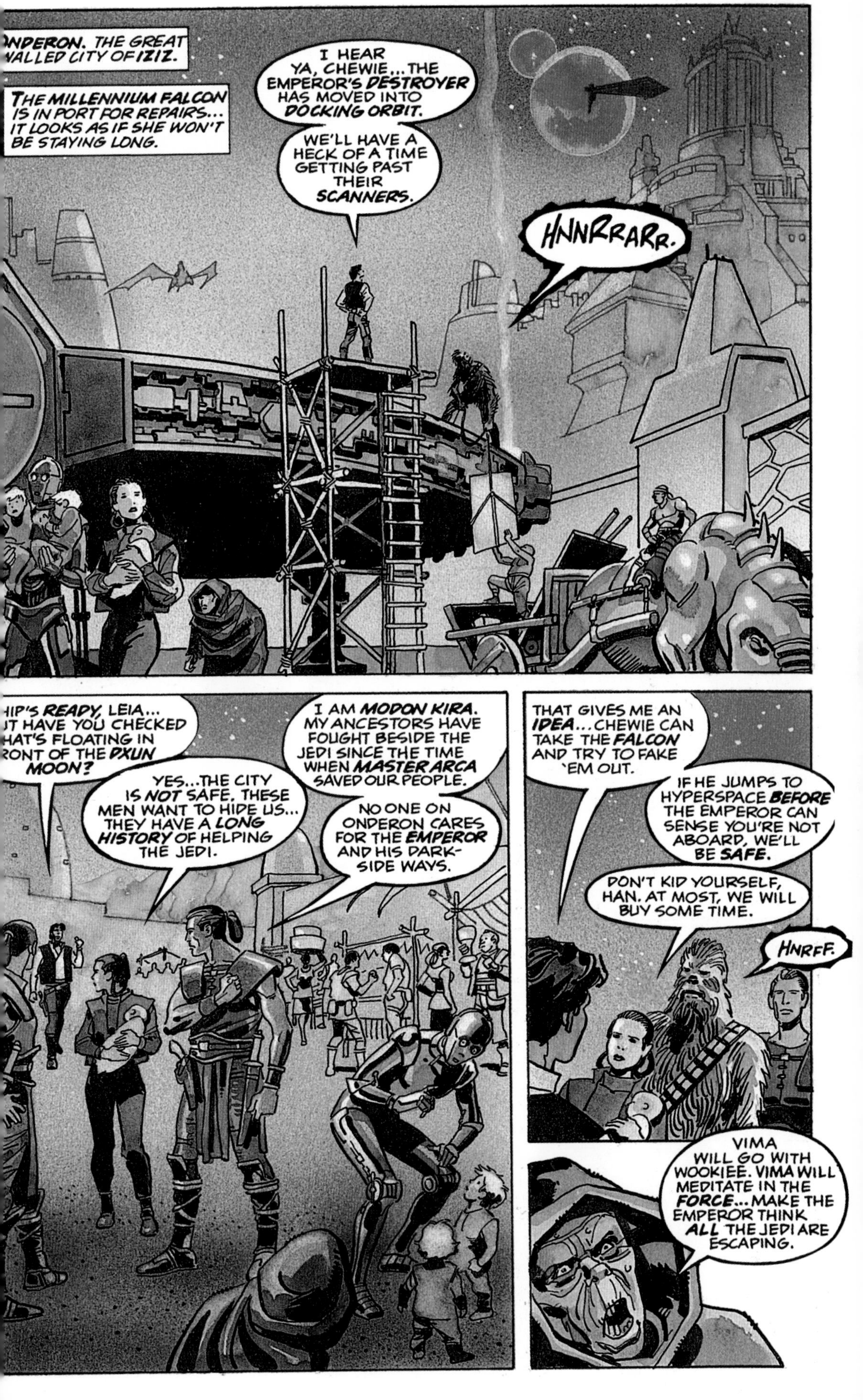
ONDERON. THE GREAT WALLED CITY OF IZIZ.
THE MILLENNIUM FALCON IS IN PORT FOR REPAIRS... IT LOOKS AS IF SHE WON'T BE STAYING LONG.
I HEAR YA, CHEWIE... THE EMPEROR'S DESTROYER HAS MOVED INTO DOCKING ORBIT.
WE'LL HAVE A HECK OF A TIME GETTING PAST THEIR SCANNERS.
HNNRRARR.
HIP'S READY, LEIA... UT HAVE YOU CHECKED HAT'S FLOATING IN RONT OF THE DXUN MOON?
YES... THE CITY IS NOT SAFE. THESE MEN WANT TO HIDE US... THEY HAVE A LONG HISTORY OF HELPING THE JEDI.
I AM MODON KIRA. MY ANCESTORS HAVE FOUGHT BESIDE THE JEDI SINCE THE TIME WHEN MASTER ARCA SAVED OUR PEOPLE.
NO ONE ON ONDERON CARES FOR THE EMPEROR AND HIS DARK-SIDE WAYS.
THAT GIVES ME AN IDEA... CHEWIE CAN TAKE THE FALCON AND TRY TO FAKE 'EM OUT.
IF HE JUMPS TO HYPERSPACE BEFORE THE EMPEROR CAN SENSE YOU'RE NOT ABOARD, WE'LL BE SAFE.
DON'T KID YOURSELF, HAN. AT MOST, WE WILL BUY SOME TIME.
HNRFF.
VIMA WILL GO WITH WOOKIEE. VIMA WILL MEDITATE IN THE FORCE... MAKE THE EMPEROR THINK ALL THE JEDI ARE ESCAPING.

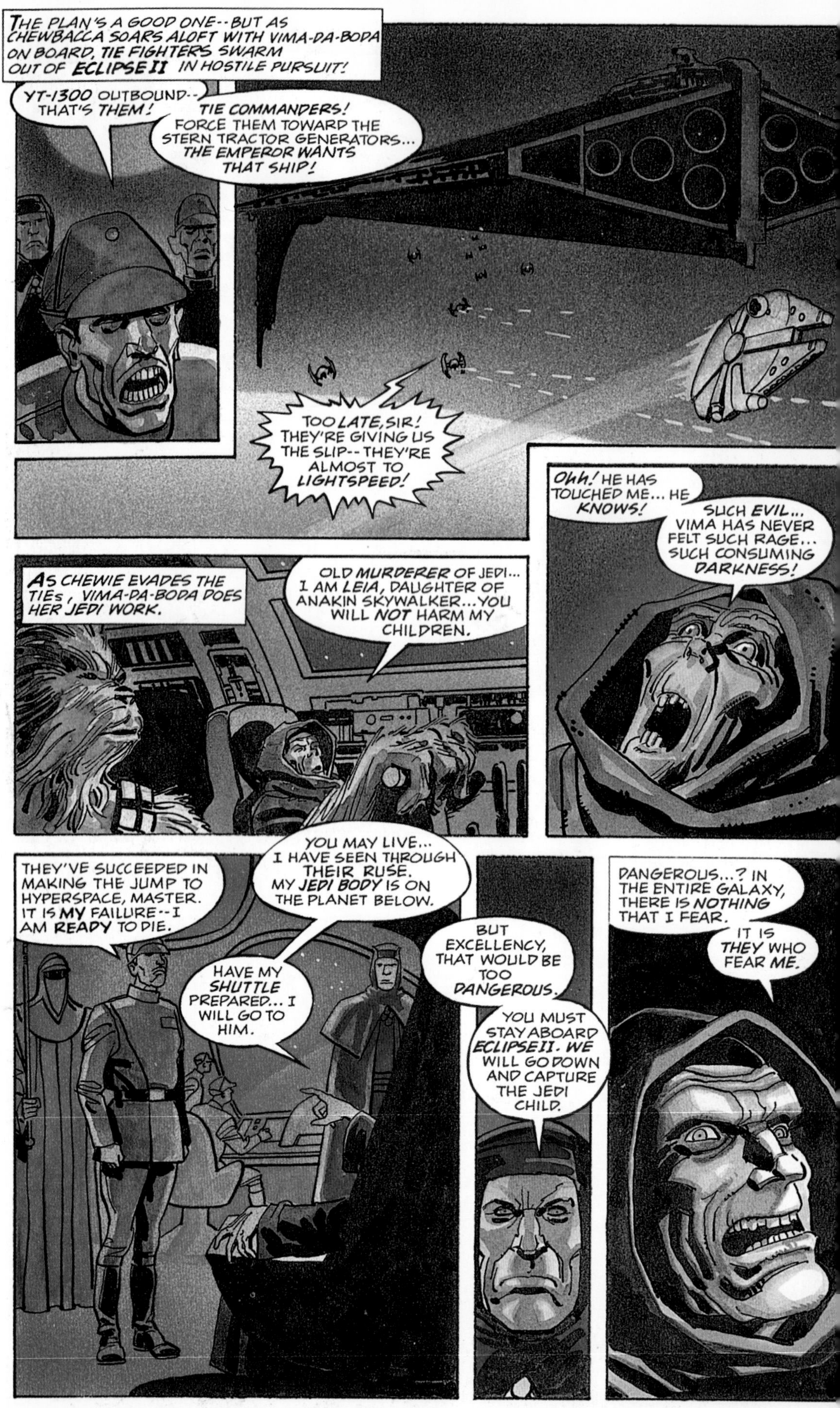
THE PLAN'S A GOOD ONE--BUT AS CHEWBACCA SOARS ALOFT WITH VIMA-DA-BODA ON BOARD, TIE FIGHTERS SWARM OUT OF ECLIPSE II IN HOSTILE PURSUIT!
YT-1300 OUTBOUND--THAT'S THEM!
TIE COMMANDERS! FORCE THEM TOWARD THE STERN TRACTOR GENERATORS... THE EMPEROR WANTS THAT SHIP!
TOO LATE, SIR! THEY'RE GIVING US THE SLIP--THEY'RE ALMOST TO LIGHTSPEED!
AS CHEWIE EVADES THE TIEs, VIMA-DA-BODA DOES HER JEDI WORK.
OLD MURDERER OF JEDI... I AM LEIA, DAUGHTER OF ANAKIN SKYWALKER... YOU WILL NOT HARM MY CHILDREN.
Ohh! HE HAS TOUCHED ME... HE KNOWS!
SUCH EVIL... VIMA HAS NEVER FELT SUCH RAGE... SUCH CONSUMING DARKNESS!
THEY'VE SUCCEEDED IN MAKING THE JUMP TO HYPERSPACE, MASTER. IT IS MY FAILURE--I AM READY TO DIE.
YOU MAY LIVE... I HAVE SEEN THROUGH THEIR RUSE. MY JEDI BODY IS ON THE PLANET BELOW.
HAVE MY SHUTTLE PREPARED... I WILL GO TO HIM.
BUT EXCELLENCY, THAT WOULD BE TOO DANGEROUS.
YOU MUST STAY ABOARD ECLIPSE II. WE WILL GO DOWN AND CAPTURE THE JEDI CHILD.
DANGEROUS...? IN THE ENTIRE GALAXY, THERE IS NOTHING THAT I FEAR.
IT IS THEY WHO FEAR ME.

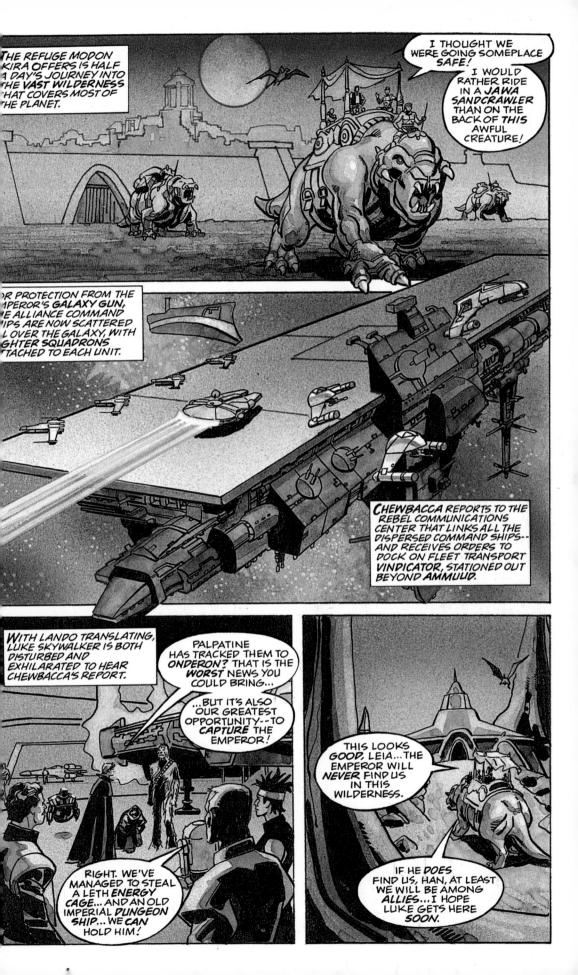

THE REFUGE MODON KIRA OFFERS IS HALF A DAY'S JOURNEY INTO THE VAST WILDERNESS THAT COVERS MOST OF THE PLANET.

I THOUGHT WE WERE GOING SOMEPLACE SAFE!

I WOULD RATHER RIDE IN A JAWA SANDCRAWLER THAN ON THE BACK OF THIS AWFUL CREATURE!

FOR PROTECTION FROM THE EMPEROR'S GALAXY GUN, THE ALLIANCE COMMAND SHIPS ARE NOW SCATTERED ALL OVER THE GALAXY, WITH FIGHTER SQUADRONS ATTACHED TO EACH UNIT.

CHEWBACCA REPORTS TO THE REBEL COMMUNICATIONS CENTER THAT LINKS ALL THE DISPERSED COMMAND SHIPS-- AND RECEIVES ORDERS TO DOCK ON FLEET TRANSPORT VINDICATOR, STATIONED OUT BEYOND AMMUUD.

WITH LANDO TRANSLATING, LUKE SKYWALKER IS BOTH DISTURBED AND EXHILARATED TO HEAR CHEWBACCA'S REPORT.

PALPATINE HAS TRACKED THEM TO ONDERON? THAT IS THE WORST NEWS YOU COULD BRING...

...BUT IT'S ALSO OUR GREATEST OPPORTUNITY--TO CAPTURE THE EMPEROR!

RIGHT. WE'VE MANAGED TO STEAL A LETH ENERGY CAGE... AND AN OLD IMPERIAL DUNGEON SHIP...WE CAN HOLD HIM!

THIS LOOKS GOOD, LEIA...THE EMPEROR WILL NEVER FIND US IN THIS WILDERNESS.

IF HE DOES FIND US, HAN, AT LEAST WE WILL BE AMONG ALLIES...I HOPE LUKE GETS HERE SOON.

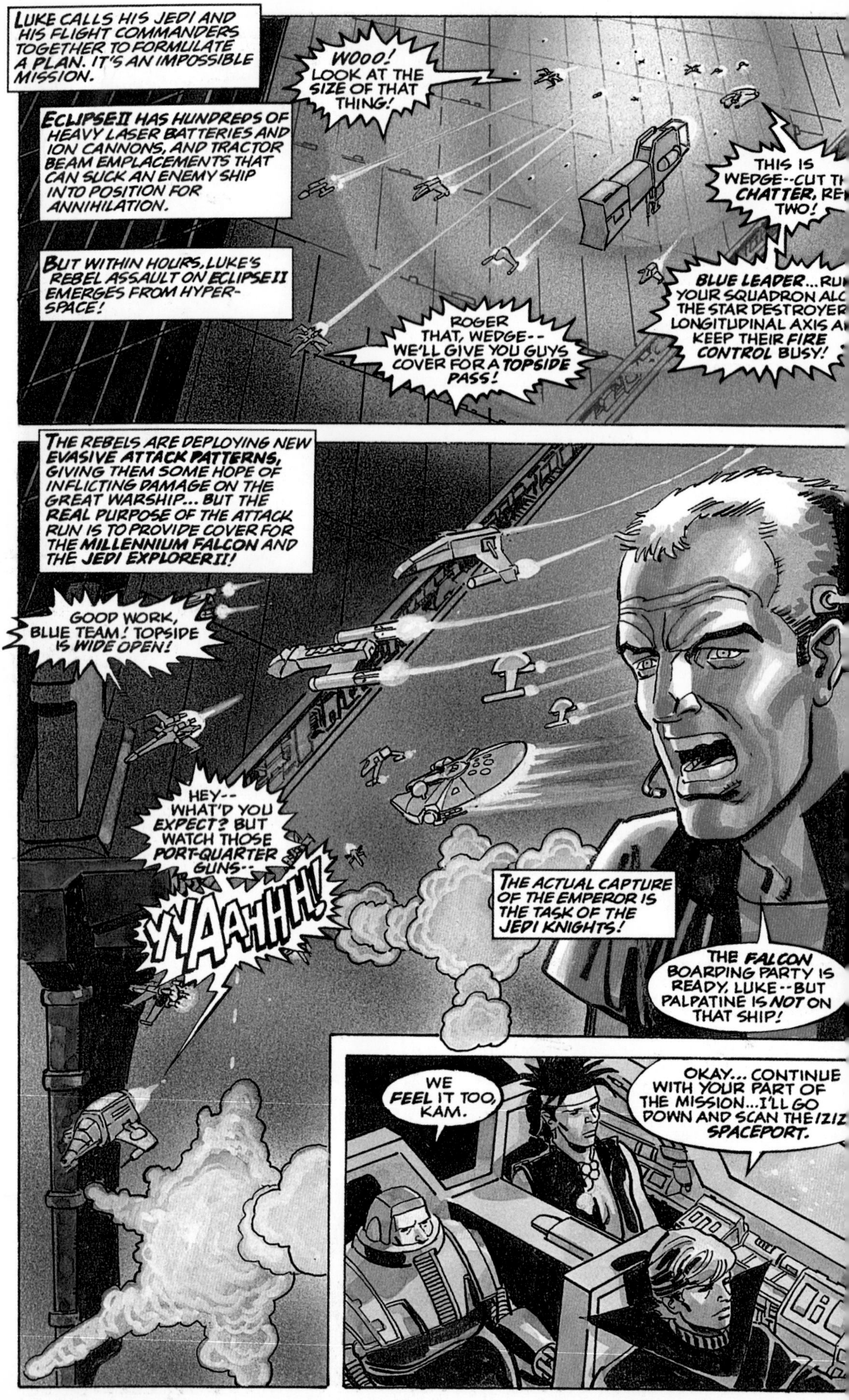

LUKE CALLS HIS JEDI AND HIS FLIGHT COMMANDERS TOGETHER TO FORMULATE A PLAN. IT'S AN IMPOSSIBLE MISSION.
ECLIPSE II HAS HUNDREDS OF HEAVY LASER BATTERIES AND ION CANNONS, AND TRACTOR BEAM EMPLACEMENTS THAT CAN SUCK AN ENEMY SHIP INTO POSITION FOR ANNIHILATION.
BUT WITHIN HOURS, LUKE'S REBEL ASSAULT ON ECLIPSE II EMERGES FROM HYPER-SPACE!
WOOO! LOOK AT THE SIZE OF THAT THING!
THIS IS WEDGE--CUT THE CHATTER, RE TWO!
BLUE LEADER... RU YOUR SQUADRON AL THE STAR DESTROYER LONGITUDINAL AXIS A KEEP THEIR FIRE CONTROL BUSY!
ROGER THAT, WEDGE-- WE'LL GIVE YOU GUYS COVER FOR A TOPSIDE PASS!
THE REBELS ARE DEPLOYING NEW EVASIVE ATTACK PATTERNS, GIVING THEM SOME HOPE OF INFLICTING DAMAGE ON THE GREAT WARSHIP... BUT THE REAL PURPOSE OF THE ATTACK RUN IS TO PROVIDE COVER FOR THE MILLENNIUM FALCON AND THE JEDI EXPLORER II!
GOOD WORK, BLUE TEAM! TOPSIDE IS WIDE OPEN!
HEY-- WHAT'D YOU EXPECT? BUT WATCH THOSE PORT-QUARTER GUNS--
YYAAHHH!
THE ACTUAL CAPTURE OF THE EMPEROR IS THE TASK OF THE JEDI KNIGHTS!
THE FALCON BOARDING PARTY IS READY, LUKE--BUT PALPATINE IS NOT ON THAT SHIP!
WE FEEL IT TOO, KAM.
OKAY... CONTINUE WITH YOUR PART OF THE MISSION...I'LL GO DOWN AND SCAN THE IZIZ SPACEPORT.

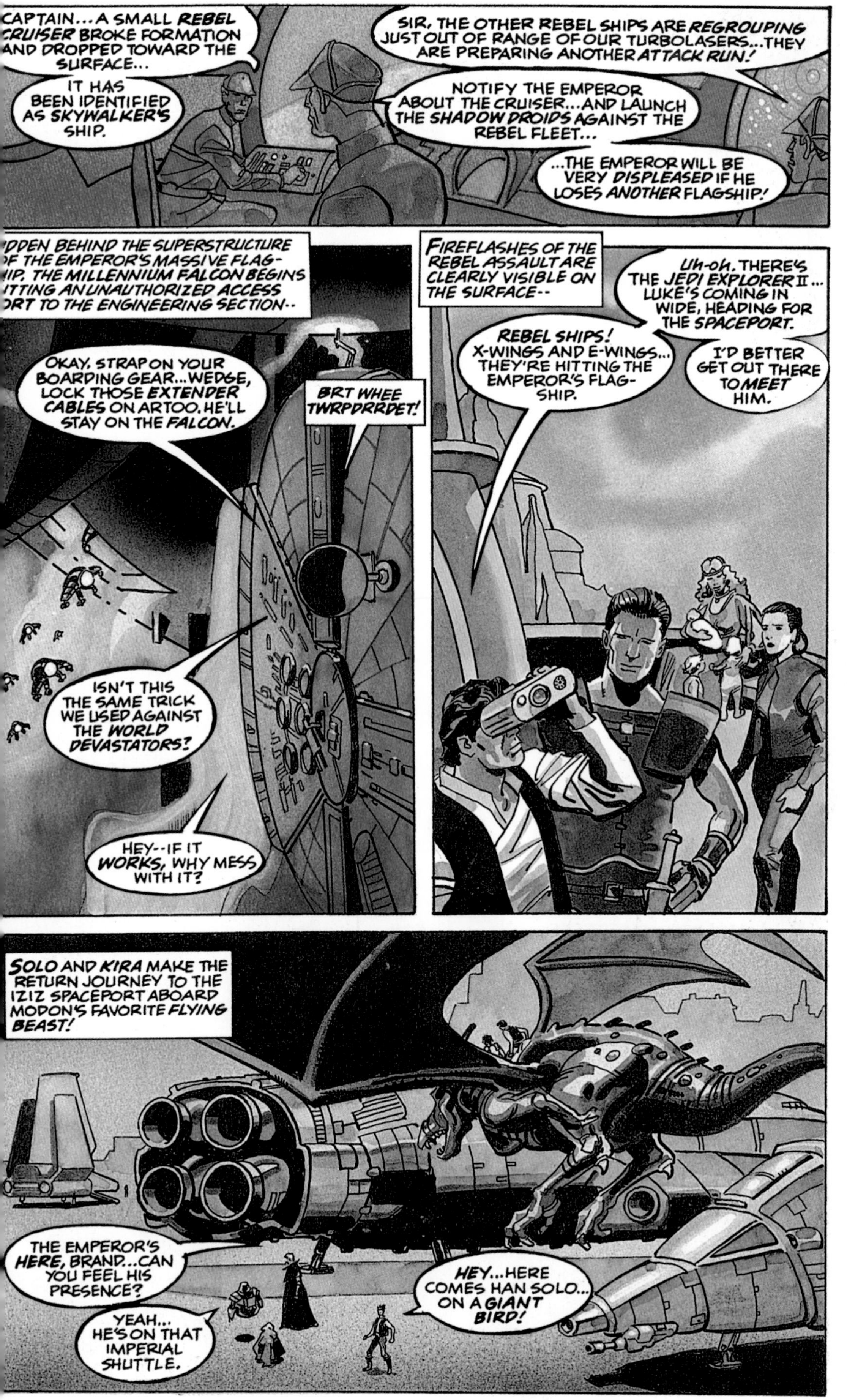
CAPTAIN... A SMALL REBEL CRUISER BROKE FORMATION AND DROPPED TOWARD THE SURFACE...
IT HAS BEEN IDENTIFIED AS SKYWALKER'S SHIP.
SIR, THE OTHER REBEL SHIPS ARE REGROUPING JUST OUT OF RANGE OF OUR TURBOLASERS... THEY ARE PREPARING ANOTHER ATTACK RUN!
NOTIFY THE EMPEROR ABOUT THE CRUISER... AND LAUNCH THE SHADOW DROIDS AGAINST THE REBEL FLEET...
...THE EMPEROR WILL BE VERY DISPLEASED IF HE LOSES ANOTHER FLAGSHIP!
DDEN BEHIND THE SUPERSTRUCTURE
F THE EMPEROR'S MASSIVE FLAG-
IP, THE MILLENNIUM FALCON BEGINS
ITTING AN UNAUTHORIZED ACCESS
ORT TO THE ENGINEERING SECTION--
OKAY. STRAP ON YOUR BOARDING GEAR... WEDGE, LOCK THOSE EXTENDER CABLES ON ARTOO. HE'LL STAY ON THE FALCON.
BRT WHEE TWRPDRRDET!
ISN'T THIS THE SAME TRICK WE USED AGAINST THE WORLD DEVASTATORS?
HEY--IF IT WORKS, WHY MESS WITH IT?
FIREFLASHES OF THE REBEL ASSAULT ARE CLEARLY VISIBLE ON THE SURFACE--
UH-OH. THERE'S THE JEDI EXPLORER II... LUKE'S COMING IN WIDE, HEADING FOR THE SPACEPORT.
REBEL SHIPS! X-WINGS AND E-WINGS... THEY'RE HITTING THE EMPEROR'S FLAG-SHIP.
I'D BETTER GET OUT THERE TO MEET HIM.
SOLO AND KIRA MAKE THE RETURN JOURNEY TO THE IZIZ SPACEPORT ABOARD MODON'S FAVORITE FLYING BEAST!
THE EMPEROR'S HERE, BRAND... CAN YOU FEEL HIS PRESENCE?
YEAH... HE'S ON THAT IMPERIAL SHUTTLE.
HEY... HERE COMES HAN SOLO... ON A GIANT BIRD!

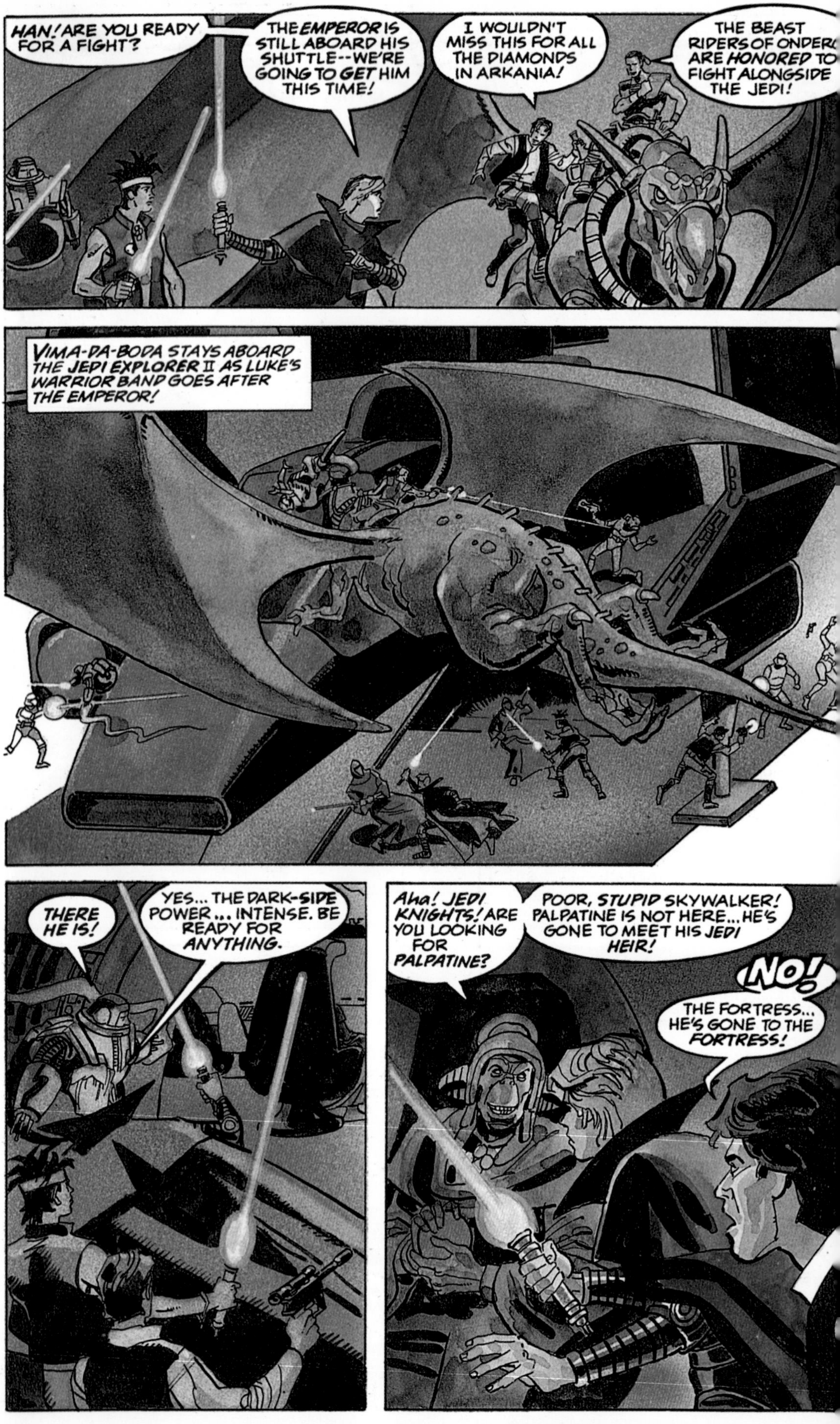
HAN! ARE YOU READY FOR A FIGHT?
THE EMPEROR IS STILL ABOARD HIS SHUTTLE--WE'RE GOING TO GET HIM THIS TIME!
I WOULDN'T MISS THIS FOR ALL THE DIAMONDS IN ARKANIA!
THE BEAST RIDERS OF ONDER
ARE HONORED TO FIGHT ALONGSIDE THE JEDI!
VIMA-DA-BODA STAYS ABOARD THE JEDI EXPLORER II AS LUKE'S WARRIOR BAND GOES AFTER THE EMPEROR!
THERE HE IS!
YES... THE DARK-SIDE POWER... INTENSE. BE READY FOR ANYTHING.
Aha! JEDI KNIGHTS! ARE YOU LOOKING FOR PALPATINE?
POOR, STUPID SKYWALKER! PALPATINE IS NOT HERE... HE'S GONE TO MEET HIS JEDI HEIR!
NO!
THE FORTRESS... HE'S GONE TO THE FORTRESS!

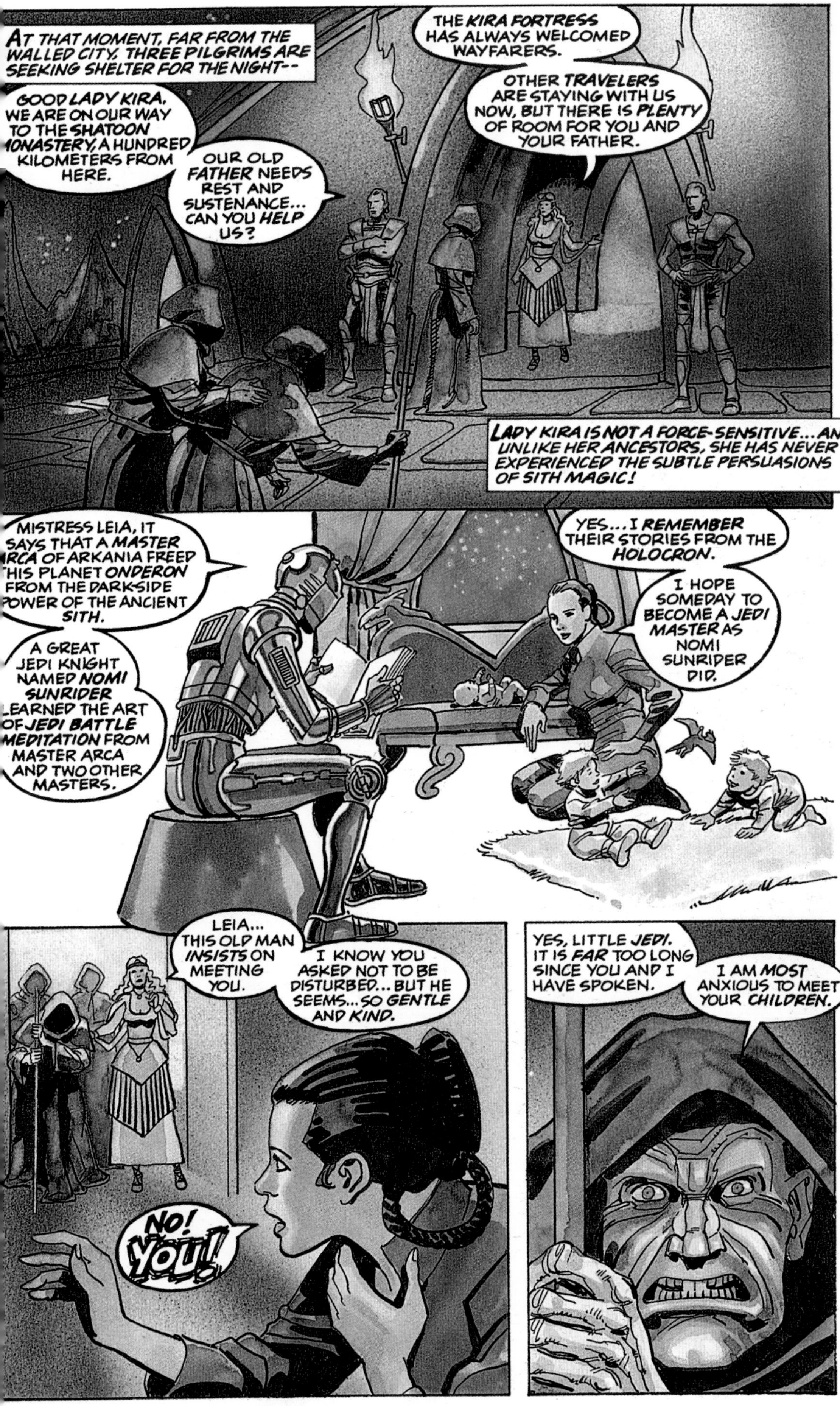
AT THAT MOMENT, FAR FROM THE WALLED CITY, THREE PILGRIMS ARE SEEKING SHELTER FOR THE NIGHT--
GOOD LADY KIRA, WE ARE ON OUR WAY TO THE SHATOON MONASTERY, A HUNDRED KILOMETERS FROM HERE.
OUR OLD FATHER NEEDS REST AND SUSTENANCE... CAN YOU HELP US?
THE KIRA FORTRESS HAS ALWAYS WELCOMED WAYFARERS.
OTHER TRAVELERS ARE STAYING WITH US NOW, BUT THERE IS PLENTY OF ROOM FOR YOU AND YOUR FATHER.
LADY KIRA IS NOT A FORCE-SENSITIVE... AND UNLIKE HER ANCESTORS, SHE HAS NEVER EXPERIENCED THE SUBTLE PERSUASIONS OF SITH MAGIC!
MISTRESS LEIA, IT SAYS THAT A MASTER ARCA OF ARKANIA FREED THIS PLANET ONDERON FROM THE DARKSIDE POWER OF THE ANCIENT SITH.
A GREAT JEDI KNIGHT NAMED NOMI SUNRIDER LEARNED THE ART OF JEDI BATTLE MEDITATION FROM MASTER ARCA AND TWO OTHER MASTERS.
YES... I REMEMBER THEIR STORIES FROM THE HOLOCRON.
I HOPE SOMEDAY TO BECOME A JEDI MASTER AS NOMI SUNRIDER DID.
LEIA... THIS OLD MAN INSISTS ON MEETING YOU.
I KNOW YOU ASKED NOT TO BE DISTURBED... BUT HE SEEMS... SO GENTLE AND KIND.
NO! YOU!
YES, LITTLE JEDI. IT IS FAR TOO LONG SINCE YOU AND I HAVE SPOKEN.
I AM MOST ANXIOUS TO MEET YOUR CHILDREN.

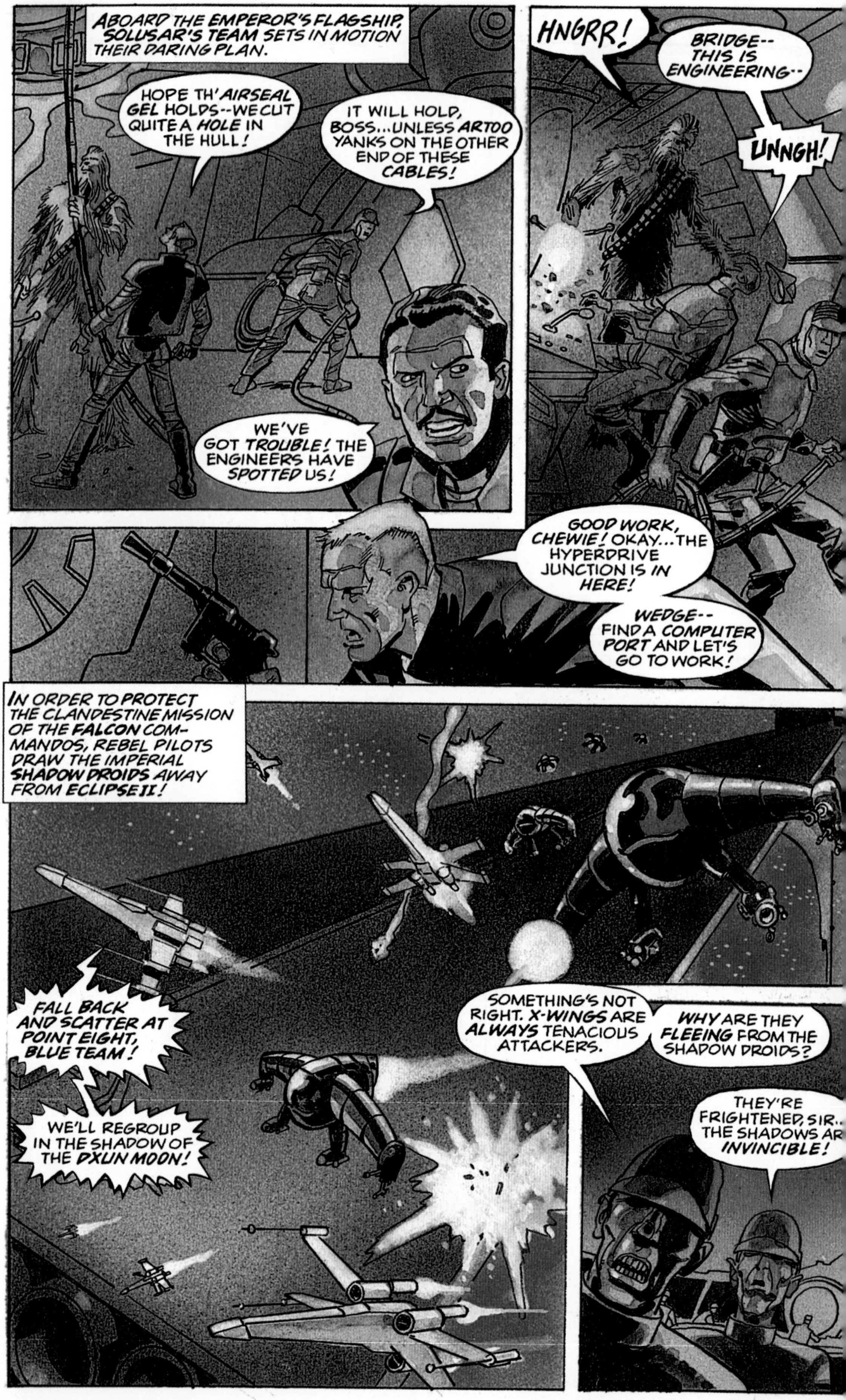
ABOARD THE EMPEROR'S FLAGSHIP, SOLUSAR'S TEAM SETS IN MOTION THEIR DARING PLAN.
HOPE TH' AIRSEAL GEL HOLDS--WE CUT QUITE A HOLE IN THE HULL!
IT WILL HOLD, BOSS...UNLESS ARTOO YANKS ON THE OTHER END OF THESE CABLES!
WE'VE GOT TROUBLE! THE ENGINEERS HAVE SPOTTED US!
HNGRR!
BRIDGE-- THIS IS ENGINEERING--
UNNGH!
GOOD WORK, CHEWIE! OKAY...THE HYPERDRIVE JUNCTION IS IN HERE!
WEDGE-- FIND A COMPUTER PORT AND LET'S GO TO WORK!
IN ORDER TO PROTECT THE CLANDESTINE MISSION OF THE FALCON COMMANDOS, REBEL PILOTS DRAW THE IMPERIAL SHADOW DROIDS AWAY FROM ECLIPSE II!
FALL BACK AND SCATTER AT POINT EIGHT, BLUE TEAM!
WE'LL REGROUP IN THE SHADOW OF THE DXUN MOON!
SOMETHING'S NOT RIGHT. X-WINGS ARE ALWAYS TENACIOUS ATTACKERS.
WHY ARE THEY FLEEING FROM THE SHADOW DROIDS?
THEY'RE FRIGHTENED, SIR.. THE SHADOWS AR INVINCIBLE!

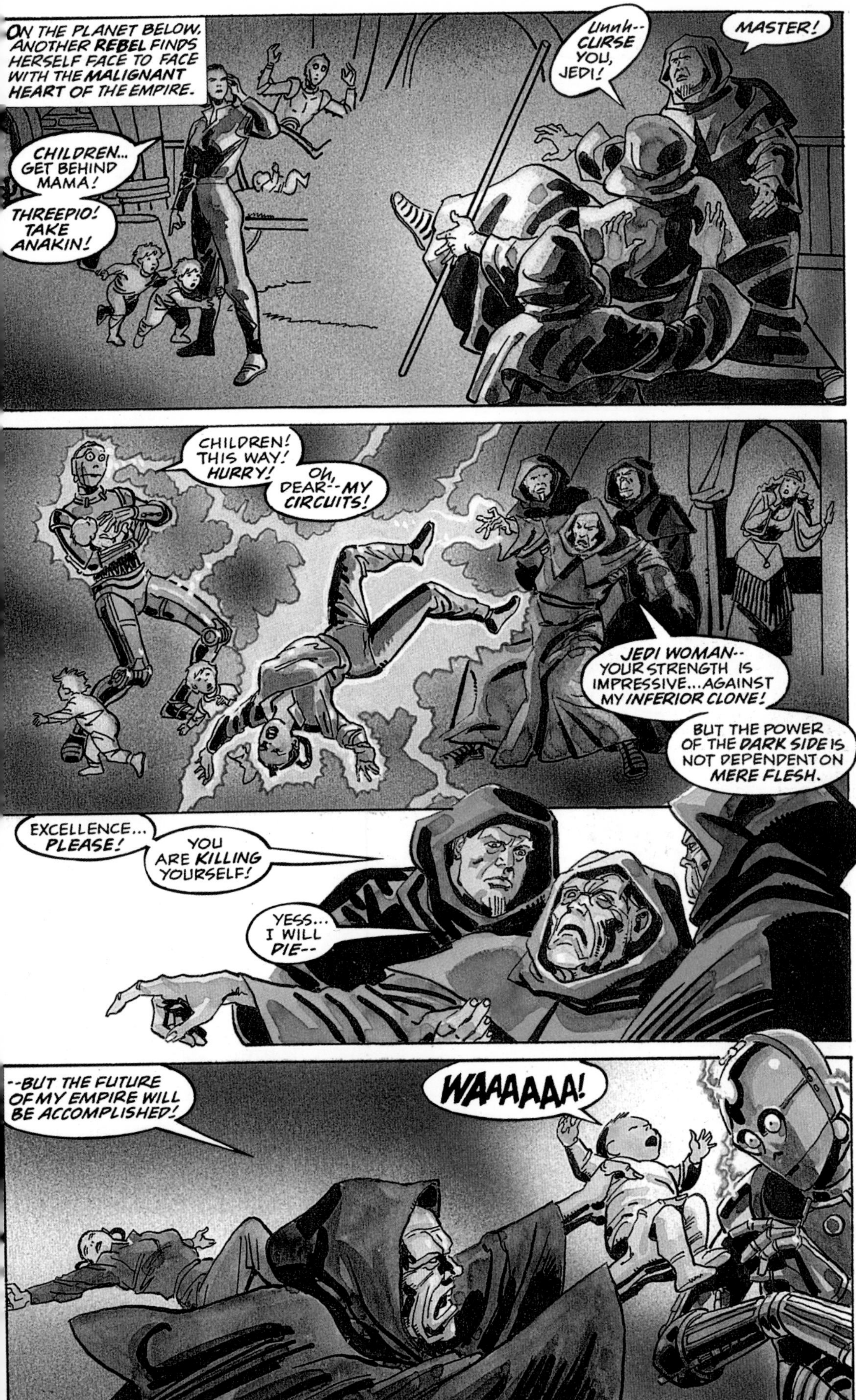
ON THE PLANET BELOW, ANOTHER REBEL FINDS HERSELF FACE TO FACE WITH THE MALIGNANT HEART OF THE EMPIRE.
CHILDREN... GET BEHIND MAMA!
THREEPIO! TAKE ANAKIN!
Unnh-- CURSE YOU, JEDI!
MASTER!
CHILDREN! THIS WAY! HURRY!
Oh, DEAR--MY CIRCUITS!
JEDI WOMAN-- YOUR STRENGTH IS IMPRESSIVE... AGAINST MY INFERIOR CLONE!
BUT THE POWER OF THE DARK SIDE IS NOT DEPENDENT ON MERE FLESH.
EXCELLENCE... PLEASE!
YOU ARE KILLING YOURSELF!
YESS... I WILL DIE--
--BUT THE FUTURE OF MY EMPIRE WILL BE ACCOMPLISHED!
WAAAAAA!

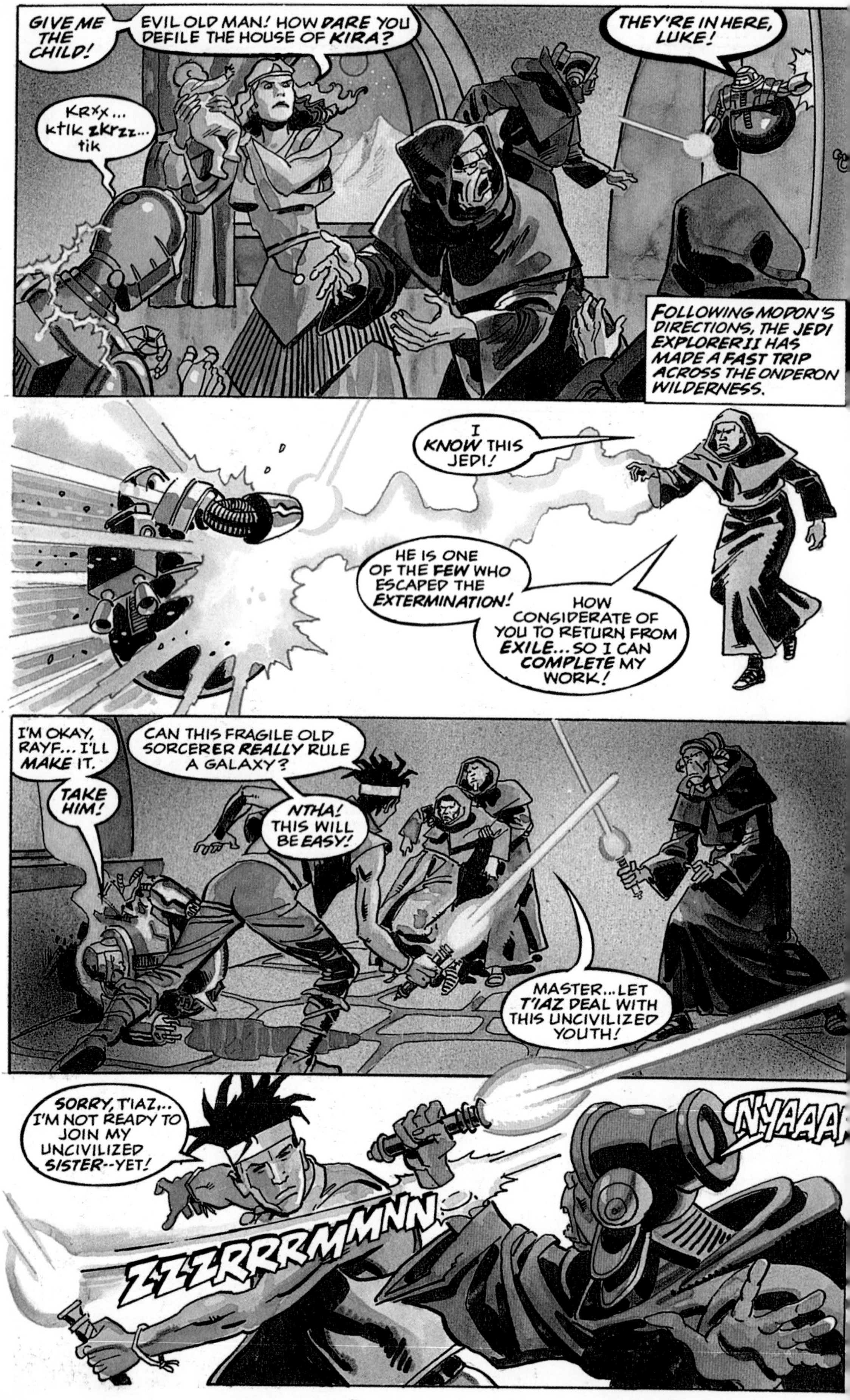
GIVE ME THE CHILD!
EVIL OLD MAN! HOW DARE YOU DEFILE THE HOUSE OF KIRA?
THEY'RE IN HERE, LUKE!
KRxx... ktik zkrzz... tik
FOLLOWING MODON'S DIRECTIONS, THE JEDI EXPLORER II HAS MADE A FAST TRIP ACROSS THE ONDERON WILDERNESS.
I KNOW THIS JEDI!
HE IS ONE OF THE FEW WHO ESCAPED THE EXTERMINATION!
HOW CONSIDERATE OF YOU TO RETURN FROM EXILE... SO I CAN COMPLETE MY WORK!
I'M OKAY, RAYF... I'LL MAKE IT.
CAN THIS FRAGILE OLD SORCERER REALLY RULE A GALAXY?
TAKE HIM!
NTHA! THIS WILL BE EASY!
MASTER... LET T'IAZ DEAL WITH THIS UNCIVILIZED YOUTH!
SORRY, T'IAZ... I'M NOT READY TO JOIN MY UNCIVILIZED SISTER--YET!
NYAAA
ZZZRRRMMNN

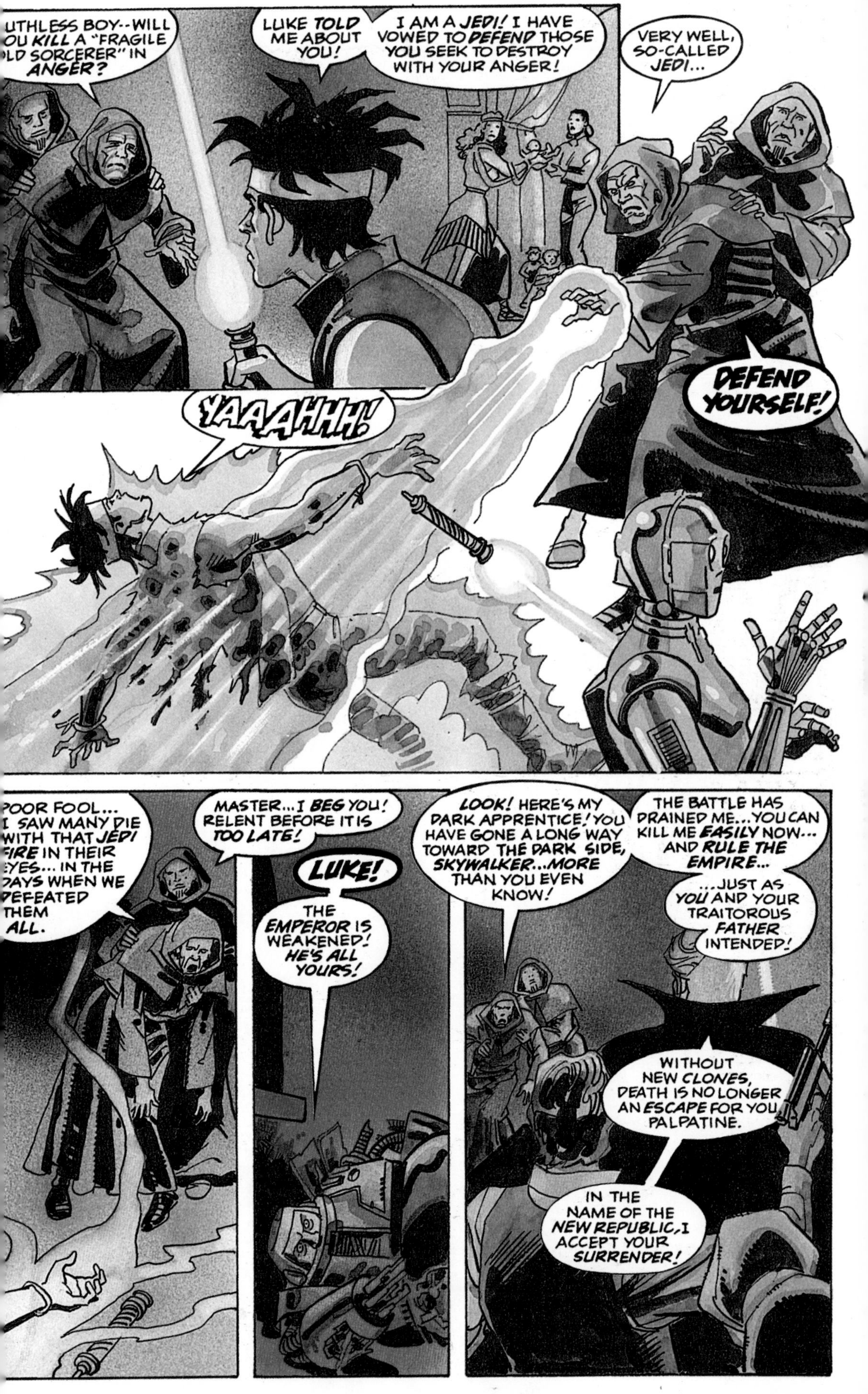

UTHLESS BOY--WILL OU KILL A "FRAGILE LD SORCERER" IN ANGER?
LUKE TOLD ME ABOUT YOU!
I AM A JEDI! I HAVE VOWED TO DEFEND THOSE YOU SEEK TO DESTROY WITH YOUR ANGER!
VERY WELL, SO-CALLED JEDI...
DEFEND YOURSELF!
YAAAHHH!
POOR FOOL... I SAW MANY DIE WITH THAT JEDI FIRE IN THEIR EYES... IN THE DAYS WHEN WE DEFEATED THEM ALL.
MASTER... I BEG YOU! RELENT BEFORE IT IS TOO LATE!
LUKE!
THE EMPEROR IS WEAKENED! HE'S ALL YOURS!
LOOK! HERE'S MY DARK APPRENTICE! YOU HAVE GONE A LONG WAY TOWARD THE DARK SIDE, SKYWALKER... MORE THAN YOU EVEN KNOW!
THE BATTLE HAS DRAINED ME... YOU CAN KILL ME EASILY NOW... AND RULE THE EMPIRE...
...JUST AS YOU AND YOUR TRAITOROUS FATHER INTENDED!
WITHOUT NEW CLONES, DEATH IS NO LONGER AN ESCAPE FOR YOU, PALPATINE.
IN THE NAME OF THE NEW REPUBLIC, I ACCEPT YOUR SURRENDER!

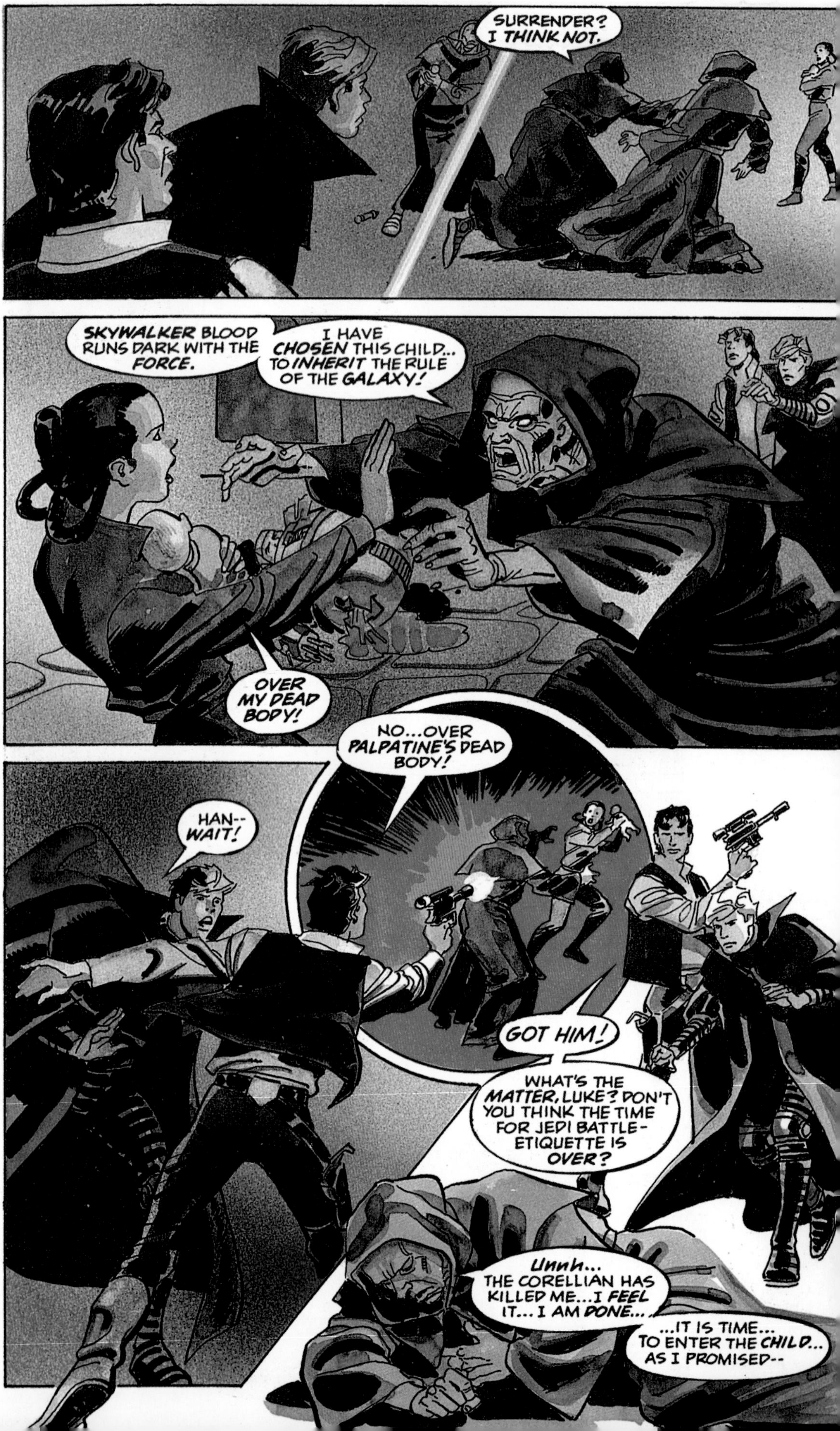
SURRENDER? I THINK NOT.
SKYWALKER BLOOD RUNS DARK WITH THE FORCE.
I HAVE CHOSEN THIS CHILD... TO INHERIT THE RULE OF THE GALAXY!
OVER MY DEAD BODY!
NO...OVER PALPATINE'S DEAD BODY!
HAN-- WAIT!
GOT HIM!
WHAT'S THE MATTER, LUKE? DON'T YOU THINK THE TIME FOR JEDI BATTLE-ETIQUETTE IS OVER?
Unnh... THE CORELLIAN HAS KILLED ME...I FEEL IT... I AM DONE...
...IT IS TIME... TO ENTER THE CHILD... AS I PROMISED--

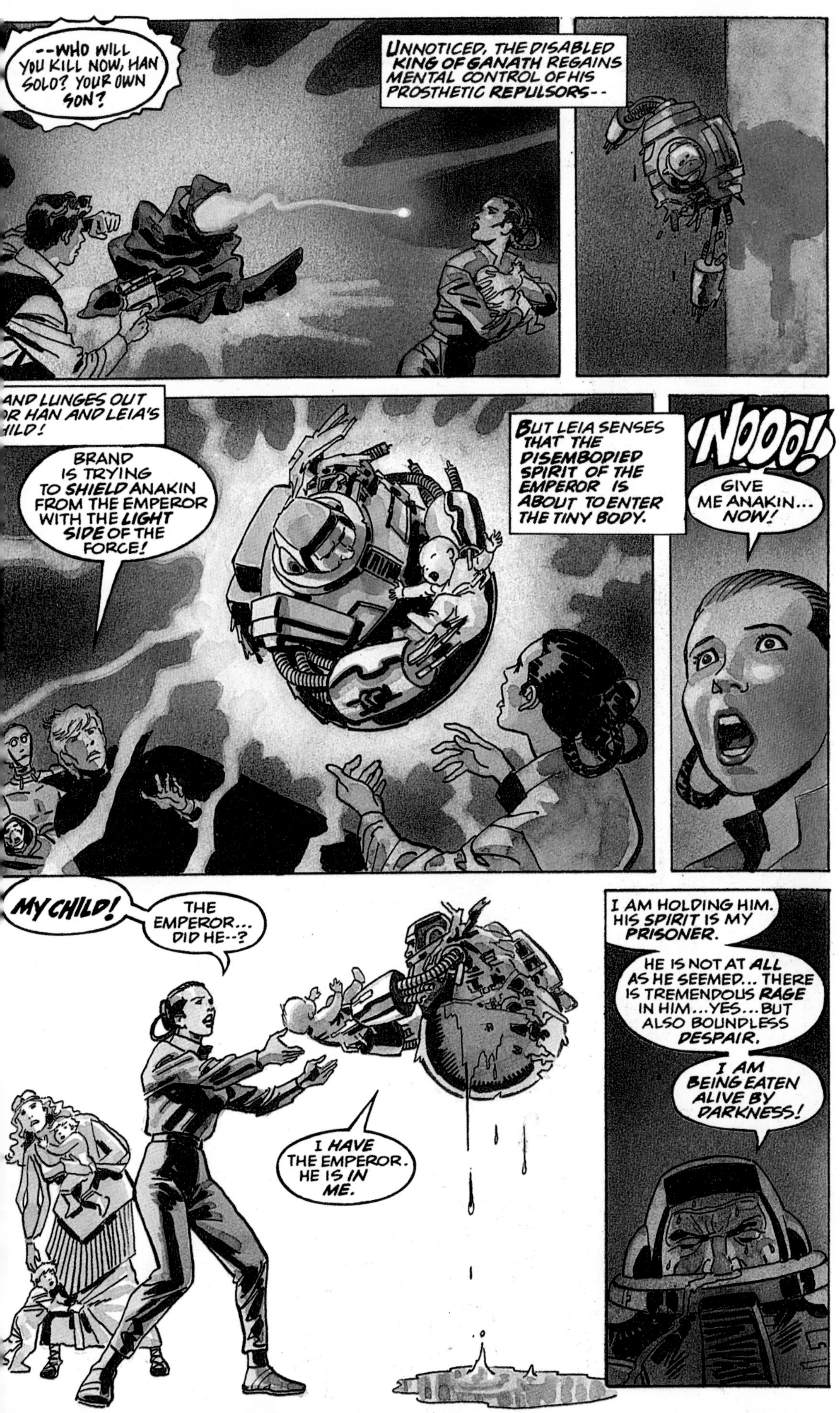
--WHO WILL YOU KILL NOW, HAN SOLO? YOUR OWN SON?
UNNOTICED, THE DISABLED KING OF GANATH REGAINS MENTAL CONTROL OF HIS PROSTHETIC REPULSORS--
AND LUNGES OUT OR HAN AND LEIA'S HILD!
BRAND IS TRYING TO SHIELD ANAKIN FROM THE EMPEROR WITH THE LIGHT SIDE OF THE FORCE!
BUT LEIA SENSES THAT THE DISEMBODIED SPIRIT OF THE EMPEROR IS ABOUT TO ENTER THE TINY BODY.
NOOO!
GIVE ME ANAKIN... NOW!
MY CHILD!
THE EMPEROR... DID HE--?
I HAVE THE EMPEROR. HE IS IN ME.
I AM HOLDING HIM. HIS SPIRIT IS MY PRISONER.
HE IS NOT AT ALL AS HE SEEMED... THERE IS TREMENDOUS RAGE IN HIM... YES... BUT ALSO BOUNDLESS DESPAIR.
I AM BEING EATEN ALIVE BY DARKNESS!

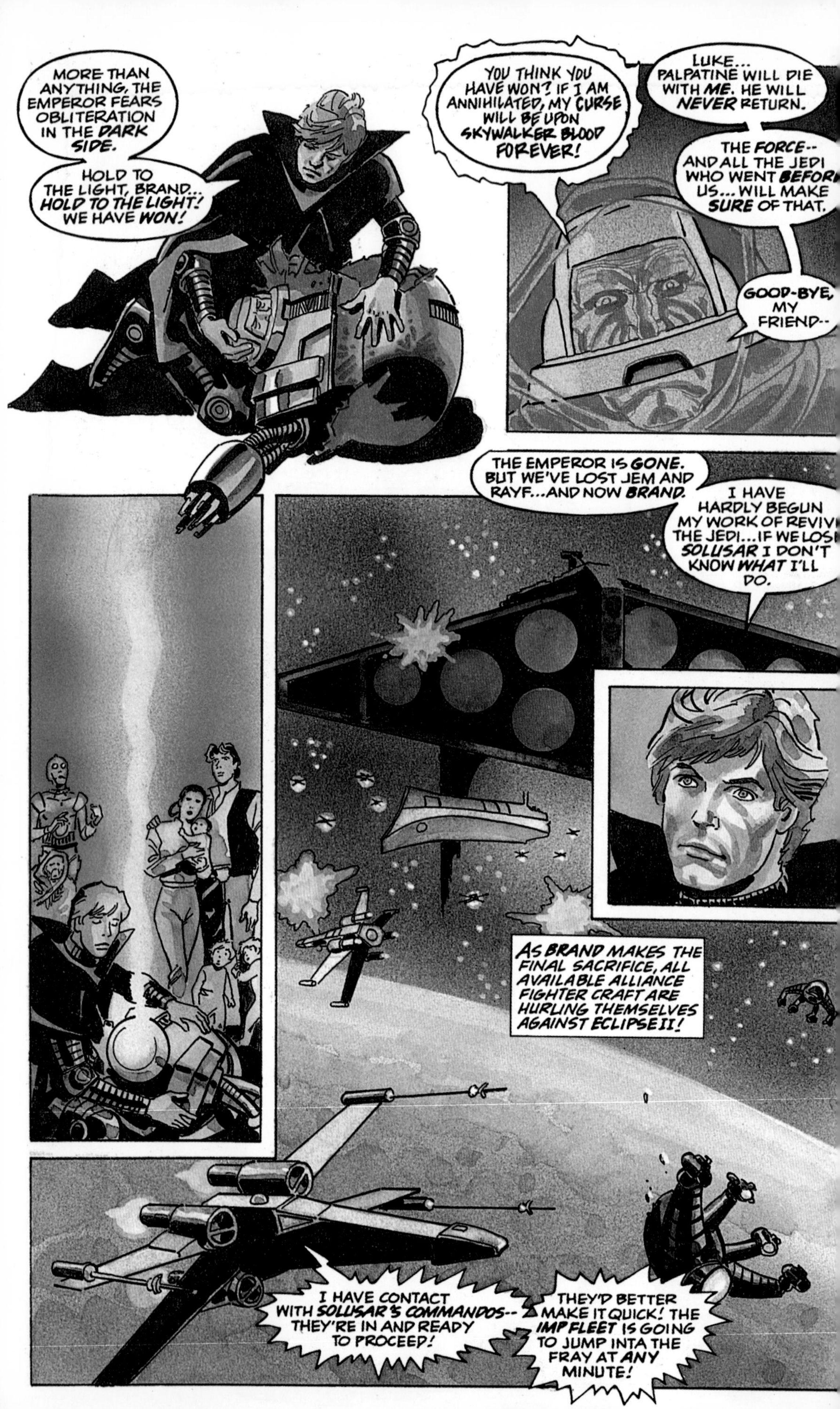
MORE THAN ANYTHING, THE EMPEROR FEARS OBLITERATION IN THE DARK SIDE.
HOLD TO THE LIGHT, BRAND... HOLD TO THE LIGHT! WE HAVE WON!
YOU THINK YOU HAVE WON? IF I AM ANNIHILATED, MY CURSE WILL BE UPON SKYWALKER BLOOD FOREVER!
LUKE... PALPATINE WILL DIE WITH ME. HE WILL NEVER RETURN.
THE FORCE-- AND ALL THE JEDI WHO WENT BEFORE US... WILL MAKE SURE OF THAT.
GOOD-BYE, MY FRIEND--
THE EMPEROR IS GONE. BUT WE'VE LOST JEM AND RAYF... AND NOW BRAND.
I HAVE HARDLY BEGUN MY WORK OF REVIVI THE JEDI... IF WE LOS SOLUSAR I DON'T KNOW WHAT I'LL DO.
AS BRAND MAKES THE FINAL SACRIFICE, ALL AVAILABLE ALLIANCE FIGHTER CRAFT ARE HURLING THEMSELVES AGAINST ECLIPSE II!
I HAVE CONTACT WITH SOLUSAR'S COMMANDOS-- THEY'RE IN AND READY TO PROCEED!
THEY'D BETTER MAKE IT QUICK! THE IMP FLEET IS GOING TO JUMP INTA THE FRAY AT ANY MINUTE!

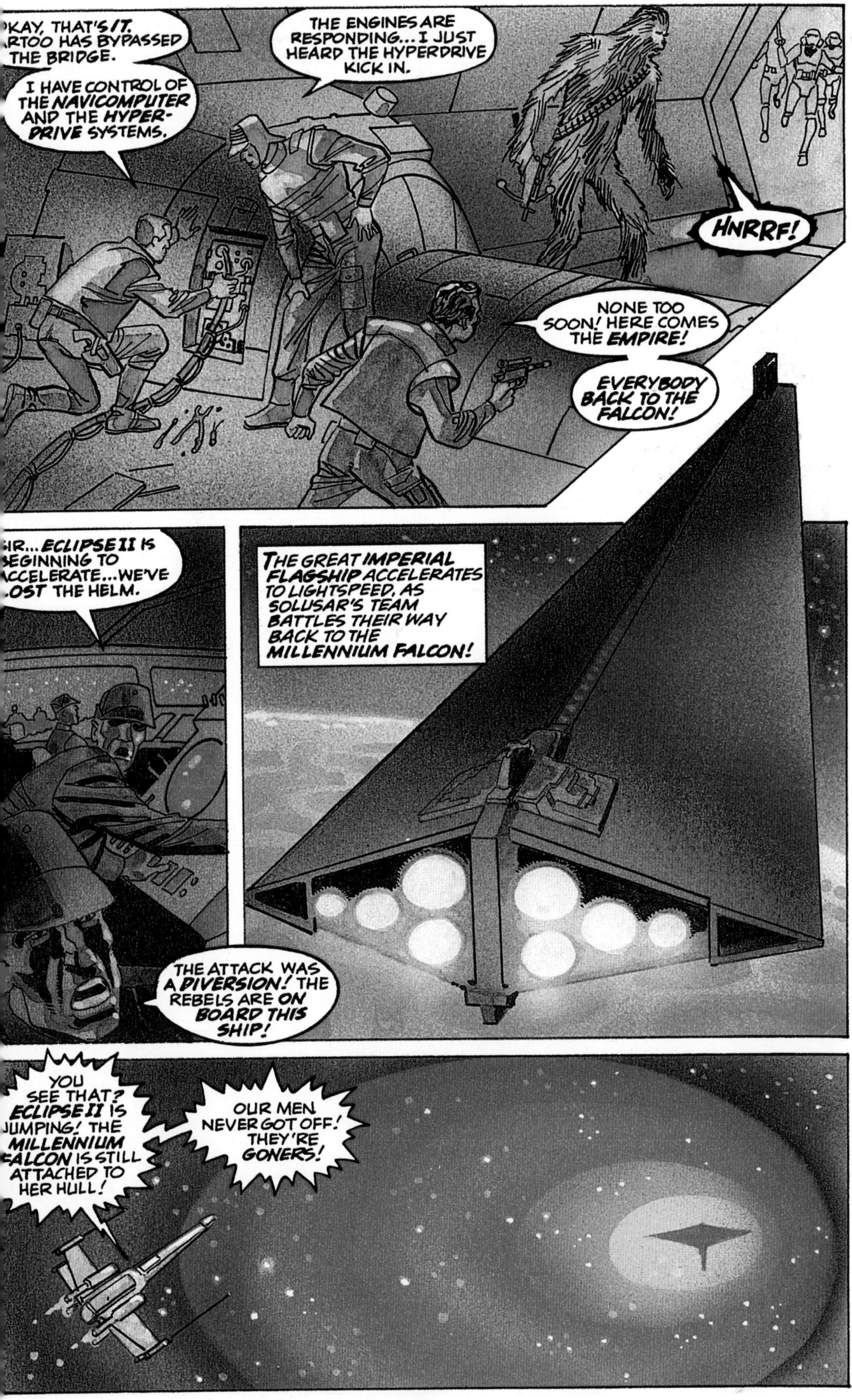

OKAY, THAT'S IT. ARTOO HAS BYPASSED THE BRIDGE.
I HAVE CONTROL OF THE NAVICOMPUTER AND THE HYPER-DRIVE SYSTEMS.
THE ENGINES ARE RESPONDING... I JUST HEARD THE HYPERDRIVE KICK IN.
HNRRF!
NONE TOO SOON! HERE COMES THE EMPIRE!
EVERYBODY BACK TO THE FALCON!
SIR... ECLIPSE II IS BEGINNING TO ACCELERATE... WE'VE LOST THE HELM.
THE GREAT IMPERIAL FLAGSHIP ACCELERATES TO LIGHTSPEED, AS SOLUSAR'S TEAM BATTLES THEIR WAY BACK TO THE MILLENNIUM FALCON!
THE ATTACK WAS A DIVERSION! THE REBELS ARE ON BOARD THIS SHIP!
YOU SEE THAT? ECLIPSE II IS JUMPING! THE MILLENNIUM FALCON IS STILL ATTACHED TO HER HULL!
OUR MEN NEVER GOT OFF! THEY'RE GONERS!

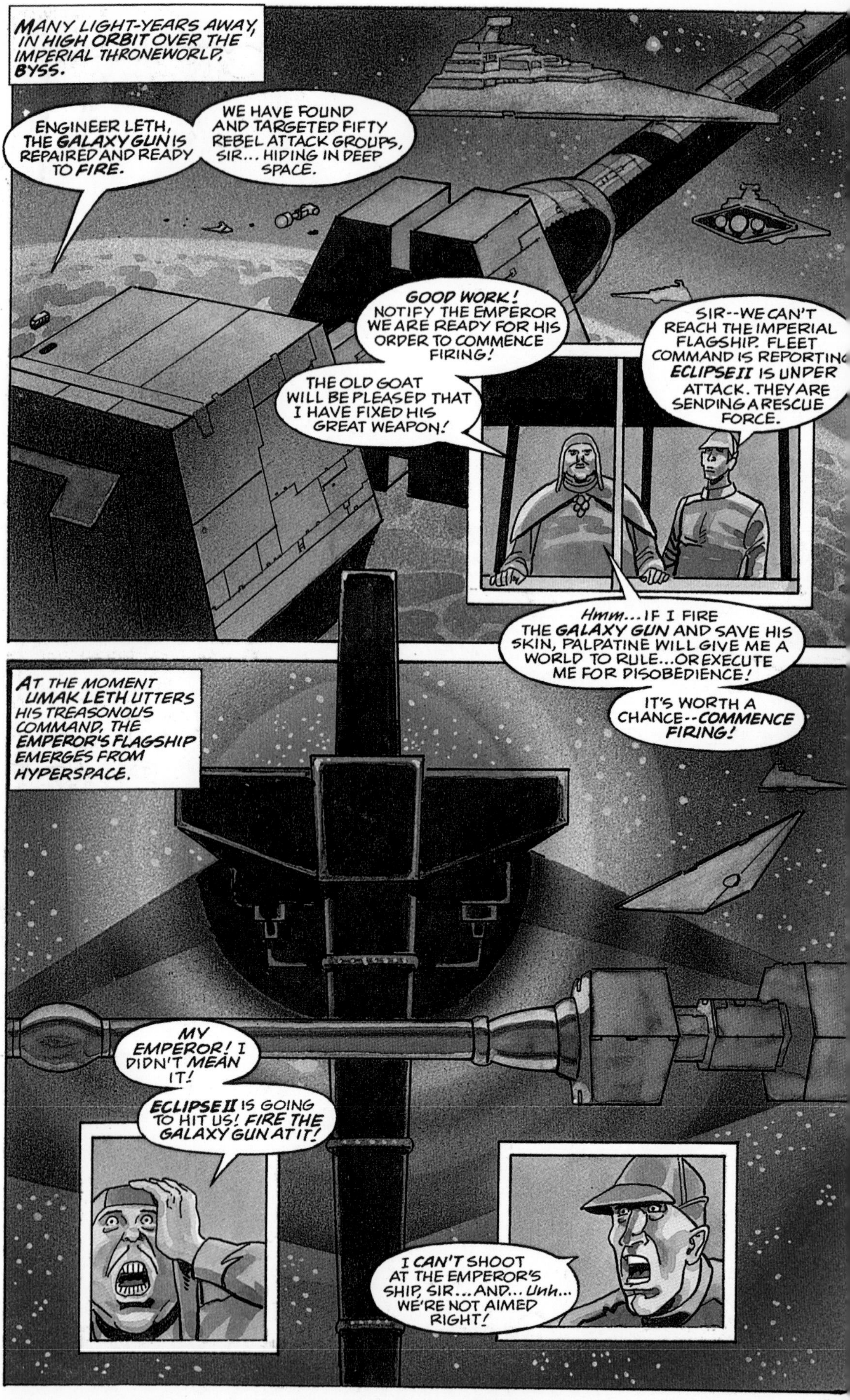
MANY LIGHT-YEARS AWAY, IN HIGH ORBIT OVER THE IMPERIAL THRONEWORLD, BYSS.
ENGINEER LETH, THE GALAXY GUN IS REPAIRED AND READY TO FIRE.
WE HAVE FOUND AND TARGETED FIFTY REBEL ATTACK GROUPS, SIR... HIDING IN DEEP SPACE.
GOOD WORK! NOTIFY THE EMPEROR WE ARE READY FOR HIS ORDER TO COMMENCE FIRING!
THE OLD GOAT WILL BE PLEASED THAT I HAVE FIXED HIS GREAT WEAPON!
SIR--WE CAN'T REACH THE IMPERIAL FLAGSHIP. FLEET COMMAND IS REPORTING ECLIPSE II IS UNDER ATTACK. THEY ARE SENDING A RESCUE FORCE.
Hmm... IF I FIRE THE GALAXY GUN AND SAVE HIS SKIN, PALPATINE WILL GIVE ME A WORLD TO RULE...OR EXECUTE ME FOR DISOBEDIENCE!
IT'S WORTH A CHANCE--COMMENCE FIRING!
AT THE MOMENT UMAK LETH UTTERS HIS TREASONOUS COMMAND, THE EMPEROR'S FLAGSHIP EMERGES FROM HYPERSPACE.
MY EMPEROR! I DIDN'T MEAN IT!
ECLIPSE II IS GOING TO HIT US! FIRE THE GALAXY GUN AT IT!
I CAN'T SHOOT AT THE EMPEROR'S SHIP, SIR... AND... Unh... WE'RE NOT AIMED RIGHT!

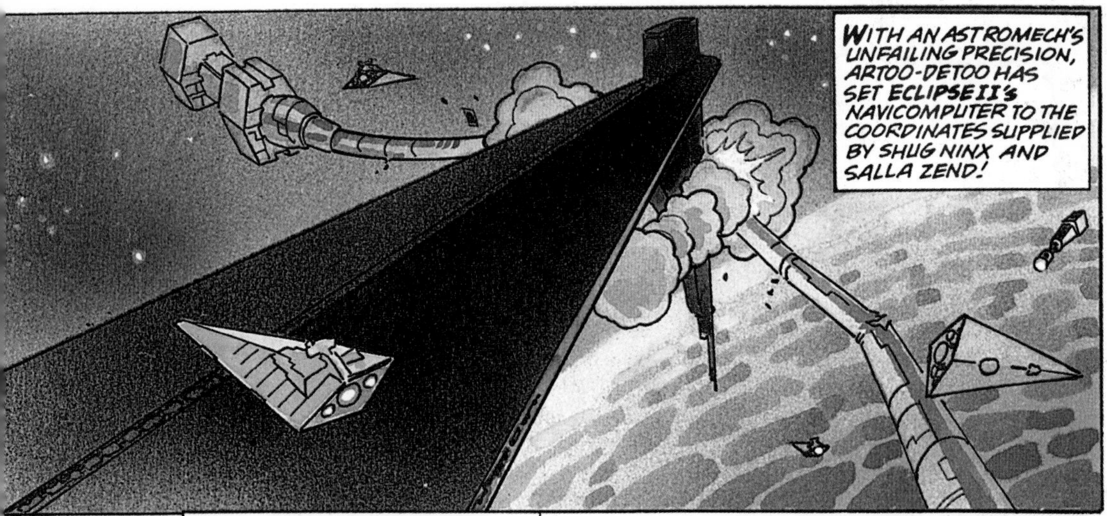
WITH AN ASTROMECH'S UNFAILING PRECISION, ARTOO-DETOO HAS SET ECLIPSE II's NAVICOMPUTER TO THE COORDINATES SUPPLIED BY SHUG NINX AND SALLA ZEND!

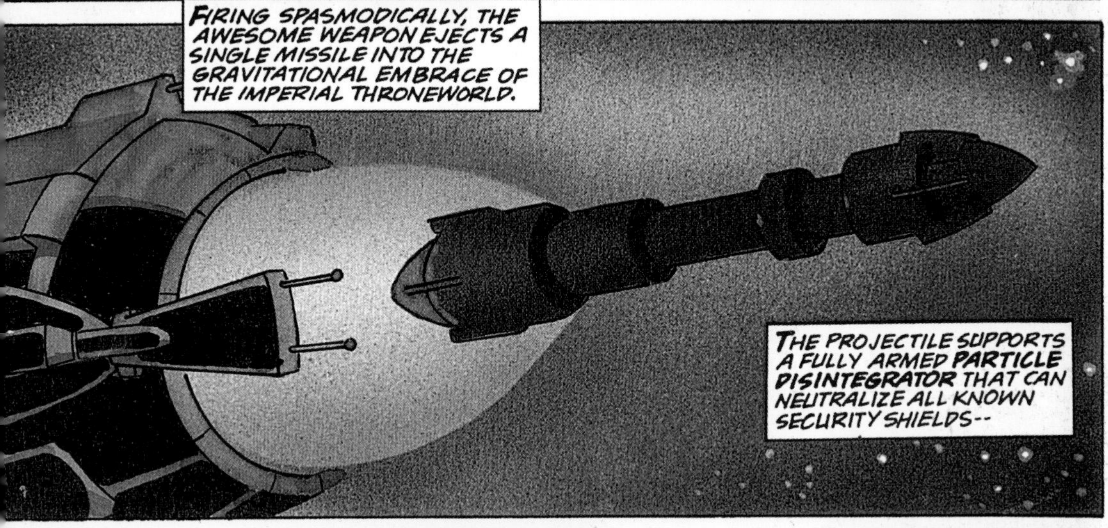
FIRING SPASMODICALLY, THE AWESOME WEAPON EJECTS A SINGLE MISSILE INTO THE GRAVITATIONAL EMBRACE OF THE IMPERIAL THRONEWORLD.
THE PROJECTILE SUPPORTS A FULLY ARMED PARTICLE DISINTEGRATOR THAT CAN NEUTRALIZE ALL KNOWN SECURITY SHIELDS--

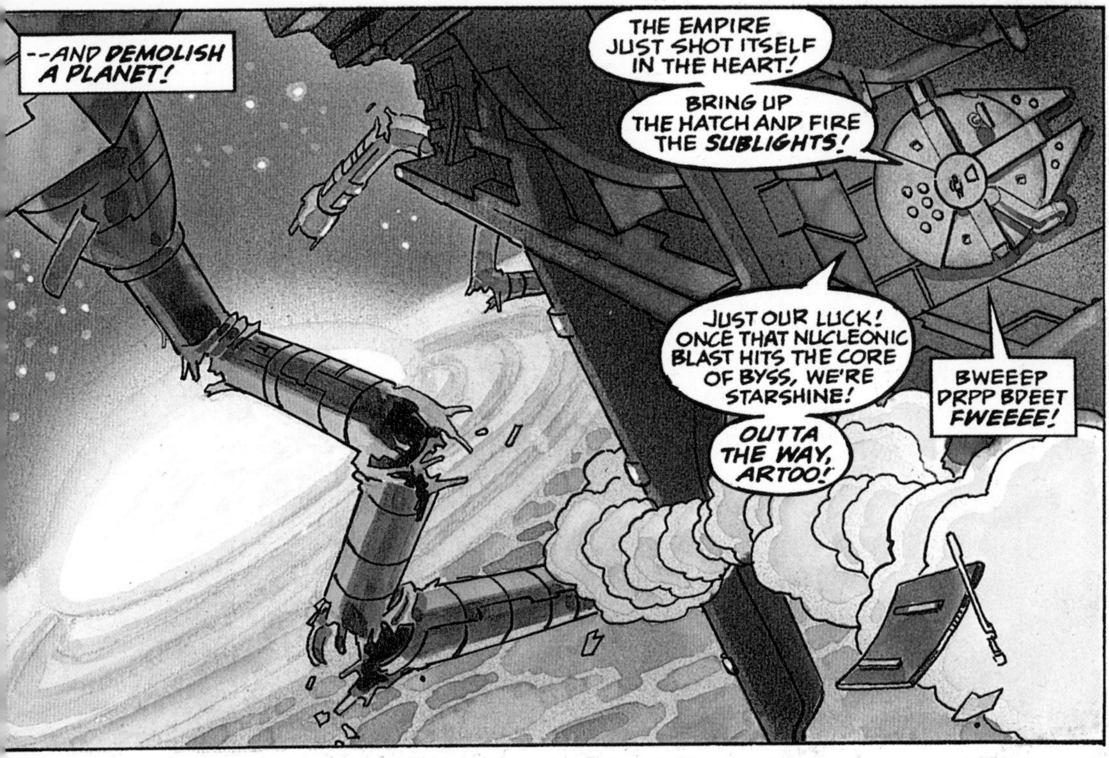
--AND DEMOLISH A PLANET!
THE EMPIRE JUST SHOT ITSELF IN THE HEART!
BRING UP THE HATCH AND FIRE THE SUBLIGHTS!
JUST OUR LUCK! ONCE THAT NUCLEONIC BLAST HITS THE CORE OF BYSS, WE'RE STARSHINE!
OUTTA THE WAY, ARTOO!
BWEEEP DRPP BDEET FWEEEE!

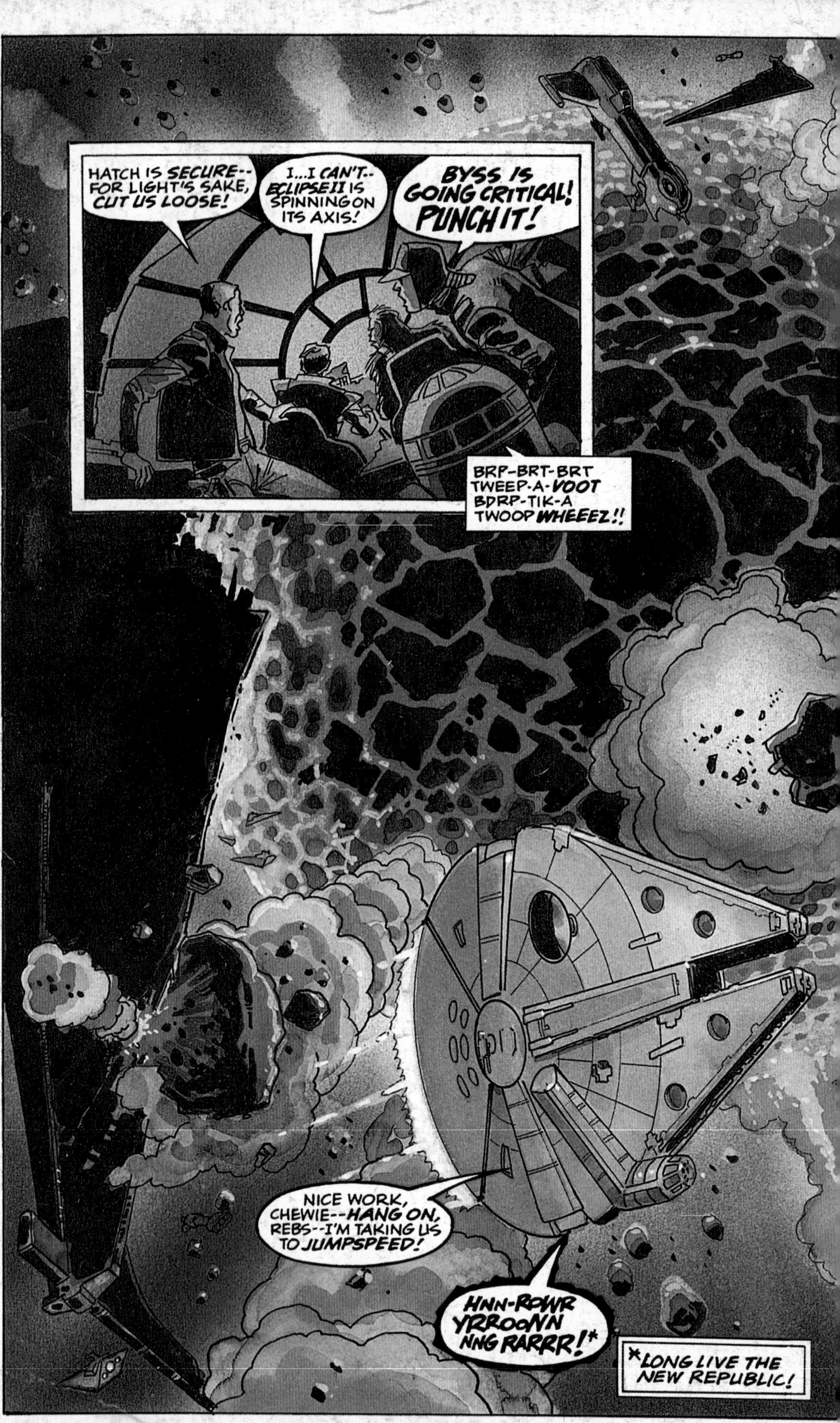
HATCH IS SECURE-- FOR LIGHT'S SAKE, CUT US LOOSE!
I...I CAN'T-- ECLIPSE II IS SPINNING ON ITS AXIS!
BYSS IS GOING CRITICAL! PUNCH IT!
BRP-BRT-BRT TWEEP-A-VOOT BDRP-TIK-A TWOOP WHEEEZ!!
NICE WORK, CHEWIE--HANG ON, REBS--I'M TAKING US TO JUMPSPEED!
HNN-ROWR YRROONN NNG RARRR!*
*LONG LIVE THE NEW REPUBLIC!